economics today-
the micro view

economics today-
the micro view

roger leroy miller
University of Washington

CANFIELD PRESS
San Francisco

A Department of Harper & Row, Publishers, Inc.
New York / Evanston / London

We gratefully acknowledge the following sources for information and quotations used in the biographical sketches:

Newsweek Magazine
U.S. News and World Report
Fortune Magazine
New York *Times* and *Times* Magazine

Business Week
Who's Who in America
Time Magazine
Current Biography

Design: *Joseph Fay*
Graphic illustration: *Ayxa Art*
Cover photography: *David Keller;* color conversion
                          by *John Hall* | San Francisco Photo Factory

ECONOMICS TODAY—THE MICRO VIEW

Copyright © 1974 by Roger LeRoy Miller

International Standard Book Number: 0-06-385455-4
Library of Congress Catalog Card Number: 73-13431

74 75 76   10 9 8 7 6 5 4 3 2 1

CONTENTS

Getting Started

ISSUE I   Illegal Activities: Marijuana, Pornography, Gambling,
Alcohol, Prostitution, Abortion   3

1   Economics: A Relevant Social Science   14

2   Markets and Microeconomics   23

Biography: *John Kenneth Galbraith: Economic Statesman*   34

3   What Makes a Market Tick?   36

ISSUE II   The Perpetual Investment Fraud: On Not Getting Rich   62

The Firm and Resource Allocation

4   Analyzing the Costs of a Business   75

ISSUE III   Crime and Punishment: The Economics of
Criminal Deterrence   89

5   The Firm in Competition   97

Biography: *Paul A. Samuelson: Economics in the Public Mind*   114

ISSUE IV   The Great Farm Ripoff: Inequities in the
Agricultural Sector   116

6   Monopoly Management   127

Biography: *Milton Friedman: The Iconoclast as Institution*   142

ISSUE V   Medical Care for All: Theory and Practice   144

ISSUE VI   The New York Stock Exchange: A Case Study in Monopoly   155

7   Not Quite Monopoly   162

ISSUE VII   Putting Advertising in Its Place: Is Advertising Bad?   174

8   Regulating the Big Ones   182

ISSUE VIII   Consumerism: Are Consumer Protection Laws Justifiable?   198

Biography: *Ralph Nader: The Fifth Branch of Government*   206

Derived Demand and Income Distribution

9	The Decision to Hire and Fire	211
ISSUE IX	Athletic Slavery: Monopoly and Monopsony in Sports	228
ISSUE X	Involuntary Servitude: Who Pays the True Cost of the Military?	237
10	Wealth, Capital, and Savings	247
Biography:	*Henry Ford II: The Consummate American Businessman*	256
11	The Distribution of Income	258
ISSUE XI	Education in Transition: Problems in the Market for Human Capital	272
ISSUE XII	Helping the Poor: Finding Alternatives to the Welfare Mess	290

Growth, Ecology, and War

12	Social Costs and the Ecology	291
ISSUE XIII	Conservation: How Should We Utilize Our Resources?	301
ISSUE XIV	The Problem of Pollution: Making Our Air Fit to Breathe, Our Water Fit to Drink	310
Biography:	*The Fox: Pollution, Principles, and Protest*	320
ISSUE XV	The Plight of Our Cities: Why Does It Take So Long to Get Around in the City?	322
13	Population Economics	330
ISSUE XVI	ZPG: Can the Earth Be Saved?	339
14	Growth and Development	346
ISSUE XVII	ZEG: Does Growth Mean Suicide?	356
15	Benefiting from Trade Among Nations	361
ISSUE XVIII	Beware of the Multinationals: The Costs and Benefits of Multinational Investment	378
Biography:	*Howard Hughes, Jr.: The Corporate Phantom*	385
16	Comparative Economic Systems	387
ISSUE XIX	China: A Case Study of a Vastly Different System	398
Biography:	*William Proxmire: Politics and Priorities*	405
17	Military Capitalism	407

TO THE INSTRUCTOR

Now, as never before, economic problems occupy the thoughts and discussions of an increasingly large segment of our population. Congressional and presidential campaigns have been waged on a foundation that centers around the basic economic problems of our times. Still, the economics programs of many universities and colleges are becoming less and less popular. Even though today's students are aware of many of the nation's economic issues, they are unwilling to study them in the abstract manner which is basic to the standard methodology in our profession. In writing *Economics Today—The Micro View* I attempted to render more concrete the oftentimes abstract and seemingly "unrealistic" theories that professional economists so widely use. The result is a modularized theory–issue text which lends itself to a variety of teaching uses.

In using this book, many instructors will find that their lecture time is best spent explaining the theory contained in the chapters, while letting the students test their understanding of the theory by reading and perhaps discussing the issues associated with it. To other instructors the opposite tack will be most usable—class discussions centered only on the issues, with reading assignments to take care of the theory.

I attempted to lay out this text in the most teachable and useful manner possible. To attract student interest, the book starts out with a discussion of illegal activities which demonstrates that economics can be applied to other than the "cut and dried" problems generally associated with it. Then a few chapters on model building and supply and demand are introduced. By this time, the student has been exposed to the basic tools of economics that he need be familiar with. As with most principles books today, I examine the competitive, monopolistic, and imperfectly competitive market situations. However, the issues that demonstrate the application of these models will, I think, be quite stimulating to the student. He is allowed, for example, to see the application of the competitive model to the buying and selling of stocks and the quest for getting rich quick. Then, he can see the monopoly model applied to the New York Stock Exchange, itself, and to the provision of medical services by the American Medical Association. Next, factor markets are introduced along with demonstrating issues concerning athletic slavery and involuntary servitude. The last part of the book is concerned with poverty; the distribution of income and wealth; growth and development; and a rather large section on ecology, zero economic growth (ZEG), and zero population growth (ZPG). There is also a discussion of international trade. The book concludes with a discussion of comparative systems, an examination of mainland China, and the problems with military capitalism. I attempted in every way possible to make the topics flow smoothly one to the other in a manner which lends itself to the usual course outline.

In addition to a comprehensive *Student Workbook,* there are numerous study aids included in the text. The first time a term is introduced it is printed in bold type with a definition. Additionally, the student will find another definition given at the end of the chapter or issue in which the term first appears. Vocabulary seems to be a stumbling block for many new students of economics, and a double dose of definitions is intended to help overcome this problem. Another useful review device is the point-by-point summary at the end of each chapter. A special study feature is that all of the graphs are self-contained. That is, the student need not refer to the text itself to understand the graphs, because a rephrased explanation is given alongside or underneath each one. There are questions for thought and discussion at the end of each chapter and issue. These questions are included so that the student can analyze certain aspects of the chapter or issue by himself.

Another learning device which I have sparingly but nonetheless repeatedly used concerns repetition of basic and important economic principles. After all, the beginning economics student does not read through a text in the same manner that a potential adopting instructor does. A repetition of familiar material serves as not only a learning device but also as part of a system of self-testing. If the student sees a supply and demand graph that appears to be similar to others already presented, he will know whether or not he has mastered the concepts inherent in that graph if he understands it at first reading. The same is true for other nongraphical concepts that economists are so fond of using. For example, a student who does not master the notion of opportunity cost is usually lost in many economic discussions because this concept seems to be so important in our analyses. For that reason, opportunity cost is repeated over and over again throughout the text, as are supply and demand curves (movements along as opposed to shifts in), the importance of expectations, the difference between average and marginal, and so on.

It is my hope that *Economics Today—The Micro View* will succeed in getting today's students more interested in the world of economics in which we must all live. I realize that I suffer from the same bias that exists in most professional economists: everything seems to lend itself to an economic explanation. Even realizing that this bias exists, it still seems that many issues facing us now have certain economic aspects which today's students should know about and be interested in. Imparting to them this knowledge and excitement is, to be sure, no easy task, but the issues approach appears to be a successful means to this end.

Because I want this book to grow and develop with the changing attitudes in our profession, I welcome any comments on any aspect of my approach, what I have written, or what I have attempted to do. I have found it extremely useful in the past to establish a dialogue with the instructors using my books, and I stand ready to answer those of you who wish to write me your opinions.

ROGER LeROY MILLER

Seattle, Washington
December, 1973

ACKNOWLEDGMENTS

A number of people helped me throughout the formation, writing, and rewriting of the manuscript for this book. Peter Frost at the University of Washington helped me immensely at the very beginning of this project. Many times he forced me to reorder and rewrite sections so that they would be easier for principles teachers to use. His constant questioning of many issues in the manuscript helped me firm up their presentation. The second draft of the manuscript was worked over assiduously and sometimes brutally by Alan E. Ellis of De Anza College, Cupertino, California, and William T. Trulove and Shik Young of Eastern Washington State College, Cheney, Washington. Oftentimes their piercing questions made me furious, but in the end the manuscript gained in clarity and completeness. Other reviewers offered very helpful comments on all or major portions of the manuscript. Norman F. Keiser and James Willis of California State University at San Jose were particularly helpful in clarifying some points in the book. Portions of the manuscript were also reviewed by:

John R. Aidem, Miami-Dade Junior College
Glen W. Atkinson, University of Nevada
Charles A. Berry, University of Cincinnati
Conrad P. Caligaris, Northeastern University
Ed Coen, University of Minnesota
Grant Ferguson, North Texas State University
Martin D. Haney, Portland Community College
Timothy R. Keely, Tacoma Community College
E. R. Kittrell, Northern Illinois University
John L. Madden, University of Kentucky
John M. Martin, California State University at Hayward
E. S. McKuskey, St. Petersburg Junior College
Herbert C. Milikien, American River College
Jerry L. Petr, University of Nebraska at Lincoln
I. James Pikl, University of Wyoming
Richard Romano, Broome Community College
Augustus Shackelford, El Camino College
Howard F. Smith, California Polytechnic State University at San Luis Obispo
Robert F. Wallace, Washington State University
Henry C. Wallich, Yale University

Most of the photographs in the book were done by Susan Vita Miller and myself. All of them were shot with a Nikon F or a Nikon F2. My colleagues inform me that all the time spent on this photography demonstrates that the concept of opportunity cost wasn't completely understood. It was, however; its computation served to confirm my feeling that photography is an expensive hobby.

R.L.M.

TO THE STUDENT

S tarting a new subject in college is always difficult. Economics, it seems, has a reputation of being unusually so. This book was written in a manner that I hope will dispel this misconception concerning what used to be the "dismal science."

My comments here on how to use this book are of secondary importance compared to the manner in which your instructor wishes you to use it. Nonetheless, I do have some suggestions for you.

In general, the issues, presented in newspaper format, are meant to complement the theoretical points brought out in the chapters. To be sure, the match is not a perfect one in every case. Not all theory in economics lends itself to an issue presentation that is both current and exciting. Many of you will find that a quick reading of the issues, without attempting to work over any points not understood completely, offers a good introduction to the particular topics at hand. Then, perhaps a quick reading of the appropriate theoretical chapter would be in order— with a rereading to go over those points not understood. The second reading of the issue, if that is thought necessary, would reveal any aspects of the theory not yet mastered. The order of these particular types of readings can be reversed to suit your own tastes or your professor's.

For review I have presented three helpful devices: self-contained graphs, definitions of new terms, and chapter summaries. You can, after having read all of the text, review what you have learned by going over one or all three of these items. The graphs are self-contained such that you need not refer to the text itself to understand them, because there is an explanation with each one. The definitions at the end of each chapter and each issue are given for all terms found in bold type throughout the text. The summaries are point by point, a format which most students find useful. You may notice some repetition of concepts, graphs, and theories. This was done on purpose. Familiar ground is easier to read and offers a test situation to find out whether you mastered the material in previous sections.

No principles book can present all views or all ramifications of the subjects treated. Therefore, you will find selected references at the end of each theory chapter and issue in case you decide to pursue further a specific topic.

To aid you in learning economics, there is a comprehensive *Student Workbook,* which contains a large number of highly useful True/False, Multiple Choice, and Essay Questions as well as crossword puzzles and short articles.

It is my sincere hope that you will become interested in the economic issues of our times not in spite of, but with the help of, your textbook.

R.L.M.

Getting Started

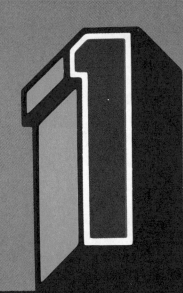

ISSUE I — ILLEGAL ACTIVITIES

Marijuana, Pornography, Gambling, Alcohol, Prostitution, Abortion

Economics Has a Lot to Say

For the beginning student in economics, it may seem strange to discover a text that includes discussions of topics such as marijuana, alcohol, abortion, or prostitution. This introductory issue demonstrates, however, that economics has much to say about topics which have traditionally been considered the province of sociologists and historians. To be sure, in many cases economics is limited in what it has to say about a particular issue or problem in society. We shall see, for example, that our analysis cannot tell us whether marijuana or prostitution or abortion should be legalized.

Economic analysis can only yield predictions and estimations of the costs and benefits associated with any particular course of action.

After examining the cases for and against the legalization of marijuana, many readers may be convinced that society would benefit from abolishing the laws against its use. Other readers may decide that society would be better off if stricter laws were enacted and enforced. Since people have varying values, different people can come up with different answers to the same issue even when given the same set of facts. Due to a strong belief against ingesting artificial stimulants or depressants, some people place a very high value on preventing others in the society from consuming alcohol and drugs. Such people might conclude that the cost of keeping marijuana illegal is outweighed by the benefit—preventing some people (but of course not all, as we shall see and as everyone knows) from consuming the drug in question.

Along the same line, economics has little to say about the morality of abortion. Economists cannot argue (as economists) whether life begins at the time of conception, at five weeks, or when the fetus quickens. Economists can present the current set of costs associated with keeping abortions illegal, and they can predict the change in these costs and/or any other ben-

efits that may arise if abortion is repealed. No statement concerning the "goodness" or "badness" of a particular course of action can be derived from the economic analysis and data presented on such issues. Value judgments are in the realm of what is called *normative* economics. Strict analysis where only theory and facts are presented is called *positive* economics. Throughout this book we shall attempt to present both types of economics, but they shall be labeled as such in each particular case. Any particular economist may have very different values than you, the student. He therefore must warn you when he is making a normative economic statement so that you can judge on your own whether your values are the same as his.

Prohibition: Alcohol and Euphoria

One of the biggest issues of today—an issue that touches the lives of a very large number of young people (and perhaps old people as well)—is the legalization of marijuana. The estimates of the number of people in the United States who have at one time tried this particular euphoric range from a low of approximately 10 million to a high of 50 million or more. The amount of literature on the subject has increased at a geo-

metric rate in the last decade. The laws in many states have recently been changed in the direction of less severe punishment for first- and second-time simple possession. Undoubtedly, the nation's collective view of marijuana has been changing. To illustrate how economics can illuminate this situation and predict future circumstances if marijuana were to be legalized, let us examine the period of alcohol prohibition and see how it parallels marijuana prohibition.

Alcohol

In 1808, Dr. Billy F. Clark met with citizens in Saratoga County who were opposed to hard liquor; they organized the first American Temperance Society. At their second convention in 1836 they added beer and wine to their list of opposed intoxicants. In the 1850s, 12 states enacted dry laws, but most of them were repealed by 1900. The temperance forces then started to gain real momentum and by 1909, five states had again gone dry. By 1919, 29 states had adopted prohibition. On August 1, 1917, the Senate approved submitting the Eighteenth Amendment to the states. This amendment, along with the Volstead Act, was the fruit of temperance efforts.

Finally, on January 17, 1920, the Eighteenth Amendment to the

United States Constitution was put into effect. It prohibited "manufacture, sale or transportation of intoxicating liquors within, or the importation thereof into, or exportation thereof from the United States ... for beverage purposes." The Eighteenth Amendment, therefore, was a legislative attempt to eliminate the *supply* of alcoholic beverages. We know, though, that there are two sides to every coin, and Congress was aware of that fact also. In 1919, while the Eighteenth Amendment was being ratified by the various states, the National Prohibition Act, or Volstead Act, was passed to enforce the amendment. This 73-section act tried to prevent trade in liquor by making it illegal to "manufacture, sell, barter, transport, import, export, deliver, furnish or possess any intoxicating liquor." Legislation therefore had also attacked the *demand* side of the alcohol question.

The days of speak-easies, the Feds, and Al Capone were upon the nation. Admittedly, hindsight is always better than foresight, but an economist would nevertheless have been able to predict many of the events that occurred during the Prohibition Era. He would have utilized the simple concepts of supply and demand along with an analysis of the risks involved in transacting illegal business. As our first introduction into the workings of economics, let's take a look at the supply and demand for intoxicating spirits.

Supply Side of the Alcohol Picture

Before the passage of the Eighteenth Amendment, businessmen entered into the liquor business if they thought as large a profit could be made in distilling, importing, exporting, wholesaling, or retailing alcoholic beverages as could be made in some other line of commercial endeavor. Take, for example, the cost involved in distilling and wholesaling bourbon. A bourbon distillery usually consists of distilling, blending, and bottling plants; each plant contains highly specialized equipment such as stainless steel tanks (where the mash is heated to convert starch to sugars), cypress wood fermenting vats, large patent or column stills, and *new* charred white oak barrels for aging.* The owner has to pay for all this equipment, and in addition he must pay his employees at least the amount that they could earn by working for someone else in a similar job.

*Old Carolina moonshiners assert that one can get by with considerably less equipment: a copper pot and worm, a section of garden hose, and some fruit jars, at a minimum. Suggested also is a rifle.

When the bourbon manufacturer goes to sell his product to wholesalers or even to retailers, if he wants to eliminate the **middle man,** he has to provide his bottles of whiskey with fancy labels that customers can use to identify his particular brand of spirits. He has to package his trademarked bottles of bourbon in cartons so that they can be transported to the buyer. In order to make wholesalers, retailers, and the public aware of his particular product, he also has to spend on some sort of advertising. When wholesalers and retailers demand his product, he either has to rent delivery trucks or purchase his own trucks. He then has to pay the wages of the drivers. To guard against losses due to theft or accident, he needs to purchase some form of insurance to cover these risks.

Before prohibition, businessmen supplied an estimated 100,000 tax gallons a year at the going price of alcohol. At this price, it was not profitable for businessmen to expand their production of spirits. But what happened to the supply of whiskey when producing and selling it became illegal? We all know that the whiskey well did not dry up despite the attempts of Congress to eliminate the source. Legislation against the manufacture, importation, and sale of alcohol merely changed certain aspects of the supply of that greatly demanded product. After prohibition, the cost of manufacturing and selling alcohol suddenly shot up. For example, any distiller faced the possibility of a stiff fine and/or jail sentence if he were caught continuing his production process. From 1920 to 1930 alone, property worth over $136,000,000 in appraised value was seized by Federal prohibition agents (71 of whom were killed while performing their duties).

One way to minimize the risk of being caught was to extend payoffs to the police and officials who were charged with preventing the illegal manufacture and sale of alcohol. In December, 1921— only one year after the start of prohibition—about 100 Federal agents in New York City were dismissed for the "abuse of permits for use of intoxicants." One New York speak-easy proprietor estimated that about 30 percent of his operating costs went for protection money to law enforcement agencies. Of course, it was no longer possible to buy insurance against the economic losses due to theft and accident. Apparently, the only insurance against theft was to pay off organized crime—the Mafia. Indeed, the Mafia's take in any individual's business dealings with alcoholic beverages was rumored to be substantial.

In brief, manufacturing and distributing spirits became illegal, the cost of doing business increased. The amount of alcohol that businessmen were willing to supply at any given price therefore had to decrease. Later on, we will translate this analytical description into lines on a graph denoting the relationship between the quantity supplied and the price that the product fetches in the marketplace. This will be the well-known *supply curve*.

The Demand Side of the Prohibition Picture

Even though the purchase and consumption of spirits became illegal after the passage of the Volstead Act, the demand for intoxicating beverages did not disappear. Before prohibition the demand for alcohol was dictated, at least in part, by people's preferences, their incomes, and the prices they had to pay for what they wanted to drink. Let's look at the aspect of price first.

We all know that the price of any product or service represents what we have to give up in order to purchase it. Give up what? you might ask. Someone buying a fifth of bourbon in 1918 would have to give up $2 of purchasing power over other goods and services that were then being sold. For the price of a single fifth of bourbon, our whiskey drinker could have

bought perhaps 12 bottles of beer, or two steak dinners, or five passes to the movies, or six new ties. The list of alternatives for the $2 purchase was large indeed. Since the higher the price, the more you have to give up of all other things, you usually find that when the price of goods or services is high, you buy less of it. This is true for legal as well as illegal goods and services. Before prohibition, the higher the price of alcohol, the less of it was sold. After prohibition, the same relationship continued to hold.

When discussing the price of anything, we should be aware of the different qualities of the same

product that can be purchased at any time. Before and after prohibition, different qualities of alcoholic beverages could be bought. Connoisseurs could perhaps tell the difference, and those who desired high quality alcohol would be willing to pay a higher price. Those who were not so insistent upon high quality would purchase cheaper spirits of a lesser quality.

Income was one of the other determinants of how much alcohol was purchased before prohibition. Usually, the higher people's income is, the more goods and services they demand. For some, when income goes up even a little bit, the quantity demanded

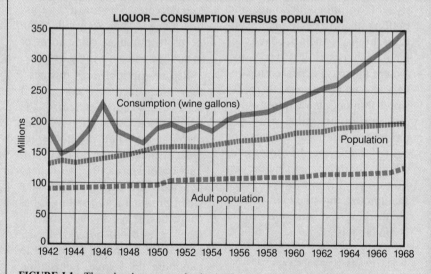

FIGURE 1-1 There has been a steady rise in liquor consumption since 1954. Because Figure 1 shows total consumption rising faster than population (the line is steeper), per capita consumption is increasing. Can you explain why so much liquor was consumed in 1946? (*Source:* Adapted from *The Liquor Handbook*, New York: C. Frank Jobson, 1969.)

jumps a lot. For others, even when income goes up a lot, the quantity demanded doesn't change much at all. Historically we have seen that as incomes have been rising, per capita consumption of spirits has increased even more. This can plainly be seen from the accompanying graph.

A third determinant of the demand for alcohol is preference. People's tastes obviously determine what they prefer; but this statement is actually a tautology. It is always correct to state that tastes determine what people buy. If I happen to prefer alcohol very very much, I may decide to forego purchasing a large amount of other goods and services in order to satisfy my urge to drink. Even if my income is very small, I may demand a much higher quantity than, say, a multi-millionaire who can obviously "afford" many times over what I could consume. His preferences are such that he chooses not to purchase alcohol, even though he has the financial ability. Economists have very little to say about what determines taste. We have not come up with any generally accepted body of theory that explains how people form preferences, and consequently no attempt has been made in this text to present a theory of preference formation. It's a fascinating topic, but one which few economists feel competent to discuss. Economists can

assume that tastes or preferences remain constant, and then they can ask what happens if the price goes up or the income goes down. In this manner we are able to develop a usable predicting theory that tells us what to expect in the future.

When prohibition made consumption of alcohol illegal, certain of the determinants of the demand for spirits changed drastically. Costs that were unknown before prohibition suddenly faced the potential imbiber. When bourbon was legal, manufacturers advertised openly the various qualities that could be found in each individual product. The prices of different brands were well known and widely publicized. The courts upheld trademark laws so that consumers were fairly certain that when they bought a particular brand, it was made by the same manufacturer. If the product was of high quality the last time it was purchased, it would most probably be of the same quality the next time. Any manufacturer attempting to sell low-quality alcohol would not be successful in such a situation unless he lowered his price accordingly to induce purchasers to buy his "inferior" product.

When prohibition came, no more advertising was in evidence. Brand names were not as numerous as before, and the possibility of fraudulent use of a brand

name was now very high. A distiller couldn't very well go to the authorities to complain about some other bootlegger using his brand name. In a phrase, the cost of information about prices and quality went up drastically after alcohol production and consumption became illegal. So, even if the price of a fifth of bourbon had remained the same, the actual cost to the imbiber went up because he was no longer sure about what he was buying. In fact, he risked the possibility of blindness or even death from drinking bootlegged liquor. Since information was so difficult and costly to come by, bootleggers could get away with producing an occasional batch of lethal bourbon—something that would have been much more difficult before prohibition. Competitors would have made sure that consumers found out about such behavior, even if bourbon drinkers didn't take the time to inform themselves.

Another cost to imbibers was the risk of being involved in a speak-easy raid. After all, consumption of spirits was illegal, even though the authorities did not arrest all whiskey drinkers during the prohibition period. In its first ten years, the enforcement of the National Prohibition Act resulted in about 550,000 arrests. One might ask which people were most likely to be caught in a speak-easy raid. Who were the people least able to find out about the best whiskey? Or, who were the people most likely to pay intermediaries to go to Canada to purchase high-quality Canadian whiskey? Obviously, we would not be surprised to learn that richer whiskey drinkers ended up with consistently high-quality bourbon and did not run a very high risk of being jailed for consuming it. As we shall point out on numerous occasions in this book, when the cost of information goes up, the people who suffer the most are usually those who are less well off. The poor are usually the ones who pay the most for our attempts to legislate morality.

The Final Outcome

What would economists predict as the final outcome? Would the price of liquor go up? Would the quantity demanded go down? Would society be better off? Very few things can be said with certainty in economics. However, predictive and analytical statements can be made with a high degree of reliability if qualifications are tacked on. We know that the cost of providing alcohol went up during prohibition because of the possibility of being fined or put in jail, because of having to pay off the police or Mafia in order to continue production or distribution, and because product differentiation was

made difficult by the impossibility of openly advertising specific brands. Hence, if everything else had remained the same, we could state that the higher costs of production and distribution would have resulted in higher prices for alcoholic beverages and less alcoholic beverages would have been demanded than before.

Everything else didn't remain the same, though. On the demand side the implicit price of purchasing spirits went up due to higher information costs and the possibility of being jailed or fined. In this case, if everything else had remained the same, less alcohol would have been demanded. We assume, for the moment, that income and preferences did remain the same. We see then that we could have predicted a *higher price* and a *lower quantity both supplied and demanded* of alcohol after the passage of the Eighteenth Amendment.

We have yet to answer the question as to whether or not society was better off after January 16, 1920. People whose values included strictures against inebriating beverages were probably better off just knowing that the Eighteenth Amendment and the Volstead Act had been passed. If, in fact, the quantity of alcohol consumed actually declined during prohibition these same people could have felt even more satisfied. If less consumption of spirits

led to higher productivity, less social unrest, fewer barroom brawls, and so on, then we could count these effects as benefits also. As for the costs to society, we must include the resources spent on increased law enforcement, court proceedings, and incarceration facilities. Also, we must not overlook the alcohol drinker's loss of happiness because of the smaller amounts that were consumed. This does not, of course, constitute an exhaustive list of the costs and benefits to society. Only after such a list is properly defined and some sort of evaluation method is applied to people's feelings can we come up with an answer as to whether society benefited by prohibition. Obviously, value judgments enter into these calculations in a very prominent manner.

Marijuana Prohibition

Cannabis sativa as well as numerous other "soft" hallucinogenics and euphorics are illegal. Even though our discussion is in terms of marijuana, it could equally apply to mescaline, psilocybin, dimethyl triptamine, tetrahydracannabinol, and a host of other drugs, but we'll reserve discussion of "hard" drugs till later.

Marijuana is one of the drug's many names. (The Bureau of Narcotics and Dangerous Drugs keeps a list of over 300 names.)

Produced from the Indian hemp plant, *Cannabis sativa*, marijuana has been known to man for 5000 years. Its first known mention is in a monograph written by the Chinese Emperor Shen Neng in 2737 B.C. Evidence suggests it was first cultivated for its fibers and used in materials for clothes. Its intoxicating effects were known, and the Chinese also used it as an anesthetic for surgery. Use was widespread by about the tenth century B.C. Herodotus, the Greek historian who lived from approximately 484 to 425 B.C., tells how natives of a region now in Siberia got high by inhaling smoke from hemp seeds thrown onto coals and hot stones.

Arabs invading Spain introduced marijuana to Europeans in the tenth century. It was used mainly by the Arabs, however, and when they returned to Africa its use died out. In the nineteenth century, the French brought samples of marijuana from Egypt, but then it was used only for experi-mental purposes by writers and scientists. The mid-nineteenth-century "Club des Hachischins," formed in Paris by poets Charles Baudelaire and Theophile Gautier, experimented a great deal with many forms of hashish and other drugs. In fact, Baudelaire's "The Artificial Paradise" as well as similar literature produced during that time was really not very popular until it was revived in this century during the emergence of the American drug scene.

Hemp was grown on American soil for its fibers as far back as the early 1600s, but use of mari-juana as a euphoric started in the 1910s and 1920s when many Mexicans came into the South-west. They grew cannabis for their personal consumption, as they had before immigrating. Apparently, the early American pioneers knew nothing of the intox-icating effects of cannabis, but many of the wagons they moved westward in were covered with cloth woven from hemp fibers.

New Orleans in the 1920s was the first large U.S. city in which marijuana was used widely. Sup-plies were shipped in from Ha-vana and Mexico. In the 20s and 30s, many crimes were attributed to the use of marijuana. The Fed-eral Narcotics Bureau instigated a big campaign to outlaw mari-juana, and by the mid-30s it was illegal in most states. The Federal Government in effect outlawed the drug in 1937 with the Mari-juana Tax Act.

State laws usually only prohibit possession or sale of marijuana. The Marijuana Tax Act of 1937 was preceded in every state by a marijuana statute—many of which were more strict than the federal law. The federal law didn't outlaw possession but enacted penalties for failures to pay $100-per-ounce taxes. However, in filing the forms (intention to purchase) to pay the tax, a person would incriminate himself under state law. In the case of *Leary vs. United States,* the act was nullified because of this "double jeopardy" Fifth Amend-ment feature.

Supply of Grass

What do we know about the cost of dealing in marijuana? For one, the risks are high and the penal-ties may be stiff. It is not surpris-ing, therefore, that the amount of profit that each particular seller of marijuana demands is ex-tremely high compared to the so-called markup on goods at grocery stores, for example. The price of a can of beans may be only a few cents more than the actual cost of that same can to the retailer. The price of a kilo of marijuana may be two or three or even four times higher than the wholesale cost. Since the risks of being caught increase with the amount of marijuana sold and since the penalties are higher for those who are caught in large deals, we would expect the markup to be highest at the bottom of the ladder of distribution. And that is exactly what appears to be the case. At the retail end, or the final rung of this ladder, street vendors selling their wares to occasional users, may impose a markup of only 20 percent. At the bottom of the ladder, however, where there is large-scale importation of marijuana from Mexico, the markup to the next highest level of distribution may be 500 percent.

Demand for Grass

Shifting now to the demand side, we find that the implicit cost of using marijuana is higher than the actual price paid for the illegal drug. Users run the risk of being caught by the authorities. Once that event occurs, there can be embarrassing court proceedings and the resultant fine and/or jail sentence. Notice here that the potential cost to any individual user increases as one's income increases. After all, if an unemployed "street person" is thrown in jail for smoking marijuana, he does not forego any income—except perhaps unemployment compensation or welfare checks. Moreover, having been caught using an illegal drug will usually not mean loss of a job for such a person if he or she happens to be working. On the contrary, a lawyer or doctor could stand to lose a large amount of income if put in jail. In addition, a lawyer would face disbarment, and a physician would lose his license. The long-run cost of such action could be as high as $100,000 or $200,000 because that person's next highest alternative income might be substantially lower than that of a lawyer or doctor. Economic analysis would therefore predict that higher income users would seek the services of intermediaries who would be paid to run the risk of obtaining the illicit drug.

Consumers of marijuana currently face relatively high information costs about the quality of the product they are buying. One does not see billboard ads advertising high quality grass. Competition among suppliers does not necessarily force out of the market those who distribute a poor grade of *Cannabis sativa*. That is not to say that poor quality stuff can fetch as much money as high quality marijuana. Rather, we expect to find a fairly large *variation* in the price charged for any particular quality in question. In a market with perfect information, only one price will prevail at a point in time for a given quality of the product and a given quantity (correcting, of course, for transportation charges). When the available information is poor, the suppliers are able to charge dif-

 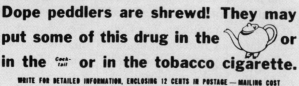

ferent prices in different parts of the market for a product of the same quality.

Legalization

What can an economist predict about the future if the sale and use of marijuana is legalized? We can merely state the reverse of the situation with alcohol during prohibition. After legalization of marijuana, we expect that the quantity supplied (at all prices that might prevail in the marketplace) would increase. The reason we expect the supply to increase is because the cost of doing business will fall. There will no longer be any risk involved. Additionally, we might expect that some economies of scale would be realized in at least the distribution of the product if not also the production. Suppliers could also provide information to consumers at a much lower cost than when marijuana was illegal. Advertising would be in evidence just as different brands of spirits are currently advertised.

The quantity demanded (at all prices) would also increase, most likely, because the actual cost of consuming the product would fall. This would partly be due to the elimination of the risk of being caught in an illegal activity. Also, as mentioned, the cost of obtaining information on the quality of the product would fall. The prob-

ability of buying really bad grass would be reduced.

What about the price of the product itself? We can predict with much certainty that the price will go down after the legalization of the drug. The forces tending to cause this decrease are on the supply side where larger quantities will be supplied than before. Since the actual cost involved in producing and distributing marijuana on a large scale are extremely small relative to the current price per unit, most economists would predict an eventual fall in the retail price after legalization occurred. As concerns legal products on the market, the long-run competition among suppliers (and demanders) eventually forces the price down to a point that more or less reflects the cost of production, including a competitive rate of return for the people investing in the business in question. This would also be the case with marijuana production and distribution. After legalization, we might hypothesize that the price would be close to what cigarettes cost today. The price might even be lower because tobacco production and sales are restricted by government control, while tobacco prices are supported by the government. However, legalized marijuana could be saddled with very high taxes as are liquor and cigarettes in most states.

Would society be better or worse off if marijuana were legalized? The same answers that were given in regard to prohibition apply here. Ultimately, the values of the individuals in the society will determine the answer to this question. One group in the economy that feels it will certainly be hurt by the legalization of mild euphorics is the liquor industry. People in the liquor industry feel that marijuana and other euphorics are *substitutes,* in the eyes of consumers, for wine and whiskey. If that is the case, the increased availability and the probable reduction in price of marijuana will lead to a reduction in the demand for alcoholic beverages. People may substitute the former for the latter.

Other Illegal Activities: Prostitution, Abortions, Gambling

You should now have sufficient ammunition to tackle the analysis of other illegal activities. Let's take prostitution for an example. Before 1945, prostitution was legal in France. But in that year, a female French politician, Madame Marte Richard, demanded that all Paris brothels be closed. She claimed that the 178 licensed houses, 1600 prostitutes serving hotels, 10,000 pimps, and 6600 ladies of the night were under-

Campfire Girls

When the Italian Parliament eliminated legalized prostitution in 1958, hopeful reformers predicted that the oldest profession was at last on the verge of extinction in Italy. They should have known better. Prostitutes evicted from the "houses of tolerance" simply set up open-air brothels alongside major highways, and now they are more conspicuous than ever. Each night, the ladies of pleasure build bonfires to warm themselves and show off their wares, and they are attended by crowds of vendors hawking coffee, sandwiches, and condoms. Because the prostitution laws are vague and lenient, the police have had little success in their efforts to clear the roads. Now, however, imaginative officials in Como and Turin have found an effective new weapon. Instead of arresting the roadside prostitutes for soliciting, the cops use the bonfires as a pretext for charging them with air pollution. Streetwalking in Italy carries a maximum penalty of eight days in jail or a $3.30 fine. Air pollution is not only an easier charge on which to obtain a conviction; it also is good for a month in jail or a fine of $135.

(Copyright Newsweek, Inc., 1972. Reprinted by permission)

mining Parisian morals and health. She also estimated that the closing of the Paris brothels would make available at least 6000 rooms for students and those who were bombed out of their homes during World War II. Impressed by her statistics, the Municipal Council of Paris gave houses of pleasure three months to close down. Using an analysis similar to the ones already developed, what would you say happened to the supply of prostitutes? What do you think happened to the demand? How about the quality of the services rendered? Who gained and who benefited from Madame Richard's campaign against the ladies of the night?*

*These particular questions might best be discussed outside classroom hours.

To make sure that you've really mastered the analysis, try to analyze what would happen if laws against abortion were repealed. Currently, most states still have not legalized abortion, except under special circumstances. The price of an illegal abortion in many states still remains quite high—$400, $600, and sometimes even $1000. It was estimated that before abortions became legal on demand in such states as Alaska, New York, Hawaii, and Washington, more than 350,000 women were admitted to hospitals in the United States with complications resulting from illegal pregnancy terminations. The estimates of the number of women who died each year from illegal abortions range from a low of 200 to a high of over 1000. Physicians and others who perform abortions risk being caught by the authorities, and the possibility of court proceedings, fines, and jail is very real.

Women who have adequate financial resources could, and still can, fly to countries such as Sweden or Japan where abortions are legal. Today, women in states that do not yet allow pregnancy terminations can travel to states that do. We predict, therefore, that women from relatively well-to-do homes have legal abortions performed. Women from homes that are less well-to-do have illegal abortions. An economist would predict that the morbidity and mortality rates among women due to abortions would mirror the distribution of income—very few women from high-income families suffer the consequences of improperly performed abortions, whereas relatively larger numbers of women from low-income families end up being injured or die from malperformed pregnancy terminations.

What happens when there is abortion repeal? Who gains and who loses? Would quacks be completely eliminated if all states were to allow the performance of abortion? How will costs for information about the availability and quality of abortionists go down after abortion repeal? These are the kind of questions the study of economics can help you to answer.

Selected References

Anslinger, H. J., & W. F. Tompkins. *The Traffic in Narcotics.* New York: Funk & Wagnalls, 1953.

Schur, E. M. *Crimes without Victims.* Englewood Cliffs: Prentice-Hall, 1965.

Goode, Erich. "The Marijuana Market." *Columbia Forum,* Vol. 12 (Winter 1967).

Hall, Robert E. *Abortion in a Changing World.* New York: Columbia University Press, 1970.

Reuben, David. *Everything You Wanted to Know about Sex but Were Afraid to Ask.* New York: David McKay, 1969, Chapter 11.

Economics–A Relevant Social Science

THE PRECEDING ISSUE started us off on our study of economic analysis and demonstrated how economics can be applied to relevant concerns of the day. In the remainder of this book, we shall treat a few other issues which include, but certainly are not limited to, the problems of poverty, the farm problem, spiraling medical costs, congestion, zero economic growth, crime prevention, consumerism, advertising, rapid transit, air and water pollution, the bald eagle, the draft, public education, health care, and zero population growth. Some students may regard the preceding discussions of marijuana, prostitution, and abortion as trivial—not getting at the crux of the issue. True, we did not come out with a program for changing unjust laws against victimless crime. We did not talk about the sociological aspects of those issues. Not a word was said about how the world might be a better place if everybody ''turned on.'' In fact, we didn't really advocate anything. But that is exactly why economics is a relevant social science. Good analysis can allow economists to separate facts and hypothesized theories from the values and preferences of those who are presenting the arguments. This is especially important if one wishes to understand, for example, political platforms of candidates running for office. In the most recent presidential campaign in 1972, bread and butter issues occupied an important share of the time of all the candidates. Politicians have used economic issues as topics for legislative debate for decades.

Economic issues continue to be examined in the press, on radio and television, and in the halls of Congress. There is little doubt that the future will be any different. Economic issues and the economic aspects of supposedly noneconomic issues will, we can all agree, continue to be important and certainly relevant.

HOW WE ANALYZE—MODELS

We have talked about prohibition against alcohol and against marijuana. We have also discussed prohibitions against abortions and prostitution. A discussion of the effects of the Eighteenth Amendment and the Volstead Act was presented, and we then indicated that marijuana prohibition could be treated in a similar manner. The legalization of abortion and prostitution were also viewed as issues conducive to the same kind of analysis. If you were able to follow the discussion and apply the analysis to each issue (taking account, of course, of any differences in institutional arrangements, products, or services sold), then you have already learned the rudiments of a **model.** Don't be worried. Mastering the rudiments of a simple economic model does not mean that you will be forced to become so sophisticated in your model building that you end up thinking in terms of mathematical equations as do physicists and engineers. Admittedly, in recent years economists have perfected their models to such an extent that they have been able to express them in terms of mathematical equations. In fact, the first Nobel prize for economics was given to two econometricians, Jan Tinbergen and Ragnar Frisch. Their contribution to economic science involved applying mathematical economic models to the real world. But more on that later when we talk about predicting economic activity.

Assumptions

Let's just briefly see what kind of assumptions and behavioral postulates you accepted when you started thinking about a simple model to analyze the effects of abortion repeal. We know first of all that some notion of a demand and a supply relationship was utilized.

Demand. We said that the higher the price of a product, the *smaller* the quantity *demanded.* Peter Minuit purchased Manhattan Island on May 6, 1626 for $39—about 3.2 cents an acre. On his salary, he probably wouldn't have wanted to buy enough land for an outhouse if he'd had to pay present-day prices of $400 per square foot. We said that the higher the price of a product, the *larger* the quantity *supplied.* If the Brooklyn Indians had received $400 per square foot, they probably would have found more islands for Mr. Minuit. Lurking behind these two seemingly innocuous postulates are a good number of assumptions concerning the way people act in different situations. If you were to be presented with all of the formal apparatus underlying the demand relationship quoted above, you would probably stop learning economics on the spot. But we do not have to go through a half dozen seemingly unrealistic axioms in order to come up with the proposition that the higher the price, the less people want to buy. For the moment we will be content with pointing out that everybody is limited in the amount of money he can spend. Hence, even if people are irrational and don't really care about the prices of the goods and services that they buy, when the price goes up, some people are not going to be able to buy as much as before simply because their budgets will not allow it. They either have to cut down on their consumption of the more expensive good or cut down on the consumption of something else.

Supply. Turning to the supply relationship, we will be content to point out that, at higher prices, suppliers find it more profitable to supply more. They can increase their production, pay for the additional costs, and still show a bigger profit. If we assume that there are at least some suppliers who aren't doing business for charitable reasons but rather to make more money for themselves, then we know that they, at least, will increase production when higher prices indicate that they can make more money by doing so.

Information Costs. A third feature of the simple demand-supply model is **information**

costs, which are a part of what we generally call **transactions costs.** It takes time and money to get good information about prices and qualities of various products. Most models that are used in economics assume *zero* transactions cost. Hence, they assume *perfect* information—just as certain theories in physics assume a *frictionless* world. We know, however, that everything is not covered with grease. Physicists' models are, nonetheless, useful in analyzing the physical world around us. Economic models which assume *zero* friction are also useful in analyzing the economic world around us. Many times, though, the assumption of perfect information and, more generally, of zero transactions cost will get us into trouble.

Legalizing Marijuana

Let's take the example of using demand and supply to predict what would happen to the price of marijuana if it were legalized. If we assumed a frictionless world, we would predict that the price would fall immediately to about the cost of production and distribution, which includes a normal or competitive rate of return for people who invest their money in this endeavor. Armed with this economic prediction, suppose we went on to analyze the actual data—that is, the actual prices paid for marijuana *immediately* after it was legalized. To our surprise, we would probably find that the price had risen, not fallen. Did our economic analysis fail? No. The problem was that we were asking the wrong question. We analyzed data right after legalization but were implicitly predicting what would happen after time had passed for adjustments. In the period just after legalization, costs will be incurred by firms setting up in the new business. Not all entrepreneurs will be aware of the potential profits in this line of activity. There are positive information costs and positive transactions costs in the world in which we find ourselves. Demanders of marijuana would know immediately if they could purchase the drug with-

out incurring the risks of going to jail or getting fined. However, potential suppliers would not be able suddenly to start producing higher quantities just because production and distribution no longer involved the risk of arrest. Thus, the day after legalization, the demand would exceed the supply and the price would rise. Only in the long run, when things settled down to a more or less normal state of affairs, could we safely predict that the price would fall to its cost of production. Throughout this book, we will constantly be stressing information costs and transactions costs. We shall see that these are important aspects of many of the key issues of today such as unemployment and inflation.

THE INFAMOUS COMPETITIVE MODEL

Probably the most well known of economic models is that of **perfect competition.** Most likely, this particular model, so often used in economics, is the cause of much disdain for the dismal science. Everybody knows that perfect competition doesn't exist. For ages economists have been applying their models of perfect competition to real-world situations that just don't coincide with the unrealistic assumptions economists often use when making their conclusions.

Did you go along with the analysis of what would happen to the price of marijuana after it became legalized? If so, then you too were guilty of applying a model of perfect competition to a real-world situation. As we shall see in later chapters, a competitive model leads us to the conclusion that the price of any good or service will be equal to its cost of production. If we were to apply a *monopoly* model, however, we could not come to that same conclusion. Rather, we would predict that the price would be in excess of the cost of production. With other models, we could come up with other conclusions. There are many, many possible models that we can apply to any particular problem. The important thing to realize is that we are, in fact, applying a *specific* model. Further, we should be aware of which model it is. Often people will switch models in mid-stream; they start out, for example, with a competitive model that assumes zero transactions costs and part-way through the analysis switch to a monopoly model with nonzero transactions costs.

TAUTOLOGIES AND TRUISMS

Another pitfall in using models for economic or any other type of analysis is the possibility of merely stating a **tautology** or **truism.** Let's say we are trying to establish the reason why 500 students decided to take Introductory Economics this year. Suppose you wanted to use a model that recognized that people have different preferences. If you stated that the reason 500 students were taking Introductory Economics is because their preferences were such that they chose to take the course, the statement would merely be a tautology. We could analyze every conceivable action by every person in the world in the same manner, and we would always be right. It is meaningless to state that people do what they are doing because that is what they want to do, because their tastes are such, or because their preferences dictate such behavior. Predictions based on that kind of model can never be refuted, or disproved. Truisms may be useful devices for debating, but they will not allow us to understand better the world in which we live. Nor will truisms allow us to predict behavior when things in the economy change.

WHEN IS A MODEL USEFUL?

Just about anything that anybody says about the world can be put in terms of a model. The model may be psychological, sociological, physiological, biological, or economic. Nonetheless, it will be a model. Within any one discipline, different people will develop or believe in different models. For many centuries most people thought that the world was flat. Using this model, they predicted that if one sailed to the edge of the world one would fall off into space. Columbus, however, applied a new model. His model, or **theory,** postulated that the world was round. He predicted that one could sail around the world and would not fall off an edge because an edge did not exist. We all know how Columbus validated the new theory. He sailed and sailed and sailed and did not fall off any edges. In other words, he refuted the flat-earth model by empirical observation.

Most people have the impression that economics is not an exact science whereas physics, for example, is. We have the idea that physical laws are somehow immutable but that economic laws are not. It is difficult to realize that everything—and I mean everything—we postulate is really a theory or model. In some sense, there is no such thing as ''truth.'' Physical ''truths'' seem true only because the theories underlying them have proven to be extremely accurate in predicting future happenings. Moreover, we have been able to apply the theories of physics, mathematics, and biology to develop real concrete ''things.'' This is not the case as regards the theories of economics. Indeed, many people will tell you that applications of economic theories have resulted in disasters for society, not improvements. Hopefully, after using this book, you will think otherwise.

If we look through the history of physics, we will find that the theories or models which survive are those which have not been refuted, those which continue to predict physical phenomena with accuracy. In certain cases, competing theories are able to survive side by side because no one has come up with one theory that can simultaneously explain the two separate phenomena. A good example of this involves the theory of light. The quantum theory explains one observed phenomenon, whereas the wave theory explains another. Neither theory explains both.

Apparently, then, the usual criterion for judging the usefulness of a model or theory is how well it predicts. If a theory predicts incorrectly, it is usually not considered to be a useful theory—however elegant it may be. Conversely, many simplistic and inelegant models predict quite well. Therefore, many economists find these models useful. When you are presented with a theory that you regard as too simple, ask yourself whether the test of predictability makes the theory useful nonetheless.

One problem that is often presented concerning types of models involves the question of whether the model is only *one* part of the economy or *all* parts. You may think that it's always better to consider as many things as possible so that nothing important will be left out. We shall attempt to show, however, that it is often necessary and *desirable* to ignore many sectors of the economy when analyzing any single issue.

PARTIAL VERSUS GENERAL EQUILIBRIUM ANALYSIS

Up to this point, we have been very selective in our economic analysis of illegal activities. We have engaged in what is called **partial equilibrium** economics. We assumed that nothing else in the system was changing while prohibition was instituted and that nothing else would change if abortion laws were repealed. But, what does **equilibrium** mean? An example will help. You may have reached a point in your life where your equilibrium weight has been established. That is, given the amount of exercise you do every day and the amount of food you generally take in, your weight will maintain itself within a few pounds of what it currently is for a long time to come. Certain forces tend to cause your weight to drop—for example, any activity which uses up calories. Other forces tend to cause your weight to in-

crease—consumption of food. These opposing forces are cancelling each other out so that your weight does not change. If you have reached an equilibrium that is *stable,* you will remain at your current weight.

There are also *unstable* equilibriums. With a little dexterity, you can probably stand a pencil with an unused eraser on its end without touching it. However, if you blow on the pencil it will fall over. When it is standing on end, it is in an equilibrium situation, but the slightest forces will cause the pencil to fall and it will never return to this situation again without your help.

In economics, we talk a lot about equilibrium analysis. In fact, our models usually start out with everything in equilibrium. Then we ask what will happen if something in the system changes. Our models usually tell us that a new equilibrium will be established, and the equilibrium in question is usually considered to be stable. That is, any movement away from the equilibrium situation will put into action forces which will cause things to go back to equilibrium.

Partial Equilibrium

What does all this have to do with partial as opposed to general equilibrium analysis? To backtrack, we said that if grass were legalized, the cost per unit would probably fall to the cost of production. That was a **partial equilibrium** analysis. First of all, we anticipated that an equilibrium was already established and a new and different one would somehow be established after legalization. Second, we ignored everything else in the economy. We didn't talk about what might happen to income; nor did we talk about what might happen to the supply of liquor, the unemployment picture, the price of cigarette paper, the changes in the supply of French wine, and so on. Partial equilibrium analysis holds everything in the economy constant except the subject under examination. In many cases, this is appropriate. If we want to analyze the effects of a tax on Zig Zag Papers, for example, we can probably ignore everything else. We don't have to concern ourselves with the effects on the pulp industry which will, in turn, affect Zig Zag Paper manufacturing. Indeed, the production of Zig Zag Papers probably accounts for a miniscule amount of total pulp production.

General equilibrium analysis considers all sectors to be important, in principle. General equilibrium analysis recognizes the important fact that everything depends on everything else. But how many "things" does "everything" encompass? The answer is obviously an *infinite* number of things because that's what the world is made up of. In the absence of some super computer with infinite capacity, no analysis can take account of everything. Thus, general equilibrium analysis usually means that more than one sector of the economy is considered. In the following chapters, we will be attempting to look at several sectors at a time when we examine monetary and fiscal policy, unemployment, inflation, and so on. Nevertheless, we cannot say that our analysis will ever be truly general. That is a physical and mental impossibility. Even so, when using partial analysis, we should make sure that we do not ignore important relationships in our model that may arise from other sectors of the economy. Even when we are aware of omitting something that may be important, we can still leave it out of our analysis without significantly biasing our predictions if we are convinced that its effect is negligible. In many instances, if not all, only empirical evidence can determine which of the omissions might be significant.

POSITIVE VERSUS NORMATIVE—REVISITED

In Issue I, we made the distinction between positive versus normative economics. **Normative economics** involves value judgments whereas **positive economics,** in principle, does not. Normative economics should not play any role in the construction (at least in the earlier stages) of the

models and theories used in this text. If, for example, I start out with a *wealth maximizing* model, I am not stating even implicitly that the pursuit of wealth is a socially or individually desirable goal. I'm not saying that those people who try to get as much wealth or income as possible are doing the "right" thing. I am merely presenting a model, an engine of analysis. That particular model may prove useless in many instances. In others, it may work well indeed. In no case will it prove or disprove that wealth maximization is "correct" behavior.

Students sometimes get mad because economics seems only to concern itself with money or material goods. Students reading this book should already have a somewhat different opinion, however. As mentioned, we are going to deal with issues like crime prevention, zero population growth, ecology, and so on. Thus, the issues economics can deal with do not always involve material goods; some of the concerns that can be treated may be in the confines of sociology, psychology, and other noneconomic disciplines. Yet, there is no way to deny the fact that economic model building or economic theorizing generally involves variables that are expressed in monetary terms. This is not because economists are fascinated by dollars and cents, but rather, because our analyses are most easily explained in such terms.

Economists like to *quantify* because quantification lends itself to refutation. If you assert that the poor in America are being exploited, there is no way anyone can really refute you. However, if you say that the distribution of income in the United States has changed every year in such a way that poor people are getting an increasingly smaller percentage of total income, someone else can try to refute you with numbers. One can look at the different percentages of national income which are going to different groups of people through time and determine whether or not your statement is correct. In short, there is a clear cut way for anyone to test your assertion.

The point is that economics is a positive

science and, as such, does not pass judgment as to the goodness or badness of the behavior characteristics that are used in its model building. Therefore, don't be upset with economics because many of its theories assume that people prefer more income to less, that entrepreneurs will seek out investments which yield the highest rate of return, and that taxpayers will take advantage of tax loopholes. You may think that people should not act in such ways. The economist hypothesizing the theory may think similarly, but that will not prevent him from using such wealth maximizing assumptions. The economist reasons that he can predict events better with these assumptions than he can without them. The test of a model's usefulness is not whether it can predict how things *ought* to be; rather, the test of any model is how well it can predict the way people will behave and the results of that behavior. Any expression of how things *ought* to be is a problem for the political process. Nonetheless, by showing costs and benefits, economists still can serve a useful purpose by pointing out the effects of alternative policies.

Definition of New Terms

MODEL: a simplified representation of how the real world works. Models can be expressed by mathematical equations, geometric graphs, or simply stated with words.

INFORMATION COSTS: the time and money costs incurred in finding out about prices and quantities of various products. Information costs are also incurred in finding out about what products exist, who supplies them, and where they can be bought.

TRANSACTIONS COSTS: the general term applied to all costs associated with any dealings in an economic system. Information costs are part of transactions costs. Additionally, transactions costs include such things as the time and money involved in writing a contract in order to purchase a house.

PERFECT COMPETITION: the most well-known economic model in use. It assumes perfect information exists.

TAUTOLOGY: a statement which is always true, otherwise known as a truism. A tautological theory can never be disproven.

THEORY: another term that is used synonymously for model. A theory is a simplified representation of the real world.

EQUILIBRIUM: equal balance between influences such as supply and demand. A stable equilibrium is one where any movement away will be met with forces which will cause things to go back into equilibrium. Economists usually talk about equilibrium prices or equilibrium quantities.

PARTIAL EQUILIBRIUM ANALYSIS: economic analysis which ignores interrelationships among all of the different things in the economy. Partial equilibrium analysis assumes that everything else in the economy remains unchanged while the circumstances surrounding a particular good or service do change.

GENERAL EQUILIBRIUM ANALYSIS: this type of analysis takes account of the numerous interrelationships among things in the economy.

NORMATIVE ECONOMICS: economic analysis with value judgments.

POSITIVE ECONOMICS: economic analysis without value judgments.

Chapter Summary

1. Economics is a relevant social science because it allows us to separate facts and hypothesized theories from the values and preferences of those presenting a particular argument. While economic analysis cannot say how things ought to be, it can point out the costs and benefits of alternative social policies.
2. All economic analysis involves either implicitly or explicitly the use of a model or theory. All models or theories are based on certain assumptions which may be implicitly or explicitly stated.
3. Many models assume that there are zero transactions costs involved in the real world. Many times, this assumption is useful, particularly if we want to predict what will happen after people have been allowed sufficient time to adjust to a change in the economic environment.
4. Information costs are the most obvious of transactions costs. Information is an economic good. As such, it requires time and money to acquire.
5. Legalization of marijuana would not lead to an immediate reduction in the price of the product because it takes time for people to adjust; that is, transactions costs are not zero. Only after a sufficient adjustment period would we predict that the price of marijuana would fall to equal its cost of production and distribution.
6. The model of perfect competition assumes zero transactions costs. That is, it assumes perfect information.
7. Tautological models or theories can never be disproven and, as such, are usually useless.
8. The usefulness of a model or theory is oftentimes judged by how well it is able to predict. Physical ''truths'' are really just theories which have proven to be extremely accurate.
9. Partial equilibrium analysis in economics uses the convenient assumption that everything else in the economy remains constant while the situation surrounding the product or service in question changes. For example, when we examine the demand and supply of marijuana, we usually ignore demands and supplies of many other goods and services. We can contrast partial equilibrium analysis with general equilibrium analysis in which many interrelationships among different parts of the economy are clearly specified.
10. Economic models do not carry value judgments. If we find it convenient to assume that people seek to maximize their wealth, we are not even implicitly stating that the pursuit of wealth is a socially desirable goal. Economics is a positive science and does not pass judgment as to the social appropriateness of behavior characteristics that are used in model building.

Questions for Thought and Discussion

1. Can you think of any physical truths that are not theories?
2. Have you experienced the use of models in other social sciences such as psychology or sociology?
3. What aspects of your life do not involve transactions costs?

4. If you were to devise a model which predicted that every time there was increased sunspot activity there would also be an increase in unemployment in the United States, would you have a "valid" theory? What would you say if, in fact, you were always right—that is, your model always predicted when there would be increased unemployment?

5. "The legalization of marijuana would lead to a reduction in its price because many of the costs of doing business would be lower. Therefore, the government should get rid of the laws against marijuana." Is this positive or normative economics?

Selected References

Maher, John E. *What Is Economics?* New York: John Wiley & Sons, 1969.

Snider, Delbert. *Economic Essentials.* Pacific Palisades: Goodyear Publishing Company, 1972.

Markets and Microeconomics

W HY DOES A person buy less when the price is higher? What happens when there is a bad year for brussels sprouts? Why are emeralds so expensive? These are some of the questions dealt with in microeconomic analysis. Although much of what is discussed on the news and in the press concerns the vagaries of such aggregate problems as unemployment, inflation, and taxation, there is also a considerable amount of interest in microeconomic topics that deal with issues on an individual basis. In fact, some economists argue that to fully understand problems like unemployment and inflation, one needs a firm foundation of **price theory**—another term for microeconomics. Now that you've had a brief introduction to what models are all about, let's build a more detailed foundation so we can better analyze the issues around us.

MAXIMIZING BEHAVIOR

We have already mentioned one possible way to analyze people's behavior. This involved a wealth-maximizing model. It was pointed out that using such a model does not mean we necessarily believe everybody is selfish, brutish, or out to screw the world. Nor does the use of this kind of model carry with it any sentiment of praise or agreement on the part of the user. In short, the use of a wealth-maximizing model carries with it no *normative* implications. Rather it can be used purely in a *positive* economics manner. We use it to derive forecasts about behavior; we then go out into the real world and see if our forecasts come true. If they do come true with regularity, then the assumptions going into our wealth-maximizing model proved useful in our quest for better understanding in predicting the behavior of individuals and groups in our economy.

Real Income

An alternative way to look at the assumptions economists use for microeconomic theory is to consider that people will attempt to make themselves better off if given the chance. That is, we assume "more" is preferred to "less." Here, we are thinking in terms of more **real income**—increased ability to consume more rock concerts, cars, books, X-rated movies, and so on.

Generally the definition of real income is nominal income or money income divided by the price level. To be more realistic in microeconomics, our definition of real income has to be expanded to take account of nonmonetary benefits of certain behavior.

Psychic Returns

One way to describe these nonmonetary benefits is in terms of **psychic returns** to individual behavior. Let's take an example. Suppose you are looking at the incomes of Ph.D.'s who are teaching in business schools. Suppose you compare their average income with the income of similarly trained Ph.D.'s who are working in the business world. What if you find that the business types are making an income that was $10,000 more than the academics? Would you automatically say that the Ph.D.'s teaching in a business school are foolish, less qualified, not wealth maximizing, or unselfish? Not necessarily. First you must look at the psychic benefits accruing to those who teach in the business school, *in addition* to their money income. In fact, you could do a very careful analysis of the two different incomes, correcting for different hours of work, different lengths of vacations, different retirement plans, and so on; you would call the resulting difference the **psychic return** to teaching in a business school. Those psychic returns must be added into the real income ascribed to the Ph.D.'s in the business school.

The concept of psychic returns is very useful in comparing different people's behavior at a point in time. However, when trying to predict the actions of groups of people after economic variables have changed, we often ignore psychic returns or at least assume that they are constant. One thing which usually cannot be disregarded, however, is the institutions in which people must operate.

INSTITUTIONAL FRAMEWORK

Let's be content for the moment to use a wealth-maximizing model to predict people's behavior. We would be foolish to ignore certain facts. One might predict, for example, that people who wanted to maximize their wealth would simply take all the wealth they could get—that is, they would steal it. By leaving the analysis at this point, one would be forgetting an important institutional fact: there are laws against stealing, and there are policemen, courts, judges, and jails to enforce those laws. Once the institutional setting is fully understood, then and only then can we be fairly confident that our analysis will be valid. We realize there are institutional barriers preventing one from stealing whatever one wants. Those institutional barriers can be translated into the particular costs of engaging in the act of stealing.

In the introductory issue of this text, we found that the costs involved in selling marijuana are higher when the drug is illegal than they would be were the drug legalized. We accounted for those costs in our supply and demand analysis. The same could be true with stealing; we can call stealing an illegal activity and attempt to predict how much stealing people will engage in. If the cost of stealing went up (for whatever reason), there would be less of it. The cost of stealing might go up, for example, if the percentage of convictions or the percentage of apprehensions were to increase.

Most of our institutional constraints result from a body of law that has come about either through precedent—the common law—or legislation. The government affects many, if not all, of the institutional constraints on our behavior. We must recognize this, and, in fact, we will see that government institutions often put restrictions on possible behavior patterns that individuals and groups can engage in.

Not only are we faced with the problem of institutional settings, but also, in using any type of wealth-maximizing model, we must remember that one of the most important constraints of all involves the depletion of the individual's budget.

SCARCITY

It goes without saying that Americans live in an age of abundance. Many people have the notion that we are so rich as a nation we could easily eliminate poverty if we wanted to do so; some feel that most goods should be free and that if we only stopped making useless, obsolete products, we could all work less and have a better life. Even the titles of various books on the market suggest that scarcity is no longer a relevant topic for economic analysis.

Unfortunately (or, fortunately, if one wants to make a living as an economist), this is not the case. It is a truism to state that, at any moment in time, the total supply of goods and services is fixed. It has to be. It may grow over time, as it has done in the past several hundred years in the United States, but we're still faced with a problem of scarcity with respect to anything that has economic importance. Take, for example, your time. You only have so much time per day. Every time you decide to use some of it to read this book you automatically give up using that time for something else. Most goods, because they're scarce, are called economic goods. They may be inexpensive, but, since they're not free,

they are, by definition, scarce. If I use something, you can't use it. If you use something, I can't use it.

Free Goods

What about free goods, such as air? Fresh air has not been a scarce good. There has been so much of it relative to the quantities demanded by the population that everybody could have as much fresh air as he wanted no matter where he was. Air was a free good everywhere, and economists had nothing to say about it. On the other hand, physicists, chemists, engineers, and other scientists have always had a lot to say about air. When air became scarce, when the supply of pure air in polluted cities disappeared, economists then started to have something to say about it. Now you buy a whiff of fresh air in Tokyo for a quarter a shot. You must move to the country to breathe freely. The economist can now step in and apply his basic tools of supply and demand to analyze the situation, for, alas, pure air is no longer a free good.

OPPORTUNITY COST

Realizing the continual and eternal existence of scarcity will make it relatively easy to understand and to apply one of the key economic concepts that pervades this entire text—**opportunity cost.** This concept has already been mentioned in the introductory issue on illegal activities. There, we referred to the potential cost of going to jail. Someone who is making a high income would forfeit that income if he were incarcerated, whereas someone out of work would forfeit no income if he were jailed. The opportunity cost of going to jail in terms of lost income is higher for the high-income person than it is for the unemployed person.

What is the opportunity cost of sitting in an

economics lecture? Since you may not be working at some money-making job, you do not have readily available the opportunity to spend one more hour on the job and get one more hour's worth of pay. However, you do have available other opportunities, such as playing tennis, or swimming, or reading a book for another class, or drinking coffee in the student union, or listening to records. The fact is, you have lots of alternatives available to you, and you can measure your opportunity cost by figuring out the value you place on the *highest* alternative among your available choices. The opportunity cost of your time is equal to its highest alternative use value. Hence, opportunity cost is sometimes referred to as *alternative* cost.

The same analytical procedure applied to the opportunity cost of people's time can be applied to evaluating the true economic cost of materials, equipment, and all products in general. We can even apply this procedure to discovering the opportunity cost of money. First, let's look at products. What is the true cost of a $600 quadraphonic 160-watt RMS amplifier? The opportunity cost of the resources that went into making the amp. Certainly the opportunity cost to *you* is equal to that price, because the $600 represents exactly what you had to give up to purchase the amplifier.

Historical Versus Opportunity Costs

Let's suppose that the amplifier was imported from Japan, and suddenly the President put a surtax on all imported goods. The retailer has the amplifier on his shelf when the surtax goes into effect. Any newly imported equipment he buys from his wholesalers will have the surtax added on; the equipment will be more expensive to him, and he will raise his prices to you, the retail customer. But what should he do about the price of the amplifier that didn't have a surtax tacked on to it? It is true that he didn't have to pay the tax, but the opportunity cost of that amplifier to him is the amount of money he could receive for it. Since all imported equipment will be higher priced

because of the surtax, he knows that other retailers will be raising their prices. If he sells the amplifier at the old price, he will be basing it on **historical costs** instead of opportunity or alternative costs. That's fine for you if you happen to get to his store soon enough.

So much for literary examples. Let's turn now to some graphic analysis. Such analyses are necessary because they greatly simplify the steps one has to go through to analyze any given problem. And once the analyses are mastered, they become invaluable. We'll start off with the concept of opportunity cost.

THE PRODUCTION POSSIBILITIES CURVE

As stated, it is a truism that, at any moment in time, the total quantity of goods and services in the United States (or in the world, for that matter) is fixed. This fact, or truism, is at the basis of the idea of opportunity cost. Since the availability of goods and services is also fixed at any moment, one has to give up something in order to have something. Just about everything has an opportunity cost. We can graphically examine the opportunity cost of a good by looking at what economists call a **production possibilities curve.**

In the following example, we will try to determine graphically the opportunity cost of producing eight-track stereo tapes. We'll divide the economy into two parts. Eight-track tapes are one good, and everything else makes up the other composite good that can be produced. On the graph that we're going to construct, we'll arbitrarily measure the production of tapes on the horizontal axis and the production of everything else (the composite good) on the vertical axis. Look at Figure 2-1. The axes are labeled as described. A zero rate of production is at the intersection of the two axes. As we move up or out on either axis, we will be indicating higher amounts of production. We can easily determine the amount of production of either good that is represented by any particular

FIGURE 2–1

REPRESENTATION OF PRODUCTION OF EIGHT-TRACK STEREO TAPES AND PRODUCTION OF EVERYTHING ELSE

If the economy is at point Z, there will be 40 million stereo tapes produced and 60 million of the composite good. Point Z is a production point.

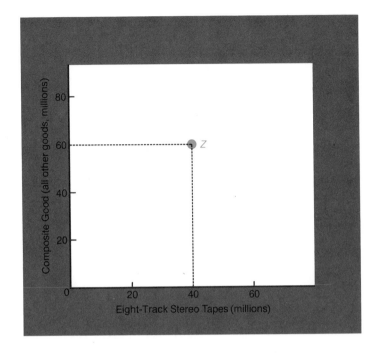

point inside the two axes. Take point Z, for example. If we drop a line to the horizontal axis, we see that it represents the production of 40 million tapes. If we move a horizontal line over to the vertical axis, we find that point Z represents a production of 60 million of the composite good. Of course, there's no way to figure out what that composite good is, or what 60 million of the composite good means, because you just can't add records and cars and cameras and clothes and everything else. The only way you can add them all up is to put prices on them. We will get to that in the example.

Let's assume it were possible to have the economy produce eight-track stereo tapes and nothing else. All the men and machines and materials in the nation would be set to work at this task. In Figure 2-2 we represent this as point A, 16.5 billion stereo tapes a year. Notice that in the last statement we added a time dimension.

Production always involves a time period. If the production time period is a week, we'll get a different figure than we would if it were for a year. For the moment, let's talk in terms of how much can be produced per year. Actually, in all of our graphs we should include the specific time period, although usually we don't do so because it will be understood. Point A represents one point on an entire production possibilities curve (schedule). It's an extreme point. Another extreme point is B, which represents how much of the composite good per year could be produced if *no* eight-track stereo tapes were made. Figure 2-2 shows this is equal to 20.4 billion of the composite good. What about the points that lie between A and B on the line we have labeled the production possibilities curve? After all, a line can be viewed as an infinite set of points. The production possibilities curve AB gives us an infinite set of possible pairs of production rates per year of eight-track

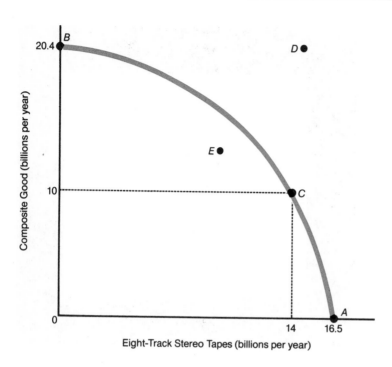

FIGURE 2–2

THE PRODUCTION POSSIBILITIES CURVE

The curve ACB represents the different production combinations of eight-track stereo tapes and of the composite good that are possible in the economy. Production is expressed on a *per year* basis. If all resources go into making tapes, 16.5 billion can be produced (point A); if all resources go into making the composite good (everything else), 20.4 billion can be produced. Point D is impossible because it lies *outside* the production possibilities curve. Point E lies inside and is therefore possible. It represents *unemployment* of our resources—men and machines. Point C lies just on the curve and represents maximum use of our resources while producing both tapes and the composite good.

stereo tapes and of the composite good. Let's look at one of those points—point C. We notice that when we move from point A to point C, the production of stereo tapes falls by 2.5 billion, whereas the production of the composite good rises by 10 billion. When we go from point C to point B, stereo tape production falls to zero, whereas the production of the composite good rises to 20.4 billion. By now you should probably be aware that opportunity cost lurks somewhere in the background.

What does it cost society to increase the production of stereo tapes from 14 to 16.5 billion a year? As seen on our production possibilities curve, the cost to society is 10 billion of the composite good. This, in other words, is the opportunity cost of increasing stereo tape output by 2.5 billion a year; this is what society has to give up. What is the opportunity cost of increasing production of the composite good from 10 to 20.4

billion per year? Obviously, it is 14 billion eight-track stereo tapes per year, or what society must give up.

The curved line AB in Figure 2-2 is sometimes referred to as the production possibilities *frontier.* Any point outside the frontier is impossible. Point D, for example, is unattainable at the moment in time for which the curve was drawn. There is no way the economy can simultaneously produce that much of the composite good and that many eight-track stereo tapes. Conversely, any point inside the curve AB (point E, for example) is always attainable. Point E, however, represents a situation of aggregate *unemployment.* The production possibilities frontier represents the maximum output society can produce. If production, nonetheless, is at point E, unemployed resources are being left idle in the nation. In 1971, for example, there were numerous unemployed resources: 6 percent of the population was without work and

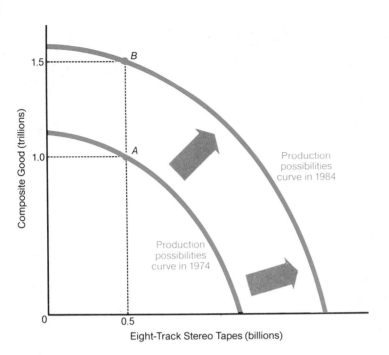

FIGURE 2-3

USING PRODUCTION POSSIBILITIES CURVES TO SHOW ECONOMIC GROWTH

The inside production possibilities curve is for 1974. At point A, 0.5 billion eight-track tapes can be produced, and 1.0 trillion of the composite good can also be made. Ten years later, in 1984, the production possibilities curve has shifted outward. Then, for example, 0.5 billion stereo tapes can be made along with 1.5 trillion' of the composite good (point B). There has been economic growth.

manufacturing was using its machines 80 percent of the time they could have been running. We were inside our production possibilities frontier.

USE OF THE PRODUCTION POSSIBILITY CURVE ANALYSIS

Besides being able to illustrate the concept of opportunity cost graphically, we can use the production possibility frontier apparatus to illustrate what economic growth means.

Economic Growth

Economic growth means many things to many people. In this chapter we'll define it as an increase in the productive capacity of the nation. We can easily demonstrate this with our production possibilities curve. Let's look at Figure 2-3. Assume

the economy is operating at point A, producing 0.5 billion stereo tapes and 1 trillion of the composite good. The production possibilities curve for the year 1984 is predicted to be to the right of that for 1974. This will be due to increases in technology, in the education of the labor force, and in inventions and innovations—to name a few determinants of growth. Since the production possibilities curve for 1984 is everywhere to the right of that for 1974, we know that we can produce more of both eight-track stereo tapes and the composite good. For example, we could continue to produce 0.5 billion stereo tapes and increase our production of the composite good to 1.5 trillion.

The way we have drawn the curves in Figure 2-3 is such that the increases in technology are equally favorable to the production of eight-track stereo tapes and the production of all other goods.

FIGURE 2–4

THE BUDGET CONSTRAINT FOR AN INDIVIDUAL

Here we are assuming that the choice for spending is between eight-track stereo tapes and drive-in movie pants. The quantity of drive-in movie pants is measured on the horizontal axis and the quantity of eight-track tapes on the vertical axis. We assume that the individual has $150 and that drive-in movie pants cost $15 a piece and eight-track stereo tapes cost $5 a piece. If he spent all of his money on drive-in movie pants, he could buy 10 pairs. That is, he would find himself at point A. If he spent all his income on eight-track stereo tapes, he could buy 30 of them; he would find himself at point B. Any combination between points A and B is possible. We draw a straight line, then, that represents the individual's budget constraint. He can be somewhere inside the line, such as at point D, if he wants to and have money left over for other things. (The individual at point D is not in equilibrium.) He cannot, however, be at point C. He does not have enough income to purchase 20 eight-track stereo tapes and 8 drive-in movie pants.

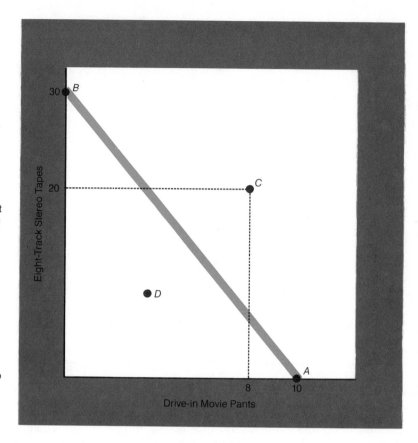

That is to say, we have shown a shift upward and outward of the production possibility curve that is equidistant at all points to the previous one for 1974. This type of growth is sometimes referred to as *balanced* because everything is affected equally.

Individual Constraints

Just as the economy faces a production possibilities frontier, a problem of scarcity—or whatever one labels our resource constraint—so, too, do individuals. You cannot spend more than your total income unless you borrow or unless you are given more income by some philanthropist. In any event, at a moment in time you certainly cannot spend more than your credit line plus what you

have in the bank and in your wallet. (You could, of course, sell some of your belongings.) You are faced with a **budget constraint.** Everybody, even the wealthiest man in the world, is faced with a budget constraint. Howard Hughes could not buy every single jet aircraft in existence because his budget would be exhausted before that. Rockefeller could not purchase all of the property in Manhattan because his budget would likewise be exhausted before that.

The Individual Represented Graphically

How can we represent an individual's budget constraint? We represented the society's budget constraint by a production possibilities curve for a specific time period. We can do a similar thing for individuals and construct their budget line. Let's do that for the trade-off between drive-in movie pants and eight-track stereo tapes. In Figure 2–4, drive-in movie pants are represented on the horizontal axis, and eight-track stereo tapes are on the vertical axis. We will assume that our slightly wacky individual has to decide between spending all of his weekly budget on one or the other of these two cherished items.

Let's say that he has at his disposal $150 per week. Drive-in movie pants cost $15 apiece. If he spent all of his money on drive-in movie pants, he could buy ten pairs; he would be at point A on the horizontal axis. Alternatively, he could buy eight-track stereo tapes. Let's say that they cost $5 apiece; he could, therefore, buy 30 of them if he chose to spend all of his $150 on eight-track stereo tapes. He would be at point B on the vertical axis. Point A and Point B are the two extremes. Anything in between those two extremes is also possible provided our individual does not exceed his budget constraint. The line between point A and B is the budget line—or, the budget constraint of our individual. He can buy any combination of pants and tapes represented by the points on that line. He can buy 21 tapes and 3 pants, or 8 pants and 6 tapes. Buying a combination on that line exhausts his whole budget of $150. He can also purchase any combination inside the line, such as D. In the inside area he will have money left over for other things.

Straight Budget Line. Why is the budget line for the individual straight, when the production possibilities curve in Figure 2–2 is bowed? The individual is such a small part of the entire situation that he cannot affect the price of eight-track stereo tapes or drive-in movie pants. The trade-off is the same whether he buys all pants or all tapes. He can get one pair of drive-in movie pants by giving up three eight-track stereo tapes. That's why the budget line is straight. The ratio of 3 to 1 remains the same no matter how many pants our individual wants to buy.

Another key difference, though, between the budget line and the production possibilities curve is that the line in Figure 2–4 represents consumption possibilities, whereas the bowed line in Figure 2–2 represents production possibilities. We could, of course, come up with a production possibilities curve for an individual, but we usually assume that most individuals work at one job. They don't try to decide whether they should work two more hours at being a pipe-fitter instead of two more hours at being a bank executive.

Outside the Line. Point C on Figure 2–4 is outside our individual's budget line. It is impossible for him to buy 20 tapes and also purchase 8 pants. His only alternative, if he wants to be at point C, is to acquire more income. He can do that, of course, by working longer hours, taking on an extra job, begging from his rich relatives, or getting a loan from some trusting banker. We'll discard the possibility of moving the budget line outward—getting more money—because that would involve changing the time span under consideration. Our budget constraint is drawn at a particular point in time, which is how it is being used in our analysis.

MARKETS—WHERE THE ACTION IS

Since the object is to find out how people react in different economic situations we shall concern ourselves with where people make their economic transactions. At this point, let's talk about markets in a little more detail. All economic transactions take place in a particular **market,** which is formally defined as follows:

A market for a good or service is the geographic area in which the price tends toward uniformity when that price is corrected for different qualities of the product or service in question and for transportation costs.

Let's take some examples to show how our definition of the market can be developed. Implicit in this definition is the idea of delineating a geographic location where the price of a good or service tends toward uniformity. Let's take potatoes. How big is the market? The production of potatoes in Minnesota may greatly affect what happens to prices and quantities of potatoes in San Francisco. Potatoes can be shipped all over the United States; in fact, we might say that the market for potatoes includes the entire United States.

What about the market for houses? They're rather difficult to move around. The seller's side of the market is obviously restricted to a small geographic location—measuring perhaps 100 feet by 50 feet in area. The buyer's market is much larger but, of course, not that large. Buyers may be looking over an entire city the size of Seattle. The market for homes in Seattle is therefore the entire city.

What about the market for stocks? Through the advent of low-cost (per unit), high-speed communications systems, the market for stocks (at least those listed on the New York Stock Exchange and the American Stock Exchange) is nationwide. Since the nation is connected with the rest of the world by similar communications systems, the market may be even extended outside our border. The buyer's and the seller's markets are probably about the same size, and that is very, very large.

Now let's go on to see the inner workings of a market.

Definition of New Terms

SCARCITY: a condition which mankind perpetually faces because at any moment in time total resources are fixed. Scarcity exists for almost all resources, including people's time.

FREE GOODS: goods which are not scarce, such as fresh air in the mountains.

OPPORTUNITY COST: the true cost of choosing one alternative rather than another. It is also called alternative cost. It represents the implicit cost of the highest foregone alternative to an individual.

HISTORICAL COST: the actual out-of-pocket cost for a good or service. Historical costs do not always equal opportunity costs. An example of historical cost is the cost that a firm puts down in its accounting statements.

PRODUCTION POSSIBILITIES CURVE: a curve depicting the maximum production possibilities for an economy at a point in time. It shows the trade-off between producing one good as opposed to another; sometimes referred to as the production possibilities frontier.

PRICE THEORY: another term for microeconomics.

MICROECONOMICS: that part of economics specializing in the study of specific economic units or parts of an economic system. In microeconomic theory we study individuals, firms, and households and the relationships between them.

REAL INCOME: generally defined as actual income divided by the price level or a price index. In microeconomic analysis we add as a factor in real income the psychic returns that individuals receive from things they do.

PSYCHIC RETURNS: nonmonetary benefits from individual behavior.

BUDGET CONSTRAINT: similar to a production possibilities curve but concerned with the consumption possibilities of an individual. The budget constraint is the maximum amount of purchasing power an individual has available.

MARKET: the geographic area in which the price of a good tends to uniformity when the price is corrected for different qualities of the good in question and for transportation costs.

Chapter Summary

1. We use a wealth-maximizing model merely as a means of analysis. There is no subjective value judgment placed on the assumptions implicit in such a model. When using a wealth-maximizing model, we assume that individuals and firms attempt to maximize their wealth or real income. They may, in fact, not be doing this or not even be thinking about wealth or real income. If our model is successful in predicting the behavior of households and firms, then we will find it useful, even though we may subjectively dislike the notion of wealth maximization.

2. A person's real income can be defined most generally as the purchasing power of his paycheck—that is, the quantity of goods and services he can buy with it. One's real income must be inflation corrected. One may also want to include the psychic returns that a person receives from a particular job; these are the nonmonetary benefits he receives. Psychic returns include all the joy and happiness that a person gets from a particular working situation. Psychic returns can also be negative, since a person can find his job very distasteful. His real income will be less than what it appears to be in such a situation.

3. Our analysis has to be couched in terms of an institutional setting. The most obvious institutional constraints result from legislation or common law. The government affects in very important ways almost all the institutional constraints on our behavior.

4. Just as the economy is faced with a budget constraint in the production of different possible types of output, the individual or household faces a constraint as to how much can be bought. The budget constraint is equal to the total purchasing power that an individual has. We usually define a budget constraint as the amount of income a person receives, but we could also add his borrowing capabilities and how much he could get if he sold some of his existing possessions.

5. In microeconomics the action takes place in markets. Markets are defined as geographic areas in which price tends toward uniformity.

Questions for Thought and Discussion

1. Do you know anybody who has no assets at all?
2. If you were to choose an alternative model for analyzing household and firm behavior other than the wealth-maximizing model, what would you choose? Why?
3. It is possible to calculate how much higher your income will be as a result of going to college and getting a college degree. Do you think the calculation will be accurate? (Hint: What about psychic returns from going to school?)
4. Can you think of institutional constraints on individual and firm behavior that are not a result of government?
5. Today many people maintain that the United States can produce so much that the basic problems due to scarcity are no longer relevant. Do you agree? Why?
6. If you were told that the wealth-maximizing model had been validated empirically, would you know what that meant?
7. Do you think human life is priceless? Why?
8. Does your answer to the previous question seem consistent with the way you empirically value your own life? What about society as a whole?

PHOTO BY JOHN AHEARN: BLACK STAR

ECONOMIC STATESMAN

John Kenneth Galbraith
Economist, Harvard University

JOHN KENNETH GALBRAITH is one of the most conspicuously public figures in American academia today, and probably the most widely read American economist. His two major books, *The Affluent Society* (1958) and *The New Industrial State* (1967), have become best-sellers. Through his writings, his work for the War on Poverty, and his commanding position in the American liberal community, Galbraith has been able to exert great influence on government economic policy.

Galbraith was educated at the University of Toronto and the University of California. He stayed in Berkeley through the 1930s as a research fellow studying price controls, both as an intrinsic aspect of the economy and as a part of government policy. After three years of teaching at Princeton University and two years as economic adviser to the National Defense Advisory Commission, in 1942 Galbraith moved to the Office of Price Administration, where he had his first taste of controversy. He later explained that most of the people around him based their ideas on an article he had written in the 1930s. He alone among them found fallacies in the article, and completely ignored it. He became so unpopular that, according to his own account, when Franklin Roosevelt accepted his resignation in 1943, "it was the most popular thing [Roosevelt] did that entire term." Galbraith then served on the editorial staff of *Fortune* magazine for five years. In 1948, he joined the faculty at Harvard University, with which he has been affiliated ever since.

During the Kennedy Administration, the President could not appoint Galbraith Secretary of the Treasury or chairman of the Council of Economic Advisers because Wall Street simply would not accept him. However, he did serve as ambassador to India for two years, where he earned a reputation as a friendly but extremely unconventional emissary who ignored State Department protocol at every opportunity. *Ambassador's Journal* (1969) is a delightful diary in which Galbraith records his attempts to hold off rampant Dullesism and the cold war mentality of the United States Information Agency.

During the remaining years of the 1960s, Galbraith moved comfortably into the most influential levels of the liberal Democratic establishment. He helped Lyndon Johnson plan the War on Poverty. In retrospect, he feels that there were two basic problems with the program: massive government aid should have been given to education and teacher-training programs, and the operating budget of the program was unrealistically low. In 1967, Galbraith became chairman of the Americans for Democratic Action, an organization which has been his major forum. He urged wage and price controls relatively early in the Nixon era, and when Nixon eventually came around on the issue, Galbraith called it a "triumph of circumstance over ideology."

One of Galbraith's major areas of interest has been the *de facto* death of the free enterprise system. The tendency toward risk minimization is an example of this process, along with government subsidy and contracting. During Joint Economic Committee hearings in 1969, Galbraith flatly stated that the major defense contractors were in reality public companies, thanks to extensive government contracting and the large amounts of government property they are allowed to use. Galbraith contended that many problems would be eliminated if these "public companies" were simply nationalized.

Galbraith is the major economist behind the view of American society as one with a highly active, expanding economy and a government willing to use fiscal tools for social-welfare purposes. He sees, in the future, the need for a well-planned technocracy to handle the economic and social consequences of technological events. In Galbraith's view, the economics profession and the society as a whole should look to the fact that our consumer-oriented society, with its concentration on accumulation, has expanded at the expense of public services. We should also examine the economic aspects of war, racism, and sex discrimination. Through it all, Galbraith has become used to waiting to see his ideas come into favor. As he once said, "I got a reputation for being unsound for urging things that now seem extravagantly trite."

What Makes a Market Tick?

L ET'S EXPLORE in greater detail those factors that determine how well a market functions. In a normative sense we say that a market functions well if the price of the product in question tends toward uniformity most of the time.

RIVALRY

One mechanism that causes the prices of different sellers to be equal is competition, or **rivalry,** among those sellers. As long as there are a few sellers out to make money, there will be some rivalry among them in the marketplace. How does this rivalry manifest itself? Advertising, whether truthful or not, is the most obvious form of rivalry. Advertising includes claims about the quality of the product and about the price at which the product will be sold. Rivalry shows up as each seller tries to undercut the price of the other guy. One might expect that sellers would keep undercutting each other until it would no longer pay—that is, until the price the seller asks is equal to what he paid for the article, plus just enough profit to keep him in business.

You may balk at this particular argument because you probably have observed many instances where sellers don't seem to be in competition. There are cases, of course, where competition does not exist, where the number of sellers is so small that, for all effective purposes, there is only one seller of the good in question. AT&T does not have too much competition in selling telephone service. We call AT&T a **monopoly,** or single seller. Later, an entire chapter will be devoted to discussing the special attributes of a monopoly market. For the moment, we'll examine a situation where there is more than one seller. Simply because you do not observe sellers competing through advertising or price cutting all the time does not mean that there is no rivalry. One might, in fact, ask individual businessmen whether they do compete and get a negative answer; this again does not mean that the forces of rivalry aren't operating. To see how these forces work, let's recall the distinction between average and marginal.

AVERAGE VERSUS MARGINAL

For rivalry to affect prices in a market, one simply assumes there is rivalry *on the margin;* that is, at least *some* sellers are trying to make more profits or get a larger piece of the action. These sellers will eventually force other sellers to toe the line.

Selling Textbooks

If some guy finds out he can sell textbooks at a lower price and thereby capture more of the market, he may go ahead and undercut every other textbook seller around. He will start getting a larger share of the market because some people—the marginal demanders—prefer to pay a lower price for a textbook so as to buy other things with the money left over. Our cut-rate seller will capture more and more of the textbook market. If other textbook sellers don't lower their prices, they will not be able to regain any of their former customers. Their profits will suffer. Some sellers may not be able to lower their prices and continue to make a profit; these are the most inefficient textbook sellers. Their production and selling costs are too high, and they may have to go out of business. The point here is that the action is on the margin. Only a few sellers need to be rivaling each other, and all other sellers will have to come around. Thus, don't be misled by some seller's apparent lack of interest in making more profits. There will be *others* who will undercut prices as much as possible.

Selling Records

Let's take another example. Say you're at a large university, and there are at least half a dozen record shops surrounding the campus. How long do you think any shop could continue to sell records, if the price charged were $1.00 more than the price at any other shop for exactly the same record? Not long. Indeed, it only takes one discounter to get the ball rolling. The discounter lets all the student buyers know that he's selling albums at cut-rate prices. If his rivals don't follow suit, he may take away enough of their business to perhaps cause them to go out of business. This is what business is all about, right?

THE MIDDLEMAN

Since we're on the topic of sellers, we should discuss the much maligned **middleman.** As the name implies, the middleman is a guy who comes in the middle of a transaction. Instead of selling directly to you, the consumer, a producer sells to a middleman who then sells the product to you. Many cooperative movements in the United States have attempted to eliminate the middleman's profits. For some reason, it is felt that anybody who merely buys a product from a producer and then sells it to a retailer is doing a disservice to his fellow men.

The Middleman's Functions

Believe it or not, the middleman may actually reduce the price of the product you want to buy. Let's look at the function of a middleman in the marketplace. The middleman takes the production of one or more suppliers; he stocks that production in a warehouse and then sells it in smaller quantities to individual retailers. He will set up a distribution system whereby he can service as many retailers as possible, providing those retailers with his wholesale goods and also providing them with information about those goods.

A middleman, therefore, serves the purposes of distributing goods and disseminating information about the goods in question. We usually find that both the producer and the retailer advertise the product. The wholesaler distributes the product to the retailer and also provides him with information about the product.

Gains from Specialization

There will always be room for middlemen in our society because there will always be gains made from **specialization.** Most people do not like to spend time doing things that other people can do better and cheaper. For example, if you wish to look for a job in your city, it may be to your advantage to go to a middleman who specializes in matching job openings with job applicants. We are referring here to an employment agent who is paid for matching up jobs with people. When you move to another city, you may employ the services of another middleman—a real estate broker. He matches up an available home with the description of the home you want to buy. Other middlemen match up produced goods with people who desire those goods. A producer typically finds that he can do better by specializing in the production of his good, while letting a middleman specialize in the matching up of the goods and the retailers.

The Middleman's Wages

Most of the profits that a middleman makes are really wages for his work. His work consists of matching different desires so that people will be better off. Producers desire to sell their products, and other people desire to buy the products. Since there are a multitude of products and different desires for different products, the middleman sector in the economy is very large indeed. By reducing information and transaction costs, middlemen are contributing to a more efficient economic

system that allows you, the consumer, to buy things at a lower cost than would otherwise be possible.

INFORMATION AND TRANSACTIONS COSTS

Let's go over the concepts of information and transactions costs once again. Every action has a cost; that cost is the opportunity cost or the alternative actions that could have been taken with the time or money or resources used. If you want to buy something, you may have to invest time and money in seeking out what you want. That is an information cost; this is a small part of what we call transactions costs, or those costs associated with exchanging property rights. The information costs associated with finding and buying a special type antique Model A Ford are probably relatively high. There simply isn't a very well defined market for Model A's these days. If, however, in another situation, you have good information about the product you want, then you will not have to invest money in obtaining any more information.

Stock Market

The best example of an item whose information costs to the buyer are perhaps the smallest of any market around is stocks. You can now press a button on a little computer outlet run off your phone and in one microsecond find out the going price of any listed stock in the big exchanges. The New York Stock Exchange will be presented as an example of a market with almost zero information costs in our next issue.

Apartment Market

Now think of a market that has very high information costs—the apartment market. It is literally impossible for you to find out about all of the available apartments in your price range without actually going to see them. You, the buyer, have to invest a lot of time and some money seeking out information so as to satisfy your desire for an apartment. Your opportunity cost is the cost you incur in obtaining that information. Your opportunity cost equals the value of the time you spend looking at apartments in its next best alternative. At the very least, you will lose leisure time—time for listening to tapes, reading, or anything else you might like to do—while you are searching for the *right* apartment. Therefore, any method that reduces information costs or transactions costs will benefit you by reducing either the amount of money or the amount of time you have to spend acquiring information.

Transactions Costs Reduced

A middleman reduces information costs to retailers. The wholesaler, or middleman, informs retailers about all of the prices of different goods he has in his warehouses. The wholesaler can tell retailers his opinions about the different qualities and so on. The wholesaler, therefore, allows the retailer to save time and money in finding out about the availability, quality, and price of various products. The wholesaler can also reduce other transactions costs to the retailer. For instance, he can ask the retailer to pay only one bill at the end of the month—even though the retailer may have bought 25 different products from the wholesaler. Had the retailer gone to individual producers, he would have written 25 different checks and kept 25 different accounts. Since the retailer has his costs reduced, in a competitive or rivalry situation, those reduced costs will be passed on to consumers in the form of lower prices.

Perhaps now you can better understand how the middleman reduces transactions costs—including information costs—and thereby allows products to be sold at a lower price. Note that if the middleman charged retailers more than he actually saved them, retailers would rather do

without him. Producers would want to do without him as well. Indeed, middlemen have existed from time immemorial, so we must conclude that their ''matchmaking'' services are more valuable than the price charged for those services. If this were not so, there would be today direct exchange between producer and customer, with no one in between. Sometimes this does occur but only for small businesses.

THE LAWS OF SUPPLY AND DEMAND

Demand and **supply curves** are the stuff of economics; we shall use them in our microeconomic analysis often; they are the bases for many predictions about people's behavior. First, let's discuss demand. Surely, a person's demand for underwear is rather different from his demand for radishes. How do we know what different demands might be? One way is by using a method called *utility analysis.*

Utility Analysis

Utility analysis is a method of talking about how people value goods and services. When referring to utility, we're not talking about a public utility, such as an electricity company, and we're not talking about the usefulness of a good or service. Rather, we're talking about the value that people *subjectively* place on things. Economists have coined the term **utility** for this type of value judgment. It is said that people gain utility from consuming the goods and services which they buy. Although we do not know exactly how to measure utility, we can still go quite a long way in our analysis without running into any problems.

Measuring Utility

Let's say we're going to measure utility in some arbitrary manner. The point is to make sure that something which gives more utility to a person

FIGURE 3–1

HYPOTHETICAL TOTAL UTILITY RELATIONSHIP

Here we have shown the quantity of beer on the horizontal axis and some measure of total utility on the vertical axis. Our total utility line is hypothesized to be straight up, equidistant from the horizontal and vertical axes. In other words, we are hypothesizing that total utility goes up and up concomitantly with the amount of beer consumed. This means you would continue to get additional utility from drinking more beer, no matter how much beer you had already consumed. Surely, this is quite an unrealistic hypothesization. (Isn't it?)

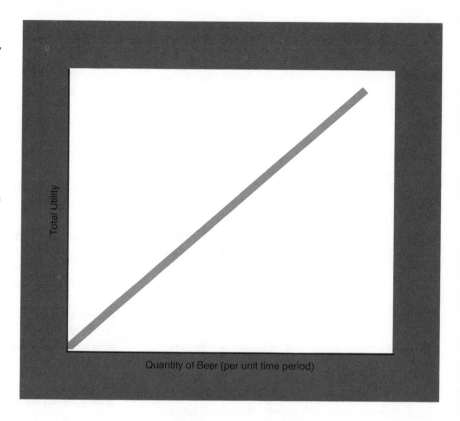

is measured as having higher utility than something else which gives less utility. Look at Figure 3–1. The horizontal axis in Figure 3–1 measures the quantity of beer. On the vertical axis, total utility is measured. We have drawn a straight line that goes up indefinitely. It is hypothesized that the **total utility** from drinking beer goes up concomitantly with the amount of beer that is consumed.

Marginal Utility

We know that Figure 3–1 is actually an unrealistic representation of people's valuation of beer. Suppose you're sitting at a tavern and someone is going to give you all the free beer you want for the next hour. You really savor the first gulp because it's such a hot day and your classes were

so boring. After you've finished the first stein, you're ready for the second. You may even like it more than the first because you're now slightly inebriated. But when you go to the third, your stomach starts to complain—as well as your kidneys. You still like it but less than the one before. Finally, when you get to the fourth stein, you can take no more. Only if somebody *pays* you to drink the fifth stein of beer, will you be willing to do so.

Here is a case where marginal theory can be applied. The first stein of beer had a very high **marginal utility;** that is, it caused a large *increase* in total utility. The second stein had an even higher marginal utility. Thus, for awhile, there was *increasing marginal utility* to beer consumption. After the second stein, however, the third one gave less utility and the fourth gave even less. There

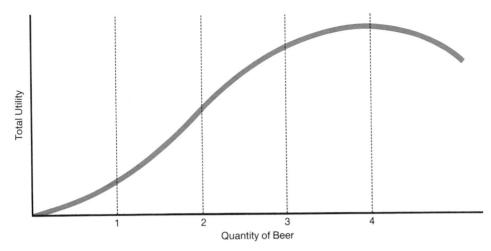

FIGURE 3-2 **BEER AND TOTAL UTILITY**

Here we show the total utility curve for the consumption of beer during an hour. At first the total utility curve is quite steep. After the second beer, it still goes up but at a slower rate. Finally, after the fourth beer, it goes down. The beer drinker is actually worse off if he drinks a fifth beer than if he didn't drink it at all, even if the beer were free.

was **diminishing marginal utility.** Finally, after the fourth stein there was *negative marginal utility*—you had to be paid to consume the fifth stein.

Graphic Analysis

Marginal utility can be represented graphically by translating our example of drinking beer onto

Figures 3-2 and 3-3. Figure 3-2 is total utility measured against beer consumption, and Figure 3-3 is marginal utility measured against beer consumption. Notice that the total utility curve slopes up until the fourth beer; after the fourth beer, it slopes down. This is because you get dissatisfaction or disutility from drinking more than four beers. Notice also that the total utility curve

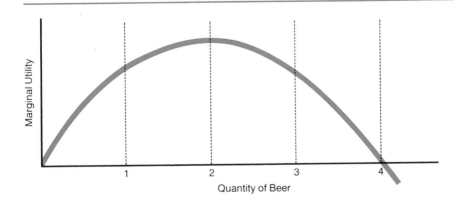

FIGURE 3-3

MARGINAL UTILITY OF BEER

Here we show the marginal utility derived from drinking beer during an hour. At first the marginal utility is increasing, but after the second beer it is finally decreasing. At four beers, it becomes zero; at the fifth beer, it would be negative and, of course, negative for any more after that.

FIGURE 3–4

HYPOTHETICAL DEMAND CURVE FOR BEER

Here we have drawn the quantity of beer demanded per month on the horizontal axis, and the price per six-pack on the vertical axis. The demand curve slopes down by virtue of the fact of diminishing marginal utility. At a lower price of beer, the last dollar spent on beer will yield more utility than the last dollar spent on economics books. In order to get the ratios in line with each other, our hypothetical student buys more beer. As he buys and drinks more beer, the marginal utility falls until the marginal utility of the last dollar spent on beer again equals the marginal utility of the last dollar spent on economics books.

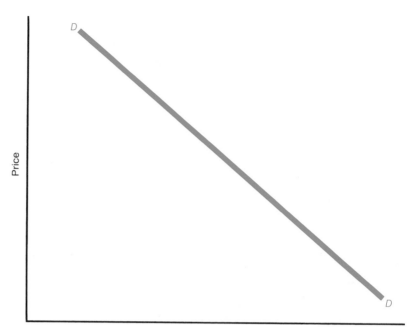

Quantity of Beer Demanded (per month)

goes up very steeply at first and then less steeply after the second stein of beer is consumed. The reason for this is that you get increasing marginal utility until your second beer, but after the second stein you get decreasing marginal utility, even though it is still positive.

THE DEMAND CURVE

How does the marginal utility theory fit in with a demand schedule? The answer is that it fits very easily. The hypothesis is that most people experience diminishing marginal utility after a certain point in the consumption of any good or service. When people are figuring out how to spend their money, they obviously buy things they want most —if, of course, they can "afford" them. Still, there has to be some way to compare the satisfaction received from one good with the satisfaction received from others. Using utility analysis we can

hypothesize that people will buy things they want in such quantities that *the marginal utility per dollar spent is the same for everything bought.*

Let's take two goods—economics books and beer. You have $50 a month to live on. You decide to spend $10.00 on economics books and spend the rest on beer. If you're happy (what else could you be with all that beer), then the marginal utility derived from the last $1.00 spent on economics books will exactly equal the marginal utility you managed to get out of the last $1.00 spent on beer.

What if the price of beer fell by half? Now that last $1.00 spent on beer will get you two six-packs instead of one. Unless you're just sick of beer, you'll get some additional utility out of that extra six-pack. Now the marginal utility per $1.00 spent on beer no longer equals the marginal utility per $1.00 spent on economics books. The marginal utility on beer is larger. How do you reduce it? By buying more beer. Since you're

FIGURE 3–5

INCREASING OPPORTUNITY COST OF STEREO TAPE PRODUCTION

We are faced with a bowed production possibilities curve. To obtain equal increases in tape production we have to sacrifice larger and larger chunks of production of the composite good. Here *BC = DE = FG;* in other words, the increases in stereo tapes are equal. But the cost of the first increase *BC* is only *AB,* while the cost of the second increase *DE* is *CD. CD* is larger than *AB.*

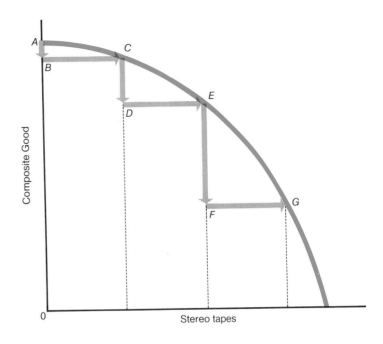

certainly getting *diminishing marginal utility,* all you need do to reduce that marginal utility is buy and drink more beer. Voila! That's one way of explaining why more of a good is demanded at a lower price. The demand curve slopes down, as in Figure 3–4.

SUPPLY

It's now time to complete our analysis by adding a supply curve. The supply curve is derived from the production possibilities curve. If the production possibilities curve is bowed, the opportunity cost of transferring productive capacity from the production of one good to the production of another good gets increasingly higher. Therefore, the only way to induce suppliers to supply more is to pay them more. Therefore, a larger supply will be forthcoming on the market at higher prices. An-

other way to look at it is that, at higher prices, producers will prefer to expand production even if it costs them more to do so.

To derive a supply curve, for example, of eight-track stereo tapes, let's go back to the bowed production possibilities curve shown in Figure 2–2. We recreate this in Figure 3–5. If no stereo tapes are being produced, we only have to give up *AB* to all other goods to get *BC* eight-track stereo tapes. The opportunity cost of producing *BC* stereo tapes is relatively small. But each time we want to produce more of them, the opportunity cost goes up and up. Otherwise stated, giving up equal amounts of all other goods yields smaller and smaller increments in stereo tape production. It should not be surprising, then, that producers want to be paid more before they will produce more eight-track stereo tapes, since the opportunity cost of production keeps going up.

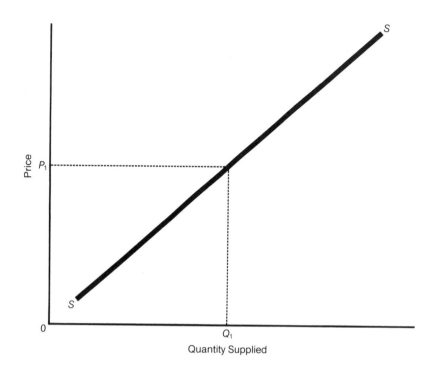

FIGURE 3–6

HYPOTHETICAL SUPPLY CURVE

The horizontal axis measures the quantity supplied and the vertical axis measures the price per quantity (measured in constant quality units). The supply schedule is upward sloping because the opportunity cost of transferring productive capacity from the production of one good into another good is increasing. Therefore, the only way suppliers can be induced to supply more is to pay them more. Moreover, at higher prices, producers will prefer to expand production even if it costs them more to do so. At a price of P_1 the quantity supplied will be Q_1. The supply schedule SS represents the minimum price at which a given quantity will be forthcoming.

We should note, however, that if the production possibilities curve were a straight line, we would be able to obtain successive increments in the production of eight-track stereo tapes without incurring increasing opportunity costs. In general, however, the opportunity costs of switching production facilities from one good into another is increasing. Hence, the only way to induce suppliers to supply more is to pay them more. Therefore, a larger supply will be forthcoming on the market at higher prices. Another way to look at it is that, at higher prices, producers will prefer to expand production even if it costs them more to do so. Our supply curve is therefore upward sloping as in Figure 3–6. Let's say that the price established in the market was at P_1. We see that P_1 intersects the supply curve at Q_1. In other words, the quantity suppliers want to sell at that price is Q_1.

PUTTING DEMAND AND SUPPLY TOGETHER

When we put supply and demand together, as in Figure 3–7, the **equilibrium price** is established at the intersection of the two curves. The underlying forces of supply and demand establish that equilibrium. At equilibrium, there is no tendency for anything to change. Demanders are happy (so to speak) with the quantity they're buying at that price; suppliers are happy with what they're selling at that price. Let's look at other points on the supply and demand diagram to find out why these points cannot exist for very long.

Excess Supply

Point *A* is on the demand curve, and, therefore, from the point of view of the demanders, it is an equilibrium. They're willing to buy that quantity and pay the particular price at point *A*. However, from the point of view of the suppliers, point *A* is not an equilibrium. Suppliers would want to supply more than the demanders wish to buy at that price. Thus, there would be an **excess quantity supplied** at point *A*. In order for suppliers to get rid of some of their extra goods, they will have to lower prices; or, alternatively, the demanders may offer a lower price to the suppliers

and still get the good they want. (Competition can work on both sides of the fence.)

Excess Demand

What about point *B*? Point *B* is on the supply curve, so there is equilibrium on the supply side of the market. At the price indicated by *B*, producers will want to supply the quantity represented by *B*. However, point *B* is at a price where people demand more goods than suppliers want to furnish. There is **excess quantity demanded.** Suppliers will find that their stocks of goods are running out faster than they anticipated; they will be able to raise their prices and still sell as much as they want to. Demanders, on the other hand, will be bidding against one another to get the available goods. They will bid the price up so that equilibrium (point *E*) is eventually established.

FIGURE 3–7

PUTTING DEMAND AND SUPPLY TOGETHER

We take the demand curve from Figure 3–4 and the supply curve from Figure 3–6 and put them together in this diagram. They intersect at point *E*, the equilibrium point. Point *E* represents an equilibrium not only for demanders but for suppliers. No other point on the diagram has such a property. For example, if we were at point *A*, there would be equilibrium for demanders—that is, they would be satisfied with paying that price to get that quantity of the good—but suppliers would not. At the price represented at point *A*, suppliers would be supplying more than demanded. Similarly, at point *B* suppliers would be happy, but demanders would be demanding more than they could get at that particular price; there would be an excess quantity demanded. If we are at point *A* or point *B* we will move toward the equilibrium point, *E*.

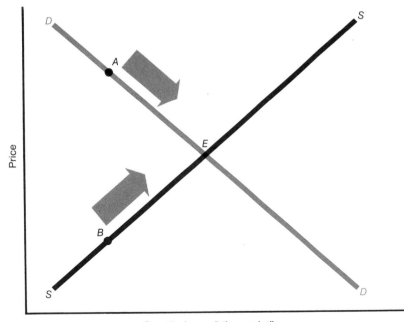

Quantity (per unit time period)

SHIFTING THE CURVES AROUND

Since we will move supply and demand curves around quite a bit in the following chapters, we had best reestablish an important point. *There is a difference between a movement along a curve and a shift in that curve.* Our diagrams are drawn in terms of prices and quantities and nothing else. This means that the demand and supply schedules are drawn while holding everything else constant. In economics you will frequently see the words **ceteris paribus.** This is Latin for "other things held constant." Suppose we state that when the price falls, the quantity demanded rises. Every time this statement is made, we should tack on *ceteris paribus* because the statement is strictly correct only when everything else (such as income, the price of other goods, tastes, technology, and so on) is held constant.

The Case of *Playboy*—Demand

Let's draw a demand curve for *Playboy* magazine. If the price were to fall from $1.00 an issue to 50¢ an issue, the quantity demanded would rise from a current circulation of, perhaps, 9 million per month to a circulation of 13 million per month. This is depicted as movement *along* a given demand schedule. (See Figure 3–8.) How would we represent a change in some outside factor such as income? Let's say that income rises by 50 percent. Wouldn't people buy more of everything, including *Playboy* magazine? In the aggregate, they probably would. We can show the effect on the sale of *Playboy* by shifting the demand schedule to the right. That is, *DD* will now move to *D'D'*. At the old newsstand price of $1.00 per issue, *Playboy* circulation would jump to 10 million per month. The increasing income shifted the

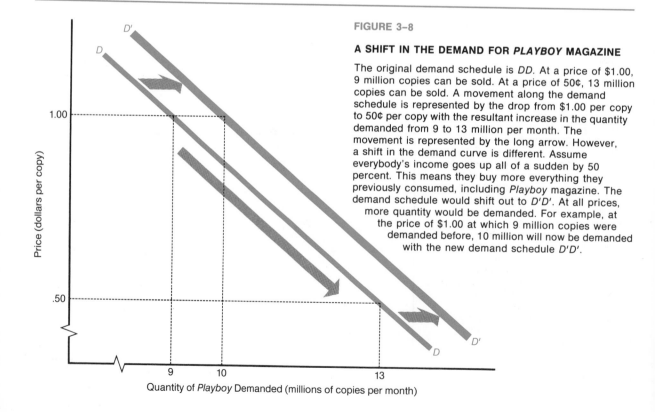

FIGURE 3–8

A SHIFT IN THE DEMAND FOR *PLAYBOY* MAGAZINE

The original demand schedule is *DD*. At a price of $1.00, 9 million copies can be sold. At a price of 50¢, 13 million copies can be sold. A movement along the demand schedule is represented by the drop from $1.00 per copy to 50¢ per copy with the resultant increase in the quantity demanded from 9 to 13 million per month. The movement is represented by the long arrow. However, a shift in the demand curve is different. Assume everybody's income goes up all of a sudden by 50 percent. This means they buy more everything they previously consumed, including *Playboy* magazine. The demand schedule would shift out to *D'D'*. At all prices, more quantity would be demanded. For example, at the price of $1.00 at which 9 million copies were demanded before, 10 million will now be demanded with the new demand schedule *D'D'*.

Price (dollars per copy)

Quantity of *Playboy* Demanded (millions of copies per month)

FIGURE 3-9

THE SUPPLY OF *PLAYBOY* MAGAZINE

The original supply schedule is *SS*. At a price of $1.00, 9 million copies will be supplied. If the price is raised to $1.50, 15 million copies will be supplied. The difference in quantity supplied represents a movement along a stable or given supply schedule, *SS*. The movement is from $1.00 to $1.50 with an increase of 9 to 15 million of quantity supplied; the movement is represented by the long arrow on *SS*. A shift in the supply schedule is different. Assume that the production costs for printing *Playboy* nudes has dropped by 10 percent. That means that Hefner can produce his magazine at a lower cost. The entire supply schedule will shift out to the right to *S'S'*. Now, for example, at a price of $1.00, instead of only furnishing 9 million copies to the newsstands, Hefner would be willing to furnish 10 million copies.

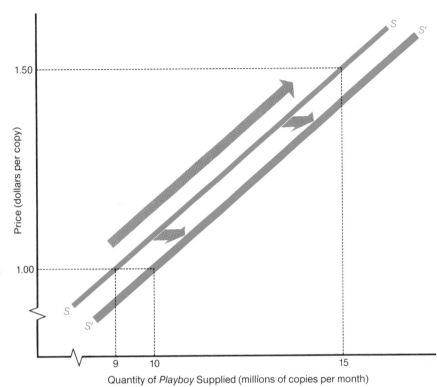

Quantity of *Playboy* Supplied (millions of copies per month)

demand schedule outward to the right. If there were a decreasing income, we would expect the demand schedule to shift inward to the left.

Let's take another situation. What if the price of *Penthouse* magazine, *Stag,* and all other soft-porn substitutes for *Playboy* increased, while the price of *Playboy* remained the same? Most likely, some people would shift their consumption pattern. Instead of buying *Penthouse,* they would buy *Playboy.* The demand schedule for *Playboy* shifts to the right when the prices of substitutes for *Playboy* go up. On the other hand, if the prices of substitutes for *Playboy* go down, we would expect the demand curve to shift inward to the left.

Supply for Playboy

Now let's do the same analysis on our supply curve. A supply curve for *Playboy* is presented in Figure 3-9. It is upward sloping. A price rise from $1.00 to $1.50 will increase the quantity supplied by Hugh Hefner from 9 million copies per month to 15 million. This is represented by movement *along* the supply schedule. Let's assume, however, that there is a breakthrough in the production process of soft-porn magazines. It is now possible to transfer full-color girlie pictures directly from the film negative to a printing plate, thus eliminating a large part of the cost of full-color reproductions for these magazines. This would in effect shift the entire supply schedule outward to the right. It would cost Hefner, say, 10 percent less on each magazine no matter how few or how many copies he printed. In order to make the same profit that he was making before, Hefner could accept a lower price for his magazines. Even at the old price of $1.00 there would

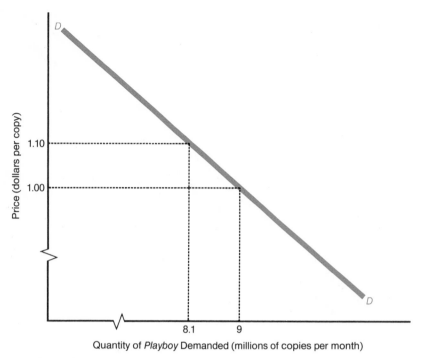

Price (dollars per copy)

1.10

1.00

8.1   9

Quantity of *Playboy* Demanded (millions of copies per month)

FIGURE 3–10

**DEMAND FOR *PLAYBOY*:
A BLOW-UP**

Here we show that at $1.00, 9 million copies will be demanded per month. A 10 percent increase in the price to $1.10 causes a decrease of 900,000 copies in the quantity demanded so that only 8.1 million are being sold per month. The price went up by 10 percent and the quantity demanded went down by 10 percent in this particular hypothetical example. Here the elasticity of demand is equal to 10 percent/10 percent, or 1.

be an increase in the quantity supplied by Hefner of, perhaps, 1 million copies per month. If, however, the supply of printing paper suddenly ran out and the only way to get paper for the magazines was to recycle it at a higher cost, a shift inward to the left of the supply curve might occur.

The importance of distinguishing between *movement along* a curve and *shifts in* a curve cannot be overstressed. You should always ask yourself which situation you are analyzing.

RESPONSIVENESS TO CHANGING PRICES

When referring to movement along a demand curve or a supply curve, we indicated that a change in the price would elicit a change in the quantity demanded and supplied. But how much

of a change in price is needed? The only way we can answer that question is by finding out something about the price responsiveness of demanders and suppliers. We would like to know how much people will change the quantity they demand or supply when there is a given change in the price.

Price Elasticity of Demand

Let's look at a blow-up (so to speak) of a small section of the demand curve for *Playboy* magazine in Figure 3–10. Here we're only looking at fairly small changes in the price. At the price of $1.00 a copy, the quantity demanded is 9 million. At a price of $1.10 per copy, the quantity demanded falls to 8,100,000. How do we relate the change in price to the change in quantity demanded? The easiest way to do this is to translate each of these changes into a percentage. The first maneuver is easy to figure out. A 10¢ increase in the price of *Playboy* represents a 10 percent increase over its original price (0.10/1.00 = 10 percent). The same is true for the quantity demanded. A 900,000 decrease from 9 million is equal to a 10 percent decrease in the quantity demanded (900,000/9,000,000 = 10 percent). Let's now put these two percents together into a fraction. We shall place the percentage change in quantity demanded on top and the percentage change in price on the bottom.

$$\left(\frac{900,000/9,000,000}{0.10/1.00}\right) = 10\%/10\% = 1$$

We end up with the number 1. But you may ask, one what? The answer is that it is a regular number with no dimensions. It is called the **price elasticity of demand.** We'll call it *e*. It is defined as the

percentage change in quantity demanded resulting from a percentage change in the price.

price elasticity of demand = *e* =

$$\frac{\%\ \text{change in quantity demanded}}{\%\ \text{change in price}}$$

To simplify matters we usually talk in terms of a 1 percent change in the price. Elasticity can also be thought of as *responsiveness*. How responsive are consumers to a change in the price of a product? In the above example, they are responsive to such a degree that a 1 percent increase in the price of *Playboy* will yield a 1 percent decrease in the quantity demanded.

Total Unresponsiveness

What if a 10 percent increase in the price of *Playboy* yielded no decrease in the quantities

---

FIGURE 3–11

PRICE UNRESPONSIVENESS FOR PLAYBOY

If people had to have their *Playboy* no matter what the price, the demand schedule would be represented by a vertical line, *DD*. Here consumers demand 9 million copies of *Playboy* per month no matter what the price is. The elasticity of demand in this case is zero. We say that the demand is completely or absolutely inelastic.

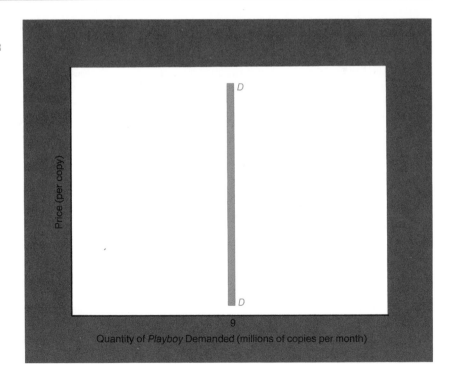

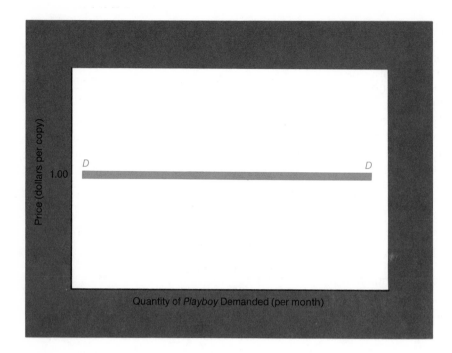

FIGURE 3–12

COMPLETE PRICE RESPONSIVENESS FOR *PLAYBOY*

Here we assume that even the tiniest increase in the price of *Playboy* will cause people to demand none of it. The demand schedule is a horizontal line at the price of $1.00. It is impossible to sell even one copy of *Playboy* at a higher price with this hypothetical demand schedule. There is total price responsiveness of demand. Here we say that the demand is completely or infinitely elastic.

demanded? Using our formula for price elasticity—that is, the percentage change in quantity over the percentage change in price—we come up with 0%/10%, which happens to be zero. If people are not at all responsive to a change in the price of *Playboy,* then they are exhibiting an elasticity of demand that is zero—total unresponsiveness. They can't do without *Playboy*. Raise the price as much as you want, Mr. Hefner, and you'll still sell the same number of copies.

We can represent zero elasticity of demand graphically. Look at Figure 3–11. Here we see that the demand schedule, instead of being the familiar downward sloping one, is absolutely vertical at 9 million copies of *Playboy* per month. No matter what the price is, people will still buy 9 million copies. Of course, this is an exaggeration; there aren't too many goods in the world that can exhibit a demand schedule such as the one in Figure 3–11. After all, at some point the budget constraint comes in. At some point, even if people are literally dying to get the good in

question, they won't be able to pay the price for it because they don't have that much income. However, many goods can exhibit elasticities that are very close to zero within a fairly small range of prices. A good example is heroin for a person who is physiologically addicted. Apparently, his demand schedule for a fix is perfectly inelastic within the constraints of his budget. He's got to have one.

Total Responsiveness

What if an increase of only 0.0000000001 percent in the price of *Playboy* caused circulation per month to drop to zero? We now see that the change in the quantity demanded has fallen from 9 million to nothing. Percentage change is, therefore, 9 million minus zero divided by 9 million, or 100 percent. When we divide the extremely small fraction, 1/10,000,000,000 percent into 100 percent, we come up with a very, very large number. In this particular case, the elasticity of

FIGURE 3-13

COMPLETELY ELASTIC SUPPLY

Here we have shown a supply curve, *SS,* which is perfectly horizontal and parallel to the horizontal axis. This supply curve shows completely or infinitely elastic supply. At the same price, an unlimited quantity will be forthcoming from suppliers. It is not necessary to offer them a higher price to get them to produce more.

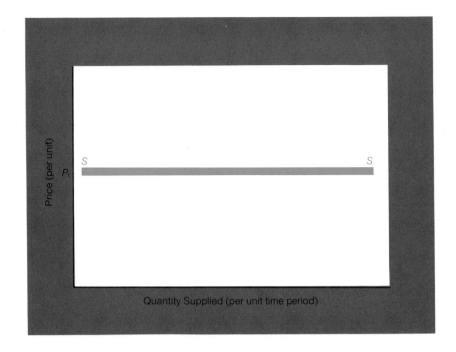

demand for *Playboy* magazine is extremely high. For our purposes, we'll call it *infinite.* The demand schedule for *Playboy* is now a horizontal line in Figure 3-12. Hugh Hefner can sell all the copies he wants at $1.00 per issue but he can sell *none* at a higher price.

The majority of demand curves in the world lie between the extremes of total *unre-sponsiveness* (zero elasticity) and complete responsiveness (infinite elasticity). Goods like automobiles, washing machines, and the like seem to exhibit somewhat elastic demands; that is, the elasticity is not infinite, but it's still greater than unity. Goods like food, wine, beer, and cigarettes seem to exhibit somewhat inelastic demands. Their elasticities aren't zero, but they're less than one.

A BRIEF RECAP

We've discussed several possible types of demand

price-quantity responses. It will be worthwhile here to categorize them in summary form:

1. A *unit elastic demand* exhibits a change in quantity demanded that is proportional to the change in price, but, of course, in the opposite direction.
2. A relatively *inelastic demand* exhibits a change in quantity demanded that is less than proportional to the change in price, and in the opposite direction. Here a 1 percent change in price leads to a less than 1 percent change in quantity demanded.
3. An *elastic demand* exhibits a change in quantity demanded that is more than proportional to the change in price and in opposite direction. Here a 1 percent change in price leads to a more than 1 percent change in quantity demanded.

Notice that we added "in the opposite direction" for each of these definitions. Elasticity of demand is always a negative number because we are assuming that the demand schedule slopes down; we also assume the quantity demanded is inversely related to the price—the higher the price, the smaller the quantity demanded; the lower the price, the higher the quantity demanded. Many times you will see elasticities of demand without a negative sign in front of them. In the preceding discussion, the elasticity of demand was put at 1 for unit elasticity. We really meant −1, but since we've always shown our demand schedules to be downward sloping, the negative sign is implicit. The estimated demand elasticities for *a few* selected goods are presented in Table 3–1.

ELASTICITY OF SUPPLY

The **price elasticity of supply** is defined in the same way as the elasticity of demand. However, all of our elasticities of supply will be positive: an increase in price will cause a larger quantity supplied; a decrease in price will cause a smaller quantity supplied. The formula of elasticity of supply, s, is the following:

$$\text{price elasticity of supply} = s = \frac{\%\text{ change in quantity supplied}}{\%\text{ change in price}}$$

If the elasticity of supply is 1, then we have a unit elastic supply. If the elasticity of supply is greater than 1, then we have an elastic supply. If the elasticity of supply is in fact infinite, we have a perfectly elastic supply, which we show in Figure 3–13.

If the elasticity of supply is less than 1, we have an inelastic supply curve. If the elasticity of supply is actually equal to zero, we have a perfectly inelastic supply curve which we represent in Figure 3–14. We can think of many examples where a supply curve exhibits perfect inelasticity. The most common example is the supply of land for all purposes. We know that we can make

TABLE 3–1

DEMAND ELASTICITY FOR SELECTED GOODS

Here we have obtained the estimated demand elasticities for selected goods. All of them are negative, although we have not shown a minus sign. For example, the price elasticity of demand for onions is 0.4. That means that a 1 percent increase in the price of onions will bring about a 0.4 percent decrease in the quantity of onions demanded. *Source:* H. S. Houthakker and L. D. Taylor, *Consumer Demand in the United States, 1929–1970* (Cambridge, Mass.: Harvard University Press, 1966); U.S. Department of Agriculture, 1954.

	ESTIMATED ELASTICITY
FOOD ITEMS	
White potatoes	0.3
Green peas, fresh	2.8
Green peas, canned	1.6
Tomatoes, fresh	4.6
Tomatoes, canned	2.5
OTHER NONDURABLE GOODS	
Shoes	0.4
Stationery	0.5
Newspapers and magazines	0.1
Gasoline and oil, Short-run	0.2
Long-run	0.5
DURABLE GOODS	
Kitchen appliances	0.6
China and tableware	1.1
Jewelry and watches	0.4
Automobiles, Long-run	0.2
Tires, Short-run	0.6
Long-run	0.4
Radio and television receivers	1.2
Sports equipment, boats,	
pleasure aircraft, Short-run	0.6
Long-run	1.3
SERVICES	
Physicians' services	0.6
Legal services	0.5
Taxi	0.4
Rail commuting	0.7
Airline travel, Short-run	0.06
Long-run	2.4
Foreign travel, Short-run	0.7
Long-run	4.0

FIGURE 3-14

COMPLETELY INELASTIC SUPPLY

Here we have shown a completely inelastic supply schedule, *SS*. It is a vertical line at the quantity *Q1*. No matter what the price, the same quantity will be forthcoming. Offering producers a higher price does not lead them to produce more.

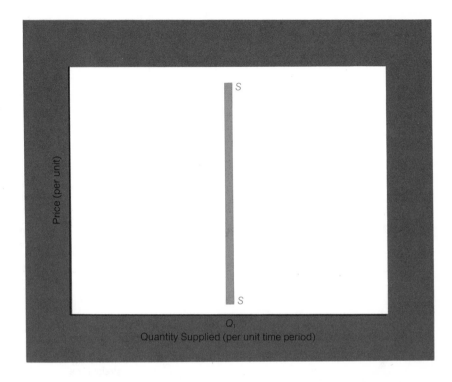

additional land by filling in San Francisco Bay and New York Harbor a little more, but we generally think of the amount of land as fixed. Any good or service that is fixed in supply has a perfectly inelastic supply schedule. The supply of fish is fixed when the boats come in and cannot get any bigger unless the boats go back out.

Can you think of cases where the supply schedule is perfectly elastic—that is, a horizontal line at a certain price as in Figure 3–13? You might be willing to sell up to 40 hours of your time at the same wage rate; if so, your supply schedule of labor hours might be horizontal at the wage generally paid to people with your education and skills. To make things even clearer, in Figure 3–15, we have presented a series of five demand schedules and five supply schedules. The figure shows the different shapes of schedules, as determined by their elasticities.

ELASTICITIES CAN AFFECT THE DEGREE OF PRICE CHANGES

For any given shift in one schedule, the elasticity of the other schedule will determine the resultant price change. Let's take the example of a stable demand curve for incense with a shift in its supply curve. If the stable incense demand curve is relatively elastic, it will have a much shallower slope than a demand curve which is relatively less elastic.

We should point out here that the degree of steepness of a demand curve or a supply curve is not, in and of itself, a measure of elasticity; elasticity is measured at a point, or at the very most, a small section of the demand or supply curve. We always talk, therefore, in terms of *relative* elasticities. We say that a demand or supply is relatively more elastic or relatively less elastic

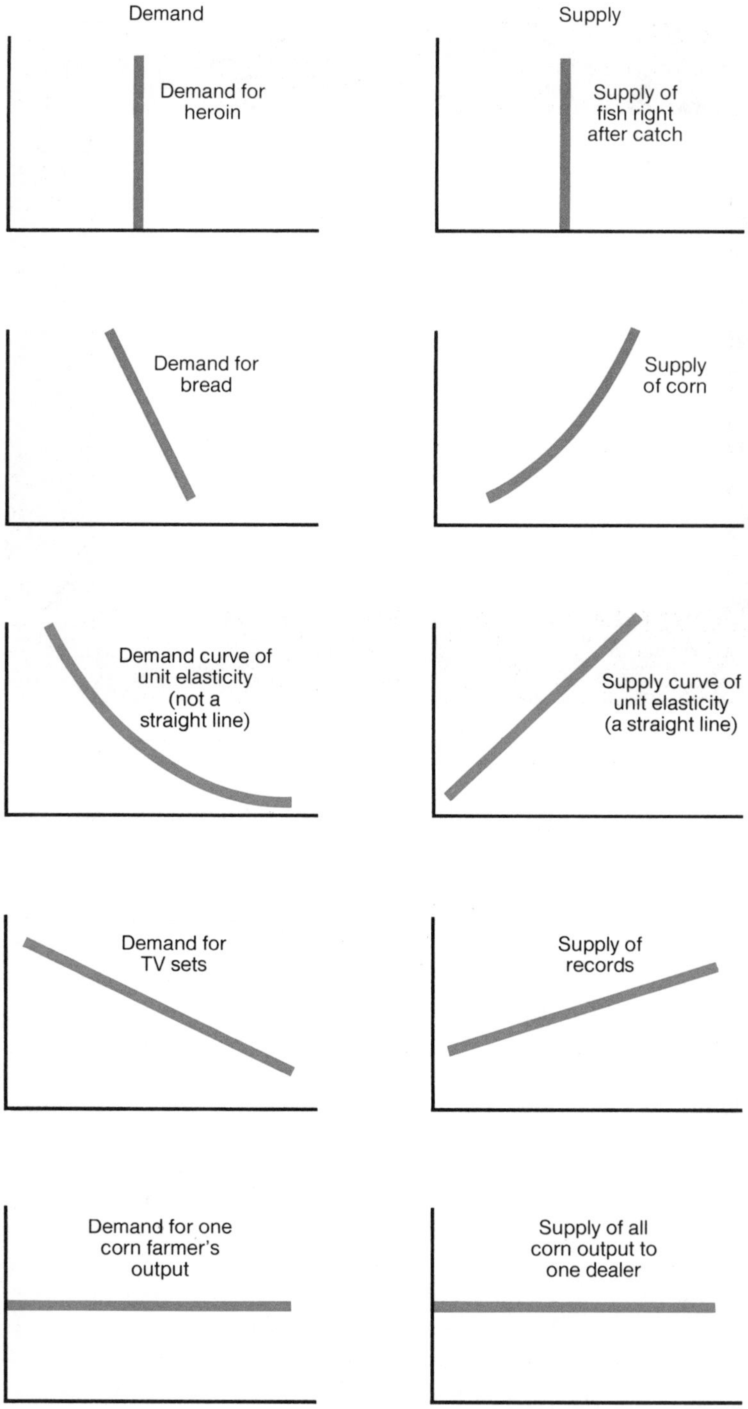

Demand	Supply
Demand for heroin	Supply of fish right after catch
Demand for bread	Supply of corn
Demand curve of unit elasticity (not a straight line)	Supply curve of unit elasticity (a straight line)
Demand for TV sets	Supply of records
Demand for one corn farmer's output	Supply of all corn output to one dealer

FIGURE 3–15

COMPLETELY INELASTIC DEMAND OR SUPPLY: The quantity demanded or supplied is completely unchanged despite any change in price. An example might be the demand for heroin by an addict, and the supply of fish right after it is caught.

RELATIVELY INELASTIC DEMAND OR SUPPLY: The quantity demanded or supplied changes less than in proportion to the change in price. For example, the demand for bread is probably relatively inelastic. We do not double our bread purchases if the price of bread falls by 50 percent. Another example for supply might be corn; the price of corn may double but corn farmers are unable in the short run to offer twice as much corn for sale.

UNIT ELASTICITY: The quantity demanded and supplied changes exactly in proportion to the change in price. The demand schedule here is not a straight line, although the supply schedule is.

RELATIVELY ELASTIC DEMAND OR SUPPLY: Changes in price result in a more than proportionate change in the quantity demanded or supplied. Many goods have elastic demand. Their sales increase dramatically when the price is lowered. Many items which are relatively easy to produce have relatively elastic supplies so that a small increase in price will bring a large increase in the quantity forthcoming from producers.

COMPLETELY ELASTIC DEMAND OR SUPPLY: Here quantity demanded or supplied at the going price is infinite. One example of this occurs in a situation where one farmer is a very small part of the market; he has to take the going price as given. At that price he can sell all the corn he can produce. On the other hand, if someone wants to buy a very small quantity of the entire output of the corn industry, that person can buy all he wants at the going price; the supply curve is horizontal.

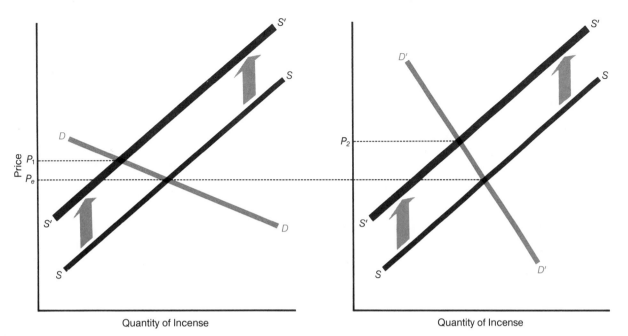

FIGURES 3–16 and 3–17 **RELATIVELY MORE ELASTIC AND RELATIVELY LESS ELASTIC DEMAND CURVES**

In these two diagrams we have shown two hypothetical demand curves for incense. In Figure 3–16 the demand curve, *DD*, is relatively more elastic than the demand curve, *D'D'*, in Figure 3–17. We start out in equilibrium with a supply schedule *SS*. In both diagrams the equilibrium price is P_e. Now the supply schedule shifts inward. (Perhaps there is a big labor strike in India.) The supply schedule is shifted to *S'S'* in both diagrams. That is, the vertical shift upward is the same as indicated by the arrows. There is a difference, however, in the new equilibrium price. In Figure 3–16, with the relatively more elastic demand, the price goes to P_1. In Figure 3–17 with the relatively less elastic demand (*D'D'*), the equilibrium price goes to P_2. P_2 is greater than P_1. For a given shift in the supply schedule, we see that the relatively less elastic demand will result in a higher equilibrium price.

than another one. Much of our discussion may be in terms of more steep or less steep supply and demand schedules, but that is really a simplified manner of analyzing relative elasticities.

In Figure 3–16, we show the relatively elastic demand curve with a given shift in the supply curve. In Figure 3–17, we show a relatively less elastic incense demand curve with the same shift in the supply curve. Both had equilibrium prices of P_e before the shift in the supply schedule. But notice that the increase in price due to the inward

shifting of the supply schedule when the demand curve is relatively more elastic is much smaller than the price increase when the demand curve is relatively less elastic. (See Figure 3–17.) That is, P_1 is less than P_2. *A price change associated with a certain change in supply will be greater when the demand is relatively less elastic than it will when the demand is relatively more elastic.*

Let's look at Figures 3–18 and 3–19. In the first figure we show a relatively elastic supply curve and in the second figure we show a relatively less

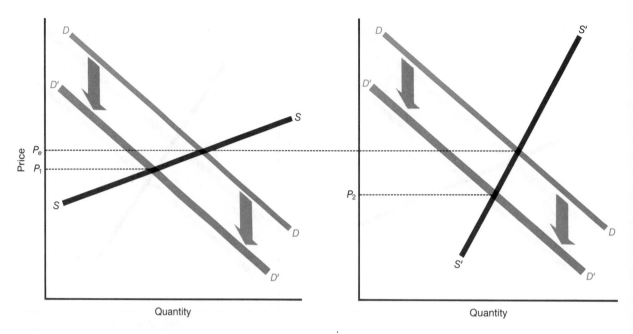

FIGURES 3–18 and 3–19   RELATIVELY MORE ELASTIC AND RELATIVELY LESS ELASTIC SUPPLY SCHEDULES

Here we have shown two hypothetical supply situations and given the results for a certain shift in the demand schedule. The quantity is measured on the horizontal axis, the price on the vertical axis. In Figure 3–18 the supply schedule is relatively more elastic than in Figure 3–19, where it is relatively less elastic. We start out with the demand schedule DD in both diagrams. The equilibrium price is the same in both diagrams, P_e. Now the demand schedule shifts in; there is a decrease in demand (less quantity is demanded at all prices). We show the equal shift by the arrows in both diagrams. With the new demand schedule, D'D', the new equilibrium price in Figure 3–18 is P_1; it is P_2 in Figure 3–19. We find that for a given shift in the demand schedule, the change in price will be greater if the supply is relatively less elastic. We see that in Figure 3–19 because P_2 is less than P_1 in Figure 3–18.

elastic one. For the given decreased demand, the price change is much greater for the relatively less elastic supply. (See Figure 3–19.) Another rule now comes up. *The price change that is associated with a given change in demand will be greater for a good with a relatively less elastic supply than it will be for a good with a relatively more elastic supply.* We should, therefore, expect to see greater price fluctuations in markets where demand or supply is relatively less elastic—and we do. We'll examine one such market later when we talk about farming.

THE LONG AND SHORT OF ELASTICITIES

Elasticities do not come out of the blue. In almost all cases, the only way we can discover the elasticity of demand or supply for a particular good is by looking at what actually happened in the marketplace in the past. That is, we have to look at real numbers. We have to come up with changes in quantities after there were changes in prices. Realizing this, we see that there are probably going to be different measures of elastic-

FIGURE 3–20

SHORT- AND LONG-RUN DEMAND CURVES FOR ELECTRICITY

Here we have drawn a supply schedule for electricity, *SS*. We have assumed that in the short run it is difficult to adjust to a change in the price of electricity. The demand schedule is therefore relatively inelastic as shown by *DD*. However, as time goes on, adjustments can be made. The demand schedule becomes relatively more elastic and pivots around to *D'D'*. In general, the longer the time allowed for adjustment, the more elastic demand will become.

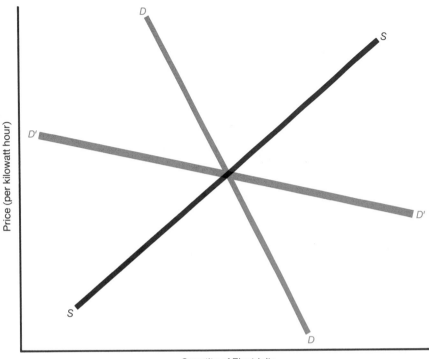

ity for different time spans. One would assume, for example, that a change in the price of the good will elicit a smaller change in the quantity demanded and supplied *immediately after* the price increase, than it would, say, after one year. One should distinguish, therefore, between *short-run* and *long-run* elasticities. Short-run elasticities are measured during the period immediately following the price change when people and firms don't have time for *complete* adjustments. Long-run elasticities are measured after people and firms have had time to adjust completely. In fact, we usually find that the demand schedule for a good in question will pivot and become more elastic if more time is allowed for adjustment.

Demand

Let's take an example. Suppose the price of electricity goes up 50 percent. In the short run, what is the only way you can adjust? You can turn the lights off more often; you can stop running the stereo as much as you used to, and so on. Otherwise it's very difficult to cut back on your consumption of electricity. In the long run, though, you can devise methods to reduce your consumption. Instead of using electric heaters, the next time you have a house built you'll install gas heaters. Instead of using an electric stove, the next time you move, you'll have a gas stove installed. You'll go out and purchase fluorescent bulbs because they use less electricity. The number of possible ways you can cut back on your consumption of electricity increase the longer you have to figure it out. We would expect, therefore, that the short-run demand for electricity would be highly inelastic, as exhibited by *DD* in Figure 3–20. However, the long-run demand curve may exhibit much more elasticity, like *D'D'* in Figure 3–20.

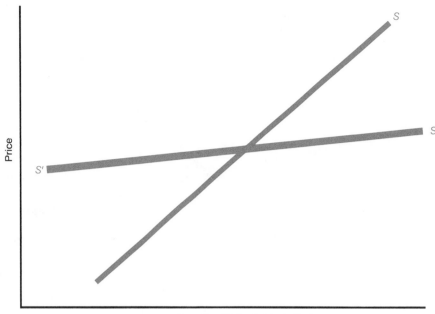

FIGURE 3-21

SHORT- AND LONG-RUN SUPPLY OF DRIVE-IN MOVIE PANTS

Here we assume that in the short run, the supply schedule for drive-in movie pants is *SS*. However, if given a long enough time to adjust—that is, if given enough time for new firms to develop and more plants to be built—the supply schedule may pivot around to *S'S'*, which is almost a horizontal line.

Quantity of Drive-in Movie Pants

Supply

The same holds for the supply curve. In the short run, the supply of drive-in movie pants may be fairly inelastic because there are only several manufacturers and they would run into increasing costs per unit of production if they tried to expand their production rate very fast. However, in the long run, more and more firms can enter the market. They might be almost as efficient as existing firms. The long-run supply curve for drive-in movie pants may nearly be the horizontal line *S'S'* in Figure 3–21. In fact, it has been asserted that in the long run, the supply curve for most manufactured goods is quite elastic because of the possibility of many new firms entering the market.

Once you distinguish between long-run elasticities and short-run elasticities, you will not be surprised to find that people's responsiveness to an increase in price is not very large immediately after the price change. As people learn to adjust and adapt to new methods of satisfying their wants, their responsiveness to the price increase will become larger. That is, the long-run elasticity of demand will be much larger than the short-run elasticity.

Definition of New Terms

RIVALRY: competition in the loosest sense of the term.
MONOPOLY: single seller of a product for which there are no good substitutes.
MIDDLEMAN: the man in the middle; the one who comes between the original producer of a product and the final retailer or consumer of the product.

SPECIALIZATION: division of activities where people end up doing more of one type of activity than any other. Complete specialization is when people do only one task. When there is specialization nobody can be self-sufficient.

DEMAND CURVE: a line showing the relationship between the prices for which a good can be purchased and the respective quantities demanded at those prices. The demand curve shows the maximum price for which a given quantity will be demanded.

SUPPLY CURVE: a line showing the various quantities that will be forthcoming from suppliers at different prices. The supply curve represents the minimum price at which a given quantity will be forthcoming; sometimes referred to as supply schedule.

UTILITY: a general term applied to the satisfaction people subjectively obtain from consuming a product or service.

TOTAL UTILITY: the total amount of satisfaction a person derives from consuming a given number of units of a product or service.

MARGINAL UTILITY: defined formally as the difference between total utility when consuming a given number of units of a good or service and total utility from consuming one less than that number. Marginal utility is the incremental utility derived from the consumption of a marginal amount of the good or service.

DIMINISHING MARGINAL UTILITY: marginal utility which is decreasing as consumption increases. Even though marginal utility may be diminishing, that does not mean it is negative. It is merely not going up in proportion to the number of units consumed.

EQUILIBRIUM PRICE: the price which clears the market, or the price at which the quantity demanded equals the quantity supplied.

EXCESS QUANTITY SUPPLIED: the difference between the quantity supplied and the quantity demanded at a price above the equilibrium price.

EXCESS QUANTITY DEMANDED: the difference between the quantity demanded and the quantity supplied at a price below the equilibrium price.

CETERIS PARIBUS: a Latin term meaning "all other things held constant."

PRICE ELASTICITY: a measure of the price responsiveness for a good or service, usually broken down into elasticity of demand and elasticity of supply.

PRICE ELASTICITY OF DEMAND: formally equal to the percentage change in quantity demanded divided by the percentage change in price. It is a measure of the responsiveness of consumers to changes in the price of a good or service.

PRICE ELASTICITY OF SUPPLY: formally defined as the percentage change in the quantity supplied divided by the percentage change in price. It is a measure of the responsiveness of suppliers or producers to an increase or decrease in the price of the product they are producing.

Chapter Summary

1. Because of rivalry in the marketplace, the prices of similar products tend toward uniformity. However, rivalry is never perfect. We may at any point in time observe different prices for the same product in different places.

2. Although the middleman is much maligned in the folklore of economics, he generally serves the purpose of minimizing transactions costs. He provides distribution and information presumably at a lower price than anyone else could. His profits are merely the wages for this work.

3. Information and transactions costs are important in market behavior. Nothing is costless. It takes time and sometimes money to acquire information about prices and

qualities of different products, where they can be bought, and from whom. Only in a frictionless world would there be no information costs.

4. It is sometimes useful to analyze household or consumer behavior in terms of utility analysis. We assume that people or households get a certain amount of utility from consuming different goods and services. Utility is a subjective measure. Nonetheless, we can talk about it in terms of marginal utility, which is equal to incremental utility from consumption of incremental units of a good or service. In general after some point people run into diminishing marginal utility of consumption. That does not mean, of course, that they should no longer consume any more of the good or service in question. If the price were zero, for example, they should continue consumption until the marginal utility actually becomes zero. Up to that point, the marginal utility is positive and greater than the cost, which we have assumed to be zero in this particular example.

5. It is sometimes useful to use marginal utility analysis to derive the demand curve for a good or service. Since we are operating in the region of diminishing marginal utility, if the price of a good or service falls, the last dollar spent on that particular good will buy more. The utility from consuming that good will increase. The marginal utility per dollar spent will increase. It will be greater than the marginal utility spent on other goods whose prices haven't changed. In order to make the marginal utility per dollar spent on all goods the same, more of the cheaper good is consumed. Because of diminishing marginal utility, increased consumption eventually decreases the marginal utility per dollar spent until equilibrium is again obtained. Thus, we see that more will be purchased at lower prices. The demand schedule will slope down.

6. If the supply schedule slopes up because of increasing opportunity cost of transferring productive resources into a particular good or service and also because at higher prices, it pays producers to produce more, even if their cost per unit of production goes up. They can still make a profit. When we put supply and demand together, the intersection of the two curves gives us the equilibrium price and the equilibrium quantity supplied and demanded. At equilibrium there is no tendency for anything to change.

7. At a price above equilibrium, the quantity supplied will be greater than the quantity demanded. There will be an excess quantity supplied. At a price below equilibrium, the quantity demanded will be greater than the quantity supplied. There will be an excess quantity demanded.

8. It is important to distinguish between a *movement along* a schedule and a *shift in* that schedule. If the price of a good falls, more of it will be demanded; we move down or along the demand schedule. However, if income goes up by, say, 50 percent, most likely more of the good will be demanded at all prices. This means there will be a shift in the entire demand schedule. The same is true for supply. However now, at a higher price, more quantity will be supplied. This is a movement along the supply schedule. If there is a new breakthrough in technology and it is cheaper to produce the good in question, more will be supplied at all prices. This is represented by a shift in the entire supply schedule.

9. We measure the price responsiveness of demanders and suppliers by elasticity of demand and supply. Price elasticity of demand tells us the percentage change in quantity demanded for a given percentage change in price (usually 1 percent). Price elasticity of supply tells us the percentage change in quantity supplied for a certain change in price (usually 1 percent). Price elasticity of demand is usually negative and price elasticity of supply is usually positive.

10. Two extremes of elasticity are completely elastic and completely inelastic. Completely elastic demand is such that, at the going price, an infinite quantity is demanded. A minute increase in price will eliminate completely the entire quantity demanded. On the other hand, with the completely inelastic demand, no matter what the price, the same quantity is demanded. On the supply side, a completely elastic supply schedule is such that at a certain price, an infinite quantity will be supplied. It is not necessary to increase price to elicit a larger quantity from suppliers. A completely inelastic supply is such that at no price will more quantity be supplied. A good example of this is fish when it comes in from the boat. No matter what the price is, the boatmen cannot offer a larger supply than they actually caught at that moment.

11. All the intermediate demands and supplies for most goods and services fall between complete elasticity and complete inelasticity.

12. Unit elasticity of demand or supply is when the quantity demanded or supplied changes in exact proportion to the change in price. Elasticities can affect price changes. For example, a given shift in the demand schedule for a relatively less elastic supply schedule will yield a larger change in price than it will for a relatively more elastic supply schedule. Moreover, for a particular shift in the supply schedule, a relatively less elastic demand schedule will yield a larger price change than would a relatively more elastic demand schedule.

13. It is important to distinguish between long- and short-run elasticity. Short-run elasticities occur immediately after a price change. Long-run elasticities occur after a time period in which adjustments have taken place. In some sense, a long-run elasticity is an elasticity measured after a complete adjustment (although complete adjustment is never possible in a changing world).

Questions for Thought and Discussion

1. Distinguish between the loose concept of competition that is equated to the notion of rivalry and the notion of competition which you had when you came into this course.

2. When cooperative grocery stores say they are eliminating the middleman and passing the savings on to you, what are they doing?

3. Many people are moving from the cities to rural areas and attempting to become self-sufficient in the production of food and clothing. Can you explain the reason for this "reverse specialization"? What would happen if everybody did this?

4. When you were deciding upon the university or college you wanted to go to, did you incur any information costs? What were they? Can you put a dollar value on them?

5. If you were to substitute one hour per week of listening to records for studying economics, would you be better off? If so, why haven't you already changed your activity schedule?

6. "I reached the point of diminishing marginal utility so I decided it was time to quit reading *War and Peace*." Analyze this statement. How would you change it to make it more accurate in terms of the way we have defined things in this book?

7. If it is true that the price elasticity of demand for heroin is, indeed, very low—if not zero—what happens when the government mounts a program to decrease the quantity of this illegal drug in the United States?

8. If the price of economics books went up by 100 percent, is there any way you could adjust your consumption of them?

ISSUE II

On Not Getting Rich

Making Money

You've probably heard of the infamous J.P. Morgan. He was supposed to have made his fortune by manipulating the stock market. You've also probably heard of men becoming millionaires overnight by making astute investments in securities. You may even have a parent who talks a lot about the stock market, follows the *Wall Street Journal,* reads the financial page of the local newspaper, talks about the prices of various stocks going up or down. Making money in the stock market seems as easy as calling up your stockbroker for the latest "hot" tips.

Getting Advice on the Market

If you want to run an experiment, try the following: look in your Yellow Pages under "Stock and Bond Brokers." Pick any one at random. Call it up. Ask to speak with a registered representative or an account executive. (In the old days, these guys were called "customers' men.") Talk to this broker as if you had, say, $10,000 to invest. Ask him for his advice. He'll probably ask you what your goals

are. Do you want income from your investment? Do you want growth in your investment? Do you want to take a chance? Do you want to be safe? After you tell him the strategy which you wish to pursue, he will proceed to tell you what the best stocks to buy are. If you ask him what he thinks the market in general will be doing over the next few months, he's bound to have an opinion, and an authoritative one at that. After all, if you want to know about what to do with your garden, you ask the man who runs the local nursery, right? If you

want to know about your car, you ask your local mechanic. That is, you seek out specialists in whatever you're interested in. Why not seek out a specialist, then, when you're interested in making money?

It may seem strange that you would waste your time and money seeking the advice of a stock broker concerning the stocks you should buy. But he is a specialist, and, in fact, you can get lots of useful information from him. He can tell you all about the stock market; he can give you quotes on all the different stocks—that is, what their prices are and how many of them were sold in the last few days and what the history

of the prices were. He can tell you about the various types of securities you can buy—common stocks listed on the big exchanges like the New York and the American, over-the-counter stocks that are sold only in very restricted sections of the country, preferred stocks, bonds, convertible debentures, puts, calls, warrants—the list goes on and on. A stock broker is the man you should ask concerning all these different avenues of investment. But he is not the one you should ask when it comes to which particular stock to buy. *The probability of his being right is no higher than the probability of your being right.* In fact, the probability of his being right is about equal to the probability of your being right. One might even take a dart and throw it at a list of stocks in the New York Stock Exchange and then pick those stocks which the dart hits. The reason behind this perhaps shocking revelation is that the stock market is the most highly competitive market in the world and information costs are perhaps the lowest of any market in existence. That is the key to understanding why any investment advice concerning *which* stocks to buy is in essence a fraud—a fraud, however, that is perpetuated by people who do *not* know that they are unable to do better than a random dart thrown at a list of stocks.

Some Facts on the Stock Market

The stock market is the general term used for all transactions that involve the buying and selling of securities issued by companies. What is a security? A security is a piece of paper giving the owner the right to a certain portion of the assets of the company issuing the security. Security is another name for stock. The most common of stocks are common stocks; these are called **equities.** A company may, for example, wish to expand its operation. It can obtain the money capital for expansion by putting up part of the ownership of the company for sale. It does this by offering stocks for sale, usually common stocks. Let's say that a company is worth $1 million. If the company wants $200,000, it may sell stocks. Suppose one man owns the company and he arbitrarily states that there are 100,000 shares of stock which he owns completely; he would then have to put out on the market about 20,000 shares of his stock which he would sell at $10 a share. He would get the $200,000 for expansion and the people who paid the money would receive 20,000 shares of his stock. They would have claim to one-fifth of whatever the company earned as profits.

There are many different submarkets within the stock market. At the top of the ladder are the big ones: the New York Stock Exchange and the American Stock Exchange. Perhaps 80 percent of the value of all stock transactions are carried out at the New York and the American. Then there are regional stock exchanges throughout the country. Then there is the national over-the-counter market and regional over-the-counter markets. These markets are somewhat less organized than the actual New York, American, and regional exchanges. The stocks are usually not traded as often in the over-the-counter market as they are on the big exchanges. Stocks in companies which are small and less well known than bigger companies are usually traded in the over-the-counter market.

Capital Gains and Losses

Stocks can go up and down in price. If you buy a stock at, say, $10 and sell it at $15, you make a **capital gain** equal to $5 for every stock you bought and then sold at the higher price. That is called an appreciation in the price of your stock which you realized as a capital gain when you sold it. If the value of your stock falls and you sell it at a loss, you have suffered a *capital loss* because of the depreciation in the market value of your stock. Some stocks pay dividends, but not all do.

Those that do pay dividends mail out checks to the stock owners. Normally when you buy a stock that has never paid a dividend, you expect to make money on your investment by the value of the stock going up. This is exactly what you would demand. If the company is making profits but not giving out dividends, it must be reinvesting those profits. A reinvestment in itself could pay off in the future by higher profits. The value of the stock would then be bid up in the market. Your profit would be by way of a capital gain rather than by dividend payments (current income from the stock that the company sends to you).

What Affects the Price of a Stock?

What affects the price of the stock? You might say that people's psychological feelings are the only things that matter. If people think a stock's going to be worth more in the future, they will bid the price up. If they think it will be worth less in the future, the price will fall. However, that is not a very satisfactory theory. What are psychological feelings based upon? Usually, such feelings are based upon the expected stream of profits that the company will make in the future. Past profits may be important in formulating

a prediction of future profits. However, past profits are bygones, and bygones are forever bygones. A company could lose money for 10 years and then make profits for the next 15.

If a company gets a new management that has a reputation for turning losing companies into winning ones, people in the stock market might expect profits to turn around and go up. If a company develops and patents a new product, one would expect the profits to go up. If a company has a record number of sales orders given to it for future months, one might expect profits to go up. Whenever profits are expected to rise, we typically find a rise in the value of the stock. That is, people bid up the price of the stock. Any information about future profits should be valuable in assessing how a stock's price will react. However, we mentioned at the very beginning of this issue that the stock market was a market in which information costs are incredibly low.

Public Information

Information flows rapidly in the stock market. If you read in the *Wall Street Journal* that International Chemical and Nuclear (ICN) has just discovered a cure for cancer, do you think you should rush out and buy ICN stock? You might, but you'll be

no better off than you would be by buying any other stock. By the time you read about ICN's discovery (which will mean increased profits in the future for the company), thousands and thousands of other people will have already read it. A rule that you should apply and one which will be explained several times in this issue is that *public information does not yield an above normal profit or rate of return.* Once information about a company's profitability is generally known, that information has a zero value in terms of being useful for predicting the future price of the stock. The only information that is useful is what we call *inside information.*

Inside Information

Suppose you happen to be the janitor at International Chemical and Nuclear? You make a habit of looking at some of the memos that are thrown in the wastepaper baskets. You've noticed recently there have been several memos about some miracle drug. Last night, you saw a memo that said: "Success! We've done it." The note was a bit crumpled, but, being nosey, you straightened it out; and now you have inside information. Assuming that the scientists and corporation officers who knew about this discovery didn't tell anybody else, you have some very valuable information.

You have it on the inside; no one else on the outside knows about it. You should go out and buy as many shares of ICN as you possibly can—borrow on your house; borrow on your car; borrow on your life insurance and anything else, because you're going to strike it rich. When other investors hear the good news later, they'll bid up the price of ICN, and you'll be able to sell out at a big profit.

Capitalization

True inside information is just that: it is information that is not generally known. Information that becomes public is *capitalized* upon almost immediately; people consider what it means for future profits and bid up the price of the stock to a level that reflects the future expected increase in profits. Information is discounted almost immediately in the stock market because it flows so rapidly. There have been studies on the value of information contained in the *Wall Street Journal* or the *New York Times,* and it turns out that this information is useless for assessing which stocks to buy. Even information about national or world events cannot tell you whether the market in general will go up or down. Reading that the Paris peace talks broke down does not give you any signals as to whether you should buy or sell in the stock market.

Studies have also been done on the profitability of information acquired by insiders in companies—that is, by corporate officers. Officers in a company are required to file statements of their transactions in their own company's stocks with the Securities and Exchange Commission, the regulator of the stock market industry. Statistical studies have shown that most of the time when insiders (corporation officers) sell their stocks, the price of the stock falls within 30 days. When insiders buy their own company's stocks, the price of the stock rises within 30 days. Obviously there is a value to having inside information. (Note that it is illegal for officers to tell outsiders any inside information which can then be used to make money in the company's stock.)

Hot Tips

What about the hot tips your broker might have? It is highly dubious that he will have inside information. After all, if it's really inside information, why would he be giving it to you? Why wouldn't he take advantage of it himself, get rich quick and quit being a stock salesman? He might get this information from his research department. Almost all stock brokerage companies have large research staffs which investigate different industries, different

companies, and the future of the general economy. These research departments issue research statements on different companies and industries in the economy. There are recommendations as to which stocks are underpriced and, therefore, should be bought. *The value of this research information to you as an investor is zero.* You will do no better by following the advice of research branches of your stock brokerage company than you will by randomly selecting stocks. This is particularly true for stocks listed on the New York and American stock exchanges. Nevertheless, the amount of research on those companies that is completed by firms, individuals, organizations, governments, and so on is indeed staggering. Since information flows so freely, by the time you receive the results of research on a particular company, you can be sure that thousands and thousands of other people have already found out. And since so many brokerage firms employ research analysts, you can be sure that there are numerous analysts investigating every single company that has shares for sale in the open stock market.

Why So Much "Research"?

Brokerage firms are in competition with each other. Their competition leads them to do research as thoroughly as possible. That means it is highly unlikely that the research one company does is going to be substantially better than the research any other brokerage firm does. In any event, even if a particular brokerage firm does do exceptionally good research, by the time you read it or your broker tells you about it, any information of value will already have been capitalized upon. That is, any information on the future profitability of the company would already have been included in the price of the particular stock. It will have gone up or down depending upon whether the information was good or bad. The price of a stock at any moment in time includes or is directly related to every piece of information that any potential or actual buyer has on the company or on competing companies in the economy. Again, information flows freely in the stock market. In a competitive market, you can't make money by taking public information and applying it to investing decisions. You can, however, expect to make a normal rate of return on your investment in the market. The normal rate of return seems to average about 8 to 10 percent per year if you randomly select some stocks and keep your money in them. This leads us to the controversial concept of the stock market as a random walk.

The Random Walk

What possibly could a random walk be? Think about your high school physics course where you talked about Brownian motion of molecules. They jumped around randomly. There was simply no way to predict where a molecule would jump next. This is exactly what happens when something follows a **random walk;** it goes in directions that are totally unrelated to past directions. If something follows a random walk, no amount of information on the past is useful for predicting what will happen in the future. The stock market would be expected to exhibit a random walk merely because it is so highly competitive and because information flows so freely. Examining past prices on the market as a whole or on individual stocks would not be expected to yield any useful information as to prices in the future. Years and years of academic research on the stock market have left little doubt that the stock market is, indeed, a random walk. (If you find out otherwise, you may be able to get rich very quickly.) However, a stock is not like a dog—which is to say, it will not eventually come home to its former price. Indeed, a stock doesn't know where its home was; it does not have a mind or a purpose. This should tell you that it

doesn't matter what has happened to a stock in the past. You can find no useable information by wasting your time examining past stock prices. To be sure, this will come as a shock to the industry's "technical analysts."

Charting the Future

Technical stock analysts believe that they can recognize patterns in stock prices. They have all sorts of special terms and ways to chart the past behavior of stocks and the average of all stock prices. They talk about "heads" and "shoulders" and "wedges" and "support" levels and "resistence" levels and so on. They will show you impressive x's and dots and dashes on sophisticated graphic charts like the one we have included here in Figure II–1. These analysts somehow think that they can predict which stocks will go up and which stocks will go down on the basis of the behavior of stock prices in the past. Our random walk theory, however, tells us that this cannot be the case.

Suppose that an analyst could make accurate predictions. How much money do you think you could make on it? If you found a chartist who knew what he was doing, other people would soon find out about him as well. As soon as enough people found out about how well his charting theory

CHARTING THE STOCK MARKET

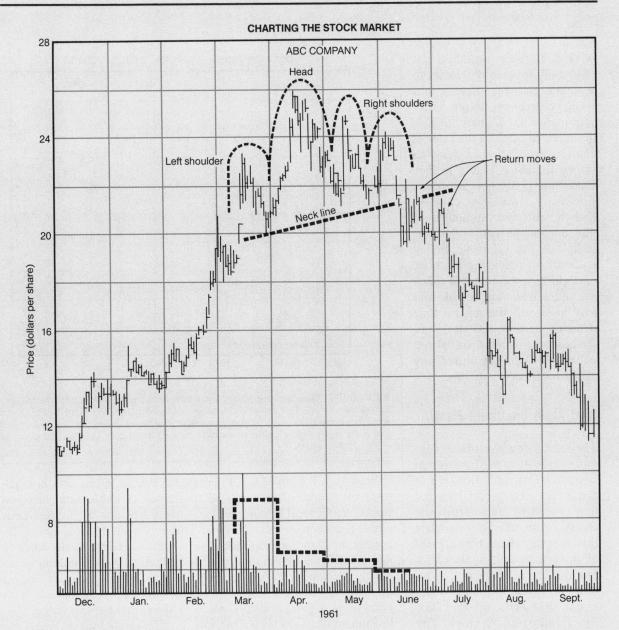

FIGURE II-1

Here we see an example of the so-called technical analysis for charting. Chartists believe that they can make some sense out of the ups and downs in the price of any particular stock or group of stocks. According to their theories, certain patterns can be recognized so that the future course of the price of the stock can be predicted. Can you make heads or tails out of the above diagram?

worked, his theory would become public information. Public information is useless for making profits in a competitive market where information flows freely. In fact, academic research on the value of charting or technical analysis has shown us that it is not, in fact, useful for predicting the future prices of stocks. A chartist, though, will swear up and down and across the valley that his technique is a valid one, that it is useful for predicting the price of stocks. If you ever meet a chartist, you might want to ask him why he is still wasting his time drawing arrows and dots and dashes and crosses on graph paper. Why hasn't he retired long ago if his theory is so good?

What About Investment Plans?

There are many investment plans and sophisticated investment counselors around. Looking at their advertising, you will see that they guarantee you a higher rate of return on your stock dollars than anyplace else. A typical piece of advertising might show, for example, the average rate of return for investing in all of the stocks that make up the Dow Jones Industrial Average. The Dow Jones Industrial Average (shown in Figure II-2) is the most widely known indication of the level of average stock prices

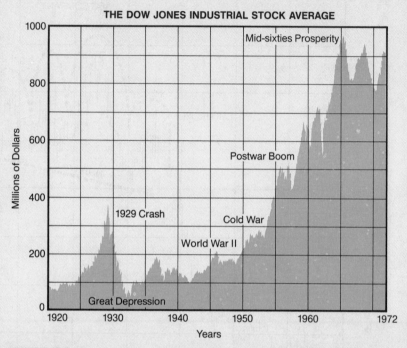

THE DOW JONES INDUSTRIAL STOCK AVERAGE

FIGURE II-2 Here we have plotted the course of the stock market over the last half century or so. The ups and downs are tremendous but the trend has been up. Wouldn't it have been nice if you could have bought in during the low points and sold at the high points! Hindsight, however, is always better than foresight, and of course much easier to assess.

in use today. It is made up of the price of 30 blue chip industrial stocks like General Motors, IBM, and other companies. If you bought the Dow Jones Industrial Average in the sense that you bought the same stocks that make up the average, you might make, on average, 8 percent a year. An investment counselor would show you that his stock portfolio made 15 percent a year. However, these investment counselors usually neglect to point out that the 15 percent rate of return does not take account of the investment counseling fees nor the trading costs for buying and selling stocks. Investment services usually do much trading: they go in and out of the market—buying today, selling tomorrow. Each time someone buys a stock, that person pays a commission to the broker. Each time someone sells a stock, he pays a commission to the broker. Thus, the more trading your investment counselor does for your account, the more trading costs you incur. In fact, in almost all cases that have been thoroughly examined, investments made through counselors do no better than the general market averages because any special profits they make are eaten up by brokerage fees and their own counseling fees.

This fact was confirmed in a study of **mutual funds.** Mutual funds take the money of many investors and buy and sell large blocks of stocks. The investors get dividends or appreciation in their shares of the mutual fund. The mutual fund, then, is a company which merely invests in other companies but does not sell any physical product of its own. You can buy shares in mutual funds just like you can buy shares in General Motors. The large study of mutual funds mentioned above concluded that mutuals which did the *least* amount of trading made the highest profits, an expected result if one understands the competitive nature of the stock market.

Is There No Way to Get Rich Quick?

The general conclusion to be reached from our analysis of the stock market is that all of the investing schemes everybody talks about are really quite useless for getting rich. That does not mean,

of course, that some people won't get rich by using them. Luck has a lot to do with making money in the stock market—just as it does with winning at poker or craps. If someone does make money with his particular scheme, it does not mean he is smart, a better investor, a wise old man, or a prophet. He is probably just lucky. He may, however, make more than a normal rate of return on his invested capital if he spends a tremendous amount of time finding out areas of unknown profit potential. But then he is spending resources—his own time. When accounting for his opportunity cost for the time spent analyzing the stock market and different companies, you'll probably find that his fantastic profits can mostly be attributed to payment for his time spent investigating.

The question still remains: how can you make money? You know you can make a normal rate of return by merely throwing a dart at the listing of stocks in the New York Stock Exchange. Pick eight stocks, for example, and just keep buying them with your investment dollars. Never sell until you need money for retirement. Over the long run you'll probably make around an 8 to 10 percent rate of return. On the other hand, you might want to pick particular stocks if you have inside information or information which is better than the tips anybody else has. In

such a case, you stand to gain more than by randomly picking stocks. Also, if you think you can somehow evaluate public information better than anybody else can, then you may want to do more than select random stocks. But before you decide whether you can evaluate better than others, you'd better think seriously about how many others there are in the world. The stock industry is huge. Why do you think that you can do better than everybody else? That is, why do you think that your evaluation of public information will be better than the market's? There is a sure-fire method of making money in the stock market but it is not by investing in stocks. Rather, it involves selling information to investors who are hungry for advice.

A Sure-Fire Scheme

What you should do is start a newsletter. Call it the *Information Systems Associated Newsletter,* or the *ISA Newsletter.* In the first newsletter, expound the virtues of your information-gathering and -evaluating investment system. Tell it like it is. Say that you're using high-speed computers to analyze all the stocks in a selected region of the country. Say that you guarantee a higher rate of return than any other newsletter service in the nation. Then make a list of, say, 100 stocks. Mail out the newsletter to everybody in your city free of charge. Follow the price of the stocks. Throw out the ones that fall in value. The next newsletter tells how successful your stock advice has been. Show how much in price all of the winning stocks have gone up. Ignore what the other ones did. Repeat the blurb on how sophisticated your computer equipment is.

Do this for three newsletters in a row. You'll be able to show, most likely, some fantastic gains in some of the stocks you recommended from the very beginning. After doing this, send a fourth newsletter which includes a little announcement stating that you must now charge people for your service; the introductory free offer is over. Charge them, say, $1000 apiece for a year's subscription. Quite a few people will buy your newsletter. After all, the stocks that you recommended have grown tremendously, right? (Recall that you ignored all the ones that didn't grow in price; you threw them out.) Once you collect all the money, you continue with the newsletter so that you won't get sued. However, people will eventually find out that your advice is no better than a random selection of stocks they could have made on their own. They will already have paid their $1000. They will be getting the product they requested, and you will be rich. In short, that's how to make money in the stock market—but don't tell a soul.

Definition of New Terms

EQUITIES: another name for common stocks; shares in a company.

CAPITAL GAINS: the difference between the price at which a stock is bought and the price at which it is sold. When this difference is negative it is called a capital loss.

INSIDE INFORMATION: information that is not public. It is usually acquired by insiders or those who have close contact with a company.

CAPITALIZATION: the process of taking account of all information about the future stream of profits for a company. This information is fully capitalized in the current price of a stock whenever the information is public.

RANDOM WALK: a theory about the movement of stock prices. In a random walk situation, the past movements of the stock have absolutely no ability to predict the future movements of that stock.

TECHNICAL ANALYSIS: a way to analyze the past course of stock prices in order to predict the future course. Technical analysis usually involves charting.

CHARTING: a type of technical analysis in which the past price of a stock or a group of stocks is plotted or charted. The results of this charting are supposed to help the chartist predict the future price of the stock.

DOW JONES INDUSTRIAL AVERAGE: the most widely known average of stock prices. It is a composite of 30 blue chip industrial stock prices.

MUTUAL FUND: a firm which buys the stocks of other firms and does not engage in the selling of products or services.

Questions for Thought and Discussion

1. If you had an extra $10,000, how would you invest it?
2. Why is the perpetual investment fraud perpetual?
3. When would it ever be worth your while to act on a "hot tip"?

Selected References

Cootner, P.H., ed. *The Random Character of Stock Market Prices.* Cambridge, Massachu-
    setts: M.I.T. Press, 1967.
Engel, Louis. *How to Buy Stocks.* 5th Rev. Ed. New York: Little, 1971.
Sprinkel, Beryl Wayne. *Money and Stock Prices.* Homewood, Illinois: Irwin, 1964.

The Firm
and Resource
Allocation

2

Analyzing the Costs of a Business

IN THE LAST chapter, the main focus was on the behavior of consumers and house-holds. To fully analyze many economic questions concerning microeconomic behavior, a theory of how businesses work is also needed. Much of this chapter will deal with some of the tools needed to complete a model of businesses. The object is to develop a model, and it will therefore be simplified. It may not be a 100 percent accurate representation of what actually goes on inside a working business. We want to be able to predict what will happen to a group of business-es—let's say to an industry—when its economic environment changes. We want to know what producers will do if, for example, the government increases taxes on business profits. We want to be able to predict what will happen if the govern-ment prevents firms from hiring college students for summer work at wages below a legal minimum. This chapter will equip us with the tools to answer these ques-tions. First, let's define what a business really is.

DEFINING A BUSINESS

What is a business? Everybody knows what a business is. It's the supermarket down the street, the head shop around the corner, General Motors, Playboy Enterprises, American Telephone and Telegraph. The list will get very large indeed if we attempt to name every business in the United States. Further, everybody knows that there is a difference between a corporate giant like General Motors and the local head shop. In terms of our analysis we will not usually make a distinction between these types of firms—except with regard to the market power they have; that is, the extent to which they control the setting of their prices. There are legal differences, of course, between *corporations, partnerships,* and *single-owner proprietorships.*

Corporations

A corporation is a legal entity owned by stockholders in the company. Stockholders are those who have purchased shares in the corporation. They are legally liable only for the amount of money they put in to buy those shares. For example, if you bought $2000 worth of General Motors stock and General Motors went bankrupt, the most you could lose was $2000. General Motors' creditors could not come pounding at your door asking for more.

Partnerships

A partnership involves two or more individuals that have joined together for business purposes but have decided not to form a corporation. In most instances, if you are a partner in a business, you can be liable up to the point where you lose all your personal wealth. That is to say, if your partnership goes bankrupt and your creditors are owed $50,000, they can legally get it from you; they could force you to sell your house in order to pay off the amount the partnership owed. Another distinction is that in a partnership, whenever one partner decides to leave the business or when one partner dies, the partnership must be dissolved and a new business must be started. A corporation, however, can last forever: the owners of the corporation may change constantly but the corporation as a legal business entity continues to live.

Proprietorships

The third form of business organization is a single-owner proprietorship. You're probably familiar with the corner grocery store that's owned by one little old man, or a gardening service owned and operated by one man, or a motorcycle repair shop owned and operated by one man. If you own a business yourself, you are legally liable for all the debts incurred by the business.

THE FIRM

We still haven't come up with a precise definition of what a business is, even though all of us have a pretty good idea. Let's define a business, or **firm,** as follows:

A firm is an organization which brings together different factors of production such as labor, land, and capital, in order to produce a product or service that can be sold for a profit.

A typical firm will have the following organizational structure: entrepreneur, managers, and workers. The entrepreneur is the person who takes the chances. Because he has taken a chance, he is the one who will get any profits that are made. He decides who to hire to run his firm. Some economists maintain that the true entrepreneur is the person who knows how to pick good managers. Managers, in turn, are the ones who decide who should be hired and fired and how the business should generally be set up. The workers, in turn, are the ones who ultimately use the machines to produce the products or services that are being sold by the firm.

The workers are paid wages. So, too, are the managers. However, it is the entrepreneurs who make profits if there are any, for profits in economics can only accrue to those who are willing to take a risk. The term profit will be used so many times in this microeconomic section that we'd better define exactly what it is.

PROFIT

Most people—businessmen included—think of profit as the difference between how much money the business takes in and how much it spends for wages, materials, and so on. In a bookkeeping sense, the following formula could be used:

accounting profits = total revenues − total costs

The trouble with this bookkeeping identification of profits is that costs are usually incorrectly figured, at least from our point of view.

Normal Rate of Return

We have now and again mentioned a *normal rate of return.* By the term we meant that people will not invest their money into a business unless they obtain a positive rate of return—unless the money put in their investment in a business pays off. Any business wishing to attract money capital must expect to pay at least the same rate of return on that money that all other businesses in a similar situation are willing to pay. For example, if somebody can invest his money in just about any publishing firm and get a rate of return on his investment of, say, 6 percent per year, then every firm in the publishing business must consider that the normal rate of return they must expect to pay out to investors is 6 percent. *This is a cost to them.* This is called the **opportunity cost of money capital.** Money capital will not stay in industries where the rate of return falls below its opportunity cost.

Forgetting Opportunity Cost

Often, single-owner proprietorships grossly exaggerate their profit rates because they forget about the opportunity cost of the time that the proprietor himself spends in the business. For example, you may know people who run small grocery stores. These people, at the end of the year, will sit down and figure out what their profits were. They will add up all of their sales and subtract what they had to pay to other workers, what they had to pay to their suppliers, what they had to pay in taxes, and so on. The end result they will call "profit." However, they will not have figured into their costs the salary that they could have made if they had worked for somebody else in a similar type job. For somebody operating a grocery store, that salary might be equal to $3.00 an hour. If that is so, then $3.00 an hour is the opportunity cost of the grocery store owner's time. In many cases people running their own businesses end up losing money in an economic sense. That is,

their profits, as they calculate them, may be less than the amount of money they *could* have earned had they spent the same amount of time working for someone else.

Accounting Profits ≒ Economic Profits

Now you should have a good notion of the meaning of profits in economics. Accounting profits, as opposed to economic profits, do not necessarily include the opportunity cost of capital invested in a business or the opportunity cost of the time that the owners of the business spend working. The term *profits* has a very special meaning in economics. It is money that entrepreneurs make over and above their own opportunity cost plus the cost of the capital they have invested in their business. Profits can be regarded as total revenues minus total costs, like the accountants think of them, but we must now include *all* costs.

In most instances, we will use a model which assumes that the goal of a firm is to maximize profits. The firm, then, is expected to attempt to make the difference between total revenues and total costs as large as possible. We are going to use this model because it will allow us to analyze a firm's behavior. Whenever that model produces poor predictions, we will examine our initial assumption that the goal of the firm is to maximize the profits. We might have to decide that the goal is to maximize the prestige of the owners, sales, the number of workers, and so on. When the firm produces its products in the quest for profit, we must ask under what constraints (conditions) it will produce. One of the most important of these is contained in the concept of diminishing returns.

DIMINISHING RETURNS

We will introduce now a very important concept in firm analysis—the concept of **diminishing (marginal) returns.** You might ask: returns to what? Returns to the use of a factor of production. You've probably heard the term *diminishing returns* used in casual conversation. Somebody might say, well, I quit studying because I reached the point of diminishing returns. Or someone else might say, I stopped going to my yoga class because I reached a point of diminishing returns. Both statements demonstrate a very loose usage of the term *diminishing returns*. The idea is, of course, that satisfaction is no longer increasing very rapidly considering the effort expended. You may, however, get diminishing returns from drinking another glass of beer, but that doesn't necessarily mean you won't drink that glass of beer. In fact, if it is free, you'll probably drink it unless the returns you receive—pleasure or utility—are negative. You will continue drinking beer until the return in terms of happiness or utility is just equal to how much you have to pay for the beer. When beer is free, you'll keep drinking until the marginal return is zero. You certainly wouldn't stop just because you had reached the point of diminishing marginal returns.

The same is true of firms in the *use* of productive inputs. When the returns to hiring more workers are diminishing it does not necessarily mean that more workers won't be hired. In fact, workers will be hired until the returns, in terms of the value of the extra output produced, are equal to the additional wages that have to be paid for those workers to produce the extra output. Before we get into that decision-making process, let's demonstrate that diminishing returns can be represented graphically and can be used in our analysis of the firm.

Measuring Diminishing Returns

How do we measure diminishing returns? The first thing is to make sure that we're only talking about one factor of production (or input). Let's say that factor is labor. Every other factor of production, such as machines, must be held constant. Only by holding all other factors of production constant can we calculate the marginal returns to using more workers. Then we can see when we reach the point of diminishing marginal returns.

Marginal returns for productive inputs are also

TABLE 4–1

DIMINISHING RETURNS: A HYPOTHETICAL CASE IN AGRICULTURE

In the first column we measure the number of workers used per week on a given amount of land with a given amount of machinery and fertilizer and seed. In the second column we give their total product; that is, the output that each specified number of workers can produce in terms of bushels of wheat. The last column gives the marginal product. The marginal product is the difference between the output possible with a given number of workers minus the output made possible with one less worker. For example, the marginal product of a fourth worker is 8 bushels of wheat, because with 4 workers, 44 bushels are produced but with 3 workers only 36 are produced; the difference is 8.

INPUT OF LABOR NO. OF WORKERS PER WEEK	TOTAL PRODUCT (OUTPUT IN BUSHELS OF WHEAT)	MARGINAL PRODUCT
0	0	
1	10	10
2	26	16
3	36	10
4	44	8
5	50	6
6	54	4
7	56	2
8	55	−1

referred to as **marginal products.** The marginal product of a worker, for example, is the increase in total product that he is responsible for when he works. The marginal productivity of labor, therefore, refers to how much increase in output on the margin labor is responsible for.

It may be that the marginal productivity of labor increases in the very beginning. That is, when a firm starts off with no workers, all it has is some machines. The firm hires one worker, but he has a hard time getting things going. When the firm hires more workers, the whole group is able to *specialize* better, and the marginal productivity of those additional workers will actually be greater than it was with the previous few workers. Soon, however, the point of diminishing returns must set in; the place will get so crowded that workers will start running into each other; they will become less productive. Managers will have to be hired to run the show.

We can use the following definition of the Law of Diminishing returns:

As successive equal increases of the variable factor of production, such as labor, are added to a fixed factor of production, such as capital, there will be a point beyond which the extra or marginal product that can be attributed to each additional unit of the variable factor of production will decline.

Diminishing returns merely refers to a situation where output rises less than in proportion to the increase in, say, the number of workers employed.

An Example

The best example of the workings of the Law of Diminishing Returns can be found in agriculture. With a fixed amount of land, fertilizer, and tractors, the addition of more men eventually yields increases in output which are smaller than the increases in the variable inputs—the number of workers. A hypothetical set of numbers illustrating the law of diminishing marginal returns (productivity) is presented in Table 4–1. The numbers are presented graphically in Figure 4–1. First

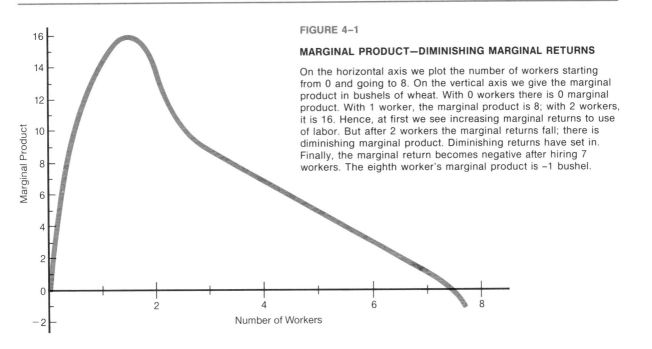

FIGURE 4–1

MARGINAL PRODUCT—DIMINISHING MARGINAL RETURNS

On the horizontal axis we plot the number of workers starting from 0 and going to 8. On the vertical axis we give the marginal product in bushels of wheat. With 0 workers there is 0 marginal product. With 1 worker, the marginal product is 8; with 2 workers, it is 16. Hence, at first we see increasing marginal returns to use of labor. But after 2 workers the marginal returns fall; there is diminishing marginal product. Diminishing returns have set in. Finally, the marginal return becomes negative after hiring 7 workers. The eighth worker's marginal product is –1 bushel.

marginal productivity (returns to adding more workers) increases. Then it decreases and finally it becomes negative. Obviously, most firms would not operate in the region of increasing marginal returns because they could probably make more profit by adding more workers. Obviously, a firm would never operate in the region where there were *negative* marginal returns because it could make higher profits by getting rid of some workers. Firms will most always be operating in the area of diminishing marginal returns.

ONE IMPLICATION OF MAXIMIZING BEHAVIOR

If a firm is profit maximizing, it will seek to utilize the various inputs it needs in a very special way. Imagine yourself as owner of a Zig-Zag factory. Let's say that you know you want to produce 100,000 units of product per month. How do you decide how many men to use, how many machines to buy, how large a building to have? The answer is that you should select the relative quantities of each input (factors of production) so as to *minimize* total costs.

Is there a way to solve this puzzle? Yes, and that way involves what economists call *optimizing* the use of your inputs. Recall how an individual would optimize his behavior. He'd buy various things so that the marginal utility per $1.00 spent on each and every item he bought would be equal. A firm does the same, but it worries about *marginal product* rather than marginal utility. The marginal product of any factor of production is simply the physical amount of production created *on the margin* by the use of that factor. Otherwise stated, marginal product of an input is the difference between total output using 100 units of the input and total output using 99 units of the input.

The marginal product of your Zig-Zag worker may be 1000 packages per month. That means if one worker quit and nothing else changed in your factory, your production would drop by 1000

units. Marginal product is also a measure of **productivity.** If your workers' marginal product grows over time, we say that their productivity is increasing.

Now what if spending $1.00 more on labor will get you 20 more units of output, but spending $1.00 more on machines will get you only 10 more units of output? What would you do? You would hire more workers or sell some machines. You should employ relative amounts of each and every factor of production so that the marginal product per $1.00 spent on each is equal. Let's say you used men, machines, and paper. You'd use them so that:

$$\frac{\text{marginal product of labor}}{\text{price of labor}} =$$

$$\frac{\text{marginal product of machines}}{\text{price of machines}} =$$

$$\frac{\text{marginal product of paper}}{\text{price of paper}} .$$

This is the least costly solution for any given level of output. We'll assume that the firm always chooses this least costly solution for whatever output level it decides upon.

COSTS

We talked about total costs and certain components of total costs. We have a much more analytical way of describing certain costs that firms must incur, and we shall see that only certain of a firm's costs are important in its decision-making process. We will get a chance here to make the distinction between average and marginal—a distinction which has been stressed throughout this entire book. Instead of talking about various costs that the firm incurs (such as those for wages, materials, rent on buildings, and so on), we will divide costs into the following categories: fixed costs, variable costs, average costs, and marginal costs.

FIGURE 4-2

TOTAL COSTS, FIXED COSTS, AND VARIABLE COSTS

On the horizontal axis of this diagram is represented the quantity of water pipes produced. On the vertical axis is represented total cost. The total cost curve is *TC*. It starts out at $2000. The fixed costs are, therefore, represented by $2000—those costs that are incurred even if the production of water pipes is zero. The difference between fixed costs and total costs is equal to total variable costs. These are all nonfixed costs for a firm. They depend on the output. In general, variable costs rise with rising output.

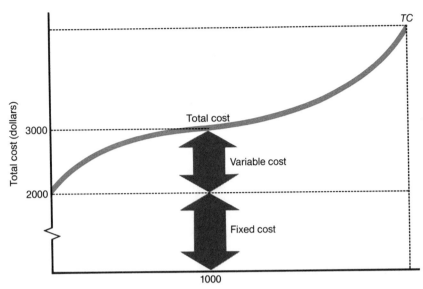

Fixed Costs

Let's look at an ongoing business such as General Motors. The decision makers in that great corporate giant can look around them and see big machines, thosands of parts, huge buildings, and a multitude of other pieces of plant and equipment that are in place, that have already been bought. General Motors has to pay for the wear and tear on these pieces of equipment, no matter how many cars it produces. It can increase production by 50 percent or decrease production by 50 percent, and the payments on its loans taken out to buy all the equipment will be exactly the same. The opportunity cost of any land that General Motors owns will be exactly the same. All costs which do not vary—that is, costs that do not depend on the rate of production—are called **fixed,** or *sunk,* costs.

There is an old saying in economics that sunk costs are forever sunk. It is hard to disagree with this truism. After all, we can't deny that what has taken place has already taken place. If a firm has

its equipment in place, that equipment is there no matter how you look at it. If a business has a lease on a building and some land that is costing $50,000 a month in rent, that cost is fixed for the duration of the lease. It is to be treated as a sunk cost; there is nothing the firm can do about it right now.

The same is true of the time that you spend waiting in a line, although it is difficult to think in terms of sunk costs when they apply to your own behavior. Even though you may have waited in a line for one and a half hours to get a new driver's license, that is no reason to tell yourself that you might as well wait it out since you've waited so long already. The hour and a half must be treated as a sunk cost; it should not influence your decision as to what to do next.

We will find that fixed costs do not enter into business decision making, at least in the short run—or during the time when changes are very difficult or costly to make.

Let's take as an example the cost incurred by a manufacturer of water pipes. His total costs will equal the cost of his rent on his equipment, the copper he buys, the glass bowls he buys, the filters he buys, the insurance he has to pay, the wages he has to pay, and so on. We can represent *total costs* as the upward sloping *TC* curve in Figure 4–2. Total *fixed* costs can be seen easily. They are equal to the point where the total cost curve starts to go up from the vertical axis. Here, the vertical axis represents total costs and the horizontal axis is the quantity of copper water pipes produced. No matter how many water pipes are produced, fixed costs will remain the same. The difference between the fixed costs and the total costs are, of course, all other nonfixed costs, which we will describe subsequently.

Total Variable Costs

As one might expect, **variable costs** are those which vary. That is, they vary with the rate of production. The most obvious variable cost is wages paid. The more a firm produces, the more workers it has to pay. Wages represent probably the largest part of variable costs. There are other variable costs, though; those include materials. For example, in building water pipes, the business has to buy more copper as it produces more pipes. Also, the rate of depreciation or the rate of wear and tear on the machines can sometimes be considered a variable cost if depreciation depends on how long and how intensively the machines are used.

Often, we want to talk about **average variable costs.** Average variable costs can be defined as all of the nonfixed costs divided by the quantity produced. Look again at Figure 4–2. At a production rate of zero, total variable costs are, of course, zero, even though fixed costs are $2000. At a production rate of 1000 water pipes, fixed costs remain at $2000, but nonfixed costs (variable costs) have increased from zero dollars to $1000 ($3000-$2000). Therefore, average variable costs equal $1000 divided by 1000, or $1.00. We will represent the average variable cost curve

on our next graph. First, however, we must cover a most well known cost—the average total cost, or unit cost.

Average Total Costs

The concept of average cost is one of the easiest to master because most people are used to figuring out averages. Average costs are defined as total costs divided by the number of units of whatever is produced. For example, if the total costs —including, of course, the opportunity cost of capital and the opportunity cost of all labor—are $10,000 for producing 5000 copper water pipes, then the **average total cost** per water pipe is $2.00.

Sometimes average total costs are called average unit costs, but the word *unit* is usually implied and need not be given. Average total costs include not only fixed costs but also payments for nonfixed costs, such as wages paid to workers. A business would, of course, like to have its average total costs as low as possible.

How do average costs for a business change as it produces more goods? Most people are familiar with the concept of mass production; it is reasoned that, with mass production techniques, the cost per unit of output can be reduced. The idea is, of course, that when a fixed amount of money is being spent on machines, the more that one can produce, the more the total fixed cost can be spread out and the smaller the average costs. Obviously, average fixed costs will become smaller as output increases. If fixed costs are $2000 to make copper water pipes, then average fixed costs for making 20,000 water pipes will be $2000 divided by 20,000, or only 10¢ per pipe. What would average fixed costs be if production increased to 200,000?

Since average fixed costs continually fall, the only way for average unit costs eventually to go up is for the other expenses—variable costs—to increase for each unit of additional production. This follows from the law of diminishing returns.

FIGURE 4–3

AVERAGE AND MARGINAL

Here we measure the output produced on the horizontal axis. Average variable costs or marginal costs are measured on the vertical axis. The average variable cost curve is shown as *AVC*. When the average variable cost curve is falling, the marginal cost curve must, by necessity, be underneath it. After all, the only way for average variable costs to fall is for the variable cost of the last unit produced to be less than the variable cost of the previous units; since marginal cost is defined as the increment in costs, it must be below *AVC*.

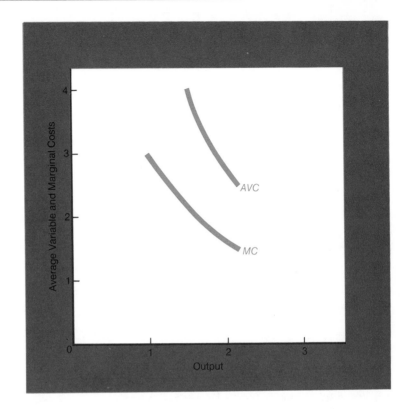

Marginal Costs

We have stated repeatedly in this text that the action is always on the margin. Movement in economics is always determined at the margin—a dictum which holds true within the firm also. Firms, according to the analysis that we will use to predict their behavior, will be very interested in their **marginal costs.** The term *marginal* means additional or incremental. Therefore, marginal costs must refer to those costs which occur on the margin, costs which result from additional or incremental changes in production rates. For example, if the production of 20,000 water pipes costs a firm $20,000 and the production to the firm of 20,001 water pipes costs it $20,000.50, then the marginal cost of producing one additional water pipe is 50¢. To find the marginal cost, one subtracts the total cost of producing all but the last unit from the total cost of producing all units, including the last one. (Actually, we can ignore the fixed cost element of total costs because fixed costs, by definition, never change no matter what the production rate.) Marginal costs would therefore be equal to the additional variable costs that are incurred because of an increase in production of one unit.

Marginal costs could also be called marginal variable costs because the only costs which are incurred by changing production rates are variable costs. However, we usually leave out the term *variable* when we are referring to marginal costs.

AVERAGE AND MARGINAL

There is a relationship between average variable costs and marginal costs. It turns out that when

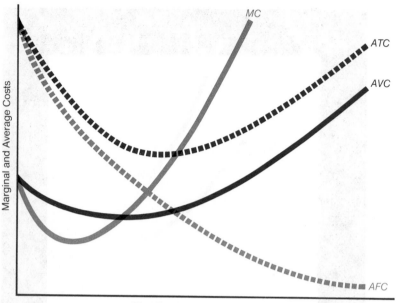

Quantity of Water Pipes Produced

FIGURE 4-4 **AVERAGE AND MARGINAL COST COMPARED**

The curve *AFC* represents average fixed costs. Average fixed costs, or *AFC*, get smaller as output increases because we are dividing a larger number into total fixed costs. Average total costs, or ATC, represent fixed plus variable costs divided by the number of units produced. Average total cost is shown to first fall and then rise. Average variable costs, or *AVC*, are shown first to fall and then rise because of the law of diminishing returns. Marginal costs are represented by the curve *MC*. They then fall as average variable costs fall. After awhile, marginal costs start to rise. Marginal costs equal average variable costs when average variable costs are at a minimum. Marginal cost also equals average total costs when average total costs are at a minimum.

average variable costs are falling, marginal costs are less than average costs. Conversely, when average variable costs are rising, marginal cost is greater than average variable cost. When you think about it a while, the relationship is obvious: the only way for average variable costs to fall is for the variable cost of the marginal unit produced to be less than the average variable cost of all the preceding units. For example, if the average variable cost for two units of production is $3.00 a unit, the only way for the average variable cost of three units to fall is for the variable costs attributable to the last unit—the marginal cost—to be less than the average of the past units. In this particular case, if average variable cost fell to $2.50 a unit, then total variable cost for the three units would be three times $2.50, or $7.50. Total variable cost for two units was two times $3.00, or $6.00. The marginal cost is, therefore, $7.50 minus $6.00, or $1.50, which is less than average variable cost of $2.50. The relationship is presented in Figure 4-3.

A similar type computation can be carried out for rising average variable costs. We know that the only way for average variable costs to be rising is for the average variable cost of additional units to be costing more than that for units already produced. But the incremental cost is the marginal cost. Therefore, in this particular case, the marginal costs have to be higher than the average variable costs.

There is also a relationship between marginal costs and average total costs. Remember that average total cost is just equal to the total cost divided by the number of units produced. Remember also that marginal cost is not affected by fixed costs. Fixed costs are, by definition, fixed and cannot influence marginal costs. The above example could be repeated substituting the term *average variable cost* for the term *average total cost*. The arithmetic would be slightly different, but the result would be the same. Marginal cost equals average total cost when the latter is at its minimum.

**FIGURE 4–5 THE EFFECTS OF
A PER UNIT TAX**

Here we redo Figure 4–4, but now
we take into account the effects of a
tax on each unit produced. The
government, for example, charges
20¢ per water pipe to the water pipe
manufacturer. This changes the water
pipe manufacturer's cost curves. The
average variable cost curve moves up
to *AVC'*, the heavy black line. It
moves up by the vertical distance
equal to the amount of the tax. After
all, the tax is on each unit of
production. That means that the
marginal cost curve will move up
also. It moves from *MC* to *MC'*. And,
finally, the average total curve, *ATC*,
moves to *ATC'*.

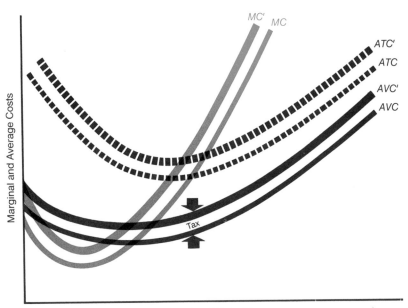

Quantity of Water Pipes

PUTTING IT ALL TOGETHER

Now we are in a position to demonstrate graphically the concepts just outlined. Let's look at
Figure 4–4. The vertical axis measures *average*
and *marginal* costs per unit. (In Figure 4–2, the
vertical axis was measuring *total* costs.) The horizontal axis again measures the quantity of output
of water pipes. Four curves have been drawn in
Figure 4–4: the average fixed cost curve, *AFC;*
the marginal cost curve, *MC;* the average variable
cost curve, *AVC;* and the average per unit or total
cost curve, *ATC*. We see that the average fixed
cost curve starts at the same place that the
average total cost curve starts on the vertical axis.
However, the average fixed cost curve continues
to fall for the entire range of the graph. This is
because average fixed costs will continuously get
smaller and smaller as we keep dividing a larger
and larger quantity of output into the same fixed
number.

In this particular depiction of cost curves, we
have drawn the average variable cost curve as
first falling and then rising; it is U-shaped. In
general, the U-shaped cost curve is not unrealistic.
(Can you think of reasons why? Remember the
law of diminishing marginal returns.)

The average cost curve or average per unit
total cost curve is also U-shaped, but it is higher
than the average variable cost curve by the
amount of average fixed costs. Notice that the
distance between the *ATC* curve and the *AVC*
curve gets smaller when more is produced. This
is because average fixed costs are getting smaller
as the rate of production gets larger.

Now, last but certainly not least, we see the
marginal cost curve which first falls and then
abruptly turns upward. The marginal cost curve,
as we said above, will be below the average cost
curves so long as the average cost curves are
falling. When the average cost curves, both total
and variable, start rising, the marginal cost curve
is above them because marginal costs will be
greater than average costs at this time.

Note the points of intersection of the marginal cost curve with the *AVC* and the *ATC* curves. Isn't there something similar about these points? The similarity is that the marginal cost curve intersects both the average variable cost curve and the average total cost curve at the *minimum* point. This should not be surprising. When average costs are falling, marginal costs will be less than average costs. When average costs are rising, marginal costs will be greater than average costs. At the point where average costs stop falling and start rising, marginal cost must then be equal to average cost. Therefore, when we represent this graphically, there will be an intersection of the marginal cost curve with the average cost curve, no matter if it be average *variable* cost or average *total* cost.

TAXING THE FIRM

It might be useful at this point to show how to represent a tax on a firm. Let's talk about a tax on each unit of production. This will be a unit tax. It is not based on the value of the output but, rather, on the mere fact that output is being produced. What do you think happens to all of those curves in Figure 4–4 when a per unit tax is put on the production of water pipes?

Let's ask ourselves what happens to fixed costs. The tax is incurred only if the firm produces water pipes. If it produces nothing it does not have to pay the tax. This means that fixed costs do not change; average fixed costs will remain the same also, so the *AFC* curve does not change. When it comes to the average variable costs, things do change. Each time a new unit is produced, the tax has to be paid. That means that the average variable cost curve will move up vertically by the amount of the tax. We show this in Figure 4–5. Since average variable cost moves up, so does the average total cost curve and by the same amount.

What about marginal costs? Marginal costs will have to move up also. The marginal cost curve, *MC,* will move up vertically by the amount of the tax on each unit of production. After all, marginal cost is defined as the increment in costs. If the firm must pay a tax when it produces one more water pipe, this means the marginal cost will go up by that tax also. We show the new curves with the tax as the heavy lines in Figure 4–5.

Definition of New Terms

FIRM: an organization which brings together different factors of production, such as labor, land, and capital, in order to produce a product or service that can hopefully be sold for a profit. A firm is usually made up of an entrepreneur, managers and workers.

CORPORATION: a legal entity owned by stockholders in the company. The stockholders are only liable for the amount of money they have invested in the company.

PARTNERSHIP: a business entity involving two or more individuals joined together for business purposes but who have not incorporated. In many instances the partners in a partnership are liable for the debts of the business to such an extent that they can lose their personal wealth if the business loses money.

PROPRIETORSHIP: a single-owner business involving only one person.

ACCOUNTING PROFITS: the difference between total revenues and total costs as perceived by an accountant; different from economic profits.

ECONOMIC PROFITS: the difference between total revenues and total costs where total costs include the opportunity cost of capital and the opportunity cost of the time that the owners of the business spend working in it.

OPPORTUNITY COST OF CAPITAL: the normal rate of return or that amount that must be paid to a capitalist in order to induce him to invest in the business.

MARGINAL RETURNS: the returns for employing additional units of a factor of production. For example, the marginal return of employing one worker would equal the increase in output after the worker was hired.

DIMINISHING MARGINAL RETURNS: usually defined as the law of diminishing marginal returns. After some point, successive increases in the variable factor of production, such as labor, added to fixed factors of production will not cause an equiproportionate increase in output.

MARGINAL PRODUCT: the same thing as marginal return. Marginal product of a worker is the amount of additional output he is responsible for when he goes to work.

PRODUCTIVITY: a loose term for the marginal product of workers. If the marginal product of a worker goes up, it is said that his productivity has increased.

TOTAL COST: all the costs of a firm combined, including rent, payments to workers, interest on borrowed money, and so on.

FIXED COSTS: those costs which do not vary depending on output. Fixed costs include such things as rent on the building, the price of the machinery, and things like that.

VARIABLE COSTS: these are the costs that vary with the rate of production. They include wages paid to workers, the costs of materials, and things like that.

AVERAGE FIXED COSTS: average costs divided by the number of units produced.

AVERAGE VARIABLE COSTS: variable costs divided by the number of units produced.

AVERAGE TOTAL COSTS: total costs divided by the number of units produced, sometimes called average per unit total costs.

MARGINAL COSTS: the increase in cost due to an increase in production. Marginal costs are defined as total costs for, say, 1000 units of production minus the total costs for 999 units.

Chapter Summary

1. When analyzing a business, we will define it as any organization which brings together different factors of production in order to produce a good or service which hopefully can be sold for a profit. Firms are typically made up of entrepreneurs, managers, and workers.

2. Accounting profits are the difference between total revenues and total costs. However, economic profits are usually different. We define economic profits as total revenues minus total costs where all costs are included. These would be in addition to everything the accountant sees, the opportunity cost of capital (normal rate of return) and the opportunity cost of the owner's time spent working.

3. The normal rate of return on capital is the yield which is necessary to keep that capital in a particular business or industry. That rate might be 7 percent or 10 percent, for example. The 7 or 10 percent yield is a cost and is not part of economic profits.

4. When all factors of production are fixed except one, that one factor can be increased. But eventually as that factor is increased, output will increase less than proportionately. This is called the law of diminishing marginal returns. At some point the marginal product attributable to an increase in the variable factor of production diminishes.

5. Marginal product is also a measure of productivity. We say that the productivity of workers has gone up if their marginal product increases—that is, if the amount of output that they can produce on the margin goes up.

6. The least cost production solution for a firm is to make equal the marginal product of every factor divided by its price.

7. A firm faces numerous costs. Economists like to separate these costs into fixed and variable, and then further into average and marginal costs.

8. Fixed costs are those which are sunk and cannot be eliminated. Average fixed costs are just total fixed costs divided by the quantity of production. Average fixed costs will forever fall.

9. Variable costs are those which vary with the amount of output. The most obvious variable cost is the cost of labor: as more laborers are hired, the wage bill goes up. Average variable costs are total variable costs divided by the number of units of output.

10. Marginal costs are those which can be attributed to an increase in production of one unit. Marginal costs are always below average costs when average costs are falling. Marginal costs are always above average costs when average costs are rising. Therefore, marginal cost is equal to average cost when average costs are at a minimum.

11. The average total cost curve is typically U-shaped. Even though the average fixed costs are falling forever, at some point diminishing returns set in and variable costs start to rise, thus causing the average total cost curve to rise.

12. A per unit tax on a firm raises the average variable cost curve, the average total cost curve, and the marginal cost curve.

Questions for Thought and Discussion

1. If opportunity costs are not entered in the accounting records of a firm, what good are they?

2. Why does the average variable cost curve and the average total cost curve have a U shape?

3. It is sometimes said that in the long run there is no such thing as fixed costs. Can you figure out why?

4. We have shown that when average costs are falling marginal costs are less than average costs and when average costs are rising, marginal costs are more than average costs. Can the same relationship be applied to average product and marginal product?

5. Why do you think the corporation is such a popular form of business organization?

6. It is sometimes said that the most important thing that matters is marginal cost. Do you agree or disagree? Why?

7. If you were setting up a new business, do you think you would expect to recoup your investment in the first year?

Selected Reference

Haynes, W. Warren. *Managerial Economics: Analysis and Cases.* Rev. Ed. Austin, Texas: Business Publications, 1969. Chapters 5 and 6.

ISSUE III

The Economics of Criminal Deterrence

The Costs of Crime

The economic costs of crime in the United States probably exceed $25 billion a year. Perhaps $6 billion of those total costs are spent on police, prosecution, courts, jails, and certain private methods of preventing crime. We see, then, that crime—both as an activity on the part of individuals and as an activity in terms of prevention on the part of the public and individuals—is big business. It may even be that this business is getting bigger. There is evidence that major felonies *per capita* have grown since the early thirties. The FBI reported that in the sixties the national crime rate rose over 100 percent for the decade. This is seen in Figures III–1 and III–2. The rise has strained the capacity of courts and police to a point which literally ap-

proaches chaos in some cities. It is estimated that in New York, for example, policemen and courts are so overworked that a man who commits a felony faces only 1 chance in 200 of actually going to jail for it.

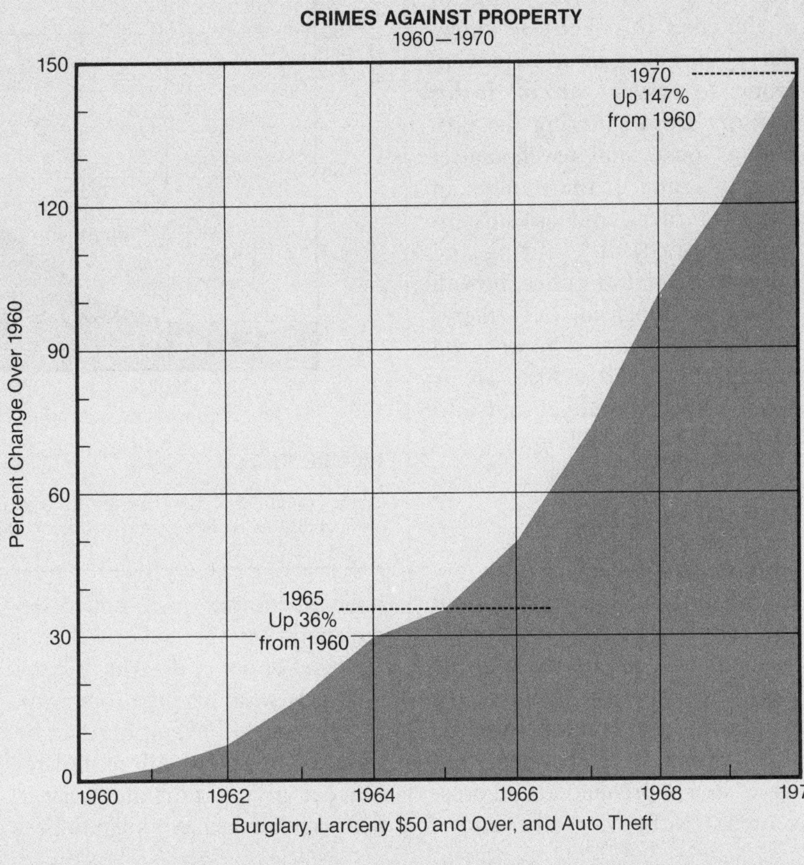

There is no doubt that crime is a complex social problem. It is a problem we have to deal with at national, state, and local levels. We will show in this issue that it is possible to analyze how re- sources can be spent optimally on preventing crime and punishing offenders. We shall use the laws of supply and demand and our analysis of how a business operates to do some theorizing about actual criminal enforcement

FIGURE III-1

The sixties saw a 147 percent increase in crimes against property over the decade. Crime has become and continues to be big business. *Source: FBI Crime Reports, 1970.*

CRIMES AGAINST PROPERTY
1960—1970

1970
Up 147%
from 1960

1965
Up 36%
from 1960

Percent Change Over 1960

Burglary, Larceny $50 and Over, and Auto Theft

procedures. Let's start our discussion with the dilemma that every police chief faces.

Constraining the Chief of Police

The head of any law enforcement department is usually faced with a fixed budget. In the city of New York, it might be $25 million. In the city of Dry Gulch, it might be $8000. In any and all cases, the fixed budget will be a constraint imposed on the behavior of the chief of police. He knows that he has been hired to prevent crime, to prevent citizens in his territory from suffering the economic, social, and psychological costs of crime. If the number of rapes, murders, and assaults increases drastically during the reign of a chief of police, he will usually be replaced. Let's therefore look at him as if he were the manager of a large firm. He is given a specific budget and told to maximize production.

Measuring Output

In this case production or output is very difficult to measure. Is it the number of robbers apprehended? Is it the decrease in the number of rapes during the chief's administration? Is it measured by the number of embezzlers that have been apprehended and prosecuted? Nobody really knows

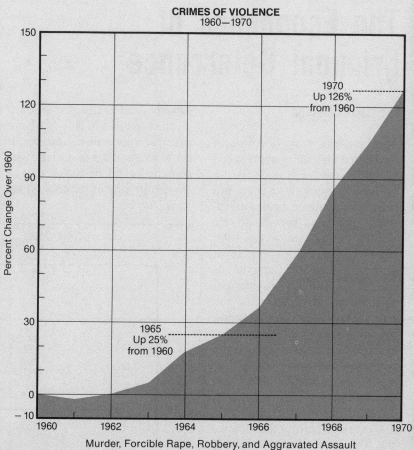

CRIMES OF VIOLENCE
1960—1970

Percent Change Over 1960

1970
Up 126%
from 1960

1965
Up 25%
from 1960

Murder, Forcible Rape, Robbery, and Aggravated Assault

FIGURE III-2

Crimes of violence have moved up 126 percent from 1960 to 1970, slightly less than the increase in crimes against property. *Source: FBI Crime Reports,* 1970.

how the output of a police department can be measured, but the chief of police does have some idea as to what his superiors want. He knows, for example, that he should not spend all of his resources giving parking tickets. Some resources have to go to preventing robberies, preventing murders, apprehending felony criminals, and so on.

Allocating a Fixed Budget

The chief of police takes his given budget, then, and decides how it should be allocated. He has to figure out, for example, how many police cars, computers, and other machines to buy and how many men to hire. Let's assume for the moment that the factors of production he wants to purchase can be divided into men and machines. If the chief finds that by spending one more dollar on machines he could obtain a higher amount of crime deterrence than by spending that dollar on men, then he should increase the proportion of the budget spent on machines. Of course, even the best of police chiefs could not hope to measure the product made available from spending an additional $1.00 either on men or on machines. He must work in much grosser figures; but the principle still holds in any event. For a given budget, the chief of police will maximize the output of his firm (police department) if he uses the different inputs, such as men and machines, in such quantities that the marginal product made possible by spending $1.00 on one input is just equal to the marginal product made possible by spending $1.00 on every one of the other inputs. The amount of crime deterrence that a chief of police can attain will be maximized with a given budget if, and only if, the marginal amount of crime deterrence made possible by $1.00 is the same for every input used in his crime preventing firm.

Eliminate Vice or Theft?

Not only is our chief of police faced with the problem of equalizing marginal products per dollar spent on all his inputs, he also has to decide how much should be spent on the vice patrol, how much should be spent on the homicide division, how much should be spent on the traffic division, and so on. Somehow he has got to allocate his fixed budget among the different divisions. Here the problem becomes somewhat more difficult. The solution will be to allocate monies so that the marginal output of each is equalized per dollar spent.

The *value* of the marginal product or output for any particular crime prevention detail is decided upon by society. If, in general, the majority of citizens are more disturbed by youths smoking marijuana than by rob-

beries, an increase in the amount of deterrence of robberies will be worth less than an equal increase devoted to stopping marijuana smokers. The chief of police most likely gets signals about the value of different types of crime deterrence from his political superiors (like the mayor). In some cities it appears, for example, that the voting public places a very high value on the apprehension of young people who behave "inappropriately." It is not uncommon to see several police cars questioning a pair of youthful, long-haired hitchhikers at just about every freeway on-ramp in some cities. But, given a fixed budget constraint, the use of police resources to apprehend illegal hitchhikers reduces the amount of resources that could be used, for example, to patrol residential districts in order to reduce the number of burglaries.

In any event, in some way or another the chief of police must allocate his budget to different departments within the police system so that the marginal product per dollar spent in each detail is equalized. Otherwise he could alter his spending among details and increase total output of his department. A change in public sentiment concerning certain crime would force a change in the chief's budget allocation. For example, if the public became less incensed about the evils of prostitution we would expect the chief of police to reduce the prostitution detail and add more men to other divisions. He would have to do this in order to equalize the value of marginal product per dollar spent on the prostitution detail with that spent in all the other departments. This relates to the law of diminishing returns. We'll assume the police department was operating in the area of diminishing returns. Therefore, a decrease in the amount of resources used to apprehend prostitutes would increase the marginal product of those resources.

The City Council

The problem faced by a chief of police in allocating his fixed budget is no different than the problem faced by a city council headed by the mayor when budget time comes around every year. There are only so many dollars in the kitty; these have to be spent for street maintenance, hospitals, and other things as well as crime prevention. The city council must attempt in one way or another to allocate parts of the fixed budget to the police department, fire department, sanitation department, and so on, in such a way that the value of the marginal products from each of these endeavors is equalized. A change in social attitude would obviously lead to a change in budget allocation. If, for instance, law and order becomes a bigger issue relative to sanitation, we would expect that the portion of the city's budget going to crime prevention would increase. This is exactly what has happened in some cases.

Deterring Crime

Some people believe that the more money spent on crime deterrence, the less crime there will be. However, it is not known what relationship there is between money spent on deterrence and the actual number of crimes that are *not* committed because of that money. It takes an extremely clever pollster to discover how many times an individual didn't break the law. We are even less certain about the effectiveness of the different methods used to deter crime. Is it best to have policemen everywhere? Or, is it best to have a system of paid informants in lieu of those policemen? Should we allow innocent parties to be apprehended and prosecuted merely because a larger absolute number of the guilty will thereby be convicted? We also have to think about the available alternatives to punishing guilty offenders. Should we allow for large fines instead of incarceration? Should we have public whippings? Should capital punishment be allowed? In terms of establishing a system of crime deterrence, we might want to assess carefully the value of different methods of supposed deterrents.

Hard Drug Problem

Let's take an example. We might suspect that the larger the potential jail sentence, the smaller the number of attempted crimes. However, this is not always correct. It appears that, for physiologically addicted drug addicts, increased penalties do nothing to deter the commission of these "crimes." Moreover, if uniformly heavy punishments is made the rule for all crimes, then we should expect to find a larger number of major crimes being committed.

Looking at the Margin

Let's look at the reasoning. All decisions are made on the margin. If an act of theft will be punished by hanging and an act of murder will be punished by the same fate, there is no marginal deterrence to murder. If a theft of $5.00 is met with a punishment of ten years in jail and a theft of $50,000 also incurs a ten-year sentence, then why not steal $50,000? Why not go for broke? There is no marginal deterrence to prevent one from doing so.

A very serious question exists as to how our system of justice can establish penalties which are appropriate from a social point of view. To establish the correct (marginal) deterrences, we must observe empirically how criminals respond to changes in punishments. This leads us to the question of how people decide whether to commit a "crime." A theory needs to be established as to what determines the supply of criminal offenses.

Offensive Supplies

Adam Smith once said:

The affluence of the rich excites the indignation of the poor, who are often both driven by want, and prompted by envy, to invade his possessions. It is only under the shelter of the civil magistrate that the owner of that valuable property, which is acquired by the labour of many years, or perhaps by many successive generations, can sleep a single night in security. He is at all times surrounded by unknown enemies, whom, though he never provokes, he can never appease, and from whose injustice he can be protected only by the powerful arm of the civil magistrate continually held up to chastise it. The acquisition of valuable and extensive property, therefore, necessarily requires the establishment of civil government. Where there is no property, or at least none that exceeds the value of two

or three days' labour, civil government is not so necessary.*

Smith is pointing out that the professional criminal is looking for income. If he is looking for income then his decision-making process could be viewed as any other. He looks at the expected returns and expected costs of criminal activity. He then compares them with the net returns from legitimate activities. The costs of crime involve apprehension, defense, conviction, jail, and so on. This is analogous to the costs that athletes may encounter when they get injured.

Viewing the supply of offenses thusly, we can come up with methods by which society can lower the net expected rate of

*Adam Smith, *The Wealth of Nations,* 1776.

return for commiting any illegal activity. That is, we can figure out how to reduce crime most effectively. We have talked about one particular aspect—the size of penalties. We also briefly mentioned the other—that is, the probability of detection for each offense. When either of these costs of crime goes up, the supply of offenses goes down; that is, less crime is committed.

Increasing the Probability of Detection

How can the probability of detection be increased? There are numerous methods—increased police activity being only one. Individuals can privately increase the probability of detecting people attempting to rob their homes. The market for individual burglar alarm systems is a burgeoning one indeed. There are also varied amounts of technologically sophisticated equipment that can be used to increase detection and apprehension. Wire tapping is one of them. This approach, however, presents a problem of infringing on individual liberties—a cost which must be reckoned with whenever it is used. It is also possible for certain "traps" to be set up so as to apprehend more criminals. For example, if money were made in a much more complicated manner, it would be more difficult

for counterfeiters to copy it successfully and go undetected.

The Courts

The probability of conviction is very important in increasing the net expected cost of commiting an illegal activity. This involves our system of courts, which today is in a sorry state. If a person knows that, even if he is apprehended, he will not be convicted, then of course the expected cost to him of commiting a crime is decreased. The likelihood of conviction is apparently an important factor in the prevention of crime. Currently, the probability of conviction for a crime is quite low in the United States. As mentioned previously, in New York City it is estimated that a man who commits a felony faces less than 1 chance in 200 of going to jail. One major reason for this is because the courts lack adequate facilities to handle the large number of cases seeking admission to the courts. The court calendars in many cities are clogged beyond belief. Many court calendars are booked for two, three, or even four years into the future. The average time lapse between filing a civil suit and getting it to trial is 40 months in New York City. What do you think happens? An overworked prosecuting attorney and his team of crime-busting as-

sistants increasingly have to arrange pretrial settlements rather than put an additional weight on the already overburdened courts. Eighty to 90 percent of criminal charges are settled before trial. Money might be spent better on streamlining court proceedings than on making more arrests. The district attorneys would not be forced to make so many "deals" with suspects. There are, of course, many inequities on the other side of the coin.

No Compensation for the Innocent

If someone is wrongfully convicted of a crime and later found innocent, he is not compensated except in rare cases for the pain, suffering, and lost income that he was caused. For example, in 1964 four youths were apprehended in New York for a suspected murder. They were convicted, but then an appellate court ruled a mistrial. They were tried three more times but no unanimous juries resulted. If they are eventually found innocent, they will most likely be paid absolutely nothing for all the years they have spent behind bars. It seems that a "just" system of justice would involve not only punishing the guilty but also full and just retribution to the innocent who are convicted of crimes they did not commit. If the court system is not faced with the full and true costs of its own mistakes,

it is not operating in an optimal manner.

Civil Suits

Courts which handle noncriminal proceedings are just as overworked as those handling criminal ones. An economically efficient system of courts would involve charging those who use the courts the full opportunity costs of that scarce resource. Instead of having to pay jurors a nominal fee for the days they spend in trial, they would be paid their full opportunity cost. And the payment would be picked up by the party who loses in the civil action. At present, taxpayers subsidize lawyers and their clients in the use of the courts. If the courts are relatively free of charge, they will be used

more often than if the lawyer and his client had to pay the full cost. This is inefficient use of resources.

The Victims

It is difficult to assess the social value that people in general place on the prevention of different types of crimes. Chiefs of police, legislators, mayors, and other officials certainly have a hard time figuring out how resources should be expended in different areas of crime deterrence. There is a possibility, though, of improving the information being used by different decision makers. Currently, there is almost no compensation to the victim or to his dependents in the case of violent crimes. If you were knocked over the head

on the street by a robber, you would probably try to sue him—if he is apprehended. But in most cases you certainly wouldn't get much money. If somebody is supporting you and that person is killed by a crazy gangster, you as the dependent would be able to collect nothing from the gangster, the state, or the government. In fact, you would probably end up paying because the criminal might be apprehended and sent to jail. You would end up paying for his care while he is in jail. In short, you get it coming and going.

A Solution—Full Liability

What is the solution? One solution might be for individual local governments to assume responsibility for the complete liability of anyone within their geographical territory. If unlimited liability were assessed against the state in the case of criminal assaults and crimes against property, then the taxpayers would find a portion of their taxes going to compensate victims of crimes. This would eventually come back through the political process as a demand for better law enforcement in those areas that were most expensive to taxpayers. Most likely, fewer resources would be spent on apprehending and convicting victimless criminals, such as prostitutes and marijuana smokers, and more resources would be spent on pre-venting robberies, assaults, rapes, and murders. We would expect a more optimal allocation of resources to prevail within police departments. Also, there may be an effort to streamline the courts in order to increase the probability of conviction. Further, our prisons may be turned into rehabilitation institutions instead of schools for improved criminal activities which increase future crime.

So far only a few states have begun to offer compensation to crime victims, and these compensations aren't overgenerous. In New York a 67-year-old tailor was savagely beaten and stabbed by a robber. He was disabled for eight months and ran up tremendous medical bills that outdistanced his insurance by a large amount. He turned to the Crime Victims' Compensation Board, which is a New York State body set up in the sixties to aid the victims of violent crimes. This board awarded him a grand total of $3133. Three thousand dollars is not much, but it is a step in the right direction. The more money that states, cities, and towns are forced to cough up for victims of crimes, the more pressure will be brought to make our entire system of criminal deterrence more effective.

Questions for Thought and Discussion

1. Do you think that poverty is a cause of crime?
2. How would you establish the amount of compensation due an innocent person who has spent time in jail because of a mistake on the part of the courts? (Hint: Start out with opportunity cost and then keep going.)
3. Why are more resources spent on preventing certain crimes and not others?
4. "The way to eliminate all crimes is to eliminate all laws." Do you agree?
5. "The determinants of crime are not economic since crime is a sociological phenomenon." What do you think of that statement?

Selected References

Cressey, Donald R. *Theft of the Nation: The Structure and Operations of Organized Crime in America.* New York: Harper & Row, 1969.

Martin, J. P., & Wilson, Gail. *The Police: A Study in Manpower.* London: Heineman, 1969.

President's Commission on Law Enforcement and the Administration of Justice. *The Challenge of Crime in a Free Society.* Washington, D.C.: U.S. Government Printing Office, 1967.

Schur, Edwin M. *Crimes without Victims.* Englewood Cliffs, N.J.: Prentice Hall, 1965.

Skolnick, Jerome H. *Justice without Trial: Law Enforcement in Democratic Society.* New York: John Wiley & Sons, 1966.

Tullock, Gordon. *The Logic of the Law.* New York: Basic Books, 1971.

The Firm in Competition

C HAPTER 4 GAVE us some tools which can be used to analyze and predict the behavior of firms in our economy. We have not yet broached the topic of how firms set their prices and how much each firm will decide to produce. To do this, we must have some information on the characteristics of the firms in question. Usually firms in our economy will be divided into two categories: those in competitive situations and those in monopoly situations. Of course, between these two categories lies an entire spectrum of possible degrees of competitiveness. For the moment, let's concentrate on a more or less perfectly competitive situation.

CHARACTERISTICS OF A COMPETITIVE INDUSTRY

Although there is no one definition for a competitive situation, most economists will agree with the following definition:

The competitive firm is such a small part of the total industry in which it operates that it cannot affect the price of the products in question.

This notion of competition relates in one sense to the number of competitors in an industry. A competitive industry usually has a large number of firms in it. Admittedly, no one knows exactly what this number must be. All that we can say is that the number must be large enough so as to insure that no single firm has control over the price of the product; the number must be large enough so that each firm in the industry is a **price taker**—the firm takes prices as given, as something that is determined outside of the individual firm.

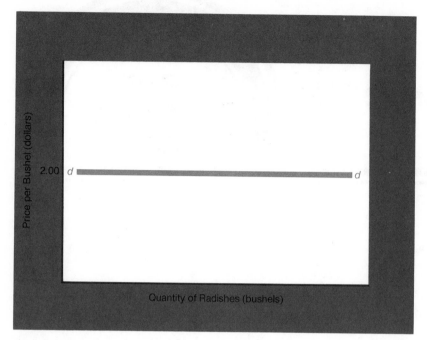

Price per Bushel (dollars)

2.00 d ━━━━━━━━━━━━━━━━━━━━━━━━━ d

Quantity of Radishes (bushels)

FIGURE 5–1

THE DEMAND CURVE FOR AN INDIVIDUAL RADISH PRODUCER

Here we assume that the individual radish producer is such a small part of the total market that he cannot influence the price of radishes. He takes the price as given. He therefore faces a horizontal demand curve, *dd* at the going market price. If he raises his price even one penny he will sell no radishes. He would be foolish to lower his price below $2.00 because he can sell all that he can produce at a price of $2.00. His demand curve is completely or perfectly elastic.

This definition of a competitive firm is obviously idealized for, in one sense, the *individual* firm has to set prices. How can we ever have a situation where firms regard prices as set by forces outside their control? The answer is that, even though every firm by definition sets its own prices, a firm in a more or less perfectly competitive situation will find that it will eventually receive no customers at all, if it sets its price above the competitive price. Let's attempt a graphic representation of the demand curve of an individual firm in a competitive industry.

SINGLE-FIRM DEMAND CURVE

When talking about the elasticity of demand, we said that, if the demand schedule was *completely* elastic and Hugh Hefner raised the price on *Playboy* by 10¢, he would suffer a drop in sales of 9 million copies, thereby reducing his circulation to zero. This is how we characterize the demand schedule for a competitive firm—it is a horizontal line at the going market price. We'll find out how that price is determined in a moment. For now, let's look at Figure 5–1. Here our example is a hypothetical demand schedule that an individual radish producer faces in the market for selling radishes. This individual's production represents a very, very small part of the total radish production in the industry. He therefore has no control whatsoever over the price he can get for his radishes. The price of radishes is $2.00 a bushel, which is where the horizontal demand curve for the individual producer lies. That is, people's demand for the radishes raised by that one farmer is perfectly elastic. If he raises his price, they will buy from some other farmer. (Why not worry about lowering the price?) We will label the individual producer's demand curve as *dd,* whereas the market demand curve will always be labeled *DD.* A perfectly competitive firm faces a completely

FIGURE 5-2

PROFIT MAXIMIZATION

On the horizontal axis we show the quantity of radishes produced per year and, on the vertical axis, the total costs and total revenues. Total revenues are represented by the straight line *TR,* and total costs are represented by the wavy line *TC.* Profit maximization occurs when the distance between total revenues and total costs is maximized. That is when profits will be largest. We find that the maximum distance occurs in this particular diagram at 25,000 bushels of radishes per year. That will be the profit-maximizing quantity to produce for our perfectly competitive radish farmer. Notice that the reason his total revenue curve is a straight line is because he can receive $2.00 per bushel for all the radishes he cares to sell.

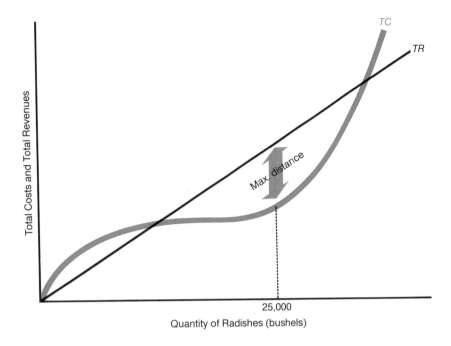

or infinitely elastic demand curve for its products; that is how we can best characterize the perfect competitor.

HOW MUCH DOES THE PERFECT COMPETITOR PRODUCE?

As we have shown, a perfect competitor has to accept the given price of his product. If he raises his price, he sells nothing. If he lowers his price, he makes less money per unit sold than he could. He has only one decision variable left to him: how much should he produce? As you might expect, we will now have to apply our model of the firm to come up with an answer. We shall use the model of *profit maximization,* and we will assume that firms, whether competitive or monopolistic, will attempt to maximize their profits—or the difference between total revenue and total cost.

Maximizing Profits

We can demonstrate a hypothetical total cost curve and total revenue curve in Figure 5-2. We're assuming this is for a competitive firm; therefore, the **total revenue curve** *(TR)* is a straight line because the price of the product does not change as the firm's output changes. If the firm sells ten bushels of radishes at $2.00 a bushel, it takes in $20.00 of revenues. If it sells twice that much, it takes in twice as many revenues, and so on. The total cost curve *(TC),* however, displays the form that we developed in Figure 4-2 in the last chapter. That is, after an initial starting point, total costs first rise less than in proportion to changes in output and then more than in proportion to changes in output.

Where will the firm end up maximizing profits? Obviously, it will maximize profits at that point on the graph where the difference between the total revenue curve and the total cost curve is the greatest. That distance happens to be, in our hypothetical example, at a production rate of 25,000 bushels per year. That is where the perfectly competitive radish producer will make the most money, if he were faced with the hypothetical total cost and total revenue curves presented in Figure 5–2.

We also should be able to use our other curves to come up with the same answer. That is to say, what can be done with total costs and total revenues can also be duplicated by using average and marginal revenues along with average and marginal costs.

Using Marginal Quantities

Let's redraw the perfectly elastic demand curve facing our radish farmer, this time adding his marginal cost curve. The marginal cost curve is computed by finding out how much total costs go up each time output is increased. When average costs are falling, marginal costs are less than average costs. When average costs are rising, marginal costs are also rising and are greater than average costs. Look at the intersection of the marginal cost curve and the perfectly elastic demand schedule, *dd*, in Figure 5–3. As you

---

FIGURE 5–3 PROFIT MAXIMIZATION FOR THE PERFECT COMPETITOR

The horizontal axis measures the quantity of radishes produced per year, and the vertical axis represents the price per bushel. The demand curve facing the perfectly competitive radish producer is *dd*—a horizontal line at the going market price of $2.00 per bushel. We have labeled *dd* also as *average revenue = price = marginal revenue*. The farmer can sell all he wants at a price of $2.00; thus, $2.00 is the average revenue. It is also the marginal revenue because he gets the same price for incremental units sold. His marginal cost curve is *MC*. The intersection of the marginal cost curve and his demand curve, *dd*, represents the point of profit maximization, that is the point where marginal revenue equals marginal cost. Look at point *A*. The farmer would not want to produce at point *A* because marginal costs are only $1.50; marginal revenue, however, is $2.00. He could make more by producing more. He would not want to produce at point *B* because marginal costs exceed marginal revenues. He therefore produces at point *E*.

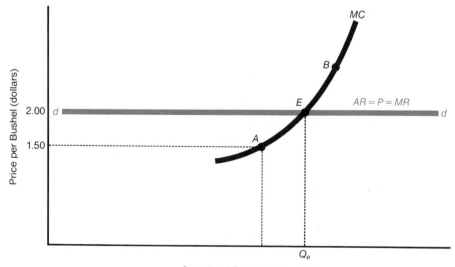

Quantity of Radishes (bushels)

might expect, since there's an intersection, something important is happening at that point. The intersection, *E,* of the marginal cost curve and the horizontal demand curve represents the point of maximum profits for the perfectly competitive firm. Let's figure out why.

Marginal Revenue. What is the amount of extra revenues (marginal revenues) that our radish farmer can hope to receive each time he sells an additional (marginal) bushel of radishes? Since he is such a small part of the market, he cannot influence the price; he must take it as given. Therefore, he knows he can receive $2.00 a bushel for every single bushel he wants to put out on the market. This means the average revenue or price he can receive is $2.00 a bushel, and the marginal revenue from increasing production is also $2.00 a bushel. **Marginal revenue** is the additional revenue our farmer can receive by selling one more bushel of radishes. It is the difference between total revenue for 100 bushels of radishes and total revenue for 99 bushels; or it is the difference between total revenues for selling 10,000 bushels of radishes and total revenues for selling 9999 bushels. *Marginal revenue represents the increment in total revenues attributable to selling one more unit of the product in question.*

Marginal Revenue = Average Revenue. We have a somewhat strange situation with our perfect competitor. The average revenue or price he receives for all the bushels he sells is equal to $2.00, and the marginal revenue he receives for selling an additional bushel is always $2.00. That is why in Figure 5–3 we have labeled the *dd* curve as the place where average revenue equals marginal revenue equals price, or $AR = P = MR$.

WHEN PROFITS ARE MAXIMIZED

Let's take a point on the marginal cost curve which is below the *dd* curve—say, point *A.* Here, the marginal cost is $1.50 a bushel. How much could our farmer hope to receive if he increased production by one bushel and sold it? He knows he can receive $2.00. Therefore, it would pay him to increase production by one more bushel. He would receive $2.00 and only be spending an additional $1.50 in marginal cost. He could make 50¢ on producing and selling that extra bushel. But why stop there? Why stop at increasing production by just one more when you're at point *A*? In fact, why not keep producing and selling until the amount of additional revenue you receive from selling one more bushel will just cover the additional costs incurred from producing and selling that bushel? Why not continue producing until marginal revenue equals marginal cost? In fact, isn't that how you will maximize your profits? Obviously it is, for if marginal cost is less than marginal revenue, you could always make more money by increasing production because the increased revenues would be greater than the increased costs.

If you were producing at a point above the *dd* curve, say at *B,* you would be making smaller profits than you could. At *B* marginal cost exceeds the price that you can receive on that additional output. You are spending more for producing that additional output than you are receiving in revenues. You would be foolish to continue producing that much. But, where, in fact, do you want to produce? You want to produce at point *E,* where the marginal cost curve intersects the horizontal demand curve because the horizontal demand curve represents not only the average revenue or price but the marginal revenue from selling one additional unit of production. You will always want to be at point *E.*

Here we have it. This is how an individual competitive radish farmer determines how many radishes he should put on the market. He knows that he can sell all of the radishes he wants at the going price. Therefore, the marginal revenue he can receive from selling any additional radishes is always going to be the market price of $2.00 a bushel. He will continue production until the cost of increasing output by one more unit would just be matched by the revenues obtainable from selling that extra unit. *Profit maximization is always at the point where marginal revenue equals marginal cost.* For a perfectly competitive firm, this is at the intersection of the demand schedule, *dd,* with the marginal cost curve, *MC.* Our profit-maximizing, perfectly competitive radish farmer will produce Q_e—no more and no less.

PROFITS AGAIN

Even though we have been talking about profit maximization in the context of a perfectly competitive situation, it turns out that in strict economic terminology a perfectly competitive firm makes *zero* profits. You may ask why any firm would want to work for zero profits. Why would businessmen even bother? Recall our definition of true economic profits. They were the returns *over and above* a normal or *competitive rate of return.* That is, *profits in economics are defined as those returns in excess of the opportunity cost of capital.* Therefore, a perfectly competitive firm might make zero economic profits, while making 7 percent accounting profits at the same time. Those 7 percent accounting profits merely represent the rate of return on investment which is necessary to keep the businessman from going into another business.

We can now graphically characterize the perfectly competitive firm's profit position by adding the variable cost curves to Figure 5–3. An average variable cost curve and an average total cost curve has been added to Figure 5–4. Notice that here the average total cost curve just touches the horizontal demand curve at the point where the marginal cost curve intersects the *dd* line. This is very important for it says that the competitive firm is selling its product at a price exactly equal to the average total per unit cost. Point *E* is also called the **break-even point** for a competitive firm. This is where total cost equals total revenue.

(Total costs equal *ATC* x quantity produced, and total revenue equals price × quantity.)

Remember here that the opportunity cost of capital is included in costs. Therefore, the break-even point here is higher than the break-even point businessmen usually refer to; they usually talk in terms of just breaking even *without* making any *accounting* profits at all, *without* being paid a normal rate of return on their investment.

SHUT-DOWN POINT

What about the average *variable* cost curve? Why is it in there? It is there for the very good reason that a firm will shut down, if it cannot at least cover its average variable costs. The **shut-down point** is at *A,* where the marginal cost curve intersects the average variable cost curve. If, for some reason, the prices go to $1.00 a bushel, which is below point *A,* then our radish farmer will go out of business because the additional revenues he can obtain (that is, $1.00 per bushel) do not even cover the additional wages he must give out to workers. If marginal revenue doesn't cover variable costs, he would be better off going out of business. Every businessman will accept this type of analysis because every businessman knows that, if he cannot at least cover the cost of his workers, he is better off going out of business because then he will only have to pay for the fixed costs, which always exist no matter what the rate of production.

ZERO ECONOMIC PROFITS

You might be wondering why the average total cost curve happens to just touch the *dd* line, or price line, exactly at the intersection of the marginal cost curve and the *dd* curve. Was that just a fortuitous happenstance, a stroke of luck? In the real world, of course, it would be pure luck to find a firm making *exactly* zero economic profits because nothing is as exact as the curves which we use to simplify our analysis of a competitive situation. Things change all the time in a dynamic world and firms, even in a very competitive situation, may, for some reason, be making nonzero profits. But usually it is reasoned that the way competition leads to zero profits is by *entry*. This brings up another market aspect that characterizes a perfectly competitive industry.

An industry which is perfectly competitive

FIGURE 5–4

PROFITS FOR THE PERFECT COMPETITOR

The quantity of radishes is measured on the horizontal axis; the price per bushel on the vertical axis. The demand curve facing the perfectly competitive radish producer is *dd,* the horizontal line at $2.00, or the going market price for radishes. The firm produces where marginal revenue equals marginal cost, or where the marginal cost curve, *MC,* intersects the *dd* line, which is also the marginal revenue line, at point *E.* We have shown that at point *E* the average total cost curve just touches the demand curve. Average total costs, then, will just equal the average revenue, or the price received per unit. This means zero economic profits will be made. Remember, though, that normal profits will be made because normal profits are the opportunity cost of capital and that is already included in our cost figures. Another way to look at it is that at point *E* total revenue equals total costs. Total revenue is just the price times total quantities sold and the price here is $2.00 per bushel. Total costs will be equal to average total costs times the quantity sold, and here we have shown average total costs to be $2.00 per bushel also. Point *E* is the break-even point in economic terminology but not in accounting terminology. The average variable cost curve is also included. We must show this in order to find out where the firm's shut-down point is. The firm's shut-down point is at the intersection of the marginal cost curve with the average variable cost curve, or point *A.* Below that point the firm cannot even cover its variable costs. It is, therefore, not worth staying in business.

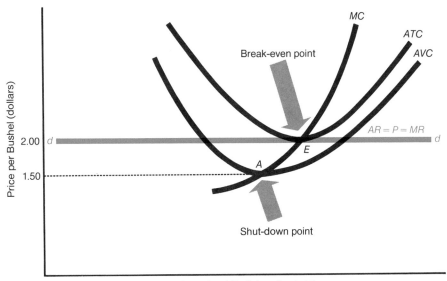

Quantity of Radishes (bushels)

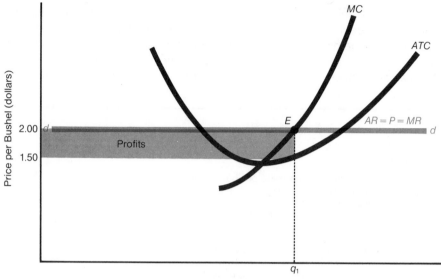

FIGURE 5–5   **SHORT-RUN ECONOMIC PROFIT**

Here we have redrawn Figure 5–4, but now we have shown the average total cost curve to be below the *dd* or average revenue line. The equilibrium quantity to be produced by this particular firm is at the intersection of the marginal cost curve with *dd*, or point *E*. At point *E*, q_1 is produced. The difference between Figure 5–5 and Figure 5–4 is that in this particular diagram, economic profits are being made. Profits are defined as the difference between total revenues and total costs. Total costs here are less than total revenues. The difference is profits, represented by the shaded area. In a competitive situation this will lead to entry by other firms. These other firms will increase the quantity supplied and therefore lower the market-clearing price. The *dd* line will eventually fall until there are no economic profits being made.

must have *no* **barriers to entry.** Other firms must be able to start a competing business without restriction. Let's look at the situation depicted in Figure 5–5. Here, the average total cost curve is below the price line; this means positive economic profits equal to the shaded area are being made by all firms. That is, all firms are getting a rate of return higher than the opportunity cost of capital. Other businessmen would soon realize this and conclude that they could make more money by changing (entering) into that field. The results of increased competition is a lowering of price because increased competition usually involves an increase in the supply of the product in question. We know from our usual supply-demand analysis that the only way a larger supply can be sold is for the price to fall. Any situation such as the one in Figure 5–5 will lead to an eventual correction by firms entering the industry. New firms will enter until nobody sees those positive economic profits. Profits will eventually fall to zero as the *dd* curve (price line) falls. This line will eventually touch the average total cost curve, where there are again zero economic profits.

THE LONG RUN

The idea behind a competitive firm having zero economic profits is obviously a *long-run concept.* That is, we know that at any moment in time, even in a competitive situation, there may be nonzero profits accruing to a large number of firms. Eventually, though, free entry will allow other firms to come in seeking these profits. This will cause the price to fall so profits will no longer be made. Then entry will stop and the situation will be stabilized.

If, on the other hand, the *dd* curve or price line lies *below* the average total cost curve, the difference is *losses* or *negative profits.* In Figure 5–6, the negative profits are represented by the heavy shaded area. After all, profits are always measured as the difference between total revenues and total costs; total revenues equal the quantity times the price, and total costs equal the quantity times the average total unit cost. The difference is profit or, in this case, losses. If this is the situation, we would expect firms to leave the industry. Firms would look for better business opportunities elsewhere, and ultimately the price would rise. The price established with a smaller number of suppliers would be higher than the price established with a large number of suppliers.

FIGURE 5–6 LOSSES FOR THE PERFECTLY COMPETITIVE FIRM

Here we have shown a situation where the competitive firm will make losses. The intersection of the marginal cost curve with the marginal revenue or *dd* line is at *E.* This competitive radish producer will produce q_1 quantity of radishes each year. He will receive total revenues equal to $2.00 per bushel times q_1. His total costs, though, will be equal to his average total costs of $2.50 per bushel times q_1. His losses are represented by the shaded area. Eventually this situation will correct itself. Firms will leave the industry; the supply will diminish; and the market-clearing price will rise. Then the individual demand schedule, *dd,* will shift upward until losses are eliminated.

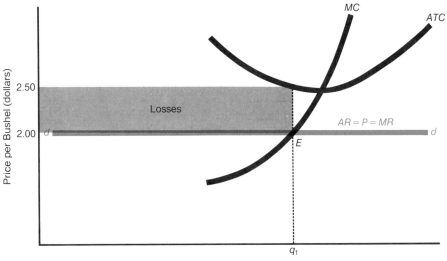

Quantity of Radishes (bushels)

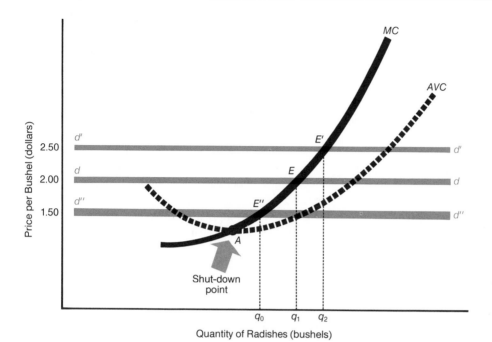

FIGURE 5–7 THE INDIVIDUAL FIRM'S SUPPLY CURVE

Here we show the marginal cost curve, *MC*, and three different individual demand curves. The first one is *dd*. If the demand curve is *dd*, the equilibrium or profit-maximizing point for the firm will be at the intersection of *dd* and *MC*, or *E*. It will produce q_1 of radishes. If, for some reason, the demand curve shifts up to *d'd'*, the new intersection will be at *E'*. He will produce q_2 of radishes. If the demand curve falls to *d''d''*, the new intersection is at *E''*. He will produce only q_0 of radishes. The supply curve, then, for the individual firm is its marginal cost curve. Actually, though, it is only its marginal cost curve above the shut-down point, or point *A*. That is at the point of the intersection of the average variable cost curve and the marginal cost curve. The firm would not want to produce at a point below *A* because the price received would not even cover the average variable costs so it would be better to shut down.

THE FIRM SUPPLY CURVE

How is the supply in the industry obtained from the individual firms' supply curves? To answer this we have to find out what the supply curve for the individual firm looks like. Actually, we've been looking at it all along. When the price was set at $2.00 a bushel, how much did the individual radish farmer produce? He produced Q_1. See Figure 5–7 where his marginal cost curve intersected the horizontal line, *dd*. What if that horizontal *dd*

line had risen to *d'd'*? Given that the marginal cost curve is rising and moving toward the right, a new intersection, *E'*, at a higher point would mean that the firm would produce more. What if the *dd* line fell to *d''d''*? The intersection would be at a lower point, *E''*, one that was closer to the vertical axis. The competitive firm would produce less. We see in Figure 5–7 three different *dd* curves representing three different going prices for radishes. Each one of them intersects the marginal cost curve at a different point. Those

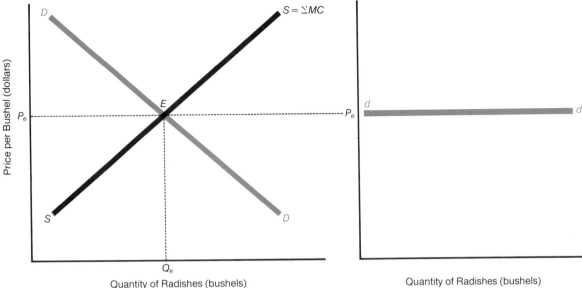

FIGURE 5-8

THE INDUSTRY DEMAND AND SUPPLY CURVE

The industry demand curve is a representation of the demand curve for all potential consumers. It is represented by *DD*. The industry supply curve is the horizontal summation of all of the individual firms' marginal cost curves. We show it as *SS* and mark it as equal to ΣMC. The intersection of the demand and supply curve at *E* determines the equilibrium or market-clearing price or going price at P_e.

FIGURE 5-9

INDIVIDUAL FIRM DEMAND CURVE

Here we have shown that the individual firm demand curve is set at the going market price determined in Figure 5-8. That is, the demand curve facing the individual firm is a horizontal line, *dd*, at price P_e.

different points represent the amounts that would be produced at each given price. *Therefore, the supply curve of the firm is exactly equal to its marginal cost curve.*

But this is not completely correct because a portion of the marginal cost curve is not part of the supply curve of any given firm. Do you know what portion that is? We said that after the shut-down point, plants will no longer operate. If the price falls below average variable costs, it will not pay a firm to continue production. Therefore, below the point where the average variable cost curve intersects the marginal cost curve, the competitive firm will no longer produce. In Figure 5-7, the true actual supply curve for our particular

radish farmer is the heavily shaded portion on the marginal cost curve that is above the average variable cost curve (above point *A*).

THE INDUSTRY SUPPLY CURVE

Now we are set to figure out what the market supply curve or the supply curve for the entire industry looks like. First of all, let's ask: What is an industry? Isn't it merely a collection of firms producing a particular product? Yes, and, therefore, we have an obvious way to figure out the total supply curve of radishes, for example. We merely add, for every price on the axis, the quantities that each firm will supply. In other words, we horizontally add up all of the individual supply curves of all of the competitive firms. But the individual supply curves are simply the marginal cost curves of each firm. Therefore, in Figure 5–8 we have drawn the industry supply curve as the horizontal sum of the marginal cost curves, where Σ stands for summation. In other words, ΣMC equals (loosely stated) the MC curve of firm No. 1 plus the MC curve of firm No. 2 plus the MC curve of firm No. 3 and so on. This is why we said that the supply curve is positively sloped.

COMPETITIVE PRICE DETERMINATION

Now we can tackle the problem of how the ''going'' price is established in a competitive market. This price is established by the interaction of all of the firms and all of the demanders. The market demand schedule DD drawn in Figure 5–8 represents the demand schedule for the entire industry—not the demand schedule for an individual firm. Price P_e is established by the forces of supply and demand at the intersection of SS and DD. Even though each individual producer has no control or effect on the price of his product in a competitive industry, the interaction of all the producers determines the price at which the product will be sold. We say that the price P_e and the quantity Q_e in Figure 5–8 is the competitive unrestricted solution to the pricing/quantity problem in that particular industry. It is the equilibrium where suppliers and demanders are content. The resultant individual dd is shown in Figure 5–9 at the price P_e.

THE LONG AND THE SHORT OF A COMPETITIVE SUPPLY CURVE

In Figure 5–8, we drew the summation of all the marginal cost curves as an upward sloping supply

curve for the entire industry. We should be aware of the possibility that a relatively steep upward sloping supply curve is really only appropriate in the short run. After all, one of the prerequisites for a competitive industry is that there are no restrictions on entry. We would expect, therefore, that, if the demand schedule shifted out to the right (there was increasing demand for the product in question), eventually more firms would enter the market so that the quantity supplied could be expanded. In fact, each time the demand curve shifts out to the right, the prices could be expected to rise. But this would mean nonzero economic profits for the current producers. Therefore, more producers would come into the market and force the price down to its old equilibrium level, if costs in the industry remained constant. Assume, however, that a larger number of firms demanding more raw materials would cause the prices of raw materials to rise somewhat. Then the average cost curve for all firms (and the marginal cost curve as well) would shift up a little. Zero economic profit would be realized at a slightly higher price than before. As shown in Figure 5–10, we would expect that, as the demand curve shifted from DD to $D'D'$, the price would jump from P_e to P_e'. Eventually the supply curve would move to the right (as new firms entered) until the price fell to P_l. The long-run supply curve would therefore be $S_l S_l$. As we mentioned before, empirical evidence suggests that the long-run supply curve for manufactured products is probably fairly elastic due to other firms freely entering industries where above normal rates of return are being earned.

WHY ECONOMISTS ARE FASCINATED WITH THE COMPETITIVE SOLUTION

Often, one will see economists using the competitive solution as the norm for what the economy should be doing, for what an industry should be doing, or for what a firm should be doing. There

FIGURE 5–10

LONG-RUN INDUSTRY SUPPLY

Here we have shown the short-run industry supply curve starting out at *SS*. The industry demand curve is *DD;* the equilibrium price starts out at *Pₑ*. Now there is a shift in demand from *DD* to *D'D'*. A shift in demand causes a rise in the equilibrium or market-clearing price to *Pₑ'* for that is where *D'D'* intersects *SS*. However, this will mean positive economic profits for the existing firms. New firms will want to enter and will indeed enter the industry, eventually driving the supply curve to *S'S'*. It will intersect the new demand curve *D'D'* at a price *Pᵢ*. When we connect the two equilibrium intersection points, *E* and *E''*, we get the long-run supply curve, *SᵢSᵢ*.

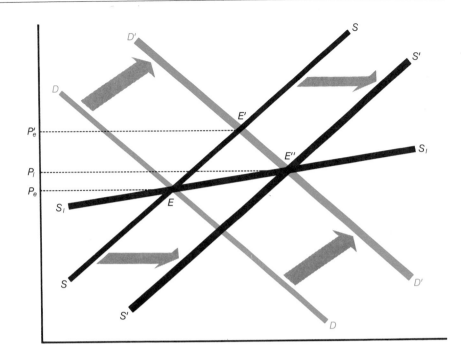

must be a reason behind this; it can't just be a whim on the part of so many economists. There is, indeed, a reason behind it, although we should be careful to distinguish between stating a factual situation and recommending policy changes because the current situation does not jibe with the desired situation. In other words, if an economist establishes the fact that a certain industry is pricing its products above the price that would prevail in a competitive situation, that is a positive economic statement. However, if the economist recommends that "something should be done" to make the industry more competitive, this is in the realm of normative economics and involves subjective value judgments. Often, economists will declare their desire for a competitive solution to an industry pricing problem without stating that this desire rests on personal value judgments.

Let's try to discover why economists are so fascinated with the competitive solution. What

does marginal cost represent? It represents the cost of increasing production by one incremental unit. Suppose a marginal cost curve shows that an increase in production from 10,000 bushels of radishes to 10,001 bushels of radishes will cost $1.50. That $1.50 represents the *opportunity cost* of producing one more bushel of radishes. It represents the opportunity cost of increasing production. Thus, we've established that the marginal cost curve gives a graphic representation of the opportunity cost of production.

The competitive firm is faced with a price that just equals the marginal cost. Herein lies the element of the "desirability" of a competitive solution. It is called **marginal cost pricing.** The competitive firm sells its product at a price that just equals the cost to society—that is, the opportunity cost—for that is what the marginal cost curve represents. The competitive solution is called *efficient*. It is not efficient in the technological or engineering sense of the word, but rather in the economic sense of the word. Economic efficiency involves a situation where it is impossible to increase total production in such a way as to increase people's *total* utility or happiness. No juggling of resources, such as labor and capital, will result in an output that is higher in value than the value of the goods and services already being produced. In an efficient situation, it is impossible to make someone better off without making someone else worse off. All resources are used in the most advantageous way possible. All goods and services are sold at their opportunity cost, and marginal cost pricing prevails throughout.

The key to understanding why economists "like" competition is because competition leads to a situation where the marginal opportunity cost is just equal to the marginal value of the good to society. Hence, if prices were raised higher than marginal costs, there would be too little produced. If prices were set below marginal cost, too much would be produced. Since in competition, price equals marginal cost, just the "right" amount of everything is produced.

IS PERFECT COMPETITION POSSIBLE?

The analytic model presented here represents a situation that may never be seen in reality. Perfect competition can only exist if information is also perfect. After all, the only way for a price to be uniform at every moment in time (corrected for quality changes and transportation costs) is for everybody to know what's happening every place else at every moment in time. Obviously, information is never perfect. In fact, the cost of trying to achieve perfect information would be prohibitive. A profit-maximizing firm will produce at the point where the additional revenues obtained from producing more goods exactly covers the additional costs incurred (where marginal revenue equals marginal cost). Similarly, if we are wealth maximizing, we would never spend more than

we get in return from improving information flows. That is, we would improve information in the marketplace only up to the point where the marginal revenue from doing so is equal to the marginal cost. That is certainly at a point well below *perfect* information.

A purely competitive industry has been defined as one with many sellers. To satisfy the criterion of perfect competition where each seller has no control whatsoever over the price of his product, we would have to have a tremendous number of firms. There are many industries where the number of firms is not extremely large and therefore individually each firm has, at least in the short run, some control over its prices. However, analyzing the industry in the *long run,* we might say that it was *tending* toward a competitive solution all the time because there were a sufficient number of firms *on the margin* attempting to increase their share of the total sales by undercutting the other firms. Notice we said that the industry might tend toward a competitive solution at all times. That is a **dynamic process**—which is to say, that it never ends. At any point in time, an investigation of the particular industry will not reveal a perfectly competitive solution, although ultimately that is where one would expect the industry to be going.

Even when an industry is not perfectly competitive, it does not necessarily follow that steps should be taken to make it more competitive so as to ensure efficiency. After all, it is not possible to change an industry's structure from noncompetitive to competitive without using resources. We will discuss some of the ways of doing this, such as legislation against noncompetitive business practices, regulation of noncompetitive industries, and others. Remember that legislation and regulation involve the use of men who could be doing something else. That is, there is an opportunity cost involved in attempting to turn a noncompetitive industry into a competitive industry. Before engaging in such a campaign, we may want to be sure that the benefits of increased competition will outweigh the costs of getting the increased competition.

The fact that we use the model of perfect competition in an economic analysis does not mean that we should hold up perfect competition as the only type of industry structure to be tolerated. Sometimes the competitive model predicts well, even in noncompetitive situations. In such cases, you may not wish to seek out some alternative theory.

Definition of New Terms

COMPETITIVE FIRM: one that is such a small part of the total industry picture that it cannot affect the price of the product it makes.

PRICE TAKER: another definition of a competitive firm. A price taker is a firm that must take the price of its product as given. The firm cannot influence its prices.

TOTAL REVENUES: the price per product times the total quantity sold.

MARGINAL REVENUE: the increment in total revenues attributable to selling one more unit of the product in question.

AVERAGE REVENUE: total revenue divided by the quantity sold. Whenever the same price is charged on all units, the average revenue equals the price.

BREAK-EVEN POINT: the point where the firm's total revenues equal its total costs. In economics the break-even point is where the firm is just making a normal rate of return.

SHUT-DOWN POINT: the point where the profit-maximizing price just covers average variable costs. This occurs at the intersection of the marginal cost curve and the average variable cost curve.

BARRIERS TO ENTRY: legal or other constraints which prevent the entrance of new firms into an industry.

MARGINAL COST PRICING: a system of pricing in which the price charged is equal to the opportunity cost of producing one more unit of the good or service in question. The opportunity cost is the marginal cost to society.

EFFICIENT SOLUTION: a situation where a shifting of resources cannot make anybody better off without making somebody else worse off.

DYNAMIC PROCESS: a situation which is always changing. We live in a world of dynamic processes. In some sense, prices are changing all the time, production is changing all the time, demand is shifting all the time. These changes make up the dynamic nature of our economy.

Chapter Summary

1. We define a competitive situation as one in which individual firms cannot affect the price of the product they produce. This is usually when the firm is very small relative to the entire industry. A firm in a perfectly competitive situation is called a price taker; he must take the price as given.

2. The firm, therefore, faces a completely elastic demand curve for its product. It can sell all it wants at the going market price. If it raises its price, it sells nothing. It will not lower its price because it would not then be making as much money as it could.

3. The firm's total revenues will equal the price of the product times the total quantity sold. Since the competitive firm can sell all it wants at the same price (the "going" price), total revenues just equal the going price times whatever the firm decides to sell.

4. The firm decides to produce and sell wherever it maximizes profits. It maximizes profits when it maximizes the difference between total revenues and total costs. We can also find out where it maximizes profits by looking at its marginal cost curve.

5. You'll remember that the marginal cost curve is that curve which represents the increment in total cost due to an increase in production of successive units. It turns out that the firm maximizes profits where marginal cost equals marginal revenue. The marginal revenue to the firm is represented by its own demand curve. This is because marginal revenue is defined as the increment in total revenues due to an increase in production by one unit. But the competitive firm can sell all it wants at the same market-clearing price; therefore, its marginal revenue will equal the price, which will equal its average revenue. The firm will always want to produce where marginal revenue equals marginal cost. If it produces above that point, marginal cost will exceed marginal revenue. If it produces below that point, marginal cost is less than marginal revenue, and it could be making more profits if it expanded production.

6. A perfectly competitive firm ends up in the long run making zero economic profits. However, it still makes a normal or competitive rate of return, since that is the opportunity cost of capital. The competitive rate of return or normal profits are included in the costs as we have defined them for the firm. The point of maximum profits for the competitive firm is therefore also its break-even point; this is where total costs will equal total revenue. Businessmen like to talk of a break-even point which does *not* include a normal rate of return as a cost. Note that this differs from the economist's notion of a break-even point.

7. The firm will always produce along its marginal cost curve, unless the price it charges to maximize profits will not cover average variable costs. This is the shut-down point. It occurs at the intersection of the average variable cost curve and the marginal cost curve. Below that point it is not profitable to stay in business, since variable costs will not be completely covered by revenue.

8. Economic profits are eliminated in a competitive situation because, in the long run, other firms will enter the industry if it is initially possible to make economic profits. These new firms increase the supply and lower the market-clearing price. Conversely, if there are economic losses (negative economic profits), firms will leave the industry thereby decreasing the supply and causing a rise in the market clearing price.

9. The supply curve of the firm is exactly equal to its marginal cost curve above the shut-down point. The supply curve of the industry is equal to the horizontal summation of all the supply curves of the individual firms. This is a short-run industry supply curve, and it is upward sloping.

10. The equilibrium or market-clearing price is determined by the intersection of the market demand curve and the industry supply curve, which is made up of all the individual firms' supply curves. That is how we determine the going price in the market.

11. In the long run the supply curve of the industry is probably quite elastic because firms can enter the industry and, therefore, cause the short-run supply curve to shift to the right.

12. The competitive solution is fascinating to economists because it is the most economically efficient one. That is to say, the competitive solution results in a situation where any change in the use of resources will result in a decrease in the economic value obtainable from a fixed amount of resources at any point in time. The competitive solution leads to what is called marginal cost pricing, where the price is set equal to the marginal cost, which is equal to the social opportunity cost of producing the good or service in question.

13. It is difficult to imagine many situations where perfect competition exists in the short run. However, in the long run we might say that there's a tendency towards a competitive solution, even if it will never be reached. That is because firms will constantly acquire new information; there will be entry and exit from the industry depending upon whether there are economic profits or economic losses.

Questions for Thought and Discussion

1. What is the meaning of zero profits in the economic sense?
2. How could a firm continue for years with negative economic profits?
3. Why would a firm be better off to quit producing if the market price were less than the average variable cost?
4. Since pure competition has never existed nor never will, why do we bother to study it?
5. "The radish farmer must receive a living price for his radishes." Discuss.
6. Is the price of radishes determined by the cost of producing them, or is the cost of producing them determined by the price?
7. If the average total cost curve lies above the demand curve, why doesn't the profit-maximizing, competitive firm produce at the point where the marginal cost curve intersects the average total cost curve? Doesn't the marginal cost curve intersect the average total cost curve at its minimum? This means the intersection of the average total cost curve and the marginal cost curve is at minimum average total cost. Is this the best place to produce?
8. Can you think of any situation where it would be better not to produce when marginal revenue equals marginal cost?
9. If you were a businessman, would you be content with just "breaking even"?
10. Do you think the concept of efficiency is in the realm of normative or positive economics?

Selected References

Knight, F.H. "Cost of Production and Price over Long and Short Periods." *Journal of Political Economy,* April 1921, **29,** 304-335.

Robinson, E.A. *The Structure of Competitive Industry.* Cambridge: Cambridge University Press, 1959.

PHOTO BY NEWSWEEK

ECONOMICS IN THE PUBLIC MIND

Paul A. Samuelson

Economist, Massachusetts Institute of Technology

" "THEY DON'T GIVE Nobel Prizes for writing text-books," commented Paul Samuelson, the 1970 Nobel Laureate in economics. Nor are Nobel prizes given for writing magazine columns, giving newspaper interviews, making Congressional testimonies, or the many other activities by which this prominent American economist is known to millions of people outside academia.

Paul Samuelson was America's first Nobel prize winner in economics; he was awarded the prize for his work in applying mathematics to broad questions of static and dynamic equilibrium and for "raising the level of analysis in economic science." This statement, which appeared in the Stockholm press, is deceptively simple. During the 1940s and 1950s, Samuelson began to synthesize economic methodology on the basis of mathematical models of almost universal applicability. He was foremost in developing mathematical model building and in expanding quantitative analysis and prediction.

Samuelson has authored many books, including *Economics: An Introductory Analysis* (1948), *The Foundations of Economic Analysis*

(1948), *Linear Programming and Economic Analysis* (1958), and a two-volume collection of articles (1967).

Of his own work, Samuelson said in his presidential address to the American Economics Association in 1961: "My own scholarship has covered a great variety of fields. And many of them involve questions like welfare economics and factor-price equalization; turnpike theorems and oscillating envelopes; non-substitutability relations in Minkowski-Ricardo-Leontief-Metzler matrices of Mosak-Hichs type; or balanced budget multipliers under conditions of balanced uncertainty in locally impacted topological spaces and molar equivalences. My friends warn me that such topics are suitable merely for captive audiences in search of a degree—and even then not after dark." Samuelson has been a popular spokesman for the economic profession. The wide circulation of his views on current economic policy, by way of his column in *Newsweek* magazine and his testimony before Congressional committees, has made him a most public "private citizen."

Although he has never held a major government economic policy post, Samuelson—true to his belief that economists should be concerned with social issues—served as adviser to both John Kennedy and Lyndon Johnson. Kennedy appointed Samuelson to head an economic task force which was to recommend means of reversing the business slump of that period. Samuelson suggested a temporary 3 or 4 percent tax cut, improved unemployment compensation, defense spending, foreign aid, federal aid to education, urban renewal, health and welfare, but no large-scale emergency public-works program. All was accepted by Kennedy, except the tax cut. Samuelson later worked on Johnson's task force which developed his Great Society program.

Samuelson has been a harsh and consistent critic of the policies of the Nixon Administration. When a GNP of $1,065 billion was predicted in 1971, Samuelson dryly suggested that the least one could do was offer the Administration the same "Christian charity" it lends Fidel Castro when he predicts a 10-million-ton sugar crop. He further stated, in testimony to the Joint Economic Committee in March 1971, that "without resolution of wage settlements and inflationary problems, even the achievement of the $1,065 billion goal would be a minor tragedy."

A strong advocate of government controls, Samuelson stated (in an interview with *U.S. News and World Report*) that we will never again have a depression like the one of the 1930s. "The big change since the 1930s is this: In the last analysis, we will not sit by and do nothing when a chronic slump is developing and threatens to feed upon itself. The Government, in a democracy, can step in to turn the tide. All the political pressures these days are for making the Government take these steps."

ISSUE IV

Inequities in the Agricultural Sector

Poor Farmers

Everyone knows there are many farmers who could be considered rather poor. At the end of the sixties, median farm income was only $6400 as compared to $10,000 for the nonfarm population. Today there are more than 1.5 million farmers with annual product sales of less than $5000 each. In fact, those 1.5 million farmers produce only 5 percent of the total output of the farming industry. Table IV-1 reveals the nature of the farming situation.

The farm problem is quite perplexing to most people. The agricultural sector is frequently referred to as the industry where technological progress has been more effective than anywhere else. Productivity has grown faster in agriculture than in any other major economic sector. Nonetheless, in terms of the percentage of the population engaged in farming, the agricultural sector is a declining industry. In Table IV-2, we see the number of farms through the years. By 1964, the number of farms was less than the number existing before the

turn of the century. Today the figure is even smaller.

The Growth in Demand for Farm Products

When we think about it for awhile, it is not surprising that the agricultural sector should decline as a proportion of the total economy. For one thing, productivity increases have been so great that the number of men needed to produce even an increasing amount has fallen. Additionally, we would expect that the rate of growth of demand for agricultural

products will fall after a country has reached a certain standard-of-living level. That country will no longer increase its spending on food products as in the past. There is a limit to how much food people can eat—even if they can "afford" a huge amount. We would expect that in developed countries only a very small part of increases in income would go into increasing demands for food.

This is exactly what empirical evidence demonstrates. Look at Table IV-3. Here we have shown the **income elasticities** of the demand for agricultural products for various countries, some developed and some less developed. We can define income elasticity in the same way we defined price elasticity. The price elasticity of demand for a product is equal to the percentage change in the quantity demanded over the per-

---

TABLE IV-1   THE DISTRIBUTION OF TOTAL FARM SALES

We see in this table that the lowest 41.2 percent of farms produce less than 3 percent of total farm sales while the top 7.1 percent of farms produce over 50 percent of total farm sales. These farmers have sales in excess of $40,000 a piece. (*Source:* Charles L. Schultze, *The Distribution of Farm Subsidies: Who Gets the Benefits* [Washington, D.C.: The Brookings Institution, 1971].)

ECONOMIC CLASS	VALUE OF SALES (THOUSANDS OF DOLLARS)	PERCENT OF TOTAL FARM SALES, 1969	PERCENT OF TOTAL NUMBER OF FARMS, 1969
I	40 and over	51.3	7.1
II	20–40	21.3	12.0
III	10–20	16.0	17.0
IV	5–10	6.3	13.1
V	2.5–5	2.4	9.6
VI	Less than 2.5	2.7	41.2

TABLE IV-2 THE NUMBER OF FARMS IN THE UNITED STATES

Here we find that the number of farms in the United States rose from 1.4 million in 1850 to a high of 6.8 million in 1935. Today there are less than 3 million farms. (*Source:* U.S. Bureau of the Census.)

YEAR	MILLIONS OF FARMS	YEAR	MILLIONS OF FARMS
1850	1.4	1935	6.8
1870	2.7	1940	6.1
1900	5.7	1950	5.4
1920	6.5	1959	3.7
1930	6.3	1964	3.2
		1972	2.9 (estimate)

centage change in the price. That is, elasticity measures the responsiveness of consumers to a change in the price of the product in question. Income elasticity will be defined as follows.

$$\text{income elasticity} = \frac{\text{percentage change in quantity demanded}}{\text{percentage change in income}}$$

We see in Table IV-3 that the income elasticity of the demand for food is much lower in wealthy countries than it is in poor countries. This means that once a country becomes fairly well developed, farmers cannot expect the demand for their product to go up as fast as the demand for other products. In the United States the income elasticity for food products is almost zero. That is, an increase in income of 1 percent yields a very small increase in the quantity of food demanded, holding everything else constant. We should be reminded that an income elasticity is defined only with everything else held constant, just as with the price elasticity. A price elasticity is measured holding income constant. An income elasticity is measured holding the price of the product constant. In both, tastes and the prices of substitutes are also held constant.

Low-Price Elasticity of Demand

Not only is the income elasticity of demand for agricultural products low; so too is the price elasticity. Whereas the low-income elasticity was important for explaining the long-run downward trend in the farm sector, the low-price elasticity of demand is important for understanding the high variability of farmers' income in the short run.

Let's compare the change in price that results from an increase in supply due to extremely good weather conditions. In Figure IV-1 we have shown the supply schedule shifting from *SS* to *S'S'*. It has shifted out to the right indicating a large increase in production. Notice that the supply schedule here is fairly vertical, indicating that the *elasticity of supply* in the short-run period under consideration is quite small. After all, once the farmers have

TABLE IV-3 INCOME ELASTICITY FOR FOOD PRODUCTS

The income elasticity of demand for food is defined as equal to the ratio of the percentage change in the quantity demanded over the percentage change in income. Here we find that this income elasticity is quite low, especially for the richer nations in the world. As real income rises, the demand for food products does not increase in proportion. (*Source:* Charles L. Schultze, *The Distribution of Farm Subsidies: Who Gets the Benefits* [Washington, D.C.: The Brookings Institution, 1971].)

RICHER NATIONS	ELASTICITY	POORER NATIONS	ELASTICITY
United States	0.08	Italy	0.42
Canada	0.15	Ireland	0.23
Germany	0.25	Greece	0.49
France	0.25	Spain	0.56
Britain	0.24	Portugal	0.60

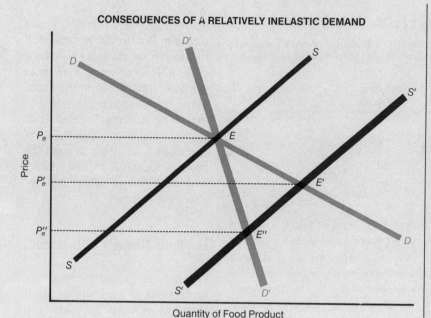

CONSEQUENCES OF A RELATIVELY INELASTIC DEMAND

Quantity of Food Product

FIGURE IV-1

Here we have established the quantity of food products on the horizontal axis and the price per unit on the vertical axis. Assume that the original supply curve is SS. It is quite steep indicating the relative inelasticity of supply in the short run. If the demand curve facing farmers were DD, a shift in the supply curve from SS to $S'S'$ due to a good year of weather would lower the equilibrium price from P_e to P_e'. However, look what happens if the demand curve is instead $D'D'$. When the supply curve shifts to $S'S'$, the new equilibrium price falls to P_e''. This accounts for the large variability in incomes of farmers during different years.

produced their crops, they can produce no more and they can produce no less—unless, of course, they decide to burn the crops.

What if the demand schedule is very elastic, such as DD? The new equilibrium price in this case will be set at the intersection of the new supply curve $S'S$ and the demand curve DD, or at point E'. The old equilibrium price was established at point E, or at a price of P_e. The new price of P_e' obviously lies below the old price.

What if the demand curve was relatively less elastic, such as $D'D'$? The new equilibrium would then be established at E'' and the new equilibrium price would be P_e'', which is even lower than P_e'. We see, then, that if the demand for agricultural products is rela-

tively inelastic, a shift in the quantity supplied will result in a fairly drastic change in the price that the agricultural products can fetch in the marketplace. This is one reason why we have seen prices in a free agricultural market changing quite drastically in response to changes in weather or in control of pestilence. The situation can be reversed, in which case the price rise will be relatively more with a less elastic demand curve than with an elastic demand curve when the supply schedule shifts inward. If for some reason there is a draught, we would expect prices to rise rather substantially due to the decreased supply in agriculture. Farmers would then be receiving high prices for their products. Although the farmers could complain about a smaller crop, they could not complain about the higher prices they could receive when selling that smaller crop.

We see therefore that the relative inelasticity of demand for agricultural products has been one of the reasons that prices and, hence, incomes have fluctuated more in agriculture than they have in other industries from year to year.

History of the Farmers' Dilemma

Before World War I, there were at least 20 years of continuous agricultural prosperity in the

United States. During the war, increased demand for agricultural products added to the "golden age of American farming." Many foreign countries demanded our agricultural products because they were using all their productive facilities to fight the war. The sharp depression in 1920 brought the golden age to an abrupt halt. Even though the economy picked up by 1921 and we were into the roaring twenties, agriculture never did share in the remaining years of prosperity. European countries stopped demanding our agricultural exports as they increased their own productive capacity in farming. The United States put high tariffs on all imported goods thereby restricting the flow of imports. Since other countries were not able to export as many goods to us as before, they were in no position to import as much from us as before. After all, exports are what any country uses to pay for its imports; the less you are able to export, the less you are able to import.

Then the Great Depression hit, and American farming was really hurt. Farm prices and farm income fell sharply. Moreover, the prices of farm products fell much more sharply than did the prices of products that farmers bought. Farmers were subjected to a price-cost squeeze. It was at this time that the beginnings of our massive farm programs were put into operation. In 1929 the Fed-

eral Farm Board was created and given a budget of $1.5 billion to begin price stabilization operations for poor farmers. The Farm Board was supposed to use the money to support the price of farm products so that farmers' incomes would not fall so much.

Then, when the Great Depression got into full swing, our current system of **price supports** came into being. Today there are some forms of price supports for wheat, feed grains, cotton, tobacco, rice, peanuts, soybeans, dairy products, and sugar. Let's see if we can

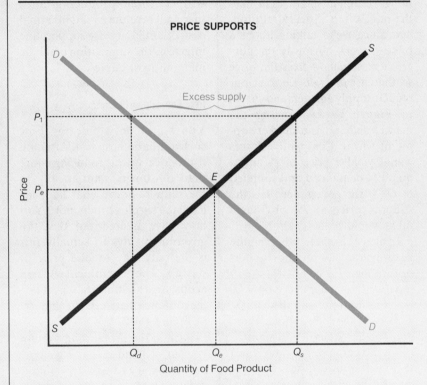

PRICE SUPPORTS

FIGURE IV-2

The quantity of the food product is measured on the horizontal axis and the price on the vertical axis. The market demand and supply curves are given by DD and SS. Equilibrium would be established at E with an equilibrium price of P_e and an equilibrium quantity demanded and supplied of Q_e. However, the government steps in and sets a support price at P_1. At P_1 the quantity demanded is Q_d and the quantity supplied is Q_s. The difference is excess supply, or "surplus" which the government must somehow take care of. It usually does this by storing the surplus or giving it away to foreign countries under one of our "food for peace" programs.

graphically analyze the effect of a price support system.

Price Supports

A price support system is precisely what the name implies. Somehow the government stabilizes or fixes the price of an agricultural product. Since we're talking about a price *support*, obviously the government somehow fixes the price so that it can't *fall*. Look at our regular supply and demand curves in Figure IV-2, showing the market demand and market supply of wheat. Competitive forces would yield a price of P_e and a quantity demanded and supplied of Q_e. If the government sets the support price at P_e, obviously there would be no change.

In many instances, however, the government has set the support price above P_e, say, at P_l. At P_l the quantity demanded is only Q_d and the quantity supplied is Q_s. That is, at the higher price, there is a smaller quantity demanded but a larger quantity supplied than at the lower price. The difference is excess supplies. Producers respond to higher market prices by producing more. That's why we show the supply schedule sloping up. At the higher prices, farmers are able to incur higher production costs and still make a profit. They will keep producing up to the point where the supported price cuts the supply curve.

(Remember that the supply curve is equal to the horizontal summation of all the marginal cost curves.) Since the government guarantees to purchase everything the wheat farmers want to sell at the price P_l, this price represents the marginal revenue. Farmers will continue producing until marginal revenue equals marginal cost, or until the price support line intersects the summation of all the marginal cost curves.

How Can Supports Last?

You might be wondering how such a situation can last. After all, if producers are producing more than consumers want to buy at the support price, what happens to all the surplus production? You may have figured out that the government buys it. (Actually, this is the only way for the price to stay up.) The government ends up acquiring the surplus wheat, or the distance between Q_s and Q_d in Figure IV-2.

Back in the fifties, things really got out of hand and the government was spending $1.1 million a day in storage costs for surplus wheat! The way the government acquires the wheat is through the Commodity Credit Corporation (CCC). The Commodity Credit Corporation is given a **parity** or fair price that it is allowed to offer for different products. Let's say that Congress has set a fair or parity price at $2.00 a bushel and

the market-clearing price where the forces of supply and demand would cause an equilibrium is at $1.50 a bushel. Farmers will sell all the wheat they can to the public at $2.00 and the rest of it—the surplus—to the Commodity Credit Corporation. In principle, the Commodity Credit Corporation merely "loans" each farmer the fair price times the number of bushels the farmer gives the CCC. The loan, however, is a nonrecourse one. That is, the CCC can never ask the farmer for the money back.

Occasionally, the forces of supply and demand will cause the unrestricted market-clearing price to rise above the fair or parity price that the CCC is offering the farmers. In such a situation the farmers would indeed pay back their loans. That is, they would pay back the CCC the money they got, take back their wheat, and then sell their wheat at a higher price on the open market.

In economics we find that the only way for a "surplus" to exist is for there to be some sort of price fixing. In an unrestricted market, a surplus can only exist temporarily. The forces of supply and demand will eliminate the surplus by causing a decrease in the price.

Who Benefits from Price Supports?

Price supports were initially instituted in order to keep incomes of poor farmers higher than they would be otherwise. The idea behind the price support is to allow farmers to earn a decent living. That's where the notion of a fair or parity price comes in. But think about it for a moment. A farmer receives income which is directly proportional to the amount of his production. If he is producing very little, even though there are price supports he will benefit only marginally. It is, rather, the very large producing farmers who benefit the most from price supports. The subsidy—the difference between the government support price and the unrestricted market-clearing price—becomes directly proportional to a farmer's production. Since we usually do not find poor farmers producing a lot, we would expect that the distribution of benefits from the price support program would mirror the distribution of the in-

come of farmers. And that it does. Look at Table IV-4. Here we have separated farmers into six categories, as in Table IV-1. We see that 7 percent of the farms in 1969 received 42.3 percent of the benefits of price support, whereas over 40 percent of the farms which had sales of less than $2500 received only 4.2 percent of the benefits from price supports. One might conclude from this small bit of evidence that the farm support program is going to help rich farmers rather than poor farmers, as originally intended.

Coping with the "Surpluses"

When the farm price support program was first instituted, the analysis presented in Figure IV-2 would not have been appropriate. During World War II, there was

an increased demand for U.S. farm products from abroad. Immediately after the war, Europe continued to demand American agricultural products, while using its productive capacity for reconstruction. The Korean war also helped to eliminate any problem of "surpluses" because of price supports. The rest of the world bought heavily from our farming production sector just in case there might be a need for large food inventories if the world broke into another war. Finally, after the Korean war was ended, the problem of excess capacity—surpluses—began to rear its ugly head.

By the mid-1950s the Commodity Credit Corporation began to stockpile larger and larger inventories of the "surplus" farm products it had purchased. By 1954 there was a slight reduction in price support levels but not enough to eliminate the rising excess supplies from the farming sector. In 1952, the CCC had purchased $1.3 billion worth of agricultural commodities. By 1955 it had purchased $6.7 billion and by 1959 almost $8 billion.

When John F. Kennedy came into office, one of his first major steps in changing farm policy was to raise support levels. We saw a substantial increase in farm income but also in potential surpluses due to the increases in the price supports. This increase in potential surpluses forced the Kennedy Administration to insti-

TABLE IV-4   THE DISTRIBUTION OF PRICE SUPPORT BENEFITS

We see that the highest economic class of farmers—that is, those with value of sales of $40,000 and over per year—make up only 7.1 percent of the total number of farms but get 42.3 percent of all price support benefits. The lowest 41.2 percent of farms receives only 4.2 percent of price support benefits. (*Source:* Charles L. Schultze, *The Distribution of Farm Subsidies: Who Gets the Benefits* [Washington, D.C.: The Brookings Institution, 1971].)

ECONOMIC CLASS	VALUE OF SALES	PERCENT OF TOTAL NUMBER OF FARMS	PRICE SUPPORT BENEFITS (PERCENT OF TOTAL)
I	40 and over	7.1	42.3
II	20–40	12.0	19.3
III	10–20	17.0	17.9
IV	5–10	13.1	11.0
V	2.5–5	9.6	5.3
VI	Less than 2.5	41.2	4.2

ACREAGE RESTRICTIONS

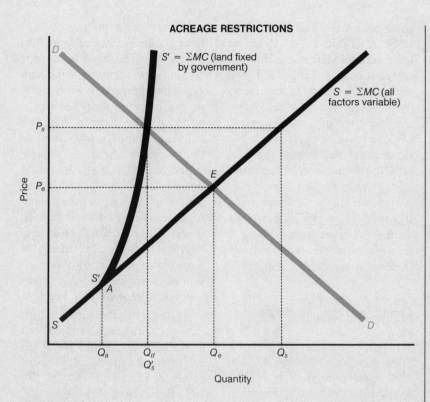

FIGURE IV-3

In an unrestricted situation we have the demand curve *DD* and the supply curve *SS*, where *SS* is equal to the horizontal summation of all the marginal cost curves of the individual farmers when all factors can be varied. The equilibrium was established at *E*—at the intersection of *SS* and *DD*—and the equilibrium price would be *Pe*. The government decides to set a support price above the equilibrium price. The support price is *Ps*. At *Ps* the quantity demanded is *Qd* but the quantity supplied would be *Qs*. There would be a surplus equal to *Qs* minus *Qd*. In order to avoid the surplus, the government restricts the amount of land that can be cultivated. When land is cultivated we get a new supply curve. It is the old one up to point *A*, and then a new one, *S'S'*. We have drawn it in such a way that it intersects the demand curve at the support price. The government could conceivably keep restricting land until this actually happens. The reason the new supply curve is steeper than the old supply curve is because land is fixed and resources that would not otherwise be used, such as more fertilizer and more machines, will now be put to work on the restricted amount of land. We can see that the supply curve actually pivots at point *A*. Before point *A* nothing happens to the supply curve because less land is used than the government allows so the restriction has no effect. In the new equilibrium situation the quantity demanded will be *Qd* and the quantity supplied will be *Qs'*, which is equal to *Qd*.

tute some fairly drastic measures to reduce the amount of production that each farmer was allowed. Even before Kennedy, a **soil bank** had been created. Through this institution the government paid farmers *not to use* land for production. There were some experiments with mandatory controls on output, but increasingly the government came to rely on direct payments to farmers not to produce. This was called *purchasing acreage restrictions*. Let's now analyze the soil bank or land conservation program in agriculture.

The Soil Bank and Acreage Restrictions

In most cases, when a farmer wants to take advantage of the price support program offered to him by the government, he has to agree to participate in the acreage allotment program. Participating farmers agree to limit the number of acres they plant, so as to reduce surpluses caused by price supports. This acreage allotment program is slightly different from the soil bank program, where the Department of Agriculture actually rents the land from farmers. The rented land could be planted in timber or cover crops but with nothing that could be sold on the food market. In the acreage allotment program there were no direct payments to farmers; the program is merely the entry fee that farmers must pay to be allowed to take advantage of price supports. In the soil bank program, the government actually gives direct payment to the farmer for *not* using part of his land, regardless of the farmer's participation in any other government program.

Let's graphically analyze the situation that occurs when the government restricts the use of land (one of the production factors in making food). Look at Figure IV-3. Here we have drawn the market demand curve and the market supply curve. Notice that the market supply curve is again labeled as the horizontal summation of all the marginal cost curves of all the farmers. Additionally, we have pointed out one very important condition—that all factors of production can be varied. That is, farmers can use whatever amounts of labor, capital, and land they want to; they can vary the proportions. If it is more profitable to use less land, the farmers will do so; they will sell part of their land. If it is profitable to use more land, they will buy more land. The same holds with all other factors. The *SS* curve is drawn under the assumption that it represents the minimum cost combination of land, labor, and capital, for producing any given quantity of the product in question. That is, it is assumed that farmers vary the proportions of their factors of production in such a way

as to minimize the cost of production for any given quantity.

In the unrestricted market the equilibrium price would be P_e and the equilibrium quantity would be Q_e. Now the government comes along and puts on a price support at P_s. If the government does nothing else, this will lead to an excess supply—that is, a surplus equal to the difference between Q_s and Q_d. In order to eliminate the surplus, the government requires more land to go into the acreage allotment program where it can't be cultivated, and the government "rents" more land to put into the soil bank. The government wants to keep taking more land out of production until finally a new supply curve will intersect the stable demand curve at a price P_s—or, the support price. Look at Figure IV-3. Here we have shown a new supply curve, $S'S'$, and we have labeled it to show that it equals the summation of all the marginal cost curves with land fixed. Why does the supply curve *pivot* upward at point A instead of shifting up? The reason is easy to see.

If farmers wanted to produce quantity Q_a, they would be at A on the supply curve. That is, an acreage restriction would have no effects, if *only* Q_a was to be produced. The same small amount of land, labor, fertilizer, and machines would be used. But after Q_a, things are different. Land cannot be added in unrestricted

quantities; there is acreage restriction. Any expansion beyond this point must come from *non-*fixed inputs. Farmers will increase the use of all other *non*fixed inputs so long as the marginal revenue from doing so is greater than the marginal cost. Since the marginal revenue from doing so is always equal to P_s because that's the government support price, farmers will increase their use of other inputs until the marginal cost just equals P_s. That's why the supply curve pivots upward. It shows, for example, that at a price of P_s, it now costs P_s to produce the quantity Q_d. Before the soil bank program was instituted, it cost less in resources.

The soil bank and acreage allotment programs lead to inefficient use of resources—not from the point of view of the individual farmer, for it is assumed that he uses his resources efficiently—but from the point of view of society. This is because the resources are being used in farming where their value is smaller than they would be if they were being used elsewhere in the economy.

Have the Acreage Allotment and Soil Bank Programs Been Successful?

As you might expect, the government did not anticipate that production of agricultural crops would fall so much less than the reduction in acreage. Farmers got rid of their worst land first and kept the best land in production. The remaining cultivated acres were worked more intensely; better seed was put in; better fertilizer and insecticides and better machines and men were used. In 1953, 80 million acres of wheat were cultivated; 1.2 billion bushels grew. In 1960, only 55 million acres of wheat were cultivated; the output, however, was 1.4 billion bushels. A 30 percent reduction in the number of acres cultivated by 1960 was accompanied by an increase of 17 percent in output. Of course, the increase in output would have been even greater had there not been soil banks and acreage restriction allotments. The government should not have been too surprised about the increase in production on less land because, at the same time it was restricting acreage, it was spending millions helping farmers improve productivity!

Tobacco

Support prices which are higher than market equilibrium entice more people into farming because of the lure of higher income. The threat of new competition was squashed by tobacco growers about three decades ago. They got Congress to pass legislation which allotted the *then current* half a million growers the right to grow

tobacco on lands that were *then* in use. Since that time, there has been no new land put into tobacco production and for a very good reason. Any tobacco that is grown on unlicensed land is taxed at 75 percent of its value. This tax is prohibitive: no potential tobacco farmer could hope to make any money if he had to pay this tax because he's in competition with all of the tobacco growers who do not have to pay it.

Perhaps, since tobacco farming is a monopoly today, you could make monopoly profits by buying some licensed tobacco growing acreage? If you think so, you're wrong. The price of that licensed land was long ago bid up to levels that yield new owners only a competitive rate of return. Who are the ones who benefited from the monopoly position granted by

Congress? The original owners who had the land at the time the legislation was passed of course; they reaped monopoly profits to the tune of $1500 to $3000 per acre because they could sell their land for more.

In addition to the restriction on acreage in tobacco growing, there are also tobacco price supports (that is, Commodity Credit Corporation nonrecourse loans), and, just to make sure that not too much reaches the marketplace, there are marketing quotas to keep output at a level consistent with price support objectives. The net results of the tobacco program have been:

1. a smaller supply of tobacco leaves than otherwise would have been grown;
2. a higher price for tobacco than

TABLE IV-5 THE BIG MONEY MAKERS IN FARMING

Here we show the amount of payments from the government to large corporation farmers in 1970. One gets the impression that the original intent of the farm program might not be in line with current reality. (*Source:* U.S. Department of Agriculture.)

STATE	FARMER	AMOUNT
California	J. G. Boswell Co.	$4.4 million
California	Giffin, Inc.	$4.0 million
California	South Lake Farms (Bangor Punta)	$1.8 million
California	Salyer Land Co.	$1.5 million
California	H. M. Tenneco	$1.3 million
Hawaii	Hawaiian Com & Sugar Co.	$1.2 million
Hawaii	Waialua Sugar Co., Inc.	$1.1 million
California	Vista del Llano Farms (Anderson Clayton Co.)	$1.1 million
Florida	U.S. Sugar Corp.	$1 million
California	S. A. Camp Farms Co.	$903,650

would have prevailed under an unrestricted market situation; and

3. a higher price for tobacco products than would have otherwise prevailed.

The Costs of the Farm Program

Two quite different costs are associated with the farm program. One involves all of the direct payments made to farmers by the nonfarm sector. There is, in other words, a transfer of income from the nonfarming sector to the farming sector. This is done in two ways:

1. taxpayers support all of the direct payments made by the government to farmers, and
2. consumers pay even more to farmers through the higher prices resulting from restrictions on acreage and from price supports.

From 1956 to 1970 taxpayers shelled out an average of $3 billion a year for direct payments to price support for agriculture. From 1968 through 1970 annual budget outlays were more than $5 billion a year. Additionally, it is estimated that in recent years actual farm prices would have been 15 percent lower in the absence of an agricultural price support program. Consumers end up paying almost $5 billion a year more for farm products than they would have paid otherwise without federal price support programs. We see, therefore, that the total cost to the nonfarm sector of our agricultural program is equal to $9 to 10 billion a year. This represents a transfer or a redistribution of income from the nonfarm sector to the farming sector. This redistribution is not insignificant, for $10 billion per year is approximately the cost of all federal, state, and local welfare programs in the United States. The farm program is indeed one of the most important public programs in existence today. The question remains whether you as a taxpayer favor this redistribution. We have given some evidence that the redistribution is not toward the less fortunate, lower income farmers. In fact, in Table IV-5, we see that there are quite a number of farming corporations receiving government subsidies in excess of $1 million a year.

The results of the farm program can be judged on the basis of whether members of the group that society intended to help are, indeed, actually being helped. Presumably there is no need (and this is, indeed, a value judgment) to "help" large corporation farmers. Their incomes are so high that any form of subsidy does not seem appropriate. The poor family farmers of the South and other marginal agricultural areas may be the subpopulation within the farming group that society wishes to help out. If this is the case, then we have a standard for evaluation, and we can observe that this goal is not being met. In fact, it is corporate business in farming that gets the vast majority of farm subsidy dollars. Using this implicit standard of the program, we can evaluate it as a complete failure. However, if your particular values allow you to agree that corporate farmers should be the subject of government charity, then the program has been a smashing success.

Definition of New Terms

INCOME ELASTICITY: percentage change in quantity demanded divided by the percentage change in income. In general, income elasticities are positive.

PRICE SUPPORTS: a system of permitting the price of certain agricultural products from falling below a support level. If the government has a price support which is above the equilibrium price, it will end up with surplus agricultural products.

PARITY: a price of agricultural products which gives the particular product a purchasing power in terms of the goods that the farmers have to buy. This price will be equivalent to what it was in some previous "good" year for farmers. A parity price is often called a "fair" price for food products.

SURPLUS: the difference between the quantity supplied and the quantity demanded. The only time a surplus can arise is when there are market restrictions keeping the price above its equilibrium price.

SOIL BANK: a government scheme to induce farmers not to use land for production. A farmer is paid to put his land in a soil bank and not use it to produce cash crops. Actually, the Department of Agriculture rents the land from the farmers for the soil bank.

ACREAGE ALLOTMENT PROGRAM: similar to the soil bank, but there is no direct payment to the farmer for not using his land. Rather, his acreage allotment is given to him as a prerequisite for being allowed to take advantage of price supports.

Questions for Thought and Discussion

1. Do you think there is an agricultural problem? Why?
2. If indeed there is a problem, is the current system helping the farmers that you would choose? What would be your alternative?
3. Do you mind paying higher prices for food in order to help out farmers?
4. On numerous occasions there will be milk strikes or potato strikes or pig strikes when the particular producers of these products refuse to sell them in order to demonstrate their desire for higher prices. Are these particular farmers acting rationally?

Selected References

Cochrane, Willard W. *The City Man's Guide to the Farm Problem.* Minneapolis: University of Minnesota Press, 1965.

Heady, Earl O. *A Primer on Food, Agriculture, and Public Policy.* New York: Random House, 1967.

Houthakker, Hendrik S. *Economic Policy for the Farm Sector.* Washington, D.C.: American Enterprise Institute, 1967.

President's National Advisory Commission on Rural Poverty. *The People Left Behind.* Washington, D.C.: Government Printing Office, 1967.

Ruttan, Vernon W., et al., Eds. *Agricultural Policy in an Affluent Society.* New York: W. W. Norton, 1969.

Schultze, Charles L. *The Distribution of Farm Subsidies: Who Gets the Benefits.* Washington, D.C.: The Brookings Institution, 1971.

Monopoly Management

T HE WORLD, of course, does not consist of purely competitive industries, and our predictions about the behavior of noncompetitive industries would be very poor if we did not take into account their special attributes. In this chapter we will present a model of a monopoly business and discuss how a monopolist decides what prices to charge and how much to produce. Fortunately, most of the analytical tools needed here have already been introduced. Before attempting any analysis at all, however, we have to understand the definition of a monopolist.

DEFINITION OF A MONOPOLIST

When hearing the words *monopoly* or *monopolist,* we usually think of gouging the consumer, selling faulty products, getting rich, and any other bad thoughts that one can have about big business. We will have to be somewhat more objective in defining a monopolist if we are to succeed in analyzing and predicting the behavior of noncompetitive firms. Although most actual monopolies in the United States are relatively big, our definition of monopoly will be equally applicable to small businesses. Thus, a **monopolist** is formally defined as a *single seller*. (This is the Greek origin of the word.)

Monopolist's Demand Curve

The term *true monopolist* refers to the original meaning of the word—single seller of *one* product or good or service. A true monopolist faces a demand curve which is the demand curve for the entire market for his good. *He faces the industry demand curve because he is the entire industry.* A single corner drugstore in a small town is therefore a monopolist just as much as a corporate giant like American Telephone and Telegraph (Ma Bell).

There are other, less pure forms of monopoly also. In the following chapter we will discuss these other forms of monopoly, such as monopolistic competition and oligopoly (few sellers). Right now we want to talk about the case where one firm produces the entire output of the industry.

Some Examples of Monopolies

Everyone is aware of at least some of the forms of pure monopoly that exist in our economy. When you turn on your lights in order to read this text, you are purchasing the output of the local monopoly power company in your area. There is only one company to which you can go to buy electric power, right? How did it get to be a monopoly? A government franchise gave it monopoly power. That is, the government certifies different electric power companies to operate in well-defined geographical areas. You and your friends could not pool your money, buy a small generator, and solicit electricity customers in your neighborhood. That is illegal; government regulations do not allow it.

When you mail a letter at the post office, you are purchasing the services of a government monopolist. Although various groups are now testing the legality of the government restricting first-class mail service to the U.S. Post Office only, for the moment first-class service is a government controlled and owned monopoly. There is a single seller of first class service, and that is the government. (First class does not of course, necessarily, refer here to high quality.)

When you dial a number on your telephone, you are using the services of a monopolist—probably your local chapter of the American Telephone and Telegraph system. And up until recently, the phone you used was produced by a monopolist because the government did not allow just anybody to produce and install telephone equipment. That is no longer the case, but it is still true that telephone services are sold by one of the largest monopolists in the country.

You're probably wondering why there has been no mention of General Motors or United States Steel. Actually, those companies do not fit into our strict definition of true monopolies. After all, General Motors does compete with other car manufacturers, both foreign and domestic. So, too, does U.S. Steel. Those companies must be classified as oligopolies—that is, companies which operate in an industry where there are only a very small number of sellers. Here, we are concerned with industries which are made up by only one seller.

ON BECOMING A MONOPOLIST

How does one obtain a monopoly? How can you, if you want to, become a monopolist? It isn't easy. There are many ways to become a monopolist but very few of them work in the long run. In the first place, for a monopoly to be able to exist there must be **barriers to entry.** That means there must be some reason why other people are barred from setting up competing companies.

Barriers to Entry

The most obvious barrier to entry is government police power. It is impossible to enter the electric utility business where someone else is already operating because the government does not allow it. The government creates the barrier to entry. It is impossible for you to set up an alternative telephone system because the government will prevent you from doing so. The most obvious barriers to entry, therefore, are legal barriers. Patents represent another type of legal barrier to entry into a business. The government grants an inventor the exclusive right to control a product for 17 years. Nobody else can produce that particular patented product unless he obtains a license or a release from the owner of the patent.

There are also other barriers to entry. It may be that the cost of setting up a new electricity company—building a dam, buying generators, stringing power lines—might be so high that it does not pay someone else to start a company to compete with an existing firm. The same is true for the telephone company. It may not be profitable for anyone to start an alternative competing system, for the start-up costs are overwhelming. In other words, this barrier to entry is excessive *capital* costs. The amount of money that you would need to produce a competing phone system is prohibitive. You couldn't get enough people to loan you their savings so that you could purchase all the necessary equipment.

Ownership of essential raw materials can also lead to a monopoly situation. The classic example involves the diamond industry. The DeBeers Company of South Africa controls almost all of the world's diamond mines. Another example might be the Aluminum Company of America, which owned almost all the basic sources of bauxite, the major ore used in aluminum production. This company was able to retain its monopoly position in aluminum apparently because of its control over this essential raw material. It would not sell bauxite to any potential competitor.

Economies of Scale

A monopoly may arise because of a phenomenon known in economics as **economies of scale.** You are probably familiar with the everyday notion of this term because it relates to *mass production.* It is generally assumed that bigger companies can produce things more cheaply than smaller companies because they can take advantage of mass production techniques. For a given amount of fixed costs, it is true that the more a firm produces, the smaller the average fixed cost. But that doesn't necessarily mean that production can continue to get larger and average total costs will therefore

continue to fall indefinitely. In fact, in diagrams we have usually shown that average total costs fall first and then rise because after a certain point there are usually diseconomies of getting bigger. In any event, true economies of scale don't involve fixed costs for they are a long-run concept. In the long run, all factors of production are variable.

We must be careful because economies of scale refers to a situation where output increases more than in proportion to the increase in *all* inputs, including men *and* machines. That is, proportional increases in all factors of production yield proportionately larger increases in output. If all inputs are increased 10 percent and output goes up 20 percent, that's economies of scale.

If economies of scale exist in an industry, we would expect that the larger the scale of production, the lower the average costs. Hence, in an industry, the firm which grows faster than the others can drive out all rivals by lowering prices as average costs fall. If true economies of scale exist in an industry, we expect only one firm to survive, and that is the one which grows the fastest.

We should be careful here to make sure that we're really observing economies of scale in the real world when looking at big companies. General Motors sells $20 billion of products a year. However, it has many plants. Apparently there is a limit to economies of scale. That limit is probably reached when production line assembly techniques start being used.

THE MONEY TO BE MADE FROM INCREASING PRODUCTION

Remember that a competitive firm has a horizontal demand curve. That is, the competitive firm is such a small part of the market that it can not influence the price of its product. Rather, it is a price taker. If the forces of market supply and demand establish the price per bushel of wheat at $2.00, then the individual firm can sell all of the wheat it wants to produce at $2.00 a bushel. The average revenue is $2.00, the price is $2.00, and the marginal revenue is also $2.00.

Marginal Revenue

Let's define marginal revenue again.

Marginal revenue equals the difference between the revenue received by increasing production one unit and the revenue received without increasing production.

In the case of a competitive industry, each time production is increased by one unit, total revenue increases by the going price, and it is always the same. Marginal revenue never changes; it always equals average revenue or price.

What about a monopolist? Since the monopolist is the entire industry, he faces the entire market demand curve. It is always downward-sloping, just like the ones we've been drawing all along. In order for the monopolist to sell more of his particular product, he must lower the price. He must move *down* the demand curve. Usually, he must lower the price on all of his units sold; he can't just lower the price on the last unit.

Here we see a fundamental difference between the monopolist and the competitor. The competitor doesn't have to worry about lowering prices in order to sell more. In a purely competitive situation, he is such a small part of the market that he can sell his entire production, whatever that may be, at the same price no matter how big his production is. The monopolist cannot do this. The more he wants to sell, the lower the price he has to charge on the last unit and the lower the price he has to charge on *all* of his units put on the market for sale. Obviously, the extra revenues he will receive from selling one more unit are going to be smaller than the extra revenues received from selling the next to last unit. Even when forgetting about everything else, you know that the monopolist would have to lower the price on the last unit in order to sell it because he is facing a downward sloping demand curve. The only way to move down the demand curve is to lower price.

Monopolist's Marginal Revenue

The monopolist's marginal revenue is going to be falling. But, it falls even more than one might think because the monopolist has to lower the price on all units, not just on the last unit produced. Since information flows rather freely, he will not be able to charge one consumer $2.00 for something and another consumer $3.00 for the same

QUANTITY OF OUTPUT (IN KILOS)	PRICE (AVERAGE REVENUE)	TOTAL REVENUE	MARGINAL REVENUE
1	$200	$200	
			$180
2	190	380	
			160
3	180	540	
			140
4	170	680	
			120
5	160	800	
			100
6	150	900	
			80
7	140	980	
			60
8	130	1040	
			40
9	120	1080	
			20
10	110	1100	
			0
11	100	1100	

TABLE 6-1

HYPOTHETICAL REVENUE FROM THE GOVERNMENT SELLING MARIJUANA

In the first column we show the quantity of output; in the second column, the price or average revenue; and in the third column, total revenues. Total revenues just equal the price times the quantity of output. Marginal revenue is shown in the last column. It is the difference between the two different total revenues when production is increased one unit.

thing. The consumer who could buy the product for $2.00 would buy lots of it and resell it to the one who was being charged $3.00 at, say, $2.50. Unless the monopolist is successful in somehow separating (discriminating between) the different markets to prevent transactions among the consumers in those market, he will have to sell all his goods at a uniform price. Therefore, when he increases production, he charges a lower price on the last unit and on all previous units. We can, therefore, define marginal revenue for the monopolist as follows:

A monopolist's marginal revenue equals the price that the last unit fetches minus the reduction in price for all the previous units times the number of those units.

This is just another way of saying that marginal revenue equals total revenue for selling one more unit minus total revenue for sales without that last unit.

Marginal Revenues from Marijuana

To drive home the concept of falling marginal revenues, we have presented in Table 6–1 a hypothetical demand schedule with total revenues and marginal revenues shown in the various columns. The demand schedule is for marijuana. It is assumed that the government has monopolized the industry; it has constructed a barrier to entry by making it illegal for private concerns to grow and distribute the drug. You can see for yourself that marginal revenue falls and is less than average revenue or the price.

This can be demonstrated graphically. In Figure 6–1, we have drawn a standard looking market demand curve for marijuana. The market demand curve is sometimes called the average revenue curve because at any point on the curve one can find out the average revenues (price) from selling that particular quantity. The marginal revenue curve lies below the demand curve, as we have explained above. Notice that at point

A the marginal revenue curve intersects the horizontal axis. After that point marginal revenues become negative.

OUTPUT AND PRICE DETERMINATION FOR THE MONOPOLIST

We still haven't found the monopoly price and quantity solution to a monopolist's decision-making problem. He has got to decide where to set his price and what quantity he should produce. Let's start off assuming that our monopolist faces no costs whatsoever in producing his product. We are simply ignoring any costs involved. Take the example of a football stadium owner. The Superbowl is coming up. How much should he charge per ticket, if the tickets cost nothing to print? You would hardly expect the stadium owner to give the tickets away. You might expect him to sell tickets at near nothing. After all, if you multiply a very small number (the price) by a very, very large number (the quantity) you can come up with sizable revenues. Notice, however, that the demand curve we have drawn in Figure 6–1 slopes down and will eventually cut the horizontal axis at some point. This means that in order to sell more than is indicated at the intersection of the demand curve and the horizontal axis (zero price), our monopolist would have to pay people to take his product. This certainly isn't any way for him to make money.

The stadium owner should be seeking to *maximize* total profits. Since he has no costs, he should be merely looking at his total revenues. He should never set a price that yielded less than a maximum. So he should never set a price that yields a marginal revenue that is negative. That is, no price below P_m in Figure 6–1 is correct for him. At a price below P_m his *MR* will be negative, thereby lowering total revenue and profits.

Look at it another way. The stadium owner has a fixed number of seats. The marginal cost

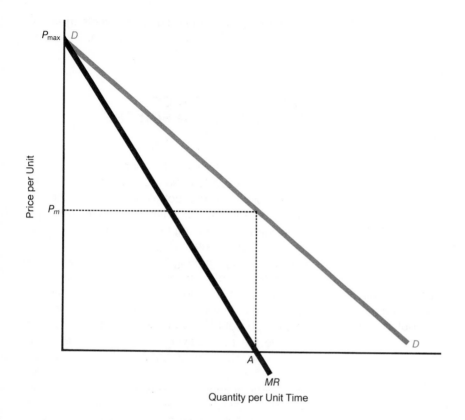

FIGURE 6-1

THE MONOPOLIST'S MARGINAL REVENUE CURVE

The monopolist faces a downward sloping demand curve. He is the single seller of the product. His demand curve is *DD*. Since the only way he can sell more units of his product is by lowering the price, the marginal revenue he receives from selling an additional unit is less than the average revenue or the price that he receives. The marginal revenue is equal to the price he receives on the last unit sold minus the reduction in price on all of the former units sold times their quantity. We have shown the marginal revenue curve as *MR* in this diagram. It intersects the horizontal axis at *A;* that is where marginal revenue equals zero. If a monopolist had no costs at all, he could figure out how much to charge to maximize profits by starting at *Pmax*, the maximum price for which he could sell one unit of his product. He could then see what happens as he charges successively lower prices. He would travel down his marginal revenue curve as he did this, going to the point where marginal revenue was equal to zero. He would charge *Pm*, for that is how he maximizes his total revenues and, since he has zero costs, his total profits. If he went to a price below *Pm*, marginal revenue would be negative; he would not be maximizing his profits because the benefit from selling additional units would be negative after *Pm*, or point *A* in the diagram. This diagram shows in a simplified manner that profit maximization occurs at the point where marginal revenue equals marginal costs. Here we have maintained that the marginal costs for our monopolist are zero—that is, they are the horizontal axis. He will produce at point *A* and sell his product for *Pm*.

of providing somebody with a seat is zero. He should continue selling seats until it is no longer profitable. It is no longer profitable when the marginal revenue falls below marginal costs, but marginal costs are zero. So seats should be sold until $MR = 0$. The way to sell more seats is to lower prices. Starting from a maximum price of P_{max} where only one seat will be sold, the stadium owner will keep dropping the price until he reaches P_m, where MR then equals zero. Up to that point, every additional seat sold will yield him positive marginal revenues. He will end up making more total profit. We say total profits here because it's assumed that the owner has no costs so he keeps everything that he takes in. (Does it surprise you now that stadium seats are priced so high when some seats aren't even sold?)

MARGINAL REVENUE AND ELASTICITY

The point on the demand schedule directly above point A, where marginal revenue becomes zero, is a very special point. For here is where the elasticity of demand is equal to unity (-1). Look at Figure 6–2. Here we see that at point A′ on the demand schedule, the point corresponding to zero marginal revenues, we have marked $e = -1$. That portion of the demand schedule to the right of point A′, we have labeled *inelastic*. That is, to the right of point A′, a change in price elicits a proportionately smaller change in quantity demanded. Contrast this with point A′, where we have said that $e = -1$. That is, the elasticity of demand is such that a change in price elicits a proportionate change in quantity demanded.

That portion of the demand curve to the left and above point A′ we have labeled *elastic*. This means that to the left of A′ a change in price will cause a proportionately larger change in quantity demanded. In our particular example, where the monopolist has no costs, we found that he would produce at point A′ on the demand

schedule. He would not go past that point because marginal revenues would become negative. Obviously, there is some relationship between elasticity and revenues.

We show that relationship graphically in Figure 6–2 and 6–3. Obviously total revenues are zero at a zero price and at P_{max} where no units are sold. Between these points, total revenues rise and then fall. The maximum revenue is where the elasticity of demand is unity as shown in Figure 6–3.

ADDING THE COST CURVES

We've assumed there were no costs involved in producing the monopoly's product. Now we'll be more realistic. When costs were zero, production was expanded until marginal revenues equaled zero. That should give you some hint as to how the monopolist will determine where he should produce. He's going to be looking at the difference between revenues and costs for each increase in production.

Let's draw in some cost schedules in our monopoly diagram. Look at Figure 6–4. Here we have the same demand schedule and the same marginal revenue curve as before, but now we have drawn in a marginal cost curve. Remember that the marginal cost curve was the key to deciding where the perfect competitor would produce. It is also the key to deciding where the monopolist will produce.

The monopolist would be smart to continue production until the additional revenues received from producing one more unit would just cover the additional costs. *The monopolist will keep producing up to the point where marginal cost equals marginal revenue.* He'd be silly to produce past that point because marginal costs will exceed marginal revenues. That is, the incremental costs of producing any more units will exceed the incremental revenues. It just wouldn't be worth his while. He'd also be silly to produce less than that

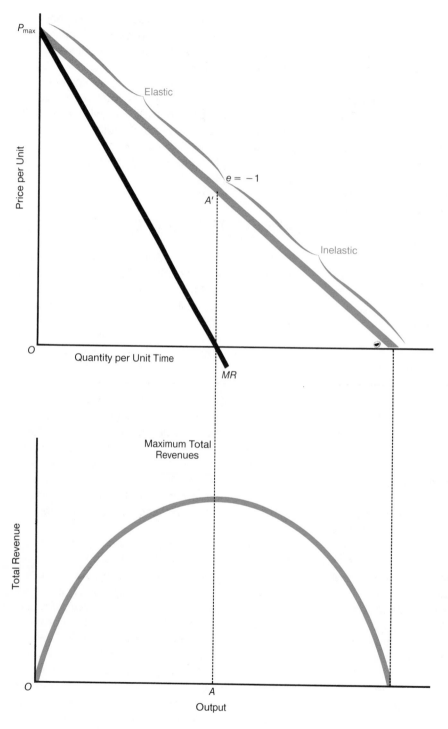

P_{max}

Price per Unit

Elastic

$e = -1$

A'

Inelastic

O

Quantity per Unit Time

MR

Maximum Total
Revenues

Total Revenue

O

A

Output

FIGURE 6–2

ELASTICITY OF DEMAND AND TOTAL REVENUES

Here we have shown the relationship between marginal revenue, the demand curve, and the elasticity of demand. It turns out that after the point where marginal revenue equals zero—that is, point A'—demand is inelastic to the right, and it is elastic to the left. At point A, demand has unitary elasticity, or –1. To the right, the monopolist would find that if he lowered price, the quantity demanded would not increase in proportion. To the left of A' as he raised price, the quantity demanded would fall more than in proportion.

FIGURE 6–3

TOTAL REVENUES AND THE DEMAND CURVE

Here we have shown the relationship between the demand curve, elasticity of demand, and total revenue. When the price is set at P_{max} in Figure 6–2, the total revenues are, of course, the lowest possible. When the price is set at zero, total revenues are zero. In between these two ends of the price possibilities scale we will find some price which maximizes total revenues. That price happens to be where marginal revenue equals zero, or at point A' in Figure 6–2. We have shown in Figure 6–3 that the maximum occurs right underneath the point where marginal revenue equals zero. If the monopolist had no costs at all he would obviously want to produce at point A, for that is where he would maximize his total revenues which, in essence, would be his total profits.

FIGURE 6-4 MAXIMIZING PROFITS WITH COSTS ADDED

Here we have shown the demand curve DD as before and a marginal revenue curve, MR. We add a marginal cost curve, MC. The monopolist will maximize profits where marginal revenue equals marginal cost; he will produce up to the point where MC equals MR, and then he will find out the highest price at which he can sell all of that quantity. The profit-maximizing production point is Q_m and the profit-maximizing price is P_m. He would be silly to produce at Q_1 for here marginal revenue would be A and marginal costs would be B. Marginal revenue exceeds marginal cost. If he increased his production by one unit, he will obviously be better off because the extra revenues will more than cover the extra costs. He will keep producing until the point Q_m where marginal revenue just equals marginal costs. It would be silly to produce at Q_2 for here marginal cost exceeds marginal revenue. The benefits from selling the extra units here are outweighed by the costs. If he were at Q_2 it behooves him to cut back production to Q_m.

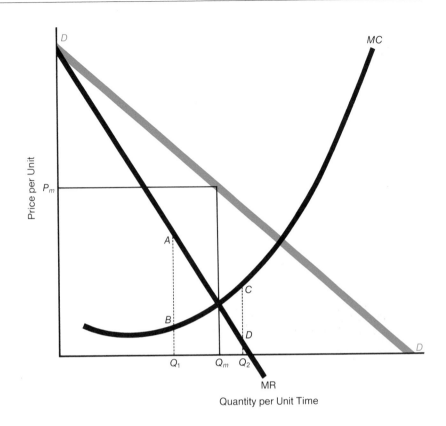

because, if he increased production by more units, he would increase his total profit because his marginal revenues still exceed his marginal costs.

Look at Q_1 in Figure 6–4. Here the monopolist's marginal revenue is at A, but his marginal cost is at B. The difference is his increase in profits on that particular unit of production. Why should he stop at Q_1? He won't. He will keep on going until he gets to the intersection of the marginal revenue and the marginal cost curve. He won't go to Q_2 because here we see that his marginal costs are C and his marginal revenues are D. The difference between C and D represents the loss that he takes on producing that additional unit. He simply won't go that far.

How does he set his price? We know he sets his quantity at the point where marginal revenue

equals marginal cost. He then finds out how much he can charge—that is, how much the market will bear—for that particular quantity, Q_m. We know that the demand curve is defined as showing the *maximum* price that a given quantity can be sold for. So our monopolist knows that to sell Q_m and no more he can only charge P_m, for that is where Q_m hits the demand curve DD. He can draw the vertical line up to the market demand curve, then reach over horizontally to the price axis to find the profit maximizing price as P_m.

FIGURING OUT PROFITS

We can now easily figure out how much profit our true monopolist will make. He has set his price

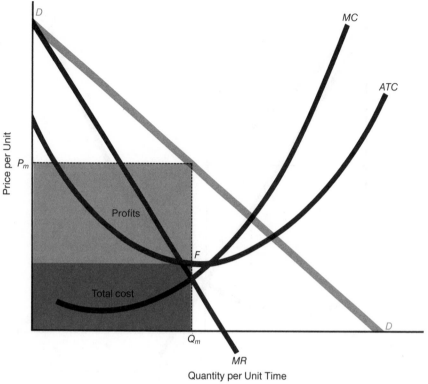

FIGURE 6–5

PROFITS FOR THE MONOPOLIST

The profit maximizing monopolist will set his production rate at Q_m and charge all the traffic will bear—that is, P_m. His total revenues equal the price times quantity, or P_m times Q_m. His total costs will equal the quantity he produces times the average total costs. Average total costs are found in this diagram at point F so the gold shaded area marked total costs are just equal to Q_m times F, where F is the average total cost. Profits are marked as the grey shaded area for they are the difference between total revenues, P_m times Q_m, and total costs, Q_m times F.

equal to P_m, and the quantity he can sell at that price is Q_m. He therefore receives total revenues equal to the price times the quantity, or P_m times Q_m. How much does he have to spend to produce all those goods? It is easy to find out: we add an average total cost curve to our diagram.

At the production rate of Q_m in Figure 6–5, the monopolist's average total cost per unit of production is at point F. Since that's the average per unit cost, we can find out what our total costs are by multiplying the average per unit cost times the quantity. This is exactly what is done graphically when the rectangle in the lowest corner of the diagram is shaded in. The difference between the total revenues and the total costs are the monopolist's profits, or the grey area. There is no way for our monopolist to make larger profits than those shown by the shaded area. *He is maximizing profits where marginal costs equal marginal reve-*

nues. If he produces less than that, he will be forfeiting some profits. If he produces more than that, he will also be forfeiting potential profits.

Actually, the same is true of a pure competitor. He produces where marginal revenue equals marginal costs because he produces at the point where the marginal cost schedule intersects the horizontal *dd* curve. The horizontal *dd* curve represents the marginal revenue curve for the pure competitor because he obtains the same revenues on all the units he sells. Pure competitors maximize profits at $MR = MC$, just as do pure monopolists. The only difference is that the pure competitor ends up making no true economic profits. Rather, all he makes is a normal competitive rate of return. This might lead you to suspect that there is a positive economic reason why monopolized industries are not considered beneficial to the economy in many circumstances.

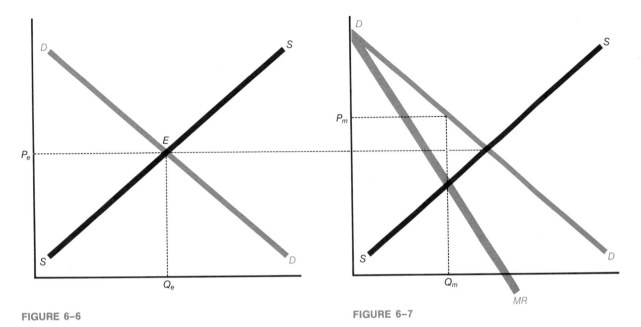

FIGURE 6-6

FIGURE 6-7

THE EFFECTS OF MONOPOLIZING AN INDUSTRY

In Figure 6–6 we have shown a competitive situation where DD is the market demand curve and SS is the market supply curve. The market supply curve is made up of the horizontal summation of all the individual supply curves of all the firms involved. Equilibrium is established at the intersection of DD and SS at E. The equilibrium price would be P_e and the equilibrium quantity supplied and demanded would be Q_e. Now we assume that the industry is suddenly monopolized. We assume that the costs stay the same; the only thing that changes is that the monopolist now realizes that he faces the entire downward sloping demand curve. In Figure 6–7, we draw his marginal revenue curve. He will produce at the point where marginal revenue equals marginal costs. Marginal cost for him is SS because that is the horizontal summation of all the individual marginal cost curves. He therefore produces at Q_m and charges a price P_m. P_m in Figure 6–7 is higher than P_e in Figure 6–6. We see, then, that a monopolist, as compared to the competitive situation, charges a higher price and produces less.

THE COST TO SOCIETY OF A MONOPOLY

Let's run a little experiment. We shall start out with a purely competitive industry where there are numerous firms, each one unable to affect the price of the product. The supply curve of the industry is equal to the horizontal sum of all of the marginal cost curves of the individual producers. Look at Figure 6–6. Here we have drawn the market demand curve and the market supply curve in a perfectly competitive situation. The competitive price in equilibrium is equal to P_e, and the competitive quantity demanded and supplied at that price is equal to Q_e. Now let's assume that some big monopolist comes in and buys up every single competitor in the industry. In so doing, we'll assume that he does not affect any of the marginal cost curves. We can therefore redraw DD and SS in the accompanying Figure 6–7. They are exactly the same as those in Figure 6-6.

What does this monopolist do when he wants to decide how much to charge and how much to produce? If he's smart, he's going to look at the marginal revenue curve. He's going to want to set the quantity produced at the point where marginal revenue equals marginal cost. But what is his marginal cost curve in Figure 6-7? It is merely SS because we said that SS was equal to the horizontal sum of all of the individual marginal cost curves. He therefore produces a quantity Q_m and sells it at a price P_m. Notice that Q_m is less than Q_e and P_m is greater than P_e. A monopolist, therefore, produces a smaller quantity and sells it at a higher price. This is the reason usually given when one attacks monopolists. They raise the price and restrict production, compared to a competitive situation. For a monopolist's product, consumers are forced to pay a price that exceeds the marginal cost of production. Resources are misallocated in such a situation. Too little resources are being used in the monopolist's industry and too many are used elsewhere.

CAN A MONOPOLIST MAKE EVEN MORE MONEY?

In our preceding discussion we assumed that the monopolist sold all his units at the same or uniform prices. However, if he can somehow *discriminate* against relatively less elastic demands, he can make even more profits. He then becomes a **price-discriminating monopolist.** This person will charge more for his product to those consumers who really desire it than he will to those consumers who have less desire for his product. He will raise the price to those consumers with less elastic demand curves.

Look at it this way. If the monopolist can somehow identify relatively less elastic demanders, he can raise his price to them and not suffer very much of a fall in the quantity they demand. If he lowers the price to consumers with relatively more elastic demands, he'll attract more buyers. They'll substantially increase the quantity demanded. The monopolist will make more revenues in both cases; he'll make more profits. Of course, he somehow has to prevent the elastic demanders who were charged a lower price from reselling the good to those who were charged a higher price.

Can you think of any examples of price discrimination? What about nightclubs that charge females less than males? It's easy to discriminate here and its pretty hard to transfer the product, right? Medical services are also hard to resell among patients. So we see doctors using price discrimination. We shall cover this in our next issue.

Definition of New Terms

MONOPOLIST: single seller.

BARRIERS TO ENTRY: barriers which prevent new firms from entering an existing industry. Some barriers might be government laws against entry, patents for research discoveries, and so on.

ECONOMIES OF SCALE: a situation where an increase in *all* factors of production brings about a more than proportionate increase in output. It is important in describing economies of scale to make sure that *all* inputs are increased proportionately. Economies of scale should not be confused with economies of mass production.

ECONOMIES OF MASS PRODUCTION: the term loosely applied to the reduction in average total costs as output is increased. Economies of mass production usually result in fixed costs being spread over a larger and larger number of units of output so that average fixed costs fall, thereby bringing down average total costs.

DISCRIMINATING MONOPOLIST: a monopolist who discriminates among classes of demanders with different elasticities of demand. He will charge a higher price to those with relatively less elastic demands than he will charge to those with relatively more elastic demands.

Chapter Summary

1. We formally define a monopolist as a single seller. A monopolist faces the entire industry demand curve because he is the entire industry. There are not too many examples of pure monopolists. In general, they have a government franchise to operate so that they can remain pure monopolists. We cite as examples electricity companies, the telephone system, and the post office. General Motors and U.S. Steel do not qualify as true monopolies under our restricted definition.

2. A monopolist can usually only remain a monopolist if there are barriers to entry; that is, if there is some reason why other firms cannot enter the industry and share in the monopoly profits. One of the most obvious barriers to entry is the government interdiction against someone else joining the fun. The government does not allow you to set up an alternative telephone system nor an alternative electric utility. Patents on a discovery can be an effective barrier to entry. A patent allows the owner of the patent to produce the product without fearing competition for a period of 17 years.

3. A monopoly could arise because of economies of scale. Economies of scale are defined as a situation where an increase in *all* inputs leads to a more than proportionate increase in output. If this were the case, then average total costs would be falling as production and all inputs were increased in order to produce the increased output. In a situation where true economies of scale exist, the first person to produce a lot and take advantage of those economies of scale could conceivably take advantage of the reduced average total cost by lowering his price and driving everybody else out of the market.

4. The marginal revenue that a monopolist receives is defined in the same way as the marginal revenue that a competitor receives. However, there is one difference. Since the monopolist faces the industry demand curve, he must lower his price in order to increase sales. He must lower his price not only on the last unit he sells but also on all the preceding units. The monopolist's marginal revenue, therefore, is equal to the price he receives on the last unit sold, minus the reduction in price on all the previous units, times the number of units.

5. The monopolist will produce where marginal revenue equals marginal cost. If he produces less than that, he is foregoing potential profits. His marginal revenue will exceed his marginal cost; thus, it behooves him to continue production. If he produces at a point after marginal revenue equals marginal cost, then his marginal cost will *exceed* his marginal revenues. The benefits from producing more are less than the costs.

6. The profit-maximizing price the monopolist charges is the maximum price he can get away with, while still selling all he has produced to the point where marginal revenue equals marginal cost. We find this price by extending a vertical line from the intersection of the marginal revenue curve and the marginal cost curve up to the demand curve and then over to the vertical axis, which measures price.

7. A straight-line demand curve can be separated into two sections. At the upper end is the elastic section, at the lower end is the inelastic section. Somewhere between is the point where elasticity is equal to –1, or unity. That can be found by extending a line vertically from the intersection of the marginal revenue curve with the horizontal axis. The point where that line hits the demand curve is the point where elasticity is unity. The elasticity is unity where marginal revenue equals zero. That is also the point where total revenues are maximized. If the monopolist had no costs at all, he would obviously want to produce where marginal revenue equals zero. That, in fact, is where he would maximize his profits because he would be maximizing his total revenues.

8. The monopolist's profits can be found easily. His profits are merely his total revenues minus his total costs. His total revenues are equal to the price for which he sells his product (the profit-maximizing price) times the quantity he has produced (the quantity found at the intersection of the marginal revenue and marginal cost curves). His total costs are equal to the quantity produced times his average total costs. The difference between these total costs and his total revenues is, as we stated, profits.

9. In general, it can be shown that a competitive industry, if monopolized, will end up with a higher price and a lower quantity supplied. That is why monopolies are "bad" in economic analysis. The reason that the monopolist will restrict production and increase price is because he will look at his entire demand curve and realize that in order to sell more units of his product, he must lower the price. He will look at his marginal revenue curve. He will find out where the marginal revenue curve intersects the marginal cost curve and that is where he will produce. Since the marginal revenue curve is below the demand schedule, we know he will produce less. Since he is producing less, he can obviously charge a higher price than in the competitive situation where more is produced.

10. If a monopolist can effectively separate out different classes of demanders, he can become a discriminating monopolist and make more total profits.

Questions for Thought and Discussion

1. It is sometimes stated that pure monopoly never exists because there are always substitites for whatever is produced. Do you agree? Why?

2. Do you think that a trade-mark gives a firm an effective amount of monopoly power?

3. Can you think of any reasons why a pure monopolist would not set the profit-maximizing price and produce the profit-maximizing quantity?

4. Will a monopolist ever produce at a point on his demand schedule that is to the right of where the elasticity is equal to -1, or unity?

5. It is often stated that the United States is run by large monopolists. Do you agree? If so, do you think you can utilize the model presented in this chapter to analyze and predict the behavior of most firms in the United States?

6. Do you think a monopolist looks at his long-run marginal revenue curve or his short-run marginal revenue curve when deciding how much to produce and what to charge?

Selected References

Adams, Walter. *The Structure of American Industry.* 4th Ed. New York: Macmillan, 1971. Chapter 11.

Caves, Richard. *American Industry: Structure, Conduct, and Performance.* 3rd Ed. Englewood Cliffs, New Jersey: Prentice Hall, 1972.

Kefauver, Estes. *In a Few Hands: Monopoly Power in America.* Baltimore: Penguin, 1965.

Robinson, E.A.G. *Monopoly.* London: Nesbit, 1941.

Schumpeter, Joseph A. *Capitalism, Socialism, and Democracy.* 3rd Ed. New York: Harper & Row, 1950. Chapters 7 and 8.

Weiss, Leonard W. *Case Studies in American Industry.* 2nd Ed., New York: John Wiley, 1971, Chapter 3.

THE ICONOCLAST AS INSTITUTION

Milton Friedman
Economist, University of Chicago

MILTON FRIEDMAN has played a unique role in the continuing battle over the role of government in the economy. He has never held a major government post, but he has heard his ideas soundly condemned by the "new economists" of the early 1960s, eventually—if cautiously— adopted by the "gamesmen" of the Nixon Administration, and then ignored shortly thereafter. Throughout, Friedman has hounded the economic watchmen about uselessly attending to invalid fiscal indices, while ignoring what he considers the one crucial factor—fluctuation in the money supply.

One of America's major conservative economists, Friedman defends the modern "quantity" theory of money: changes in the amount of money in circulation shape short-run economic events. In his testimony before the Joint Congressional Economic Committee in 1959, Friedman said that the Federal Reserve Board, instead of tightening money during booms and loosening money during recessions (which doesn't work because of the lags), should simply increase the supply of money at a steady rate of 4 percent, "month in and month out, year in and year out."

An ideal economy, according to Friedman, is based on a free-market model; government's role should be little more than the maintenance of optimal competitive conditions. This concept has two important corollaries, both of which stand solidly in opposition to "liberal" economic thought in this country: (1) the obligation of the business community is the maximization of profit with direct responsibility to the stockholder; and (2) the economy is not a tool of social betterment, to be manipulated by the government in pursuit of so-cial-welfare goals. Friedman explained, in "The Social Responsibility of Business is to Maximize Profit" (*New York Times Magazine,* 1970), that the use of corporate profits for environmental protection, safety and quality-control devices, and so on represents a direct tax on the stockholder; a board of directors which "levies" such a tax is acting as a legislative body. The way certain companies have timidly received the demands of consumer groups is, to Friedman, completely at odds with the valid economic role of the corporation. "When I hear businessmen speak eloquently about the 'social responsibility of business in a free enterprise system,' I am reminded of the wonderful line about the Frenchman who discovered at the age of 70 that he had been speaking prose all his life."

In Friedman's view, it is dangerous to regard the economic sector as a cure for social problems. It drives economists into roles of oracles and social magicians. As Friedman stated: "I believe that we economists in recent years have done vast harm—to society at large and to our profession in particular—by claiming more than we can de-liver."

Friedman would, nonetheless, like to apply many of his free-market concepts to other areas of the society. He has written eloquently of the need for an all-volunteer army. He opposes pro-tective tariffs, feeling that America has a good deal to gain by encouraging imports. "If Japan exports steel at artificially low prices, it is also exporting clean air. Why shouldn't we take it?" Other aspects of Friedman's approach are his distaste for subsidies (especially farm) and price supports, and his dislike of government mandates for safety equipment in automobiles. He also advo-cates abandoning social security and welfare, to be replaced with a negative tax (a cash subsidy for those citizens in the lowest income group).

During Senator Barry Goldwater's unsuc-cessful bid for the Presidency in 1964, Friedman served as chief economic adviser. He and the Senator agreed in wanting a reduction in govern-ment spending, opposing tax manipulation or spending control as economic levers or weapons, and proposing an annual 5 percent reduction in taxes over a five-year period. Friedman also ad-vised Nixon on economic matters during his cam-paign for the Presidency in 1968, but Nixon broke with Friedman's theories when he instituted the wage and price freeze.

Whether the American economy—nurtured on government contracts, production guidelines and quotas, and wage and price controls—will ever turn in the direction Friedman. proposes is not as important as Friedman's advocacy role in the economics establishment. Paul Samuelson said three years ago: "To keep the fish that they carried on long journeys lively and fresh, sea captains used to introduce an eel into the barrel. In the economics profession, Milton Friedman is that eel."

ISSUE V
MEDICAL CARE FOR ALL

Theory and Practice

Spiraling Costs of Medical Care

The woeful lack of adequate health care for large segments of the American population has been decried by Congressmen, Presidents, laymen, and even doctors. There have been many suggested solutions to our health care crisis, some of which have already been enacted in the form of Medicare and Medicaid. Even more comprehensive medical care insurance plans have been demanded by several Senators.

In addition to the problems of inadequate supplies for medical care, concerned legislators and citizens could not help noticing the spiraling costs of obtaining what medical care is available. In Figure V-1, we show the Consumer Price Index and a price index of health care services, which has risen considerably faster than the Consumer Price Index. This means, of course, that the relative price of health care services has been rising. Subsequently, we shall present some plausible explanations for this phenomenon. As one of his Phase II price stabilization actions, President Nixon nominated a

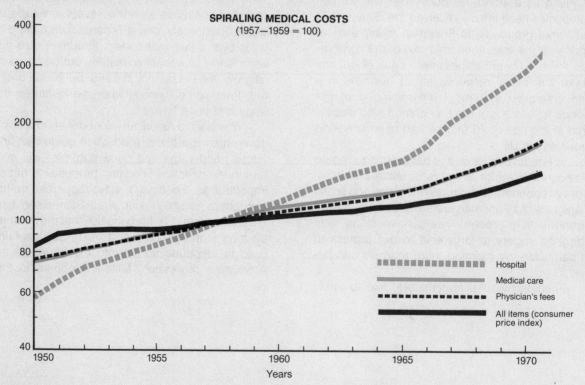

SPIRALING MEDICAL COSTS
(1957–1959 = 100)

Legend:
- Hospital
- Medical care
- Physician's fees
- All items (consumer price index)

Years

FIGURE V-1

Medical prices have risen faster than the average prices of all other goods. (*Source:* U.S. Dept. of Labor.)

number of people to serve on a committee to oversee medical care prices. His hope was that this committee could encourage and perhaps obtain some price restraints on the part of the medical care industry. The success of Nixon's committee has not been overwhelming. Americans are still facing ever-increasing costs in health care services.

Medical Care Expenditures

The expenditures for medical care in the United States have increased dramatically in the last four or five decades. We spent only $4 billion on medical care in 1929; we increased our spending to $40 billion by 1965, and it is over $70 billion today. In 1929, expenditures on medical care represented 4 percent of total national spending, but today's expenditures represent 7 percent. We can say, therefore, that the demand for medical care has been *income elastic.* As real incomes rose, Americans demanded not just more medical care, but more than in proportion to the rise in real income. While the proportion of total spending going to medical care has risen, the prices of medical care services have also risen. Since 1947, for example, health service costs rose at an annual rate of 3.5 percent, substantially higher than the annual percentage increase of all other prices in the economy.

For this to occur, the demand schedule for medical services must have shifted faster than the supply schedule of those services. We see this depicted in Figure V-2. Here we find that over time the demand schedule for health care has shifted from *DD* to *D'D'*. At the same time, the supply schedule has shifted from *SS* to *S'S'*.

The shift in the supply schedule is much less than the shift in the demand schedule. The new equilibrium is at *E'*, with a higher price than the old equilibrium of *E*. The key, then, to understanding why the price of medical services has risen more rapidly than other prices is to find out *(a)* why the demand schedule shifted

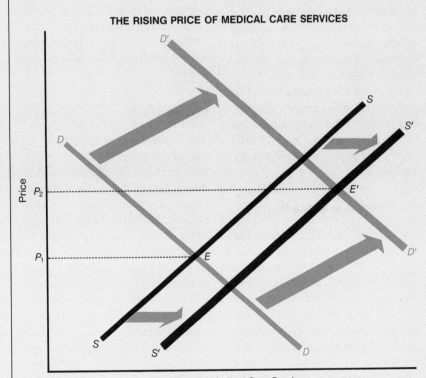

THE RISING PRICE OF MEDICAL CARE SERVICES

FIGURE V-2

Here we see that the demand schedule for medical care services has been shifting outward faster than the supply schedule. Twenty years ago the demand and supply schedules were *DD* and *SS* and the price was *P₁*. Since then, the demand schedule has shifted to *D'D'* and the supply schedule to *S'S'*. The new equilibrium price is *P₂*, which is higher than *P₁*.

to the right so fast, and *(b)* why the supply schedule shifted so little. That is exactly what we will do in this issue. We will then discuss the possibilities for universal medical care for everyone in the United States.

The Supply of Medical Care

Medical care consists of a number of items including, but not limited to, the services of physicians, nurses, and hospital staff, hospital facilities, maintenance of the facilities, medications, and drugs. We will limit our discussion in this issue to what determines the supply of the most important input (at least up till now) into the total medical care package—physicians' services.

The Production of Medical Doctors

In 1972, 50,000 people took the Standard Medical School Admissions Test; only 12,000 were accepted in medical schools. Applicants to Harvard's Medical School run almost 3500, but the class size remains at less than 150. Some students apply to as many as ten different medical schools, and when turned down reapply two or three times. The number of students who don't apply because they know the odds are so much against them is probably two or three times the number who actu-

ally do take the chance. Why is there such a large discrepancy between those who want to go to medical school and those who are accepted? If you compare the number of students who wish to attend law school with the number of students who actually go, the discrepancy is small relative to the medical school situation. The reason for this discrepancy is not hard to find; the number of medical schools in the United States is severely restricted and the number of entrants into those schools each year is similarly restricted.

Restrictions

The question is: restricted by whom? In principle, restriction on the number of medical schools is due to state licensing requirements which universally prohibit proprietary medical schools (schools run for profit). Also, it is difficult for a university which does not have a medical school suddenly to start one. A university can start a graduate department of romance languages without asking anybody, and it can start a law school without asking anybody. However, unless the medical school is accredited by the state, the graduates are not even allowed to take the licensing exam required for practicing medicine.

To understand why such restrictions have been put on medi-

cal schools, we only have to read the statements of Dr. John H. Knowles in an article in *Saturday Review*, August 22, 1970:

At the turn of the century, the AMA [American Medical Association] stood at the forefront of progressive thinking and socially responsible action. Its members had been leaders in forming much-needed public health departments in the states during the last half of the nineteenth century. It formed a Council on Medical Education in 1904 and immediately began an investigation of proprietary medical schools. Because of its success in exposing intolerable conditions in these schools, the Carnegie Foundation, at the AMA's request, commissioned Abraham Flexner to study the national scene. His report in 1910 drove proprietary interest out of medical education, established it as a full university function with standards for admission, curriculum development, and clinical teaching. Our present system of medical education, essentially unchanged since the Flexner (and AMA) revolution—and acknowledging its current defects—was accomplished through the work of the AMA. Surely this contribution was and is one of the finest in the public interest.

The Past

Looking back to the first decade in this century, we find there were 192 medical schools. By 1944 that number declined to 69. The number of physicians per 100,000 people dropped from 157 in 1900 to 132 in 1957. Perhaps the American Medical Association and the so-called Flexner report lauded by Dr. Knowles were responsible for the reduction in the rate of growth of the supply of physicians. At least, this appears to be the case.

The AMA Wins Out. The American Medical Association was started in 1847. It represented then and still does represent existing practitioners in the field of medicine. From the period of 1870 to 1910 there was a struggle between the AMA and medical educators over who should control the output of doctors—that is, who

should control the number of doctors allowed to practice. This became a battle over who should control medical schools themselves. We know the American Medical Association won the battle. It essentially has complete control over medical education in the United States. In order for a medical school graduate to become licensed in any particular state, he must have obtained a degree from a "certified" medical school. The certification is nominally done by the states themselves; however, in all cases the states follow exactly the certification lists of the American Medical Association. If, for example, the American Medical Association were to decertify a particular medical school, you can be sure the state involved would also decertify that same school. Graduates coming out of that decertified school would find themselves barred from legal medical practice.

The Flexner Report. The regulation and certification of medical schools was, in all probability, based on the outcome of the famous Flexner Report. In 1910, the prestigious Carnegie Foundation commissioned one Abraham Flexner to inspect the existing medical education facilities in the United States. Flexner's recommendations resulted in the demise of half of the existing medical schools of the day. He asserted

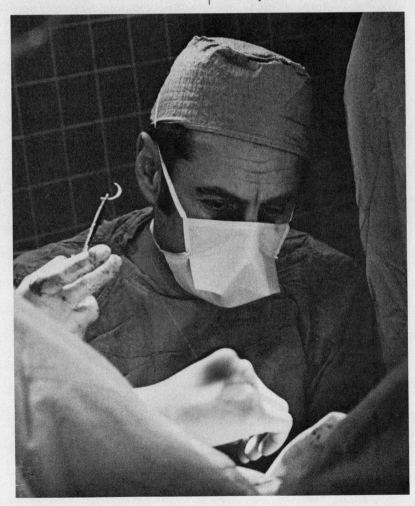

that they were unqualified to teach medical education. It is interesting to note that Flexner had absolutely no qualifications himself for deciding which medical schools were to be rated class A. Flexner was not a physician; he was not a scientist; and he was never a medical educator. He had an undergraduate degree in arts and was himself the owner and operator of a for-profit preparatory school in Louisville, Kentucky. Moreover, his evaluation of existing medical schools consisted of a grand inspection tour—nothing more, nothing less. Sometimes Flexner evaluated an entire school in one afternoon. The way he decided whether a medical school was qualified was by estimating how well it compared with the medical school at Johns Hopkins University.

It is also interesting to note that Flexner was examining the *inputs* and not the *output* of these particular schools. Instead of finding out how well or how qualified the doctors were who *graduated* from different schools, he looked at how doctors were taught. This would be equivalent to your instructor giving you a grade on the basis of how many hours you spent studying rather than how well you did on the final exam (even though you might find that preferable).

Discrimination. Flexner's endeavors not only caused the number of medical schools to drop by half, but they also caused greater discrimination against blacks and women. Whereas the number of white medical schools fell by half from 1906 to 1944, the number of black medical schools went from 7 to 2 and the number of students admitted to the surviving two schools decreased. This should not surprise anyone reading the Flexner Report where he states in all seriousness:

A well taught Negro sanitarian will be immensely useful; an essentially untrained Negro wearing an MD degree is dangerous. . . . The practice of the Negro doctor will be limited to his own race.

The number of women physicians reached a high point in 1910, just before the recommendations of the Flexner Report were put into effect. In 1940, the number of women physicians was less than it was in 1910.

Discrimination in medical schools is not hard to understand. After all, the number of applicants greatly exceeded and continues to exceed the number of vacancies. One easy way to ration out the available supply of slots in medical school is to weed out those persons with distinct characteristics like sex and race. One would also expect that the ability to discriminate increases as the discrepancy between the number of applicants and the number of available positions grows larger. Indeed, this is exactly what happened.

Why Did the AMA Seek Control?

It is not hard to find the motive behind the AMA's desire to control medical schools. We merely need quote from the former head of the AMA's Council on Medical Education, Dr. Beven, who said in 1928:

In this rapid elevation of the standard of medical education . . . the reduction of the number of medical schools from 160 to 80, there occurred a marked reduction in the number of medical students and medical graduates. We had anticipated this and felt that this was a desirable thing. We had . . . a great oversupply of poor mediocre practitioners.

Dr. Beven's statement can be rephrased to the effect that, if the supply falls, the price will therefore rise. On the other hand, if the supply increases, the price will fall. If we look at Figure V–3, we can see that the reduction in the number of physicians during this period resulted in the supply curve of physicians shifting to the left. The demand curve was at least stable if not increasing. Therefore, the price of the physicians' services went up, thereby allowing them to make higher incomes.

RESTRICTING THE SUPPLY OF DOCTORS

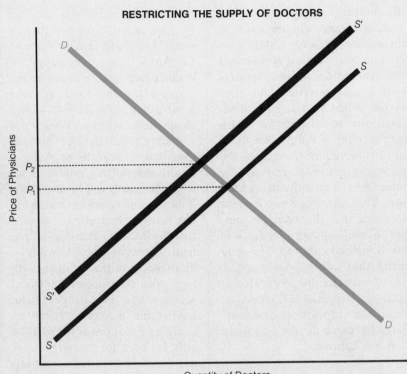

FIGURE V-3

Here we see that the AMA's successful attempt at restricting the supply of doctors shifted the supply schedule from *SS* to *S'S'*. Even with a stable demand schedule, the price of physicians would go up. That is, their income would increase.

AMA's Motives Not Satisfied

If we look at the American Medical Association's avowed motives, we realize that even those were not satisfied. The AMA maintained that the qualifications of many doctors were deficient—that is, the public was being serviced by doctors who were doing damage to unsuspecting patients. The idea behind medical school licensing was to weed out the most unqualified students and to eliminate the possibility of an unsuspecting sick person being treated by an inadequately trained, yet licensed doctor. It is strange, therefore, that the AMA did not seek in 1910 to analyze the qualifications of the current crop of physicians. The closure of one-half of the medical schools resulted in the elimination of a *future* supply of supposedly unqualified doctors. The then current supply of supposedly unqualified doctors was allowed to continue practicing until retirement or death. Further, the then current generation of unsuspecting citizens were to seek the aid of whoever happened to have an M.D. degree before the implementation of the recommendations of the Flexner Report. Somehow this type of behavior does not seem consistent with the AMA's desire to raise the quality of medical services in the United States.

Moreover, it is difficult to understand why doctors are not re-examined periodically if they wish to continue practicing. Even a brilliant medical student from a very excellent medical school could become very lax in his medical practice and be unqualified after a period of years. Since there is no recertification procedure, the public can still be subject to the malpractices of unqualified doctors.

Additionally, it is not obvious that the quality of medical care actually consumed by the public increased as much as the AMA professed. After all, there are two ways of obtaining medical services. One is self-diagnosis and self-treatment. The other is reliance on the medical care industry. If the price of a physician's diagnosis and treatment goes up, then one might expect that the quantity demanded would fall. An increased reliance on self-diagnosis and self-treatment would result. People would only decide to go to doctors after their symptoms became alarming. It may be that the increase in quality and, therefore, price of doctors' services resulted in a decrease in the *total* quality of medical care utilized because physicians were consulted less often. Moreover, we must presume that some people might forego the services of a licensed physician in favor of some alternative method which may be of "inferior" quality, such as naturopaths or faith healers. When the price of the services of licensed physicians goes up, there is an increase in the demand for substitute healing services.

Jumps in Demand—Medicare

Another reason for large increases in the price of medical care relates to jumps in demand that aren't a function of rising real income. Prior to the imposition of Medicare ("free" medical care for the aged), the congressional estimates of the cost of that particular program were many times less than the actual cost turned out to be. There is an easy explanation for

this, and it partially involves the practice of *price discrimination* in the medical profession. Before we get into this, we must realize that the demand for medical services is both income elastic and price elastic. When Medicare was instituted, the actual price of health care services to many were drastically lowered. In some cases, the price was reduced to zero. As the price fell, the quantity demanded rose. The quantity demanded rose so much that the available supply of medical care services was taxed beyond capacity. The only thing that could give was the price, and price did go up. Hospital room charges have skyrocketed since the imposition of Medicare—but this is not the only thing that has happened.

Price Discrimination

Previous to Medicare, a large percentage of poor older patients were given free medical treatment. In other words, physicians did not charge these patients. After the imposition of Medicare, physicians did charge them. The patients still paid nothing, but the government started paying for what the patients had previously received free. The explanation of the change in the behavior of physicians has to do with their ability and desire to price discriminate.

We have discussed price discrimination in the context of a

monopoly. The same model can be applied to the medical profession. Doctors have a monopoly; the AMA controls the supply of doctors and, therefore, can be analyzed as a monopolist. Let's take a particular physician who wishes to maximize income. (We are not assuming this is actually his motive; rather, we are applying a wealth-maximizing model to see what the results will be and to see if those results conform with what has actually happened.) Assume that the doctor is charging all patients the same price. Obviously, he makes sure that patients with high price elasticities for medical services are discouraged from buying the medical services by charging equal prices for what he sells. He does not discourage very many potential patients with less elastic demands because, by definition, they are not very price responsive.

The doctor now decides he might get more income if he charged some patients lower prices and other patients higher prices for the same services. Let's assume that he can separate the relatively less price-elastic demanders from the relatively more price-elastic demanders. One easy way to do this is to separate patients by their incomes. Apparently, high-income people have relatively lower elasticities of demand for medical services than do low-income people. If the doctor lowers his price to low-income

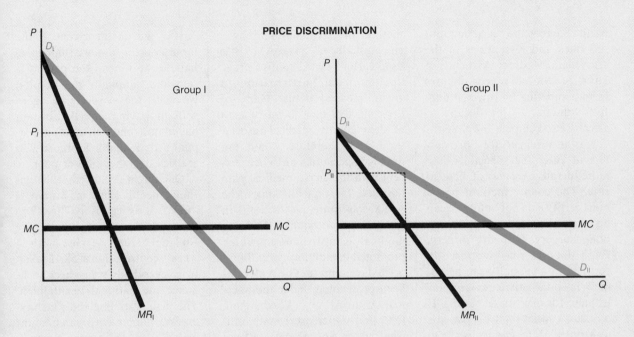

PRICE DISCRIMINATION

FIGURE V–4

Here the smart doctor has separated his patients into those with relatively less elastic demand curves (group I) and those with relatively more elastic demand curves (group II). Profit maximization occurs when marginal revenue equals marginal cost. Therefore, our doctor sets his marginal revenue equal to his marginal cost in each individual category. We find that he sets a price of PI for group I and a price of PII for group II. Those with the relatively less elastic demands end up paying more than do those with the relatively more elastic demands for the same service. In such a situation the doctor maximizes profit more than he could, if he weren't able to price discriminate.

people—that is, those with elastic demands—his total revenues from these people would increase because the quantity demanded will rise more than in proportion to the decrease in price. If he raises the price charged to high-income or less-elastic demanders, the total revenue will also rise. The quantity demanded will not fall as much as the increase in price.

Graphic Analysis

We see how our doctor does this in Figure V–4, where two separate market demand curves for his services have been drawn—one less elastic and one more elastic.

We assume he has a constant (horizontal) marginal cost curve. He will charge a higher price for the less elastic demanders than for the more elastic demanders. You might be asking yourself: How can a doctor act as a monopolist? He's in competition with many more doctors. Unless he is in a small city where no other doctor is practicing, he will not be able

to price discriminate in a competitive situation. Other doctors will, in fact, undercut his expensive services to high-income patients. Eventually only a uniform price per constant quality unit can prevail in a competitive industry. Doctors, if left to their own devices, would actually be in competition with one another and price discrimination could not occur. So goes the reasoning, but the rules and regulations of the American Medical Association have prevented many doctors from competing by price cutting. It is "unethical" for doctors to advertise to compete for patients.

It is also difficult for price cutters to enter the specialties, the more lucrative aspects of medical care. The county medical board must certify a doctor before he can be allowed to specialize in, say, bone surgery or heart surgery. Even doctors who are already certified in a specialty can be denied hospital privileges as punishment for overt price cutting. If a doctor cannot send his patients to a hospital, he cannot perform lucrative operations unless, of course, he can do them in his office.

Fighting the Group Health Plans

Given that the American Medical Association has followed a policy which we can equate with price discrimination, it is not surprising that the AMA has fought tooth and nail against prepaid medical plans, such as Kaiser, Group Health, and Ross-Loos. With these medical plans, everybody is charged the same for the same thing. These plans are all prepaid; the charges are not a function of subscribers' incomes. There is no way to price discriminate as there is with the typical "fee for service"

method of payment that physicians usually use. The AMA has used various tactics to discourage doctors from participating in group medical plans. Many of these doctors have been run out of their county medical associations and, therefore, could not practice specialties anywhere except with the group medical plan hospital. In some instances, the AMA was quite unsuccessful in its attempts to squelch budding medical establishments which promoted competition and didn't price discriminate. The AMA has been prosecuted under the Sherman Antitrust Act in Washington, D.C. and under other state antitrust acts; nonetheless, about one-third of the states have declared group health plans illegal.

National Health Insurance

Is a national health insurance policy the answer to our medical care problem? This is what many Senators and numerous laymen think should be done. After all, it has apparently worked in England where there was a limited national health insurance scheme in effect from 1911 to 1948. In 1948, the present comprehensive national health plan was devised. Anybody in England can go to one of Britain's 23,000 family doctors and receive whatever health care is needed without

paying the doctor a cent. If the family doctor is not equipped to handle the illness, the patient is sent to a nationally run hospital where he sees a specialist, again without paying directly. Britain has almost one-half million hospital beds available for those who are sick, whether rich or poor.

One might ask whether the national health plan in Britain is "free." It is certainly "free" to most people, although they pay for the "free" service with a weekly contribution of $2.12 taken from everybody's paycheck to finance the national health plan. The plan costs England's taxpayers $4.5 billion a year, an amount which represents more than 10 percent of all public expenditures. The weekly contributions of individuals employed only covers 10 percent of the costs, and the rest is made up from taxes. Thus, medical care in England clearly is not free: it is paid indirectly via taxes that the government collects.

No matter *who* pays for medical care, the costs still have to be borne by *someone*. Don't think that medical services would somehow be sent from heaven if a national, all-inclusive health insurance plan were passed in the United States. Part of your taxes would go to pay for health care. To the extent that you took advantage of "free" health care, you would be repaid for your contribution. To the extent that you received more services than what you paid for, you would be obtaining a subsidy from those taxpayers who received less than what they paid for. Actually, this is a form of redistribution of income—not necessarily from the rich to the poor—but from the more healthy to the less healthy.

Britain's national insurance plan has not been without its problems. Currently many doctors a year are leaving the country in search of greener pastures. The wages paid by the British government are not sufficient to keep all of the doctors satisfied with England. This would be a potential problem for the United States if a similar plan were instituted here. Our doctors couldn't find better jobs in other countries, but they could work less.

Let's assume that a national health care act was passed by Congress and anyone could obtain a physician's services if he wanted—no matter what his income. The patient would not be billed directly. Rather, physicians would bill the government. If the government refused to pay what the physicians asked, then we might find that the quantity of health care in the United States would actually fall as physicians decided to work fewer hours because the rate of return for working more hours was not sufficient. Another possible response to maximum rates for, say, office visits would

be for physicians to cut down on the number of minutes spent per patient. This is apparently what has happened in certain circumstances. It has been discovered that a few doctors have made in excess of $200,000 a year in Medicare and Medicaid payments. The only way this can be done is by seeing a large number of patients each day; and the only way a doctor can see a large number of patients each day is by spending fewer minutes with each patient. Notice, however, that some patients still may be better off than they were before Medicare. If they had not been seeing a doctor at all, they have improved their lot even with only a few minutes of a doctor's attention at the government's expense.

The Real Problem

Apparently, there would still be a problem about adequate medical care even if a national health plan were passed in the United States. No doubt, the supply of hospitals can be expanded. The supply of medical equipment can be expanded, and the supply of nurses can be expanded. But the supply of licensed physicians is controlled by the American Medical Association. We will find our current medical crisis ameliorated only if the supply of doctors is allowed to expand.

Many suggestions have been made for increasing the supply of doctors, and the AMA has seen fit to take some of these suggestions to heart. For example, larger numbers of paramedics are being trained to assist physicians in medical tasks which do not require a high degree of training. Further, there has apparently been some loosening up of the standards for entrance into medical schools.

One proposal involves elimination of licensing from medical school. Instead, there would be a licensing procedure at the *output* stage in the production of medical services. Potential doctors would have to pass a national examination before entering practice, and no questions would be asked about the doctor's training. This is similar to the bar examination that a potential lawyer must pass in order to practice in a particular state. The same examination given to potential doctors would also be given to practicing doctors at certain time intervals. In this manner, we would be assured that the supply of doctors would not deteriorate in quality. The current crop of doctors would write the examinations. They would know that with an extremely difficult examination, fewer doctors would enter the profession, but also fewer of their own colleagues would be able to pass the exam and continue in practice.

Questions for Thought and Discussion

1. In almost all cases doctors with whom you come in contact will vigorously deny that the AMA has actually harmed the welfare of the nation by restricting the supply of doctors. Doctors will maintain that it is necessary to keep the quality of medical services as high as possible. Do you agree? If so, why shouldn't the argument hold for other products and services?
2. "Poor people would rather have low quality, low priced medical care than no medical care at all." Evaluate.
3. "The problem is not that poor people need medical care, but rather that they do not have the money to buy it. Therefore, it is a problem of a maldistribution of income." Evaluate.
4. Would you rather get medical services in England or in the United States? Does your answer depend on your income?
5. Small rural towns have difficulty in getting a doctor to live and work in them. Why? Can you think of a solution?

Selected References

Kessel, Reuben. "Price Discrimination in Medicine." *The Journal of Law and Economics,* October 1958, **1,** 20-53.

Kessel, Reuben. "The A.M.A. and the Supply of Physicians." *Law and Contemporary Problems,* Spring 1970.

Rayack, Elton. *Professional Power and American Medicine.* New York: World, 1967.

ISSUE VI THE NEW YORK STOCK EXCHANGE

A Case Study in Monopoly

Price Fixing

It may seem paradoxical that the New York Stock Exchange will be viewed as a case study in monopoly. After all, we have pointed out how fantastically competitive the stock market is, given the low cost of transactions and the speed with which information is transmitted throughout the market. But the paradox is easy to explain. There is an almost perfectly competitive market in the buying of stocks; however, the selling of securities has for some time involved a monopoly. The New York Stock Exchange may be viewed as a private club which does not allow just anyone to enter—or, at least, this was so in the past. We will find out in this issue that the monopoly power of the New York Stock Exchange has allowed member firms to reap monopoly profits. We will also find that the price-fixing agreements made by the members of the Exchange lead to a situation of uniformity in services offered by the brokerage firms. This will become clearer later on. First, let's review a little history on the Exchange, or the "Big Board," as it is sometimes called.

History of the Exchange

The present Exchange developed from informal outdoor gatherings of securities and commodity traders. We are all familiar with some of the spectacular successes of tycoons such as the Morgans and the Goulds. We are concerned here not with individual fortunes, but rather with how the New York Stock Exchange originally came about as a monopoly in the field of buying and selling securities for the public.

On May 17, 1792, a group of 24 brokers signed a statement that has become known as the Buttonwood Tree Agreement:

We the undersigned, brokers for the purchase and sale of public stocks, do hereby promise and pledge ourselves to each other that we will not buy or sell from this date for any person whatever, any kind of public stocks at a rate less than one-quarter of one percent commission on the specie value, and that we will give preference to each other in our negotiations.

Here we see the essential element of a monopoly arrangement. First, prices for sale of brokerage services were fixed and, second, the individual signatories of the statement agreed to give preference to one another in negotiations. So, the agreement estab-

lished a cartel with a monopoly price for the services sold and there was an agreement of noncompetition among the members of the cartel so that price cutting would not occur.

After the Buttonwood Agreement until 1817 the organization of 24 brokers remained quite informal and business continued to be transacted in the streets or in coffee houses in the Wall Street district. Finally, in February 1817, the informal group gave themselves a name—the New York Stock and Exchange Board. A new constitution was drawn up; a rented office was declared the center of transactions. All meetings henceforth were held in strictest secrecy; nonmembers were not allowed to listen.

The "Curbstone Crowd"

As one could expect, nonmembers wanted to transact business, too. The New York Stock and Exchange Board did not (and still doesn't) have *complete* control over all of the brokerage business in the United States. Nonmembers congregated outside the rented office and became known as the "Curbstone Crowd." Since the Crowd was a source of competition for the members of the Board, a new resolution was drawn up to squelch this competition. Members of the Board were not allowed to transact business for anyone who was not a member

without charging the full commission rate. At that time there was an air of secrecy around the actual transaction prices for stocks bought and sold. As a consequence, transaction and information costs were quite high relative to what they are today in the stock market.

The "Curbstone Crowd" of competitors grew larger and larger. Finally, by 1869 this set of rivals, otherwise known as the "Open or Regular Board," merged with the "Big Board," and the consolidated organization became known as the New York Stock Exchange (NYSE). Just before the merger, both organizations changed their rules to allow the sale of their membership rights. When the new constitution of the NYSE was drawn up, this provision allowing for sale of **seats,** as they are called, was included and continues to this day. For a fairly long period of time, the New York Exchange attempted to prevent rival exchanges building up in different sections of the city and the country from receiving stock quotes from the Big Board. The courts finally decreed that other exchanges had the right to these stock quotations from Western Union.

The American Stock Exchange

A rival (but not so rival) organization got started with the bless-

ings of the New York Stock Exchange. It consisted of a group of brokers who dealt with stocks that were not listed on the New York Board. In 1910, this curb group of brokers officially organized as the New York Curb Market Association. The Association's constitution was approved by the Board of .Governors of the New York Stock Exchange. Expectedly there was a prohibition in this constitution against members of "the Curb" trading securities listed on the NYSE.

The Curb Market Association has grown and prospered since 1910. In 1921 a new constitution was drawn up, and the club was renamed the New York Curb Market. In 1929 it changed its name to the New York Curb Exchange. In 1953 it became known as the American Stock Exchange. It still is subservient and dependent upon the New York Stock Exchange.

The New York Stock Exchange has maintained its dominant position in the securities market in the United States. Of the almost $1 trillion of securities exchanged every year, the NYSE accounts and controls well over 80 percent.

The Monopoly Profits on the New York Stock Exchange

Since membership is limited on the New York Stock Exchange, we would expect that the only people

benefiting from the monopoly position of that exchange are the member firms. This is, in fact, exactly what we find. We can use the theory of monopoly presented in the previous chapter to analyze what has happened in the NYSE. With a fixed number of members and a fixed minimum commission rate schedule, we see that the members of the NYSE are essentially participating in a cartel. Any member of the cartel would therefore be expected to earn profits that are supernormal, or above competitive levels. The commission rates or prices charged for services are fixed so we would expect that each member's profits would depend upon how much business he has. How much business he has, in turn, depends upon the demand for trading securities. It is not a function of the price he charges in the sense that he is not allowed to vary that price. He cannot expect to get more business by lowering the price because, if he attempts to do so, he can lose his membership on the Exchange. Competition via prices is not allowed. The constitution of the Big Board prevents any member from engaging in price competition with other members of the Exchange.

Free Entry Means No Monopoly Profits

If there were free entry into the business of selling securities, we would expect that no monopoly profits would prevail in the long run. This is exactly what we should expect to see for nonmember security brokers. They will only be obtaining a competitive rate of return for their investment. These outsiders, or nonmembers, would certainly like to obtain the profits made available by being a member of the NYSE cartel. There is a way for nonmembers to become members: they can purchase the membership from someone who is already part of the club. But what would you expect nonmembers to be willing to pay for a seat on the New York Stock Exchange? What would you expect members to be willing to accept for giving up their right to membership in the New York Stock Exchange?

Valuing a Seat

The answer to these last two questions involves figuring out what the value of a NYSE seat is. The value of the seat is obviously going to be equal to the monopoly profits over time that a member can expect to obtain via his membership in the club. If nonmembers or outsiders didn't think that membership was valuable and allowed for monopoly profits, then one would not expect them to pay anything for membership. Rather, they would be content with remaining nonmembers because they could obtain just as high a rate of return as members. We find, however, that the prices actually paid for membership in the Exchange by nonmembers have exceeded zero ever since the seats were offered for sale. And nonmembers have a very easy way of finding out whether it is profitable to be a member. All they have to do is see how profitable current member firms really are. Moreover, for a given volume of business at fixed commission rates, the smaller the number of seats, the more valuable each seat will be because its owner will partake of a larger piece of the pie of monopoly profits.

The number of seats on the Exchange was set at 1100 until 1929. At that time the Exchange expanded the number to 1375. The current number of seats is 1366. Obviously, if nonmembers thought that the number of available seats would increase drastically, they would be hesitant about paying anything because

they would not know what percentage of the monopoly profits would be available to them in the future.

Estimated Monopoly Value

How would a prospective nonmember firm get a feel for the monopoly value of the membership he wanted to buy? Since he knows that he would get a fixed amount of profit on each sale of a security because of the minimum fixed commission schedule, he will be interested in the total volume of transactions. One of the ways that he can figure out the monopoly value of a seat on the Exchange is by looking at the actual level of transactions—that is, the volume of transactions that occurs on the Exchange. It is not surprising that there is a high correlation between the actual price of seats on the Exchange and the volume of transactions in the New York Stock Exchange. When the market was really booming in 1968, seats on the Exchange were going for prices in excess of one-half million dollars. During the down days of the 1969-70 recession, when the volume of business on the Exchange had dropped drastically, these same seats were selling at prices around $100,000. Several statistical studies have shown that the relationship between volume of trading and the

price of Exchange membership is highly correlated, thus confirming, to some extent, the concept of the Exchange as a monopoly.

The Effect of Minimum Commission Rates

Even though the Board of Governors of the New York Stock Exchange can fix a minimum commission rate schedule that all members must adhere to, the Exchange cannot or at least has chosen not to eliminate all forms of *nonprice* competition among its membership. We are referring here to all of the various increases in the *quality* of services that may be offered by member firms in their quest for a larger share of the total volume of business. Put yourself in the position of a member of the Exchange. You are not allowed to advertise that your firm can sell stocks at a lower commission rate; you are not allowed to advertise that if a customer comes to you, you'll give him a good deal in terms of the price he pays for the services you are selling. Rather, you have to seek out other forms of enticing the customer (stock buyer or seller) to deal through you instead of through one of your competitors. There are many ways of doing that. You may be even familiar with some of these methods if you've ever had occasion to see the literature that stock brokerage houses send to current and potential customers.

Since only the price is fixed, an increase in the quality of service is a reduction in the price of a constant quality unit of brokerage service. We expect, therefore, that competition among member firms will lead to increases in quality—that is, to nonprice competition. This is exactly what we see.

Research Galore

Every member firm has a research department. These research departments analyze trends in the economy, trends in the market, and individual companies and industries. Their analysis goes into special newsletters and research reports, which are furnished free of charge to current and potential customers. We see, then, that research efforts which are given away "free" to customers are really a form of nonprice competition. There are other forms of competition also. Brokers can have instant quotations of all the stocks if they are willing to pay for sophisticated electronic equipment. Brokers can offer to manage your money at a very low fee or at no fee at all because they know they will make it up in the commission rates when they buy and sell stocks for you. The point is that a fixed minimum commission schedule leads to various forms of nonprice competition as individual members of the monopoly cartel arrangement attempt to obtain higher absolute profits. We would expect, therefore, that if there were no constraints on nonprice competition, it would reach the point where increased costs would eliminate all of the monopoly profits that were due to membership in the New York Stock Exchange.

Some Restrictions

We know, however, that the Governors of the Exchange will not allow complete, unmitigated nonprice competition. They restrict competition enough so that some monopoly profits are still gained in Wall Street by member firms. Notice, however, that you, as an outsider, would not be able to share those monopoly profits. If you attempted to purchase membership, a current member would probably only be willing to sell it to you if you paid him the full value of all the expected monopoly profits that he could make by remaining a member. Since you pay him the full value of those profits, all you will be left with is a normal rate of return. Of course, he may underestimate the future stream of monopoly profits and, when he does, you will be the lucky purchaser who captures some of them. However, you could overestimate these future profits and end up losing money. The same could be said for any business you buy. If the person who owns the business underestimates the future stream of profits, then you will be the one who benefits and vice versa. This, of course, happens all the time because we live in a world of uncertainty. No businessman knows exactly how much income his business will make in future years.

No Diversity in Quality

Another aspect of minimum rate schedules is that diversity in the supplying of brokerage services is almost nonexistent. After all, brokers cannot lower the prices of their services. They cannot offer cut-rate services. If you as an individual want to purchase brokering services—that is, you want somebody to buy and sell your stocks—you cannot get a "good deal" by shopping around. Rather, you must pay the same price everywhere. Why, then, would you be willing to take a lower quality product at the same price that you could get a higher quality product? Most likely, you wouldn't. Therefore, competition forces all member firms to offer ancillary services to potential and current customers.

Even if you personally happen to know that the stock market is highly competitive and therefore think that the best thing to do is buy a random selection of stocks, you cannot tell that to a broker and buy a cut-rate (less costly) product from him. He must charge you the same as he charges somebody else on whom he lavishes thousands of research papers and hours of advice. In other words, you're stuck with "high quality" services in the brokerage business. If you don't somehow take advantage of them, you will in effect be subsidizing all those "lucky" investors who do.

Negotiated Rates

In the last few decades, more and more large institutions have been springing up which trade in very large blocks of stock. For example, insurance companies have lots of funds to invest in the stock market. *Mutual funds* take in money from investors, purchase large amounts of stock, and then distribute the profits to the mutual fund members. Banks usually have trust departments with lots of money, part of which goes for common stocks. These are the so-called **institutional investors;** they are not private individuals but, rather, institutions using the money of many private individuals. For many years the New York Stock Exchange had a fixed minimum rate schedule that covered the purchase of one share all

the way up to the purchase of as large a number of shares as is conceivable.

On the cost side, we would not expect a brokerage house to incur twice as much cost for selling one million dollars' worth of General Motors stock as for selling only a half million dollars' worth. It turns out that the costs of brokering do not go up in proportion to the number of shares sold or the number of dollars involved. Numerous institutional investors trade in large blocks of stock; they, therefore, started to complain that they were getting a bad deal from the New York Stock Exchange. So-called third markets opened up; that is, nonmember brokers set up a mechanism whereby large institutional investors could trade large blocks of stocks at commission rates substantially below what would have been paid on the New York Exchange for the same transaction.

These large institutional investors then started clamoring for Big Board membership for themselves. This would be a way for them to eliminate the high sales costs of trading large blocks of stock. If they were members themselves, they would merely pay the fixed commission rate to themselves. The only costs they would actually incur were those they really had to pay to do the transacting. They would not be giving any monopoly commission

profits to member firms. The Board of Governors of the New York Stock Exchange fought the institutional issue for a long time. As one way to appease institutional investors, the Exchange decided to allow negotiated rates on sales of stock in excess of a half million dollars. When that rule came into being, investors (usually institutions such as mutual funds and insurance companies) who wanted to buy or sell a half million dollars or more of stock could negotiate with different brokerage houses for the actual rate paid. We would expect that such negotiation would lead to a price which just covered the cost of doing the business.

After this experiment with negotiated rates proved successful, the Exchange—apparently in concordance with the Securities and Exchange Commission—decided to lower the negotiated rate barrier from $500,000 a transaction to $250,000 a transaction and even down to $100,000 a transaction. Some member firms who felt themselves more efficient than others declared that they would like to see negotiated rates all the way down to the smallest transaction. This would, of course, eliminate the cartel as such. Only if price cutting is not allowed can a cartel remain an effective monopoly and, thereby, earn monopoly profits for its members.

Definition of New Terms

SEAT: term denoted to membership in the New York Stock Exchange. The seats are sold—that is, memberships are sold—openly at a competitive price.

NONPRICE COMPETITION: competition by other than price, such as by changing the quality or the amount of services offered.

INSTITUTIONAL INVESTORS: large institutions which invest huge sums of money. These institutions may be mutual funds, insurance companies, trust funds, or banks.

Questions for Thought and Discussion

1. "Fixed commission rates are necessary to prevent destructive competition in the securities brokerage business." Evaluate.
2. It is usually difficult to maintain a monopoly for a long period of time. How do you think the New York Stock Exchange did it?
3. "It is necessary to prevent large institutional investors from being able to purchase seats on the New York Stock Exchange in order to prevent situations of conflict of interests. That is, if institutional investors are allowed to have a seat on the Exchange, they will want to buy and sell stocks just to generate the commissions." Do you agree? What model are you using?
4. In the recession of 1969-70, many brokerage houses went bankrupt. Many observers maintained this meant even higher commissions should be charged for brokerage services (buying and selling stocks). Do you agree?

Selected References

Neil, H. B. *The Inside Story of the Stock Exchange.* New York: B. C. Forbes, 1950.
Ney, Richard. *The Wall Street Jungle.* New York: Grove Press, 1971.

Not Quite Monopoly

U P TO THIS POINT two extremes in market structure have been discussed—a competitive structure and a pure monopoly one. It was mentioned that there are variations between these two extremes. In this chapter we will discuss several of these variations. However, cut and dried models are not now possible because the theories of *oligopoly* and *imperfect (monopolistic) competition* are not as definitive as the theories of pure competition and pure monopoly. At any rate, the supposed harm to the buying public caused by oligopoly and imperfect competition has been decried by numerous Congressmen and consumer advocates—including, of course, Ralph Nader. We will have a chance to analyze some of the recommendations and findings of the Nader study group on antitrust enforcement later on. That group comes out very strongly against industries where economic power is concentrated in a very few large firms.

OLIGOPOLY

Two fairly distinct kinds of concentrated economic power shall be discussed in this chapter. The first one is **oligopoly.** We define oligopoly as a market structure characterized by a few firms with a rather large amount of interdependence among them. Presumably, each oligopolist makes his own pricing policies with an eye on how his rival producers will react. The main characteristic of oligopoly is that any change in one firm's output or price influences the profits and sales of his few competitors. This leads one to predict that an oligopolist will attempt to anticipate the impending changes in pricing and output policies of other firms before he decides to change his own policies.

You can probably think of quite a few examples of an oligopolistic market structure. The automobile industry is dominated by three large firms—Chrysler, Ford, and General Motors. The steel industry has numerous firms but the top four account each year for more than 60 percent of the industry's ingot capacity. Economists maintain that these major firms must take account of the reaction of the others each time a change in pricing policy is contemplated. One of the most blatant empirical observations we find in oligopolistic industries is that when one large company changes its prices, others follow suit immediately.

In Table 7–1 we see that there are quite a number of industries where the percent of the industry output produced by the first four firms exceeds 80 percent. The firms in all of these industries are usually called oligopolies. One should be aware, however, that merely because the four firms in each of these industries produce a large amount of the industry output does not necessarily lead us to the conclusion that "something" should be done. In fact, one of the most surprising aspects of attacks against oligopolies is that very little proof is given as to the detrimental effects of such an industry structure. Merely because we define an industry as oligopolistic does not mean we have said anything about what an alternative market structures could be and what the costs of getting to those alternatives might involve.

OLIGOPOLY VERSUS *PURE* FORMS OF MARKET STRUCTURE

We know what the demand curve facing an individual competitor looks like; it is merely a horizontal line established at the going market price. The individual competitor cannot influence the price of the product he sells. He takes it as given; he is a price taker. On the other hand, we know what the demand curves individual monopolistic firms are because a monopolist *is* the entire industry. The demand curve he faces is merely the market demand curve. He can influence the price of his product. In fact, if he wants to sell more, he can do so by lowering his price. He is a price setter, not a price taker.

What about an oligopolist? He does not face a horizontal demand curve because he is a large part of the market and can probably influence the price. He does not face the entire market demand curve because he does not sell the entire output in the market. A graphic characterization of an oligopolist's demand curve is not easy. Even

TABLE 7–1

INDUSTRY CONCENTRATIONS

This table shows the percentage of total output produced by the largest four firms in selected concentrated industries. (*Source:* United States Senate.)

INDUSTRIES	PERCENT OF INDUSTRY OUTPUT PRODUCED BY FOUR LARGEST FIRMS
Primary aluminum	100
Passenger cars	99
Locomotives and parts	97
Steam engines and turbines	93
Sewing machines	93
Electric lamps (bulbs)	92
Telephone and telegraph equipment	92
Gypsum products	84
Synthetic fibers	82
Cigarettes	80

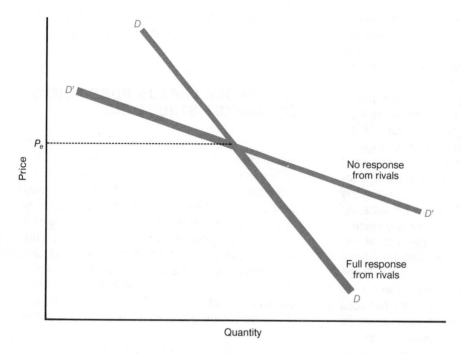

FIGURE 7–1

THE KINKED DEMAND CURVE

Assume that the equilibrium price is somehow established at P_e. The oligopolist knows that if he lowers his price, his rivals respond. That means that he faces a fairly inelastic demand curve, *DD*. If he raises his price, he knows that his rivals may not respond. Therefore, he will lose a lot of customers. By raising his price, he faces the demand curve *D'D'*. The kinked demand curve then becomes *D'D*, or the heavily shaded line.

though there are a few theories floating around and we present one of them below, bear in mind that there are numerous critics of any theory of oligopoly, no matter what the theory looks like.

The Kinked Demand Curve

Some economists believe that, rather than a horizontal demand curve or a downward sloping demand curve, oligopolists face a downward sloping *kinked* demand curve. Look at Figure 7–1. The oligopolist is selling at P_e. If he lowers his price he knows his competitors will follow suit. So the demand curve he faces is *DD*. It is relatively inelastic. Lowering his prices will not make him very many new customers because all his rivals will be charging the same low price. But if he raises his price, the oligopolist will face demand curve *D'D'*. All his rivals may *not* follow suit. His higher price will send his customers fleeing to his lower

priced rivals. Thus, *D'D'* is more elastic than *DD*.

We might put *DD* and *D'D'* together to form a kinked demand curve *D'D*. It may not pay the oligopolist to change price if he is profit maximizing at the kink. Only if his marginal cost curve changes drastically, will he want to change prices.

One of the problems with the kinked demand curve is that we have no idea how the existing price, P_e, came into being. Seemingly, if every oligopolist faced a kinked demand curve, it would never pay, in a stable environment, for him to change prices. The problem is that the kinked demand curve does not show us how supply and demand originally determined the going price of an oligopolist's product.

Models of Oligopoly

Through the years, numerous oligopoly models have been developed. The kinked demand curve presented above is just one of them. All of these models involve some assumption about how other firms will react when one oligopolist changes his prices.

Cournot. The first model that was presented to the economics profession dates back to the research of a French economist, Monsieur Cournot, who published his theory in 1838. Cournot's model involved only two sellers of a product. This is formally called a *duopoly* (two sellers). It is a rather naive model, for Cournot assumed that each duopolist would ignore the possibility that the other would change output. He assumed that both duopolists were profit maximizing but that neither thought the other guy could possibly change the picture. Cournot presented the model in a step by step situation. First, one duopolist would increase his output; then the other would increase his, and so on. Each firm would take the other firm's output as given and choose the output that maximized its own profit.

Edgeworth. One of the critics of the Cournot model was Professori Edgeworth, who presented his new theory of oligopoly in an Italian economics journal in 1897. Edgeworth felt it was better to assume that firms believe their competitors will hold price constant, rather than quantity. In contrast to Cournot's model, Edgeworth's theory predicts a process of successive price cutting, sometimes loosely referred to in economics as predatory pricing. Eventually, though, the process reverses itself and prices start to rise again. The Edgeworth model predicts oscillating prices within a specified region.

Some people have tried to use Edgeworth's rather naive model to explain gasoline prices. Have you ever noticed that in some cities gasoline prices seem to change quite often? However, rather than successive steps down and successive steps up, we usually find that after several days or weeks of price cutting by various gas stations, suddenly *all* prices jump back up to the *previous*

high levels. This particular type of behavior does not fit in very well with the predictions of the Edgeworth model.

Why the Models Are Naive

These models are considered to be extremely naive because they assume that the oligopolist does not learn by doing. Essentially, there is an assumption that the firm continually makes the same mistake. In Cournot's model, the firm assumes that his rival's output will remain constant. In Edgeworth's model, the firm assumes that his rival's price will remain constant. But the oligopolistic entrepreneur would eventually figure out that those were incorrect assumptions on his part. More sophisticated models of an oligopoly have included the *theory of games*. Each firm tries to figure out the other firm's strategy. Based on what he thinks the other firms are going to do, the oligopolist attempts to figure out his own strategy. The theory of games has proven to be useful in restructuring the oligopoly problem. However, no one has yet derived specific predictions from the game theory models about how oligopolists will actually behave.

If there are so few producers in the oligopolistic industry, why don't they get together and produce as a monopolist would? After all, we know that a pure monopoly structure is the one that allows the largest profits to be made for selling any particular good or service. This leads us to a discussion of the possibility of **collusion.**

COLLUSION AND CARTELS

Let's say there are only two firms in an industry. It is a duopoly situation like Cournot used. Since firms presumably are not so naive as Cournot envisioned, they must realize there is a lot of interdependence. The advantages of collusion must, therefore, seem obvious. If the two firms can get together, they will decrease uncertainty; they perhaps can prevent entry into their industry;

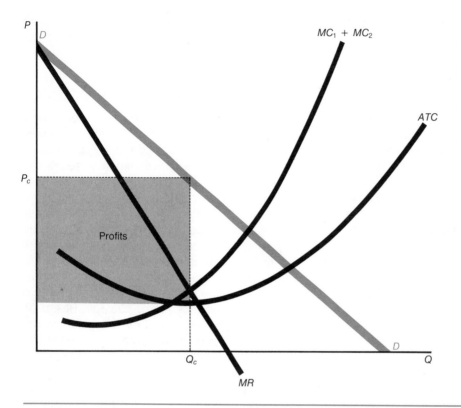

FIGURE 7–2

COLLUSION TO MAXIMIZE PROFIT

Here we have assumed that two firms get together and collude. Their marginal cost curve then becomes MC_1 plus MC_2. We assume that they have the same average total cost curves. They will set the quantity supplied at Q_c and set the price at P_c. Their total profits are equal to the shaded area, which they will split half and half.

and—last but not least—they should be able to make more profits.

Let's assume for the purposes of analysis that the two firms in our oligopolistic industry both have exactly the same cost curves. We see in Figure 7–2 that a market demand curve is drawn, DD. The combined marginal cost curves are presented in MC_1 and MC_2. Now, since the oligopolists are working in concert, they will want to set the price where marginal cost equals marginal revenue. That is at point E and therefore the price they set will be P_c and the quantity they sell will be Q_c. There will be no problem here because we have assumed that each firm has exactly the same marginal cost curve. Their profits will be equal to the heavily shaded area, and they will merely split them half and half. The price that is set maximizes the total profits for both firms together

and neither firm has any complaint about where price should be set because they are both faced with the same cost curves. They collude because they make more profits acting as a joint monopoly than by competing with each other.

Problems with Large Numbers

The problem gets a little more sticky when there are more than two firms. However, if we merely sum all of the marginal cost curves together we can still find the profit maximizing price and quantity for the entire industry in collusion. In many cases, as we shall see, it is difficult for a large number of firms to maintain a collusive agreement. However, if there are legal sanctions, large collusive arrangements can be made openly and formally. Then they are called a **cartel**.

Cartels

Legal cartels are found in many European countries. The United States, however, prohibits most collusive agreements under the Sherman Antitrust Act, which dates back to before the turn of the century. Despite the fact that cartels are illegal, many attempts have been made at forming them in the United States. The most blatant attempt that received the largest amount of publicity involved the great electrical conspiracy cases. Back in 1960, the Justice Department finally charged a large number of electrical companies with price fixing and divvying up the market for certain electrical products such as switching gear and circuit breakers. Many of the price-fixing agreements were reached during meetings at the conventions of the National Electrical Manufacturers Association. Some agreements were made through telephone calls and written memos sent from executive to executive in different companies. Elaborate coding techniques were used in order to keep the agreements secret. Obviously, the executives knew that what they were doing was illegal.

Legal Cartels. Some industries in the United States are involved in legal cartels. One such industry is air transport. Airlines flying transatlantic routes are members of the International Air Transport Association, which agrees on uniform prices for transatlantic flights. Until recently, it was very difficult to charge below the uniform price. In fact, only one company, Icelandic Airways, did so for a long period of time. As punishment, it was forced to land only in Luxembourg because Luxembourg was not a member of the International Air Transport Association. An Icelandic Airlines flight could not, for example, land in London or Paris.

The Cartel's Job. The job of the cartel is not merely to set the price that will maximize the joint profits of all its members, but also somehow to distribute those profits to the different members. In the previous examples of a duopoly, there were two firms who both had similar cost curves. They did not disagree on what the price should be, and they would both split the pot evenly. What happens when there are numerous cartel members—each having a different marginal and average cost curve? If the cartel seeks to maximize total cartel profits, it will set one price and allocate production to each firm so that the marginal costs of all firms are equal. This means that firms which are inefficient and have higher marginal costs would not be able to produce as much as firms which are more efficient and have lower marginal costs. The inefficient firms will be unhappy because they will have lower total profits than the efficient firms. The political process involved in allocating production among firms in a cartel is difficult indeed. You would presume that those firms which were the best bargainers and had the most influence would receive the largest production quotas, even if total cartel production costs increased. Empirical observations on cartels which have worked for any period of time have revealed that production rates have usually been allocated according to each firm's production rate in the past. Also, there have been geographical distributions of sales. Firms were allowed to produce for certain regions only. Certainly, it is a difficult task to run a cartel without any snags. Even in theory we would predict that cartels are going to be shaky.

CARTEL INSTABILITY

When there are many firms in a cartel arrangement, there are always going to be a few that are unhappy with the situation. There will always be those who will want to cheat on the cartel by charging a lower price than the one stipulated by the cartel. If there are geographical allocations of sales for each member firm in the cartel arrangement, any change in regional demand patterns will cause those cartel members who lose sales to be unhappy; other members will be picking up sales somewhere else in the country. We

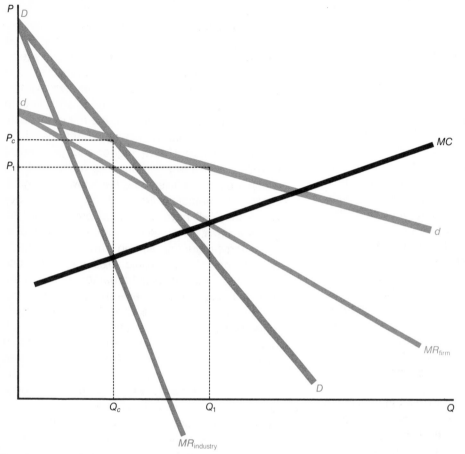

FIGURE 7-3

CARTEL INSTABILITY

Here we show the demand curve facing the industry, or all the members in the cartel, as *DD*. The cartel marginal revenue curve is *MR*industry and the marginal cost curve is *MC*. The cartel sets its profit maximizing at Q_c and charges a price of P_c. Now look at the individual member's demand curve, *dd*. His marginal revenue curve is *MR*firm and it intersects the marginal cost curve at Q_1. He can lower his price to P_1 and sell a lot more units because individually he faces such a relatively elastic demand curve (assuming, of course, that nobody else cheats on the cartel also).

would expect the unhappy members to either require a bribe on the part of the happy members or to cheat on the cartel arrangement by cutting prices and seeking customers outside their stipulated region.

Let's see if we can graphically demonstrate why any individual cartel member would be tempted to cheat, to cut prices clandestinely. Let's take a cartel that has quite a few members. In addition, let's look at a member who is producing a very small percentage of the total output of the cartel. He is almost like a perfect competitor because the individual demand curve that he faces if he cheats on the cartel is going to be very elastic.

Look at *dd* in Figure 7-3; we have drawn it almost horizontally. Assume *MC* for all members are the same. Cartel profit maximization is when *MR* = *MC*, or at price P_c. Our one member produces Q_c. Now our small price cutter looks at the potential payoff from cheating on the cartel. If he cuts his price from P_c to P_1 without anybody else in the cartel knowing it, he stands to increase his sales from Q_c to Q_1. Since his demand curve is so elastic, that small drop in price will result in a very large increase in his total revenues. The lure of such increases in revenues is probably too tempting to cartel members for a cartel to last forever.

There will always be cartel members who figure that it will pay them to cut prices, to break away from the cartel. Each firm will try to do this, thinking that the others will not do the same thing. Obviously, though, when a sufficient number of firms in the cartel try to cheat, the cartel breaks up. We would expect, therefore, that as long as the cartel is not maintained by legislation, there will be a constant threat to its very existence. All of its members will have a large incentive to price cut, and, once a couple of members do it, the rest might follow. We find numerous examples of cartels breaking up: even the electrical conspiracy seemed to be quite unstable, since the agreements did not tend to last too long. Apparently, over-capacity in the industry led numerous participants in the conspiracy to chisel in order to increase their profits. Because of the overcapacity, they felt they could do it without incurring very large production costs and therefore the potential profits from doing so seemed great. Apparently, one collusive agreement after another had to be reached because each preceding one broke down.

Indeed, cartel instability is not confined to business firms. Have you ever noticed how short-lived a housewives' boycott of supermarkets is? There are so many members in that particular cartel that it is difficult for one of them not to "cheat" and actually go out and buy some food from the supermarket. It is impossible to police the large number of housewives involved, and, as expected, these cartel arrangements never last.

IMPERFECT OR MONOPOLISTIC COMPETITION

In the beginning of this chapter, another possible noncompetitive industry structure was mentioned; that was **imperfect** or **monopolistic competition.** Back in the 1920s and 1930s, economists became increasingly dissatisfied with the polar extremes of market structure—competition and monopoly. Theoretical and empirical research was instigated to develop some sort of middle ground. The most popular and, at least for awhile, well-received theory was that of monopolistic competition. This theory was presented by Harvard's Edward Chamberlin who wrote *The Theory of Monopolistic Competition* in 1933.

Chamberlin defined the monopolistic competition structure as one in which there are a relatively large number of producers offering similar but *differentiated* products. The most obvious situation is reflected by the plethora of brand names for such things as toothpastes, soaps, and gasolines. Should you buy Crest, Colgate, Gleem, Macleans, Ultra-Bright, Stripe, Close-Up, or any of numerous other brand names? Each firm has a small monopoly because it has product identity. The differences between the similar products may indeed be very small. However, Chamberlin still presumed that each producer selling his differentiated product faced a gently downward sloping demand curve. The producer was such a small part of the industry that he did not face the total industry demand curve, nor did he face a large part of it like an oligopolist does. He wasn't a perfect competitor and, therefore, did not face a perfectly horizontal, completely elastic demand curve. Each monopolistic competitor has some control over the price of his product; but that control is very little because the availability of substitutes—other brand names—is very large. Chamberlin found it useful to group together all firms producing similar products and call them a *product group.* Obviously, the way we combine firms into different product groups has to be arbitrary; there is no way of deciding how close substitutes must be in order to be included in the same product group. But Chamberlin did assert that meaningful groups could be formulated.

Key Assumption

One key assumption in Chamberlin's theory was that the number of firms in each product group was large enough that every firm could expect its actions to go unheeded by all the other firms

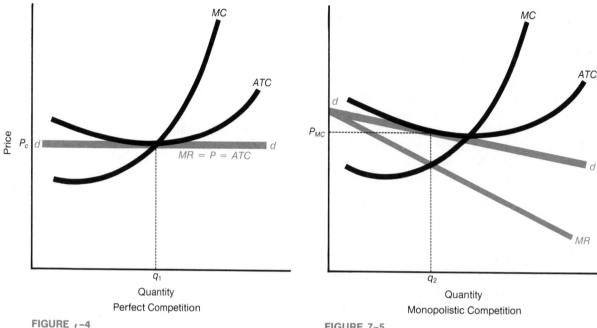

FIGURE 7–4

FIGURE 7–5

COMPARISON OF PERFECT COMPETITOR WITH MONOPOLISTIC COMPETITOR In Figure 7–4 the perfect competitor has zero economic profits. His average total cost curve is tangent to the demand curve DD just to the point of intersection of the marginal cost curve. The price is set equal to marginal cost and the price is P_c; there are zero economic profits. However, with the monopolistic competitor in Figure 7–5, there are zero economic profits also because the average total cost curve is tangent to the individual monopolistic competitor's demand curve, dd, at the point where production occurs. The price, however, does not equal marginal cost, and the monopolistic competitor does not find himself at the minimum point on his average total cost curve.

in that particular group. In other words, no retaliatory measures are expected. Notice that this is different than the oligopolistic situation, where interdependence is usually presumed. Additionally, Chamberlin assumed that both the cost curves and the demand curves for all of the firms would be the same in each group. Notice here that this is a very restrictive assumption: since the products are, by definition, differentiated, would we not

expect their demand and cost curves to be somewhat different?

Zero Profits

Since there is free entry into a monopolistically competitive industry, zero economic profits are going to result. The price will be just equal to the long-run average total cost. That is, price equals cost; there is no profit. Monopolistic competition leads to zero profits just as does perfect competition. But since each firm faces a slightly downward sloping demand curve it produces *less* than what a competitive firm would produce. Compare Figure 7–4 with Figure 7–5.

HOW HAS CHAMBERLIN'S THEORY FARED?

A number of economists have pointed out sometimes serious, sometimes not so serious, problems with Chamberlin's theory. We mentioned one of the problems before. The definition of the product group must be completely arbitrary. It has been pointed out that the number of firms in a product group could be one or many. If you don't know how to distinguish the firms that should be in a product group from the firms that shouldn't, then how can you talk about a particular industry being monopolistically competitive? You can't.

We also pointed out another problem. Chamberlin assumed that each firm in the product group faced a similar demand and cost curve. However, that is only possible if they are selling exactly the same product, and one of the attributes of a monopolistically competitive industry is that the products are differentiated. If they are differentiated, they must be facing different demand and cost curves. Finally, some economists claim that there are very few if any markets that we can look at in the real world where all of Chamberlin's assumptions hold. This is not surprising, for his assumptions were, indeed, very stringent. One of the most caustic critics of Chamberlin's work, Chicago's George Stigler, once stated: "In the general case, we cannot make a single statement about economic events in the world we sought to analyze . . . [but] many such statements are made by Chamberlin."[*]

[*]George Stigler, *Five Lectures on Economic Problems* (London: Longmans Green, 1949), pp. 18-19.

Definition of New Terms

OLIGOPOLY: a market situation where there are only very few sellers. Each one knows that the others will react to changes in prices and quantities.

CONCENTRATION RATIO: a measure of the amount of concentration in an industry. Typically, the concentration ratio is computed by finding out the percentage of the value of shipments accounted for by the leading four firms in an industry. If this percentage is high, the industry is very concentrated.

COLLUSION: a situation in which several firms get together and collude about prices and/or quantities and/or territorial boundaries for their individual sales. Collusion may be overt or implicit.

CARTEL: a formal collusive arrangement among firms. In some countries cartels are legal. In the United States most cartels are illegal.

IMPERFECT COMPETITION: otherwise called monopolistic competition. A situation where there are a large number of firms producing similar but not exactly identical products. There is easy entry into the monopolistically competitive industry. Toothpaste and soap are good examples of monopolistically competitive industries.

Chapter Summary

1. Between the extremes of competition and monopoly there lie numerous in-between situations. We covered two of those in this chapter: oligopoly and monopolistic competition.

2. Oligopoly is a situation where there are several firms. Each one knows that its rivals will react to a change in price. Oligopolies are usually defined as those in which the four firm concentration ratio is relatively high, for example, in excess of 70 or 80 percent. That means that we would classify all industries in which the leading four firms produced 70 or more percent of the value of shipments each year.

3. There are many theories of oligopoly, none of which seems to be totally satisfactory in explaining the behavior of oligopolistic firms. Cournot came up with a naive theory which assumed that the firms did not learn that their rivals could act in a way that would change the situation. Edgeworth came up with something similar.

4. Oligopolists may want to collude in order to form a monopoly to make monopoly profits. When large numbers are involved, the collusion is called a cartel.

5. Cartels are inherently unstable because the pay off from cheating is quite high. The individual firm in the cartel faces a relatively less elastic demand curve than the cartel taken as a whole. Assuming that nobody else will cheat, one cheater can make out quite well. All individuals in the cartel may think the same way and, therefore, the cartel will break down. Cartels can last if they are legal and sanctioned by the government. For example, the International Air Transport Association is a cartel which has lasted a long time, but on occasion even then was threatened with a breakup because of members who wanted to "cheat."

6. Monopolistic competition is a theory developed by Edward Chamberlin at Harvard University. He referred to industries where there were specific product groups in which different companies had slight monopoly powers due to a slightly differentiated product. Examples might be toothpastes and soaps. The monopolistic competitor ended up with zero economic profits because there's free entry into the industry. However, according to Chamberlin the monopolistic competitor did not produce where price equalled marginal costs and, therefore, did not produce at the minimum point on the average total cost curve.

Questions for Thought and Discussion

1. Between the extremes of competition and monopoly there lie numerous in-between structures. Which one do you believe prevails?

2. If you believe the kinked demand curve theory, how could you ever explain a change in the price of an oligopolist's product?

3. Since every member of the cartel knows that together they can maximize profits better than they can when apart, why do members keep trying to cheat on the cartel and, therefore, make it break up?

4. Do you think it is sufficient for a group of firm owners to get together and discuss prices for collusion to be effective?

5. In some European countries all sales must go through a central agency. In such a situation, is it possible to cheat on the cartel?

6. Do you buy soap on the basis of brand or price? Does it make any difference?

Selected References

Adams, Walter. *The Structure of American Industry.* 4th Ed. New York: Macmillan, 1971. Chapters 2, 3, 5, 7, 8, and 9.

Chamberlin, Edward H. *The Theory of Monopolistic Competition.* 8th Ed. Cambridge, Mass.: Harvard University Press, 1962.

Galbraith, John K. *American Capitalism.* Boston: Houghton Mifflin, 1956. Chapters 7 and 9.

Mansfield, Edwin. *Monopoly Power and Economic Performance.* 3rd Ed. New York: W.W. Norton, 1972.

Robinson, Joan. *The Economics of Imperfect Competition.* New York: St. Martin Press, 1969.

ISSUE VII

Is Advertising "Bad"?

The War Is On

In 1972, the Federal Trade Commission (FTC) was restructured, and the war against deceptive advertising was stepped up. The Commission's new chairman, Miles Kirkpatrick, proclaimed as he was taking over the FTC: "The little old lady of Pennsylvania Avenue [the FTC] has taken off her tennis shoes and has put on cleats." The cleats have been digging into, for example, deceptive TV advertisers. Once a company has been proven a sinner by the FTC, it is required to "correctively" advertise. By early spring of 1972, the FTC had issued almost a dozen orders calling for corrective advertising.

One of the FTC's most famous cases involved Profile bread—that fantastic stuff that was supposed to be less fattening than its competitors. The fact of the matter is that Profile was merely sliced thinner than other breads. The producer was forced to publicly admit this in advertisements he had to pay for himself. Now the FTC is calling on other advertisers, industry by industry, to give it documentary proof of all advertising claims made to the public. Before we can analyze the desirability and the effects of the FTC's new war against advertis-

ing, we should probably distinguish between the two types of advertising.

Types of Advertising

One type of advertising involves informing potential customers about the availability of new products and the qualities and prices of new and old products. This type of advertising is usually called **informative advertising.** Then there is another type of advertising which must be used because everybody else in an industry advertises; this is called **competitive advertising.** You are probably familiar with many types of competitive advertising. The cigarette industry is a clear-cut example. All of the cigarette manufacturers advertise widely,

spending perhaps a half billion dollars per year. However, there's no evidence that taken together their advertising increases the amount of cigarettes smoked in the United States. Individually, each producer of cigarettes is required to advertise because all of his competitors advertise. If he fails to advertise, he will go out of business. But if he does advertise, he will make no more profits than he is already making. Advertising seems to be a prerequisite for merely making a normal rate of return.

Much of the advertising you see is, of course, of the informative type. The grocery store ads in your newspaper, the ads for new products in magazines, the used car ads on TV, and so on, are all forms of informative advertising. Instead of checking the prices of specials at five different supermarkets, you can look at the ads in your local newspaper to find out where you can get the best buys for the things you want. Advertising is a way of reducing the costs of searching for the lowest price possible, and in this context advertising reduces transactions cost to you, the consumer. Competitive advertising, on the contrary, seems to have no redeeming virtues—at least, not at first glance. This type of advertising appears to be a social waste. We'll discuss this argument subsequently because it is exactly the one used by the Federal Trade Commission in its attempts to prosecute the large cereal manufacturers.

Why So Much Advertising Seems "Bad"

You're probably fully aware of how painful it is to watch commercial television programs or listen to AM radio stations. There are so many advertisements on some programs that you can barely maintain the story line of the movie you're watching or of the program you're listening to. Many of the ads seem to be an insult to your intelligence. Therefore, advertising inherently seems "bad." However, isn't it the *form* of the advertising and the *amount* of advertising that you are subjected to that really bothers you, rather than advertising *per se?* The reason you find so much advertising on radio and TV is because of the particular method by which radio and TV airwaves are allocated.

Radio and TV Transmission

In most states it is impossible for somebody to set up a TV station and sell programs on a pay-as-you-watch basis; pay TV is usually illegal. It is impossible for individual program producers to charge only those people who want to watch their programs. Consequently, the only way radio and TV stations can usually survive is by being paid to use part of programming time for ads. You do not find ads in movie theaters (except perhaps at intermission in the drive-in) because theater owners can charge people individually to watch each movie that is shown. There is no need on the part of theater owners to obtain advertising revenues; and, further, the advertisers themselves can reach a much larger audience through radio and TV.

The opposite situation is found in France, for example. Radio and TV are government monopolies in that country, paid for by taxes. Almost no advertising is allowed. Thus, when you go to see a movie in France, you are subjected to one-half hour of continuous ads.

The reason, then, that advertising seems so obnoxious is not because it is inherently a bad thing, but rather because of the peculiar restrictions on how radio and TV signals can be generated. In order to exist, station owners have to accept lots of advertising because they aren't allowed to charge consumers directly.

Billboards

You probably also dislike most of the ads you see on the highway. Billboards ruin the scenery, and this kind of advertising also seems "bad." Billboards do, however, offer some information. The reason such advertising exists is because nobody seems to own the property rights to the scenery, and advertisers feel the money spent on billboards is well invested. Even if someone did own the rights to the scenery, it would be very difficult for him to charge individuals to look at his scenery. Since no one has figured out a way to do that, we find individual landowners reaping the benefits from allowing billboards on their land. Meanwhile, passing motorists and tourists are annoyed by the destruction of the natural scenery.

Deceptive Advertising

The question as to whether deceptive advertising should be allowed is a normative question which we can never answer using economic analysis. However, the competitive model we have previously employed indicates that, when there is competition among various producers, those producers who use deceptive advertising will eventually go out of business. We would expect, for example, that if a women's hosiery manufacturer advertised snag-proof nylons at a higher price than other snaggable nylons, and his ads were in fact lies, he would eventually be found out. Some customers would stop purchasing his hosiery, particularly if they had to pay more than the price of another

product that was actually similar. Since the manufacturer would be incurring expensive advertising costs, he would have to obtain more business in order for his advertising to pay off.

An argument can be made that the adjustment period between the time a producer starts to use false advertising and the time the public actually discovers it may be so long that such types of advertising should be prohibited.

This is an empirical question and cannot be answered by using economic theory alone. We know, however, if there is regulation against deceptive advertising, some uncertainty will be reduced; some information costs will be reduced to some consumers. Those consumers will no longer have to worry about being taken in by a phony ad, and they can spend less of their time scrutinizing the ads that are put before them.

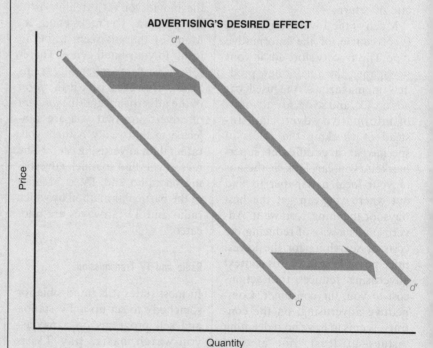

ADVERTISING'S DESIRED EFFECT

FIGURE VII-1

The firm which advertises hopes that the advertising will shift the demand schedule for its product to the right. In other words, before advertising the demand schedule is at *dd*; after advertising takes place, the demand schedule hopefully will shift to *d'd'*.

The Why of Advertising

Since advertising takes money, businessmen are only going to engage in advertising if they think they will profit from it. We expect, therefore, that advertising will only be undertaken when the marginal revenue exceeds the marginal costs of advertising. In an economic sense, what busi- nessmen actually hope to do when they decide to advertise is make high profits. One way to do that is to increase their volume of business. Basically, through advertising a businessman wishes to *shift* the demand curve for his product to the right. This is shown in Figure VII-1. Then at the same price he can sell a larger quantity of his product. (He may also be con- tent if advertising prevents the demand curve from shifting *in*.)

Since the effects of advertising are usually felt over a period of time, it might be better to analyze advertising as an investment rather than as a current business expense. And this is probably the way most businesses view it. Since it is an investment, the firm must decide whether the rate of return on that investment is adequate. This will depend upon the alter- native uses the business could find for that particular amount of money. The business finds the rate of return by looking at the in- creased sales that were made pos- sible by the advertising campaign over a period of time.

Another alleged reason for ad- vertising is that the subsequent increased sales can lead to econo- mies of scale. This is possible only if the economies of scale outweigh the advertising costs. Look at Fig- ure VII-2. Here we find that the hypothetical average total cost curve without advertising is *ATC*. With advertising, it is *ATC'*. If production is at point *A,* then average total costs will be ATC_1. If advertising campaigns shift de- mand and production to point *B*, then average total costs will fall to ATC_2. The reduction in average total costs will more than out- weigh the increased expenses due to advertising. If, in fact, the ad- vertising campaign was not suc- cessful and demand and produc-

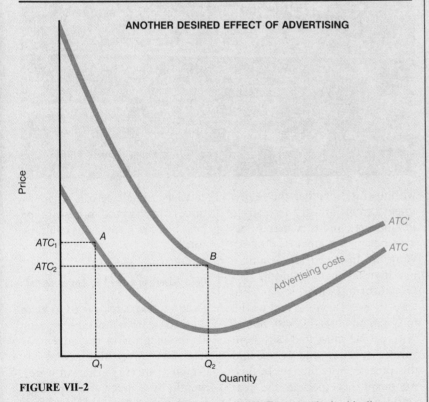

ANOTHER DESIRED EFFECT OF ADVERTISING

FIGURE VII-2

Advertising may be able to more than pay for itself. For example, in this diagram we start out on the average total cost curve *ATC* at point *A* with production of Q_1. Here average total costs are ATC_1. Advertising is added and the average total cost curve shifts up to *ATC'*. However, we move out to point *B* with the quantity produced of Q_2 and an average total cost of only ATC_2, which is lower than ATC_1.

tion remained where they were, then the businessman would stop advertising. It would not be profitable to continue.

The FTC Versus Kellogg's Cornflakes

When the Federal Trade Commission went before Congress to ask for appropriations one of the claims made was that the Commission could reduce the price of cereals by 25%. One FTC staff member told United Press International: "If the cereal business became more competitive, say like the produce section of grocery stores, the consumer might save 25% or at least 15%." According to this same FTC staff member, markups on cereals are high because cereal manufacturers "suggest" retail prices which give grocers a mark up of 20 percent. Let's look at some of the charges the FTC brought against the cereal manufacturers. We shall also examine some of the manufacturers' responses to the claims against them.

Are Potential Entrants Barred?

Among other things, the FTC maintains that large advertising expenditures by the four leading cereal manufacturers prevent competition from *potential* entrants. According to the FTC, these high advertising costs effec-

tively bar anybody else from entering the cereal business, and, therefore, the industry is a monopolistic one.

When looking at this argument,

we must ask whether the ready-to-eat cereal industry is really a monopolistic industry merely because there is a great deal of advertising. In a *perfectly* competitive industry there would be perfect information flows at zero costs. However, in the real world, information costs do exist. Somehow, people must find out about various products and prices, and this process costs money. In fact, we might say that, in the real world, advertising goes along with competition. A monopolist, however, by definition, would not *have* to advertise his product because he wouldn't have to compete with

anybody else. Thus, we might question the FTC argument on this point.

For its part, the cereal industry maintains that advertising allows retailers to sell cereals at lower prices than would otherwise be possible. Let's see if this could be true.

Does Advertising Lead to Lower Costs?

Ready-to-eat cereals used to have marked seasonal swings in consumption prior to the advent of television advertising. Sales increased during the summer months by as much as 100 percent over winter sales. However, after the cereal manufacturers started advertising on TV in the early 1940s, winter sales picked up relative to summer sales. Manufacturers assert that, due to the smoothing of the consumption pattern brought about by increased advertising, there were savings in costs. According to the cereal manufacturers, at least, advertising lowers costs to consumers.

Industry spokesmen claim that prices would be higher if manufacturers were not allowed to advertise. Due to advertising, increased consumer demand has motivated retailers to carry more complete lines of cereals from each big manufacturer and to make sure the shelves are always stocked. The cereal companies now do not have to provide personnel or equipment for servicing stores. Presumably, they have been able to pass on their savings to retailers who, in turn, pass the savings to consumers. (The retailers' savings, however, would partially be offset by *their* increased costs for checking the shelves.)

The data furnished by cereal companies seem to support their contention that advertising has led to a lower expense. Distribution and selling costs accounted for 35 percent of sales revenues prior to 1940. In the sixties, these same costs only accounted for 25 percent of sales revenues.

Spreading Fixed Costs

Cereal manufacturers have also used more conventional, theoretical lines to defend their advertising practices. They have maintained that advertising allows manufacturers to sell greater quantities, which means fixed costs will be spread over a larger number of units of sales. Average total cost falls and the consumer can get a lower priced product. It is also maintained that products which are rapidly sold result in increased revenues per any given amount of shelf space—and shelf space is, after all, a commodity like anything else. The more profitable the shelf space is, the better off the store is. According to the reasoning, retailers therefore would not need a large markup on advertised products because these products turn over faster.

It must be granted that the FTC's case against cereal manufacturers is far from obvious. Nevertheless, the basic desire to reduce advertising expenditures in cereals has been supported by a large segment of the population. Indeed, it seems as if the case against advertising has been stamped upon the minds of layman and politician alike. Let's briefly go over some additional arguments that can be made against advertising.

Other Arguments against Advertising

Many critics of advertising do not accept the argument that expanded production through advertising makes for a lower unit cost. These critics contend that much advertising is self-cancelling, as in the cigarette industry. Even though each advertiser must continue to spend money on flashy billboards and magazine ads, the tobacco industry as a whole gets no additional customers with all members advertising at once. Moreover, if advertising can cause a firm to realize gains from mass production through increased growth, it seems that at some point the firm will incur diseconomies of scale. If economies of scale are really at question, surely there must be other ways for the firm to expand production to achieve these economies. The firm could spend its advertising money on research and development in order to make a better product that was wanted by more people. The results would be at least as good if not better than those obtained from advertising.

Critics also contend that advertising expenditures divert human and other resources away from much more pressing needs. Advertising, in short, gives rise to a misallocation of resources. The most telling argument along these lines is the claim that advertising causes people to consume more private goods and fewer "public" goods—such as schools, hospitals, better streets, and so on. Although the critics may be right, we should realize that private businesses are not the only ones who advertise. Look at the amount of advertising done by universities in need of funds; look at the amount of advertising that the government uses to ensure us we are being well cared for.

Advertising has also been attacked as the means by which producers can create artificial wants. Numerous books have been written about how advertising subtly and not so subtly alters the ways we think and the things we desire to consume. Analyzing this particular contention is difficult because economics can say very little about the creation of wants. However, we do know that advertisers compete, and, therefore, it would seem to be quite difficult for one manufacturer to induce consumers to buy a product they didn't want, when numerous other manufacturers were attempting to do exactly the same thing. Moreover, there is plenty of advertising for nonconsumption—that is, for savings. How many times do you see ads on TV and in the newspaper about new savings and loan associations wanting your money? And don't we see ads for U.S. Savings Bonds? The fact is we find ads asking us to do everything imaginable with our income and our time. Thus, the question is whether some forms of advertising are more persuasive than others, and, if so, does one particular industry have a monopoly on that form of advertising? This is a question no one has yet answered.

A Final Note

Actually, the most telling complaint is that advertising is deceptive. People feel that it is an affront to their intelligence when advertisers make absurd claims about the qualities of their products. But this is really not an indictment of advertising *per se*. It is an indictment of dishonesty and not advertising. We could be equally upset with political speeches because we know that politicians rarely carry out *in toto* their campaign promises.

We also have to ask ourselves, if ads are so obviously deceptive, who is actually fooled by them? If no one is fooled, then why should we bother? If some people are fooled, then the question is: how do we regulate advertising? This is a thorny problem. Whom can we trust with the job of censoring ads? We are very reluctant in this country to trust anyone with the job of censoring what we read in newspapers, magazines, and books. Although it does not seem such an obvious extension, we might be wise to think about who we want to censor advertising.

One way to counter deceptive and fraudulent advertising is to make firms fully liable for all damages incurred by those who are hurt as a result of the firm's advertising. If, for example, you could show that a false ad cost you $500, you would be able to sue and collect $500.

Definition of New Terms

INFORMATIVE ADVERTISING: a type of advertising which actually gives information that is useful to consumers.

COMPETITIVE ADVERTISING: advertising that is not informative but is necessary to the survival of an industry such as cigarette manufacturing.

Questions for Thought and Discussion

1. The American Medical Association maintains that only highly qualified doctors are given licenses to practice. However, advertising by doctors is prohibited by the AMA. Is this consistent?
2. Why do firms spend so much money on advertising in situations where the advertising cancels itself out, such as with cigarettes or soaps or toothpastes?
3. Do you think that you would be better off as a consumer if all advertising were banned? Don't forget to take into account all costs and all benefits of such a law.
4. If advertising can create wants, how does one distinguish between those firms or industries that are successful in creating wants for their particular products and those firms or industries that are unsuccessful?

Selected References

Adams, Walter. *The Structure of American Industry.* 4th Ed. New York: Macmillan, 1971.
Backman, Jules. *Advertising and Competition.* New York: New York University Press, 1967.

Regulating the Big Ones

IN OUR DISCUSSION of monopolies, it was mentioned that there are actually very few examples of *pure* monopolies. In fact, almost all monopolies are supported or regulated by the government. It was also pointed out, however, that certain conditions lead to **natural monopolies.** In such instances, Adam Smith's "invisible hand," which supposedly leads to maximum total happiness, is amputated. In order to restore at least a facsimile of that lost hand, government regulation steps in to protect consumers from the undesirable effects of monopoly. In this chapter, we will treat two separate issues involving monopolies. One is government regulation of natural monopolies and of industries deemed so important to the public good that they must be overseen. The second topic is antitrust legislation and theory. Antitrust legislation is another alternative to preventing monopolization in restraint of trade. Whereas regulation allows government to directly intervene into the decision-making processes of the regulated industries, antitrust legislation and enforcement seek to prevent monopolies from occurring in the first place and, therefore, to obviate the need for regulation.

ONE WAY FOR A MONOPOLY TO ARISE

In many industries, a tremendous amount of capital is required to produce the product or service in question. Think about how much money you would have to have to start an electric utility or a telephone company. Once you've started, however, the *marginal cost* of providing service is relatively small. Thus, in industries where large capital requirements are needed just to get the ball rolling, average fixed costs fall dramatically with higher and higher production rates. That is,

FIGURE 8-1

THE COST CURVES THAT LEAD TO A NATURAL MONOPOLY

Here we have shown the average total cost curve falling over a very long range of electricity production rates. The marginal cost curve is, of course, below the average cost curve when the MC is falling. A natural monopoly might arise in this situation. The first firm who could expand production before anybody alse would be able to take advantage of the lower average total cost curve. This firm would drive out all rivals by charging a lower price than the others could sustain at their higher average total costs.

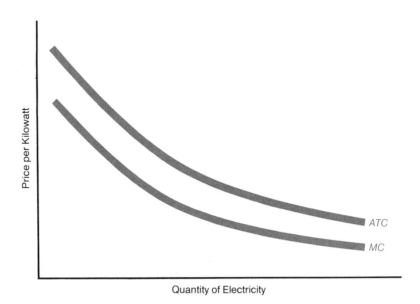

the average total cost curve would be downward sloping throughout a very large range of production rates.

In Figure 8-1, we have drawn a downward sloping average total cost curve for electricity. When the marginal cost curve is falling, it is below the average cost curve. The marginal cost curve, therefore, has been drawn below the average total cost curve. Since average costs are falling over such a large range of production rates, we would expect that only one firm could survive in such an industry. That firm would be the natural monopolist. It would be the first one to take advantage of the decreasing average costs; that is, it would expand production faster than other firms. As its average total cost curve fell, it would lower prices and get increasingly larger shares of the market. Once that firm has driven all other firms out of the industry, it should set its price to maximize profits. Let's see what this price would be.

A monopolist will set his price where marginal revenue is equal to marginal cost. Let's draw in the market demand curve, DD, and the marginal revenue curve, MR, in Figure 8-2. The intersec-

tion of the marginal revenue curve and the marginal cost curve is at point A. The monopolist therefore would produce quantity Q_m and charge a price of P_m.

What do we know about a monopolist's solution to the price-quantity question? Compared to a competitive situation, we know that consumers end up paying more for the product and, consequently, they purchase less of it than they would under competition. In addition to these drawbacks, the monopoly solution is inefficient; the price charged for the product is higher than the opportunity cost to society. That is, people are faced with a price which does not reflect the true marginal cost of producing the good. For the true marginal cost is at the intersection A, not at price P_m. Look at Figures 6-6 and 6-7 in Chapter 6. These figures demonstrate that, if a competitive industry were suddenly monopolized, the output would be restricted and prices would be raised. Thus, if we could somehow arrive at a competitive solution, prices would be lowered and the output would be increased relative to the monopoly situation.

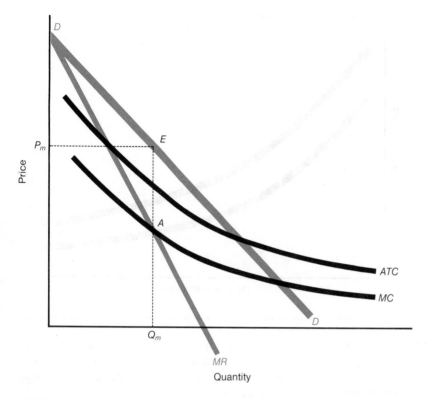

Price

Quantity

FIGURE 8–2

PROFIT MAXIMIZATION

The profit-maximizing natural monopolist here would produce at the point where marginal cost equals marginal revenue—that is, at point *A* which gives the quantity of production *Q*$_m$. The price charged would be *P*$_m$.

REGULATING THE NATURAL MONOPOLIST

Let's assume the government decides to make the natural monopolist produce at the competitive solution. Where is that competitive solution in Figure 8–3? It is at the intersection of the marginal cost curve and the demand curve, or point *A*. Remember, the marginal cost curve represents the supply curve in the competitive industry. Now the regulatory commission forces the natural monopolist to produce at quantity Q_1 and sell the product at a price P_1. Let's see now how large the monopolist's profits will be. Profits, remember, are the difference between total revenues and total costs. In this case, total revenues equal P_1 times Q_1, and total costs are equal to average costs times the number of units produced. At Q_1, average cost is equal to P_2. Average costs are higher than the price that the regulatory commission forces our natural monopolist to charge. Profits turn out to be losses which are equal to the shaded area in Figure 8–3. Thus, regulation which forces a natural monopolist to produce at the competitive solution would also force that monopolist into negative profits. Obviously, the monopolist would rather go out of business than be subjected to such regulation.

Subsidization

How do we get out of such a dilemma? There are several possible answers. The first one that comes to mind is to have the government force the natural monopolist to produce at the competitive solution and then subsidize him. That is, the

FIGURE 8–3

REGULATING NATURAL MONOPOLIES

If the regulatory commission attempted to regulate the natural monopolies so that a competitive solution would prevail, the commission would make the monopolist set production at the point where the marginal cost curve intersects the demand schedule because the marginal cost schedule would be the competitive supply schedule. The quantity produced would be Q_1 and the price would be P_1. However, the average total costs at Q_1 are equal to P_2. Losses would ensue equal to the shaded area. It would be impossible for a regulatory commission to force a natural monopolist to produce at a competitive solution because losses would eventually drive the natural monopolist out of business.

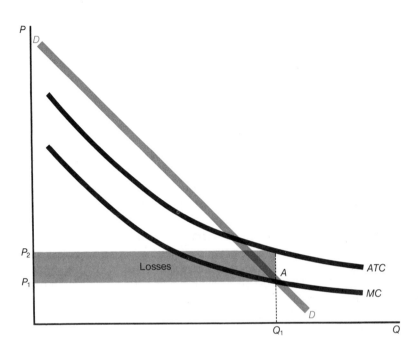

government should give the monopolist a subsidy that will allow him to break even (after, of course, he has included a normal rate of return to his investment). The subsidy in this particular case would have to be equal to the difference between P_2 and P_1; it would have to match the natural monopolist's losses.

Price Discrimination

Another possible solution is to allow the monopolist to *price discriminate*. This means he would charge different prices to different customers who have different elasticities of demand for his product. He would charge a lower price to those who have very elastic demands and a higher price to those who have relatively less elastic demands. If he is allowed to perfectly discriminate, he will travel down the demand curve, making everybody who buys his product a marginal buyer. The monopolist will extract all the money he can from

everybody who is interested in purchasing what he has to sell. Essentially, then, the demanders with relatively less elastic curves would allow the monopolist to recover sufficient revenues to cover his costs. You might say that those with less elastic demands would be subsidizing those with more elastic demands.

As mentioned in previous chapters, any monopolist can make more money if he can discriminate among the demanders of his product. Assume the monopolist is not discriminating and charging everyone the same price. He now begins to discriminate. First, he raises the price to less elastic demanders and lowers the price to more elastic demanders. When he raises the price to less elastic demanders, the total revenue received from them will rise because the fall in the quantity demanded is proportionately smaller than the increase in price. On the other hand, when he lowers the price to more elastic demanders, total revenues from them will rise. The increase in the quantity demanded will be proportionately greater than the decrease in price. The monopolist, therefore, makes out in both areas, and his total revenues will rise. The telephone company, for example, price discriminates against businesses and in favor of residential customers. Essentially the same service costs more if a business wants it than if a household orders it.

Even though allowing a natural monopolist to discriminate would result in more production than would obtain in the nondiscriminating case, most regulation does not condone such discrimination. It is usually felt to be unfair because those with less elastic demands are forced to pay more than those with more elastic demands, and problems of equity arise. We should note, however, that many regulated utilities do price discriminate. The charge for first class service on airlines is greater than the cost to them in additional expenses. Additionally, airlines have special student fares not available to nonstudents.

Electric utilities also price discriminate. It is usually true that an industrial firm's demands for electricity is more elastic than the residential demand for electricity. After all, industrial concerns can, if the price becomes too high, generate their own electricity. Residential consumers do not usually have this option. We therefore find that residential rates are higher than industrial rates. Whereas it could be argued that the cost of servicing residents is higher than the cost of servicing industrial users, the difference in cost does not seem to account for the entire difference in price. When prices to different people vary because of different costs involved in serving these people, the situation is called **price differentiation**—as opposed to price discrimination.

Selling the Rights to Produce

The last alternative to regulating a natural monopoly is actually selling the right or franchise to have the monopoly. Let's say the government knew that the generation of electricity was a natural monop-

oly. Rather than allow a monopolist to have his geographical service area decided for him, the government could first offer the right to generate electricity to the highest bidder. The bid in this case would be a stipulation of how *low* the businessman could go in setting a price for electricity. Some would say they could sell electricity at 10¢ a kilowatt; some would say 7¢ a kilowatt; some would say 5¢ a kilowatt. How low do you think the lowest bid would be? For an answer, let's go back to the theory of competition. In a perfectly competitive setting, each firm will produce where marginal cost equals the price or average revenue (which is also equal to marginal revenue, since the price is the same on all units). The average total cost curve just touches the price line at the point of intersection with the marginal cost curve. This is the nature of competition. There are zero economic profits. If the average total cost curve did not touch the price line, but was lower, that would indicate positive economic profits. Because there is free entry in a competitive industry, the entry of new firms would lower the price line to the point where it would, in fact, touch the average total cost curve. Economic profits would be eliminated.

We would expect, therefore, that if there were competitive bidding for the right to operate a natural monopoly, the lowest price-of-service bid would just equal the average total cost of providing that service, where cost included a normal rate of return. The businessman who was awarded the franchise would produce at quantity Q_2 and sell the product at price P_2 in Figure 8–4. He would not have to be subsidized, and he would not be restricting production as much as a monopolist would. That is, he would be producing more than the natural monopolist. This is obviously not the competitive solution for the competitive solution presumably would be where the marginal cost curve (the supply curve) intersects the demand curve. We know that the competitive solution is ruled out since, at that point, costs exceed revenues.

FIGURE 8–4

SELLING THE RIGHTS TO PRODUCTION

Here we put up the rights to produce the product of the natural monopoly to the highest bidder. The bidding will force the price to the point where it just covers average total costs, where costs include a normal rate of return. The price of the product will then be P_2. It will not be the competitive solution, which we showed in Figure 8–3 which would result in losses for the natural monopolist. P_2 would lie below the monopoly price but above the competitive price.

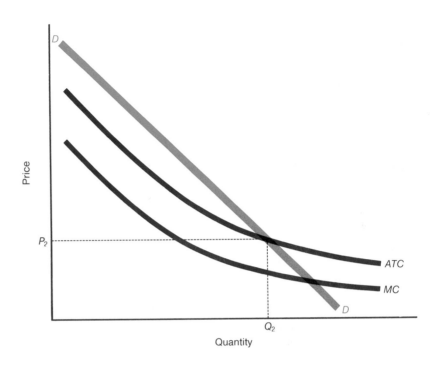

METHODS OF REGULATING MONOPOLIES

Since the government has decided to regulate the natural monopolies in our economy, it is faced with the problem of deciding how to regulate. There are many possibilities and we will only name a few. We will then talk about the problems involved and some of the more common methods of regulation.

Cost of Service

One way of regulation is to attempt to keep a lid on prices—that is, to keep prices at the level that would prevail in a competitive situation. This is usually called **cost-of-service regulation.** The regulatory commission only allows the regulated companies to charge prices that are in accordance with the actual cost of providing the services to

the customer. This was the standard practice for many years in the regulation of natural gas. Natural gas companies had to demonstrate exactly what their costs of service were, and it was on these costs that prices were based. It is no easy matter for any company, including regulated monopolies, to come up with an estimate of the costs involved for every service that they provide.

How does one allocate **joint costs** to several products or services which may be sold? For example, the post office can build a large building to handle incoming and outgoing mail. The post office sells various services: first class, air mail, parcel post, second class, third class, and fourth class mail. All of those different classes of mail service utilize in some way or another the services of the building that the post office constructed. How can the post office attribute parts of the joint cost of the building to the various classes of services it provides? The answer is that it can't.

The only way to allocate joint costs is in an arbitrary way.

A reasonable expectation would be, therefore, that regulated monopolies which are forced to present costs of services in order to establish rate schedules would allocate more of the joint costs to services provided to less elastic demanders than to services provided to more elastic demanders. In other words, we would expect the regulated monopoly to attempt some form of price discrimination. This could be done if the monopoly is successful in putting more of the burden of joint costs onto the less elastic demanders. They would not reduce quantity demanded very much so total revenues would rise.

Controlling the Rate of Return on Investment

Another method of regulation involves allowing the regulated companies to set prices which ensure a normal or competitive rate of return on the investment in the business. (The investment in the business is usually called its *equity.*) Assume that for the regulated monopoly in question the rate of return to investing in a competitive industry with similar risks is 12 percent per year. The regulatory agency will attempt to keep the rate of return to the investment in the regulated monopoly at 12 percent per year. Therefore, in requesting rate changes, the regulated monopoly must demonstrate to the regulatory commission that the proposed rate schedule will just allow investors in the company to obtain a 12 percent rate of return. In order for the company to do this, it has to establish what its costs are going to be. In many instances, the regulatory commissions will allow the company to show what its costs were in an historic test year. Some regulatory commissions will allow a company to establish what its costs will be in a future test year. In any event, there is the problem of allocating joint costs again, and there is the problem of which costs should be included in the computations and which

costs shouldn't. As you can well imagine, the rate-making proceedings that are carried out before regulatory commissions for most public utilities are extremely complicated. One sometimes wonders if the regulators themselves even understand all of the technical material presented to them.

Many critics of this particular type of regulation point out that if the percentage rate of return on investment is fixed, then the regulated companies will have perverse incentives to overinvest. After all, the object of the game is to maximize total profits. If the rate of profit that can be earned on investment is fixed, then why not increase capital investment to get higher *absolute* profits? Although regulated companies staunchly deny that this actually happens, economic theory would predict that the ratio of capital to labor in regulated monopolies would be higher than it would be without regulation.

It has also been pointed out by critics of regulation that when pecuniary or money profits are limited by regulation, unexploited monopoly profits may remain. How can the management of these regulated companies take advantage of those unexploited profits? One way is to increase their nonpecuniary gains from working in those companies. One can think of a thousand ways to do this. Managers can hire pretty secretaries, have lavish offices, do a lot of entertaining at the company's expense, work shorter hours, have innumerable underlings do every conceivable task for them, drive company cars that are large, roomy, and always new, and so on.

Problems with Inflation

Regulation based on rate of return to investment will always run into problems in inflationary periods, particularly in cases where rate schedules were pleaded on the basis of costs that occurred in a past year. If the costs of operating a regulated monopoly are rising along with all other prices in an inflationary economy, a rate schedule based on a previous year's costs will be insufficient in future years. That is, rates based on historic costs will turn out to yield a lower than normal rate of return in future years when costs will have risen. This has been particularly burdensome to the public utilities in the United States since 1965 when inflation soared to heights that no one had been accustomed to. Up to that time, many regulated utilities had been asking for price *decreases* due to improved technology and economies of scale. After 1965, however, the improvements in their technology and any other increases in their general productivity were swamped by the increases in the costs of doing business due to the general inflation in the economy.

The utilities had to start asking for price increases. You can imagine that regulatory commissions which were used to granting price *decreases* would be against the idea of price *increases*. Many public utilities began to face serious capital problems by the beginning of the 1970s. They were faced not only with higher labor costs but with higher money capital costs. Many of those companies had issued bonds in the past to get money for plant expansion at interest rates of 3, 4, and 5 percent. Many of those bonds were coming due, and they had to be paid off. The utilities then had to replace them with bonds that cost them 7, 8, and 9 percent. Their money capital costs were therefore increasing along with their labor costs. The price of physical capital was going up, too. Increased ecological awareness forced many utilities, particularly in electricity generation, to add expensive pollution control equipment to their facilities.

QUALITY OF SERVICE

A major problem with regulating monopolies concerns the quality of the service or product involved. Consider the many facets of telephone service: getting a dial tone, hearing other voices clearly, getting the operator to answer quickly, having out-of-order telephones repaired rapidly, putting through a long distance call quickly and efficiently. The list goes on and on. In fact, it is probably without end. But regulation of the telephone company usually deals with the prices charged for telephone service. Of course, regulators are concerned with the quality of service, but how can it be measured? Indeed, it cannot be measured very easily. Therefore, it is extremely difficult for any type of regulation to be successful in regulating the *price per constant quality unit.* Certainly, it is possible to regulate the price per unit, but we don't really know that the quality remains unchanged when the price changes. And if regulation doesn't allow prices to rise, quality of service can be lowered.

We must not overestimate the monopoly power which an obvious monopolist has. Nothing has a completely inelastic demand schedule; rather, most things do have substitutes in one form or another. It may be true that electricity for some uses does not have a substitute, but electricity for other uses does. For example, you can heat your house with gas, oil, or electric space heaters. You can cook either with gas or with electricity. You can have a gas water heater or an electric water heater. And industrial users can generate their own electricity. There are perhaps fewer substitutes for telephone service, but there are still many: letters, person to person communication, and telegrams.

And in some cases a supposed natural monopoly is not a natural monopoly at all. The post office is a good example. There are numerous entrepreneurs waiting to compete with the U.S. Post Office. So far they have only been successful in delivering bulk mail. Attempts at selling first-class mail service by private companies have been met with legal injunctions. Apparently, in this instance, the money capital costs necessary to start out in the post office business are not large enough for our natural monopoly argument to hold.

Regulation of natural monopolies will always

have its problems. Regulation of whole industries that supposedly affect the public interest also has problems. We shall treat several of these industries in subsequent issues. Right now, it might be useful to briefly indicate what can happen when prices are regulated in an otherwise relatively competitive situation.

REGULATING PRICES—THE CASE OF THE AIRLINES

The airline industry could now be quite competitive. The Civil Aeronautics Board (CAB), however, regulates the rates which commercial airlines can charge for their services. The CAB also regulates the routes that are awarded to the different airlines. If an airline wishes to fly a route that it is not already scheduled to fly, it must petition for that route. If it wishes to abandon service on a particular route, it must petition for that also.

The idea behind regulating the rates of commercial air carriers presumably is to prevent a monopoly rate from being charged and alternatively to prevent "destructive" competition. The idea behind CAB regulation is theoretically to provide the consumer with low-cost, high-quality air travel possibilities. We can see, though, that some detrimental effects result from across-the-board price regulation in the air transport field.

Nonprice Competition

There are quite a number of airline companies in the United States. In many cases, there are several competing airlines flying the same route. Between the West Coast and Honolulu, there are at least six competing companies flying to and from Honolulu and between different major West Coast cities. Between New York and San Francisco or Los Angeles, there are at least four competing airlines. Since there is more than one company flying between two cities, we would expect some sort of competition among the different companies. However, this competition has to take a very special form. The Civil Aeronautics Board does not allow companies to compete on the basis of price, so the airlines attempt to lure customers away from other airlines. They do this with improvements in the quality of service, which can be altered in many ways. Obviously, there can be prettier stewardesses, better looking stewards, more champagne, better meals, wider seating, nicer music, instant computerized reservation scheduling, free additional travel arrangements, and so on. Occasionally, we find such quality wars among the airlines. For a while there was a "lounge" war among airlines going between the West Coast and the East Coast. One airline started offering a lounge for its tourist-class customers. For a while it was taking away business from the other airlines, until they found ways to offer the same service. Then another airline started to offer live entertainment in its first-class lounge. And so went the lounge war. The CAB usually attempts to stop these wars before they get out of hand and will prohibit certain improvements in quality when it feels the time is ripe.

Timing of Flights

Another aspect of quality service is the timing of flight take-offs and landings. Naturally, it would be better if you could leave New York at 4 in the afternoon and arrive on the West Coast at 8 P.M. than if you had to leave at 12 midnight and arrive at 3 in the morning. Moreover, an airline will probably seem more attractive if it has a larger number of flights leaving from your city than if it has a smaller number. The airlines have figured this out, and therefore competing airlines fly out of the same place at the same time headed for the same destination. In Los Angeles you might find four different airlines leaving within one hour of each other, all going to the East Coast.

Most probably, all of those planes are not full. In fact, the airlines could be expected to add planes at different times until it was no longer worth their while. They would add planes until the marginal cost of doing so just equalled the marginal revenue. That's why four half-empty planes leave Los Angeles at the same time, all headed for New York. A utilization rate of 50 percent seems to be about the break-even point for airlines. Thus, competition forces them to keep adding planes until the average load factor is 50 percent.

The Civil Aeronautics Board can set prices, but it has a difficult time preventing competition via changes in quality. If price competition were allowed, however, there would be decreases in certain quality aspects of air transportation. There would probably be a reduction in the number of flights per day between big cities. But cut-rate economy classes would be offered, and it would be possible to travel at a lower cost between major cities in the United States. However, it might be impossible to travel by air at all between small cities. Under regulation, many companies are forced to maintain such unprofitable routes in order to be allowed to maintain profitable ones. In effect, then, those customers who use the airlines on the profitable routes are subsidizing those who travel the unprofitable routes.

ANTITRUST POLICY

It is the expressed aim of our government to foster competition in the economy. To this end, numerous attempts at legislating against business practices which seemingly destroy the competitive nature of the system have been made. We will briefly discuss some of the major antitrust acts in operation today and then concern ourselves with the actual implementation of monopoly-busting legislation.

The idea behind antitrust legislation should be obvious: if the courts can prevent collusion among sellers of a product, then a monopoly price will not result; there will be no restriction of output if the members in an industry are not allowed to join together in restraint of trade. Remember that the competitive solution to the price-quantity problem is one in which no *economic* profits are being made. The price of the product produced in a competitive situation is equal to its opportunity cost. If, for some reason, positive economic profits are being made in a competitive situation, free entry into the industry will force the price down to the point where there will no longer be any economic profits. Of course, members of the industry will still make a normal rate of return on their investment.

There are numerous ways to stifle competition. We've talked about collusion among potential competitors and about price-fixing, particularly as concerning the electrical manufacturers' conspiracy. There are also other ways to limit competition. Potential competitors can voluntarily decide to not compete by agreeing to sell only in a specified geographical area. There can be limits to the amount of output that each cartel member is allowed to produce. Supposedly, large, well-financed companies can use predatory pricing (a situation where the price of the product is reduced to below its cost) to drive out potential competitors. The idea behind predatory pricing is that the big, well-heeled businessman can drive out his rivals by forcing them to operate at a loss. Since he has more resources available, he can outlast his smaller competitors. He then raises his prices when all the competition is gone.

All of these restraints to trade are deemed illegal in one way or another in the United States. The precedent for our legal antitrust laws can be found in the body of English common law. During the nineteenth century in the United States there was extensive private litigation which drew on and even expanded English common law notions of restraint of trade.

The Sherman Act

The first major antitrust act which was passed by Congress was the famous Sherman Act of 1890.

The most important provisions of that act are:

Section 1: Every contract, combination in the form of trust or otherwise, or conspiracy, in restraint of trade or commerce among the several states, or with foreign nations, is hereby declared to be illegal.

Section 2: Every person who shall monopolize, or attempt to monopolize, or combine or conspire with any other person or persons to monopolize any part of the trade or commerce . . . shall be guilty of a misdemeanor.

Notice how vague this particular act actually is. No definition is given for the terms *restraint of trade or monopolization.* Despite this vagueness, however, the act was used to prosecute the infamous Standard Oil trust of New Jersey. Standard Oil of New Jersey was charged with violation of Section 1 and Section 2 of the Sherman Antitrust Act. This was in 1906 when Standard Oil controlled over 80 percent of the nation's oil refining capacity. Among other things, Standard Oil was accused of predatory price cutting to drive rivals out of business and also of obtaining preferential price treatment from the railroads for transporting Standard Oil products, thus allowing Standard to sell at lower prices.

Standard Oil was convicted in a district court. The company then appealed to the Supreme Court, which ruled that Standard's control of and power over the oil market created "a *prima facie* presumption of intent and purpose to maintain dominancy . . . not as a result from normal methods of industrial development, but by means of combination." Here, the word *combination* meant taking over other businesses and obtaining preferential price treatment from railroads. The Supreme Court forced Standard Oil of New Jersey to break up into many smaller companies.

The ruling handed down in the Standard Oil case came about because the judges felt that Standard Oil had used "unreasonable" attempts at restraining trade. The court did not come out against monopoly *per se.* The fact that Standard Oil had a large share of the market did not seem

to matter; rather, according to the Court, the problem was the way in which Standard acquired that large market share. In any event, antitrust legislation was started in the name of the Sherman Antitrust Act and was used to break up one of the largest trusts in U.S. business at that time.

The Clayton Act

The Sherman Act was so extremely vague that in 1914 a new law was passed to sharpen the antitrust provisions of the Sherman Act. This law was called the Clayton Act. It prohibited or limited a number of very specific business practices, which again were felt to be "unreasonable" attempts at restraining trade. Some of the more important sections of that act are listed here.

Section 2: [It is illegal to] discriminate in price between different purchasers [except in cases where the differences are due to differences in selling or transportation costs].

Section 3: [Producers cannot sell] on the condition, agreement or understanding that the . . . purchaser thereof shall not use or deal in the goods . . . of a competitor or competitors of the seller.

Section 7: [Corporations cannot hold stock in another company] where the effect . . . may be to substantially lessen competition.

Notice that these provisions outlaw practices which tend to "substantially" lessen competition. It is not very clear, however, what the term *substantially* actually means. How are the courts to interpret this word?

Robinson-Patman Act

Section 2 of the Clayton Act was later amended by the Robinson-Patman Act which was passed in 1936. The Robinson-Patman Act was aimed at preventing producers from driving out smaller competitors by means of selective discriminatory pricing cuts. The Robinson-Patman Act prohibits special cut-rate deals for services rendered "unless such payment or consideration is available on proportionally equal terms to all of their customers." It further prohibits sellers from performing services for customers, unless such services are available to all on "proportionately equal terms."

Other Laws

There are numerous other antitrust acts, many of which serve to exempt certain business practices from antitrust legislation! One of those is the Miller-Tydings Act that was passed in 1937 as an amendment to Section 1 of the Sherman Act. This act allowed for "fair trade" agreements. A fair trade agreement is something that you are probably all familiar with. A manufacturer can specify to all of the people who sell his product that they cannot sell it below a listed or "fair trade" price. This is what is called **resale price maintenance.** It is illegal for firms to lower the price of the product if the manufacturer has invoked a fair trade price. One would think that this type of fair trade agreement would violate antitrust laws aimed at preventing price fixing. Nonetheless, the Miller-Tydings Act made this type of price fixing legal. Some states skirted the Miller-Tydings Act by passing their own legislation which allowed retailers to cut prices on fair-traded goods. If you look at advertisements for stereo equipment from different big stores around the country, you will notice that stereo stores advertising from Washington, D.C. will usually put on their ads "no resale price maintenance" or "no fair trade laws here." These retailers are merely advertising the fact that they will cut prices on nationally fair-traded brands of stereo equipment.

THE ENFORCEMENT OF ANTITRUST LAWS

The enforcement of antitrust laws has been rather uneven. Of course, there have been many spectacular cases brought and won by the government, such as the case against the electrical companies' conspiracy in the early 1960s. Use of the Sherman Act did allow the government to break up the Standard Oil trust, and the government also broke up the American Tobacco Company. By and large, though, governmental efforts to prevent problems of monopoly have been concentrated in preventing mergers. A merger occurs when two companies join together and become one legal entity. It is very difficult for large companies today to merge without first seeking permission from the Justice Department of the U.S. Government. Often, the Justice Department will deny the merger on the grounds that it will seriously lessen competition.

We would expect that the uneven enforcement of antitrust laws reflects the political atmosphere more than anything else. Certain administrations are committed to big business; others are committed to doing as much as they can to thwart big business. For a while in the late 1960s and early seventies, there was vigorous antitrust legislation against **conglomerates.** A conglomerate is a company which has many subdivisions dealing in totally different products. International Telephone and Telegraph (IT&T) is a good example of how a conglomerate can get into numerous diverse fields of interest. It produces and sells houses, radios, books, insurance, hotel services, and rental car services. It is now a multibillion dollar corporation. In 1972, there was a scandal concerning IT&T and the Antitrust Division of the Justice Department. Apparently, there was going to be an antitrust proceeding against the large conglomerate, but certain dealings between government officials and the company's management allowed for an out-of-court settlement.

Even though the attack on conglomerates seems obviously necessary to many students of antitrust policy, the empirical evidence as to the monopoly power of such large corporations is not overwhelming. In fact, a Presidential Commission on Antitrust Activities failed to support any attacks against conglomerates. It is alleged that conglomerates are so big that they can wield market power in the separate submarkets in which they operate.

However, it is not obvious that IT&T, merely because it is so large, has market power in renting cars. After all, there are numerous car rental companies in competition with IT&T's Avis Rental Company. In fact, the competition seems to be getting even stronger as other rental companies "try harder" and as local rental companies pop up around the country.

WHEN TO PROSECUTE?

Even if we accept the premise that monopolies should not be allowed, how can the government come up with a policy rule that will help determine which mergers should be stopped? How can the government decide which companies should be dissolved? How will it know which business practices actually restrain trade? There have been numerous attempts by government officials and by interested academicians to derive specific policy rules. One of the most prevalent rules states that the *concentration ratio* in a particular industry should not become too large. The concentration ratio is defined as the percentage of total industry output accounted for by a few leading firms—say the first four or five. No one knows, though, what this magic number should be. Does monopolization of the industry start when the four-firm concentration ratio becomes 50 percent, 60 percent, 70 percent, or 80 percent?

Another way to assess the degree of monopoly power that an individual firm possesses may be to look at its profits. If the profits are higher than the "normal" rate of return elsewhere, then presumably that company is making monopoly returns. However, it is difficult to find out what those profits really represent. They are accounting profits and, therefore, do not include risk or inflation. The empirical findings on profits are usually for very short periods of time and may not demonstrate that the industry is tending toward a zero economic profit. Suffice it to say that it is difficult to establish any readily observable statistical procedures for establishing when antitrust enforcement should be attempted.

There is also a problem involved with attempting new legislation to increase competition in our economy. The legislative process usually alters any such suggested legal additions to our institutional framework. Numerous critics of antitrust legislation have come up with what they consider better pieces of legislation than those existing now. However, even if the legislation which they recommend is exactly what it should be for bettering our competitive system, by the time it goes through the legislative mill, it will be vastly different. Moreover, legislation which calls for increased enforcement of antitrust laws leads to increased costs on the part of government and the firms involved. Only when we are convinced that the costs will be outweighed by the benefits might we presume to proceed with our action.

Definition of New Terms

NATURAL MONOPOLY: a monopoly that arises out of the peculiar production characteristics in the industry. Usually a natural monopoly arises when production of the service or product requires extremely large capital investments such that only one firm can profitably be supported by consumers. A natural monopoly usually arises when there are large economies of scale.

PRICE DIFFERENTIATION: differences in price which depend on differences in cost, distinct from price discrimination, which is not a function of costs but rather a function of relative elasticities of demand.

COST-OF-SERVICE REGULATION: a type of regulation which is based on allowing prices which reflect only the actual costs of production and do not include monopoly profits.

JOINT COSTS: costs which are common to several products for a firm. The post office, for example, could be using the same building to service first class, third class, fourth class, and air mail. It is difficult to allocate joint costs to various separate services or products that use them.

RATE-OF-RETURN REGULATION: regulation which seeks to keep the rate of return in the industry at a competitive level by not allowing excessive prices to be charged.

RESALE PRICE MAINTENANCE: sometimes called "fair trade laws," a system whereby the manufacturer stipulates a specific retail price and the retailer is not allowed to sell the product at a lower price. Certain states have outlawed retail price maintenance because it is a form of price fixing; it prevents price competition.

CONGLOMERATES: a large firm which is composed of numerous smaller divisions, each one in a different field. A conglomerate may be in automobile leasing, farming, airline travel, investment, and a dozen other types of economic activities.

Chapter Summary

1. Traditionally, there are two ways of regulating monopolies. One is actual regulation by some commission; the other is by way of antitrust laws.

2. Regulation usually involves a natural monopoly which arises when, for example, the average total cost curve falls over a very large range of production rates. In such a situation, only one firm can survive. It will be the firm which can expand production and sales faster than the others to take advantage of the falling average total costs.

3. If regulation seeks to force the natural monopolist to produce at the point where the marginal cost curve (supply curve in the competitive case) intersects the demand curve, the natural monopolist will make losses because when average total costs are falling, marginal costs are below average total costs. The regulators are faced with a dilemma. They can get out of this dilemma by (a) subsidizing the natural monopolist, (b) allowing him to price discriminate so as to prevent losses, or (c) selling the rights to produce so that the price will be set equal to average total costs, where there will be zero economic profits.

4. There are several ways of regulating monopolies, the most common being on a cost-of-service basis or a rate-of-return basis. With a cost-of-service regulation, the regulated monopolies are allowed to charge prices which reflect only reasonable costs. With a rate-of-return regulation, the regulated monopolies are allowed to set rates so as to make a competitive rate of return for the equity shareholders.

5. In any type of regulatory procedure, there is always a problem of keeping the quality of the product constant. If a price is regulated it may be possible for the regulated monopoly to lower the quality of its product in order to effectively raise the price above that which the regulators desire.

6. The airlines industry is a good example of what can happen with price regulation. Since the airlines cannot compete on the basis of price, they compete on the basis

of nonprice or quality aspects of their product. This is why we find so many airlines leaving the same airport going to the same destination exactly at the same time of day, even though none of them are filled to capacity. That is also why we find that different companies will schedule their flights at prime times to bid away each other's customers. Hence, we get a tremendous amount of congestion at airports during the best times of the day.

7. Antitrust legislation is designed to obviate the need for regulation. The major antitrust acts are the Sherman Act, the Clayton Act, and the Robinson-Patman Act.

8. While the legislation against monopolies may, in fact, be comprehensive, the enforcement of this legislation has been extremely erratic in the history of antitrust.

Questions for Thought and Discussion

1. If regulation were unsuccessful and the regulated monopolies were able to do exactly as they wanted to, how would the consumer lose out? Do you have any idea how we could measure his losses?

2. If regulatory commissions are so against price discrimination, why do we, in fact, see price discrimination in almost all regulated industries?

3. It has been argued that if the Civil Aeronautics Board did not guarantee monopoly returns for airlines traveling between profitable routes which usually involve big cities, these same airlines would have to discontinue their unprofitable routes between smaller cities. Assume that this is true. Would you still favor the elimination of monopoly profits in the airlines industry?

4. Is there any way for regulation to be completely comprehensive and to take account of all aspects of the product or service being sold?

5. Our antitrust laws prohibit price fixing; yet for many years many state bar associations set minimum fee schedules for lawyers. This is a form of price fixing. To date it has not been prosecuted by the U.S. Justice Department. Can you think of a reason why?

6. Some economists maintain that conglomerates do not endanger competition because they involve the merging of totally unrelated companies. Others point out, however, that such mergers provide conglomerates with greater financial power and greater market power in general, thereby lessening competition. Which side do you agree with? Why?

7. During President Nixon's Phase II price stabilization policies, the Price Commission came out with some rules for certifying rate increases requests by electric utilities. Many electric utilities maintained that if the rate increases were not granted, black-outs and brown-outs would result in the United States. Do you think there is any truth in that statement? What is the relationship between price increases and the ability of an electric utility to meet its energy demands?

Selected References

Berki, Sylvester E., Ed. *Antitrust Policy, Economics and Law.* Lexington, Mass.: D.C. Heath, 1966.

Green, Mark, et al. *The Closed Enterprise System.* A Report by the Nader Study Group on Antitrust Enforcement, New York: Grossman, 1972.

Kahn, Alfred E. *The Economics of Regulation.* Vol. 1 and 2. New York: John Wiley & Sons, 1970.

Leonard, William N. *Business Size, Market Power, and Public Policy.* New York: Thomas Y. Crowell, 1969.

MacAvoy, Paul W., Ed. *The Crisis of the Regulatory Commissions.* New York: W. W. Norton, 1970.

Stelzer, Irwin M., Ed. *Selected Antitrust Cases.* 4th Ed. Homewood, Illinois: Irwin, 1972.

Wilcox, Clair. *Public Policies toward Business.* 4th Ed. Homewood, Illinois: Irwin, 1971.

ISSUE VIII

CONSUMERISM

Are Consumer Protection Laws Justifiable?

Let the Buyer Beware

Until recently, the public and the government were content to allow Adam Smith's famous invisible hand to maximize the welfare of the nation. Times have changed, however, and the dictim *caveat emptor*—let the buyer beware—no longer seems to be appropriate. The age of consumerism is upon us. Heralded by the exposés of Ralph Nader and his Raiders, picked up by presidents and politicians, and furthered by contin-

ued popular support, active control of business practices by the government has become a reality in practically every state in the Union. Business can no longer assume that it is the buyer's responsibility to find out whether a product is safe, whether food is healthful, or whether advertising has been fair. The age of consumerism has brought a reversal of roles: the businessman must be the one to make sure that his product is safe for consumption. If he fails in this task, he can now be sued and even put in jail.

DRAWING BY ED FISHER; © 1970
THE NEW YORKER MAGAZINE, INC.

"That ought to satisfy Ralph Nader!"

Consumer Protection Agencies

Throughout the country consumer protection agencies have been popping up like wildflowers. There are probably 25 states that have consumer protection offices or departments. Over 40 states have consumer fraud or protection agencies within the state attorney general's office. Five states even have consumer agencies in the governor's office. Cities also have organized consumer protection units. In addition, county offices and local private groups exist, and there is even a Consumer Affairs Aide to the President.

These consumer protection agencies and advocates do a lot. Usually, they handle complaints filed by consumers about unsafe products or against fraudulent practices by businessmen. New York City's Consumer Affairs Department, with a budget in excess of $3 million, has attacked truth-in-lending problems, unfair past-due bill collection procedures, deceptive sales techniques, and misleading advertising. At one time, the New York City Consumer Affairs Department issued almost 100 summonses to 16 large supermarkets when the businesses ignored new regulations to post unit prices of all their products.

Many consumer agencies push for legislation aimed at protecting the consumer. The enactment of unit-pricing laws and truth-in-lending laws, the enforcing of more stringent controls over building contractors and shady car dealers, and the processing of complaints against automobile repairmen, mail order operations, and other suspected shysters are some of the accomplishments of these consumer groups.

Now there is even an "anticorporation" corporation, organized on behalf of consumers everywhere. Called the Public Equity Corporation, it was formed to bring suit against other corporations which pollute the environment and defraud customers. It is too soon to tell how successful the corporation will be, but its very formation is more evidence of how numerous and how serious consumer advocates have become. Let's turn now to an analysis of the effects of consumerism.

Straight Economics

What does standard price theory have to say about the "need" for legislation to prevent businessmen from defrauding the public with unhealthy food, unsafe products, and unsubstantiated advertising claims? Price theory tells us that the forces of market competition should obviate any need for regulation. Let's take an example. Suppose that, unknown to you, there is a fraudulent TV repairman in your neighborhood. When

your set goes on the blink you call him in. He says a lot more is wrong with your TV set than actually is. You, however, have no way of knowing whether he's telling the truth because you do not possess the necessary technical information. If you believe him, you are defrauded. He charges you a higher price than you "should" be charged. He takes your set, repairs it at a cost of about $5.00, brings the set back to you, and gives you a bill for $95. He tells you three transformers had blown out and 14 transistors had to be replaced. You may cry in anguish, but you pay the bill anyway. You have been defrauded.

The fact is, however, in economic analysis, it matters little whether you have been lied to. You pay the same amount one way or the other. You still got a bill for $95.

If there's any competition, fraudulent, high-priced repairmen would be expected to lose all their business. The competitive process takes time, however, and information costs are not zero. Nonetheless, according to our standard theory, competition among repairmen will *eventually* lead to elimination of "dishonest" repairmen, since people will seek out the honest ones in time.

We know that competition will act faster in certain circumstances. In this particular one, if we are in a community which has a relatively stable or fixed citizenry we

would expect that the dishonest repairmen would be run out of business faster than if the community in question were unstable with lots of people leaving and others moving in. In the former, neighbors would all know which guys were the crooks. In the latter, the crooks could go to the unsuspecting newcomers to get business. We would expect, therefore, that there are fewer dishonest repairmen in small towns than in large cities. For in the former, there is very little movement of population compared with the latter.

We would also expect manufacturers of TV sets to try to do something about reducing the repair costs of their products. After all, the higher the price you have to pay for repairs, the higher the price of service per unit time that you get from your set. If the price per constant quality unit of service is artificially high due to costly repairs, then we would expect TV manufacturers to have an incentive to reduce the need for repairs in their machines. This would reduce the price and increase the demand for TV services.

The Need for Protection

Why, then, is it necessary today to have consumer protection? First, even if we assume that competition will *eventually* lead to the elimination of fraudulent TV repairmen, the adjustment time may be unacceptably long from a social standpoint. It may be socially cheaper for consumer protection agencies to take action and make spot checks on businesses suspected of defrauding the public.

One instance in which consumer protection may now be more necessary than in the past is when the population becomes more transient. In such a situation people would not know about dishonest businessmen. The adjustment time needed for the eventual elimination of fraud would be greatly lengthened and, from a social standpoint, unacceptable.

There are additional reasons why information costs have increased and adjustment times have, therefore, become longer. Presumably, as products become more complex, it is more difficult for consumers to understand what they are buying. Therefore, consumers are easy prey for unscrupulous businessmen because they cannot understand the technical jargon the salesman uses. Another area in which consumers may be unable to protect themselves pertains to the ingredients in food products.

The Case of the Fat Wienie

For a number of years now, consumer protection agents, particularly the President's Aide on Consumer Affairs, have been concerned about the fat content in hotdogs. When the hotdog manufacturers wanted to raise the fat content, the President's Consumer Aide fought tooth and nail against them; consumer advocates also rallied to prevent hotdog manufacturers from increasing the amount of chicken meat in hotdogs. Let's use our standard microeconomic model to analyze this situation.

Economic Analysis

As with TV sets, we can also talk about the price per constant quality unit in the case of hotdogs. The price of hotdogs should be viewed as the price of a constant quality unit hotdog. If the price of hotdogs remains the same and the fat content increases, then the price per constant quality unit has gone up, assuming, of course, that the actual meat content of a wienie is important to the consumer.

Let's assume that the value of hotdogs to consumers is based both on taste and on food content. Assume also that increasing the fat used in the hotdog does not change taste but does reduce food value. Thus, the true price of the hotdog goes up if manufacturers increase fat content. What does our standard supply and demand analysis say will happen? At a higher price with an unchanged demand curve, a smaller quantity will be demanded. But if this is the case, why would manufacturers want to raise the price? Obviously, the supply and demand curves must not remain stable; either the supply curve shifts in or the demand curve shifts out so that the equilibrium price is higher than it was in the past. (This is obviously going to be true in an inflationary setting, but that's a macroeconomic issue.)

Let's take an individual firm, and assume for the moment that consumers are unable to assess the food value of hotdogs. If fat content does not alter taste, wouldn't a profit-maximizing producer try to make hotdogs that had 99.99 percent fat? Only the skin would be nonfat. If it could charge the same price and lower the cost of production, this profit-maximizing firm would make more profits. This is not the case, however, because obviously fat content *does* alter the taste; consumers can, at least on the margin, discover how much food value there is in a hotdog; and there is competition among wienie producers.

Marginal Analysis

The point that must be brought out here is that some sort of competition can exist if there is information *on the margin*. We must distinguish carefully between the average and the margin. The average consumer of wienies may not know what he is buying and not care, but there are marginal consumers who do take note. For example, dormitories and schools are usually highly critical of the food value that they buy—but not the taste, right? They will not be fooled by higher percentages of fat in hotdogs. They will realize that it is an increase in the price per constant quality unit.

Consumer protection in the form of preventing hotdog manufacturers from increasing the fat content of their wienies can serve the purpose of increasing information in the marketplace and *decreasing* uncertainty. The search costs to the buying public can be reduced. One might wish, though, to assess the costs of such consumer protection as well as the benefits. Moreover, one might distinguish between what one thinks people *should* buy and what people actually do buy. Such questions are in the realm of normative economics.

Truth in Labeling

An alternative policy might be to enforce accurate labeling of the contents of food products. Then each consumer could buy exactly what he wanted and would know exactly what he was buying. Government regulation could seek to improve information about products rather than restrict their various characteristics to some governmentally "acceptable" norm.

Unsafe at Any Speed

It might be said that the current consumer movement started off with Ralph Nader's book, *Unsafe at Any Speed,* a lambasting critique of the automobile industry and of General Motors in particular for its production of the apparently unsafe Corvair. (The Corvair is no longer being produced.) Partially as a result of Mr. Nader's unending assault on the unsafe automobiles being produced in Detroit, we now have a set of safety standards which automobile manufacturers must comply with when producing their cars. These safety standards involve collapsible steering wheels, dual brake systems, over-the-shoulder seat belts, padded dashes, and crash absorbing bumpers. The list of required safety features is growing. The apparent result is that we are now driving safer cars than we did ten years ago. Let's see what economic analysis can say about product safety regulations such as those imposed on automobiles.

Changing Quality

We should again be careful to distinguish between the price per unit and the price per constant quality unit. Obviously, when an automobile is made safer, its quality is increased for most people. If the nominal price were to remain the same, the price per

constant quality unit would fall as quality increased. When viewed in this respect, safety is no different than any other aspect of a product. We can view the demand for safety the same way we can view the demand for ornamental trimmings on a car. In this instance, remember that our object is to apply an economic model which will predict well. We use as simple a model as possible to answer the particular question at hand. The question in this case happens to be whether the effects of safety legislation actually protect the consumer.

Commission on Product Safety. The President's Commission on Product Safety once said: "The exposure of consumers to unreasonable product hazards is excessive by any standard of measurement." The Report of the Commission also indicated: "Many hazards . . . are unnecessary and can be eliminated without substantially affecting the price to the consumer." If the President's Commission is correct and many safety hazards could be eliminated at substantially no cost to the producer or the consumer, then we must conclude that people do not care about safety. After all, if people wished to have safer products, then profit-seeking producers would be motivated to provide safety aspects for their products, since the costs for doing so would be negligible. However, we know that nothing is free; even safety has a cost. If we make cars safer, as we have been doing, the price of those cars will go up. It takes men and machines to make products which will last longer and which will be safer to use. This is a general rule which we can assume holds in most cases.

If a car has to have an airbag passive-restraint system to protect its occupants in a collision, then the car will probably cost more. In fact, the industry has estimated the cost of airbags will be several hundred dollars per car. From what we know about the resultant price of a product when the costs of production go up, we might say that safety legislation is essentially equal to a tax on products. The tax is only *nominally* paid by the manufacturer. The consumer will pay most of it.

Consumer Sovereignty. Our competitive model would say that in the past the existing level of product safety was the one desired by consumers since they were the ones who actually determined what was produced. This model of **consumer sovereignty** may not be appropriate in certain circumstances, although it could conceivably be appropriate in many others. There is a tricky question as to whether consumer sovereignty actually exists. Do consumers determine what kind of products are made, or do produc-

ers? Do consumers, through their choice of products, determine what is actually produced and sold? If *not,* then there is an argument for product safety legislation. If consumers do not have control even in the long run over what they are actually sold, then producers may be selling products that are either unsafe or lack the greatest utility possible.

Costs and Benefits

To assess the advisability of a consumer protection program which involves product safety standards, we might want to look at the costs as well as the benefits of such programs. In the case of the automobile, a study has been done for the President which reveals that the costs of increased

car safety will not be met by an equal amount of benefits.

In 1972, a fourteen-man panel prepared a report entitled "Cumulative Regulatory Effects on the Cost of Automotive Transportation." The report pointed out that safety and pollution control equipment now required for 1976 model cars will add around $800 to the price of what the car would have cost in 1971. The panel concluded that the costs were not worth the benefits. It suggested that the so-called passive-restraint system of quick inflating airbags should be abandoned and, in their place, well-known, time-tested, three-point over-the-shoulder safety belts be devised so that the engine would not start unless they were fastened. The panel also pointed out numerous projects which could be instituted to eliminate roadway hazards. For example, for a cost of $1600 per mile we could place empty oil drum crash cushions, break-away signs and lightpoles, and other safety devices on our highways. This would come to about $6 billion, but it would give off safety benefits that would be well in excess of that figure.

Safety Costs

We should be fully aware of the fact that any increase in safety usually entails higher production costs and ultimately higher costs to the consumer. The question comes up as to whether the consumer benefits from the improvement of the products he buys if he has to pay more for them. If, however, the adjustment time to a competitive solution (including increased safety) seems extraordinarily long, then there may be a case for safety legislation.

There is certainly a case for safety legislation when it involves so-called **third party** or **external effects.** If you have faulty brakes, you can run over a pedestrian as a result. Here, the pedestrian is an external party to your decision to drive with faulty brakes. There was no way for him to get you to fix your brakes. Certainly you will be forced to compensate the injured pedestrian, or his dependents if he is killed, as the accident was purely due to your negligence.

However, in most instances, the compensation to the injured party is less than the injured party would have demanded before the fact of the accident. Thus, in order to avoid excessive third party effects of faulty products, safety legislation may be appropriate. Such legislation would involve requiring good tires, good brakes, cars without knife-edged hood ornaments, windows which do not distort vision, and so on.

Safety May Decline

Let's assume that people demand a certain level of safety in their cars. When they are forced to buy an over-the-shoulder seat belt, they suddenly feel safer because they know that, in case of an accident they will face a lower probability of being seriously hurt. Therefore, they drive faster in order to maintain their desired level of safety. This is particularly true with something like passive-restraint systems such as airbags. There is nothing that the occupant of a car can do to eliminate the safety feature of airbags, whereas there is something he can do with an over-the-shoulder seat belt: he doesn't have to put it on. With airbags, however, the driver feels he can increase the recklessness with which he drives and still maintain his formerly desired level of safety.

This argument may seem far-fetched, but there are probably some of you who do, in fact, feel safer with a combination lap and over-the-shoulder seat belt and a large head restraint behind you. Would you perhaps be less timid when driving if you didn't have all of that safety paraphernalia? The statistics from Sweden show that in the last few years no one who was wearing an over-the-shoulder belt has been killed in an accident at speeds of under 65 miles an hour. That's certainly impressive evidence that the probability of dying in an automobile crash is lower if you wear an over-the-shoulder belt. Might you not take a few more chances, given that new information? If the answer is yes, then the wild argument just presented does, indeed, have some relevance.

What Can Be Said about the Consumer Movement?

The consumer movement will have measurable benefits to the extent that it increases the amount of product information made available and to the extent that this information has a positive value to consumers. So long as the cost of providing the new information is less than the value to the consumers—from a purely economic cost-benefit point of view—the consumer movement will increase overall economic happiness. To the extent that the consumer movement leads to restrictions on product design and production, costs and benefits are much less obvious. The cost not only includes the increased price of the products due to safety requirements, but also the reduction in general consumer utility because of the lower quantity demanded.

The benefits can obviously be measured by the reduction in the number of product-related accidents and in the reduction in uncertainty about certain products. From an economic cost-benefit point of view, it is not obvious that any particular piece of consumer protection legislation which restricts the choice of products bought and sold leads to a net benefit or a net loss to society. That is an empirical question and each separate piece of consumer protection safety legislation must be analyzed on its own terms. No general blanket statement can be made.

Definition of New Terms

CAVEAT EMPTOR: let the buyer beware.

CONSUMER SOVEREIGNTY: a notion that the consumer registers his preferences in the market place by his dollar votes. In a competitive economy, competition among suppliers will force them to adjust their particular production to whatever consumers demand.

THIRD PARTY EFFECTS: sometimes called external effects; effects of a decision which bear on a third party who is not part of the decision-making process. When you buy a car from the dealer, you may make an agreement with him that is satisfactory between the two of you. However, if the brakes are faulty, you can run down a third party who is not part of the agreement.

Questions for Thought and Discussion

1. Many people contend that consumer sovereignty no longer exists in the United States because we do not have a competitive world. Do you agree? Why? What bearing does this have on consumerism?
2. Ralph Nader's study group has shown that the Volkswagen is presumably a relatively unsafe car. Why do so many people still ride in Volkswagens?
3. It has been suggested that by 1985, only cars which meet very strict safety requirements will be allowed to drive on highways. All other cars will be restricted to city streets. Will you be better or worse off after this legislation is passed?
4. Do the requirements for sturdy bumpers relate to the safety of automobile occupants?
5. If all cars are required to have extensive safety features, do you think that the relatively less wealthy in the United States will benefit equally with the more wealthy?

Selected References

Nader, Ralph. *The Volkswagen: An Assessment of Distinctive Hazards.* Washington, D.C.: Center for Automobile Safety, 1971.

Stanford, David. *Who Put the 'Con' in Consumer?* New York: Liveright, 1972.

Tomerlin, John, "Ralph Nader vs. Volkswagen," *Road & Track,* April, 1972, pp. 25-33.

WIDE WORLD PHOTOS

THE FIFTH BRANCH OF GOVERNMENT

Ralph Nader

Founder, Center for the Study of Responsive Law

RALPH NADER has been described as a public official never elected by anyone, an unmonitored watchdog accountable to no one, an institution unto himself. These observations could also describe Nader's major targets—the corporation executives, the utilities, the ineffective regulatory agencies, and the advertising media. Nader's focus for the past ten years has been an anti-institutional one. He has attacked the paradox of "crimes" which are severely punished when committed by individuals, but ignored or even subsidized when committed by corporations. His research has described the detailed way in which he feels free enterprise has become a slogan rather than an economic mode of operation.

While at Harvard Law School, Nader first became conscious of the trend for bright young lawyers to go into the lucrative fields of corporation and tax law. After receiving his degree, Nader began practicing law in Hartford, Connecticut, specializing in automobile accident cases. By 1963 he had compiled a collection of data which he thought refuted the myth that all accidents were caused by careless drivers. He discovered that the auto industry was sitting on plans for "safety cars'' while pushing dangerous cars onto an un-suspecting public.

Two years later, *Unsafe at Any Speed* was published; probably few books have had as immediate and serious an impact on American industry. Its primary target was General Motors—the Chevrolet division in particular. With case studies and detailed engineering data and specifications, Nader had compiled a devastating attack. The company hired a private detective to trail Nader, tried to trap him into compromising situations with attractive young women, and generally harassed him at every turn. But General Motors could not have selected a less vulnerable target: Nader's idea of relaxation is ''sitting down to discuss anthropology.'' Nader then sued GM, bringing even more attention to the book, and was awarded $280,000, money he used to continue his fight against harmful corporate practices.

The book and subsequent trial established Nader's reputation as an uncompromising, incorruptible, skillful fighter. Nader created The Center for the Study of Responsive Law, now composed of groups of lawyers, statisticians, scientists, doctors, and other specialists who have produced exhaustive reports on almost all facets of industrial production, federal regulation, and state government policy in the United States. Nader has earned the devotion of his underpaid staff, and he is consistently cited in public opinion polls as one of the few Americans in public life that young people trust and respect.

At least five major regulatory and consumer protection laws can be ascribed directly to Nader's efforts: the Motor Vehicle Safety Act (1966), a direct result of *Unsafe at Any Speed;* the Wholesome Meat Act (1967); the Natural Gas Pipeline Safety Act (1968); the Coal Mine Health and Safety Act (1969); and the Occupational Safety and Health Act (1970). Nader has also produced a series of books on some of the federal regulatory agencies; he and his staff found absenteeism, featherbedding, inefficiency, incompetence, and a lack of commitment at the highest levels of the Federal Trade Commission and other agencies.

A staff report on the state of Delaware explored the broad political and economic influence of the DuPont Corporation which, in the view of the authors, completely compromises any semblance of a free market economy and electoral freedom in the state. And though it swallowed hard, the DuPont Corporation spent $450.00 to obtain some copies of the report.

The oldest argument against Nader is that he would sell the free enterprise system down the river to a series of mega-agencies with absolute regulatory power. ''Where is the free enterprise system?'' he asks. ''I'm trying to find it. Is it the oil oligopoly, protected by import quotas? The shared monopolies in consumer products? The securities market, that bastion of capitalism operating on fixed commissions and now provided with socialized insurance? They call me a radical for trying to restore power to the consumer, but businessmen are the true radicals in this country. They are taking us deeper and deeper into corporate socialism—corporate power using government power to protect it from competition.''

Derived Demand and Income Distribution

The Decision to Hire and Fire

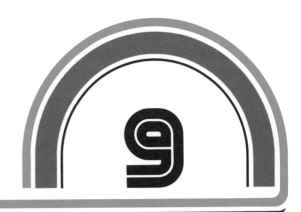

W HEN A FIRM decides to fire an employee, the employee usually suffers. The costs of unemployment are not insignificant in our economy. Conversely, when an employer decides to hire a new worker, the worker usually feels he's better off; otherwise, he probably would not have accepted the job. If employers are willing to pay higher wages to workers, those workers are also obviously better off. If employers can get away with paying very low wages, then perhaps the employers will be better off, making higher profits. How much people are paid and the extent to which their labor resources are used are crucial issues in economics for they determine who is rich and who is poor. These factors determine what percentage of national income goes to wages and what percentage goes to interest, profits, and dividends.

Before tackling the problem of analyzing the distribution of income, we first have to come up with a model that predicts how much of a particular input firms will demand and what price they will pay for it. In our discussion, we shall consider only one variable factor of production—labor. We will assume all other factors of production are fixed; in other words, the firm has a fixed number of machines but can hire or fire workers.

A firm's demand for inputs can be studied in much the same manner as we studied demands for outputs in different types of market situations. Again different types of market situations shall be examined. Our analysis will always end up with the same conclusion: a firm will hire employees up to the point where it isn't profitable to hire any more. It will hire employees to the point where the marginal revenue of hiring a worker will just equal the marginal cost. The best way for us to start out is to assume that everything is perfectly competitive.

A COMPETITIVE MARKET

Let's take as our example a prerecorded tape manufacturer who is in competition with many other similar companies selling the same kind of product. Assume that the laborers hired by our tape manufacturer do not need to have any special skills. This firm sells its product in a perfectly competitive market and also buys its variable input—labor—in a competitive market. The firm can influence neither the price of its product nor the price that it must pay for its variable input; it can purchase all of the labor it wants at the going market wage without affecting that wage. The "going" wage is established by the forces of supply and demand in the labor market. The demand is made up by all of the individual firm demands. Because our single tape maker is such a small part of the total demand for labor, he cannot influence the wage rate.

CONSTANT FACTOR COSTS

The cost of adding one more worker to the production line is the same whether our tape maker hires 50 workers or 500. Thus, he faces a constant marginal input cost (cost of a factor of production) which is exactly equal to the wage rate set by market forces that are out of his control. Since he can do nothing about the wage rate, the only variable he has left to play with is the total number of workers. That is, he takes the wage rate as fixed and decides how many workers he should hire, given that fixed wage rate. As you might expect, it will be profitable for him to hire more workers as long as they can make him more profits. When additional workers don't bring in more profits, our tape maker will stop hiring. It's fairly easy to figure out at what point hiring should stop.

Marginal Product. To find the point at which hiring stops, we have to know the additional output or **marginal product** of each worker. We'll assume that all workers have the same education and ability. They can all do the same type of job with the same results; each worker, by himself, can produce the same amount; and each is paid the same wage. But each worker does *not* work alone. They work together to produce the tapes, and a new worker may not be able to produce as much as his co-workers.

Think about this: we are assuming that everything else is held constant, which means that, if our tape maker wants to add one more worker to an assembly line, he's got to crowd all the existing workers a little closer together. This is so because he did not increase his capital stock (the assembly line equipment) at the same time he increased his work force. Therefore, as we add more workers, each one has a smaller and smaller fraction of the available capital stock to work with. If you have one worker using one machine, adding another worker usually doesn't double the output because the machine can only run so fast and for only so many hours per day. This notion was introduced previously in connection with diminishing marginal returns. The returns from adding more of a variable factor of production first rose, then fell, and finally became negative.

Thus, for a variable factor of production, such as labor, the increased output made possible by hiring additional workers may be expected to get smaller. The increased output made possible by an additional worker is called the worker's marginal product. If ten workers can produce 1000 tapes and 11 workers can produce 1090 tapes, then the marginal product of the eleventh worker is 90 tapes. Be careful here, because we are assuming the only thing that varies is the number of workers. That's how we find out their respective marginal physical product, or what their particular productivity is. In fact, a worker's *productivity can be defined as a worker's marginal product.*

Value of Marginal Product. We now know that as more workers are added, their marginal product falls. We still really can't figure out how many workers our tape maker should hire. He wants to hire workers as long as the additional tapes each worker produces are *worth* more than the wages the worker receives. That way the manufacturer ends up making a profit. But it is difficult to compare a physical product, such as the number of tapes, with a wage rate that is expressed in dollars. We somehow have to translate the physical product into a dollar value. This is easily done by multiplying the physical product times the market price of the tapes. If the eleventh worker's marginal physical product is 90 tapes and each tape sells for $3.00, then the value of the worker's marginal product (VMP) is 90 times $3.00, or $270. If that is his value of marginal product per month and his wage rate per month is only $250, it behooves our tape maker to hire him, for the difference between his wage rate and his contribution to total revenues **(value of marginal product)** is going to be $20.

Rule for Hiring

We are now ready to formulate a general rule for the hiring decision of a firm. *It should hire workers up to the point where their wage rate just equals the value of their marginal product.* If the firm hired more workers, the additional wages would not be covered by additional increases in total revenue. If the firm hired fewer workers, it would be forfeiting the contributions that additional workers could make to increasing total profits. A simple example is outlined in Table 9–1, which shows that the number of workers the firm should hire is 12 because at that point the value of the workers' marginal product just equals the going wage rate. We can plot the numbers in Table 9–1 on a simple graph. This graph is called *the value of marginal product curve.* Notice that it is downward sloping. As more workers are hired, the value of a worker's marginal product decreases for only one reason: diminishing returns. The price of the tapes remains the same because the firm is selling in a competitive market. The firm is a price taker and cannot influence what the market price actually is.

Using Figure 9–1 we can find out how many workers our firm should hire. First, we draw a straight line across from the going wage rate which is determined by demand and supply on the labor market. This intersects the value of marginal product curve at 12 workers. The intersection, *E,* is where the wage rate is equal to the value of marginal product. We can use the value of marginal product curve as a *factor demand curve,* assuming only one variable factor of production and competition in both the buying of the variable factor and the selling of the product.

TABLE 9–1

THE VALUE OF MARGINAL PRODUCT

Here we show the number of workers in the first column. In the second column, we show their marginal product per month. For example, when we add 1 worker to an already existing work force of 8 workers, the marginal product falls from 111 tapes per month to 104 tapes per month. We find out in the third column the value of the marginal product of each worker. We multiply the marginal product times the price, which in our example is $3.00 per tape. Here we have assumed that the wage rate is $250 per month. In such a situation, the rational employer will hire only 12 workers for then the value of marginal product is just equal to the wage rate or monthly salary.

NUMBER OF WORKERS	MARGINAL PRODUCT	PRICE OF TAPE X MARGINAL PRODUCT = VMP
7	118	354
8	111	333
9	104	312
10	97	291
11	90	270
12	83	250
13	76	228

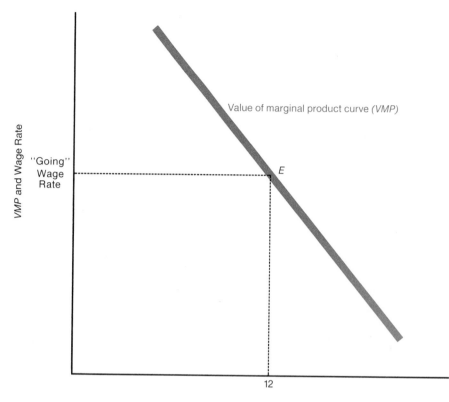

FIGURE 9-1

VALUE OF MARGINAL PRODUCT CURVE

Here we have plotted the value of marginal product curve from Table 9-1. On the horizontal axis of this diagram is the number of workers hired. On the vertical axis is the value of marginal product and the wage rate ($250 per month in this figure). We find out how many workers our firm will want to hire by putting in the wage rate that is established by the forces of supply and demand in the entire labor market. The employer in a competitive situation takes this wage rate as given. He then hires workers up to the point where the value of marginal product equals the wage rate. In our case, it is 12 workers.

DERIVED DEMAND

Notice that this demand curve is *derived,* for the tape maker does not want to purchase the services of workers just for the services themselves. This is different than, say, a consumer's desire to buy his product. The product is bought because it will give satisfaction. Factors of production are rented or purchased not because they give satisfaction *per se,* but because they can be used to produce products which can be sold at a profit. The value of marginal product curve will shift whenever there is a change in the demand for the final product that the workers are making. If, for example, the market price of tapes goes down, the value of marginal product schedule will shift inward to

VMP′, as shown in Figure 9–2. If the market price of tapes goes up, the value of marginal product schedule will shift outward to the right to *VMP′′.* After all, we know that *VMP* equals *MP* times price. If price falls, so, too, does *VMP;* at the same going wage rate, our tape manufacturer will then require less workers. Conversely, if price rises, *VMP* will also rise, and our tape maker will demand more workers.

INPUT DEMAND CURVE FOR ALL FIRMS TAKEN TOGETHER

An individual firm's value of marginal product curve is also its demand schedule for the variable

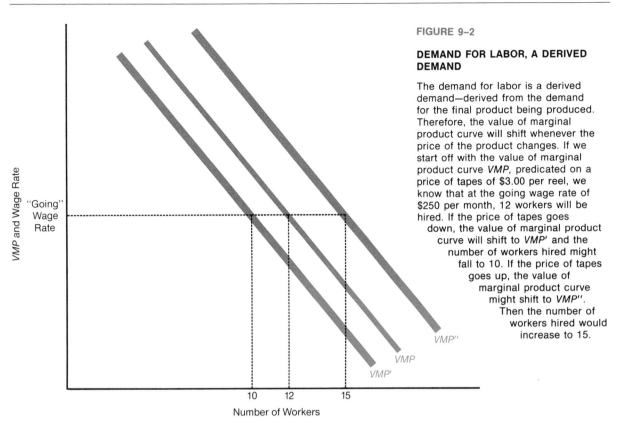

FIGURE 9–2

DEMAND FOR LABOR, A DERIVED DEMAND

The demand for labor is a derived demand—derived from the demand for the final product being produced. Therefore, the value of marginal product curve will shift whenever the price of the product changes. If we start off with the value of marginal product curve *VMP*, predicated on a price of tapes of $3.00 per reel, we know that at the going wage rate of $250 per month, 12 workers will be hired. If the price of tapes goes down, the value of marginal product curve will shift to *VMP'* and the number of workers hired might fall to 10. If the price of tapes goes up, the value of marginal product curve might shift to *VMP''*. Then the number of workers hired would increase to 15.

factor of production—in our example, labor. Is it possible to add up all of these separate business demand curves for labor and come up with a market demand curve for labor? The answer is no because one important aspect of the demand for input has been forgotten. We must remember that this is a derived demand. It is derived from the demand for the final product that is being produced. Therefore, if all firms together react to a reduction in the price of labor (the wage rate) by hiring more workers and producing more of the good, the only way *all firms combined* will be able to sell that increased production is by lowering the price. If the supply curve of the prerecorded tape industry shifts out to the right, the equilibrium price that will be established for

tapes will be lower than it was before. As we go from a wage rate of $4.00 an hour to $3.00 an hour in the tape industry, we cannot simply look at how many more workers each individual firm wants to hire, because then we would be *overestimating* their total demand for labor. As firms hire more workers and expand production, the price of tapes will start to fall. That will shift the value of marginal product curve inward to the left, which means that, for the tape industry as a whole, the increased employment will be less than we would have predicted by looking at the original *VMP* curves for each firm. *The price responsiveness for the market is less than the price responsiveness for each individual firm after there has been a price change in a factor of production.*

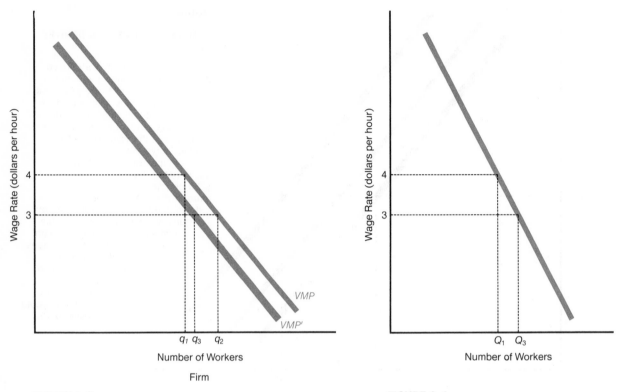

FIGURE 9–3

FIGURE 9–4

THE FIRM AND MARKET DEMAND CURVES FOR LABOR

In Figure 9–3 we draw the value of marginal product curve for the individual firm. They start off at *VMP*. The going wage rate is $4.00 per hour. The total quantity of workers demanded by the firm is therefore q_1. We add up all of the individual demands for workers at that wage rate and find it is equal to Q_1 in Figure 9–4. Now the wage rate falls to $3.00 per hour. The value of marginal product curve dictates that q_2 number of workers would be hired by the firm. But all firms do the same thing. Therefore, when they all increase production the price of the product has to fall in order for all the goods to be sold. This means that the value of marginal product curve will shift down to *VMP'*. At a wage rate of $3.00 per hour, the quantity of workers demanded will fall from q_2 to q_3 for the firm. We add up all of the q_3 quantities for all firms and find out that the market demand for labor at a price of $3.00 per hour is Q_3. Notice that the market demand curve for labor in Figure 9–4 is more elastic than the individual firm demand curve for labor in Figure 9–3.

We can see this in Figure 9–3. The original value of marginal product curve for the firm is *VMP*. At a wage rate of $4.00 an hour, it demands quantity q_1 of workers. Let's now add all the firms together and put their total demand for workers at a wage rate of $4.00 on the accompanying

graph in Figure 9–4. Total market demand for the quantity of workers is therefore Q_1. That means that at a wage rate of $4.00, the entire industry demands Q_1 workers.

Now we assume that the market wage rate falls to $3.00. On the original *VMP* curve our firm will demand q_2 workers. But, when it hires more workers, it produces more; so, too, do all the other firms in the industry. But all of this increased production cannot be sold without lowering the price of the product. Therefore, we have to draw a new *VMP* curve, which we will call *VMP'* and which is constructed using a *lower* price for the product. Now we see that the new equilibrium demand for workers by the firm is q_3 when the wage rate drops to $3.00 an hour. We find out all of the workers now demanded at this lower wage rate and plot it in Figure 9–4. It happens to be at quantity Q_3. Notice one important thing: *the market elasticity of demand for an input is smaller than the firm elasticity of demand for the same input at the market price for the input.*

Our hypothetical derived demand schedule for the variable input labor has been drawn with the assumption of a certain elasticity of demand for labor.

We really don't know the exact elasticity of the demand for labor, but there are a few rules of thumb that can be followed for a general idea. It is important to know labor demand elasticity if we want, for example, to forecast the employment (or unemployment) effects of a new union movement in a specific occupation. We should be aware of some of the determinants of this elasticity and not merely assume it is the same for all industries and for all types of inputs. A long time ago, a well-known economist named Alfred Marshall came up with some determinants of the elasticity of demand for an input. We will briefly go over them now.

DETERMINANTS OF DEMAND ELASTICITY FOR INPUTS

There are basically five determinants of the price elasticity of demand for an input.

1. The easier it is for a particular variable input to be substituted for by other inputs, the more price elastic the demand for that variable input will be.

2. The greater the price elasticity of demand for the final product, the greater the price elasticity of demand for the variable input.
3. The greater the price elasticity of supply of all other inputs, the greater the price elasticity of demand for a particular variable input.
4. The smaller the proportion of total costs accounted for by a particular variable input, the lower its price elasticity of demand.
5. A determinant which was not mentioned by Marshall is that the price elasticity of demand for a variable input will usually be larger in the long run than in the short run.

A Closer Look

Let's look at the first determinant. It seems obvious to expect that, if one particular input can be substituted very easily for another, then an increase in the price of one input will lead to greater use of the other input which did not go up in price. Look at an example where two inputs are equally useful and are equally productive in doing the same job. Sleeping bag manufacturers can use either plastic or metal zippers on their bags. Right now both types of zippers are equally usable, equally expensive, and are used, let's say, in equal proportions. For some reason, the price of plastic zippers rises by 20 percent. How many plastic zippers do you think the firm will use? Probably none; it will switch to metal zippers because they work just as well. On the other hand, thread is absolutely necessary for sewing the seams of the sleeping bags, and it cannot be substituted for by anything else. We would expect the elasticity of demand for thread to be very low indeed. A rise in its price would not lead to a very large decrease in quantity demanded because there are no other inputs which can be used instead.

The second determinant of factor demand elasticity is the elasticity of demand for the final product. This second determinant of input price elasticity is probably the easiest to understand since we have already seen that the demand for an input is a *derived* demand. Since it is derived from the demand for the final output, we would expect that the elasticity of the derived demand would mirror the elasticity of the demand for the final product.

Assume the elasticity of demand for electricity is very low. If the wages of skilled workers in the electricity industry are forced up by strong unions, the companies can pass on the wage increases to customers in the form of higher prices. But since the elasticity of demand for electricity is relatively low, customers will not reduce the quantity of electricity demanded by very much. The electricity companies will lay off very few workers. Thus we see that the low elasticity of demand for the final product leads to a low elasticity of demand for factors of production. The converse is also true.

The third determinant is the price elasticity of supply of other inputs. This determinant is probably somewhat less obvious. We know what the elasticity of supply of an input is all about: it is defined as percentage increase in the quantity supplied of an input which results from a 1 percent increase in the price of that input. Now think about the possibility of all other inputs having very high price elasticities of supply. That means a very small increase in their price will yield a very large increase in quantity supplied. If this is the case, then the demand for the variable input in question will be more price elastic than usual because the industry as a whole can obtain much more of all the other inputs by offering a slightly higher price. The competition from other inputs is therefore greater, and, hence, the price elasticity for the variable input under study must be relatively higher.

The fourth elasticity determinant is the proportion of total costs accounted for by the input under study. The fourth determinant merely points up the conclusion that if a factor of production accounts for only a very small part of the total cost of the product, any given price change will not affect total costs by much. Take the example of electricity as an input into manufacturing. On average, the cost of electricity accounts for less than 1 percent of the total cost of manufactured goods. Let's assume that it accounts for exactly 1 percent; let's say that electricity prices go up by 100 percent. This, however, would only add 1 percent to the total costs.

The fifth determinant concerns the difference between the short run and the long run. The long run is usually defined as the time period during which businessmen adjust to a change in their business environment. As pointed out previously, the longer time there is for adjustment, the more elastic the curves will be. This assertion holds for input demand curves as well. The longer the time allowed for adjustment to take place, the more responsive firms will be to a change in the price of a factor of production. Particularly in the long run, firms can reorganize their production process to minimize the use of a factor of production which has become more expensive relative to other factors of production.

WHAT HAPPENS WHEN THERE IS MORE THAN ONE VARIABLE INPUT?

We have developed a firm and a market demand curve for one factor of production. It was assumed that labor was the only factor of production which could be varied. However, we must be careful in situations where other factors of production can also be varied. Then we have to worry about the value of marginal product schedule shifting around. The use of more labor, for example, may involve the increased use of new machines which will in turn change the value of the marginal product of labor. There may be inputs used instead of labor, so that when labor is increased, their use will be decreased. Their value of marginal product curve will therefore go up, and the value of marginal product curve for labor will go down.

These interrelationships do not prevent us from deriving a fairly accurate demand schedule at the firm level for a particular variable input. We won't attempt to do so here because the arithmetic gets a little messy. Suffice it to say that the demand schedule at the firm level for a particular input will still continue to slope downward and to the right as we would expect.

MONOPOLY

Thus far, we've considered only a perfectly competitive situation, both in selling the final product and in buying factors of production. Now we'll consider other possibilities. One situation occurs when the firm buys factors of production in a competitive market but sells its product in a monopolistic situation. Remember that a monopolist faces a downward sloping demand curve for his product; thus, if he wants to sell more of his product, he will have to lower the price *not only on the last unit but on all preceding units*. The marginal revenue he receives from selling an additional unit is continuously falling as he attempts to sell more and more. Now, in reconstructing our demand schedule for an input, we must account for the facts that *(a)* the marginal *physical product* falls because of the law of diminishing

returns as more workers are added, and *(b)* the price received for the product sold also falls. We have to take account of both the diminishing marginal physical product and the diminishing marginal revenue. First, we shall redo Table 26-1, taking account of the fact that the per unit price of the final output falls.

In Table 9–2, we see that the change in total revenues gives us the **marginal revenue product** (MRP). This is what we wanted, for it gives the firm a quantitative notion of how valuable additional workers and additional production actually are. In Figure 9–5, the marginal revenue product curve has been plotted. Just as the *VMP* curve is the input demand curve for a competitor, the *MRP* curve is the input demand curve for a monopolist.

Why does the *MRP* curve represent the monopolist's input demand curve? It is because our profit-maximizing monopolist will continue to purchase workers as long as he can make profits. He makes profits as long as the additional cost of more workers is more than outweighed by the additional revenues from selling the output of those workers. When the wage rate just equals these additional revenues, he stops hiring. That is, he stops hiring when the wage rate is equal to the marginal revenue product.

TABLE 9–2

MARGINAL REVENUE PRODUCT

Here we show in column 1 the number of workers. In column 2 is the total product made, while column 3 shows the marginal *physical* product on the change in total product. Since we're looking at a monopolist, we notice that the price per unit in column 4 falls as more product is sold. Total revenues are given in column 5. Marginal revenue product of each new worker is presented in the last column. It is merely the change in total revenues, and it can become negative.

(1) NO. OF WORKERS	(2) TOTAL PRODUCT	(3) MARGINAL PRODUCT	(4) PRICE OF PRODUCT	(5) TOTAL REVENUES (2) × (4)	(6) MARGINAL REVENUE PRODUCT
11	5	5	$3.00	$15.00	$15.00
12	9	4	$2.00	$18.00	$ 3.00
13	12	3	$1.50	$18.00	$ 0.00
14	14	2	$1.00	$14.00	-$ 4.00

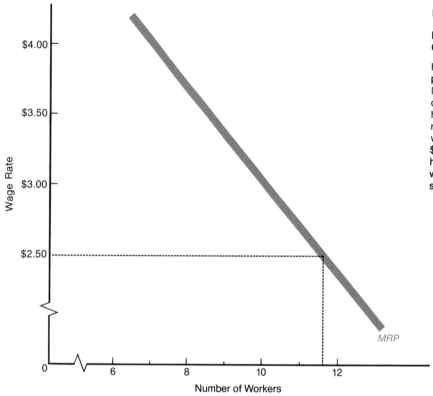

FIGURE 9–5

MARGINAL REVENUE PRODUCT CURVE

Here we plot the marginal revenue product from Table 9–2. It is labelled *MRP*. The monopolist decides how many workers to hire by hiring just enough to make marginal revenue product equal to the going wage rate. If the going wage rate is $2.50, the monopolist would want to hire somewhere between 11 and 12 workers. (How could he obtain the services of half a worker?)

MONOPSONY: A BUYER'S MONOPOLY

Having looked at the possibility of a monopoly in the selling of the final product, let's now go back to the assumption that the firm is a perfect competitor in the product market. Assume again that the firm cannot alter the price of the product it sells; it faces a horizontal demand curve for its product. However, we shall now assume that the firm buys a large proportion of a particular input. While this situation may not frequently occur, it is useful to consider. Let's think in terms of a "company town." There are numerous examples in the mining industry. One company not only hires the miners but also owns the businesses and hires the clerks, waiters, paymaster, and all other personnel. This buyer of labor is called a **monopsonist,** which is Greek for "single buyer."

Again, the monopolist faces a downward sloping demand curve. If he wants to sell more units, he has to lower the price on the last unit and on all of the other preceding ones. He therefore has to look at his marginal revenue curve to find out how much he gains by selling more units of his product. Now think in terms of the monopoly buyer—the monopsonist. He will face an *upward sloping supply curve.* The *market* supply curve has also generally been shown as upward sloping. Usually, however, firms don't face the market curve; they can buy all the workers they want at the going wage rate and thus usually face a fairly horizontal supply curve of factors of production.

FIGURE 9–6

MARGINAL FACTOR COST CURVE FOR A MONOPSONIST

The monopsonist demand curve for labor is his value of marginal product curve—assuming he's in a competitive product market. Since he is a monopsonist, he faces an upward sloping supply curve instead of a horizontal one as in the previous situation. He therefore knows that to hire more workers he has to pay higher wage rates. He looks at a marginal factor cost curve, *MFC*, which slopes up and which is above his supply curve, *SS*. He finds out how many workers to hire by seeing where his marginal factor cost just equals the value of marginal product. That is at point *E*. He therefore hires Q_m of workers and only has to pay them W_m in wages.

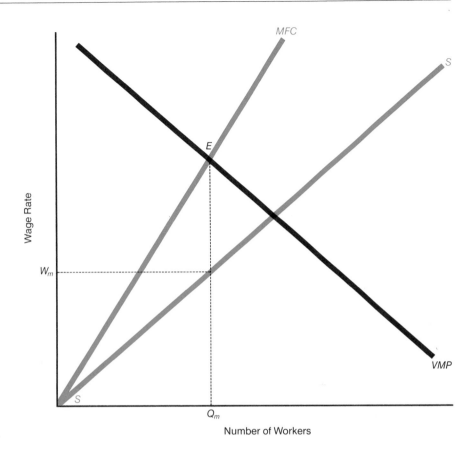

What if a firm does face an upward sloping supply curve? What does this mean to a monopsonist in terms of the costs of hiring extra workers? It means that if he wants to hire more workers, he has to offer higher wages. Only if he faces a horizontal supply curve would things be otherwise. Our monopsonist cannot hire all the labor he wants at the going wage rate. If he wants to hire 10 percent more workers, he may have to raise wages 3 percent. Not only does he have to raise wages to attract new workers, but he also has to raise the wages of all his current workers. He therefore has to take account of these increased costs when deciding how many more workers to hire.

Marginal Factor Costs

To find out how a monopsonist decides the number of workers to hire, we need to look at the supply and demand for labor. Let's first look at the supply curve of labor drawn in Figure 9–6. It slopes upward. We have also drawn another curve above the supply line. It is labeled **marginal factor cost** curve, or *MFC*. This means the curve is similar to a marginal revenue curve, only now it is for buying rather than selling. The *MFC* curve indicates the increased costs that are incurred when a monopsonistic firm wants to hire more of the variable input labor. It lies above the supply curve because whenever a monopsonist wishes to hire one more worker not only does he have to pay a higher wage to that worker but he also has to raise wages for all the other workers. The marginal factor cost for that last worker is, therefore, his wages plus the increase in all of the wages for all the other existing workers.

An Example

Let's take a simple example. Assume that our monopsonist has ten workers. He pays them each $100 a week. That means his total wage bill is $1000 per week. Let's say that, since he faces an upward sloping supply curve of labor, if he wants to hire one more worker, he has to pay that worker $101 in order to entice him to work. But he also has to pay more to all the other workers. They're not going to stand by and see a new worker make more than they do. Our monopsonist, therefore, has to pay them each $1.00 a week more. The increase in cost due to hiring one more worker is equal to his wage rate, $101, plus the increase in all the other wage rates, or $10 ($1.00 times 10). In this particular example, the marginal factor cost for hiring one more worker is equal to $101 plus $10, or $111 a week.

We still haven't found out how the monopsonist determines the number of workers he wants to hire. He does this by comparing his demand curve for labor with the marginal factor cost curve for labor. How does he get his demand curve? Since he is perfectly competitive in selling his product, his demand curve for labor is just the value of his marginal product curve. This is drawn as VMP in Figure 9–6. To decide how many workers to hire, our monopsonist looks at the intersection of the marginal factor cost curve and his demand curve for labor. This tells him how many workers to hire, for this is the point at which the marginal cost of hiring a worker is exactly equal to the value of the marginal product produced by that additional worker. The next question is: how much is our monopsonist going to pay these workers? In a normal situation, he would be faced with a given wage rate in the labor market. But since he is a monopsonist, he can

determine the wage rate himself.

Now that he has decided on the number of workers he wants to hire, the monopsonist sets the wage rate so that he will get exactly that quantity supplied to him by a captive labor force. We find that that wage rate is W_m.

There would be no reason for the monopsonist to pay the workers any more than W_m because, at that wage rate, he can get exactly the quantity he demands. The quantity he demands is established at the intersection of the marginal factor cost curve and his demand curve for labor—that is, at the point where the marginal revenue from expanding employment just equals the marginal cost of doing so.

ABUSING THE MONOPSONY MODEL

The monopsony model has been used as a justification for **minimum wages.** A minimum wage is a wage level legislated by states, cities, or the federal government. It is illegal for employers to pay their employees less than that wage. In Figure 9–7, the firm's demand for labor schedule has been drawn as its value of marginal product curve because we're considering that it is selling its product in a competitive market. We have also drawn in the supply curve of labor and the marginal factor cost curve that the monopsonist actually faces because he is the only buyer of that labor supply. If he wants to get more labor, he has to raise wages, not only for the additional workers but also for all the preceding ones. The marginal factor cost curve is always above the supply curve. The desired level of employment from the monopsonist's profit-maximizing point of view is at the intersection of the marginal factor cost curve and the value of marginal product curve. That is, the monopsonist will desire q_m number of workers. To get q_m number of workers, he only has to pay W_m.

Now suppose a minimum wage was established at W_r. We draw a horizontal line at W_r. It

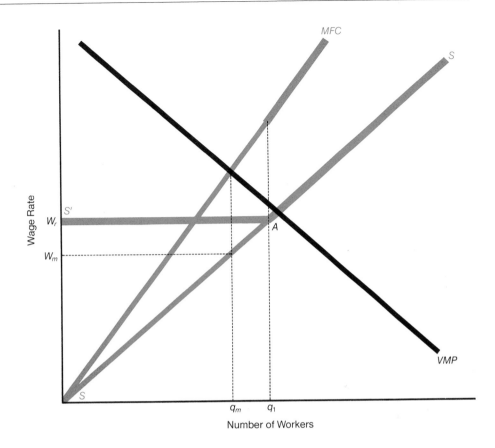

FIGURE 9-7

MINIMUM WAGES AND THE MONOPSONY MODEL

Here we assume there is a monopsonist. He looks at his marginal factor cost curve and in the absence of restrictions would hire q_m workers and pay them a wage rate of W_m. However, if minimum wages are set, it is possible that we can get the monopsonist to hire more workers at a higher wage rate. Assume that the minimum wage rate is set at W_r. What is the effective supply curve now? It is equal to the horizontal line from W_r until that line hits the old supply curve, SS. The new supply curve, then, is $S'S$. What is the marginal factor cost curve for this situation? For the horizontal part of the supply curve, the marginal factor cost curve is also equal to the horizontal line. But when the supply curve starts to slope up at point A, the marginal factor cost curve jumps up to its original line. We have shown that as the heavily shaded part of MFC. How many workers does the monopsonist hire in this minimum wage situation? He'll hire the number of workers that allows him to set marginal factor cost equal to value of marginal product. That's at q_1 where the marginal factor cost curve jumps up to its higher level. The minimum wage in this situation causes an increase in the quantity of workers hired from q_m to q_1.

will extend to and then merge with the supply curve. The monopsonist now faces a new supply curve, starting at W_r, moving horizontally until W_r hits the old supply curve, and then merging with the old curve. We have drawn it as $S'S$ in our graph.

What is his new marginal factor cost curve? It is also the horizontal portion of the new supply curve—that is, the horizontal portion at the minimum wage rate, W_r. When the minimum wage rate line hits the old supply curve, we're also back to the old marginal factor cost curve. The new marginal factor cost curve therefore jumps up to coincide with the old one; as can be seen, it is discontinuous.

How do we figure out what quantity of workers the monopsonist will demand when there is a minimum wage rate slapped on him that is higher than the wage rate he has been paying? Obviously, we're going to want to find out that point at which his marginal factor cost is just equal to the value of the marginal product of the additional workers. We find in Figure 9–7 that this happens to be where the new marginal factor cost curve—the horizontal line at P_m—jumps up to meet the old marginal factor cost curve. This is where marginal revenue equals marginal cost in hiring workers. Employment will now expand from the original level of q_m to q_1. Here is a situation where a rise in wages results in an increase in employment, contrary to the normal situation. The imposition of a minimum wage rate will cause employment to expand. It will benefit workers, not only those who already have a job, but others who will be hired.

The monopsony argument for minimum wages might, in special circumstances, apply to a company town. However, it is difficult to imagine that a sufficient percentage of the labor force would actually be employed in a company town so that an increase in minimum wages throughout the nation would cause an increase in employment. Even if we take a very broad definition of what a company town is, we find that the fraction of the labor force employed in a monopsonistic situation is very small indeed. For example, one researcher found that the fraction of counties in the United States where the 30 largest firms employed 50 percent of the labor force was extremely small.

Moreover, the minimum wage applies to the lowest paid, least skilled workers in our economy. All other workers are making wages well above the minimum. It is equally hard to imagine that any firms actually have to offer higher than the going wage rate to get more unskilled workers. Hence, the firms affected by the minimum wage law could hardly be considered monopsonists.

Another important objection to the monopsony argument in favor of minimum wages is the assumption that employers will not be able to discriminate among workers. The argument assumes that employers will have to raise wages to all workers. Given the ingenuity of entrepreneurs, one could imagine that minimum wages as applied to most monopsonists (in fact, if there are any) would not greatly affect the overall wage rates paid to the monopsonist's workers.

BILATERAL MONOPOLY

Now let's assume that in the labor market we have a single seller selling to a single buyer. In other words, we have a monopolistic seller of labor (one that can exert an influence over wage rates) facing a monopsonistic employer (one who can also affect wage rates). This is an extreme example, but it occurs quite often. For example, the major league baseball club owners confronted the major league Baseball Players Association in the spring of 1972, and we had a bilateral monopoly situation. Often, large industrial unions will meet large industrial employers, and, again, we have a bilateral monopoly situation.

The bilateral monopoly is depicted in Figure 9–8. The monopolistic employer faces an upward sloping supply curve of labor. He therefore looks at his marginal factor cost curve which is above his supply curve in order to determine how many workers he wants to hire. The intersection of his demand curve for labor, which is his marginal revenue product curve, is at Q_m. He would therefore like to hire Q_m workers and pay them just

FIGURE 9-8

BILATERAL MONOPOLY IN THE LABOR MARKET

Here we show a monopsonist buying labor from a monopolistic seller of labor. The monopsonist might be a big company, and the monopolist seller of labor might be a union. The monopsonist wants to hire Q_m workers where the marginal factor cost curve intersects the marginal revenue product curve. He would like to pay a wage rate of W_m. However, the union wants to set a wage rate of W_u, where the wage rate is just equal to the marginal revenue product. The solution here is logically indeterminate. Bargaining will, however, lead to an intermediate solution with the wage rate between W_u and W_m and the quantity of workers hired probably greater than Q_m.

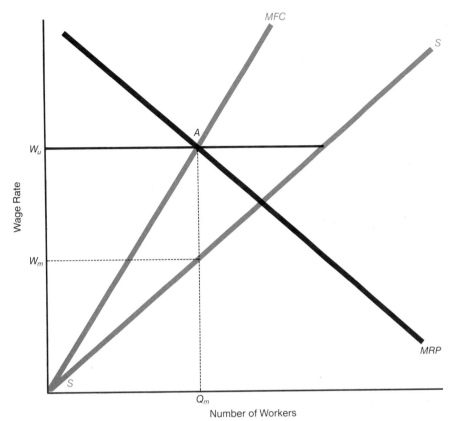

enough so that they're willing to work. That wage rate would be W_m. On the other hand, the monopolistic seller of labor, say a strong union, would presumably like to have a much higher wage rate. For example, the monopolistic seller would like to establish a wage rate at W_u where the marginal factor cost curve intersects the marginal revenue product curve. The union would like to extract all of the money possible from the monopsonistic employer. Therefore, it would want a wage rate just equal to the marginal revenue product of its workers. The outcome of the bilateral monopoly situation is logically indeterminate.

We should point out, however, that if the monopsonistic employer were completely successful, the quantity of workers hired would be Q_m. If the union were completely successful, the quantity of workers would also be Q_m. We know, therefore, that the outcome of bargaining will result in a higher level of employment. This is somewhat the argument of countervailing power, where the union countervails the power of the monopsonistic employer. The result may be closer to a competitive wage rate, W_c, and a competitive quantity of producers utilized, Q_c, than in either of the extreme cases where one or the other side of the bargaining table has complete monopoly power.

Definition of New Terms

MARGINAL PRODUCT: the output that an additional worker is responsible for. The marginal product of the worker is equal to change in total output that can be accounted for by hiring him, holding all other factors of production constant.

PRODUCTIVITY: usually defined as the worker's marginal product.

VALUE OF MARGINAL PRODUCT: the marginal product times the price at which the product can be sold in a competitive market.

DERIVED DEMAND: demand derived from the final product being produced.

MARGINAL REVENUE PRODUCT: the marginal product times the marginal revenue.

MONOPSONIST: single buyer.

MARGINAL FACTOR COST: the cost of using more of a factor; that is, the additional cost of using a factor.

MINIMUM WAGE: a legal minimum wage rate below which employers cannot pay workers.

BILATERAL MONOPOLY: in the labor market, a situation where a single seller of labor confronts a single buyer or monopsonist.

Chapter Summary

1. In a competitive situation where the firm is a very small part of the entire product and labor market, the firm will want to hire workers up to the point where the value of their marginal product just equals their going wage rate.

2. In such a situation, the value of marginal product curve for the individual firm is equal to the firm's demand curve for labor. However, the summation of all the value of marginal product curves does not equal the market demand curve for labor. The market demand curve for labor is less elastic because of the fact that as more workers are hired, output is increased and the price of the product must fall, thereby lowering the value of marginal product.

3. The demand for labor is a derived demand, derived from the demand for the product produced.

4. The elasticity of demand for an input is a function of several very obvious determinants including the elasticity of demand for the final product and the elasticity of supply of other factors of production. Moreover, the price elasticity of demand for a variable input will usually be larger in the long run than it is in the short run because there is time for adjustment.

5. In a monopoly situation, the demand curve for labor is no longer the value of marginal product curve, but is the marginal revenue product curve which is derived from the marginal physical product of workers times the marginal revenue. It slopes down, just like the value of marginal product curve, but is usually steeper.

6. In a situation where there is only one buyer of a particular input, a monopsony arises. The single buyer faces an upward sloping supply curve and therefore must pay higher wages to get more workers to work. He faces a marginal factor cost curve which is upward sloping and above his supply curve. He would hire workers up to the point where the value of marginal product equals the marginal factor cost. Then he would find out how low a wage rate he could pay in order to get that many workers.

7. Often the monopsony model is used to justify a minimum wage, which in the situation of monopsony will result in greater employment at higher wages.

Questions for Thought and Discussion

1. Unions want to raise wages. Does the theory developed in this chapter tell us anything about the possible employment effects of "excessive" wage increases?

2. Since the demand curve for labor is the value of marginal product curve in a competitive situation, more workers would be hired if the value of marginal product curve shifted to the right. This can be accomplished by either raising the marginal product or increasing the price of the product sold. How can workers help in shifting the *VMP* curve to the right?

3. Many businessmen maintain that they have no idea what the value of marginal product is for their workers, that they just hire their workers at the going wage rate and hire as many as they "need." How can you reconcile the theoretical presentation in this chapter with what businessmen say they do?

4. Look back at the five determinants of the price elasticity of demand for inputs. After reviewing them, figure out where you would want to unionize—that is, where you would think unionization could have the most effect.

5. Look at the outcome of some bilateral monopoly situations. Can you tell who had the better hand?

6. The minimum wage law has been called "the most anti-Negro law on the books." Why? Discuss.

Selected References

Cartter, Allan M., & Marshall, F. Ray. *Labor Economics: Wages, Employment, and Trade Unionism.* Rev. Ed. Homewood, Illinois: Richard D. Irwin, 1972.

Galenson, Walter. *A Primer on Employment and Wages.* 2nd Ed. New York: Random House, 1970.

Rees, Albert. *Economics of Trade Unions.* Chicago: University of Chicago Press, 1962.

ISSUE IX

Monopoly and Monopsony in Sports

Fighting the System

"A salesman can shift from one company to another but an athlete is bound in slavery." Such were the words of basketball superstar Spencer Haywood who, at 20, became the youngest player in professional basketball. In 1971 Mr. Haywood was involved in a suit against the National Basketball Association (NBA). That association said that he could not play in the NBA until the following season because the class with which Mr. Haywood had entered college had not yet graduated. This is the so-called "four-year rule" that professional basketball leagues have imposed upon their member teams. No member teams are supposed to take young basketball stars out of college. Therefore, they are not allowed to let them play until four years after they enter college, even though the players may already have quit school. Mr. Haywood countered the NBA's ruling with a $6 million antitrust suit. In 1970 baseball star Curt Flood filed an antitrust suit against professional baseball leagues. He argued that the so-called "reserve clause," which binds players to work ex-clusively for the teams which own their contracts, was in violation of antitrust legislation.

Do the rules of the game justify Spencer Haywood's contention that players are bound in slavery? Is there any reason to think that antitrust action should be applied to professional leagues? Does the reserve clause effectively limit the wages that professional players receive? These and other questions will be answered in this issue. We will be able to apply the monopsony and monopoly models introduced in previous chapters.

Unrestricted Labor Market

To fully understand the effect of, say, the reserve clause, we should review how a labor market works when there are no restrictions.

"*He earns one million dollars, and you're excited!*"

DRAWING BY RICHTER; © 1971
THE NEW YORKER MAGAZINE, INC.

Let's take the example of an unrestricted market for babysitters. Suppose one babysitter charges considerably less than the "going" price for babysitting. She will soon find that there are many new requests for her services. If she is not willing to put extra hours into babysitting, she will have to decide *(a)* to refuse the additional work, or *(b)* to raise her prices so that certain customers, present or potential, will not be interested in obtaining her services. On the other hand, a babysitter who wants work is free to lower her price. In short, babysitters can compete among themselves to maximize their own individual income. Not all babysitters may do this, but those *on the margin* do.

Coping with Excess Demand

Let's assume that a particular babysitter gains a reputation for being not only responsible but also a real charmer with children. Since she will have a full schedule, a customer might have to offer some incentive to gain her services on a regular basis. She might be persuaded to either work longer hours or drop one of her former customers.

The usual form of inducement is higher wages, although incentive might come in some non-monetary form. In any case, people who employ such tactics are competing among themselves to

obtain a babysitter. Although not all people may do this, again those *on the margin* do.

We have just described the workings of a competitive market in babysitting. The babysitters are free to vary their price and hours and customers are free to vary the price (wage) offered and the quantity of service demanded. Theoretically, babysitters end up getting the wage that just equals the value of their services. That is, *they are paid the value of their marginal product*. Buyers of babysitting services end up paying for the opportunity cost of those services—no more, no less. They pay the value of the babysitter's marginal product.

Restricting the Market

What would happen if all families in an area decided to institute a "babysitters reserve clause?" The reserve clause would require each babysitter to work for only one family or one group of families. The babysitter could not work elsewhere unless the owner of her contract decided that he wanted to sell or trade the contract. Now one crucial aspect of the competitive market has been eliminated: babysitters cannot seek out the most advantageous job opportunities or compete for business. Certainly, such restraint might prevent babysitters from maximizing their own income. This reserve clause could leave the sit-

ters worse off than they would have been with freely competitive conditions.

Collusion

If all of the families in an area formed a cartel—that is, if these families colluded and agreed not to compete among themselves—one could be fairly certain that the babysitters would be paid less than the value of their marginal product. They would be exploited by the *monopsony* power of the families. The group of families would represent the single buyer of babysitter services. Competition in the babysitting market would be stifled on both sides: among the sellers and among the buyers of babysitting services. Of course, it is difficult to imagine that such a cartel would actually work. The incentive to cheat in a cartel arrangement is extremely great. There would also be a problem of how to take care of new families that moved into the area.

The Baseball Market

The pure folly presented in the above discussion becomes stern reality in the world of baseball. Before signing initially with a major league team, a baseball player obviously owns his own baseball talent. He has the right to offer his services for sale to any ball club he wants. However, once he signs with a major league club, he can no longer negotiate for the sale of his services with any other club in the league in which he plays or in a competitive league. He does, nonetheless, have the right to refuse to play. So in that sense, the reserve clause does not lead to complete slavery.

Reserve Clause

The **reserve clause** is written into every contract that is ever given to a baseball player. It requires that any major league club which wishes to acquire the services of another major league club's player must purchase his contract from the current owner. In this sense, once the player has signed a contract with a major league team, he has signed away part of the rights to his own baseball talents. The club owning the player's contract can reserve the player for its own use even though other teams might be willing to pay that particular player more than he is actually receiving.

Drafts

The reserve clause is coupled with a system of **drafts.** When baseball teams want to hire fresh college stars, they do not compete among themselves for the right to use the services of individual players. Rather, they use a draft system.

The worst team in each league is given the first choice. Obviously, the first choice will be for the best college baseball players. The next worst team has second choice; the third worst team has third choice, and so on. The key provision of the draft system is that no team can bargain with a player who has been drafted by another team. Therefore, the draft system, coupled with the reserve clause, eliminates the possibility that two or more teams would bid for the same star athlete. Apparently, much of the player's bargaining power is reduced.

"Need" for Restrictions?

What is the reasoning behind such a system of purchasing players' talents? If you ask people in the leagues, they maintain that the reserve clause and the draft system are "reasonable and necessary" to maintain the stability of the game. This is exactly how Federal Judge Irving Ben Cooper ruled in the summer of 1970 when he was reviewing Curt Flood's antitrust suit against baseball. Presumably the wealthiest clubs would be able to hire all the best players. Therefore, baseball teams contend that the reserve clause is essential for the game because it allows for an even distribution of good players among all teams. If the draft and reserve clause system were disallowed, the richer

teams would bid away the best talent, games would be lopsided, bored spectators would quit buying tickets, and poor teams would become even poorer.

Although this argument sounds plausible at first glance, it does not hold up for two reasons. First, look at any industry. Do we find rich firms buying up all of the best workers and thus making the manufacturing game lopsided? Hardly. Firms, and baseball clubs too, can always borrow money to invest in good workers and good players if the potential payoff from doing so is high enough. Obviously, if only one good (rich) team existed, the payoff from building a competing good team would be high enough to allow a club to borrow money (or sell additional stock) in order to do so.

Second, it is in the best interest of all teams that there be a fairly even distribution of good players among them. How much gate attendance do you think the L.A. Dodgers would have if they bought all of the best players and, therefore, won every single game of every season? Certainly, the attendance would be poor. Why would anybody want to go see the supercompetent L.A. Dodgers trounce all of the crummier teams? There would be no suspense; the game would be won even before it started. It would, therefore, be in the best interest of the L.A. Dodgers to allow other

teams to bid away some of its better players. The owners of the L.A. Dodgers would maximize their wealth position if they allowed other teams to get better so that game results would not be foregone conclusions. Gate attendance would, therefore, rise.

Is the Distribution of Good Players Altered?

The question that we should be asking is whether the reserve clause actually changes the distribution of good players among teams. If it doesn't change the distribution of players among teams, then we must seriously doubt the contention that the clause is necessary. We will find that no matter who owns a player's contract—whether he owns it or his team owns it—the distribution of players among teams will remain the same.

The easiest way to see why is to consider two examples. To start off, assume that there is no reserve clause in existence. We have a player who is receiving a wage rate of $20,000 a year from the Dodgers. The Giants decide to offer him $21,000 a year. If $21,000 is more than the value of this player to the Dodgers, they will not increase his salary; they will allow the Giants to bid him away. If, on the other hand, his services to the Dodgers are worth more than $21,000, he will be extended a counteroffer large enough to make him stay in Los Angeles. Then, when there is no reserve clause, the player will end up playing for the club that most highly values his services.

Now let's take an example where the reserve clause is in effect. Assume the same player is working for the same salary with the Dodgers. The Giants decide to offer the Dodgers $1000 a year for this player's contract. If negotiations succeed, the Giants will end up paying $21,000 a year for the player, of which $20,000 is actually paid to the player under the original contract and $1000 is paid to the Dodgers. If the $1000 per annum exceeds the player's net value to the Dodgers after paying his $20,000 a year salary, then it will be in the Dodgers' best interest to sell his contract to the Giants. On the other hand, if this particular player is worth more to the Dodgers than $21,000, which is equal to the $1000 offer from the Giants plus this player's $20,000 salary, it will refuse to sell his contract.

We see, surprisingly enough, that, when subject to the reserve clause, the condition under which this player will be transferred to the Giants is exactly the condition under which he will decide himself to transfer to the Giants when not subject to the reserve clause. He transfers to the Giants if the Giants find his services more valuable than the Dodgers *whether or not the reserve clause is effective.* We must conclude that the reserve clause does not cause a different distribution of players among teams than would obtain

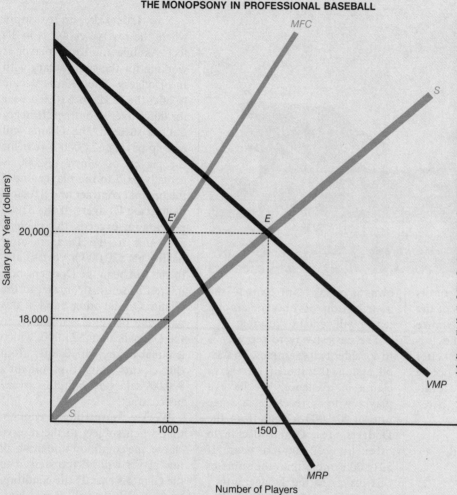

THE MONOPSONY IN PROFESSIONAL BASEBALL

FIGURE IX-1

Here we represent the number of players in the entire baseball industry on the horizontal axis and the salary per year on the vertical axis. The demand curve for players is represented by the marginal revenue product curve, *MRP,* because the baseball club owners have banded together to form a monopoly. These baseball club owners face an upward sloping supply curve, *SS,* and therefore look at their marginal factor cost curve, *MFC.* They decide how many players to hire at the intersection, *E',* where the marginal factor cost curve and the marginal revenue product curve intersect. They hire 1000 players and pay them a salary of $18,000 per year. In an unrestricted or competitive situation, the equilibrium intersection would be at *E* with 1500 players working for an average salary of $25,000 per year.

otherwise. This is a surprising result, indeed, but it does serve to discredit the absurd allegations of baseball club owners. The reason they want to keep the reserve clause is so that they will be the ones, rather than the players themselves, who reap the benefits of exceptional players' services.

Monopsony Needs Monopoly

This is a classic monopsony situation. However, the only way it can persist is for there to be some sort of monopoly in the baseball business. After all, competition among teams would cause the starting salaries of players to go up. For a while "side payments" or bonuses were paid to new players. But then the draft system was inaugurated under which no such payments are allowed. The impact of the reserve clause on players' salaries was, for quite a time, augmented by the effects of a compact between the National and American Leagues *not* to compete for each other's players. Such an arrangement would obviously suggest a potential for a third league to bid the best players away from the other two by offering higher salaries. However, no third U.S. league could have succeeded because players who might have signed with it would be barred forever from the American and National Leagues. Apparently not enough players are willing to take this chance and no other major league appeared.

The reason that baseball can get away with such obvious restraints of trade is because Supreme Court Justice Oliver Wendell Holmes wrote a decision in 1922 which said that pro baseball was outside the scope of federal antitrust laws. The decision pointed out that baseball games were not trade or commerce in the accepted uses of these words. He supposed that Congress had not intended to subject baseball to antitrust regulation. He went on to say that baseball exhibitions were purely local affairs to which the interstate transportation of players was merely incidental. Again in 1953 the Supreme Court reviewed the antitrust implications of baseball's restraints of trade. Then it did not even examine the underlying issue

of interstate commerce; instead, it reaffirmed Holmes' earlier decision. The Court stated: "That decision determines that Congress had no intention of including the business of baseball within the scope of the federal antitrust laws."

There is no doubt today that baseball is big business. By the beginning of the 1970s, there were 30 million baseball fans paying over $80 million to watch their favorite team struggle. In their homes, hundreds of millions of people watched or listened to the games. The major networks paid almost $40 million for exclusive broadcast rights, and total baseball revenues exceeded $130 million per year. It was estimated that the total value of all the team franchises exceeded $200 million, or about $8.5 million per team. The case of the Seattle Pilots illustrates how large the monopoly profits can get. The Pilots were brought to Seattle for a price of $5.5 million. That included the contracts on 30 players and the franchise itself. Only one year later, the Seattle Pilots were sold for almost $11 million.

Graphic Analysis

The professional baseball world fits very nicely into the monopsony model developed previously. We can show how much the players are losing by the monopo-

lization and consequent ability of the clubs to act as monopsonists in the hiring of baseball players. Look at Figure IX–1. Here we have drawn the value of marginal product curve for all baseball players, but we are assuming that the teams have banded together to form a cartel arrangement sanctioned by the Supreme Court rulings. Therefore, the teams will look at their marginal revenue product curve, MRP, and not their VMP curve. We've also drawn the supply curve of baseball players, but that is not what the teams will look at. They will look at the marginal factor cost curve, MFC. They're acting as monopsonists. A competitive situation would find us at point E. Here the players would obtain a salary of, say, $25,000 apiece on average, and there would be, perhaps, 1500 professional players. However, the equilibrium wage rate is established by the baseball monopoly first equating the marginal revenue product with the marginal input expenditure point E'. That determines the quantity of players demanded. Then the teams figure out how much they have to pay to get that quantity. We'll say they happen to pay $18,000. Therefore, we see that the monopolist clubs end up paying their players less than they would in a competitive situation; likewise, they also end up employing fewer players than they would in a competitive situation.

Football Too

Football isn't much different from baseball. There is a draft system which Senator Sam J. Ervin, Jr. of North Carolina once equated with arrangements that "are comparable to the newspaper profession deciding that a college journalism graduate could either work for the newspaper in Anchorage, Alaska, at the salary offered or not work at all." From 1919 to 1960, there was only one professional football league, the National Football League (NFL). Then, in 1960 the American Football League (AFL) appeared on the scene. As you might have expected, the players' salaries promptly skyrocketed. Bonuses were being offered in astronomical sums to get college superstars to play in the competing AFL. Competition among the AFL and NFL destroyed any monopsony power that the NFL once had. When the NFL ruled the scene, teams could only "draft" players and that was it. No competition by way of larger salary offers was allowed.

Finally, after six years of "competition" the AFL and NFL decided to merge. The way the merger was obtained showed the astute political capability of the football league commissioner "Pete" Rozelle and the league owners. Remember that only baseball was exempt from antitrust legislation—football was not. In order to get legislation around the House Antitrust and Monopoly Subcommittee, a bill allowing the merger between the AFL and NFL was tacked on as a rider to an investment tax bill—a strategic move worked out by Representative Hale Boggs, a Democrat from Louisiana.* Senator Ervin said of that legislation the unavoidable conclusion was that the measure was railroaded through the Congress. The AFL-NFL merger, by precluding the need to compete for players, has obviously held the salary of players lower than they would have been under freely competitive conditions.

Finally Basketball

In late 1971 there were hearings in the Congress as to whether the two professional basketball leagues should be allowed to merge. For 22 years basketball had only one professional league —the National Basketball Association (NBA). Then, in 1967 the American Basketball Association (ABA) was formed. Not surprisingly, until that time, basketball players were getting the lowest pay of all professional team athletes. A reserve clause exists in basketball but it was only effective as long as the National Basketball Association was unchallenged. When the ABA was formed, players' salaries skyrocketed. Then, when the ABA and the NBA attempted to merge, a temporary injunction against the merger was granted to the NBA Players' Association. By the time you read this book, legislation may have been passed to allow these two professional leagues to merge and become one. They will then have a common draft; no bonuses will be allowed; and basketball players can be assured that they will be exploited by the monopolist club owners. Players will be paid a monopsony price instead of a competitive price for their services.

The attempt at a merger came about after one of the most expensive battles for bodies ever to occur in the history of the ABA and NBA. In late spring of 1971, ABA club owners were going after the draft choices of NBA club owners; NBA club owners were going after draft choices of ABA club owners. Some seven-foot college stars were reportedly being offered in excess of $2 million from competing clubs. The draft system was falling apart because of the competition between the two leagues, but the players didn't

---

*Curiously enough, New Orleans got a new franchise that year and was also the site of the Superbowl.

mind at all. That was the time when the four-year rule was first violated. The four-year rule essentially assures the collegiate teams that none of their superstars will be bid away by more wealthy professional clubs. The rule essentially allows a "farm" system to be used that is very inexpensive for the professional clubs. Actually, it costs them no out-of-pocket expenses at all. In addition, the colleges are certainly happy about the four-year rule because, no matter how good a player becomes, he cannot be bid away by professional teams.

The example of the disruption within the professional basketball leagues demonstrates the necessity of a monopoly being instituted in order for a *monopsony* price to be paid to professional players. This is true whether it is in basketball, football, or baseball. If there is no monopoly where rules can be enforced against competitive bidding for valuable players, competing teams will use all sorts of methods to get the best players.

Conclusion

Professional sports are big businesses; they are owned by men who have invested large sums of money and who wish to make profits on their investments. Many onlookers maintain that there is nothing wrong with professional sports clubs being business concerns, but these onlookers feel that sports should operate under the same laws as other businesses. The trustbusters have taken on professional sports to that end. Senator Warren G. Magnuson of Washington introduced for several consecutive years a bill which would include baseball under the Sherman Antitrust Act. Senator Sam Erwin and Representative Emanuel Celler of New York introduced identical bills in the Senate and the House which would strip professional basketball and professional football of their antitrust exemptions. It appears that the time may be ripe for introducing more competition into professional spectator sports. Whether you think that is "good" or "bad" must ultimately depend upon your particular value judgment. The distribution of players among competing clubs will not change, as we explained above. However, the distribution of total earnings from the game of baseball will change: the players will get higher salaries and the clubowners will get smaller profits.

Definition of New Terms

RESERVE CLAUSE: a clause in the contract of a professional athlete which essentially transfers the ownership of his playing talents to the first club which hired him. He is reserved to them and cannot change unless they want to allow him to change. They can trade him just like any other asset they own.

DRAFT: a system of choosing new players for professional teams. In a draft system teams are not allowed to bid for the best players by offering higher amounts of money. Rather, they draft players in a peculiar sequence. The worst teams are allowed to have the first choice.

Questions for Thought and Discussion

1. Some baseball players support the reserve clause. They maintain that if it did not exist, competition among teams would drive salaries so high that many teams would go out of business. If this reasoning is correct, which kind of players should support the reserve clause: the best ones or the worst ones?
2. Do you think that professional sports should be exempt from antitrust laws? Why?
3. Professional teams have agreed not to seduce college stars away from college until four years after they enter. Why do you think professional teams agree to this? (Hint: What services are colleges providing professional teams?)
4. A few college players have started to go to work for Canadian teams. What are the implications for the future of professional sports in the United States?

Selected Reference

Rottenberg, Simon. "The Baseball Players' Labor Market." *Journal of Political Economy,* June 1956.

ISSUE X

Who Pays the True Cost of the Military?

The Draft

Various forms of military involuntary servitude have existed throughout the history of the United States. The military draft was with us for almost two centuries, being first used during the War for Independence. In 1777, the colonies of Virginia and Massachusetts used conscription. In February of the following year the benign Congress recommended that the other colonies follow suit. However, France was kind enough to send us troops and therefore it was unnecessary for a general draft to be instituted. In April of 1862 the Confederacy started universal conscription, and by 1863 the North was required to pass the Enrollment Bill.

The Civil War

Things were different, though, at least in principle, during the Civil War. Anybody who was drafted could "buy" someone else to go in his place. The method of conscription was arbitrary, but the final determination of exactly who would go to war was somewhat more flexible. A doctor who was drafted had the option of paying off someone else to replace him. Presumably, if the going price for replacements was below the doctor's opportunity cost as a civilian, he would profit from such a transaction and would therefore find someone to go in his place. Many arrangements of this sort were negotiated. There were, as today, many workers who did not earn as much as a doctor could; their opportunity cost being lower than the doctor's, such persons might agree to be replacements for a certain price. Quite understandably, there were relatively few doctors, lawyers, or other highly paid civilian employees fighting in the Civil War. During Vietnam, it was possible to buy one's way out of the draft, but the price was relatively high: one could either go to jail or escape to Canada. Most likely, the implicit cost involved in choosing one of these two alternatives exceeded the price it would have taken to induce someone else to go in one's place.

Allocation Efficiency

Since a person's contribution to the economy can be roughly indicated by his salary (presumably workers are paid the value of their marginal product), when conscripted men were allowed to pay someone else to go in their place during the Civil War, a more *ef-*

"*For heaven's sake, you'll get your appropriation, General! But first we have to go through our deliberations, don't we?*"

ficient allocation of resources resulted. Men who were highly paid in civilian occupations stayed in those jobs; men whose value of marginal product was lower found it more advantageous to stay in the army or offer to replace someone else. Men worked or fought where their services were of most value in economic terms. By doing so, they maximized the value of economic output. Efficient allocation of resources means maximizing the value of economic output obtained from a given amount of inputs.

From Inefficient to Efficient Allocation

We can look at efficiency in another way. Inefficiency exists whenever machines and men are being used in such a manner that their full potential for contributing to the output of the economy is not being realized. We know, then, that a change from an inefficient to an efficient allocation of resources results by definition in an increase in output. However, this increase in output does not mean that everybody will be better off when moving from an inefficient to an efficient solution. We know that all changes in the economy carry with them certain costs. Those who incur these costs are worse off. In theory, though, the increase in output made possible by going from an inefficient to an

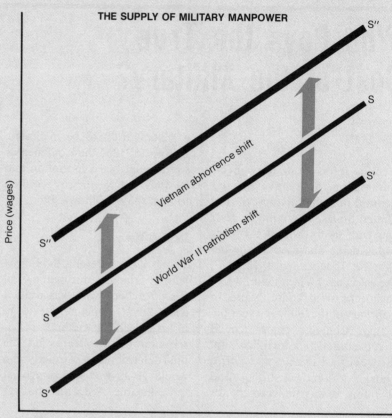

FIGURE X-1

The supply curve of military manpower slopes up and to the right as depicted by *SS*. There may be shifts in the supply curve in times of extreme patriotism such as during the World War II that might have shifted down to *S'S'*. However, at other times such as during Vietnam and Indochina, it might have shifted up to *S"S"*.

efficient solution allows those who bear the costs of the change to be fully compensated. It is difficult to imagine, however, that sufficient institutional mechanisms exist that can actually carry out the "side payments" distribution problem.

The Supply Curve of Military Men

We should be able to derive a typical supply curve for military men in the same manner we would derive a supply curve for any other factor of production. In this particular case, we presume there are three types of workers in our economy. The first type can really get into the military scene. They are men who like the discipline and the structure of the Army. Army life would appeal to them. At one time or another, you have probably met people of this temperament. These people would be willing to go in the Army at exactly the same pay (or less!) that they could make in a similar civilian occupation. After all, the Army offers to them *psychic* returns that they cannot receive outside of the military establishment.

The second type of worker is one who has the opposite temperament: he does not like the idea of the strict military life. He must be compensated for going into the Army; he therefore would require a premium over and above what he can make as a civilian, if he were to join the Army.

The third type of person is the one whose moral or religious convictions prevent him from ever joining or participating in the military machine. He apparently would not join the Army at any price, although this is a pretty drastic statement. In any event, the premium that would have to be paid for him would be outrageous and probably not worth it to the Army machine.

We find, therefore, that the supply curve SS of military men is upward sloping as we have shown in Figure X–1. This is a fairly realistic representation of what the military machine faces when it wants to obtain the services of potential workers. The supply curve could, of course, shift around in time of national emergency. One would expect that patriotism would have caused the supply curve to shift down and to the right to $S'S'$ during World War II. We might hypothesize that the supply curve would have shifted up and to the left to $S''S''$ during Vietnam and Indochina. For the moment, though, let us assume that the supply curve is

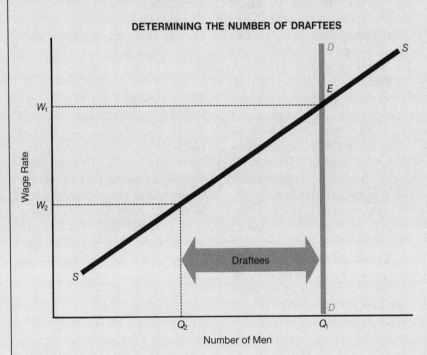

DETERMINING THE NUMBER OF DRAFTEES

FIGURE X–2

Given a particular supply curve, SS, the military may decide that it demands or it "needs" a specific number of military men. We draw the demand curve as DD, a vertical line at the quantity Q_1. If it offers a zero wage rate, then it has to draft the entire amount, Q_1. If it offers a wage rate of W_1, then it will have to draft no one for it will be paying the equilibrium wage rate. If it establishes a wage rate of W_2, then it must draft the difference between Q_1 and Q_2.

stable and does not move. What, then, do we know about the demand for military men?

The Demand for Soldiers and the Need to Draft

How can we characterize the demand curve for military men? Let's assume for the moment that the leaders in the Pentagon merely decide how many men they "must" have. We therefore put in a vertical demand curve *DD* in Figure X–2. The quantity demanded is Q_1. The intersection of the demand curve with the supply curve is at a wage rate of W_1. If the Army decides to set wages at zero, then the necessary amount of men that have to be drafted is obviously equal to the full quantity demanded, or Q_1. However, we know that the government is more magnanimous than that; in the past, it has set a wage rate in excess of zero. Let's say it sets a wage rate of W_2. The quantity supplied at that wage rate—that is, the number of volunteers—will equal Q_2. The difference between Q_1 and Q_2 is the quantity of men who must be drafted, the quantity of men who will enter into the military's form of involuntary servitude. They, however, will be partly compensated because they will be paid something, even though it is obviously much less than necessary

to induce them to volunteer. If the Army were willing to pay W_1, it would get just the number of men it needed.

The case against a draft as compared to an all volunteer Army involves a number of economic arguments concerning the costs of the draft. We are now well equipped to analyze them. So let's go through some of these cost arguments. They involve costs that often go unnoticed and frequently aren't mentioned by Pentagon officials.

The Unnoticed Costs of Involuntary Conscription

Let's simplify our assumption somewhat and be quite unrealistic. We'll assume that the Army is run as if it were a business and talk about managers who hire and fire "workers" and who allocate part of their fixed yearly budget to pay for machines instead of men.

Incorrect Relative Prices

When the Army gets soldiers at a wage rate lower than that which would induce them to join of their own free will, the military managers are obtaining incorrect information about the true costs of their operation. Because labor is artificially underpriced due to the fact that the military can draft,

military management ends up using fewer machines and more men than they would have otherwise. That is, the labor to capital ratio is inefficiently high. Now, why does military management do this? The decision is usually made along the following lines. At a given price for men, the military managers must consider the possibility of adding machinery either to aid the men or to replace them in certain jobs. For example, if an additional computer would allow one man to do the work that two men would have done otherwise, military managers must look at the *relative prices* of the computer and of the men in order to decide rationally if the machine should be rented (or bought). Let's say that one man costs $200 a week and that one computer rents for $100 a week. The computer will obviously be rented because it eliminates the need for one man at $200 per week. The savings to the manager is therefore $200 minus the cost of the machine, which is only $100, or $100 per week.

Now consider what would happen if the price of the man falls to $90 per week. It is no longer worthwhile to rent the computer for the purpose of saving one man—that is, for the purpose of saving manpower. This is exactly what happens in the military because draftees are, in fact, paid far below their "going price" on the labor market, or the price that would induce them to volunteer. We know then that the military is using "too many" men and using "too few" machines. Conscription results in a higher than optimal men/machine ratio in the military. This results in higher costs to society than is necessary. The optimal men/machine ratio would require fewer total resources to produce the same amount of military output, whatever that might be. (It is a curious problem as to how one measures the output of the military. We all know how it was done in Vietnam, but it is not obvious that enemy body counts are an accurate or appropriate tool for figuring out the quantity or value of military output.)

Turnover Costs

A large cost to any employer is the necessary training of new workers (**turnover costs**). Every time an employer loses an old worker and hires a new one, he discovers that there are costs involved with the changeover. When he is training a new worker, that worker's output is much less than was the old worker's. When he is training a new worker, there is more spoilage; the employer usually has to employ the services of an experienced worker in order to coach the newer one. He has to get the payroll computer to

forget about the worker that quit and add on the worker that was just hired. The list of turnover costs goes on and on, and the Army faces these turnover costs also.

In the past, conscription was usually for a period of only two years. In all likelihood, if the Army had been composed entirely of volunteers obtained in the same way that firms hire their workers—that is, by offering adequate wages—then the turnover time would have been longer than two years. In fact, since we know that the Army would have certainly paid much higher wages than those they've offered in the past, management would have made more effort to insure that the turnover time was substantially longer than two years. In this manner, the Army could have saved some very real costs. After all, when a soldier comes into the service, he is "green" and must be trained. Training involves the use of resources such as machines and other men's time. When the draftee's two years are up, someone else must be trained to fill his spot at additional cost.

Inefficiency of Intramilitary Resource Allocation

Even within the Army, we find that the draft results in an inefficient allocation of men's talents. One rarely sees college-trained

men washing latrines in the civilian world. Why? Because usually college-trained men can be used more profitably doing other jobs. Employers benefit from placing their workers where the workers' training adds to productivity and hence profitability. We expect workers to be placed where they contribute most to the output of the firm, but this is not necessarily the case in the Army.

All draftees are obtained at the same wage rate whether or not they are functional illiterates or engineering Ph.D.'s. We would expect, nonetheless, there would be some incentives for military management to use draftees as effectively as possible, just as businessmen would want to use their employees as effectively as possible. However, in the Army the signals about where different workers should be used are not as apparent as in the civilian world. In civilian life, we find highly differentiated salaries for different quality workers. These highly differentiated salaries are unmistakable signals. To hire a Ph.D., an entrepreneur must pay more than he pays for a high school dropout—at least usually! It therefore behooves the employer to get the most for his money by putting the Ph.D. to work at a job where he is most productive.

There is an additional inducement to the military establishment not to use draftees as effectively as possible. For many years, the Army used a system whereby prospective soldiers were offered a choice of training schools. Usually, the volunteers filled most of the available slots in these schools. The result, to give one example, might be that an unskilled high school dropout who volunteered would be trained as a radar technician, while a draftee already trained in electronics would be put to work at some simple job where his skills remained wasted.

Who Gets Drafted?

There are three possible kinds of draft systems, all of which have been used in the United States at one time or another. The first one we mentioned was instituted during the Civil War and it can be called a **mercenary draft.** It involves the possibility of draftees hiring substitutes from among those who have not been drafted. The second form of draft is the one that we have used throughout most of the history of military involuntary servitude in the United States. It is called an **exemption draft.** There is a large number of eligible draft-aged men, all of whom need not be drafted to fulfill the military demand for men. Therefore, some system is set up whereby people

of draft age can obtain deferments. You all know what those deferments were in the past: educational status, occupational skills, large number of dependents, and so on.

The last method of draft is a **lottery draft.** The required number of soldiers are selected at random from the eligible pool. Presumably, there are no exemptions. Actually, even with the lottery system in the United States, there have always been certain types of exemptions, but it became harder to obtain them.

We know that under the system of mercenary conscription during the Civil War, men whose opportunity costs were very high found it profitable to pay other people to go in their stead. We would expect that during the Civil War very few high-income men actually fought in the war. In fact, that is exactly what happened.

College Deferments

One might think that under the exemption system such biases would not occur. However, the facts of the situation were more or less the same. Under the exemption system, college students and highly skilled workers in "critical" jobs were deferred from military conscription. Who do you think goes to college? It is hardly the poor blacks from Alabama or the poor whites from Appalachia.

Usually the distribution of college-bound students mirrors the distribution of income. Very few poor kids end up in college; and very few of the poor end up in "critical" draft-exempt jobs because those jobs require training that is usually obtained in college. Therefore, under the exemption draft few well-to-do-men entered the Army. If they did, it was usually as a relatively highly paid officer, certainly not as a draftee at $80 a month. The exemption draft would be composed of the relatively less well-to-do members of society.

Exemptions Lead to Efficiency

Notice, however, that the exemption draft does allow for higher economic output than a pure lottery system which requires everyone who is chosen to actually serve. Typically the value of marginal product of college students and those men in critical occupations is higher than for most non-college-aged persons who are not attending school and men who have not been well trained and are not in "critical" occupations. It is therefore to the benefit of the total economic output that the exemption system allows highly trained individuals not to be drafted. However, a draft exemption also makes going to college more "profitable," thereby causing a misallocation of resources.

The problem of equity is obviously ignored here. It does not seem "fair" for college students to be deferred while their less fortunate cohorts are forced to "serve." Be that as it may, this is a question which cannot be answered by economic analysis. It boils down to a value judgment: is the fairness of an absolutely random system of drafting worth the cost of reduced output?

The Lottery

One would have imagined that a lottery draft in the United States would have resulted in a more equitable distribution of draftees among the draft-aged population. However, the lottery may only have somewhat eased the "inequitable" distribution that existed with the pure exemption system. It did not eliminate it completely. Even after the institution of the lottery system, it was still possible to find loopholes in the draft law in order to avoid being drafted. If one had a sufficient amount of money to hire good lawyers, good doctors, or good psychiatrists, one could escape the draft.

The True Cost of the Military Machine

Everybody knows what it costs to run an army. Just look at the $80 to $100 billion defense budget

that is presented to the Congress each year. This, however, is hardly the *true* cost of the military machine. The true cost of using any resource in our society is its opportunity cost. Here, we shall try to analyze what the true cost of a draft system really is.

Opportunity Costs

The economy suffers an opportunity cost for every man drafted that is *totally independent of what draftees are paid in the Army.* Obviously, the true cost to society of a draftee is what he could be earning as a civilian. If a civilian is paid $20,000 a year by his employer, we can usually presume that the employer is obtaining at least that amount in services. Most employers will not pay more than

the value of the marginal product of their employees. If the employee demands more than his *VMP,* the employer will probably terminate the working arrangement. It will not pay him to pay more than the employee's value of marginal product. Now, let's assume that this same $20,000-a-year man is drafted. What is the economy giving up? It's giving up at least $20,000 worth of civilian productive services a year in order to obtain what is likely to be a much smaller amount in military services. That $20,000 a year is the true annual cost of this man's entrance into military involuntary servitude. The piddling $2500 a year that the man may earn in the Army has nothing whatsoever to do with what his true cost actually is.

Implicit Tax

Now the question arises: if the Army pays only such a small fraction of the true opportunity cost of draftees, who pays the rest? We know that the draftees themselves bear the burden of what we call an *implicit tax* on them. How big do you think that implicit tax is? If you think about it a moment, it is at least as large as the difference between what the draftee *could* earn as a civilian and what he is being paid in the Army. In most instances, you would expect that it is even larger than that. Very few men who are drafted would consider joining the Army at the same pay they were receiving in the civilian world. The Army would have to pay them more. Therefore, the tax on draftees is even larger than merely the difference between Army pay and civilian pay.

We all suffer somewhat, though, because the induction of a $20,000 a year technician into the Army where he is paid $2500 a year and where the value of his marginal product is lower (but perhaps not as low as his Army pay) will end up reducing the total civilian output in the economy. You could argue that this is an overstatement of the true cost of the military because military service "makes men out of boys." It also presumably makes good

citizens out of bad ones, and community leaders out of juvenile delinquents. Of course, there may be cheaper ways of attaining these "goods."

Given what we know about the distribution of those who serve under the draft system, we should be able to figure out what the distribution of the implicit tax actually might be. We would find that it was highly favorable to the rich and highly unfavorable to the poor, mainly because of the exemptions (real and pseudo) that are available to higher income draft candidates. With a lottery system, the tax is borne somewhat more by the rich because it is more difficult for them to evade military conscription.

Switching from a Draft to an All Volunteer Army

First of all, we must realize that in order for a draft system to be turned into an all volunteer army, the wages offered potential soldiers must be raised up to the point where the quantity demanded by the military machine is just matched by the quantity supplied. If our previous analysis of the implicit cost to the draft is correct, we would expect that the changeover from a draft army to a volunteer army would mean the following.

1. The ratio of men to machines would decrease.
2. Turnover rates would fall, together with all the associated costs.
3. Soldiers would be placed where their skills would contribute the most to the military—that is, in economic terms where the value of their marginal product was highest.

Objections to an All Volunteer Army

Our presentation of the costs of the draft and the benefits of switching to an all volunteer army ignored a number of mostly non-economic complaints that some people have against a full-fledged mercenary military. We will go through some of those arguments; we will not be able to analyze these issues fully in economic terms, however, because they do involve value judgments.

Most people think that an all volunteer army is costing much more than a draft army. This, of course, is not true. The real cost of an army is the opportunity cost of all the men and machines it uses. Society pays this cost whether the men are involuntarily conscripted or whether they are offered a high enough wage to induce them to join. The Army, of course, would prefer that the true cost be hidden because then society would be more likely to support a larger military.

The decision whether to have a volunteer army is really a decision about who should bear the costs. With a draft system, the economic burden is shared in a small part by the taxpayers and in great part by the draftees. With a volunteer army, only the taxpayers are paying the cost because there are no draftees. There is no implicit "draft tax." We expect now that the number of productive resources used to obtain the same military output has fallen since we changed from a draft system to an all volunteer system because of the three alterations listed above.

There is a fear that an all volunteer army is dangerous because it is no longer controlled by civilians. Seymour Melmen, who wrote *Pentagon Capitalism* in 1970, said that he fears a powerful professional military elite, an army of mercenaries, who would constitute a threat to the democratic processes in the United States. The increased probability of a military takeover would not be worth the potential benefits from going to an all volunteer army. There is also the possibility that our professional army will be composed of officers and enlisted men whose primary allegiance would be to their senior officers

and not to the nation. For many people, this is a disconcerting prospect.

Lastly, many people believe that an all volunteer army will end up composed of minorities and the poor. The reason they think this is because untrained and uneducated men will find the military more attractive than civilian employment. They will therefore join and outnumber the more well-to-do and, most probably, white volunteers. However, this is

not necessarily what might happen in the long run. After all, as military wages and working conditions are improved by military managers, minorities and poor whites may find themselves competing with more well-to-do whites who have the advantage of more education and more training for Army jobs. It is not necessarily a foregone conclusion that the proportion of minorities in the military will rise.

Definition of New Terms

TURNOVER COSTS: the costs associated with the changing of employees to do particular jobs. Turnover costs might include such things as redoing employee records, training new employees, and so on.

MERCENARY DRAFT: a draft system which involves the possibility of draftees hiring substitutes from among those who have not been drafted.

EXEMPTION DRAFT: a draft system in which a large number of eligible men can obtain deferments for various reasons, such as educational status, occupational skills, and so on.

LOTTERY DRAFT: a draft system in which men are selected at random through a lottery. Not all draft-aged men are therefore inducted.

Questions for Thought and Discussion

1. Can you think of any more objections to a volunteer army?
2. In time of war, especially an unpopular one, the wage rate necessary to fulfill the manpower demands of the military machine may be quite high. Does that mean that an all volunteer army is unfeasible during war time?
3. If you were going to be drafted, how much would you be willing to pay in order to avoid induction?

Selected References

Melman, Seymour. *Pentagon Capitalism.* New York: McGraw Hill, 1970.

Miller, James C., Ed. *Why the Draft?* Baltimore: Penguin Books, 1968.

Oi, Walter Y. "The Economic Cost of the Draft." *American Economic Review,* May 1967.

Report of the President's Commission on an All Volunteer Armed Force. Washington, D.C.: U.S. Government Printing Office, 1970.

Wealth, Capital, and Savings

10

SOME PEOPLE HAVE lots of wealth: yachts, big houses, several cars, big bank accounts, stocks, bonds, and businesses. Some people have very little wealth. One question is: how do people obtain wealth? Why is it that some men have more than others? What's the difference between wealth and income? Do savings enter into this picture? These are some of the questions we will answer in this chapter. Let's first make sure we know what we mean when we're talking about wealth.

WEALTH

Wealth includes more than tangible objects, such as buildings, machinery, land, cars, and houses. People are wealth also. They have skills, knowledge, initiative, talents, and comprise what is called the human wealth part of our nation's **capital stock.** When we talk about the stock of capital we are now referring to things that can generate utility to individuals in the future. A fresh, ripe tomato is not part of our capital stock. It has to be eaten before it gets rotten and after it's eaten it can no longer generate utility. The nonhuman aspect of our capital stock has a market value of over $3 trillion. It's hard to hazard a guess as to what the human aspect equals because human beings don't usually sell themselves like capital goods.

People can invest in themselves, however. That is, they can engage in human capital investment. One increases his future productive ability by investing in training or schooling. By going to college, you are sacrificing current consumption in order to be more productive later on and make your human capital worth more.

Once you acquire a particular skill or additional education, it is embodied in you: no one else can take it away. Your parents, for example, can either invest in your education or invest with the same money in the stock market in your name. Either course of action leads to a larger capital stock for you.

In a subsequent issue, we shall go into greater detail about the human capital market in relation to public education. Now we will turn our attention to the nonhuman aspect of our capital stock and find out how it occurred and how it can be increased, or decreased for that matter.

HOW TO GET WEALTH

Let's say that you have no wealth at all except your body, and even that may not be too obvious. Anyway, you decide to get a job. You start making income. How do you acquire wealth? If you spend everything that you make, you won't be able to get any wealth at all. That is, if you consume everything, nothing will be left over with which to acquire nonhuman wealth, such as cars, stereos, stocks and bonds, houses, and so on. Thus, the only way you can obtain wealth is by saving—that is, by not spending your income on perishable goods. You have to buy durable goods or you have to lend your income to someone else in exchange for the promise to be repaid in the future plus interest. At this point, we should probably make the distinction between perishable goods and nonperishable or durable goods.

Durable and Nondurable Goods

Economists usually call goods that are used up in the very near future nondurables. When used by consumers, these are also called consumer nondurable goods. Examples are food, movies, trips to Europe, pencils, and cigarettes. These are goods that are bought for nonwealth-increasing purposes. On the other hand, durable goods can-

not be used up right away. They last; they give utility in the future. These durable goods, like houses and cars and stereos, are also called capital goods. It is the durable or capital good which adds to one's wealth position.

Savings

We mentioned that the only way to acquire wealth was to save. Saving is the process of nonconsuming part of one's current income. Whether you know it or not, any time you buy something that lasts—that is, any time you buy a durable or capital good—you are actually saving. That means that people who go out and buy houses and cars aren't really spending all of their money in the sense that they are consuming all their income; they are actually saving part of it because they will receive the services from the houses and cars they bought well into the future. One of the easiest ways to realize that the purchase of durable goods is actually a form of saving is to see what happens when you go to the bank to take out a loan.

Net Worth

The loan officer will try to determine your **net worth** position. That is, he will try to determine how much wealth you own outside of your body. He will ask you whether you have any stereos, cameras, cars, and things which could be sold if you were in a pinch. In other words, he will treat your durable goods as part of your net worth or wealth position. If you recently saved up money to buy a car, your wealth position would be higher than if you had not bought the car but, rather, had spent the money on a Caribbean vacation. In determining your wealth position, the bank loan officer does not ask you how many trips to the Caribbean you took. There is no way if you default on your loan that he could get you to sell a trip you already took. Obviously, a trip you already took has no market value for it is a consumption good already consumed. You have already consumed it. Nobody else can have it. It should be pointed out here that, when referring to wealth and capital, we have been talking about what we call a **stock.** We should always distinguish between a stock and a flow, which we will do in the next section.

STOCKS AND FLOWS

When the bank loan officer tries to determine your wealth position, he tries to determine how much you are worth at a point in time. The wealth that you have is a stock. (Note here we're not talking about a stock in a company.) Lots of other things are stocks, too, such as the building you might own. Stocks are defined independently of time although they are assessed at a point in time. A car dealer can have a stock or inventory of cars on his lot which may be worth $500,000. A timberman may have five acres of $3000 trees; he then has a stock of trees.

On the other hand, the income you make is a flow. A **flow** is an on-going concept, a stream of things through time. It is a certain number of things per time period. You receive so many dollars a week or so many dollars per month or so many dollars per year. The number of trees which grow in a forest is a flow of trees; it is a certain number of trees per time period, such as a year. The number of cars that a car dealer sells per week is a flow. Flows, in other words, are defined for a specific period of time.

If you want to add to your stock of wealth or capital, you must save. That is, you must not consume part of your income. The act of saving is a flow which makes your stock of wealth larger. You should not confuse the act of saving with how much you have in savings. Savings is another stock concept which is akin to wealth as we have defined it. You might have $5000 in a savings account. You have a stock of $5000 of accumulated savings. If you want to increase that stock, you have to save more. You have to add a flow of saving to your stock of savings.

There is a big difference, for example, between a millionaire and someone who makes a million dollars a year. The person who makes a million a year is probably much richer than the former. The millionaire has a stock of wealth worth $1 million; however, the man who makes $1 million a year has a flow of income equal to $1 million—year in and year out. He could easily save a big chunk of that million dollars each year to add to his wealth or savings so that in time he would be much more than a mere millionaire. He could become a multimillionaire in very short order. It is possible to translate a flow of income or saving into a stock of wealth. We do this by a procedure called present value discounting, which we will describe now.

PRESENT VALUES

If someone gave you the choice of receiving $1 a year for the rest of your life or $20 today, which would you prefer? You would probably be hard-pressed to figure out which was the better deal. It's hard to assess the value of dollars coming in at the end of each year, year in and year out. A dollar ten years from now certainly will not be as desirable as a dollar today. You know, of course, that a dollar 50 years from now is not as good as a dollar today. In fact, you might even be dead fifty years from now so the dollar would do you no good at all. The point, however, is that you should value dollars today more than you value dollars tomorrow. You have to *discount* future dollars in order to figure out what they're worth to you today.

Discounting is a term we apply to the procedure of reducing *future* values in order to show how much they are actually worth today. We reduce them by a discount factor which depends upon the discount rate we've used. The discount rate we use is some interest rate. Let's say that you could take your money and put it in a savings and loan institution. At the savings and loan institution you might get a 5 percent rate of return on your savings. If you put in $1 today, you would get $1.05 a year from now. The discounted value of $1.05 using a discount rate of 5 percent is only $1. Or, put another way, the discounted value of $1 one year from now is about 95¢, if you could get a 5 percent yield in a savings and loan association. You could put your 95¢ in today and get about $1 in a year. A dollar two years from now would be worth even less. You could put in about 91¢ today and have a dollar two years in the future. The point is that *a dollar received in the future is worth less than a dollar received today.* In Table 10–1 we show various present values of future dollars at the end of specified years for particular interest rates. The higher the interest rate (that is, the higher the amount you

could actually get on a savings account if you invested your money in it), the lower the value of dollars in the future. Moreover, the further in the future you get those dollars, the smaller the present value.

ANNUITIES

We still haven't answered the question of whether you would want to take $20 today or have $1 a year for the rest of your life. What if you could put that $20 in a savings account? If it yielded 5 percent, you could get a dollar a year forever. So at an interest rate of 5 percent, and assuming you will live quite a while, you would be indifferent between receiving $20 or receiving what we call an **annuity** of $1 a year forever. However, if you

TABLE 10–1

PRESENT VALUES OF A FUTURE DOLLAR

Each column shows how much a dollar received at the end of a certain number of years in the future (identified on the extreme left-hand or right-hand column) is worth today. For example, at 5 percent a year, a dollar to be received 20 years in the future is only worth 37.7¢. At the end of 50 years, it isn't even worth a dime today. To find out how much $10,000 would be worth a certain number of years from now, just multiply the figures in the columns by 10,000. For example, $10,000 received at the end of ten years discounted at a 5 percent rate of interest would be equal to $6140.

YEAR	3%	4%	5%	6%	8%	10%	20%	YEAR
1	.971	.962	.952	.943	.926	.909	.833	1
2	.943	.925	.907	.890	.857	.826	.694	2
3	.915	.890	.864	.839	.794	.751	.578	3
4	.889	.855	.823	.792	.735	.683	.482	4
5	.863	.823	.784	.747	.681	.620	.402	5
6	.838	.790	.746	.705	.630	.564	.335	6
7	.813	.760	.711	.665	.583	.513	.279	7
8	.789	.731	.677	.627	.540	.466	.233	8
9	.766	.703	.645	.591	.500	.424	.194	9
10	.744	.676	.614	.558	.463	.385	.162	10
11	.722	.650	.585	.526	.429	.350	.134	11
12	.701	.625	.557	.497	.397	.318	.112	12
13	.681	.601	.530	.468	.368	.289	.0935	13
14	.661	.577	.505	.442	.340	.263	.0779	14
15	.642	.555	.481	.417	.315	.239	.0649	15
16	.623	.534	.458	.393	.292	.217	.0541	16
17	.605	.513	.436	.371	.270	.197	.0451	17
18	.587	.494	.416	.350	.250	.179	.0376	18
19	.570	.475	.396	.330	.232	.163	.0313	19
20	.554	.456	.377	.311	.215	.148	.0261	20
25	.478	.375	.295	.232	.146	.0923	.0105	25
30	.412	.308	.231	.174	.0994	.0573	.00421	30
40	.307	.208	.142	.0972	.0460	.0221	.000680	40
50	.228	.141	.087	.0543	.0213	.00852	.000109	50

thought you could get 10 percent if you invested or saved that $20, you would prefer getting the $20 today rather than $1 a year. After all, at a 10 percent rate a year, you could get $2 a year in interest: you'd obviously be better off.

In Table 10–2 we show the present value of an annuity of $1 that will be received at the end of each year. Various interest rates that could be used for assessing that annuity and various time periods are shown. You can see that the higher the interest rate, the lower the value of the annuity. That's because at higher interest rates, the present value of a dollar in the future is worth less than at lower interest rates. At higher interest rates, rather than having an annuity, you would often be better off getting some lump sum payment today. This is similar to the first example where you'd be better off by getting $20 today rather

than by getting $1 a year forever if the interest rate exceeded 5 percent.

Now you see how a future stream of income can be translated into a present value of wealth figure. Businessmen determine how much they should pay for an investment by similar procedures. They look at expected profits on a potential investment through the years and discount them back to the present. That tells them how much the investment is actually worth and how much they should pay for it. If the person selling the investment wants more than the present value of the discounted future profits, it probably would be a mistake for our businessman to buy it.

Let's take a specific example. Assume that a McDonald's Hamburger stand was expected to yield a profit of $10,000 for 50 years. How much would a businessman pay for that McDonald's

TABLE 10–2

PRESENT VALUE OF AN ANNUITY OF ONE DOLLAR

Here we show the present value of $1 received at the end of each year for a specified number of years. For example, the present value of a dollar received at the end of each year for 10 years at an interest rate of 5 percent would be $7.72. If it were received for 50 years, it would have a present value of $18.30.

YEAR	3%	4%	5%	6%	8%	10%	20%	YEAR
1	0.971	0.960	0.952	0.943	0.926	0.909	0.833	1
2	1.91	1.89	1.86	1.83	1.78	1.73	1.53	2
3	2.83	2.78	2.72	2.67	2.58	2.48	2.11	3
4	3.72	3.63	3.55	3.46	3.31	3.16	2.59	4
5	4.58	4.45	4.33	4.21	3.99	3.79	2.99	5
6	5.42	5.24	5.08	4.91	4.62	4.35	3.33	6
7	6.23	6.00	5.79	5.58	5.21	4.86	3.60	7
8	7.02	6.73	6.46	6.20	5.75	5.33	3.84	8
9	7.79	7.44	7.11	6.80	6.25	5.75	4.03	9
10	8.53	8.11	7.72	7.36	6.71	6.14	4.19	10
11	9.25	8.76	8.31	7.88	7.14	6.49	4.33	11
12	9.95	9.39	8.86	8.38	7.54	6.81	4.44	12
13	10.6	9.99	9.39	8.85	7.90	7.10	4.53	13
14	11.3	10.6	9.90	9.29	8.24	7.36	4.61	14
15	11.9	11.1	10.4	9.71	8.56	7.60	4.68	15
16	12.6	11.6	10.8	10.1	8.85	7.82	4.73	16
17	13.2	12.2	11.3	10.4	9.12	8.02	4.77	17
18	13.8	12.7	11.7	10.8	9.37	8.20	4.81	18
19	14.3	13.1	12.1	11.1	9.60	8.36	4.84	19
20	14.9	13.6	12.5	11.4	9.82	8.51	4.87	20
25	17.4	15.6	14.1	12.8	10.7	9.08	4.95	25
30	19.6	17.3	15.4	13.8	11.3	9.43	4.98	30
40	23.1	19.8	17.2	15.0	11.9	9.78	5.00	40
50	25.7	21.5	18.3	15.8	12.2	9.91	5.00	50

Hamburger stand? Look at Table 10–2. We have to multiply everything by 10,000 because the table is only in terms of receiving an annuity of $1 per year. The only way we can figure out what the McDonald's Hamburger stand is worth is by deciding upon an appropriate rate of interest for discounting purposes. The discount rate will be determined by what we could do with our money if we invested it in something else. Let's say we thought we could make 10 percent. At an interest rate of 10 percent, $1 per year for 50 years is worth $9.91 dollars today. Therefore, $10,000 every year for 50 years is worth, at a 10 percent interest, $9.91 times 10,000 or $99,100. If the prospective buyer of the McDonald's wanted more than $99,100, it wouldn't be worth while to buy the hamburger stand. If he wanted less than this amount, it would.

THE NATURE OF COMPOUND INTEREST

We've been talking about discounting dollars in the future. Now it's time to talk about **compounding** dollars into the future. If you decide to add to your capital stock or wealth position by not consuming all of your income, you can take what you save and (loosely speaking) invest it. You can put it in the stock market or you can buy bonds—that is, lend money to businesses. You could also put it in your own business. In any event, you might expect to make profit or interest every year in the future for a certain amount of time. In order to figure out how much you will have at the end of any specified time period, you have to *compound* your savings yield and, just as in discounting, you have to use a specified interest

TABLE 10–3

ONE DOLLAR COMPOUNDED AT DIFFERENT INTEREST RATES

Here we show the value of the dollar at the end of a specified period after it has been compounded at a specified interest rate. For example, if you took $1 today and invested it at 5 percent, it would yield $1.05 at the end of the year. At the end of 10 years, it would be equal to $1.63, and at the end of 50 years, it will be equal to $11.50.

YEAR	3%	4%	5%	6%	8%	10%	20%	YEAR
1	1.03	1.04	1.05	1.06	1.08	1.10	1.20	1
2	1.06	1.08	1.10	1.12	1.17	1.21	1.44	2
3	1.09	1.12	1.16	1.19	1.26	1.33	1.73	3
4	1.13	1.17	1.22	1.26	1.36	1.46	2.07	4
5.	1.16	1.22	1.28	1.34	1.47	1.61	2.49	5
6	1.19	1.27	1.34	1.41	1.59	1.77	2.99	6
7	1.23	1.32	1.41	1.50	1.71	1.94	3.58	7
8	1.27	1.37	1.48	1.59	1.85	2.14	4.30	8
9	1.30	1.42	1.55	1.68	2.00	2.35	5.16	9
10	1.34	1.48	1.63	1.79	2.16	2.59	6.19	10
11	1.38	1.54	1.71	1.89	2.33	2.85	7.43	11
12	1.43	1.60	1.80	2.01	2.52	3.13	8.92	12
13	1.47	1.67	1.89	2.13	2.72	3.45	10.7	13
14	1.51	1.73	1.98	2.26	2.94	3.79	12.8	14
15	1.56	1.80	2.08	2.39	3.17	4.17	15.4	15
16	1.60	1.87	2.18	2.54	3.43	4.59	18.5	16
17	1.65	1.95	2.29	2.69	3.70	5.05	22.2	17
18	1.70	2.03	2.41	2.85	4.00	5.55	26.6	18
19	1.75	2.11	2.53	3.02	4.32	6.11	31.9	19
20	1.81	2.19	2.65	3.20	4.66	6.72	38.3	20
25	2.09	2.67	3.39	4.29	6.85	10.8	95.4	25
30	2.43	3.24	4.32	5.74	10.0	17.4	237	30
40	3.26	4.80	7.04	10.3	21.7	45.3	1470	40
50	4.38	7.11	11.5	18.4	46.9	117	9100	50

rate. Let's go back to the simple case of putting money in a savings and loan association that yields 5 percent per year. At the end of one year, you have $1.05. At the end of two years, you have $1.05 plus 5 percent of $1.05, or $0.0525. That means that at the end of two years you have $1.1025. This goes on at three years, four years, and so on.

The Power of Compounding

The power of compound interest is, indeed, truly amazing. Look at Table 10–3. Here we show $1 compounded every year for 1 to 50 years at different interest rates. At an interest rate of 10 percent, $1 at the end of 50 years will equal $117. This means, if you inherited a modest $10,000 when you were 20 years old and put it in an investment which paid 10 percent every year compounded, you would end up at 70 years of age with $1,170,000. Now it's not so hard to understand how some people become millionaires. It usually doesn't take much brains or business acumen to get a 10 percent rate of return on your savings. If somebody would have invested in the stock market 50 years ago, he would have received a lot more than 10 percent. There are a number of people around who inherit moderate amounts of money when they are quite young. If this money is put in the stock market and left there to compound itself, it grows to quite unbelievable amounts after 30 or 40 years. One should be careful about analyzing the astuteness of elderly millionaires; they could have been very conservative, done nothing with the money they inherited except put it in the stock market and leave it there. No business sense would be needed at all and the person could easily become a millionaire by the time he's 65.

The power of compound interest should also tip you off as to the true worth of many investment schemes. Take high-priced paintings. Often art dealers will tell you that paintings are good investments. They will cite, for example, a Picasso that somebody purchased for only $5000 and then sold for $15,000. You have to find out, however, when it was purchased. Usually, if you look at the length of time the person held the painting, the actual gain in value might be very modest, say only 3 percent a year. After all, if the painting cost $1000 in 1950, at a 3 percent compound interest, it would be worth over $2000 in 1975. The person who sold it in 1975 could boast that he doubled his investment, while he probably could have done better if in 1950 he had put his $1000 into a savings account that yielded 4 or 5 percent; he would have done even better if he had put his money into the stock market because then he would have had a rate of return of 8 to 12 percent. Usually paintings yield a lower rate of return than savings accounts or the stock market because people get some consumption pleasure out of having the paintings in their houses. They are, therefore, willing to receive a lower rate of return than they would if they had put the money in some other type of investment.

THE UNKIND TRUTH

Even though the power of compound interest is indeed staggering, particularly at higher interest rates, the fact remains that the only way to increase wealth is to not consume all of what you make as income. Unless you plan on inheriting something or stealing wealth from others, you will not be a wealthy person if you consume everything you earn. The larger the percentage of your income you decide to save, the larger your wealth will be in the future. The better the investment you put your money in, the higher the rate of return will be and, again, the larger your wealth will be in the future. You do have the option of investing in your own personal human wealth or capital and that's exactly what one does by going to college. You will be wealthier because of this investment since your productivity and, hence, the wage rate you will make in the future will be higher.

Definition of New Terms

CAPITAL STOCK: the sum total of all human and nonhuman wealth in the United States. Included are buildings, machinery, land, cars, houses, the productive talents of human beings.

NET WORTH: the difference between the assets and liabilities for an individual or a business. Your net worth position can be found by adding up the value of everything you own and subtracting the amount you owe. The difference is your net worth.

STOCK: the quantity of something at a point in time. An inventory of goods is a stock. A bank account at a point in time is a stock. Stocks are defined independently of time although they are assessed at a point in time. Different from a flow.

FLOW: something defined per unit time period. Income is a flow which occurs per week, per month, or per year. Consumption is a flow. So is saving.

PRESENT VALUE: the value of something which occurs in the future. The present value of a dollar tomorrow is less than a dollar today. Present values are obtained by discounting future dollar figures.

DISCOUNTING: the procedure used to reduce future values to their present values. Discounting requires the use of a discount rate which is the interest rate that is decided upon as appropriate for each particular case.

ANNUITY: a specified income payable at stated intervals for a fixed period.

COMPOUNDING: the process of allowing the interest on an investment or savings to yield interest itself, thereby being compounded.

Chapter Summary

1. The total wealth of the United States consists of the nonhuman wealth and the human wealth, the human wealth being the productive capacities of individuals.

2. The only way to obtain wealth besides stealing it or inheriting it is by not consuming everything that you make. In other words, you have to save to acquire wealth. Your wealth is then your accumulated savings.

3. It is useful to distinguish between stocks and flows. A stock of wealth is something that you have accumulated that you can measure at a point in time. You obtain a flow of income, however, for a specific period. Your income is so many dollars per week or per month. Your saving is also a flow concept. You save at a rate of so many dollars per week or per month or per year. On the other hand, your savings is a stock, the result of your past saving.

4. In order to assess the value of future dollars, it is necessary to reduce those future dollars by discounting them to the present value; discounting requires using an appropriate interest rate.

5. Compound interest is exceedingly powerful. A small amount of money left in a savings account at 5 percent a year ends up being quite a large amount of money at the end of 50 years.

Questions for Thought and Discussion

1. In some universities and colleges you can receive loans at very low interest rates relative to what you would have to pay in the open market. If you could borrow money at 5 percent per year on these special loans even though you didn't need it, do you think it would be worthwhile to take advantage of it? Why? (Hint: Could you earn more than the 5 percent interest, if you invested the money?)
2. If you decide to save all of your income over the next two years, what happens to the value of your wealth position right now? In one year? In two years?
3. Are there any people around with no wealth at all?
4. Would you rather be given $1 million today or $100,000 a year for the rest of your life?

WIDE WORLD PHOTOS

THE CONSUMMATE AMERICAN BUSINESSMAN

Henry Ford II
Industrialist

HENRY FORD II is a businessman who can do exactly as he pleases because, as he says, "my name is over the door." And he has done just that—from giving $50,000 to a Detroit ghetto recreation center to promoting change in his company, his city, and the country's business community. He had the privilege of being descended from one of America's wealthiest industrial families, but he also had to face the task of turning a money-losing organization into a major industrial power.

Between 1929 and 1941, the Ford Motor Company was on the brink of financial collapse. Edsel Ford, Henry Ford II's father and titular president of the company, was only a figurehead and the senile Henry Ford was actually steering the sinking ship. The company was foundering because of mismanagement, poor cost control, and antiquated production methods. In 1945, Henry Ford agreed to make his grandson president of the company. Although the younger Ford had little formal training, he knew the advantages of strong, trustworthy counsel. He brought in the "Whiz Kids," a group of sharp, ambitious men who were willing to apply modern technological and managerial techniques to the problems of the company. "I knew it could be turned around; it never occurred to me I couldn't do the job," said Ford at the time. He fired hundreds of top management personnel and brought in former General Motors men who decentralized and reorganized the company along the lines GM had perfected over the preceding decade.

One of Ford's major problems has been with the United Auto Workers (UAW). He had generally succeeded in his determined efforts to improve relations with Walter Reuther's men, but the Ford Motor Company remains a particularly tempting target for UAW strike action. Nonetheless, Ford has actively defended his company's interests in labor negotiations. He charged that the 1964 UAW job-security demands amounted to featherbedding and an undermining of the efficiency of the industry.

During his first eight years in the presidency, Ford made capital investments totaling an extraordinary $1 billion. The company acquired Philco Corporation in 1961, which turned out to be a profitable move toward electronics and defense contracting. Ford's high and low points have been associated with auto models. The Edsel, introduced in 1957, became one of the major disasters in the history of the industry, selling only 110,000 units in three years and incurring a loss of $250 million for the company. The Maverick and Mustang, though, have had substantial success on the market.

Because of his interest in urban renewal of the depressed sections of Detroit, his backing of the Ford Foundation, and his position (by default) as the most "concerned" of America's big automakers, Ford is considered a model of enlightened corporate management. According to Ford, we are in "the worst domestic crisis since the Civil War," and we must "make some basic changes in our schools, our housing, our welfare system. We also need to make basic changes in our employment practices—in whom we hire, how we hire, and what we do with people and for people after they are hired." As early as the 1940s, Ford ordered his managers to hire blacks and members of other minorities. After the Detroit riots of 1967, Ford opened two hiring centers in the ghetto, recruiting the hard-core unemployed— those who had never worked and who were often illiterate and ex-cons. Ford gave them bus fare and lunch money until they received their first paycheck. Most started at $3.25–$3.80 per hour as sweepers, stockboys, assemblers, or press operators. Now about half of the work force at the River Rouge plant are blacks.

But many have discovered the limits of this image. Ford refuses to read Ralph Nader's *Unsafe at Any Speed,* a book that strongly attacks the design failings of auto manufacturers. In response to the proposed "safety cars," Ford said, "If you want to ride around in a tank, you won't get hurt. You won't be able to afford one though . . . ." He also balks at safety legislation, maintaining that "if you start by law to fool around with model changes, to tell the industry it must do this, that or the other thing within a period of time in which it cannot be done . . . you upset the whole cycle of this industry."

Areas such as safety and antipollution programs still take minor roles in the Ford budget. Ford's "social concerns" are those which relate directly to the running of a profitable corporation—jobs, employment security, stable wages. His success is evident. When Henry Ford II took over, the company was losing $10 million a month; in 1969 it earned $546.5 million on sales of $14.8 billion.

The Distribution of Income

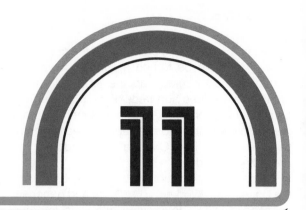

11

E VERYONE KNOWS there are lots of rich people around, and everyone knows there are lots of poor ones, too. However, not many of us know why some people make more money than others. Why is the **distribution of income** the way it is? Economists have devised different theories to explain why some people make more income than others. In this chapter, we will present some of those theories. Additionally, we can present some of the more obvious institutional reasons why income is not distributed evenly in the United States.

INCOME DISTRIBUTION—PAST AND PRESENT

The easiest way to talk about the distribution of income is to divide income earners into separate categories. Let's rank all income earners and divide the total into five equal parts. So doing, we can talk about how much the bottom fifth makes compared to the top fifth, and so on. We see in Table 11–1 that in 1947 the bottom fifth of the population was receiving 5.0 percent of total personal income, while the top fifth was reaping 43.1 percent. Today, the figures haven't changed very much, as is shown by the data for 1971.

LORENZ CURVE

We can graphically represent the distribution of income by the use of what is called a **Lorenz curve.** Look at Figure 11–1. On the horizontal axis we measure the accumulated percent of families. Starting at the left-hand corner there would be zero families. On the right-hand corner we would have 100 percent of the

FIGURE 11–1

THE LORENZ CURVE

The horizontal axis measures the accumulated percent of families going from 0 to 100 percent. The vertical axis measures the accumulated percent of income going from 0 to 100. A straight line at a 45° angle which cuts the box in half represents a line of perfect income equality where 25 percent of the families get 25 percent of the income, 50 percent get 50 percent, and so on. Normally, though, the Lorenz curve is not a straight line but, rather, a curved line as shown. The difference between perfect income equality and the Lorenz curve is the inequality gap.

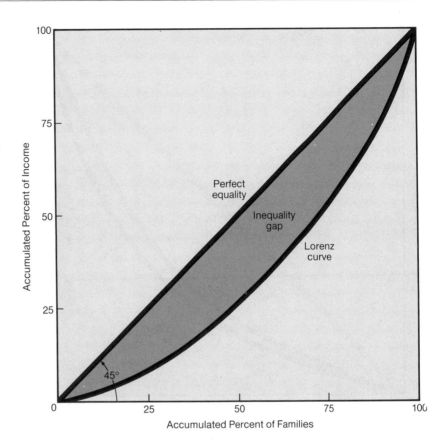

families, and in the middle we would have 50 percent of the families. The vertical axis represents the accumulated percent of total income. On the bottom we would have zero income, and on the top, 100 percent of all income. In the middle we would find 50 percent of total income. We expect, therefore, that the line between the lower left-hand corner and the upper right-hand corner of the Lorenz box (a 45° line) would represent perfect equality. At the middle of the box we would have

TABLE 11–1

THE DISTRIBUTION OF INCOME, 1947 TO 1971

Here we cut up households into fifths and show the lowest fifth to the highest fifth. The distribution of income has not changed very much since just after World War II. (*Source:* Department of Commerce.)

PERCENTAGE OF HOUSEHOLDS	PERCENTAGE OF NATIONAL INCOME	
	1947	1971
Lowest 5th	5.0	5.4
Second 5th	11.8	12.3
Third 5th	17.0	17.8
Fourth 5th	23.1	23.8
Highest 5th	43.1	40.7
	100.0	100.0

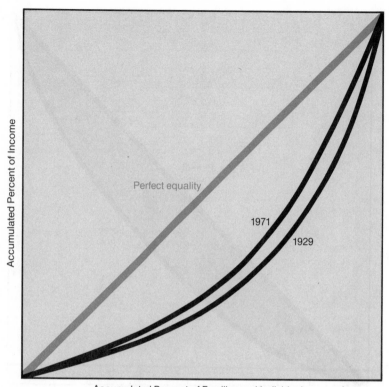

Accumulated Percent of Income

Perfect equality

1971

1929

Accumulated Percent of Families and Individuals

FIGURE 11–2

LORENZ CURVES OF INCOME DISTRIBUTION, 1929 AND 1971

We notice that the Lorenz curve has come slightly in toward the straight line of perfect income equality since 1929. *Source:* U.S. Department of Commerce.

50 percent of the families obtaining 50 percent of total income. Of course, no real world situation is such that there is perfect equality of income; no Lorenz curve will be a straight line of perfect equality as presented in Figure 11–1 but rather will be the curved line.

We see in Figure 11–2 that the actual distribution of income in the United States is certainly not equal. Compared to 1929, however, it is improving (a value judgment) in the sense of becoming more equal. It might be interesting to compare the United States today with other countries in the world. We see in Figure 11–3 that the Lorenz curve for Sweden is closer to the straight line than is the curve for the United States. Just as we would have expected, Sweden has a more equal distribution of income than we do. This has been

accomplished in Sweden by extremely progressive taxes. On the other hand, we see that the distribution of income in Thailand is much more unequal than in the United States. The bottom 80 percent of families receive less than 40 percent of all income, whereas the top 10 percent of families receives more than 40 percent of all income. This is a typical pattern in underdeveloped nations where the vast majority of people are extremely poor and where the few on top are extremely rich. In most underdeveloped countries, there is almost no middle class.

As an aside, it might be noted that the more industrialized a nation becomes, the larger is the percentage of national income that is paid in wages. In less developed countries, much of the national income goes to rent, interest, and profits,

FIGURE 11–3

INTERNATIONAL COMPARISONS OF INCOME DISTRIBUTION

Here we show the Lorenz curves for the United States, Sweden and Thailand. As can be expected, Sweden has a Lorenz curve which is closer to the straight line of perfect income equality than that of the United States. Sweden has a much more progressive set of income taxes. Thailand, on the other hand, has a much more unequal distribution of income. *Source·* U.S. data from U.S. Department of Commerce. Data for Thailand from *Statistical Yearbook of Thailand.* Data for Sweden from *Statistical Abstract of Sweden,* 1968.

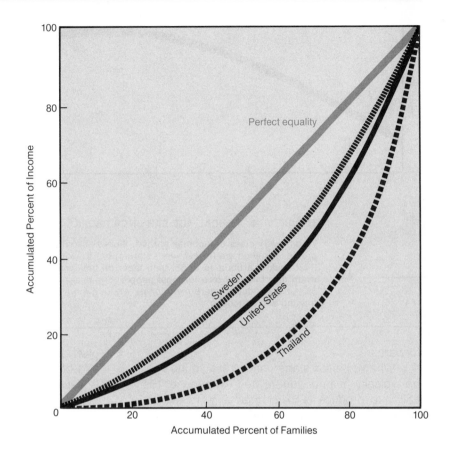

whereas in countries such as the United States, Britain, France, Germany, Sweden, and the rest of Western Europe, the majority of national income does not originate from capital but, rather, from labor services. In the United States today, for example, over three-fourths of national income is paid in wages; less than one-fourth is paid as returns to investment in land, buildings, companies, and so on.

THE AGE-EARNING CYCLE

Within every class of income earners, be it the lowest or the highest, there seem to be regular cycles of earnings behavior. Most people earn much more when they are middle aged than when they are either younger or older. This is called the **age-earnings cycle.** Every occupation has its own age-earnings cycle and every individual will probably experience some variation from the average. Nonetheless, we can characterize the typical age-earnings cycle graphically in Figure 11–4. Here we see that at age 25 the lowest income is made. Income gradually rises until it peaks around 45 to 50. Then it falls until retirement when it becomes zero—that is, earned income becomes zero although retirement payments may then commence. The answer as to why there is such a regular cycle in earnings is fairly straight-

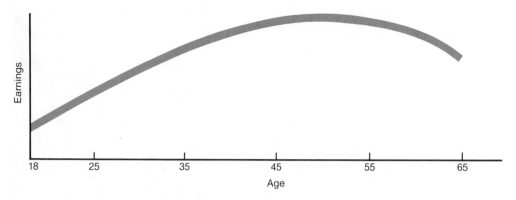

FIGURE 11–4 TYPICAL AGE-EARNINGS PROFILE

Within every class of incomes earned, there is usually a typical age-earnings profile. Earnings are lowest when starting out to work at age 18 and reach their peak at around 45 to 55, then taper off until retirement at around 65 when they become zero for most people. The rise in earnings up to age 45 to 55 is usually due to more experience, working longer hours, and better training and schooling.

forward.

When a person starts working at a young age, he typically has no work-related experience. His ability to produce is lower than a more experienced worker. That is, his productivity is lower. As he becomes older, he attains more training and more experience. His productivity rises, and he therefore is paid more. Moreover, he starts to work longer hours, in general. At the age of 45 or 50 productivity of individual workers usually peaks. So, too, do the number of hours per week that are worked. After this peak in the age-earnings cycle, the detrimental effects of aging usually outweigh any increases in training or experience. Moreover, hours worked usually start to fall for older people. Finally, as a person reaches retirement age, his productivity and hours worked fall rather drastically relative to, say, 15 or 20 years earlier.

As an additional note, we can abstract from the issues of general shifts in the entire age-earnings profile and inflation. Inflation and general increases in overall productivity for the entire work force will raise the typical age-earnings profile as given in Figure 11–4 upward. Thus, even at the end of the age-earnings cycle, when the worker is just about to retire, he would not receive a really "low" wage compared with what he started out with 45 years earlier. His wage would be much higher due to inflation and other factors which contribute to rising wages for everyone, regardless of where they are in their age-earnings cycle.

Now we have some idea why individuals will experience different incomes at different times in their lives, but we have yet to explain why different people are paid different amounts of money for their individual labors. One way to explain this is to fall back onto our marginal productivity theory developed in Chapter 9.

MARGINAL PRODUCTIVITY THEORY

When trying to find out how many workers a firm would hire, we had to construct a value of marginal product curve. We found out that as more workers were hired, the value of marginal product fell since the marginal productivity of the work force would fall due to diminishing returns. If the forces of supply and demand established a certain wage rate, workers would be hired until the value of their marginal product was equal to the wage rate. Then the hiring would stop. This suggests what a person can expect to be paid in the labor market. In other words, *he can expect to be paid the value of his marginal product.* This, of course, assumes that there are good information flows and that everything is competitive.

Process of Competition

In most situations the value of marginal product theory gives us a rough idea of what workers will be paid. In a competitive situation with mobility of labor resources (at least on the margin), workers who are being paid less than the value of their marginal product will be bid away to better employment opportunities. Either they will seek better employment themselves or employers in an attempt to lower labor costs will try to find workers who are being paid below the value of their marginal product. This process will continue until workers are paid no less than the value of their marginal product. In general, employers will not want to keep workers if the workers' wage rate is greater than the *VMP.* In such a situation it would pay an entrepreneur to fire or lay off those workers who are being paid more than the worth of their contribution to total output. It would be unusual, then, to find situations where large numbers of workers were being privately employed at wages exceeding their *VMPs.* (This assertion may not hold for government employment situations.)

Full Adjustment Is Never Obtained

You may balk at the suggestion that people are paid the value of their marginal product because you may personally know individuals who are seemingly worth more than they are being paid. This, in fact, may happen because we do not live in a world with perfect information. Employers cannot always seek out the most productive employees available. It takes resources to research the past records of potential employees, their training, their education, and their abilities. You may know musicians, artists, photographers, singers, and other talented people who are being paid much less than more well-known, publicized "stars." But this does not mean that marginal product theory is invalid. This merely indicates that information is costly. It is not always possible for talent scouts to find out exactly who the next superstars are going to be, which means that lots of potential stars never fulfill their dreams.

If we accept value of marginal product theory, then we have a way to find out how people can, in fact, earn higher income. If they can manage to increase the value of their marginal product, they can expect to be paid more. Some of the determinants of marginal product are innate intelligence, schooling, experience, and training. These are means by which marginal product can be increased. Let's examine them in greater detail.

Intelligence. This factor is obviously the easiest to explain and the hardest to acquire if you don't have it. Innate intelligence can be a very strong, if not overwhelming, determinant of a person's potential productivity. If one is born without "brains," he has a smaller chance of "making it" in the economic world than does an individual who is born smart. The determinants of intelligence are, of course, not a topic for economic discussion. It is no longer believed, however, that intelligence is purely innate. Some sociologists and educators think that intelligence can be changed by the environment. Nevertheless, whether a change in intelligence due to a "better" environment leads to higher incomes in the future is a debatable and as yet untested contention.

Schooling. This is another obvious method of increasing one's marginal product. Schooling is usually placed under the heading of "investment in human capital," a topic we will go into later. For the moment, suffice it to say that schooling or education improves one's productivity by increasing the human capital one has available for use in the labor market. If you have been taught to read, write, work with mathematics, understand scientific problems, do engineering, drafting, lay out advertisements, design clothes, or edit manuscripts, you obviously are of more value to a potential employer than a person who is illiterate and unknowledgable about anything except manual labor. It is merely a statement of the fact that schooling often increases a person's value to a potential employer. If anything, schooling usually allows an individual to be more versatile in the things he can do.

Experience. Additional experience at particular tasks is another method of increasing one's productivity. Experience can be linked to the well-known *learning curve* that almost everyone experiences when he does the same task over and over. Take an example of a person going to work on an assembly line at General Motors. At first he is only able to screw on three bolts every two minutes. Then he becomes more adept and can screw on four bolts in the same time plus insert a rubber guard on the bumper. After a few more weeks he can add even another task. Experience allows him to improve his productivity. The better people learn to do something, the quicker they can do it and the more efficient they become. Hence, we would expect on any task that experience would lead to higher rates of productivity. Therefore, we would expect that people with more experience would be paid more than those with less experience.

Training. Training is similar to experience but is more formal. Much of a person's increased productivity is due to on-the-job training. In many instances there are training programs for new workers. Here workers learn to operate machinery, fill out forms, and do other things they will be required to do on the new job. On-the-job training is perhaps responsible for as much an increase in productivity as is formal schooling. And, in fact, on-the-job training is an alternative to formal schooling, one that should not be completely ignored.

There are, of course, other determinants of people's incomes which we have not yet discussed. One of the most fascinating is the uniqueness of people's individual resources. If you have a unique resource in yourself, such as a singing voice, a beautiful face and body, a creative mind, or an athletic prowess, you may be able to earn "surplus" income or **economic rents.** But, of course, in your attempt to capture those rents, you will run into much risk, which is what we shall talk about now.

EARNING TOO MUCH

Some people earn "too" much. That is, they are paid more income than would be required to get them to do the amount of work they actually perform. These people are receiving what economists call economic rents. These rents have nothing to do with the rents that must be paid on apartments. *Economic rents are a kind of surplus, a surplus of income over and above what is required to get someone to do a specified kind and amount of work.*

How can you possibly get into a situation where you are paid more than you actually require to do the work that someone wants you to do? Well, all you have to do is have a unique resource. Just ask Bob Dylan, or the Rolling Stones, or Joan Baez, or Catherine Deneuve, or Joe Cocker, or Marlon Brando, or Jane Fonda. They are making fantastic incomes. Most likely, they would be willing to work for less if they had to. But they don't have to, and the reason they don't have to is because the demand for their special talents is relatively high. No one else can take their place.

FIGURE 11–5

ECONOMIC RENTS ACCRUING TO BOB DYLAN

If we assume that Bob Dylan's supply curve of concerts is a vertical line at, say, two concerts per year, then the economic rents that Bob Dylan would receive would equal the price, *P1*, times the quantity of concerts that he gave.

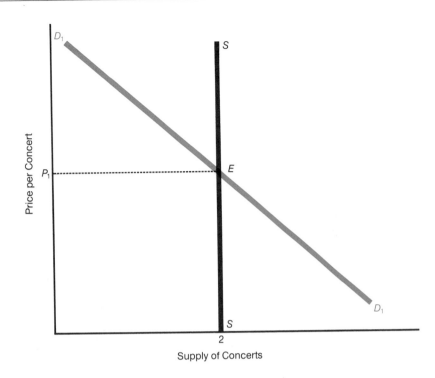

That is, there are very few substitutes for people who have unique resources or unique talents.

We can formally define economic rent for workers as the portion of the price that is paid for a person's labor services which does not influence the amount of those services offered. If, for example, the supply curve of Bob Dylan's talents was the vertical line in Figure 11–5, then the amount of economic rent he would receive would be exactly equal to whatever he was paid. If the demand curve happened to be D_1D_1, the rent he would receive would equal the intersection price times the quantity of services he offered. That is because here he would presumably be willing to offer that same amount of services at a zero price.

Economic Rent Cannot Be Eliminated

There is no way to get rid of economic rents or economic surplus. The demand and supply curves intersect at the point *E* in Figure 11–5. *Economic rent serves a rationing function.* The only way that people can obtain the services of Bob Dylan is by bidding them away from someone else. Since a lot of people want to bid for the same services, the price goes up, and the economic rent that Bob Dylan receives goes up accordingly. Since price serves as a rationing mechanism, it has to be high enough to allocate a scarce resource. If we do not allow price (wages) to rise to the point where supply just equals demand, then some other form of rationing must be used.

Joan Baez's Curious Habit

A good example of this concerns a peculiar habit of singer Joan Baez. Often she requests that her concert tickets be sold at $2 or $3 a piece and no higher. However, the quantity of tickets demanded at that relatively low price far exceeds the quantity available for any given performance. We find that fans will line up a day in advance in order to get the low-priced tickets. Instead of paying a higher *money* price to get in the door to see Joan Baez, devoted fans will pay a combination of a time cost and a relatively low price for the actual tickets. The point is that when the price is below the market-clearing one, some form of rationing must take place. In this particular example, it is a long wait in line.

People who attempt to make extraordinary incomes on the basis of their artistic talents usually start out at the bottom making almost nothing. The Beatles were a relatively poorly paid Liverpool rock group for a number of years before they made stardom and started collecting economic rents. During those Liverpool years they probably could have made more money in some alternative occupation, such as driving a truck.

Risk Factor

A high risk is involved with occupations that promise fantastic incomes. There are a lot of super beautiful $80-a-week waitresses and car-hops in Hollywood. These budding starlets could probably make more money if they did office work in another city. However, they want to take a chance of making it big, of breaking into the movies or singing. Many would-be actors, actresses, singers, musicians, painters, photographers, and authors voluntarily remain relatively poor throughout their lives because they do not seek alternative employments where they could make more money. Rather, they attempt to eke out a living doing bit parts, for example, or writing infrequently published short stories in the hopes that eventually they will break into the big times. If they do break into the big times, you can be sure that they will make economic rents, that they will be paid more than is required to get them to work. But that's what makes them take the risk in the first place.

EXPLOITATION AND DISCRIMINATION

Exploitation and discrimination also affect the distribution of income. Even with equal educational achievement, both in quality and quantity, certain disadvantaged groups may not and empirically do not receive incomes equal to those of other groups. We know, for example, that urban nonwhite males earn approximately 40 percent less than urban white males. We know that blacks obtain lower rates of return, on average, from investing in college education than do whites. Are minority groups, and especially blacks, being exploited? Are minority groups being discriminated against in the labor market? Before we can answer these questions, we have to come up with a fairly straightforward definition of these two terms.

Exploitation

The economists' definition of **exploitation** is somewhat more restrictive than the everyday connotation. We usually say that a person is being exploited in the selling of his labor services if he is being paid less than the value of his services to his employer.

How can exploitation exist in the labor market? First of all, lack of information could allow it. If employees (on the margin) are ignorant of better job opportunities, they may be exploited by employers. Another possible method of exploiting laborers is by restricting entry into an industry. Professional sports leagues prevent the entry of competing leagues which would thereby bid up the price of professional athletes. We say that players may be exploited because of the monopsony power of the single existing major league employers. In fact, there is pretty good evidence that this is actually taking place. Another possible cause of exploitation is restricted mobility. If a lawyer is prevented from practicing in states other than the one where he now works, he may be exploited because he is not allowed to go where the value of his services and his potential income is highest.

Note, however, that we have talked about the possibility but not the certainty of exploitation. Stress should be placed on the possibility, because the lack of information, the lack of free entry, and the lack of mobility do not offer *prima facie* evidence of exploitation. More evidence is needed.

In terms of information, *all* employees concerned must be unaware of the facts, not just the average employee. We know, for example, that non-English-speaking immigrants arriving in America could be exploited only when they first set foot on shore because afterwards there were brokers who specialized in providing them with translated information. Competition among brokers for immigrants assured that non-English-speaking employees received wages equal to the value of their marginal product. (It should not be forgotten that the value of their marginal product was, on average, lower than for the native born because the ability to use English increased productivity.) The point that is made here is that information may not be obtained directly by the employee himself, since competition among employers will provide sufficient information, at least at the margin, to insure nonexploitation.

The mere lack of free entry into a new industry is not a surefire way to exploit workers. Those participating in the restrictive side of the market must also agree *among themselves* not to compete with one another. This is exactly what has happened in the professional sports leagues. There is a draft system which prevents teams from bidding against each other. If this draft system did not exist, there would be incentives for individual teams to compete for the best players. Players would therefore be no longer exploited; they would receive incomes equal to the value of their services to club owners.

In sum, exploitation requires restriction on information, entry, and mobility plus additional arrangements that will insure that such restrictions affect *all* employees.

Discrimination

How can we define discrimination now that we have analyzed exploitation? Discrimination is usually taken to mean about the same thing as exploitation, but it may also include not being able to find a job and not being able to buy certain products, such as housing in particular neighborhoods. Usually we say that an employer has a "taste for discrimination" when he acts as if there were nonmonetary costs associated with the hiring of blacks or other minority group members. This type of behavior would lead to lower income for blacks than they would receive otherwise. In fact, there is quite a bit of evidence of discrimination in the labor market, particularly in restricted situations such as those caused by union activities.

In a theoretical and empirical study of discrimination against blacks, Professor Gary S. Becker found that discrimination was related to a number of readily observable variables. Here, discrimination is defined by wage differentials not accounted for by different *VMPs* between whites and blacks in similar job situations. Becker found the following relationships.

1. Discrimination is positively related to the relative number of blacks and whites. For a given sized city, the larger the proportion of blacks, the more discrimination there will be. This is sometimes called the "propinquity" theorem. Further, discrimination is more prevalent when large numbers of blacks are involved in nonmarket activities such as attaining a formal education. This means that the larger the number of blacks relative to whites, the more discrimination we would expect to see.
2. Discrimination is less evident for those seeking temporary as opposed to permanent work.
3. Discrimination is greater for those who are older and better educated.

4. Discrimination has deterred blacks from entering professions such as law because of their competitive disadvantage in arguing before white juries.

Becker also found that black incomes were reduced by 16 percent because of discrimination against them.[*]

There appears to be quite a bit of discrimination against blacks and other minorities in the acquiring of human capital. That is, the amount and quality of schooling offered blacks has been detrimentally inferior to that offered to whites. We find that even if minorities attend school as long as whites, their scholastic achievement is usually less, for they typically are allotted more meager school resources than their white counterparts. Analysis of census data reveals that a large portion of white/nonwhite income differentials resulted from differences in both the quantity of education received and the scholastic achievement which is a function more or less of the quality of education received. One study showed that nonwhite urban males receive between 23 and 27 percent less income than white urban males because of lower quality education. This would mean that even if employment discrimination is substantially reduced, we would still expect to see a difference between white and nonwhite income because of the low quality of schooling received by the nonwhites. We say, therefore, that, among other things, blacks and certain other minority groups, such as Chicanos, suffer from too small an investment in human capital. Even when this difference in human capital is taken into account, there appears to be an income differential that cannot be explained. The unexplained income differential between whites and blacks is often attributed to discrimination in the labor market. Until a better explanation is offered, we will stick with the notion that discrimination does indeed exist in the labor market.

[*]See Gary Becker, *The Economics of Discrimination*, Rev. Ed. (Chicago: University of Chicago Press, 1971).

INVESTMENT IN HUMAN CAPITAL

Investment in human capital is just like investment in any other thing. If you invest in a building, you expect to reap a profit later on through receiving a rate of return for your investment. You expect to receive some reward for not consuming all of your income today. The same is true for investment in human capital. If you invest in yourself by going to college rather than working and being able to spend more money, you presumably will be rewarded in the future by a higher income and a more interesting job. This is exactly the motivation that usually underlies the decisions of many college-bound students to obtain a formal higher education. Undoubtedly, there would still be students going to school even if the rate of return to formal education was zero or negative. After all, college is fun, right? (And it's certainly better than going to work.) But, we do expect that the higher the rate of return to investing in oneself, the more investment there will be. Indeed, we find that the investment in a college education does pay off. Look at Figure 11–6. Here we show the age-earnings cycle of grade school graduates, high school graduates, and college graduates. The age-earnings cycle jumps up for each increase in formal education. The investment in human capital pays off.

To figure out what the rate of return to an investment in a college education is, we first have to figure out what the costs of going to school are. The main cost is not what you have to pay for books, fees, and tuition but, rather, the income you forego. *The main cost of education is the income foregone or the opportunity cost of not working.* That may amount to as much as $5000 to $10,000 a year. In addition, of course, you have to pay for the direct expenses (or, rather, your parents do in many cases). Of course, not all students forego income during their college years. Many people work part-time. Taking account of those who work part-time and those who are supported by state tuition grants and other schol-

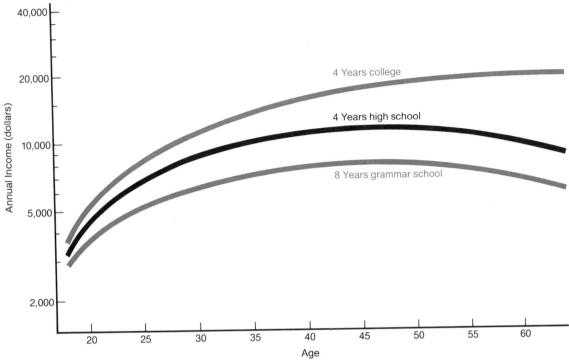

FIGURE 11–6

AGE-EARNINGS PROFILE FOR SELECTED DEGREE HOLDERS

The figure demonstrates how the age-earning cycle jumps up for each increase in formal education. It is obvious that the investment in human capital eventually pays off. *Source:* U.S. Department of Commerce, Consumer Income, Series P60, No. 74.

arships, it turns out that the average rate of return of going to college is somewhere between 8 and 12 percent. This is not a bad rate of return. It's certainly more than you could get by putting money in a savings account. It's about equal, in fact, to the rate of return you would receive by randomly selecting stocks in the stock market. Of course, this type of computation does leave out all of the consumption benefits you get from attending college. College is not *all* pain even though economics sometimes is. Also omitted from the calculations is the change in one's personality after going to college. You undoubtedly come out a different person (for better or for worse we do not know). However, most people who go through college think that they better themselves both culturally and intellectually, as well as increasing their marginal product so they can make more income. How does one measure the benefit from expanding one's horizons and one's desire to experience different things in life? Certainly, this is not easy to measure, and these types of benefits from investing in human capital are not included in our normal calculations.

The fact that the rate of return to investing in human capital is higher than one can get by putting money in a savings and loan association does not mean, however, that everybody "should" go to college. And it does not mean that there "should" be more public higher education for more people. There are many problems with education today, as we shall see in the following issue.

Definition of New Terms

DISTRIBUTION OF INCOME: the way that income is distributed in a particular country. For example, a perfectly equal distribution of income would find that the lowest 20 percent of income earners would make 20 percent of national income whereas the top 20 percent would make 20 percent of national income also. The bottom 50 percent of income earners would receive 50 percent of national income.

LORENZ CURVE: a geographic representation of the distribution of income. A Lorenz curve which is perfectly straight represents perfect income equality. The more bowed a Lorenz curve, the more inequally income is distributed.

AGE-EARNINGS CYCLE: the regular earnings behavior of an individual throughout his lifetime. The age-earnings cycle usually starts with a low income, builds gradually to a peak at around 45 to 55, and then gradually curves down until it becomes zero at retirement age.

ECONOMIC RENTS: that amount of payment for an individual's services over and above what the individual would be willing to accept to provide that same quantity of services. Sometimes called surplus.

EXPLOITATION: the payment to a person of wages or income that are less than the value of his services to the employer.

Chapter Summary

1. The distribution of income in the United States has remained fairly constant since after World War II. The lowest fifth of income earners still receive only about 5 percent of total personal income while the top fifth of income earners receive over 40 percent.
2. We can represent the distribution of income graphically. The extent to which the line is bowed from a straight line shows how unequal the distribution of income is.
3. Most individuals face a particular age-earnings cycle or profile. Earnings are lowest when starting out to work at age 18 to 24. They gradually rise and peak at about 45 to 55, then fall until retirement. The reason they go up is usually because of increased experience, increased training, and working longer hours.
4. Marginal productivity theory of the distribution of income indicates that workers can expect to be paid the value of their marginal product. For this theory to be exactly correct, we must have competition with fairly minimal information costs. Otherwise there will always be people who are being paid more or less than the value of their marginal product.

5. The value of marginal product is usually determined by innate intelligence, schooling, experience, and training.
6. Some people can be paid economic rents if they have a unique resource, such as a beautiful singing voice, a beautiful face or body, or a creative mind. Economic rents or surplus cannot be eliminated because they serve a rationing function.
7. Exploitation can be defined as a situation where a worker is paid less than his value to his employer. Exploitation may occur in situations where monopsony power exists on the part of the employer, where information is restricted, or where entry into the industry is also restricted.
8. Discrimination is usually defined as a situation where a certain special minority group is paid a lower wage for the same work than other groups.
9. You can invest in your own human capital by going to school. The investment usually pays off for the rate of return is somewhere between 8 and 12 percent.

Questions for Thought and Discussion

1. What kind of changes do you think will tend to make the distribution of income more equal?
2. Do you think that exploitation and discrimination are responsible for the unequalness of the distribution of income in the United States? If not, what are the main determinants?
3. Do you think that in a capitalistic system there will always be rich people and poor people?
4. "If we took all of the income in the United States and all of the wealth and divided it equally among everybody in the country, within 10 years rich people would be rich again and poor people would be poor again." Do you agree?
5. "To each according to his needs, from each according to his means." What kind of distribution of income would result from such a system?

Selected References

Becker, Gary. *The Economics of Discrimination*. Rev. Ed. Chicago: University of Chicago Press, 1971.
Budd, Edward. *Inequality and Poverty*. New York: W.W. Norton, 1968.
Ferman, Louis A., Kornbluh, J.L., & Haber, A., Eds. *Poverty in America*. Rev. Ed. Ann Arbor: The University of Michigan Press, 1968.
Harrington, Michael. *The Other America: Poverty in the United States*. Rev. Ed. New York: Macmillan, 1970.
Soltow, Lee, Ed. *Six Papers on the Size Distribution of Wealth and Income*. New York: Columbia University Press for the National Bureau of Economic Research, 1969.
Will, Robert E., & Vatter, Harold G., Eds. *Poverty in Affluence*. 2nd Ed. New York: Harcourt, Brace & Jovanovich, 1970.

ISSUE XI

Problems in the Market for Human Capital

Finances Falling

You are going to college. So you are investing in yourself; you are investing in human capital. You expect to see your investment yield a positive rate of return in the future. That is, you generally expect to make more income with a college education than you would with just a high school diploma. You have probably made the right decision for yourself. When you were younger, you had no decision to make at all; it was made for you. Education from the ages of around 8 to 16 is mandatory in just about every state in the Union. Today there are problems in education, both at the lowest levels where it is compulsory, and at the highest levels, where it is purely voluntary. Local school districts are finding themselves without sufficient funds to cope with a growing demand. Private universities are finding themselves without sufficient funds to meet rising costs. So, too, are public universities where such things as open enrollment have increased the number of minds to be taught, while at the same time legislators have been paring budgets to the bare minimum. In

this issue we will examine the human capital market in general and review specific suggestions for ameliorating the crisis in education at all levels.

The Market for Human Capital

If you want to go out and buy a house, a car, a business, you usually can obtain a loan to do so. You can get someone else, such

as a bank or finance company, to loan you the funds to purchase a capital good or asset. There is a well-developed market for investing in physical capital so there is a well-developed capital market in the United States. If you want to get a loan for your car, you typically put up the car you are buying as **collateral** for the loan—that is, as a guarantee that the loan will be paid off. If you default on your debt, the creditor can repossess your car and sell it to pay off whatever is owed. If you want to borrow money to start a business, you will usually be required to put up some sort of collateral, such as stocks that you have in General Motors or IBM. The point is that you can eventually find somebody who is willing to loan you money to invest in something that you want to buy.

This is not the case if you decide that you want to invest in your own human capital. If you want to increase your future earnings potential and your future productivity by acquiring additional training or schooling above the high school level, you often will find that you cannot obtain a loan to do so. This is so because there is no well-developed market in human capital. If someone loans you money to go to college, he does not have claim on your body or claim on you as a human being. If you default in the loan, he can perhaps attempt to recoup the money he lent you by attaching some of your assets. But what if you have none? What if you decide after having gone to college that you want to drop out? The person who loaned you the money has no way to make you pay. He has no claim on you as a person.

There was a time when there was a well-developed market in human beings. Aside from the period of slavery which we won't discuss here, there was voluntary servitude in the form of **indenture.** Way back when the colonies first started rolling, Europeans could obtain passage to the New World if they promised to work for the provider of the passage for a period of five to seven years. They were indentured for that period of time. If they broke their agreement, they would be brought back by the authorities to continue in their jobs. At that time, property rights in human beings were honored. Today they are not. And today we find that obtaining loans for increasing one's productivity by additional schooling is difficult.

Cost of College

Since it is hard to get a loan to invest in human capital, one must be able to work his way through college, get money from a fellowship or scholarship, or obtain money from parents or relatives. We would expect that at least those who receive money from

home are relatively well to do. In fact, that is actually what we find. Although the trend is changing, for many years higher education was restricted to children from more wealthy families. The reason is not hard to find. What is the cost of going to college? Part of the cost is involved in books and tuition, although for many public schools the tuition is very small. The major cost is *foregone income,* and foregone income for a poor person looms much larger in the decision-making process than for a relatively well-to-do person. When there are no parents around to support one during the college years, it is difficult to survive even if tuition is very small. Even though the payoff from getting a college degree is something on the order of $200,000 additional income during a person's lifetime, children from poor families cannot manage to forego their income during the four years of college.

Improving the Human Capital Market

There are numerous possible ways for improving the market in human capital. Any action that does improve this market will also improve the distribution of the benefits from higher education. That is to say, if somehow the market in human capital is made more perfect, more children from lower income families will end up

going to college and receiving the benefits from higher education. The government has attempted in a very minor way to correct some of the imperfections in the market for human capital. There are National Defense Education Act loans which some students may obtain at relatively low interest rates. In fact, these interest rates are lower than those prevailing in the general credit market. There are also certain banks which will give loans to students at relatively low interest rates because the government guarantees these loans. However, both of these attempts at improving the human capital market are small relative to the total market itself.

One suggestion has been made that the government extend the market for human capital by providing for a system of loans to anybody who wants to obtain one to go to school. The loan would be made at market rates of interest and would have to be paid back every year after the student left college and was earning income. The Internal Revenue Service could be apprised of a student's past borrowing record and therefore could automatically deduct a certain amount every year that income was made until the debt was repaid. Alternatively, a person's contribution to Social Security could be reduced by a certain amount each year to pay off his loan. He would then face a smaller retirement fund from

Social Security and would have to make it up in some private manner using a private retirement fund. He would be more likely to be in a position to do that if he goes to college anyway because he will make so much more income.

The amount of money that had to be repaid each year could be structured in a sliding scale. At lower incomes, very little would have to be paid; at high incomes, quite a bit. If no income was made, no money would be owed. It is also possible to extend this system of loans to provide for payment to the universities themselves for the full cost of educating each student. It is clear that something, perhaps not necessarily along these lines, will have to be done in the future because universities are all feeling a definite financial pinch.

Financing Higher Education

The financial crisis in higher education shows no signs of abating. Costs have increased dramatically in the last several decades for both private and public schools. Tuition has not increased commensurately and the result has been deficits that are sometimes staggering. In 1972, New York University faced a $7 million deficit, and the University of Southern California faced a $1.2 million deficit. There have been nu-

merous suggestions for helping out financially troubled schools. Most of them have centered on a call for more money from state and federal governments, particularly from private universities who already have tuitions which far exceed those that students going to public universities must shell out. It is not hard to understand why enrollments in private

schools are falling relative to enrollments in public schools. For example, tuition at New York University runs almost $3000 while the State University of New York charges less than $600 per year and the City College of New York is absolutely free.

To help out some of the private institutions, states have started giving the institutions grants for

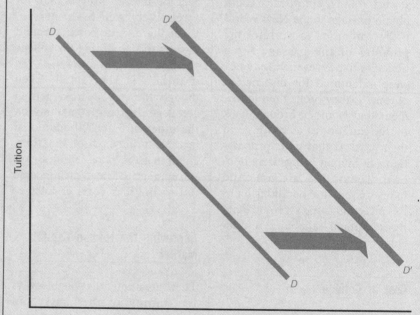

HOPED-FOR SHIFT IN THE DEMAND FOR PRIVATE SCHOOLS

Tuition (vertical axis)

Quantity of Students (horizontal axis)

FIGURE XI-1

Private schools want public colleges and universities to raise their tuition so that it is equal to the true cost of educating each student. The rise in the price of this substitute for private universities would shift the demand curve for them from *DD* to *D'D'*. At any given tuition level, there would be a larger quantity of students desiring to go to private schools.

each B.A. that they generate. For example, Maryland pays private colleges $500 for every B.A. turned out; New York pays private schools $400. Clearly that is not enough, or at least it is not enough in the eyes of the people who run private universities. They have asked many of the states to raise the tuition at public schools to cover the full cost of education there. If this were done, the demand for private institutional facilities would obviously increase because the relative price would fall. That is, the price of going to a private school relative to attending a public school would decrease.

Another way to look at the situation is that when the price of the substitute goes up, the demand curve of the other good or service shifts outward to the right. We see this in Figure XI-1. Here the demand curve for private education shifts out to the right so that, at the same price, more is demanded, just as the administrators in private schools would wish.

The suggestions of private school administrators also fall in line with the idea of making students pay for the full cost of their education. This seems an anathema to many citizens who think that public education should be "free." However, we know that in a world of scarcity, nothing is free. The cost of educating a youth is about the same whether he goes to a private school or a public school. And that cost is not, at the moment, fully borne by the person receiving the benefits.

External Benefits

It has sometimes been argued that higher education should be subsidized (and that is exactly what we are doing now) because it generates externalities. That is, the benefits that the individuals obtain in the education received are not the only benefits that society receives. Society receives *additional* benefits in the form of a more educated public, a public which will vote better, commit less crime, and so on. Whether a college education generates a sufficient amount of these externalities to justify subsidization is debatable. The subsidized research at universities certainly generates positive benefits but of what size we do not know. One thing we can be certain of is that in cases of specialized training, there are very few, if any, externalities involved. If you decide to become an engineer, you obtain very special training that is different from the general education referred to in the last few sentences. You obtain the benefits of that training by earning a higher income in the future. It is therefore hard to justify subsidization of specialized education on the externality grounds that are often mentioned.

Opportunity Banks

Be that as it may, we still have to solve the problem of financing higher education. We could work out an "opportunity" bank similar to the loan system described in the previous section. The opportunity bank concept has been endorsed by the Presidential Panel on Educational Innovation. The plan basically involves setting up a public or private agency which would loan money to students to cover living costs and tuition fees for a specified number of years. These tuition fees could then be set equal to the full cost of providing the education. The student would sign papers agreeing to pay back a set percentage of his earnings in excess of some base for each $1000 he received from that particular agency. The base would be his estimated average earnings without any additional or special training.

The pay back could be calculated in such a way as to make the program finance itself. And it could be withheld from current income or be remitted at tax time through the IRS. The Presidential Panel made some preliminary estimates which suggest that such a lending agency could be self-sustaining if repayment were 1 percent of gross income for each $3000 borrowed and the term of repayment was 30 years. Less ambitious plans, but similar in nature, have been inaugurated at two major universities, one of them being Yale.

Many people balk at such a suggestion because higher education no longer is "free" to needy students. However, it never was and nothing ever is free to society, at least. And in fact, current "free" higher education is most often not used by the lowest income students, but rather by middle income or higher income students. An opportunity bank such as the one described above would eliminate the problem of financing at the individual level. It would also ameliorate the problem of financing the schools themselves. The individuals who benefited from a college education would, in fact, be the ones who paid the costs. No subsidization would be necessary.

Vouchers for College

Another possibility, and one that has already been tried, is a voucher system for colleges. College-aged students could be allotted a specific amount of money every month or every year which they could cash in at the school of their choice. This is what we've called the G.I. Bill. We had it after World War II, the Korean war, and the Vietnam war. Instead of giving grants directly to universities, the grants are given directly to the students and the students decide to spend the money at the

educational institution of their choice. Many colleges and universities object, of course, to this type of arrangement because they would rather have control over the funds themselves. The same is true at the grammar school, junior high, and high school levels. The concept of giving parents the money to spend at the school of their choice is anathema to public school officials and teachers, which brings us to lower level education and the problems it has been facing.

Primary and Secondary Education

Primary and secondary schools are finding themselves in trouble, too. Both private and public schools are having a hard time meeting their commitment to educate the nation's youth. Everybody, whether he wants to or not, pays for primary and secondary education. In most states, he pays for it through a property tax. The tax he pays depends upon the particular assessment and tax levy in his particular location. But it is a function of the value of his house and property. The more expensive a house, the higher the taxes paid. It is an unusual situation because the homeowner is forced to pay for public education whether he wants to or not, and, more importantly, whether he sends his kids to public schools

or to private schools. Morever, the parent is unable to purchase the particular quality of education he wants unless, of course, he decides to send his children to private school.

Private Schools

A parent will send his child to a private school only if he thinks that the additional price is more than matched by the benefits he and his children will receive from the private education. For the parent who decides to send his child to private school, the total price of educating his child is actually quite staggering, for he is already paying for the public education he is not using. Additionally, he must pay for the tuition at the private school. As property taxes have increased to pay for higher costs of education, even though the cost of private education may have remained the same, the full cost of private education will have gone up. Consequently, we find that an increasing number of private secondary schools are going out of business. One count in 1970 showed that 200 had gone out of business in a period of four years. This means that the public schools in turn become more crowded.

New Court Cases

There have been numerous suggestions for improving the financial status of public education at

the primary and secondary level. Recent court decisions have required certain states to somehow eliminate the discriminatory aspects of using the property tax as the only method of financing public education. It is discriminatory in the sense that children who are in districts with low property values will end up with less money per pupil spent on education. In districts where there are higher property values, there will be more money spent per pupil. Most people are well aware of the fact that the richer suburbs spend more for education than do the poor inner-city ghetto areas.

Apparently, the courts are tending toward the direction of forcing an equalization of per pupil expenditures throughout the districts of a state. Obviously,

those districts with the lowest per pupil expenditures will be forced to spend more on public education. Thus, even more funds are going to be needed in the future. Some experts have demanded that the states take over the financing of public education in order to equalize per pupil expenditures. Other experts have maintained that the federal government should step in and use its taxing power to provide uniform funds to all school districts throughout the nation. There are other ways of financing education. And, in fact, some of them are radical in the sense that they have not been tried until recently. Some means are similar to the suggestions for financing higher education. We will discuss a few of the most prominent ones now.

The Voucher System

Instead of the federal government or the states or the individual school districts providing education, these government bodies could provide educational vouchers. The voucher would be given to the parent. It would state that the parent could take the voucher and turn it in at a *bona fide* school of the parent's choice and the school would then be able to turn in the voucher to the government for whatever payment was decided upon—let's say $1000 a year. Parents could presumably send their children to any school they wanted to, be it private or public. This means public schools would have to compete with private schools. Also, many more schools would come into being as private entrepreneurs responded to parents' demands for improved education for their young.

Right now it is very difficult for most parents to obtain an education for their children that is different or better than the one offered in public schools. Many people in America are quite discontent with the educational program now in existence in their own school districts. Unless, however, they are willing to come up with several thousand dollars for private education in addition to the taxes they already pay for public education, they can do little about changing the educational atmosphere.

The voucher system would change all that. With educational vouchers, even the poorest families could seek out the private education they thought was best for their children. In this manner, there would be equal spending on every child with no discrimination against children on the basis of where they live. Parents who want to spend more than the voucher allowed could do so. Parents who wanted to spend less could not. Therefore, a minimum level would be specified but a maximum would not, just as in the current system, but with much more flexibility. The Office of Economic Opportunity decided to sponsor a voucher system in a school district near San Jose, California, several years ago. Unfortunately, it restricted the vouchers to use only in public schools; no private schools qualified. A large element of competition was therefore eliminated in the experiment. The outcome of the experiment will not tell us whether a voucher system would actually serve to improve our primary and secondary education system.

Performance Contracting

Another method of improving primary and secondary education is to utilize **performance contracting.** A private institution takes on the responsibility of educating certain youngsters and of making them attain a certain performance level at the end of a stipulated time. If the performance level is attained, the private contractor is paid a certain amount of money by the government. If the performance level is not attained, the private contractor is paid nothing. He either performs or goes out of business. One would expect that here the profit incentive would cause the contractors to attempt to be as innovative as possible in teaching students the requisite skills in the shortest amount of time and with the least amount of effort. The government has sponsored several performance contracts in a couple of cities in the United States with mixed results. It is too early as yet to decide whether this is a valid and viable method of putting more flexibility into our educational system while at the same time allowing for improvements in the quality of education.

What Is the Right Amount of Education?

We all take it for granted that more education is better than less. That is probably true for any individual and certainly if that individual receives his additional education "free." But for society as a whole, and indeed for individuals, more education may be worse than less education. That is, more education may be socially nonoptimal in the sense that more education may cost more to society than society receives in benefits. We all probably agree that children should be educated until 16 or 18. It is much less certain a statement to say that people should be educated from the ages of 18 to 22. There is no doubt we are committed to providing education for all children through high school, and there is probably little doubt that this is socially optimal. However, after high school the problem is not so simple.

True, it is sometimes simple for the individual to decide. He looks at the rate of return he will receive from going to college and decides whether it will be worthwhile. He also includes all the consumption benefits he receives from going to college. After all, college is not all work, is it? And, in fact, at an individual level, there are certain benefits to be derived from learning how to enjoy art, music, books, travel, and other things that are often missed by those who go to work immediately after graduating from high school. These are all benefits from the college experience and they typically do not enter into the monetary calculations that economists make when they decide what the rate of return is to investing in those four years. But those consumption benefits that college students as individuals receive are peculiar to them as individuals and not to society as a whole. Therefore, from society's viewpoint, it is the individual himself who should pay for any consumption benefits obtained during college years.

The question then remains: should society encourage and, indeed, subsidize higher education to make sure that more young people continue after high school? Don't ask yourself or your college friends for the answer because you obviously are the beneficiary of the current level of subsidization to higher education; you cannot be expected to give an unbiased answer. You can't expect your parents to be any more objective. After all, they receive benefits from the prestige of having college graduates as sons and daughters. Moreover, you can't expect state legislators to know the answer either. Many of them, college graduates that they are, feel the words of a famous man: "An uneducated young man may rob a single train whereas an educated man may end up robbing the entire railroad."

Definition of New Terms

COLLATERAL: security pledged in payment for a loan.

INDENTURE: a system of binding a person under contract to work for another person over a period of time, usually 7 years, in return for passage to the New World.

VOUCHER SYSTEM: a system of giving educational vouchers to parents or students for them to use at the school of their choice instead of financing the schools directly.

PERFORMANCE CONTRACTING: a system of payment to private enterprise schools if they succeed in getting their students to achieve a certain level of competence.

Questions for Thought and Discussion

1. Is public higher education provided to a large percentage of students from poorer families?
2. Who should pay for higher education: The student? His parents? Or society?
3. Is it possible to have better education without spending more money on education?
4. Assume that all education is offered "free" to all individuals. Should every rational young person take advantage of "free" education?
5. The Carnegie Commission reported in 1972 that at least 300,000 and perhaps as many as 900,000 college students "shouldn't" be in school. What did the Commission mean?

Selected References

Becker, Gary S. *Human Capital: A Theoretical and Empirical Analysis with Special Reference to Education.* New York: Columbia University Press for National Bureau of Economic Research, 1964.

Hechinger, Fred M. "School Vouchers: Can the Plan Work?" New York Times, June 7, 1970, Section E-11.

"Investment in Human Beings." *The Journal of Political Economy,* **70** (Supplement, October 1962).

National Society for the Study of Education. *Social Forces Influencing American Education.* 60th Year Book. Part 2. Chicago: University of Chicago Press, 1961.

Thurow, Lester. *Investment in Human Capital.* Belmont, California: Wadsworth, 1970.

ISSUE XII

Finding Alternatives to the Welfare Mess

Poverty Still Around

Throughout man's history mass poverty has been an accepted inevitability. However, this nation and others, particularly in the Western world, have sustained enough economic growth in the last several hundred years that *mass* poverty can no longer be said to be a problem for these fortunate countries. As a matter of fact, the residual of poverty which still remains in the United States appears to be bizarre—an anomaly. How is it that there can still be so much poverty in a nation of so much abundance? Having talked about the determinants of the distribution of income, we now have at least some ideas on why some people are destined to remain low income earners throughout their lives.

There are methods of transferring income from the relatively well to do to the relatively poor. As a nation, we have begun an attempt to redistribute income from the wealthy to the poor.

Today we are saddled with a vast array of welfare programs that are set up for that reason and that reason alone. However, we know that these programs have not been entirely successful. The relative distribution of income has not changed appreciably in the last 30 or 40 years. Are there alternatives to our current welfare system? Is there a better method of helping the poor? To answer these questions we must first examine how the current system actually works.

The Welfare Mess

Current welfare programs are a labyrinth of state and local legislation. Nonetheless, over 90 percent of national welfare payments are made through programs that are partly or largely federally funded. Each month perhaps 8 to 10 million persons are given some form of welfare. These recipients include:

1. 3 million who are over 65, blind, or otherwise severely handicapped;
2. 4 million who are children in the Aid for Dependent Children program, whose parents do not or cannot provide financial support;
3. 1.5 to 2.5 million who are the parents of children on Aid to Families with Dependent Children (AFDC). Of these,

"You might be eligible for AFDC. Of course, that may be supplanted by FAP, but we might be able to get something from OASDHI. In any event there should be some PA for you."

over 1 million are mothers and the rest are fathers. About two-thirds of the fathers are incapacitated.

Public Assistance

Public assistance programs are designed to meet, at least partially, the needs of only certain categories of the poor. Among public assistance programs, there are: Aid to Families with Dependent Children, old age assistance, aid to the permanently and totally disabled, aid to the blind, and a general assistance program. Only about one-third of poor families and one-quarter of poor persons receive public assistance (PA). Many of the poor do not receive PA because they fail to pass the so-called "means tests." These are tests which the state uses to compare a budget plan of expenditures with potential resources of the persons applying for aid. In the past, poor people often could not obtain public assistance because they failed to meet local or state residency qualifications. Of course, there are many who do not know their possible eligibility, and some are frightened off by the stigma they feel is attached to going on relief. There are many more poor people who receive no public assistance merely because they do not fall into one of the prescribed categories.

Disparity of Payments

Different states pay different amounts for different public assistance programs. Take, for example, the AFDC program. State and local governments contribute on average about 45 percent of the costs of supporting this program. Each state sets the level of grants for its own residents. We find, therefore, that monthly payments range from a low of perhaps less than $10 in Mississippi to a high of over $60 in New York City. AFDC programs cost approximately $3 billion a year. In many states and cities the case loads are increasing, particularly in times when unemployment is high. As can be expected, the burden of welfare and of the increase in case loads falls principally on our central cities, particularly New York, Chicago, St. Louis, Detroit, Cleveland, and Los Angeles. Examination of our current programs provides one with an insight into the relatively high cost of giving away money under certain systems and the disadvantages of doing it in such a manner.

Disadvantages of Current Public Assistance

The amount of paperwork involved in providing public assistance is indeed appalling. In many cities, five, six, or even seven copies of each form must be made and filed. Welfare workers have to go out to interview prospective and current welfare recipients in order to make sure that they are eligible—to find out if, indeed, the recipients are spending their welfare money in the correct way. In most welfare situations, it is not possible, for example, for the recipients to have phones. That is considered a frivolous expense. Moreover, and perhaps even more appalling, is the fact that many welfare programs are cut off once a person who receives money finds a job—no matter how poor the pay for that job might be. Until recently, all amounts earned on outside jobs by adult welfare recipients were deducted directly from the welfare payments they would have otherwise received. This practice was required at one time by federal law.

Incentives Not to Work

How do these rules affect the incentive to seek part-time or full-time employment for welfare recipients? Most likely, the laws have succeeded in reducing the work effort on the part of welfare recipients. Put yourself in the unenviable position of someone on public assistance. You know that if you find a job for a few hours a week, your welfare payment will be reduced by exactly the amount you make. In such a situation the rate of return to working rather than not working is zero. In fact, you would have to find a job that paid you quite a bit more than what you get for doing nothing and remaining on public assistance. Otherwise, it really wouldn't pay you to work. New York City finally started to experiment with a program that allowed welfare mothers to keep the first $85 of earnings each month and a percentage of the amounts above that. This particular type of system, at least, does not generate an incentive *not* to work as did previous systems.

Man in the House Rule

An additional, somewhat disconcerting feature of most public assistance programs is that the money is cut off if both parents live in the same household. In other words, in some states one parent has to be absent from the home for the family unit to be eligible for AFDC. This is called the **man-in-the-house rule** and was intended to prevent payments to children who have an alternative potential source of support. But what would such a rule actually encourage? Most likely it fostered the breakup of homes and perpetuated reliance on welfare. The irritation caused by this rule has been aggravated in some states by regular searches of recipients' homes to ferret out violations.

Some cities have actually employed "spies" to snoop around AFDC homes to make sure a man is not present.

This sort of degradation of one's human dignity is another detrimental aspect of the current public assistance programs. In some cases, the amount of questioning that welfare recipients have to go through in order to receive their payments is appalling. In Chicago, for example, welfare workers are usually required to ask mothers who apply for AFDC monies to explain when, with whom, and how they last had intercourse.

In addition to public assistance, there are social insurance programs which to some extent provide income redistribution from the more well to do to the less well to do.

Social Insurance

For the retired and unemployed, certain social insurance programs exist which provide income payments in prescribed situations. The most well known is Social Security, which includes what has been called old age, survivors, disability and health insurance— or OASDHI. This is essentially a program of compulsory saving financed out of compulsory payroll taxes levied on both employers and employees. One pays

for Social Security while working and receives the benefits later on in life after retirement. The benefit payments are usually made to those reaching retirement age. When the insured worker dies, benefits accrue to his survivors which include his widow and his children. There are also special benefits that provide for disabled workers. Over 90 percent of all employed persons in the United States are covered by OASDHI.

Since it is a social insurance program that is supposedly paid for by the workers themselves, the actual size of the benefit payment varies according to the amount that the worker has contributed to the program, to the number of his dependents, and so on. In 1972, there were more than 25 million people receiving OASDHI checks averaging about $130 a month. Benefit payments from OASDHI redistribute income to some degree. However, benefit payments are typically not based on the recipient's need. A participant's contribution gives him the right to benefits even if he would be financially secure without them. In fact, Social Security appears to be a system whereby the relatively young subsidize the relatively old. One pays in when one is younger and receives payment when he is older. Social Security is not really an insurance program, however, because one is not guaranteed that the benefits he receives will be in line with the contributions he has made. The benefits are legislated by Congress. In the future, Congress may not be as sympathetic toward older people as it is today. It could legislate for lower benefits instead of higher ones.

Medical Care

Social Security now provides for medical care in the form of Medicare and Medicaid. The first Medicare program was passed in Congress in 1965. It provides for compulsory hospitalization insurance covering up to 90 days for each "spell of illness." The beneficiary pays the first $52 for each period of hospitalization and nothing more. The financing of the program comes out of OASDHI payroll taxes. Medicare and Medicaid have turned out to be much more expensive than originally anticipated, and the payments each worker has to pay into that program are increasing.

Unemployment Insurance

Lastly there is unemployment insurance which is not provided for by the Social Security Act of 1935. In other words, there is no federally operated program of unemployment insurance. It is left to the states to establish and operate such programs. Right now all of our 50 states have these programs, although they vary widely in the extent and amount of payments made. Programs are basically financed by taxes on employers. These taxes average less than 2 percent of total payrolls. When a worker finds himself unemployed, he may become eligible for benefit payments. The size of these payments and the number of weeks that they can be received vary from state to state. In 1970 over 2 million workers were obtaining unemployment payments that averaged about $50 a week. Currently, about 60 to 70 million people are covered by unemployment compensation.

Have We Been Successful?

If we look at how many people are in poverty today, we might be fooled into believing that our income redistribution plans, some of which have been outlined here, have been successful. First of all, we have to set a poverty line. Let's take a poverty line of $3000 for a family of four measured in 1959 purchasing power. If we use this standard, a third of Americans were poor in 1935; little more than 20 percent were poor in 1959; and today only 10 percent are poor. If this trend continues, we will eliminate poverty by 1980. But you know very well that this is not what will happen. The poverty line does not stay still. *Poverty is a relative concept.* Today's poverty would have been considered opulence 200 years ago. Further, poverty in the United States is greater than the average income level in almost every other country in the world. In 1980 when we will supposedly have eliminated poverty in this country, most people will think there are still a large number of poor people around. As stated several times before, the distribution of income has not changed very much in the last 30 or 40 years. The bottom 20 percent of the income earners are still getting between 4 and 5 percent of the income, just as they did in 1930. We are currently transferring about $45 to $50 billion a year to poor people with little effect in redistributing income. One alternative to the present welfare system is negative income taxation which we will now discuss. So far, this system holds the greatest promise as a method of redistributing income in the United States without incurring many of the detrimental aspects of our current system.

Negative Taxes

The individual income tax system would be used as a vehicle for closing at least a portion of the poverty income gap. By way of negative taxation, the difference would be made up between the actual income of poor families and the income that society stipulates as its poverty line. The money would be paid directly out of the federal Treasury according to a schedule based on family size, actual income earned, and other attributes. Notice here that we're not talking about setting up a new system; we're talking about an extension of an existing already, fully computerized income taxation set-up.

With a **negative income tax**, a family of four, for example, making an income of $1000 might be said to have a poverty income gap of $2000. Their income is $2000 below a poverty line of $3000. The $1000 of earned income also falls below the total of personal tax exemptions and minimum standard deductions which are allowed under current income tax laws. Under current laws, each person is allowed, say, $750 exemption for each member of the family. For a family of four, total exemptions would be $3000. In this particular situation, with an income of only $1000, there would be $2000 of unused exemptions. This is the negative base to which one would apply a tax rate to compute a negative tax. In this particular example, the negative taxation base would be $2000. If the negative tax rate was 50 percent, then the family would receive a check for $1000. Let's look at Table

XII–1. In the second column, we show family income before any allowances. Then we show poverty income gaps assuming that the poverty line is $3000. In the fourth column, we find out how much the people would receive, if the negative income rax rate were 50 percent.

The Difference Between PA and Negative Taxes

You might be wondering what the difference is between negative taxation and public assistance. With negative taxation, the taxpayer may have income and still receive a tax benefit as an income supplement necessary to raise his standard of living. He will still have an incentive to work. This incentive is directly related to how carefully defined the level of negative tax is. We can be fairly certain that the work effort of a man or woman will be related to the rate at which the negative tax benefits fall as earnings rise. The

faster benefits fall, the less incentive there will be for people to work. The slower they fall, the more incentive there will be for people to work, but, of course, the less redistribution of income there will be. This particular negative income tax system is not exactly the same thing as a guaranteed income. A guaranteed income would be, say, $3000 to anyone who didn't work. Here there would be no incentive for people to work unless they wanted to make considerably more than $3000 because once they made more than $3000, they would receive nothing. The negative income tax system generates less incentive for *not* working than would a pure form of guaranteed income.

Making Up the Entire Gap

One disadvantage of this example of a negative income tax program is that it does not bridge the poverty gap completely. Any family

---

TABLE XII–1 BRIDGING THE POVERTY GAP COMPLETELY

Here we use a minimum income of $3000. The caption for Table XII–2 on the next page illustrates how to use this table.

(1) MINIMUM INCOME	(2) EARNED INCOME	(3) POVERTY INCOME GAP	(4) NEGATIVE INCOME TAX (50% OF GAP)	(5) TOTAL INCOME
$3000	0	$3000	$1500	$1500
3000	$1000	2000	1000	2000
3000	2000	1000	500	2500
3000	3000	0	0	3000

whose income falls below the poverty line is partially compensated for that deficiency, but not wholly. One way to make sure that no one earns below a certain poverty line while not destroying the incentive to work is to raise the minimum income for the negative income tax. Look at Table XII–2. Here we have shown $6000 as the minimum income, and we have applied the 50 percent negative tax rate to the resulting higher deficits. Notice that total income never falls below $3000. Of course, the income subsidy is quite a bit larger than that shown in Table XII–1. Every family with some earned income will be subsidized to the extent that total incomes will all exceed the minimum level of $3000. In other words, people who are not "poor" will be getting some subsidy.

Workfare

In the fall of 1969 the Nixon administration proposed a new antipoverty program that was to replace state administered public assistance. His administration structured his "workfare" program in a manner that was supposed to provide an incentive for people to work rather than take public assistance. The main feature of this program involved a Family Assistance Plan (FAP). As originally conceived, it would have provided $500 per year for the first two members of a family plus $300 for each additional member. Nixon also proposed that the federal Food Stamp program be expanded. (Can you think of a good reason why he would want to give out food stamps instead of money?)

Under FAP, the first $720 per year of income could be made without losing any FAP payments. Then cash benefits from FAP would fall by 50 percent for any income earned in excess of $720. However, in 1971 and 1972, proposed changes in the FAP program were such that, if enacted, the incentive to work would in fact not be maintained very much.

The key to Nixon's originally conceived program was the emphasis on work. He originally stated that mothers with children under 6 who applied for FAP benefits would have to register with state employment agencies for training or suitable employment. There would have been an expansion of day-care facilities so that dependent children could be taken care of so as to free their mothers for participation in the labor force. One wonders if this particular aspect of the program is indeed cost effective. It may turn out that the wages that mothers can earn are not large enough to justify the cost of day care for their children. It may be that welfare mothers have a comparative advantage in doing just that—taking care of their children instead of working for someone else. If a welfare mother has four children and is *forced* to put them all in day care, the state may end up paying more for their care than the mother can actually make in the labor force. As can be ex-

TABLE XII–2

Here we have shown a minimum income of $6000. In column 2 we show the earned income from zero to $4000; in column 3, the difference between earned income and minimum income. Then we apply a negative income tax rate of 50 percent to come up with the negative income tax payment, or income subsidy, in column 4. Total income is therefore column 2 plus column 4, which is given in column 5.

(1)	(2)	(3)	(4)	(5)
MINIMUM INCOME	EARNED INCOME	POVERTY INCOME GAP	NEGATIVE INCOME TAX (50% OF GAP)	TOTAL INCOME
$6000	0	$6000	$3000	$3000
6000	$1000	5000	2500	3500
6000	2000	4000	2000	4000
6000	3000	3000	1500	4500
6000	4000	2000	1000	5000

pected, when Nixon announced his program, there was heated debate about the concept of forcing welfare mothers to work.

A Final Note

Even the most hard-hearted citizen will probably agree that certain forms of poverty should be eliminated. Even the most misanthropic of us will agree that people unable to earn income because of disabilities should be provided for. Those who do not like to see poverty in the midst of plenty want to have a much more comprehensive program of income redistribution from the rich to the poor—even if the poor are working. Currently, we have a complex, often ineffective system of helping those in need and of helping many who are not in need, such as the bureaucrats who run these programs.

Few economists will agree on the "correct" approach to income redistribution. It is certain, however, that we have been quite unsuccessful in effecting any real redistribution of income in the United States. Moreover, we have probably perpetuated with our public assistance programs a class of welfare recipients who are encouraged to remain unemployed. It is quite clear that there are other alternatives to the current welfare mess. President Nixon provided his Family Assistance Plan as one possible alternative, but there are others. All plans will cause some deterioration of the incentive to work. That is an inescapable fact and the cost that society must bear for any type of income redistribution. Apparently, however, society thinks the cost of such programs are outweighed by the benefits.

Definition of New Terms

PUBLIC ASSISTANCE: programs designed to meet, at least partially, the needs of certain categories of the poor. Public assistance programs include Aid to Families with Dependent Children, old age assistance, and others.

MAN-IN-THE-HOUSE RULE: a rule that usually has been applied to families in order that they become eligible for Aid to Families with Dependent Children. There can be no man in the house if AFDC is to be given.

NEGATIVE INCOME TAX: a system of transferring income to the relatively poor by way of taxing them negatively—that is, giving them an income subsidy depending upon how far below a minimum income their earned income lies.

Questions for Thought and Discussion

1. Do you think poverty is a relative concept or is there an absolute standard on which we can judge whether people are poor?
2. What method of eliminating poverty do you favor? Why? Is it economically efficient?

3. "We have socialism for the rich and free enterprise for the poor." Explain.
4. Do you believe in forcing unemployed workers to take any job given to them?
5. If a negative income tax program were instituted, would it be necessary to have special welfare programs or special subsidy programs for individual groups in the economy?

Selected References

Hamilton, David. *A Primer on the Economics of Poverty.* New York: Random House, 1968.

Kershaw, Joseph A. *Government Against Poverty.* Washington, D.C.: Brookings Institution, 1970.

Levitan, Sar A. *Programs in Aid of the Poor for the 1970s.* Baltimore: Johns Hopkins University Press, 1970.

Theobald, Robert, Ed. *Guaranteed Income.* New York: Doubleday, 1965.

Wilcox, Clair. *Toward Social Welfare.* Homewood, Illinois: Richard D. Irwin, 1969.

Growth, Ecology, and War

Social Costs and the Ecology

T ODAY THERE SEEMS to be an appalling amount of air, water, noise, and visual pollution. At first glance, it seems that the free market solution to the problem of allocating our scarce resources has gone awry. In fact, as pollution increases, so, too, do people's fears that the free working of supply and demand will bring about the ultimate destruction of our world as we know it. Perhaps, there is a way we can alter some of the existing signals in our market economy so as to bring about a more rational use of our resources and a less polluted environment. We will see in this chapter that some fairly straightforward improvements could be made in the institutional set-up in our economy which might bring about the desired reduction in pollution. We will examine some of the most pressing ecological issues after this chapter. Before we can really understand what economics has to say about these issues, we must establish why some economic agents (polluters) can do harm to our environment without paying for the consequences. We shall start off our discussion with the distinction between social costs and private costs.

SOCIAL VERSUS PRIVATE COSTS

Thus far, we've been dealing with situations where the costs of an individual's actions are fully recognized and, indeed, quite explicit. When a businessman has to pay wages to workers, he knows exactly what his labor costs are. When he has to buy materials or build a plant, he knows quite well what it will cost him. When an individual has to pay for fixing his car, or pay for a pair of shoes, or for a theater ticket, he knows exactly what his cost will be. These very explicit costs are what we term *private costs.* Private costs are those borne solely by the individuals who incur them. They are *internal* in the sense that the firm or household must explicitly take account of them.

Social Costs

What about a situation where a businessman can dump the waste products from his production process into a nearby river? Or what about instances where an individual can litter a public park or beach? Obviously, a cost is involved in these actions. When the businessman pollutes the water, people downstream suffer the consequences. They drink the polluted water and swim and bathe in it. They're also unable to catch as many fish as before because of the pollution. In the case of littering, the people who bear the costs are those who come along after our litterer has cluttered the park or the beach. The scenery certainly will be less attractive. We see that the cost of these actions are borne by people other than those who commit the actions. That is to say, the creator of the cost is not the bearer. The costs are not internalized; they are external. When we add *external* costs to *internal* or private costs, we come up with **social costs.** They are called social costs because society in general bears the costs and not just the individuals who create them. Pollution problems and, indeed, all problems pertaining to the environment may be viewed as situations where social costs are different than the private costs. Since some economic agents don't pay the full social costs of their actions, but rather only the smaller private costs, their actions are socially excessive.

Polluted Air

Let's ask ourselves why the air in cities is so polluted from automobile exhaust fumes. When automobile drivers step into their cars, they bear only the private costs of driving. That is, they must pay for the gas, maintenance, depreciation, and insurance on their automobiles. However, they cause an additional cost—that of air pollution—which they are not forced to take account of when they make the decision to drive. The air pollution created by automobile exhaust is a social cost which, as yet, individuals do not bear *directly.* The social cost of driving includes all the private costs plus the cost of air pollution which society bears. Decisions that are made on the basis of private costs only will lead to too much automobile driving or, alternatively, too little money spent on the reduction of automobile pollution.

EXTERNALITIES

When private costs differ from social costs, we usually term the situation a problem of **externalities** because individual decision makers are not *internalizing all* of the costs which society is bearing. Rather, some of these costs are remaining external to the decision-making process. We might want to view the problem as it is presented in Figure 12–1. Here we have drawn the market demand curve for product X. We have also drawn a supply curve for product X. The supply curve, however, is equivalent to the horizontal summation of all the individual marginal cost curves that include only internal or private costs. The intersection of the demand and supply curves as drawn will be at price P_e and quantity Q_e. However, we will assume that the production of good X involves externalities that the private businessmen did not take into account. Those externalities could be air pollution or water pollution or scenery destruction or anything else of that nature.

In any event, we know that the social costs of producing X exceed the private costs. We can show this by drawing the supply curve $S'S'$, which is above the original supply curve SS. It is above that original curve because it includes the externalities, or the full social costs of producing the product. Now the "correct" market equilibrium price would be P_1 and the quantity supplied and demanded would be Q_1. We see that the inclusion of external costs in the decision-making process

FIGURE 12–1

ADDING SOCIAL COSTS

Here we show the demand for good X as DD. The supply curve is shown as SS, which is equal to the horizontal summation of all the individual marginal cost curves of the firms producing that good. These individual marginal cost curves only include internal or private costs; they do not include any social costs which might be pollution in the air or water. If the social costs were included and added to the private costs, the supply curve would shift up to S'S'. In the uncorrected situation, the equilibrium price would be Pe and the quantity demanded and supplied would be Qe. In the corrected situation, the equilibrium price would rise to P1 and the quantity demanded and supplied would fall to Q1.

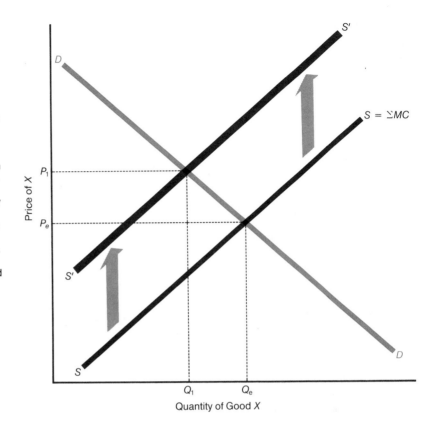

CORRECTING THE SIGNALS

would lead to a higher priced product and less of a quantity supplied and demanded. We can say, therefore, that in an unrestricted situation where social costs are not being fully borne by the creators of those costs, the quantity produced is "excessive."

We can see here an "easy" method of reducing the amount of pollution and environmental degradation that now exists. Somehow the signals in the economy must be changed so that decision makers will take into account all of the costs of their actions. In the case of automobile pollution, we might want to devise some method whereby motorists were taxed according to the amount of pollution they caused. In the case of a firm, we might want to devise some system whereby businessmen were taxed according to the amount of pollution they were responsible for. In this manner, they would have an incentive to install pollution abatement equipment.

When you think about it, however, it may not be appropriate to levy a *uniform* tax according to physical quantities of pollution. After all, we're talking about social costs. Such costs are not necessarily the same everywhere in the United States for the same action. If you drive your smelly, belching car in the middle of the Mohave Desert, you will probably not inflict any damage on anyone else. No one will be there to complain; the natural cleansing action of the large body of air around you will eliminate the pollution you generate to such an extent that it creates no economical harm. If a businessman pollutes the water in a lake that is used by no one except him and the lake is, in fact, inaccessible to everyone except him, the economic damages he creates by polluting may be negligible.

Essentially, we must establish the size of the *economic damages* rather than the size of the *physical* amount of pollution. A polluting electric steam-generating plant in New York City will cause much more damage than the same plant in, say, Nowhere, Montana. This is so because the concentration of people in New York City is much higher than in Nowhere. There are already innumerable demands on the air in New York City, so that the pollution from smokestacks will not naturally be cleansed away. There are millions of people who will breathe that smelly air and thereby incur the costs of sore throats, sickness, emphysema, and even early death. There are many, many buildings which will become dirtier faster because of the pollution, and many more cars and clothes will also become much dirtier. The list goes on and on, but it should be obvious that a given quantity of pollution will cause more harm in concentrated urban environments than it will in less dense rural environments. If we were to establish some form of taxation in order to align social costs with private costs and force people to internalize externalities, we would somehow have to come up with a measure of economic costs instead of physical quantities.

PROPERTY RIGHTS

Now let's find out why there will be a divergence between social costs and private costs. Why do certain situations create externalities, while others do not. For an example, consider some of the things you own. Suppose you own a bicycle. If someone comes along and somehow alters it unfavorably by slashing the tires or bending the

spokes, you can, in principle, press criminal charges or at least civil charges and recover damages. The damages you recover would at least be equal to the reduction in the market value of your bike. The same goes for a car, if you own one. Anyone damaging your car is liable for those damages. The courts will uphold your right to compensation.

Common Property

What if you live next to a stinky steel factory? The air around you—which is something that you have to use—is damaged. You are also damaged by breathing it. However, you do not necessarily have any grounds for stopping the air pollution or for obtaining compensation for the destruction of the air around you. This is so because you do not have *property rights* in the air surrounding you, nor does anyone else. Air happens to be a *common property resource.* Herein lies the crux of the problem: whenever property rights are indefinite or nonexistent, social costs may be different than private costs, particularly in the situations we will outline below. This is as you would expect. When no one owns a particular resource, people do not have an incentive to consider their particular despoliation of that resource. In fact, a person would be foolish to do so. If one person decides not to pollute the air, there will be no general effect on the total level of pollution. If one person decides not to pollute the ocean, there will still be the same general amount of ocean pollution, provided of course that the individual is a small part of the total number of polluters.

When property rights are in existence, individuals have legal recourse to any damages sustained through the misuse of their property. When property rights are well defined, the use of property—that is, the use of resources—will generally involve contracting between the owners of those resources. If you owned any land, you might contract with another person so that he could use your land for raising cows. The contract would most likely be written up in the form of a rental agreement. We can probably predict that whenever contracting becomes exceedingly expensive or difficult, social and private costs will diverge. Whenever contracting is relatively costless, social costs and private costs will end up being one and the same thing as we shall see. In fact, this is why externalities are only problems in certain areas of activity in our society. We don't worry about social and private costs with the majority of all the activities that go on in our economy because almost all of what goes on involves contracting among individuals and the transference of property rights.

WHEN PROPERTY RIGHTS DO NOT EXIST

Surprisingly enough, even when property rights do not exist, it is sometimes possible for private costs to equal social costs. In such situations, there is no misallocation of resources. Let's take a simple example. Suppose you live in a house with a nice view of some lake. The guy living below you plants a tree. Over the years the tree grows larger and larger, and eventually it starts to cut off your view. In most cities, nobody has property rights to views; and therefore, you usually cannot go to the courts for relief. You cannot file suit against your downhill neighbor for obstructing your view.

Contracting

You do have an alternative, however. You can, as it were, bribe your neighbor (contract with him) to top his tree (make it shorter). What kind of bribe would you offer him? You could start out with a small money figure and keep going up either until he agrees or until you reach your limit. Your limit will be equal to the value you place on having an unobstructed view of the lake. The neighbor will be willing to top his tree if the payment is

at least equal to the reduction in property value due to a stunted tree. In this manner, you make him aware of the social cost of his action; you inform him of the social cost of his growing a large tree which blocks your view and thereby lowers the value of your property. But you do this in a rather odd way—essentially, you bribe him. Nonetheless, he is still informed of the true cost of his actions. Alternatively, your neighbor could come to you and ask you how much you would be willing to pay to have him top his tree.

For fun, let's see if things would be different when property rights were actually vested in views. Let's say that the property right to your view was vested in you. Therefore, anybody destroying your view would have to pay the consequences. In this particular case, the downhill landowner would have to bribe you to be able to let the tree grow higher than you want it to. The bribe to you would have to be at least equal to the reduction in the value of your property because of an obstructed view. (This will, of course, be a measure of the value of the view itself.) If the downhill landowner doesn't offer that high a bribe, he will have to top his tree because you will not go for his bargain.

Opportunity Costs

Now let's change the situation. Assume that he has the property right in your view—a strange situation indeed but actually equivalent to the example where no one had the property right. If he has the property right in your view, will things be any different from when you had the property right? If you think so, you're wrong. Just because he now owns the view does not mean he will ignore the cost he is imposing on you. After all, he would be giving up the opportunity of perhaps making some money in a deal with you. He could gingerly walk to your house and ask you how much you would be willing to pay to have him top his tree. If you were willing to pay enough, he would do so. If not, he would leave it as is.

In other words, your neighbor would take account of the *opportunity cost*. This is the key to understanding why private costs will equal social costs in all three of the above situations—in the first instance where there were no property rights, in the second case where property rights were given to the uphill landowner, and in the third case where property rights were given to the downhill landowner. In each and every situation, opportunity costs exist and will be taken into account. The contracting involved is relatively simple: only two parties are concerned and verbal agreements could be made relatively easily. This particular example leads us to a strange but, nonetheless, correct conclusion:

When transactions costs are minimal, it does not matter who has the property rights in the resources under study. They will be used in exactly the same way.

Otherwise stated:

The allocation of resources does not depend on who has property rights if transactions costs are small.

Wealth Distribution

Note that the distribution of wealth will differ. *The person who gets the property rights to some resource that was formerly common property will obviously be better off, as his wealth will be higher.* In the above example, if a large untopped tree is more valuable than the view of the uphill landowner, the tree will not be topped. Think about this. In the case where the uphill landowner had the property right in the view, he will accept a bribe that is at least equal to the reduction in his property value due to the large tree. The downhill landowner will offer a sum that does not exceed the increase in his property value due to an untouched tree. If the view is more valuable than the untouched tree, he will not be able to bribe the uphill landowner; he will have to top the tree.

On the other hand, if the downhill landowner has the property rights in the view, he will have to be bribed to top the tree. If the increased value of the unobstructed view leads the uphill landowner to offer a sum which is greater than the value of an untouched tree to the downhill landowner, the downhill landowner will accept the bribe and top the tree. In either case, the resource—the view—will be used such that it generates its highest economic value.

When Transactions Costs Are High

Our example so far is pretty simple. It only involves two people and the contracting or transactions costs are small. What about a case where the transactions costs aren't so small? Take the example of a factory polluting a city of several million people. It would be difficult for the several million people to get together to somehow bribe the factory into reducing its pollution. The transactions costs here would be extremely high. Therefore, we cannot predict that private costs will equal social costs for the factory. This is probably true with many environmental problems.

There are indefinite property rights which in and of themselves are not always a problem if contracting can be done easily. However, when large numbers of people are involved, contracting is difficult, and, in many instances, the actual costs are hard to measure and/or the creators of those costs are difficult to identify. If ships are spilling excess oil into the ocean, how do we police them to find out which ones are doing it? The costs of such policing may be high. This discussion of property rights leads us to another possible solution that might help solve our environmental problems.

PINPOINTING PROPERTY RIGHTS

Instead of attempting to tax polluters in proportion to the economic damages caused by their pollution, we could define property rights more precisely so that contracting would have to take place. As concerns the view of the lake, it did not really matter who had property rights in the view. In fact, indefinite property rights really were inconsequential to the outcome of the situation except, of course, with reference to the wealth positions of the individuals. This is not the case with other environmental problems. For example, we might want to make factories liable for the pollution that they create. When we do that, we are implicitly vesting property rights in the common property resources of water and air surrounding the factories. The individuals living there will implicitly be the owners of the air and water. The factory will therefore be liable for the use of water and air in a manner which imposes costs on others.

In a sense, this is not really "fair." After all, a common property resource is, by definition, owned by everyone. We would be arbitrary in assigning property rights in a common property resource to the homeowners, just as we would be arbitrary in assigning the property rights to the factory. But, due to the fact that it is easier to make the individual factory owner pay, we still might want to go ahead with this arbitrary assignment of property rights. In essence, the government will have to act in behalf of the homeowners when dealing with the polluting factory. The government will somehow have to come up with the value of the economic damages that the factory's pollution is causing and require that the factory make due compensation or install pollution abatement equipment. The compensation would have to be distributed to the homeowners in a manner that reflected the economic cost sustained by each of them. That, of course, is a difficult problem. It might be simpler to use the "bribe" money to clean up some of the pollution caused by the factory instead of trying to compensate the losers (the individual homeowners). Note here that the optimal level of pollution is not zero. The optimal level is that point where the social benefits of further reducing pollution just equal the social costs of doing so.

WHAT ABOUT EXTERNAL BENEFITS?

So far, we've discussed external costs that were not internalized by individual decision makers. We should note that there are also situations with external benefits. In cases where the social benefits of an action exceed the private benefits, we would expect that individual decision-makers would do too little of such an action from society's point of view. In fact, it is often argued that many endeavors involve large social benefits which are not internalized. It is further argued that government subsidization of such activity is in order. This is often the argument used to justify public education. An educated citizenry presumably votes more wisely, commits less crime, and so on. Therefore, it behooves society to furnish "free" public education to all.

Many times the mere fact that an external benefit exists does not economically justify government subsidization of the activity. A well-dressed, attractive female generates a considerable amount of external benefits which no one pays for. Does that mean that we are underproducing attractive females? Should the government subsidize sexy clothes and alluring make-up so that more females can generate more external benefits? Well-developed males also generate external benefits, but should the government, therefore, subsidize gyms? When someone has a beautiful garden, passers-by benefit from that garden yet do not pay anything. Does that mean that we should subsidize beautiful gardens so that there will be more of them?

The key to understanding when an external benefit is relevant is in finding out whether those people who are benefiting from the externality would be willing to pay, on the margin, for one more unit. For example, it is argued that when electricity wires are put underground, more people than just the property owners benefit. People driving or walking in a neighborhood that has no overhead wires benefit because they are looking on a more beautiful neighborhood. That does not, however, necessarily mean that underground electricity wires should be subsidized (paid for by the government instead of the property owners). We would somehow have to find out if people who do not live in the area would nonetheless be willing to pay something for the privilege of seeing the neighborhood without electricity wires. If they are unwilling, then in this particular situation it is probably not economically meaningful to consider the externality problem as a real problem.

EXTERNAL BENEFITS AND NONPAYERS

When external benefits exist, we usually find that those who obtain those external benefits cannot be excluded from obtaining them. Otherwise, the benefits wouldn't be external; they would be internal. A theater can generate external benefits if, in fact, there is no way to exclude viewers. After all, once the picture is being shown, everybody can benefit from the picture as long as there is sufficient space. But since theater owners like to capture profits, they construct walls and doors to exclude nonpayers. The exclusion of nonpayers is important to making sure that all benefits from an action are internalized.

This is not the case in all situations. Consider, for example, fireworks displays. They can be seen for many, many blocks around, and it is difficult to exclude nonpayers. Here is a case where social or external benefits actually exist because nonpayers will not be excluded and can get value from the production of a fireworks display. However, businessmen in general are quite ingenious in finding ways to exclude nonpayers. To the extent that they are successful, we need not worry about external benefits. Football stadiums have high walls; theaters have closed doors, and so on. However, there are situations where, even though it is relatively costless to exclude nonpayers, it might be more socially beneficial if no one were excluded.

PUBLIC GOODS

There is a class of goods which economists have labeled **public goods.** With such goods, the amount that one individual uses of the good or service does not take away from the amount that any other individual can use the good, *once it has already been produced.* If you write a poem, anybody can read the poem without preventing anybody else from doing the same thing. If you develop a theory, anybody else can use the theory without reducing other people's use of that theory. The marginal cost, once the good or service is produced, is zero. Indeed, pricing on the basis of marginal cost, we would see that once the good is produced there is no price!

This is the situation with television and radio signals. Once they are produced, they are a public good. Anyone who wants to use them can do so without taking away from any other person's ability to use them. Further, the cost to the television or radio generating station is zero when a new person decides to use the waves. The marginal cost of providing TV or radio programs, once they are produced, is usually zero; and, in that sense, the price should be zero. However, if the price were zero, then you would not expect much to be produced, would you? Entrepreneurs usually don't like to sell their products at a zero price.

In such cases, and for most public goods, there has to be some way to transfer the public good into a private good. Otherwise, the government will have to take on the production itself. In the case of television, we now have a *semi* public good because television stations allow advertisers to buy time. The advertising pays for the production of the signals. You pay for the TV programs you watch when you buy the products that are advertised. If you buy none of the products advertised on TV, then in essence you are being subsidized by those people who do. In the case of national defense, another classic public good, government has taken on the production of the service. (With that particular public good, it would be very expensive to exclude nonpayers from the benefits.)

Sometimes there are ways of transferring a public good into a private good by setting up a system which will exclude nonpayers. That's exactly what cable television or pay-TV is all about. Anybody who does not pay does not obtain the TV signal, or if he does, it is scrambled. If this were the case, we would not have to see so many commercials on television because we would pay directly for the service.

The area of public goods is new in economics and not very well defined. At this point, we can say that it is usually inappropriate to blindly carry over the principles we have laid out for private goods to goods which are public. We have, however, established a fairly comprehensive theory in this chapter which we can apply to various ecology issues. We shall turn to these issues next.

Definition of New Terms

SOCIAL COSTS: costs of an action which include all those that society bears. Social costs are different from private costs in some situations where externalities are involved.

EXTERNALITIES: effects on third parties which are not taken into account by individual decision makers. An externality to the production of steel might be the pollution put into the air that the individual steel maker does not have to pay for.

COMMON PROPERTY: property which is owned by no one, which can be used by all.

PUBLIC GOODS: goods for which the marginal cost of an additional person using them once they have been produced is zero. National defense is a good example of a public good.

Chapter Summary

1. Up until this chapter we have been dealing with situations where the costs of individual actions are fully recognized. These are called private costs and they are borne privately by people who transact any exchange in the economy. In some sense they are internal to the firm or the household and must explicitly be taken care of.

2. In some situations there are social costs which do not equal private costs. That is, there are costs to society which exceed the cost to the individual. These social costs may include such things as air and water pollution, for which private individuals do not have to pay. Society, however, does bear the costs of these externalities.

3. One way to analyze the problem of pollution is to look at it in terms of an externality situation. Individual decision makers do not take account of the negative externalities that they impose on the rest of society. In such a situation, they produce "too much" pollution.

4. It might be possible to ameliorate the situation by imposing a tax on polluters. The tax, however, should be dependent upon the size of the economic damages created rather than upon the physical amounts of pollution. This tax, therefore, will be different for the same level of physical pollution in different parts of the country because the economic damages differ depending upon the location and the density of the population.

5. Another way of looking at the externality problem is to realize that it involves the lack of definite property rights. We are talking about common property resources such as air and water. No one owns them and, therefore, no one takes account of the long-run pernicious effects of excessive pollution.
6. In situations where transaction costs are minimal, the same allocation of resources will result whether the property in question is common or privately owned. The distribution of wealth, however, will change depending upon who is allowed to effectively assume property rights over the common property.
7. External benefits arise when individual actions create positive benefits to other individuals without those other individuals having to pay for the positive benefits. It is often thought that whenever external benefits exist, subsidization is required to reach an optimal production of them.
8. In economics we have a body of theory devoted to public goods. These are defined as goods for which the cost of providing service to an additional individual is zero, once the good has already been produced. National defense and radio and TV signals are examples of public goods.

Questions for Thought and Discussion

1. Are there any actions which you engage in for which no external benefits or costs arise? What are they?
2. Invitingly dressed members of the opposite sex generate positive external benefits. Should the government subsidize such clothing?
3. If you were in a jury and a houseowner was suing an airport for noise pollution, in whose favor would you decide? Would it depend on who got there first, the homeowner or the airport? Does this bother you?
4. If you were the economic consultant to a nation that was just created, would you tell the government to prohibit private property rights in land or allow private property rights? Why?
5. Is it true that property rights often interfere with human rights?
6. When Charles DeGaulle was ruler of France, he decided to not support NATO. Do you think there was a free rider problem involved here? Why? Is NATO a public good?
7. It is possible to prevent nonpayers from receiving TV signals without a large cost. That is why pay-TV is feasible technologically. Does this mean that pay-TV will not be a public good?

Selected References

Coase, Ronald H. "The Problem of Social Costs." *Journal of Law and Economics* (October 1961).
Coase, Ronald H. "The Federal Communications Commission." *Journal of Law and Economics* (October 1962), 111-140.
Kneese, Allen V. *Economics and the Quality of the Environment.* Washington, D.C.: Resources for the Future, April 1968.
McKean, Roland M. *Public Spending.* New York: McGraw Hill, 1968. Pp. 67-75.

ISSUE XIII

How Should We Utilize Our Resources?

The Debate

Conservation is a loaded word, there is no doubt. The first head of the U.S. Forest Service, Gifford Pinchot, felt that "conservation means the greatest good for the greatest numbers, and that for the longest time." Members of the Sierra Club and the Wilderness Society believe that the government should take a vastly increased interest in preserving our natural wilderness areas and in preserving Mother Earth in general. Some businessmen might think that the Sierra Club members are fanatical and unknowledgeable about the economics of conservation. After all, trees have to be cut to make houses, and iron ore has to be taken out of the ground to make steel for buildings. There are economic aspects to the conservation question which we can apply to finding out what the real issue is all about. Let's see if we can put these economic aspects to work.

What Conservation Really Means

Let's look carefully at the quotation from Gifford Pinchot. We should ask whether this is really an operational definition of conservation. Is this really what conservationists believe should be the *modus operandi* of the government in conserving our natural resources? The answer is probably not. Think about it for a while.

Limited Resources

We know that at any moment in time, the total amount of resources in the United States is fixed. Therefore, with the exception of public goods, whatever you use of a resource, your friends cannot use. Whatever your friends use, you cannot use. This makes it difficult to talk about the greatest good for the greatest number, and this is what economists refer to as erroneous and impossible double maximization. It would be like saying you want the best for the least. Either you seek out the highest quality product you can buy for a given price, or for a given quality you seek out the lowest priced brand. A firm either takes production as given and tries to minimize costs, or it takes costs as given and tries to maximize production. The same holds for conservation. It is impossible to have the greatest good for the greatest number because what one person has, another person doesn't have.

Also consider the clause, "and that for the longest time." What does this mean? What could it possibly lead to in terms of the use of resources? Doesn't it imply that no resources should be used at all today and forever after? That, of course, is how we use our resources for the longest time—by never using them up at all! We can keep all the coal in the ground

from now to eternity by never taking any out. But does conservation mean that we should limit the amount of resources we use so that they will last the longest? If so, we should stop consuming resources today. Then our grandchildren and their grandchildren and their grandchildren will inherit the largest amount of natural resources.

An Operational Definition

Another definition of conservation must be found if we are to have a rational, objective standard with which to judge current actions involving our natural resources. Let's take a simple example of an acre of land which has some trees on it. Suppose you are the owner of that land. How should you decide whether to cut the trees or let them grow? If you decide to cut the trees, when should you cut them and how many should you do it to? Should you cut one tree, two trees, or all the trees?

Let's make the problem simple and assume that the trees are located in an area that no one ever sees. We will assume you get no pleasure from the mere fact of owning trees. You are a wealth maximizer and look only at the monetary return to the piece of property that you own. If you wanted to maximize wealth, you would decide how to use your

trees by looking at how profitable it would be to either cut them or let them grow. That's a hard decision but really no different from the decisions facing any property owner. He must decide the optimal use of his resource. With natural resources, this also involves the optimal *timing* of the use of the resource.

If you thought you could build a road to your stand of trees and then charge campers a certain amount of money to use the area, you would consider this as an alternative way to use your resource. You could also cut down all the trees today, sell them on the open market, and receive a certain price per tree. If you waited another year, you could sell them on the open market and you'd perhaps receive a different price. Since the trees would have grown during that time, there would be more board feet of lumber to sell. Obviously, if you thought that the price was going to rise in the future and the trees were going to grow bigger, you might want to wait to cut them. But obviously you shouldn't wait forever. At some point, you will maximize your net wealth position by cutting the trees or, if camping becomes very lucrative, by making your tree stand into a private campground. The point is that you must compare the benefits from not cutting trees with the costs of not cutting trees. The benefits of not cutting is the fact that they could be used as a campground. Moreover, if you do not cut, you might get a higher price for them in the future.

Your costs are the opportunity costs of not cutting the trees and selling them for what you could get. If, for example, you could sell them for $1 million this year and invest that money in a comparatively risk-free government bond which yielded a 6 percent rate of return, the opportunity cost of not cutting the trees is going to be equal to 6 percent of $1 million, or $60,000. The combined benefit of not cutting the trees—that is, the benefit of a potential higher price in the future with bigger trees to sell—must at least equal the $60,000. Otherwise, you would cut the trees right away. (You also have the alternative of cutting now and then replanting. You might want to sell the timberland with small young trees on it.)

Discounting

In order to maximize the value of a piece of property that has natural resources on it, you should time your use of those resources so as to maximize the *discounted* value of the resources. Let's review the concept of discounting. If you get a dollar today, it's worth a dollar; but if you get a dollar one year from now, in today's terms, it is not worth $1. It is worth less. You must discount tomorrow's dollar back to today to find out what it is really worth to you. After all, today's dollars could be put in a savings and loan association to earn interest. If somebody said you had to pay them one dollar a year from now, you might be able to put 95¢ in the bank and earn interest so that in one year, you would be able to pay the dollar. Thus, *costs which are borne in the future are less of a burden than those which must be paid today.*

The same is true of benefits. In this particular case the benefits will be the income received from cutting the timber. Money that is forthcoming a year from now will be worth less than money today. Even if you didn't want to invest the money you have today, you would be better off having it today than in the future because you have the opportunity to invest it or spend it during the interim. *Benefits are worth less the further away they are in the future.* If you have an acre of trees, you will estimate how much money you will receive for each time profile of cutting them. (You could sell the land and trees, too.) It may turn out that you should never cut them if, in fact, the money you can make from turning the acre into a private campground exceeds the money you can make from cutting the trees. That, in fact, has happened in this country. As public campgrounds (for which users are usually charged a below market-clearing price) become more and more crowded, private campgrounds become more attractive to individuals and therefore more and more private campgrounds have sprung up throughout the United States. There was a 15 percent increase in such campgrounds from 1970 to 1971.

Conservation Defined Operationally

Conservation now takes on a very definite meaning. The definition we shall use will be that *conservation means the optimal timing of the use of our fixed amount of resources.* What does optimal timing involve? This merely means utilizing resources in such a way that the present value of the streams of net benefits from those resources is maximized. We can apply this definition to many of the problems of conserving our natural resources. Let's do that now.

Depletion of Nonrenewable Resources

There is much concern about using up all of the natural gas under this earth. There's also much concern about using up all of the iron ore, coal, oil, or any of the other minerals and resources that are found in the earth which cannot be renewed (or renewed only very slowly). This is not the case, of course, with trees: we can always plant more trees. But lots of resources cannot be renewed. Many conservationists believe that because they cannot be renewed, their use should be limited. Using our newly found definition of conservation, we can agree that the use of such resources should indeed be limited, but not to the degree of never using them. After all, if the coal in the earth is never used, the present value of that coal will be zero. We'll never obtain any benefits from it. Neither will our grandchildren nor their grandchildren because they will never be able to use it to furnish energy. If it will never yield a benefit in the future, then there is nothing to discount, and present value is zero. The question really is: how fast should we use our coal? How fast should we use our natural gas? Inevitably, we will eventually run out of many of our natural resources if we consume them at some constant rate forever. Any finite use of resources will eventually deplete nonrenewable resources unless their quantity is infinite. The only thing that holds true is that the slower we use them, the longer they will last. But how do we decide the rate at

which we should actually use these resources?

Correct Timing

Again, we can go back to a wealth-maximizing situation. Now we will want to assume that it is the wealth of the entire world that is important. Here we can use our same criterion. The value from nonrenewable resources is maximized if they are used at different periods in time so that the net present value of these resources is highest. You might immediately scream "Bloody murder" at this criterion, for it leads to an eventual depletion of the kinds of resources that you are familiar with. Let's take the case of natural gas. It is true that we may eventually run out of natural gas if we continue using it. First of all, we will not continue using it at its same rate if the Federal Power Commission allows the price to rise as a reflection of the interaction of supply and demand. As the price of natural gas becomes higher, people will seek less expensive alternatives. This is one key to understanding why there is a limit to how much of a natural resource will be used. After some point, the resource becomes so expensive that nobody uses it any more. In fact, we may never run out of natural gas because it will become prohibitively expensive to take it out of the ground. People will use substitutes.

Using Substitutes

The use of substitutes is another key to understanding why it might be better to use up some of our natural resources rather than limit their use today. If we do not use natural gas, for example, we will use oil, coal, or some other form of energy. If we restrict the production and consumption of any one of our natural resources, we can be sure that some others will be used more intensively or other substitutes will be developed. That means that they will be used up faster than otherwise. It is impossible to conserve *everything* because that means that we would have to cease to exist. It is also somewhat naive to talk in terms of conserving only one or a selected few natural resources because then other resources will be used up more quickly. If, in fact, we want to maximize the benefits from our available resources, we would be wise to use up the cheapest ones first and then go on to the more inaccessible and less readily available ones. This can perhaps be best illustrated by an example.

Using Too Little May Mean Less for the Future

Assume that the government has a million dollars to invest in the economy. What if the government decides to invest the million dollars in a project that yields a rate of return of 5 percent and the rate of return in the private (nongovernmental) sector is 10 percent? Future generations will not be better off by the government investment. They would inherit a larger capital stock—that is, more wealth—if the government had not used the million dollars, which it would have gotten from the private sector in the first place, and allowed the private sector to use it in private investment where it would yield a rate of return of 10 percent. The same goes for use of natural resources.

If we decide to use a combination of natural resources that has a higher cost than some other combination, we will be cheating future generations, not helping them out. It may be that if we decide to use less natural gas and more oil, for example, the wealth that future generations will inherit will be less than it would be otherwise. We will be doing future generations a disfavor by being "conservationist-minded." Admittedly, this is a hard concept to accept because it does mean allowing nonrenewable resources to be depleted if that is in fact the cheapest way to provide consumption and investment that the present generation wishes to engage in. But acting in any other way would leave future generations worse off, contrary to the notion of most conservationists. Conservation cannot mean limiting the use of our resources; it has

to mean maximizing the benefit from our limited resources.

Who Benefits from Conserving the Wilderness?

Conservationists like to maintain that preservation of wilderness areas is for everybody—for the good of all, for the rich man and the poor man. We will see, however, that this may not be the case. Before we examine the distribution of benefits among the population, we have to realize what the preservation of wilderness areas actually involves.

Remember that every action has a cost in that opportunity costs

are always involved. This cost does not have to be explicitly stated or even understood for it to exist. We live, unfortunately, in a world of limited resources—in a world of trade-offs. If we realize that every alternative course of action involves a certain set of costs, then we can ask who will bear these costs. If we look at preservation of our natural ecology, we see that there are going to be costs involved.

What is the opportunity cost of preserving in its pristine beauty an area of wooded hillsides? The opportunity cost will include what could be done with the land for campgrounds and for logging. In the case of campgrounds, the people who bear the costs of pre-serving the area as wilderness rather than as campsites are those who like to camp but not those who like to backpack.

More Expensive Wood Products

When looking at who bears the cost of not using the wooded area for forest products (for logging), we find that it is everyone who likes to buy houses, or other wood products, or wood product substitutes for that matter. After all, when fewer forest areas are opened up for logging, the supply of lumber will be smaller than it could have been. We see in Figure XIII–1 that the demand schedule for wood products has shifted to the right due to increasing population and income, but the supply schedule remains stable because wilderness areas are not opened up for logging. We would expect that the equilibrium price of wood products would rise from P_1 to P_2. Houses become more expensive, whether they are made out of wood or nonwood. This happens because the price for a wood house is higher than it would otherwise be so people substitute nonwood houses. The demand schedule for nonwood houses shifts to the right and the price of such houses also goes up.

Benefits

There are obviously going to be benefits from preserving the wil-

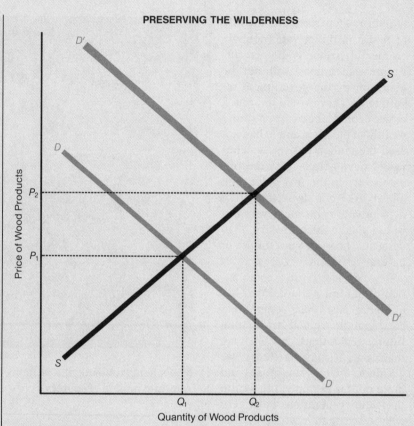

PRESERVING THE WILDERNESS

FIGURE XIII–1

Here we have shown the quantity of wood products on the horizontal axis and the price of wood products on the vertical axis. We assume that due to increases in population and income, the demand curve for wood products shifts from DD to $D'D'$. However, due to the maintenance of wilderness areas, the supply schedule of wood products does not increase. The price of wood products therefore rises from P_1 to P_2. Houses become more expensive as a result.

derness. There will be increased areas for backpacking in a pre-served area. People who like to backpack can enjoy hunting and fishing there. Moreover, benefits are bestowed upon those who do not themselves want to backpack, hunt, or fish but would, nonethe-less, pay something to keep the wilderness for their children.

Now we come down to the cru-cial question. Who bears the cost and who reaps the benefits from conserving wilderness areas in their natural state? This is an em-pirical question and we can only find out by examining actual data. There have been some very limited studies on who uses wilderness areas. It has been found that in general backpackers are fairly well educated and earn considerably more than the average American. We might, therefore, tentatively conclude that the benefits from conserving wilderness areas will be bestowed upon the better educated and the more highly paid members of society. Now, what about the costs? We said before that those who like to camp will be denied camping areas. It has been found that people who use tents, trailers, and camper trucks are, on average, less well educated and earn less than backpackers. We would expect that there would be a trade-off, then, of recreation facilities used by lower income people (campers) in favor of those used by higher income people (backpackers). Additionally, there will be those who suffer from higher housing costs. We know in general that the poor will suffer more than the rich because housing expenditures are a larger fraction of the budget of poor people.

The meager evidence that we have so far on the distribution of benefits and costs due to conservation of wilderness areas leads us to the rather annoying (a value judgment, to be sure), highly tentative conclusion that it is the relatively well-to-do who benefit and the relatively less well-to-do

who bear the costs. One might want to consider that this type of income redistribution is the reverse of what people usually consider as appropriate.

The Vanishing Bald Eagle and Other Endangered Species

We are now faced with the danger of eliminating many species of wild animals. The bald eagle is only one of them. Among others, there are the condor, the blue whale, and the bighorn mountain sheep. Why are people concerned about the survival of whooping cranes and alligators but are not worried about the disappearance of dogs and chickens? No one is concerned about whether there will be a sufficiently large number of cows in the future, or a sufficient number of horses or pigs or rabbits or cats. No one is worried because these animals are private property. People have a vested interest in preserving the species and in making it as large as will be profitable. This is not the case with wild animals.

No one owns bald eagles. In fact, it would be difficult to vest property rights in them because it is very hard to keep track of where they go. If somebody owned all the bald eagles, it would cost him a fortune to police his property. He would have a difficult time preventing his eagles from being killed by poachers,

even though he would have legal right to suing the killers. The same is true for blue whales, condors, bighorn mountain sheep, and so on. They are all in a sense common property. It never pays anyone to be conservationist-minded with these wild animals. If, for example, you were out in the woods and you had the choice of shooting a bighorn mountain sheep or not shooting it, what difference do you think it would make on the total population of that species whether you took one course of action or the other? It would make very little difference. Your single action has little effect on the total population of bighorn mountain sheep—which is why people despoil a common property. That is also why we find many vanishing species of wild animals that are valued highly by some of us.

How to Protect Wild Animals

What would be the solution to saving these vanishing species? How would we protect wild animals? One solution would be to vest property rights in them, and, for some species, this is not difficult. This would be a particularly thorny problem with migrating animals, however, because it's so hard to even attempt to enforce property rights in them. On the other hand, if people own the land that wild animals graze on, then the wild animals could become part of the property in addition to the land. In this manner, the owners would have a vested interest in preserving the species (most likely). Anybody who violated the owners' property rights would be sued for damages.

This is exactly what has happened in the northwestern part of the United States. Some entrepreneurs bought an island and called it Safari Island. They imported rare animals as well as more common animals and started to raise them. The owners charge hunters a very high price to come on the island to stalk these animals. Concerned wild animal lovers have raised a big stink over Safari Island; however, it seems that such an endeavor is exactly what is needed to preserve species of rare animals. If the entrepreneurs who own the island want to make money, they must insure themselves of a continual supply of animals. One way to do this is to breed the animals on the island. In this manner, there is no further elimination of any endangered species. Rather, hunters must pay for the right to hunt these animals and the entrepreneurs who own them will continue to breed them to insure their continued existence. It seems like Safari Island is just the thing to give an alternative to hunters who feel the need to kill wild animals. Instead of going out and killing those endangered animals that are common property, hunters have an alternative where they pay for the right to shoot animals which are private property. Agreed, many people do think the idea is repulsive. But given that many people do engage in the sport, is it not generally better for the animals that property rights be vested in some of them so that the species can be preserved?

Ocean Rights

The extension of private property rights to ocean waters might also solve the problem of vanishing fish species and vanishing aquatic mammal species. Vesting property rights in ocean waters would have been a losing proposition a hundred years ago; it would have been impossible to police one's property. However, things have changed, and we now have relatively cheap electronic sensing equipment which can be used to police large areas of water to insure that property rights are not violated. In fact, the problem of vanishing fish species could be solved by parcelling out the ocean's water to various countries. These countries would therefore have property rights in specific locations and there would be no common property problem.

We would still be faced with migrating fish species, but they can be fairly easily monitored nowadays. That means that we could alternatively vest the property rights in specific species where they spawned or where they were at a certain time of year. People would buy and sell property rights in fish so that we would be insured that they would not be treated as a common property. There would be no problem of overfishing because owners of the fishing rights would want to insure the future of their profitable piece of property. They would not allow overfishing as is done today.

Today we resort to a mass of artificial restrictions on the efficiency of fishermen in order to insure that not too large a catch is taken out. That is how we attempt to maintain the viability of any given species of fish. And now some countries have decided that they are not going to allow overfishing by other countries' vessels. We find that Ecuador and Peru have set 200 mile property right limits on the waters surrounding their shore lines. The United States has never recognized this 200 mile limit. In fact, we only recognize a 12 mile limit, the same as we have around the United States. However, the extension of property rights to ocean waters is probably one of the most fruitful lines of endeavor that can be used to solve the problems of the conservation of aquatic species. That is how we will insure that the future of most of the world's aquatic population will not be one of total extinction.

Definition of New Term

CONSERVATION: the optimal timing of the use of our limited resources such that their present value is maximized.

Questions for Thought and Discussion

1. If we extended our territorial limits in ocean waters all the way up to the territorial limits of other nations, what would happen to the doctrine of "freedom of the seas"?
2. If private property rights were standard to all ocean waters, does that mean that only the nation which owned a particular segment of the ocean would be allowed to use it?
3. Do you think that there is a relationship between property rights and economic incentives even in a socialist country?
4. If the dodo bird had been privately owned, do you think that it would have become extinct? If dinosaurs had been owned by someone, do you think they would have been exterminated? Why?
5. In comparing a private lake with a public lake, what do you think the average age of the fish caught would be in the private one as compared with the public one? In which lake do you think there would be overfishing?
6. Would you favor $10,000 fines for anyone caught shooting a bald eagle? A condor? Or a bighorn mountain sheep?

Selected References

Crutchfield, J. A., & Pontecorvo, G. *The Pacific Salmon Fisheries.* Baltimore: Johns Hopkins University Press, 1969.

Ehrlich, Paul R., & Ehrlich, Anne H. *Population, Resources, Environment.* 2nd Ed. San Francisco: Freeman, 1972.

Schwartz, William, Ed. *Voices for the Wilderness.* New York: Ballantine Books, 1969.

ISSUE XIV

THE PROBLEM OF POLLUTION

Making Our Air Fit to Breathe, Our Water Fit to Drink

Is the End Coming?

Lake Erie is dying; certain rivers are fire hazards, and every year beaches become fouled from oil spills. The air in Gary, Indiana, is said to be as thick as pea soup, while the smell of the smog in Los Angeles on a *good* day makes unaccustomed visitors sick to their stomachs. Most surely, air and water pollution have become part of our everyday lives.

How bad is the problem really? What caused it? How can it be improved? These are questions we shall deal with in this issue. They are some of the most pressing issues of our times because pollution of air and water has already reached the point where many scientists believe irreversible damages may cause national disasters.

Is the Problem as New as It Seems?

We all seem to think that the problem of pollution is something new to the sixties and seventies, but this is not the case. London had smog for well over a century because its inhabitants burned

soft coal. Los Angeles has been smog-filled for many, many years, and Pittsburgh used to be dark during the day in some sections of the city. In fact, we know there's always been some pollution because it is impossible to produce anything without waste by-

products. However, in the past what appeared to be the natural cleansing action of the earth's waters and air was able to cope with the waste products that man created. Until the last 10 to 20 years, the level of pollution in most parts of the United States was apparently not over the level that could be tolerated by the vast absorptive capacities of water and of air. It seems this is no longer the case. Population increased by 24 million between 1960 and 1970, and it is projected to increase by the same amount during this decade. There has also been an in-

"We're lucky. This stream could be next to a paper mill instead of a brewery."

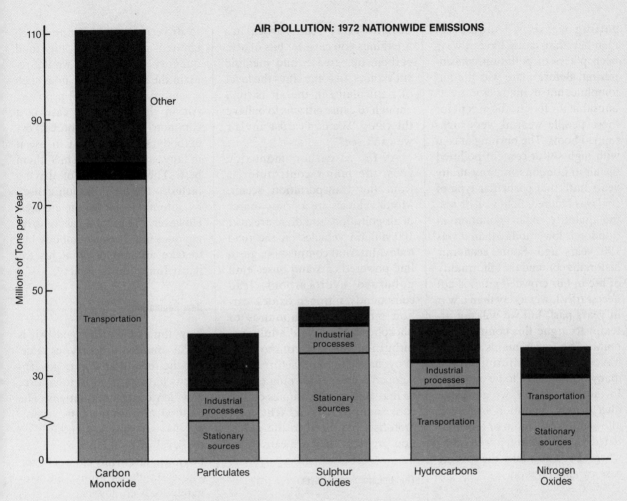

FIGURE XIV-1 Here we find that in 1972 there were over 110 million tons of carbon monoxide spewed out into the air. Over 60 percent of that was accounted for by transportation. Transportation also accounted for a large part of hydrocarbon emissions and nitrous oxide emissions. *Source:* U.S. Department of Health, Education and Welfare.

creased concentration of people in urban areas. This has been a trend that started ever since the beginning of our country. Right now, over half of the population is crowded into 1 percent of our land, and two-thirds crowd themselves onto less than 10 percent of the land. In these urban environments, there are many manufacturing plants, power plants, and transportation facilities, which are so highly concentrated that the natural environment can no longer absorb our waste products.

Even though the air and water pollution problem seems to be

getting worse, we should remember that cities have always
been places of pollution concentration. Before there was the automobile, horses made city streets
unusable for foot traffic except for
those people wearing very high-
topped boots. The burning of coal
with high sulfur content polluted
the air in London for many, many
years until that particular type of
coal was banned. Believe it or not,
the quantity of air pollution in
London is lower today than it was
100 years ago. Some economic
historians contend that the quality
of life in our crowded cities is not
necessarily lower today than it was
in years past, but we will not attempt to argue this controversial
point. The fact remains that we
have levels of pollution which
many of us believe to be too high.
In the last chapter, we got some
idea of why pollution has been
allowed to grow more or less una-
bated in our country and elsewhere. Let's now take the specific
case of air pollution.

Air Pollution

We see in Figure XIV–1 that
the largest physical quantity of
pollution consists of over 110 million tons of carbon monoxide, of
which over 60 percent is generated
by transportation: cars, buses,
planes, and so on. We are show-
ered with 30 million tons of par-

ticulates every year. Particulates
are things you can see: bits of ash,
carbon, oil, grease, and metallic
substances. In some cities the level
of particulates in the air is high
enough to cause citizens to believe
the cant: "We don't trust any air
we can't see."

As far as carbon monoxide
goes, the major contributor is
from the transportation sector.
Motor vehicles are a prime source
of air pollution, and there are over
100 million vehicles on the road
today. Internal combustion, gaso-
line-powered cars and buses emit
unburned hydrocarbons, lead
compounds, nitrogen oxides, carbon monoxide, compounds of
phosphorus, lead, and additional
unburned organic compounds.
Why haven't manufacturers developed a cleaner burning engine
so that auto exhaust fumes do not
choke our precious air? Why don't
motorists pay heed to the pollution problem they are causing?

The Unpaid Social Costs

The answers to these questions are
easy. Until very recently, auto
manufacturers and motorists were
not forced to pay the costs they
imposed on the rest of society by
stinking up our air. Anybody who
got into his car could ignore the
pollution problem he was adding
to. In any event, his single contribution is, for all practical purposes, negligible. If he decided not

to drive or use an engine which
emitted no pollution, the total
quantity of pollution would remain the same because he is such
a small part of the total problem.
Air in this particular case is a
common property resource; everybody seems to want to use it
in any manner that suits them
best. The social cost of driving
includes the air pollution caused
by internal combustion engines.
However, the private cost of driving does not, because nobody has
to take account of what his exhaust fumes do to society.

New Regulations

Now things have changed. Air is
still a common property resource,
but the federal and state governments have stepped in to enforce
emission control regulations. The
Federal Government, for example, has set specific standards on
the level of pollutants which can
be emitted from any car's exhaust.
These standards apply, unfortunately, only to new cars and it is
quite obvious that they will not
eliminate the problem completely
because of all the older cars on
the road. Moreover, unless there
is some system whereby cars are
checked periodically to make sure
that their engines have been tuned
properly and to make sure that
their exhaust control systems have
not been disconnected, we will
probably not drastically alter the

level of air pollution caused by vehicles. In any event, automobile manufacturers have been hastily developing cleaner burning engines and have even been experimenting with external combustion cars, such as steam engines.

No-Lead Gas

The development of no-lead fuel created one potential way to eliminate some forms of air pollution from automobiles. The lead or ethyl in high-octane gasolines for high-compression engines contributes substantially to air pollution. Therefore, it has been suggested that the lead content of gasoline be taxed. This particular method of pollution control was dropped in favor of requiring all cars to be built with engines that could run acceptably on low-octane, no-lead fuel. (These engines would have low compression ratios.) This particularly affected the performance of foreign imported cars which historically have relatively higher compression ratios than American engines. Here we find again that reduction of pollution is not costless.

People pay in reduced car performance in order to help eliminate pollution. When Mercedes-Benz came out with an eight-cylinder sports car, it turned out in some tests to be slower than the previous year's six-cylinder model. This happened because the new government standards requiring cars to be able to run on no-lead gas forced the compression ratio to be reduced so much that the car had a much slower engine. This is a good point to remember. *Elimination of pollution will always involve a cost.* In order to find out the entire cost, we must be careful to ferret out all of the ways individuals end up paying for pollution abatement.

The Future of the Auto

What does the future hold for the automobile? Perhaps we will have electric cars in the future; but even here we will not eliminate all pollution. After all, an electric car's batteries have to be recharged with electricity, and that electricity has to be generated somewhere. When it is generated, the process of generation will itself cause pollution. In fact, electric power plants account for almost one-half of the emissions of sulfur oxides and one-fourth of the emissions of particulates in our air. Let's see what we can expect to happen in that sector of the economy in order to ease our pollution problem.

Electricity Generation

The generation of electricity has been doubling every ten years. At the beginning of the decade, over 16 billion kilowatt hours were generated. Ten years earlier, less than 8 billion kilowatt hours were generated. It is estimated that at current relative prices for electricity, by the year 2000, there will be a demand which is six or seven times what it is today.

Right now most electricity is generated in steam power plants that burn fossil fuels. That is, some form of fuel such as oil, coal, or natural gas is burned to generate steam which runs large turbines that then create the electricity for the nation. In the process of burning fossil fuel—except, of course, for natural gas which burns with almost no pollution at all—sulfur oxides and particulate matters are injected into the air.

Clean Air Act. The government has stepped in to force electric power companies to account for the pollution they create by generating their product. The Clean Air Act was passed in 1970 and is the most stringent air quality measure that has ever been legislated. This act provides for setting up standards for stationary polluters, such as electric utilities. The standards will be based on what emission control capabilities are currently technologically feasible. Some states have gone further than the Clean Air Act by requiring that the sulfur content of the fuel burned must be 1 percent or less. The Nixon Administration suggested a sulfur content tax but later changed its mind and opted for a tax on the sulfur emissions. This is obviously a much more economic way of controlling pollution. We really do not care what input goes into generating power, but we do care what the output is in terms of pollution content. A sulfur emissions tax will allow producers to find out the most efficient ways of eliminating pollution. This may be by burning lower sulfur content fuel; however, it may also turn out to be by installing pollution abatement equipment on the smokestack or something of that nature.

Inefficiency of Uniform Sulfur Tax. The legislation on sulfur emissions was also realistic about

the fact that the economic costs of pollution in general differ according to where the costs occur. It would be economically inefficient to set uniform sulfur emissions taxes everywhere in the United States. The same physical quantity of pollution in New York City is most likely much more economically damaging than it is in the middle of Arizona. A uniform sulfur emissions tax set at the average level of economic damage caused by this form of pollution would result in "too much" pollution in New York City and "too little" pollution in the middle of Arizona. This may shock you because you might have the idea that no amount of pollution should be allowed. (The word

should, however, automatically makes this a value judgment.) You may desire to have as clean an environment as possible, no matter what it costs you, but, of course, you know that this is not correct either. If a clean environment meant that everyone would do absolutely nothing but sit in the country and contemplate their navels, you would probably object and say that some pollution should be allowed. The question is how much pollution "should" be allowed. In economics, we can talk about the optimal level of pollution; it certainly is not zero. *The optimal level of pollution* (and this is not a value judgment) *is at the point where the social cost of improving the environment just a little bit more exceeds the social benefit from doing so.* If, for example, you have obtained a 98 percent reduction in sulfur emissions out of an electric power plant, it may cost much more than it's worth to eliminate the remainder. The social benefits would not be worth the social costs.

Other Stationary Polluters

Industrial plants also generate different forms of air pollution just like electric power plants. They contribute to about 20 percent of the national tonnage of carbon monoxide, hydrocarbons, particulates, nitrogen oxides, and sulfur oxides. Apparently the major problems come from iron and steel mills, chemical plants, oil refineries, nonferrous metal smelters, and pulp and paper mills. Why have these plants gotten away with polluting the air so much in the past? Again, the problem is one of their not being required to take social costs into account—social costs being their private costs of production plus the damage they bestow on the rest of society by polluting the air. In effect, in the past the full costs of industrial products were not borne by those who bought the products. Rather, they were also partly borne by those who suffered the ill consequences of air pollution. Usually these were not

one and the same people. If they were, there would be no problem.

Now with the implementation of the Clean Air Act and various state and local regulations, industrial polluters are being required to eliminate little by little the pollution they cause. Undoubtedly, products made through a process that requires large expenditures for pollution abatement equipment will become relatively more expensive than other products. The purchasers of these more expensive products will start to bear the full social costs of production. Again, it should be pointed out that a uniform standard based on physical quantities of air pollution would not be optimal in an economic sense. It would probably be more economically efficient for localities to set their own pollution standards in order to take account of the peculiarities of the surrounding environment. Beverly Hills, California may wish to require zero amounts of physical pollution. Detroit, Michigan may want to encourage businessmen to build in that city; therefore, it would not set a very stringent pollution standard. People who do not like high levels of pollution would be able to move to cities comprised of other people with similar tastes. Those cities would have pollution abatement standards that were much stricter than other places in the United States. Such is the world of air pollution.

Now let's look at the problem of water pollution, which lends itself to a parallel analysis.

Water Pollution

In 1970 the government issued a report indicating that millions of Americans may be drinking water with potentially hazardous contamination. A while back there was a mercury scare: certain types of fish had such high levels of mercury they were presumably unsafe for human consumption. The mercury they obtained was from effluent discharged by industrial plants.

The components of water pollution are quite numerous and complex and in many cases hard to identify and isolate. Among the pollutants are inorganic and chemical compounds. These include fecal bacteria, lead, arsenic, barium, cadmium, chromium, and selenium. An additional type of water pollutant that we will talk about concerns heat. This is called thermal pollution and is known to disturb the ecology in surrounding waters. This type of pollution relates, in particular, to the electric utility industry which wants to build a large number of nuclear power plants that may heat the surrounding water.

One collective measure of water pollutants that scientists often talk about is Biological Oxygen Demand (BOD). This is a measure of the dissolved oxygen in water which is required before any organic polluting matter can be biologically degraded. Thus scientists refer to manufacturing plants which generate pollution that contains a certain number of pounds of BOD per day. The larger the BOD for a given quantity of water, the less likely it will be that the water can cleanse the pollution away naturally.

The Harm from Water Pollution

There are numerous medical reasons for wanting to eliminate or reduce the level of water pollution in the United States. Certain types of pollution, such as the sewage of human beings and livestock, may cause increased disease. There are also synthetic organic chemicals like pesticides, which may be directly harmful to both human beings and nonhumans such as fish.

Certain forms of inorganic chemicals and minerals destroy aquatic life. They also produce excessive hardness in water; they will corrode metals, and, in many cases, they are poisonous if taken in large enough quantities. Additionally, if radioactivity is contained in water, it may in fact be harmful not only to present but to future generations as well. This is a particular problem for nuclear power plants.

Municipal Wastes. Municipal sewage is still a major source of BOD and suspended solid pollutants. While it is true that rivers no longer carry visible lumps of human excrement, they do continue in some cases to be highly contaminated because of the relatively unprocessed sewage that is put into them. In fact, there are currently well over 1000 municipalities in the United States which do not treat their sewage at all before dumping it into a river or lake. In 1970 the Federal Water Quality Administration indicated that almost 40 percent of the nation's sewage treatment systems were inadequate.

There are two types of waste water treatment—primary and secondary. The first refers to removal of solids, grease, and scum. Over 30 percent of municipalities provide only primary treatment. The second type of treatment involves the controlled degradation of microorganisms of organic matter. But even secondary treatment does not remove such things as nitrogen and phosphorus which come from detergents.

The Federal Government estimated that $25 billion would have to be spent between 1970 and 1975 in order to achieve what they call "adequate" levels of primary and secondary treatment of municipal wastes. However, we know this figure really doesn't mean anything because the standards

which the government sets are as arbitrary as the standards that you or I could have set. The fact is that the purer we want our water, the more expensive the process will be. At some point it becomes prohibitively expensive to continue making the water purer.

Unfortunately, the decision as to how much money should be spent on sewage treatment in a municipality is totally unrelated to the economic damages caused by relatively untreated sewage. If a city lives on a river and dumps untreated sewage into the river, it does not bear the consequences. Rather, it is the downstream users of the river that do. If there are only two cities involved, it may be possible for the downstream city to bargain with the upstream city to provide more sewage treatment. However, in cases where there are large numbers of polluters on a river, it may be difficult to find out which cities are doing the polluting. The policing costs would be very high, even if some agreement were reached. Again, we are talking about a common property problem. Here, the resource is a moving body of water that, in most cases, nobody owns. The Federal Government wants all rivers and lakes to be clean enough to swim in by a specified year—say 1980 or 1985. This amounts to a uniform purity requirement that all municipalities will have to comply with. Again, such a uniform requirement runs into problems of economic inefficiency. It may be better to devote resources to cleaning up only selected rivers instead of trying to make all of them fit for swimming. Some rivers may have so many industrial plants on them that no one would want to swim in them anyway. So it would be economically inefficient to require that the polluters on those rivers stop all water pollution activities.

Heating the Water. When a large body of water is heated several degrees, it sometimes changes the balance of the aquatic ecology. Certain fish cannot survive in warm water. They will perish or move to other areas if possible. Other fish thrive in warmer water and will therefore become more populous when the water is warmed. How does water get warmed in large bodies? If you put a large nuclear power plant on the ocean, it sends out billions of gallons of heated water into the surrounding waters. This heated water will raise the average temperature all around. Impounded water behind dams also heats up relative to free flowing rivers.

Cost-Benefit Analysis

Thermal pollution is thought to be "bad" by environmentalists. In fact, they brought a suit against the Baltimore Gas and Electric Company and stopped at least temporarily the construction of a nuclear power plant on Chesapeake Bay. The interveners, as they are called, pointed out that the National Environmental Policy Act of 1969 required that government agencies had to require environmental statements from companies and individuals seeking project clearance. In this case, the government agency which has to okay all the permits for building nuclear power plants is the Atomic Energy Commission (AEC). Until the Calvert Cliffs decision (a label taken from the area where the nuclear power plant was being built), the Atomic Energy Commission did not require very detailed environmental statements from electric utilities requesting nuclear power plant permits. Now the AEC must require utilities to go into a comprehensive and quantitative **cost-benefit analysis** of the power plant they propose to build.

Obviously, the costs that a utility has to consider are not only the private costs it will incur, but also the social costs it will force on society. The interveners in the Calvert Cliffs case maintained that thermal pollution would have killed many fish and therefore destroyed commercial and recreational fishing in that area. If this is indeed the case, then some monetary value must be placed on a fish kill.

The Calvert Cliffs decision has brought to the forefront the need to use comprehensive cost-benefit analysis when deciding to undertake a project that can seriously alter the environment. A nuclear power plant is such a project—and so is a highway, a fossil fuel steam generating plant, a dam, and many other government and private projects. Now it appears that there must be a reckoning of all costs and all benefits from proposed projects, and this reckoning must be, so far as is possible, quantitative. In other words, it is no longer possible for environmentalists to maintain that the status quo of the ecology is priceless and should not be altered. Rather, they have to come up with a dollar figure; somehow they have to estimate the implicit value that people place on cold water in Chesapeake Bay and the results thereof. This also allows those seeking projects clearance to do a quantitative assessment of the costs and benefits involved. The benefits of relatively cheap nuclear power may be large indeed. In fact, when one considers the alternatives available for power generation, it may be that the costs of generating power in a nuclear power plant are less than the costs of generating power in a coal-fed or oil-fed steam generating plant. In order to find out if this is indeed the case, one would have to consider all possi-

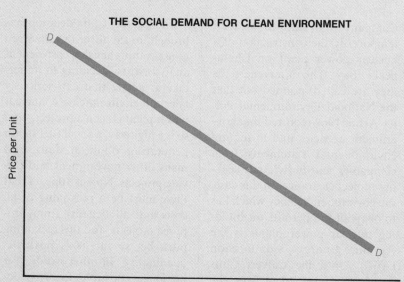

THE SOCIAL DEMAND FOR CLEAN ENVIRONMENT

Price per Unit

Quantity of Clean Environment

FIGURE XIV-2

We see that the social demand curve for a clean environment slopes down just like any other demand curve. More of a clean environment will be demanded at lower prices, but at higher prices—increased pollution abatement costs—less of it will be demanded.

ble economic damages that are incurred by each form of power generation. In the case of fossil fuel plants, there is air pollution and water pollution. In the case of nuclear power plants, there is thermal pollution and radiation pollution. Nuclear power plant builders maintain that the radiation surrounding a nuclear power plant is less than what we naturally incur in our daily lives. Of course, there is the possibility of a nuclear disaster if one of the power plants were to overheat or if something of that nature were to occur. The utilities maintain that the probability is so small as to be negligible, but if a disaster ever happened the consequences would be large indeed.

Will There Ever Be an End to Air and Water Pollution?

Is it too late? Are we already headed for disaster? Or can we assume that somehow pollution abatement will turn the tide and allow us in the future, or at least our children or grandchildren, to live in a cleaner environment? Apparently, we have indeed not gone "too" far. We can improve our environment but it does take resources, and we will have to spend part of our income in the process. A clean environment can be treated just like any other good or service. Presumably there is a collective demand curve for a cleaner environment and there is a supply curve. Figure XIV-2 shows that the social demand curve for a clean environment slopes down just like all demand curves. At a higher price, a clean environment is less desired than at a lower price. The cost of cleaning the environment seems to rise; the supply curve is upward sloping. We would expect that if somehow an optimum solution were reached, we would still have some pollution in the air and in the water, but it would be the quantity desired by the public. We would have a certain level of pollution clean-up demanded by the public at the price the public had to pay. Again, this may be upsetting to some people who wish to see our environment perfectly cleaned up. But that would be prohibitively expensive, and not many people are willing to pay the costs. They would rather live in a not-so-perfect environment and have that extra income to spend on other things. We can't simultaneously have a perfectly clean environment and the current amount of goods and services that we consume because at any moment in time we are faced with a fixed amount of resources. Environmental clean-up involves a trade-off with other goods. We see that scarcity follows us wherever we go.

Definition of New Terms

COST-BENEFIT ANALYSIS: a procedure that can be used to analyze the net benefits accruing from a particular action. In cost-benefit analysis all costs are laid out from now on into the future as are all benefits. These costs and benefits are discounted back to the present and the costs are subtracted from the benefits; we come up with a net present value benefit figure. If the net benefits turn out to be negative, then the project or action probably is not justifiable.

Questions for Thought and Discussion

1. What does it mean to say that the optimal level of pollution is not zero? Do you disagree? Why?
2. Is it ever possible for the consumer not to pay for the costs of pollution?
3. In a world of polluters, what would happen to a businessman who decided to spend the money to reduce pollution on his production process?
4. Why would some people prefer to live in a polluted environment?
5. Who would benefit from a reduction in smog in Los Angeles?

Selected References

Dales, J. H. *Pollution, Property and Prices.* Toronto: University of Toronto Press, 1968.
Goldman, Marshall I., Ed. *Controlling Pollution.* Englewood Cliffs, N.J.: Prentice Hall, 1967.
Kneese, Alan V. *Economics and the Quality of the Environment.* Washington, D.C.: Resources for the Future, April 1968.
Kneese, Alan V., & Bower, B. T. *Managing Water Quality: Economics, Technology, Institutions.* Baltimore: Johns Hopkins University Press, 1968.
Ridker, R. G. *Economic Costs of Air Pollution.* New York: Praeger, 1967.

POLLUTION, PRINCIPLES, AND PROTEST

The Fox

Pollution Protester

THE ENVIRONMENTAL MOVEMENT of the late 1960s and early 1970s has brought about some significant changes in the way Americans think about business. In general, business has warded off procedures to enforce antipollution legislation, while broadcasting threats of catastrophic unemployment if present production methods are curtailed. These tactics are being questioned, however, by members of the labor force and by public figures such as Ralph Nader, Edmund Muskie, and Barry Commoner. Meanwhile, a professional enigma who lives near Chicago in Aurora, Illinois, has been stating his own views in a very dramatic way.

He calls himself "The Fox," both in honor of his beloved Fox River, which flows through Aurora, and as an effective analogy to his operating strategy. The Fox River is a mess, and its namesake (who once enjoyed fishing there) has been watching with despair the prolonged death of the river from industrial wastes. His neighbors occasionally commented on the problem, ignored it, or at most wrote to their Congressman; but The Fox decided to *do* something about it, starting in 1969.

His plan of action was the most significant aspect of his success in attracting attention and substantial news coverage. The Fox did what every citizen who has ever taken a serious look at what is happening to the environment wants to do. He put homemade "stoppers" on filthy smokestacks, dammed up sewage pipes spewing unprocessed waste into public waterways (generally a federal offense), and in his most theatrical moments actually invaded corporate offices. By pouring foul-smelling liquids on plush carpets, dumping dead skunks on manicured lawns, and terrifying secretaries all over the Chicago area, The Fox brought his indignation to the feet—quite literally—of the men and organizations he considered responsible. His actions, though not by any means effective in halting pollution or encouraging corporate respect for common people, gave the appearance of effectiveness because of their frontal assault technique.

This unknown protester leaves messages at the scene of the "crime," explaining his purpose and simply signed "The Fox." Technically his actions are illegal under the malicious mischief and trespass statutes, but he does not consider himself a criminal. In a telephone interview with *Newsweek* magazine, planned so as to protect his anonymity, The Fox said: "Who's breaking the law anyway? Do you know where I got that raw sewage I dumped at U.S. Reduction [a Chicago-based company operating an aluminum plant in Aurora]? I just went down to the Fox River and took what came out of their pipes."

When The Fox invaded U.S. Steel's Chicago headquarters, his action drew much attention because he had planned for newspaper coverage through the Chicago *Daily News*. He emptied some samples of U.S. Steel's sewage output onto the carpet and quickly vanished. Again, The Fox contends that U.S. Steel is in no position to criticize his untidy demonstration. "They keep saying that they aren't really polluting our water. If that's true, then it shouldn't hurt rugs, right?"

The Fox has more or less retired, but his actions elicited startling contrasts in corporate response to antipollution measures. The U.S. Steel executives who returned from lunch that afternoon in 1970 were furious upon discovering the aftermath of the protest, and they were determined to get to the bottom of the outrage. In comparison to this indignant response were the bland replies of six steel companies warned by the Interior Department in 1969 about impending indictments for violating federal water-quality laws. A U.S. Steel spokesman commented: "We could be shut down any time, I suppose. But it is very unlikely. After all, this is the biggest steel mill in Chicago and in the state of Illinois. Technically, it's a matter of whether government agencies want to accept a practical solution and say, 'O.K., clean up pollution as fast as you can,' or whether they want to get tied up with prolonged lawsuits which will have no particular effect."

What the government must forgo in the way of drama and headlines in the fight against pollution, The Fox certainly gained in his brief and intense campaign. He probably did not regret his lack of clout with the U.S. Steel Corporation, U.S. Reduction, or any of his other "victims." Hopefully, he was satisfied that he had made his point.

ISSUE XV
THE PLIGHT OF OUR CITIES

Why Does It Take So Long to Get Around in the City?

The Bad News

Our urban areas present us with an exasperating paradox. On the one hand, incomes are highest in the cities; opportunities are greatest; and entertainment possibilities are the most varied. On the other hand, the crime rate is the greatest in the cities; living conditions in the ghettos are appalling; and the income levels of ghetto dwellers are often below the poverty line. Pollution is usually at its highest where people are most concentrated, and congestion on the streets is overwhelming at rush hour in our larger urban areas.

Apparently, things are getting worse in the cities. Nonetheless, it is expected that our population will continue to become more urbanized. Way back in the year 1800, over 90 percent of the population lived in rural areas, mostly on farms. Today, three-fourths of the population lives in urban areas, and, as shown in Table XV-1, the Census Bureau estimates that by 1980, almost 80 percent of the population will be living in cities. The benefits from living in cities seem to outweigh the costs, however, because there appears to be no end to the amount of growth that urban areas will experience in the future.

To understand why cities develop, we have to learn a little bit about what economists have started to call the economics of *agglomeration*. (Don't shudder too violently at this atrocious word. Perhaps you can think of a better one.)

Why We Have Cities—Agglomeration Economics

It turns out that the primary determinant of the quantity and quality of such things as cultural activities associated with any particular city is the number of people who live there. We would expect that there would be a greater variety of activities in Chicago, New York, Los Angeles, or San Francisco than in Tulsa, San Jose, Madison, or Lafayette. This is just an extension of Adam Smith's famous observation that *specialization depends on the size of the market*. When the market is larger, there will be more specialization and, hence, more variety. This is an example of what has become known as **agglomeration economies.** This is just a fancy way of saying that there are economies of scale in certain activities.

TABLE XV-1 URBAN POPULATION IN THE UNITED STATES

In 1790 the urban population in the United States was a mere 5 percent of the total. It is projected that by the year 1980 the urban population will grow to almost 80 percent of the total population. (*Source:* U.S. Bureau of the Census.)

YEAR	RURAL AS A PERCENT OF TOTAL POPULATION	URBAN AS A PERCENT OF TOTAL POPULATION
1790	95	5
1810	93	7
1830	91	9
1850	85	15
1870	75	25
1890	65	35
1910	54	46
1930	44	56
1950	36	64
1973	26	74
1980	21	79

As the number of people, houses, cars, and so on increases, there is a proportionately greater increase in cultural offerings. Considering agglomeration economies, we would expect that people will want to live close enough to each other to support the things they like, such as restaurants and athletic teams.

There are also some good hard-nosed business reasons for people wanting to locate near one another. Transportation costs are usually smaller, the shorter the distance one has to travel. Taking this into account, we can perhaps explain how metropolitan areas tend to have cores or centers in which the largest sources of employment and cultural activities are located. The pattern of development of cities has been successive rings around a center core of the city—each ring being less densely populated the further one gets from the core. This is how many of our major cities have developed. In recent years, however, there has been a dramatic change. Suburbs have started to become cities within themselves, as many suburbanites find that they do not like working in the core of the city because of the congestion, high crime, pollution, and so on. In many instances, agglomeration economies may be more than offset by the problems associated with high-density living. And in some areas the

"This is your flying traffic reporter. Traffic is normal in all directions."

living is extremely high density. Harlem has almost 70,000 people per square mile!

Problems in the City

Cities are obviously facing tremendous problems today. We've mentioned many of these problems, and there are certainly others that are not related to economics. In this issue, we will spend most of our time discussing why there is so much congestion on city streets and what solution can be proposed for alleviating that congestion.

Congestion

Try to drive a car in downtown Manhattan at 5 o'clock on any weekday evening. Try to do the same thing in Chicago or St. Louis or San Francisco or in just about any big city. Congestion is a problem that is sometimes overwhelming. You can do absolutely nothing when you get stuck in your car in a traffic jam. You can abandon your car (and then get fined), but otherwise you're stuck. In most cities congestion is a problem that occurs only during selected hours of the day. You can, most likely, drive anywhere you want at 3 in the morning in any city in the world without running into traffic problems. The problem of congestion usually limits

itself to peak periods of street use. It is a *peak-loading* problem, where the system is overloaded during the morning and afternoon rush hours. And there doesn't seem to be much incentive on the part of the individual drivers to change the situation.

Private versus Social Costs

When someone gets in his car to take a drive in the city at rush hour, he incurs the private costs of driving—that is, he incurs the cost of gas, oil, maintenance, insurance, and so on. He also incurs a time cost: the longer he is held up in traffic, the more expensive it becomes to drive. This time cost is directly related to the driver's opportunity cost. It is more expensive for a $100,000 a year busy executive to get stuck in downtown Manhattan than it is for an $80 a week clerk. The executive's opportunity cost is much higher

than is the clerk's. This does not mean, of course, that they both won't become equally annoyed.

There are other costs that our driver creates but does not incur. There is the cost to other drivers caused by his slowing them down. If traffic is moving smoothly but one additional car will cause a tie-up, then the driver of that additional car imposes a time cost on everybody else. Additionally, he imposes costs on all those who want to drive but don't because they know the streets will be congested. As yet there is no way people can bribe this driver to stay off the road so they can drive without congestion. Nor can he offer to stay off the streets. A contract would be difficult to create and to enforce. This question is whether there's a way out of this dilemma. Is there a way to make private costs equal to social costs? There is, and it is called **peak-load pricing.**

Peak-Load Pricing

Let's take the example of a toll bridge that goes into a city. It is crowded perhaps four hours out of the day. During that time cars creep along at five miles an hour taking a half hour to cross the bridge. The nonpeak crossing time is ten minutes. This is a typical peak-load problem. The bridge is uncrowded during the rest of the day. The next question is whether there are ways to discourage people from using the bridge during peak periods. One way involves a *surcharge,* or an additional charge, for use during that time. In this manner, drivers would be faced with a truer representation of the marginal cost of using the bridge during peak periods. That marginal cost involves preventing other people from getting on the bridge and slowing down people who are already on it. Toll bridges, however, are usually not priced in this manner.

Usually, exactly the opposite occurs in most cities that have toll bridges. Instead of charging a higher price during peak periods, a lower price is charged by way of special commuter tickets that are lower priced than the regular tickets. Commuter tickets are mainly purchased by businessmen and workers who use the bridge exactly at peak hours. This is an example of reverse peak-load pricing. If we assume that the elasticity of demand for the services of the bridge is not completely zero, a decrease in the price encourages *more* use. We therefore have more people on the bridge at peak periods than we would if we had no system of lower priced commuter tickets. On the other hand, you can be sure that if the price for peak-time use of the bridge were raised sufficiently high, there would be no peak-period problem. Commuters would start using more car pools. Some downtown businesses would find it advantageous to allow their employees to come and leave at other than the normal periods, thereby saving their employees the peak-period price on the bridge. People casually going into the city over the bridge would alter their schedules so as to avoid peak periods. In other words, there would be a change in the transportation habits of those who used the bridge.

Peak-Period Pricing and Income Distribution

You might be upset by the thought of charging a higher price to commuters who have to come at peak periods because you might maintain that they are the ones least able to afford the penalty fee. That, in fact, may be true. Remember, though, that the higher peak-load price is really a reflec-tion of the true, higher marginal cost of using the bridge at rush hour. At any rate, it is difficult to find out what people can really afford, which is not the issue here anyway. We are discussing methods of eliminating congestion around our urban areas, and our object is to discover the optimal use of resources. Here, the resource in question happens to be a bridge. A peak-load pricing system will discourage use of the bridge during peak periods. If you think that some people will not be able to afford the increase in price, then you are really concerned about the current distribution of income—which is a separate issue from the allocation of resources.

It is usually best to separate the problems of how to use our resources and how to distribute our income within the United States. If one devises a system which uses resources efficiently, there will always be more income to redistribute than if one attempts merely to redistribute income by altering the existing allocation of resources. In simpler words, attempting to improve the conditions of poor people by keeping down the prices of the products they buy will result in an inefficient allocation of resources. We would have more total income if prices were not artificially manipulated. The most economically efficient way to help needy people is to give direct income transfers, as outlined in our discussion on welfare programs.

Mass Transit—Another Solution

One of the most frequently proposed solutions to our congestion problem in the cities is mass transit. That is, railways, subways, and buslines. In fact, there has been a real renaissance in mass transit systems throughout the world.

Fortune magazine found that in 1972, 19 cities were building new subways, and 23 others, including London, Tokyo, and New York, were adding to existing systems. Planners throughout the world estimate that when all of their systems are finished, there will be 12.5 billion passengers a year riding subways. Through its Urban Mass Transportation Assistance Act of 1970, the U.S. Congress provided $3 billion in federal funds for constructing subways.

Congress stated that it intended to appropriate an additional $7 billion later. We see in Table XV–2 that the world's subways are going to start carrying a lot of people.

Subways are not cheap. They typically cost almost $6 million a mile to install, and many are more expensive because soil conditions are so bad that pilings have to be driven, water has to be drained, and so on. In Washington, D.C., the subway system will have 98

TABLE XV–2

THE WORLD'S SUBWAYS

Here we find that in 1972, 19 cities were building new subways, and 23 others were adding to existing systems. When all of these systems are finished there will be 12.5 billion passengers a year riding them. (*Source: Fortune,* February 1972, p. 124.)

EXISTING SYSTEMS	PASSENGERS PER YEAR (EST.)			NEW SYSTEMS UNDER CONSTRUCTION	
Athens	85,000,000	Budapest	20,000,000	Amsterdam	50,000,000
Berlin (East)	80,000,000	Hamburg	175,000,000	Antwerp	NA
Buenos Aires	270,000,000	Kiev	100,000,000	Brussels	10,000,000
Chicago	160,000,000	Leningrad	370,000,000	Cologne	40,000,000
Cleveland	15,000,000	Lisbon	500,000,000	Frankfurt	NA
Glasgow	20,000,000	London	675,000,000	Hanover	15,000,000
Haifa	5,000,000	Madrid	535,000,000	Helsinki	135,000,000
Mexico City	225,000,000	Milan	60,000,000	Kharkov	NA
Montreal	130,000,000	Moscow	1,505,000,000	Munich	50,000,000
Peking	NA	Nagoya	120,000,000	Prague	NA
Philadelphia	75,000,000	New York	1,300,000,000	San Francisco	50,000,000
Tbilisi (U.S.S.R.)	60,000,000	Osaka	455,000,000	Santiago	550,000,000
		Oslo	25,000,000	São Paulo	510,000,000
EXISTING SYSTEMS BEING EXTENDED		Paris	1,175,000,000	Sapporo	70,000,000
		Rome	20,000,000	Seoul	40,000,000
Baku (U.S.S.R.)	40,000,000	Rotterdam	30,000,000	Stuttgart	NA
Barcelona	200,000,000	Stockholm	180,000,000	Vienna	165,000,000
Berlin (West)	220,000,000	Tokyo	1,360,000,000	Washington, D.C.	350,000,000
Boston	95,000,000	Toronto	150,000,000	Yokohama	35,000,000
				TOTAL	12,505,000,000

miles of service and will cost $3 billion. It will be one of the most expensive single public works projects ever undertaken in the United States.

However expensive subways seem to be, many engineers are convinced that they are the long-run solution to the urban congestion problem. The Subdirector and Secretary General of Compania Metropolitano de Madrid, Señor Rafael Balero del Rio, maintains that "subways are the solution to the problem, the only solution." In London, it was concluded by a group of engineers that it would take an 11-lane highway to transport the 25,000 commuters who could be served hourly by a new subway line. However, some economists are not so optimistic about the future of mass transportation. In fact, some studies have shown that mass transportation will never be effective at replacing the auto and stopping congestion if current conditions exist into the future. And what are those conditions? They involve the fantastic amount of subsidization that is presented to private automobile drivers.

Subsidizing the Automobile

Highway travel that is most immediately competitive with mass transit—rush hour commuting in automobiles by private citizens—is

subsidized to such an extent that mass transit may never be able to stand on its own two feet. Urban motorists pay very little of the true cost of driving their cars to the city. For example, they do not pay for urban street maintenance and repairs, street cleaning, snow removal, traffic signals, or traffic police.

Most of these costs are incurred by all citizens paying taxes because they are generally paid for out of city revenues. Additionally, urban motorists who park in the streets use valuable land for which they pay no rent or property taxes as must other people who occupy scarce land. Only a small parking meter fee is charged. Motorists use all of the capital invested in city streets but pay no tax comparable to the property or corporation income taxes imposed on users of these other forms of capital. Ad-

ditionally, when cities decide to improve streets and highways, the money is often borrowed and the interest cost is subsidized by the Federal Government.

Further, the peak user of highways and streets is subsidized the most since he is the one for which capacity is ultimately geared. In most cities, for example, it was found that freeways, expressways, and other arterials leading into the city were fully occupied only 10 to 20 percent of the time. But the size of these highways is geared toward those few hours of the day when they are filled. Anybody who does not use the highways at peak periods is therefore subsidizing those who do, and the subsidy is quite large. All bond issues that are passed for expanding commuting facilities are aimed at improving traffic conditions at peak hours of use—not at off-peak hours of use. This means if you, in your city, approve a bond issue or approve higher taxes to pay for another bridge into the city, in effect you will be paying for the peak-periods users' privilege of continuing to come into the city at a rapid speed during rush hours.

Some Solutions

We might want to figure out some way to have people's private costs better reflect the actual social costs of their driving. One way of eliminating peak-period problems was mentioned above. That is, by charging peak-period prices which exceed nonrush-hour prices for the use of a toll bridge or road. Under this plan the people who create the rush hour problem would be paying more than those who don't. On freeways or expressways, the problem is a little different because there may be too many on-ramps and off-ramps to effectively police a particular system of roads.

There are still other alternatives. People could be encouraged to use car pools, thereby eliminating a certain number of cars at rush hours. One way of doing this is by fining all drivers in certain express lanes who do not have at least two other people in their car or, in the same vein but in the opposite direction, by allowing cars filled with three or more people to get a reduced price for a toll bridge or toll road. This is exactly what is happening in San Francisco on the Bay Bridge. There is a special lane for those cars with four or more people, and these cars go over the bridge free. You'd be surprised how many car pools are springing up in San Francisco to take advantage of this reward system.

Additionally, it will be necessary to levy adequate specific charges on motorists who use high-cost facilities that become congested. You are automatically charged for long-distance, self-dialed telephone calls, and you are charged different prices at different times of the day and on different days of the week as a reflection of peak-period problems. Thus, it is cheaper to dial on Sunday than it is to dial Monday through Friday. As yet, we do not have available electronic methods to charge motorists for using congested areas. There are such things as electronic surveillance devices which will automatically record the passage of different cars over specified spots in a city. However, while this is a feasible technique that could be used in the immediate future, it does pose problems for individual privacy. The whereabouts of people could be tracked very easily using such a system. If we were not sure that the agency using the system was going to keep the billing data secret, we might be concerned about the possible use of this device to spy on citizens without their knowing it. However, the same comment is true for telephone use, at least for long-distance calls.

The Other Problems of the City

Automobile congestion, while a major urban problem, is, of course, not the only problem that needs a solution today. Many cities seem overcrowded because of too many human beings. The ghetto schools are bursting at the seams; the hospitals can hold no more; and the sewage systems are overflowing. The garbage dumps are filled to capacity. An examination of each of these problems would require at least a separate issue for each one. Therefore, we will not go into these problems here. We can point out, however, that if overcrowding in the cities is really a problem, we should not encourage people to move to the cities. Right now, we are doing this by making many of the services in the cities available at a lower cost than society actually incurs. New York City is a prime example: it is forever involved in a budget problem, and, just like many other big cities with similar problems, it keeps asking for more money from the Federal Government. Perhaps from society's point of view, we would be better off if cities such as New York charged the full cost of their municipal services so as to discourage people from living in them. In this manner, we would have less crowding in urban areas and perhaps more incentive for people to remain in rural areas or to move out of the city to less crowded districts. Then our big cities might become livable.

Definition of New Terms

AGGLOMERATION ECONOMIES: the economies of scale that come about because of an increased size of the market in urban areas and an increased density of population.

PEAK-LOAD PRICING: pricing which accounts for the fact that during peak periods of using a resource, such as a toll bridge or freeway or streets, the marginal cost for each individual's use is higher because of the congestion that is caused. Peak-load pricing involves a surcharge or an additional charge for use of the resource during a peak period.

Questions for Thought and Discussion

1. Do you favor a reduction in the gasoline tax so that less money will be available for building more roads? Why?
2. If New York City is such a horrible place to live, why do so many people remain there?
3. Do you think that increased urbanization leads to increased crime? If so, would you predict that countries with higher population densities would have more crime? (In fact, there seems to be no correlation between population density of countries and each country's crime rate relative to other countries.)
4. Should the automobile be banned in all urban areas? Who would be hurt? Who would gain?

Selected References

Bish, Robert L. *The Public Economy of Metropolitan Areas.* Chicago: Markham, 1971.

Culbertson, John M., Ed. *Economic Development: An Ecological Approach.* New York: Alfred A. Knopf, 1971.

Durr, Fred. *The Urban Economy.* Scranton: Index Educational Publishers, 1971.

Jacobs, Jane. *The Economy of Cities.* New York: Random House, 1969.

Mishan, E. J. *The Costs of Economic Growth.* New York: Praeger, 1967.

Netzer, Dick. *Economics and Urban Problems.* New York: Basic Books, 1970.

Phelps, E. S., Ed. *Private Wants and Public Needs.* Rev. Ed. New York: W. W. Norton, 1965.

Schreiber, Arthur F., et al., Eds. *Economics of Urban Problems: Selected Readings.* Boston: Houghton Mifflin, 1971.

Population Economics

13

JUST ABOUT EVERYBODY has heard at one time or another that there is a population explosion. Myriad books and articles have been written on when the world will come to an end if we don't cut back on the growth of population. The arithmetic of population economics is not hard to figure out, but it is deceiving as we will see in this chapter and in the following issue which concerns itself with the Zero Population Growth movement. What we want to do in this chapter is to present some information about how demographers—people who study population—measure trends in people growth. We also want to concern ourselves with which economic variables determine fertility and mortality. If we can figure what determines the birth rate and the death rate, as it were, then perhaps we will be better equipped to analyze the arguments presented by those in Zero Population Growth (ZPGers).

THE ARITHMETIC OF POPULATION GROWTH

Demographers like to look at the difference between birth rates and death rates. They calculate for a given country and a given year what is called the **crude birth rate**—the number of babies born per 1000 people in the population. Then they look at the **crude death rate,** which is the number of deaths per 1000 people in the population. When you subtract the crude death rate from the crude birth rate, you come up with the increase in population in that year. If we divide that by 10, we'll get the result as a percentage, and we will have the rate of increase of the population. Let's look at a few examples. In Table 13–1, we have listed the crude death rate and the crude birth rate for several countries. The difference is divided by 10, and we find that the rate of increase of population of the countries listed varies from 3.69 percent per year to as low as –0.03 percent per year in East Germany.

The rate of growth of population is not, therefore, just a function of the birth rate, but it is also a function of the death rate. We would expect that any improvement in death control, as it were, would lead to an increase in population growth. In fact, if death "decontrol" proceeded at a faster pace than birth control, we could still have a rapidly growing population even though birth control methods were being used.

Doubling Time

Population experts like to translate rates of population growth per annum into what is called the **doubling time.** In other words, if the population of Luxembourg is growing at 0.4 percent a year, how many years will it take for the population to double? In the case of Luxembourg, this would take almost 175 years!

In Table 13–2 we see the doubling time for population for the world and for selected countries. A good rule to use to figure out the doubling time is *the rule of 72*. If you divide the percentage rate of increase in population into 72, you come up with an approximate doubling time. In our example of Luxembourg, the growth rate of population is 0.4 percent a year. Thus, 72 divided by 0.4 equals 180 years, just about the figure we came up with before.

Doubling times are fascinating numbers because if we extend them indefinitely into the future, we find that the population of very small Latin American countries will increase until there are so many people there will no longer be a place to walk. The countries will literally be covered with people. Even if the doubling time is 175 years as in Luxembourg, if you extend that rate of growth far enough into the future the result is one

TABLE 13–1

BIRTH AND DEATH RATES AND RATE OF INCREASE OF POPULATION FOR SELECTED COUNTRIES

In column 2 we show the crude birth rate per 1000 people in each of these countries. In column 3 we show the crude death rate. Column 4 is the difference between the crude birth rate and the crude death rate, divided by 10. It represents the percentage rate of increase per year of the population. (*Source:* Statistical Office of the United Nations.)

COUNTRY	CRUDE BIRTH RATE	CRUDE DEATH RATE	RATE OF INCREASE
U.S.	17.7	9.5	0.82
Australia	20.0	9.1	1.09
Canada	17.6	7.3	1.03
Costa Rica	36.2	6.5	2.97
Denmark	14.6	9.8	0.48
France	16.7	11.3	0.54
Germany—East	14.0	14.3	–0.03
Iceland	20.7	7.2	1.35
Israel	26.1	7.0	1.91
Mexico	41.6	9.4	3.22
Pakistan	49.0	18.0	3.10
Poland	16.3	8.1	0.82
So. Africa			
White	23.6	8.8	1.48
Other	40.0	14.4	2.56
Sweden	13.5	10.4	0.31
USSR	17.0	8.1	0.89
Venezuela	43.6	6.7	3.69
Vietnam	27.7	6.4	1.13

horrendously large number. That's one of the reasons Zero Population Growth people are so adamant about the necessity of limiting the number of births not only in countries where the populations are unbelievably dense, as in Hong Kong, but also in countries where population is much less dense.

Net Reproduction Rate

Demographers also like to talk in terms of **net reproduction rates.** These rates are calculated on the basis of the total number of female children born to every 1000 mothers. If every mother has exactly one daughter in her lifetime, then the net reproduction rate will be exactly equal to 1. What do you think will happen to the population? It will remain stable, neither decreasing nor increasing (assuming life expectancy doesn't change). If mothers tend to have more than one daughter throughout their child-bearing years, then the net reproduction rate will be in excess of 1 and the population will grow.

The net reproduction rate is probably the most important statistic to look at when you want to find out what the future holds for a particular country. Japan is a good example. There the crude birth rate is about 17 per 1000, and the crude death rate is about 6.5 per 1000. The rate of growth in population is therefore in excess of 1 percent per annum. Even a 1 percent annual growth rate in population leads to a doubling every 72 years. But Japan really isn't worried about that. In fact, Japan's worries are in the opposite direction. The net reproduction rate is now less than 1 in Japan. The Japanese have legalized abortion and also widespread birth control. Given that the net reproduction rate is less than 1, after a few more years of growth, the Japanese population will begin a long steady decline. In fact, by extending net reproduction rates into the future forever without any change, you would find that the population of Japan will eventually disappear.

TABLE 13–2

THE DOUBLING TIME FOR SELECTED COUNTRIES' POPULATIONS

Here we show how many years it takes for each country's population to double. The range is immense, from Venezuela's 19 years to Sweden's 232 years. (*Source:* Statistical Office of the United Nations.)

COUNTRY	DOUBLING TIME
U.S.	93
Albania	26
Australia	62
Canada	70
Costa Rica	23
Denmark	150
France	133
Iceland	47
Israel	35
Luxembourg	175
Mexico	21
Pakistan	22
Poland	82
So. Africa	
White	46
Other	28
Sweden	232
USSR	72
Venezuela	19
Vietnam	62

Some time ago, Japanese businessmen were publicized as complaining that their profits were going to fall in the future because of a diminishing labor supply. They would have to start paying higher wages in order to have a sufficient number of workers.

IS THERE AN OPTIMUM POPULATION?

How do we know when our population should be stabilized or when the world should not be allowed to get any larger? Those in Zero Population Growth believe that the world is already overcrowded. Some people—including Dr. Paul Ehrlich, the man who wrote *The Population Bomb* and started it all in the United States—think that the population of the United States should fall to 50 million. For Ehrlich, that is the optimum population. In economics, however, we have to be somewhat more precise about what is considered optimal. Economists have come up with their own idea of how large the population should be. This, of course, is a normative statement, but if we want to translate it into a positive statement, we can merely employ the term *optimum population* without any connotations of its being good or bad or something that must be attained.

Most certainly, there are diminishing returns in population control. In order to establish the optimum population, we should look at the contribution of new workers to total output divided by population. Obviously, an increased labor force can always produce more goods and services—or at least almost always. This means that the larger the population, the larger the labor force and, hence, the larger the output. But total output is deceiving. Total output in an economy could be very large indeed, while the population could be extremely poor. This could happen if output per capita were very small. We can present a definition of the optimum population as follows: *the optimum population is reached when real output per capita is maximized.*

If you decide that real output per capita is the criterion to use when judging the actual size of an optimum population, then from a strictly subjective point of view, you would advocate a government policy toward population growth which ensures that population remains where real output per capita is maximized. That, in fact, is a very definite and objective criterion which you could use to determine birth control and death decontrol policy. However, you have to realize that a value judgment is also being used. Someone else could come up with another goal, and it would be just as valid from an economic point of view. If an advocate of Zero Population Growth believes that the best population size is one which allows 99 percent of the United States land to be uninhabited because he feels that open spaces are the most important thing in the world, then his decision to limit population is based on a value judgment which is equally as valid as yours.

WHERE THE PEOPLE ARE

It is interesting to note that even though population seems to be exploding all around us, the centers of population are really the only places where this is the case. Historically, we find that people move to where jobs are. Jobs are usually at ports or places where there are many natural resources. After transportation became relatively cheap, people started to live where they wanted to, and jobs then followed the people. There must be some attraction to the city, however crowded it may be, because that is where people are going. Indeed, the percentage of people in urban centers has increased from 5 to 74 percent in the last 185 years. Additionally, in the United States, population has shifted out of the central areas to the South and to the West. The South and the West happen to have more agreeable climates.

If people did not find benefits from living in large cities, there would probably be a much more

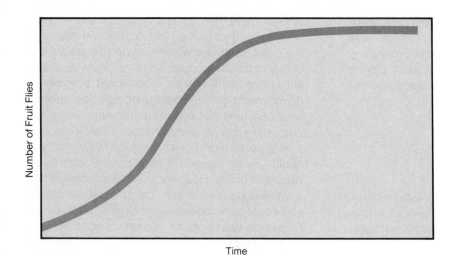

FIGURE 13–1

S CURVE FOR FRUIT FLY POPULATION

The population of fruit flies in a container might grow very rapidly at first but then level off and reach its natural limit at some specific number. The growth in population looks like an S curve as depicted in this diagram.

Number of Fruit Flies

Time

even dispersion of the population throughout our entire land area. Presumably, if this were the case, there would be less concern over the population explosion. Indeed, one need only take a drive across the United States or a plane trip in good weather to realize how sparsely populated these United States really are. But this is not to say that we should or should not do something about population growth. Rather, the paucity of people in the wide-open spaces merely serves to demonstrate that overpopulation may really only be a problem in overcrowded urban environments.

POPULATION PROBLEMS FOR NONHUMAN SPECIES

If we were to examine population growth in other animal species, we would find that there are natural limits to the total population that a particular species can obtain. An experiment can be run with a pair of willing fruit flies in a small enclosure. At first, the population grows by leaps and bounds. It runs up at a geometric rate: first 2, then 4, then 8, then 16, and so on. If this geometric progression of the fruit fly population were extended way into

the future, we would find that their mass would eventually overcome the earth. However, this geometric growth rate does not continue for very long. Eventually it peters out because there just aren't enough resources for the flies to continue growing.

S Curves

In our particular example, one resource that holds the fruit flies back is the size of the container. For other populations, it might be the food supply. In any event reproduction slows down, and at some point a ceiling is reached. The growth curve for the fruit fly population in our container can be plotted as an S, as shown in Figure 13–1. The ceiling is called the *natural population limit*. It is determined by the supply of the resources that are needed for survival.

Getting Out of Hand

In Figure 13–2, the growth line of population has for some reason just kept going up and up and up. This is exactly what seems to have happened with the world population. Instead of slowing

FIGURE 13–2

THE S CURVE FOR HUMAN BEINGS GONE AWRY

Here we show what has happened to the population of human beings in the world. Instead of following a typical S curve where the natural limit is reached after a while, there seems to be no end in sight.

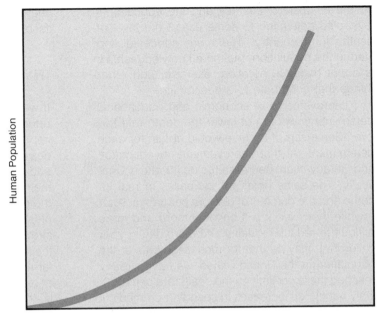

down, the growth rate has actually increased. Doubling time has fallen from 2000 years to 1000 years to 500 years, down to its present 35 years. However, we know that there has to be a ceiling somewhere. As one famous economist characterized the earth, it is a spaceship; it can only hold so many people for it has a fixed amount of space and a fixed number of resources.* Population obviously cannot continue to grow forever.

WHY HAS THE S CURVE GONE AWRY?

Man's population growth has, according to some, departed from the S curve. The natural population limit seems to be way into the future. One of the most obvious reasons for this departure lies in

*But we can live under and above ground, too. The Second Law of Thermodynamics would seem to indicate that the earth is an open system.

our ability to alter our environment—an ability that fruit flies do not possess. Medical science happens to be something that changes the course of population. We have been successful in decreasing the crude death rate tremendously in the last few decades. We have also been extending our medical knowledge to underdeveloped countries where the birth rate has remained the same for many, many years but where the death rates have fallen drastically. The rate of growth of population in those countries has consequently increased dramatically.

Numerous studies have been done on what determines the death rate in different countries. The economic determinants of that variable are quite obvious. We would expect that the larger the real income per capita, the lower would be the death rate because people would spend more money on more nutritious foods, medical care, and the like. We would also expect that the larger the number of doctors per capita, the lower would be the death rate. Literacy and the educational level also determine to some extent the level of deaths in a country. The more educated and literate the population, the more knowledgeable it is about hygiene, nutrition, exercise, and other things that contribute to a healthy life.

Improvements in economic and educational determinants would not lower the death rate forever. Some sort of S curve would obtain for each determinant. At first improvements in education and literacy might decrease the death rate dramatically. The same holds for increases in real income and the number of doctors per capita. After a while, however, it will become more and more difficult to reduce mortality and morbidity in your children. It may be that for most segments of the population in the United States, we have already reached the lower limit on the death rate per 1000. Only very large increases in spending on medical care could lower the death rate even further. This, of course, is not the case in underdeveloped countries where life expectancy is still extremely short by American standards and where infant mortality is very high by world standards.

BIRTH CONTROL

Even before the advent of modern birth control techniques, couples still had ways to determine the number of children they would have. When marriage occurs at a later age in life, the birth rate will be lower. Celibacy, of course, is always an effective method of birth control, and it doesn't require modern techniques.

In any event, economists have found that fertility rates or birth rates can be explained by various economic variables. This is especially true in Western countries where birth control is widely practiced and relatively inexpensive. The more inexpensive birth control methods become, the fewer unwanted babies there will be. We might discover how couples decide how many offspring

they want by looking at children in an economic fashion.

INVESTING IN CHILDREN

If we treat children as an investment, the rate of return to that investment would most likely be an important determinant of how many children were desired. This is especially true for agricultural societies where children become productive members of the family at a very young age. In the past, it was not uncommon for 5- and 6-year-olds to start picking cotton, olives, grapes, or strawberries on the family farm. Most probably, the higher the price of the farm products, the more farm babies would be desired because the rate of return to having children would be higher—that is, the value of their marginal product would rise.

It is quite ludicrous now, however, to consider children as an investment (at least in the United States). Some parents do, nonetheless, get a return on their ''investment'' later in life when their retirement is provided by their children. This is increasingly rare, though, because of Social Security and other retirement plans that parents have paid into throughout their lives.

Children as Consumption

It might be more appropriate to consider children as a consumption good. We would expect, therefore, that the normal determinants of the quantity demanded would prevail. What are these determinants? In the main, they are the price of the good and the income of the demander. There will be an income elasticity of the demand for children and also a price elasticity. The price elasticity most likely is negative; that is, the higher the price of raising children, the lower the quantity demanded. The income elasticity is positive, but it may be less than unity. As real incomes go up, the quantity of children demanded may not go up in proportion. In any event, we can easily determine the cost of raising children and this is exactly what the Insurance Institute of America has done.

Cost of Children

Surprising as it may seem, the cost of raising children through college has risen to about $35,000 per child (undiscounted). That means that if a parent decides on having a child, the parent knows that the $35,000 of income which he could have used himself will be used to raise the child. This, of course, does not indicate the total cost of raising children, as any parent can vouch for. There is a tremendous time cost involved. The higher the wage rate that a parent makes, the higher the opportunity cost of the time that must be devoted to the child. This perhaps is where the term "a millionaire's family" comes from. The millionaire's family is one boy and one girl—only two children. It becomes too expensive in terms of opportunity cost for the high income man to have more children in his family. (He could, of course, purchase the services of a surrogate father at less than his opportunity cost. But then what's the use of having children?)

Given the rapidly rising cost of higher education and the larger and larger portion of young people attending college, one would expect that *ceteris paribus* the number of children desired should fall. For this or for some other reason, the net reproduction rate in the United States has done just that: zero population growth may be a reality in the United States within the next few decades, if the trend in net reproduction does not reverse itself. In fact, in the long run, our current reproduction trend may lead to below ZPG. This fact should make Zero Population Growth addicts quite happy. They aren't convinced, though, as we shall see in the next issue.

Definition of New Terms

CRUDE BIRTH RATE: the number of births per 1000 people in a population.

CRUDE DEATH RATE: the number of deaths per 1000 people in a population.

POPULATION RATE OF GROWTH: the crude birth rate minus the crude death rate divided by 10; the percentage rate of growth per year in a population.

DOUBLING TIME: the number of years it takes for the population in a specific country to double.

NET REPRODUCTION RATE: the number of daughters born to every mother. When the net reproduction rate is one, the population will remain stable.

Chapter Summary

1. The arithmetic of population growth is rather simple. To find out the rate of increase in population per year in percentage terms, we subtract the crude death rate from the crude birth rate and divide by 10. We can translate the rate of increase in population into a doubling time, which is equal to the number of years it takes the population to double.

2. The easiest way to find out the doubling time of a population is to use the rule of 72. We divide the percentage rate of increase of population into 72 and come up with an approximate doubling time.
3. Another important population statistic is the net reproduction rate. When it is equal to 1, it means that one mother has one female child and the population will remain stable.
4. The optimum population will occur when the real output per capita is maximized.
5. People are increasingly moving to the cities. Urban centers account for about 75 percent of all the population in the United States.
6. While animal species reach a natural population limit, human beings apparently have not reached one yet. The S curve of population growth has turned out to be an incorrect predictor of human population. One of the reasons is because of the drastic increases in preventing the premature death of human beings.
7. We might explain fertility rates using economic variables. The children of agricultural societies can be looked at as an investment because by the age of 5 or 6 they become productive. However, in an industrial society such as ours, children are much more a consumption item.
8. Just like any other consumption item, the demand for children should be a function of income and the price of raising them. The price of raising children has been increasing rapidly.

Questions for Thought and Discussion

1. Do you think that human beings will necessarily procreate until they reach the natural population limit?
2. East Germany has a negative rate of population growth. Do you believe that this is because the death rate is greater than the birth rate or because of other reasons? What are they?
3. Can you think of criteria upon which the optimal size of the population can be based? What are they?
4. "The $750 tax exemption for dependent children should be eliminated because it encourages large families." Do you agree? Why or why not? If you do not agree, why do you think that the demand for children is price inelastic?

Selected References

Ehrlich, Paul and Anne. *Population, Resources, Environment.* 2nd Ed. San Francisco: W.H. Freeman, 1972.
Hardin, Garrett. *Population, Evolution and Birth Control.* 2nd Ed. San Francisco: W.H. Freeman, 1969.

ISSUE XVI

Can the Earth Be Saved?

Filling up the Globe

The members of Zero Population Growth (ZPG) obviously have something to be concerned about. And, indeed, they are not alone in their concern. The following advertisement appearing in the May 1972 issue of *Playboy* gives some indication of the sense of urgency in the ZPG campaign against overpopulation.

It was fun while it lasted. But the party's almost over. Mother Earth has had enough.

Every day of every year almost 350,000 babies are born on the Earth.

That means a net increase of 70 million people each year. 70 million extra mouths to feed. 70 million new bodies to clothe and comfort. The Earth can't handle it alone. It needs your help.

Consider the alternatives to over population. And what smaller families would mean to your world.

Bring the Earth back to the way it ought to be. Clear skies. Clean water. And just enough inhabitants to assure a comfortable ride through eternity.

Please consider all the good you can do. Please consider all the good we can do together.

Please consider Zero Population Growth.

It is, indeed, disturbing, isn't it? An increase of 70 million people a year on the face of this earth. There's got to be a limit somewhere, and, in fact, someone figured out that the earth presumably can accommodate 20 million times its present population. Living conditions, however, would be somewhat strange, as there would be 120 people per square meter enclosed in a 2000 story building covering the entire earth. And, at our present growth rate, it would take us less than 900 years to reach that far-from-enviable situation. (Think of all the friends you could have over.) By that time, of course, we would be able to export additional bodies to other planets or other solar systems.

The ZPG movement does not reflect the dawning of a totally new consciousness in world ecology. Indeed, the very groundwork for ZPG's current *modus operandi* was laid by various colorful personalities from the past. Thomas Malthus was one such figure, whom we shall discuss now.

Copulatory Economics

Back in 1798 a persuasive parson named Thomas Robert Malthus published his *Essay on Population*. Basically Malthus set forth a doctrine which predicted that food would grow at an arithmetic rate—1, 2, 3, 4, 5, 6, 7, 8, and so

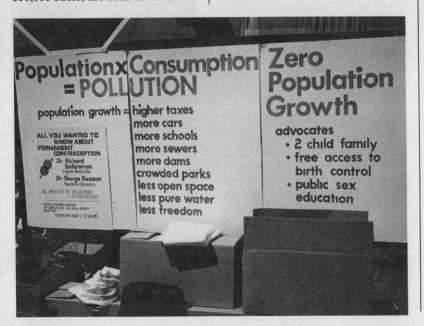

on. Population, however, would grow at a geometric rate—2, 4, 8, 16. We're all familiar with what happens when something grows at a geometric rate. If you took a single grain of barley and placed it on a chess board and then allowed it to grow geometrically once for every square that was on the board, by the final square you would have about 18,500,000,000,000,000,000 grains of barley —which is almost a billion tons. Geometric growth is indeed a delightful discovery.

Malthus figured that population would grow as long as there is food and as long as income is rising. He looked at some past population growth rates and found that men have an insatiable urge to mate and beget their own. Parson Malthus reasoned that there's a fixed amount of resources on the earth. It is true that additional population brings additional labor to work on those resources, but, because of the law of diminishing returns, additional labor working on a fixed amount of land will not result in proportional increases in output. Output will go up but not by as much as the increase in population and the labor force. Malthus reasoned that labor would be added to the fixed amount of land until living standards were reduced to a subsistence level—a level that would keep everybody on earth at the brink of starvation. Malthus, of course, *ignored increasing technology.*

Malthus' theory was that population would inevitably expand to its natural or fixed limit. That is, the physical limitation to population would be reached at least every so often, and there would be crises which would always prevent the natural limit from being exceeded. Those crises would be in the form of famines; large numbers of people would die. Essentially Malthus was treating the human species as if it were just like any other species. Recall our example of the fruit flies in the last chapter. They would multiply until the conditions for reproduction were so bad that the population would reach its natural limit. The long-run equilibrium level for fruit flies is at the maximum attainable limit. The same is true for every other nonhuman species. Malthus thought people would constantly expand to some fixed natural limit.

Population Control

If the worries of Zero Population Growth people, the neo-Malthusians, are indeed justified, then it follows that some sort of population control program should be instituted. This, in fact, was the conclusion reached by the Commission on Population Growth and the American Future after two years of exhaustive study. The Commission opted for a goal of population stability in future years. The Commission chairman, John D. Rockefeller, III, asserted that all of the goals of population stability could also be justified in terms of other objectives not related to population. Rockefeller was referring to the goals of improved education, cleaner environment, increased standards of living, and better health. The commission argued for a two-child family at most for Americans. (A while back the originator of Zero Population Growth, Paul Ehrlich, suggested that the average number of children per family should be one in

The Optimal Family Size?

order to reduce the size of the population from its current 200 million plus.)

The Commission noted that if current immigration rates continue, foreign born persons will account for 25 percent of the nation's future population growth. Some of the commissioners argued that immigration should be restricted as part of a total effort to reach population stability. This recommendation, of course, goes against the "melting pot" ideology of America.

Concerning the dispersion of population within the United States, the commission called for a plan to foster growth in smaller communities so that there will be less crowding in the larger urban areas. Right now there is a current immigration level of 400,000 a year to our largest centers of population density, such as New York, Chicago, and Los Angeles.

One of the most controversial conclusions of the Commission on Population Growth and the American Future was the call for more liberal abortion laws, for government financing of abortion, and for including abortion benefits in health insurance programs. We would expect that as the price of abortion falls, the quantity demanded will rise. It is therefore not without forethought that the Commission suggested such a method to help stabilize the population. The problem of whether abortion should be allowed is not economic.

The rest of the commission's recommendations are listed here.

1. Increase efforts in population and sex education, particularly in the schools.
2. Eliminate restrictive laws that prevent minors from being given contraceptive information and services.
3. Eliminate any restrictions on voluntary sterilizations for women and men.
4. Increase federal spending for research aimed at improving means of birth control.
5. Extend and expand existing federal programs that provide family planning information.

These are just some of the schemes that can be used for stabilizing the population. We'll assume for the moment that there will be nothing done to reduce the number of deaths. There are also other schemes, and it might be interesting to talk about a couple of them now.

Schemes for Reducing Population Growth

The American economist, Kenneth Boulding, an academician very much concerned about ecology and population problems, has suggested that the way to stabilize population might be to give every child when it is born a ticket allowing it to have one child at any time in the future. These birth tickets could be traded—that is, bought and sold—or given away. We would expect that a birthright market would develop. People who wanted to remain celibate, homosexuals, unmarried or married people without desire for children would all want to sell their birth tickets. People who wanted to have more than their allotted share of children would want to purchase the tickets. We would expect that a lively market in birthrights might develop, much as the stock exchange has developed.

What would happen as soon as the net reproduction rate fell below 1—that is, as soon as the net reproduction rate were such that the population would begin to decline? The price of birthrights would fall to zero. Let's see how this can be explained graphically. Look at Figure XVI-1. Here we show the supply curve of birthrates as a vertical line SS. When the demand curve crosses it, there will be a positive price for the tickets at P_1. But if the demand curve shifts to $D'D'$, the price will be zero.

The birthright concept that Boulding suggests is obviously a controversial one because it involves population control rather than voluntary birth control. It would be illegal for anybody to

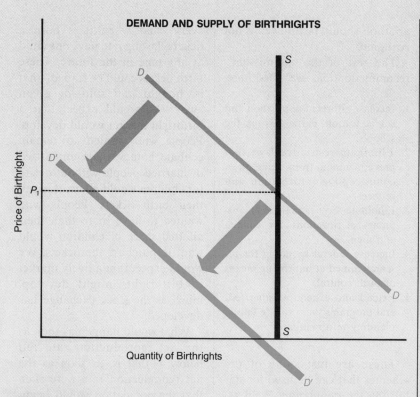

DEMAND AND SUPPLY OF BIRTHRIGHTS

FIGURE XVI-1 Here we assume that the government sets the number of birthrights at a fixed amount so that the supply curve is the vertical line, *SS*. So long as the demand curve is somewhere such that it intersects the supply curve above the horizontal axis, the price of birthrights will be positive. Once the supply curve shifts from *DD* to *D'D'*, however, the price of birthrights will fall to zero. That's when the net reproduction rate falls below 1.

have a child unless he had a ticket for having a child. (One wonders what the punishment would be if a person were caught procreating without the appropriate tickets.) Even the notion of a widespread, readily available, and perhaps subsidized birth control technique runs into a tremendous amount of controversy for religious and other reasons. But currently, birth control is, in fact, voluntary. To some extent it would become involuntary if we were to sell tickets for births because if one did not have a ticket, she or he would be forced to practice birth control. The counterargument is, of course, that anybody who wanted to have more children than their allotted number could, in fact, have them if they were willing to purchase the tickets. That would mean that they would be forced to spend part of their income to buy those tickets; they would have to give up consuming something else. This, of course, is just one means of raising the price of having children and, therefore, reducing the quantity demanded.

Population and the Ecology

Zero Population Growth people believe that the only way to prevent increasing amounts of pollution is to check our rapidly growing population. In fact, some maintain that the underlying cause of pollution is too large a population. In the ad appearing in *Playboy,* the assumption is that, if we stabilize our population, we will have "Clear skies. Clean water." There is a problem with this line of reasoning which you should be aware of. Population is figured as the cause of many of our environmental problems, but, when you think about it, it really isn't.

If we had a population of one-half our current size but the income per capita was double what it is today, don't you think that more or less the same level of pollution would prevail? The level of total production would remain the same. Given our current set of institutions—property laws, pricing systems, and so on—we would expect that the same level of pollution would prevail regardless of population (within limits, of course) because pollution output is a function of consumption levels and consumption levels are a function of income or real standards of living. The problems of despoiling our environment really are not problems of overpopulation. The problems of conservation, ecological destruction, pollution, and so on were covered in previous discussions. It turned out that much of the problem of pollution is due to the fact that nobody owns natural resources such as air and water. It is perhaps misguided, then, to think that without solving the common property problem, or the problem of equating social costs and private costs, that the reduction in population growth would somehow create a cleaner environment. In fact, we would imagine that if property rights became more indefinite, we could have more pollution with a smaller population even if income fell.

Crowding

One of the inevitable consequences of the population explosion is overcrowding. In fact, all one need do is try to get to work on the subway at 8 in the morning in New York City to find out what crowding is all about. All one need do is travel to Hong Kong to see how closely people can pack themselves into a restricted space. But are these really the problems of overpopulation?

The density per square mile in the United States is quite small relative to other countries in the world. Therefore, does the United States face a problem of overcrowding due to a population explosion? Probably not. Rather, the United States faces a problem of too many people in too concentrated an area. That is, we find that 98 percent of the people live on 2 percent of the available land. We know, of course, that lots of the land in the United States is uninhabitable, but much is left over that generally does not have people living on it. Perhaps instead of attempting to control the population, one would wish to control the location of the population in order to ameliorate overcrowding in big cities.

What is amazing is the fact that big cities are becoming more and more crowded despite the horrendous distresses that are created by them. Of course, when you think about it, it should not be too surprising. *Specialization is a function of the size of the market.* How many operas, symphonies, and playhouses can be supported in small rural towns? Even when you go to a relatively large city, you cannot always find what you want in terms of entertainment and cultural activity. Seattle is one of the largest cities in the United States, but the variety of cultural activities available to its inhabitants is unbelievably small relative to what is available in, say, New York City. This may explain why people like to live in New York City despite the tremendous cost of doing so: The benefits are also tremendous—thousands of restaurants, hundreds of theaters, and everything else imaginable for one to do. (We won't go into some of them.)

An Unexpected Result of ZPG—A Geriatric Population

If we accept the premises of Zero Population Growth advocates, then our population should indeed stabilize. If we accept some of the more radical suggestions, such as the one that Paul Ehrlich made in a *Playboy* interview some years back, then we should have a net reproduction rate of less than 1 so that population will decline to about 50 million people in the United States. A consequence of either course on the age structure of the population is a little talked about and less understood aspect of population control.

Right now, the median age in the United States is somewhere between 20 and 30. As the population expands, the median age falls, as you would expect. However, if we were to go to a stable population, the median age would jump by a full ten years. That is, it would lie somewhere between 30 and 40. Some demographers estimate that it would be 37. There would be an aging of the population and if we were to go from our current 200 million plus to Ehrlich's desired 50 million, the age distribution of the population would be skewed dramatically toward older people. That is, the median age would go from its current 27 to 37 to 47 or even to 57, depending upon how fast we would reach the magic number of 50 million. The thought of a geriatric population may be somewhat discomforting to you, but, of course, that is a noneconomic problem. In any event, we would find that there would be less chance for rapid advancement in the job market. There would be very few young people who were successful, as they can be now, and there would be almost no presidents of corporations who are in their thirties as we find currently. Everything would become much more stabilized in terms of job advancement. Perhaps the benefits from population stabilization or reduction would be worth the costs. But in any event, the costs just mentioned will be there and there is no way to avoid them. The age structure of the population must change;

it's an arithmetic certainty if we stabilize the population. No doubt the country will be a much less exciting place to live in, unless, of course, medical science rapidly improves the mental and physical well-being of older people so that the aging of the population will not be as noticeable.

Depopulation

While the United States concerns itself with limiting population growth, there are other countries in the world which have concerned themselves with how to *increase* population growth. Believe it or not, populating is a problem in certain countries of the world such as France.

France has had a population "problem" for many years. There have been various methods to increase the average family size and thereby prevent France's total population from declining. The government has even given special family allowances to encourage larger families. The trend in family size was increasing for a few years after World War II and after incentives were presented to French families, but then family size started to go down again. The government decided to increase family allotments and to use other monetary methods to encourage larger families. For most countries, it is a frightening proposition to think of the population size

actually getting smaller. This, of course, is not the case in India, Pakistan, or some other non-Western nations.

In any event, France's methodology for increasing family size should give us a hint as to what might be done in the United States to encourage smaller families, if indeed that is what we want to do. Currently, there is an incentive to have larger families. It is done by way of a $750 deduction per dependent that is allowed when paying income taxes. For every child in the family, the parent is allowed to deduct $750 from income before he computes his income taxes. Obviously, an elimination of this deduction would raise the price of having children. We would expect (at least on the margin) there would be fewer children born because of the increase in price. Perhaps Zero Population Growth sympathizers might suggest that this be a start toward finding out what the natural population growth rate in the United States would be without any special inducements. It may turn out that there will be no need to worry about a population explosion because the natural reproduction rate would be 1.

The United States Today

In early 1972, the U.S. Census Bureau produced evidence that young Americans are moving toward a state of generational equilibrium. That is, the net reproduction rate in the United States is falling to 1, even without the institution of the suggestions of Zero Population Growth people. Married women between the ages of 15 and 24 that were interviewed by the Census Bureau in 1971 expected to have an average of only 2.4 children. In 1967, the same faction of mothers thought they would have an average of 2.9 children. When demographers figure in how many unmarried women there will be, the expected birth rate might dip as low as 2.2. The birth rate required for married women to attain population stability, or ZPG, is 2.1, the 0.1 being necessary to take account of deaths. Perhaps in the next few years the problem of the population explosion, at least in the United States, will no longer be discussed because, in fact, we will have reached a net reproduction rate of 1. There will then be no need for a ZPG movement.

Questions for Thought and Discussion

1. How could we enforce population control?
2. Why should we believe modern day Malthusians when Malthus himself was proven wrong?
3. How can Paul Ehrlich maintain that the optimum population in the United States is 50 million?

Selected References

Brunner, John. *Stand on Zanzibar.* New York: Ballantine Books, 1968.

Ehrlich, Paul. *The Population Bomb.* New York: Ballantine Books, 1968.

Hardin, Garrett. *Population, Evolution and Birth Control.* 2nd Ed. San Francisco: W. H. Freeman, 1969.

Growth and Development

14

N OT ONLY AMONG individuals but among nations, there exist the haves and the have-nots. The world is one of developed, less developed, and underdeveloped nations. Some are growing at fast rates; others at slow rates. Economic growth is obviously an important policy variable which concerns the governments of all nations. Today in the United States there is an increasing clamor for *reducing* our current economic growth rate. We will touch upon this in greater detail in the following issue. In the present chapter, we shall discuss the general theory of growth and development. Zero economic growth may seem desirable to many in the United States. However, underdeveloped countries in the world are still struggling for economic growth to reach what we in America would consider a decent standard of living. Therefore, even if the United States were suddenly to decide to quit growing economically, underdeveloped nations would still want to know what policies they should pursue to increase their rate of economic growth so that their citizens could enjoy the fruits of economic progress and attain higher standards of material living. This is why the theories of growth presented in this chapter are still important today.

DIFFERENT RATES OF GROWTH

We see in Table 14–1, that the per capita incomes in different countries in the world today vary widely. So, too, do the growth rates in per capita income, or in GNP, however we wish to look at it. The United States is at the top of the list in terms of per capita income. However, the United States is not the fastest growing country in the world and indeed has had one of the lower growth rates around. You will notice that the growth rates do not differ by very much: 1, 2, 3 or so percentage points. You might want to know why such small differences in growth rates are important. What does it matter, you could say, if we grew at 3 percent or at 4 percent per year?

It matters a lot—not for next year or the year after—but for the future. The power of compound interest is overwhelming. Now let's see what happens with three different growth rates: 3 percent, 4 percent, 5 percent. We start out with $1 trillion, which is approximately equal to the gross national product of the United States at the beginning of this decade. We put the year 1971 as our start. We then compound or grow this $1 trillion into the future at these three different growth rates. The difference is huge. In 50 years, $1 trillion becomes $4,380,000,000,000 if compounded at 3 percent per year. Just one percentage point more in the growth rate—that is, 4 percent—results in a GNP that almost doubles that amount. Two percentage points difference in the growth rate—that is, 5 percent per year—results in a GNP of $11,500,000,000,000 50 years from now. Obviously, there is a great difference in the results of economic growth for very small differences in growth rates. That is why nations are concerned if the growth rate falls even by a very small amount in absolute percentage terms.

It is often asserted that the reason income and wealth in the United States is so great relative to other countries is because we were endowed with such a large amount of valuable natural resources. This, however, is not a necessary nor a sufficient condition for rapid economic growth.

NATURAL RESOURCES AND ECONOMIC GROWTH

In the first place, a large amount of natural resources are not sufficient to guarantee economic growth. Many Latin American countries are fantastically rich in natural resources. They, however, have not been overly successful in exploiting those resources through efficient economic activity. Natural resources must be converted to useful forms. Even in the United States, the Indians had more natural resources available to them than we have now, but they were unable to increase their standard of living or experience economic growth. They were poor for centuries and centuries.

Only if we include people in the category of natural resources can we say that natural resources are required for economic growth; obviously, *people* must devise the methods by which

---

TABLE 14–1

PER CAPITA GROWTH RATES AND INCOME

Here we show the per capita income in 1969 for selected countries and the average annual rate of growth of GNP per capita from 1960 to 1968. Notice that there is no correlation between income per capita and the growth rate. (*Source:* Statistical Office of the United Nations.)

COUNTRY	INCOME PER CAPITA (1965)	AVERAGE ANNUAL RATE OF GROWTH OF INCOME PER CAPITA (1960–1968)
U.S.	4664	3.7
Argentina	828	1.6
Brazil	337	1.1
Canada	2997	3.5
Dominican Republic	290	−0.6
France	2783	4.4
Greece	858	6.3
Iran	295	4.7
Italy	1548	4.3
Korea (South)	227	6.2
Uruguay	650	−0.9

other natural resources can be converted into useable forms. This is where the United States was more fortunate than other countries, particularly those with similar natural resources. (We also benefited from large capital investments from England and other Old World countries.) The founding fathers of our nation were a biased sample of the people on earth at that time. Many of the "criminals" who were transported to the colonies were guilty of such crimes as religious heresy, going into debt, evading economic laws made by the government, and disagreement with the government itself. Thus, we see that many of the people who came to the United States were those who either wanted to or who were forced to escape regimentation by a much more structured society in the Old World. These are just the type of people who would attempt to devise new methods to utilize the natural resources in America. And that they did.

This is not to say, of course, that if we transplanted a cross section of Americans to some Latin American country, the growth rate in that country would suddenly take off. However, we can assert that the United States required more than just abundant natural resources to reach its current level of development; it required people who could devise ways to form those resources into something useful for man. Underdeveloped nations will also require this type of human resource.

CAPITAL ACCUMULATION

It is often asserted that a necessary prerequisite for economic development is a large capital stock—machines and other durable goods which can be used to aid in the production of consumption goods and more capital goods in the future. It is true that developed countries have, indeed, larger capital stocks per capita than underdeveloped countries. It is also true that the larger the capital stock for any given population, the higher the possible rate of economic growth. This

is basically one of the foundations for many of the foreign aid programs that the United States and other countries have engaged in. We and other nations have attempted to give underdeveloped countries additions to their capital stocks so that they, too, may grow. However, the amount of capital that we have actually given to other nations is quite small: a steel mill here, a factory there. The relationship between the capital stock and growth is sufficiently important for us to spend another section on it. But before we do that, let's look at a perceptive and controversial concept of growth aired by a president of the International Finance Corporation, Mr. Robert L. Gardner.

Let us briefly examine some of the frequently cited causes of underdevelopment and slow economic growth.

It is often claimed that geography and natural resources are determining. They . . . are important . . . but resources lie inert and have no economic worth except as people bring them into use. It is easy to attribute the progress of the United States to its wide expanse and abundant physical resources. However, other areas—in Latin America, Africa, Asia—have comparable natural wealth, but most of it is still untouched. On the other hand, there are countries in western Europe with limited fertile land and meager mineral deposits, yet they have achieved high levels of economic life. . . .

Perhaps most often lack of capital is blamed. In the first place, there is in most developing countries more potential capital than is admitted. But large amounts are kept outside, because of political instability and depreciating currency at home. Over the post-war period immense sums have been made available to the developing areas. Some of these funds have been well applied and have produced sound results, others have not. . . .If [foreign aid] is applied to uneconomic purposes, or if good projects are poorly planned and executed, the result will be minus, not plus. The effective spending of large funds requires experience, competence, honesty and organization. Lacking any of these factors, large injections of capital into developing countries can cause more harm than good. The test of how much additional capital is required for development is how much a country can

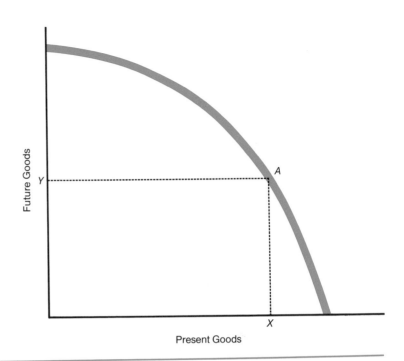

FIGURE 14-1

THE TRADE-OFF BETWEEN PRESENT GOODS AND FUTURE GOODS

Here we show the production possibilities curve between present goods and future goods. If we want to have more goods in the future, we have to sacrifice goods today. In other words, there has to be more saving if we are to have more future goods. At a point in time—for example, if we were at point *A* in this diagram—we could consume *X* present goods and we would have *Y* future goods.

effectively apply within any given period, not how much others are willing to supply.

I am, therefore, forced to the conclusion that economic development or lack of it is primarily due to differences in people—in their attitudes, customs, traditions and the consequent differences in their political, social and religious institutions.

Mr. Gardner is perhaps overstressing the human element in the question of growth and development. However, he does point out that lack of natural resources and lack of capital is really not the main deterrent to development. If Gardner is correct, then underdeveloped nations would be wise to invest more of their efforts in the population rather than in the capital stock. That is to say, underdeveloped nations would possibly grow faster if there was a larger investment in human capital than there was in physical capital. The education of the population, as well as training both on and off the job, might do more to improve the development of the third world than would

devoting all efforts and resources to increasing the capital stock. Nonetheless, there is a distinct and well-defined relationship between the possible rate of growth of an economy and how large its capital stock is.

Capital and the Rate of Growth

Let's look at a production possibilities curve for the country as a whole. We want to find out the trade-off between goods today and goods tomorrow, or between present consumption and future consumption. Therefore, we label the horizontal axis as present goods and the vertical axis as future goods, as seen in Figure 14-1. The production possibilities curve, as you will remember, represents the *maximum* amount of each of the two goods that a nation can produce at any point in time. If, for example, we were at point *A* in Figure 14-1, we could with our present resources consume *X* amount of present goods and *Y*

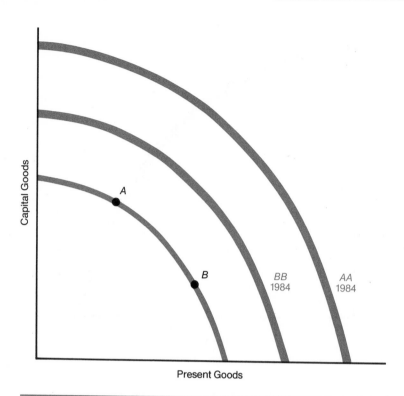

FIGURE 14–2

THE IMPORTANCE OF CAPITAL FOR GROWTH

Here we show a production possibilities curve with two points on it, A and B. At point A we are consuming less today and providing more consumption for tomorrow in the form of capital goods. At point B we are consuming more today and providing less in the form of future consumption by saving and investing in capital goods. If we operate at point A, we may end up on a production possibility curve of AA in 1984. However, if we are at point B, we may end up at a production possibilities curve of only BB in 1984. In other words, there will be less growth during the next decade if we consume more goods today instead of saving and investing in capital goods which provide for more future consumption.

amount of future goods. We see that by decreasing the amount of present goods, we can increase the amount of future goods. This, of course, means that if we consume less today, we will end up consuming more tomorrow. We have to sacrifice present consumption in order to have more future consumption.

Each individual, of course, is faced with this decision. It is a decision he must make with respect to how much he wants to save. If he wants to have a lot of future consumption, he cuts back on his current consumption; he saves more. He puts more of his income in a savings and loan association or in the stock market so that later on, perhaps when he retires, he will be able to consume more than otherwise. In terms of the economy as a whole, the decision as to whether there should be present consumption or future consumption ends up being a decision as to whether there should be more movies and food consumed or more buildings and machines constructed today. When you decide not to consume but to save part of your income, you will perhaps put it in a savings and loan association. That money will then be available to borrowers for new housing. You might also invest your savings in a new company or in the expansion of an old one. In this way, the money that you save ends up providing the money capital for businessmen so that they can construct and purchase physical capital—machines and equipment.

WHY IS CAPITAL IMPORTANT?

The size of the capital stock determines the amount of income that can be produced at any point in time. Obviously, if there are very few machines around which can be used to make goods and services, we will be able to make less and our income will be lower. The more machines there are, the more income can be generated. Therefore, the larger the capital stock, the larger the income pie. But how does the capital stock grow? It grows by people making the decision not to consume today but rather to save and invest. The more saving and investment there are as a percentage of total income, the higher will be the capital stock. And therefore, the higher will be possible future income. We can perhaps demonstrate this decision using our production possibilities curve again.

In Figure 14–2, we have drawn a production possibilities curve for 1973. Again, we have labeled the horizontal axis as present consumption. But the vertical axis is now labeled capital goods. Capital goods are just another way of talking about future consumption. We would expect that if our economy is operating at *A,* where there are relatively more capital goods being produced than at *B,* the production possibilities curve in 1984 would be farther to the right than it would be if we were producing at B. We have labeled the outside curve *AA* and the middle curve *BB.* Obviously, the rate of growth starting from point *A* is greater than the rate of growth starting from point *B.* The pie gets potentially larger the more people are willing to save today. In fact, we might be able to increase the rate of growth in the United States drastically if we somehow increased the saving rate of the population. This could be done by government taxation. In other words, taxes could be increased and the proceeds from those increased taxes could be put into investment goods which would yield increased income in the future. Let's now turn from investment to saving.

SAVING DECISIONS

Saving decisions are based on lots of things. However, the key determinant is what we call a person's **personal discount rate.** If you just can't wait to consume all of the income you make, you have a relatively high discount rate. If you can wait longer and are not so impatient, you have a relatively low discount rate. The lower your discount rate, the more you'll be willing to save at any given yield on those savings. Whenever your personal discount rate exceeds the yield you can get on savings, you will not save; you have to be offered a yield which is higher than your discount rate. Otherwise you'll be better off by consuming today. The saving behavior of economies taken as a whole therefore depends upon the collective discount rate of the population and the average rate of return to saving. (The government, of course, can cause forced saving by increasing taxes, but that's another matter.)

Limit to Growth

We would expect, therefore, that there is some limit as to how much the country can grow. That limit will be set by available technology and by the amount of saving the population wants to have. Notice here we are not talking about accumulated savings but about a *rate* of saving—that is, how much out of current income people want to sock away for a rainy day. It is often stated that poor people in underdeveloped countries cannot save because they are barely subsisting. This, in fact, is not actually true. Many anthropological studies of villages in India, for example, have revealed that saving is in fact going on, but it takes peculiar forms that we don't recognize in our money economy. In some places, capital accumulation may involve storing dried onions. In any event, saving does take place, even in the most poverty stricken countries.

The Poor Save Too

We can look at it this way. Even if you are very, very poor and just barely making a living, you know that sometime in the future you will no longer be able to work. You will either reach mandatory retirement or you will become so unproductive that nobody will be willing to hire you. Your income stream will be cut off. Unless there is a benevolent government around or charities which will take care of you, you will face starvation unless you have accumulated savings. Therefore, you must decide today how much of your current meager income you want to set aside for those retirement years when you can no longer work. Unless it is literally true that you will starve if you reduce your current level of consumption by a very small amount, you probably will attempt to save a little bit, however small, out of your meager income. Most people would rather reduce current consumption by a small amount so as to be able to at least exist after they can no longer work. If they did not reduce their consumption at all, they might face certain starvation as soon as their income stream fell to zero.

Saving, after all, is a method by which individuals can realize an optimal consumption stream throughout their expected lifetime. The word *optimal* here does not mean adequate or necessary, but rather the most desirable, from the *individual's* point of view. If the individual faces the constraint of very low income for all of his life, in most cases, he will still want to provide some savings to live with when he can no longer work.

THE USE OF SAVINGS

Merely because a population is willing to save does not mean it is guaranteed a high economic growth rate. People in underdeveloped countries sometimes save a tremendous amount. But what do they do with their savings? Often they hoard their savings in the form of gold or precious metals because they are uncertain about the safeness or the rate of return they can make if they invest their savings in a new business enterprise or a savings and loan association. Recall that a person will save, if his personal discount rate is less than the rate of return he can make on savings. He

can make a rate of return on savings by purchasing gold if the price of gold has gone up in the past. Even if it hasn't gone up a person may wish to take part of his income and purchase gold so that he will have at least some asset to sell when he is no longer working. This is why we find so much hoarding of gold in underdeveloped countries. For centuries, gold has been one of the few assets which has never lost its value. It hasn't always appreciated in price, but it has rarely decreased in value. A country such as India is perhaps worse off when so many people put their savings into gold, for gold does not generate future production. If Indians who saved were to put their money into savings and loan associations, India's capital stock would be larger because the money could then be loaned out to businessmen for investment. India's growth rate would also be higher. This brings us to the relationship between private property rights and growth rates.

PROPERTY RIGHTS AND THE RATE OF GROWTH

If you were in a country where bank accounts and businesses were periodically expropriated by the government, how willing would you be to leave your money in a savings account or to invest in a business? Certainly you would be less willing than if such things never occurred. A good rule of thumb is: the more certain private property rights are, the more capital accumulation there will be. People will be willing to invest the money that they do not spend in endeavors which will increase their wealth in future years. They have property rights in their wealth which are sanctioned and enforced by the government. In fact, some economic historians have attempted to show that it was the development of well-defined private property rights which allowed Western Europe to increase its growth rate after many centuries of stagnation. The ability and certainty with which one can reap the gains from investing also determine the extent to which businessmen in *other* countries will invest capital in underdeveloped countries. The threat of nationalization which hangs over most Latin American nations probably prevents a massive amount of foreign investment that might be necessary to allow these nations to become more developed.

HUMAN CAPITAL

The role of physical capital and the savings necessary for it to be created is an important determinant of economic growth. However, the development of, and investment in human capital is equally important. Even large infusions of foreign physical capital into underdeveloped countries will not necessarily increase the rate of growth or increase the standards of living in those countries unless that foreign capital is put to good use. The only way it can be put to good use is to have trained personnel who know how to use it. When Castro nationalized all of the foreign capital holdings in Cuba, he acquired for his country many billions of dollars worth of machinery, buildings, and equipment. However, the growth rate in Cuba has not appreciably increased since Castro came into office. Notice here we are not talking about the social well-being of the population, for that is not easily measured. Rather, we are referring to the standard economic concept of growth as an increase in GNP per capita, or an increase in per capita income. Castro's government could not take full advantage of all of the physical capital which it inherited because it did not have sufficient

human capital. Most of the trained technicians who were running the plants left the country. Many of these plants continue to sit idle. They rust away and are, in fact, completely useless to the Cuban people without technicians to run them.

WHAT HOPE FOR THE THIRD WORLD?

As you might have guessed from reading this chapter, there is no clear-cut guaranteed model of economic growth that we can apply to underdeveloped nations so that they, too, may become developed. This does not mean there is no hope for the future of the third world. Perhaps economists will become better attuned to the actual determinants of growth in different situations so that specific models can be made and applied in specific situations. The economics of development and growth is perhaps one of the less well-defined disciplines in the entire study of economics. That, of course, does not mean that there is.a paucity of "development" literature. On the contrary, the number of books written on the subject could fill several rooms. We list a few of the more interesting ones at the end of this chapter. You should be warned, however, that in no case is there a generally accepted theory of economic development. The majority of economists will agree with basic price theory or microeconomic notions, but the same cannot be said of almost all the literature that has been written on economic growth. Many deep disagreements still exist.

Definition of New Terms

PERSONAL DISCOUNT RATE: the rate at which you as an individual discount future pleasure or future consumption. If you have a high personal discount rate, then you will want to consume a lot today because you don't want to wait until tomorrow. If you have a low personal discount rate, you will be willing to wait in order to have more consumption in the future. You will be willing to save more.

Chapter Summary

1. Just as there are different levels of per capita income in the world, there are different rates of growth. There seems to be no correlation between the level of per capita income and the rate of growth, however. It is the rate of growth that we are concerned with in this chapter.
2. A slight difference in the compound rate of growth ends up causing a tremendous difference in the per capita income or GNP many years in the future. For example, a jump from a 3 percent to a 5 percent per year rate of growth results in, at the end of 50 years, a difference in total income of almost 250 percent.
3. While natural resources are important for allowing economic growth, we must include in the concept of natural resources people and their productive services in order to come up with factors necessary for economic growth.
4. Even though people are important, so is capital accumulation or capital from other countries. In fact, we find that the more saving there is today, the larger is the capital stock and the larger will be the amount of possible future consumption. Hence, in economies where the people save a large percentage of their income, we would expect, *ceteris paribus,* a higher rate of growth than in economies where people do not save so much. The use to which this capital is put is also important. If it is not used for investments which allow for future production and consumption, then the rate of growth may not be high merely because the rate of saving is high.
5. It is important to note that saving is a way to reach an optimal rate of consumption throughout one's life. Therefore, even poor people may want to save in order to provide for future consumption when they are no longer working and making an income.
6. Some economists believe that the more well-defined property rights are, the greater the rate of growth will be because individuals will have an incentive to accumulate and conserve capital.

Questions for Thought and Discussion

1. Do you think Latin America is going to be better off by discouraging foreign investment through numerous nationalizations and expropriations of foreign property? Why?
2. Many underdeveloped countries put extreme restrictions on the purchase of foreign made luxury goods. Do you think that this is a helpful policy for increasing the rate of growth in these countries?
3. If you were the economic policy advisor to an underdeveloped country, where would you suggest the government start investing? Why?
4. Many people contend that in most underdeveloped countries, the population is too poor to be able to save. Go back to our definition of saving as a way to distribute consumption optimally throughout one's lifetime. Do you think it is true that poorer people are unable to save as much as rich people in percentage terms? What is the relevant determinant of desired saving?

Selected References

Bruton, Henry J. *Principles of Development Economics*. Englewood Cliffs, New Jersey: Prentice Hall, 1964.

Dowd, Douglas F., Ed. *America's Role in the World Economy*. Boston: D.C. Heath, 1966.

Hagen, Everett E. *The Economics of Development*. Homewood, Ill.: Richard D. Irwin, 1968.

Higgins, Benjamin. *Economic Development*. New York: W. W. Norton, 1968.

Johnson, Harry G. *Economic Policies toward Less Developed Countries*. Washington, D.C.: The Brookings Institution, 1967.

Rostow, W. W. *The Stages of Economic Growth*. 2nd Ed. New York: Cambridge University Press, 1971.

ISSUE XVII

ZEG

Does Growth Mean Suicide?

Stopping GNP

We've noted some of the various theories that explain why nations grow, and we've shown some of the strategies underdeveloped nations might want to follow to increase their rate of economic growth so that their inhabitants might enjoy higher standards of living. Recently, though, the cry has been heard that economic growth should be stopped. Ecologically minded scientists, laymen, academicians, and public officials have declared that we must end our fetish with GNP growth. They argue that growth in GNP should be stopped because it depletes our natural resources, pollutes our environment, and makes us into materialistic money-grubbers. Furthermore, lurking somewhere in the future is a maximum limit which will be reached sooner or later. A fast growth rate in GNP just makes us reach it sooner. Then GNP will fall, and living standards will go down instead of up.

To Zero Economic Growth enthusiasts, there is no hope. Those concerned with the environment attack GNP as a digital idol worshipped by materialist gluttons. GNP measures, of course, only the output of goods and services. It

ignores the pollution and industrial grime that growth generates.

So some maintain there must be a limit to growth. In fact, in the hands of several scientists the computer has shown that growth

will reach a limit. An 18-month study sponsored by the somewhat unknown Club of Rome arrived at this very conclusion, which we will discuss now.

The Limits to Growth

Look at Figure XVII-1. It's pretty wild, isn't it? But the conclusion,

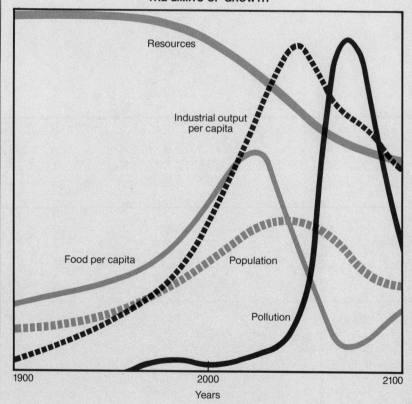

THE LIMITS OF GROWTH

Resources

Industrial output per capita

Food per capita

Population

Pollution

1900 — 2000 — 2100

Years

FIGURE XVII-1 Here we look into the twenty-first century. The prediction is that even though we will have ample natural resources, sufficient pollution controls, and better birth control, we will still run out of food. Malthus revisited. *Source:* Potomac Associates.

if those lines mean anything, is that food supplies are going to prove inadequate, even with ample natural resources, pollution controls, and a falling population. The question is: who drew those curves and how did they do it? Several scientists at the Massachusetts Institute of Technology set up many mathematical equations using information on what determines industrial output, food production, pollution, population, and so on, and the relationships between these factors. A big computer was then used to calculate and project the behavior of each of these trends as they related to each other.

The M.I.T. computer forecasted dramatic events for the world if the current trends in these variables continued. Before the year 2100, the world as a system would reach a point where the population could no longer be supported by existing resources. These grim findings apparently hold even if important advances are made in birth control and food production, in natural resources output and pollution control.

The equations show exponential (geometric) growth for everything except food production. Even breakthroughs in technology will not prevent the final collapse of the world. Take, for example, one computer run that the M.I.T. scientists experimented with. This is the one which actually underlies the funny curves shown in Figure

XVII-1. Those curves assumed that recycling technology would reduce the input of raw material per unit of output to 25 percent of the amount now used. It was also assumed that birth control would eliminate all unwanted children. Additionally, pollution would be 75 percent below its present level. What happens? Resources are sufficient; that's no problem. But the growth of industry is so great that higher output soon offsets the 75 percent decline in pollution. That is, even with the smaller amount of pollution per unit of output, the tremendous increases in output result in an overwhelming absolute amount of unwanted waste. Population, of course, even when all unwanted pregnancies are eliminated, gets out of hand so that there is a food crisis. Even increases in agricultural technology apparently will not save us. There will still be overuse of land which will lead to erosion causing food production to drop. This, at least, is what the computer predicted.

The M.I.T. authors of *Limits to Growth* point out that, even if there are tremendous scientific breakthroughs, they must be matched by equally dramatic changes in the world's social institutions. Otherwise, these breakthroughs, whether they be birth control devices or high grain yields, will not be effectively distributed to those in need of them. Needed changes won't appear.

Limits to the Limits to Growth

The study by M.I.T. scientists on the limits to growth presents us with a frightening perspective of what might occur in the future. However, it seems only fair that the deficiencies in the study itself should be mentioned. We have had enough doomsday foreseers in our history to warrant our being suspicious of any new ones. After all, Malthus predicted disaster over 150 years ago and it has yet to come.

Relative Prices

An economic fact that you are all aware of by now was completely forgotten in the world model established by the scientist-authors. When specific resources become scarce, their price goes up. People are motivated to find substitutes or, if necessary, to do without the more expensive goods and services. That's something that many ecologists seem to forget, but it is an immutable economic fact of life. If a good becomes scarcer, the supply curve shifts inward. With a stable demand curve, we expect a rise in price. The quantity sold falls as we see in Figure XVII-2. If timber becomes more scarce, we would expect that its price would rise and substitutes would be found. The same holds for steel, coal, copper, or anything else. The history of any economy is in part a history of how changing relative

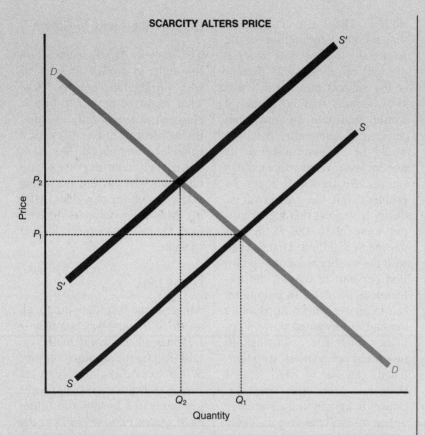

SCARCITY ALTERS PRICE

FIGURE XVII-2 If some particular resource becomes scarcer, its supply curve will shift from *SS* to *S'S'* and its price will rise from *P₁* to *P₂*. The quantity demanded and supplied will fall from *Q₁* to *Q₂*. This change in the relative price of those resources which become more scarce is something that modern-day doomsdayers do not discuss.

prices reflect relative scarcity. Production and innovation respond to such changes in relative prices. If the price of steel goes up because iron ore is becoming more scarce and more expensive, more attempts will be made at finding steel substitutes. Perhaps there will be an increased use of plastics. In any event, such is the way of the economic world.

Consider also that economic growth does not necessarily have to involve wasting resources or generating tremendous amounts of pollution. There is some growth that may not involve any pollution at all. For example, the increased use of computers like the one used to come up with the dire predictions in the *Limits to Growth* may involve almost no pollution at all relative to the dramatic increases in economic growth made possible by increased computer capacity. Additionally, we would expect that increased pollution controls would cause producers to learn to recycle their unwanted by-products. If this pollution abatement involves much higher costs, consumers will end up being faced with higher prices. They will alter their consumption accordingly. We would expect that products and services which do not involve pollution in their production and which therefore do not involve increases in relative prices will experience increased demand. In this way pollution will be reduced, not increased as growth continues.

Growth Rates

Another suspicious characteristic of the 18-month study on the limits of growth is that our problems were prophesied as growing at an exponential or geometric rate whereas our ability to solve those problems was only supposed to grow at an arithmetic rate. That's exactly the same kind of reasoning that led Malthus to predict the continual crises in the world due to lack of adequate food supply for a growing population. The population was growing exponentially or geometrically whereas the food supply was only growing arithmetically. Somehow that just hasn't seemed to have been the case and perhaps it may not be the case in the future either.

What If ZEG Were to Become Reality?

How does one stop economic growth? It's fairly simple to make suggestions on how to stop population growth—birth control, abortion, and the like—but what about those new machines that are being built every year? What about rising real incomes? Zero economic growth means that machines would be built only to replace worn out ones; no net additions to our capital stock would be allowed. How does the world go from growth to a so-called steady-state equilibrium? Advocates of zero economic growth really haven't a viable methodology for the world to follow. In any event, there are serious implications for the inequality of income, not only within countries but throughout the world, if in fact economic growth comes to a standstill.

Income and Equality

If industry growth is halted in underdeveloped countries, we would expect that the disparity between their standards of living and our own, for example, would

be maintained forever—a fact strongly voiced at a 1972 U.N. ecology conference in Stockholm. Within the United States itself, income differentials might presumably remain the same. And since income would not be growing, the poor would have no hope for ever extracting themselves from their poverty dilemma. Growth, after all, is a sort of substitute for equality of income. We know that as long as there is growth, there is hope for those who are not well to do; they know that things will get better.

Moreover, if we are to clean up our environment, we are going to have to use resources to do it. If growth is stopped, where will these resources come from? Will they come out of current standards of living? Somehow it is doubtful that people would be willing to give up such a large share of their current income for the Great Cleanup. With growth we will have more resources to do that Great Cleanup; without growth, we will have less. It's as simple as that.

Growth as Suicide

If the M.I.T. computers are correct, we are indeed in for trouble. If the findings are at all accurate, they raise staggering questions. And to these questions, hopefully, we will find answers. But in the meantime we must realize that

growth in the past has never proceeded in a simple-minded, exponential fashion. Growth may, in fact, be suicidal, but the human race apparently is not, or at least has not been since its incipience. We're still around, and the world population continues to grow despite the multitudinous doomsday reports that have been published in the last several hundred years. Perhaps what we should do and what the ultimate result of the ZEG furor may be is to look at different parts of growth.

We can look at the sectors of our economy that are growing and attempt to ascertain whether this growth is warranted in terms of the net social cost-benefit analysis on different parts of our total growth; we can then determine which sectors of the economy should be slowed down. It may be that certain types of growth should be speeded up. Certainly we would want the growth in pollution-solving technology to be speeded up. Perhaps we would want to slow down growth in certain resource-consuming activities. However, this usually happens of its own accord for when these resources become scarce, their price goes up relative to other resources, and people shift their activities to other sectors of the economy. This is the nature of economics. We see it happening around us time and time again.

Questions for Thought and Discussion

1. If all externalities were taken care of in whatever manner necessary, would there be anything wrong with economic growth?
2. Can an M.I.T. computer ever be wrong?
3. How do you explain to a ghetto resident that economic growth should be stopped?

Selected References

Barnett, H., & Morse, C. *Scarcity and Growth.* Baltimore: Johns Hopkins University Press, 1963.

Boulding, K. E. *Economics as a Science.* New York: McGraw Hill, 1970.

Meadows, D. H., et al. *The Limits to Growth.* New York: Universe Books, 1972.

Mishan, E. J. *The Costs of Economic Growth.* New York: Praeger, 1967.

Mishan, E. J. *Technology and Growth.* New York: Praeger, 1970.

Benefiting from Trade among Nations

15

T HE MYTHS OF international trade have been with us for a long time, at least since Abraham Lincoln spouted his now famous words:

If I buy a Nikon I have the camera and the Japanese have my money. If I buy a Kodak, I have the camera and Americans have the money.

Most people regard trade as a gain when they are able to buy cheaper foreign products but as a loss when they see workers put out of jobs because of foreign competition. In this chapter, we hope to ferret out the real issues involved in international trade. It is certainly true that you as a consumer gain from cheaper foreign products. It is also true that employees and stockholders in industries hurt by foreign competition end up losing. The question is: Are the gains from trade worth the costs?

PUTTING TRADE IN ITS PLACE

Trade among nations must somehow benefit each nation more than it costs the nation. We find that the volume of world trade has been increasing at a compound growth rate of between 5 and 10 percent per year for quite a while. In 1800, world trade was a mere $1.3 billion in terms of current purchasing power; just before the Great Depression, it reached almost $70 billion. That figure was again reached in 1950. Today, as seen in Figure 15–1, world trade on average exceeds $300 billion a year. If countries were not all gaining from this increased world trade, the volume would not be growing at such a fast rate. For the most part,

FIGURE 15–1

WORLD TRADE

World trade has grown rapidly over the last decade or so. In 1972, it had reached the $300 billion mark. (*Source*: U.S. Department of Commerce.)

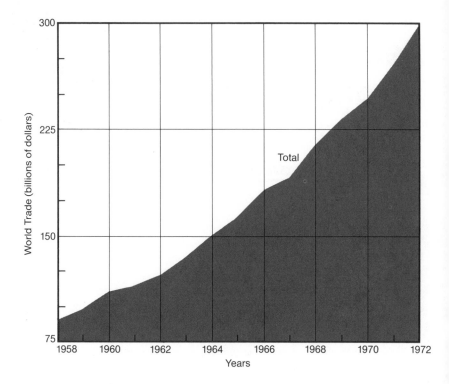

the transactions involved are voluntary between individual citizens in different countries.

Table 15–1 demonstrates that the size of international trade in different countries varies greatly when measured as a percent of GNP Some countries export and import more than one-third of their GNP. The United States ranks at the bottom of the list. In fact, the United States is the only Western country that would suffer very little if foreign trade were completely stopped. The change, however, would not go unnoticed.

If Foreign Trade Stopped

If imports stopped, tea and coffee drinkers would have to switch to Postum or Pero. Chocolate would be out of the question; you'd have to switch to carob. You would have no bananas, no pepper, no Scotch whiskey. A large percentage of other

TABLE 15–1

WORLD TRADE IN DIFFERENT COUNTRIES

Here we show the amount of world trade in different countries expressed as a percent of their GNP. The United States is the lowest on the list, where world trade represents only 5 percent. The Netherlands, on the other hand, is at the top of the list where world trade is a whopping 44 percent of GNP. *Source:* U.S. Bureau of Commerce.

COUNTRY	% OF GNP
Netherlands	44
Belgium-Luxembourg	36
Sweden	25
Canada	22
West Germany	21
United Kingdom	18
Italy	18
Japan	11
United States	5

categories of products is also imported. For example, Mr. T. C. of New York asked the *Playboy* Advisor, "Is it true that few radios are now made in the U.S. and that the bulk of them are imported?" The *Playboy* Advisor answered: "Approximately 88% of the home radios, 50% of the black and white TV sets, 42% of non-rubber footwear, and an estimated 96% of the motorcycles sold in the U.S. during 1971 were imported."*

Many of our raw materials come from other countries. Over 90 percent of the bauxite from which we make aluminum is of foreign origin. All of our chrome, cobalt, and the vast majority of our nickel, platinum, tin, and asbestos are imported. If the world's trade stopped, we wouldn't be able to drink French wine; we wouldn't see Italian movies; and we wouldn't drive VWs.

Exports

Imports, of course, make up only one-half of the story. We pay for our imports either by our exports or through an extension of credit by other countries. Much employment goes into our export industries. One-fifth of our cotton, 25 percent of our grains, and 25 percent of our tobacco are shipped abroad. A third of our sulfur and one-fifth of our coal is sold in foreign countries. Over one-seventh of our auto production, 25 percent of our textile and metal work machinery, and 30 percent of our construction and mining machinery go overseas. Additionally, there are perhaps 35 other industries in which at least 20 percent of the output is regularly sold abroad. All told, there are three to four million jobs involved in the export end of production.

Of course, if world trade ceased to exist, all of those jobs wouldn't be lost. All of the types of goods imported wouldn't vanish from our shelves since we would alter our own production to take account of the situation. New industries would spring up to provide substitutes for the imported goods. Workers who lost their jobs in

Playboy, April 1972, p. 58.

export industries would find themselves temporarily unemployed but might get a job later as we readjusted.

Voluntary Trade

The fact is, though, that we do engage in foreign trade, and we do it for only one reason—because we benefit from it. All trade is voluntary, and a voluntary exchange between two parties has to benefit both of them. Otherwise the exchange would not take place. The reasoning behind this argument is so simple that it often goes unnoticed by politicians who complain about foreigners "underselling" us by offering relatively cheap foreign goods. Let's explore the mechanism which establishes the level of trade between two nations. We will need first to develop a demand schedule for imports and a supply schedule for exports.

DEMAND AND SUPPLY OF IMPORTS AND EXPORTS

Again, let's limit our considerations to two countries. We shall try to calculate graphically how many gallons of wine Americans will desire to import every year. We do this by deriving the **excess demand schedule** for wine. The left-hand portion of Figure 15–2 presents the usual supply and demand curve for wine in the United States. We draw consecutive price lines starting at equilibrium and going down. At the equilibrium price of $2.00 per gallon, there is no excess demand or excess supply for U.S. wine. In the right-hand portion of the figure, we have drawn the price $2.00 and the *excess* demand of zero. That is, at $2.00 per gallon, there is no excess demand for wine. If $2.00 were the world price of wine, Americans would not buy any wine from foreigners. (In our two-country model, we're assuming the world is comprised of France and the United States.) Therefore, at the price of $2.00 per gallon, no wine trade would take place between these two countries.

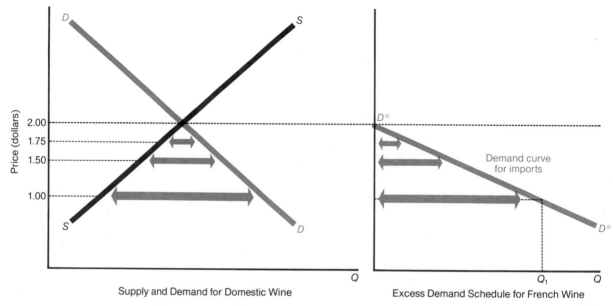

Price (dollars)

2.00
1.75
1.50

1.00

Supply and Demand for Domestic Wine

Excess Demand Schedule for French Wine

Demand curve
for imports

FIGURE 15–2   DERIVATION OF IMPORT DEMAND SCHEDULE

On the left-hand side of the diagram, we draw the domestic demand and supply schedules for wine. The demand schedule is *DD;* the supply schedule is *SS.* The equilibrium price is at $2.00. At $2.00 per gallon, there will be no excess demand for wine; therefore, the demand for imports would be zero. However, at a price of $1.00, there will be an excess demand for wine. The excess demand is represented by the longest arrow. We transfer that arrow to the right-hand side of the graph to show the excess demand for wine at a price of $1.00. The excess demand for wine is, in other words, the demand for imports of wine. If the world price were $1.00, we would demand the quantity Q_1 of imported wine. The excess demand curve for French wine slopes down, starting at the equilibrium price for domestic wine—in this case $2.00.

Imports

But what about prices lower than $2.00? Take a price of $1.00. At a price of $1.00, there is an excess demand for wine in the United States. This is represented by the distance between the domestic supply curve and the domestic demand curve (the heavy arrow in Figure 15–2). We take that distance (the heavy arrow) and transfer it, at that price level, to the right-hand side of the figure. Here we draw the excess demand for wine at price $1.00 (the amount of wine represented by the length of the arrow). The length of the arrow is the same on both sides of the graph. We could continue doing this for all different prices below the price of $2.00. We will come up with

an *excess demand schedule for wine.* Whatever the world price is, we can find out how much the United States will import. If the price is established at $1.00, for example, we will bring in imports equal to Q_1. As we would expect, the excess demand schedule for imports is downward sloping, like the regular demand schedule. The lower the world price of wine, the more imports we will buy.

Exports

What about the possibility of the United States exporting wine? Europe, in fact, is starting to drink California wines. The situation is depicted graphi-

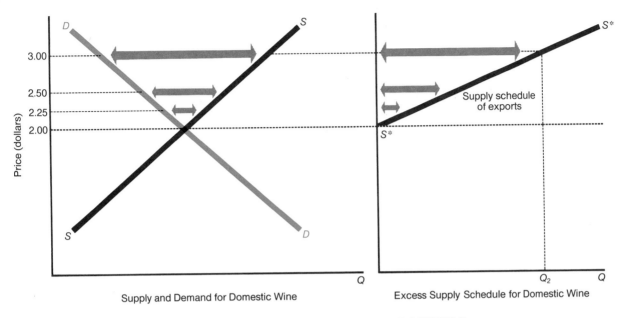

FIGURE 15–3   **DERIVATION OF EXPORT SUPPLY SCHEDULE**

The domestic demand and supply of wine is shown in the left-hand side of the figure. At an equilibrium price of $2.00, there is no excess demand nor excess supply of domestic wine. In the right-hand portion of the graph, we show the excess supply of wine. At prices higher than $2.00, there is an excess supply of wine. The excess supply is represented by the bold arrows. We transfer these bold arrows over to the right-hand graph to derive the quantity of excess supplies for exportation purposes. In this manner, we derive the supply schedule of exports. It is S^*S^*. It slopes upward like all supply schedules. If, for example, the world price were $3.00, we would export the quantity Q_2 of wine to other countries.

cally in Figure 15–3. Let's look at prices above $2.00. Take a price of $3.00. Here the *excess supply* of wine is equal to the amount represented by the distance between the demand curve and the supply curve (again represented by the bold arrow). The excess supply curve for purposes of wine export is shown in the right-hand portion of the figure. The supply curve of exports slopes up, like all the other supply curves. At a price of $2.00, there are no exports from the United States. At a price of $3.00, however, there are exports, and they are equal to the amount represented by the length of the heavy arrow. Thus, if the world price rises above $2.00, the United States would become a net exporter of wine. The

higher the world price, the more wine we will export. The lower the world price, the less wine we will export. Below a price of $2.00, we will start importing. The **zero trade point,** then, is $2.00. This means that at a world price of $2.00 we will not engage in world trade.

THE QUANTITY OF TRADE IN FOREIGN COUNTRIES

We can draw the graph for France, our trading partner, in a similar manner. However, we have to establish a common set of measurements for the price of wine. Let's do this in terms of dollars,

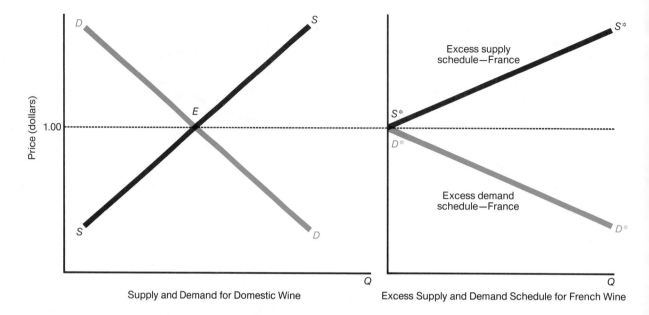

FIGURE 15–4   DERIVATION OF FRENCH EXCESS DEMAND AND SUPPLY OF WINE

The left-hand side of the graph presents France's domestic demand and supply curve for wine at an exchange rate of 20¢ per franc. The domestic equilibrium price of wine in France translates into $1.00 per gallon. At $1.00 per gallon, France will neither have an excess demand nor an excess supply of wine. At higher prices, it will have an excess supply—that is, it will export wine. At lower prices it will have an excess demand—that is, it will import wine. Therefore, on the right-hand side of the graph, we have drawn France's excess supply schedule and excess demand schedule. The export schedule is S*S*, and the import schedule is D*D*.

and let's say that the exchange rate is 20¢ for one franc. We shall place the excess demand schedule for imports and the excess supply schedule for exports on the same graph. Figure 15–4 shows a standard supply and demand schedule for French wine in terms of dollars per gallon. The equilibrium price of French wine is established at $1.00 per gallon. At a world price of one dollar per gallon, the French will neither import nor export wine. At prices below one dollar, the French will import wine; at prices above one dollar they will export wine. We see in the right-hand portion of Figure 15–4 that the excess supply schedule of French wine slopes up starting at $1.00 per gallon. The excess demand schedule

for imports of wine slopes down, starting at $1.00 per gallon.

INTERNATIONAL EQUILIBRIUM

We can see the quantity of international trade that will be transacted by putting the French and the American export and import schedules on one graph. The zero trade point for wine in America was established at $2.00 per gallon, whereas in France it was established at $1.00 a gallon. We see in Figure 15–5 that the excess supply schedule of exports in France intersects the excess demand schedule for imports in the United States at point

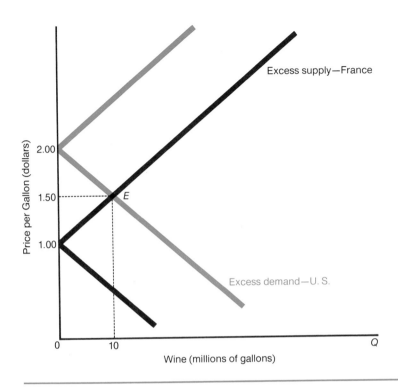

FIGURE 15–5

INTERNATIONAL EQUILIBRIUM

We plot France's excess demand and supply schedule along with the United States' excess demand and supply schedule. France's excess supply schedule intersects our excess demand schedule at point *E*, which establishes an equilibrium world price of wine. That world price is $1.50, which will be the price of wine everywhere. America will import ten million gallons of wine at that price and France will export ten million gallons of wine.

E with an equilibrium world price of wine of $1.50 per gallon and an equilibrium quantity of trade of ten million gallons per year. Here we see how much and the terms under which trade takes place. The amount is determined by the excess demand and supply schedules in each country and the point at which they intersect each other. If the tables were turned and America's no-trade point was below France's no-trade point, then America would be exporting wine and the French would be importing it.

THE GAINS FROM TRADE

We can once again establish the fact that there are gains from trade between the United States and France. Let's look at the United States first. After we started trading with France, the price of wine fell from $2.00 per gallon to $1.50 per gallon

and the quantity demanded increased. We were able to increase our consumption of wine. Additionally, domestic wine production fell so the resources released in those firms going out of business could be used elsewhere. The increased satisfaction we got from the additional wine was less than the cost to us in resources foregone. We are better off.

So, too, are the French. Their *consumption* of domestic wine falls but their domestic *production* increases. The difference goes to the United States in the form of exports. With those exports the French can now purchase U.S. imports, the value of which to Frenchmen will be *larger* than the resources foregone to make additional wine for export to the United States. The point is that both countries gain in the free-trade situation. If, however, both countries had a no-trade point at the same price, there would be no gains and no reason to trade. There would, in fact, be no trade.

Comparative and Absolute Advantage

The reason there are gains from trade lies in one of the most fundamental principles of economics: a nation gains by doing what it can do relatively best. The United States benefits by *specializing* in only those endeavors in which it has a **comparative advantage.** Let's take an example to demonstrate this concept.

William Howard Taft was perhaps the best stenographer in the world before he became President; he had an **absolute advantage** in stenography. When he became President, by definition he also had an absolute advantage in being President. As President he did not specialize in stenography, even though he was the best. The advantage to him and to the nation of devoting all his time to being President was much greater than the loss of his stenographic output. His comparative advantage lay in presiding over the nation, not in taking dictation at 220 words per minute.

In general, people discover their own area of comparative advantage by contrasting the return from doing one job with the return from doing another job. An executive in a large corporation may have an absolute advantage in doing 15 different tasks for that company. For example, he may be able to type better than all of his secretaries, wash windows better than any of the window-washers, file better than any of the file clerks, and carry messages better than any of the messengers. His comparative advantage, however, lies in being an executive. He knows this because he is paid more for being an executive than he would be paid for any other job. The company willingly pays his salary as an executive because the value of his output in that job is at least as large as the salary paid to him. They would not pay him the same amount if he wanted to be a typist. In fact, they could probably pay ten typists combined and still be paying out less than the amount of his salary.

The key to understanding comparative advantage lies in the realization that total resources are fixed at any moment in time. You only have so much time in a day. A nation has only so many men and machines. An individual, a company, or a nation must decide how it will allocate its available resources at a given moment. No one can use a resource in two different jobs at the same time. Even if companies or nations are *absolutely* better at doing everything, they will still specialize in only those tasks in which they have a comparative advantage. For in that specialization they maximize the returns for the use of their time and resources. The United States may have an absolute advantage in producing computers and roller skates in the sense that we can produce both goods with fewer man hours of labor than any other nation in the world. However, we let other countries produce roller skates because our comparative advantage lies in producing computers. We gain from exchanging the computers we produce for the roller skates produced by other countries.

Comparative Advantage and Opportunity Cost

We can relate the concept of comparative advantage to the ever-present concept of opportunity cost. In fact, understanding comparative advantage will give you an important insight into all relationships involving exchange among individuals or among nations. Comparative advantage emphasizes the fact that cost means opportunities which must be foregone. If the United States decides to produce roller skates, it foregoes part of its opportunity to produce computers because the time and resources spent in producing roller skates cannot simultaneously be used in producing computers. The basic reason for the existence of comparative advantage among individuals, companies, and countries lies in the fact that opportunity costs vary. Therefore, it costs less for different parties to engage in different types of economic activities. Opportunity costs for different countries vary just as they vary for different individuals. Let's examine some of the reasons why opportunity costs and, hence, comparative advantages differ among nations.

DIFFERING RESOURCE MIXES

We know that different nations have different resource bases. Canada has much land relative to its population, whereas Japan has a very large population relative to its land. All other things being equal, one would expect that countries with relatively more land would specialize in products that require much land. One would expect Australia to engage in sheep raising but not Japan, because the opportunity cost of raising sheep in Japan would be much higher. Since land in Japan is scarce, its use represents a higher opportunity cost.

There are also differences in climates. We would not expect countries with dry climates to grow bananas. Such facts of life, however, do not always prohibit a country's actions. Watermelons require tremendous amounts of water; they are, nonetheless, grown in Arizona. (The reason for this has to do with the fact that the Federal Government subsidized water to watermelon growers in that state.)

ADVANTAGEOUS TRADE WILL ALWAYS EXIST

Since the beginning of recorded history, there have been examples of trade among individuals. Since these acts of exchange have usually been voluntary, we must assume that individuals generally benefit from the trade. Individual tastes and resources vary tremendously. As a consequence, there are sufficient numbers of different opportunity costs in the world for exchange to take place constantly.

Taken as individual entities, nations have different collective tastes and different collective resource endowments. We would expect, therefore, that there will always be potential gains from trading among nations. Further, the more trade there is, the more specialization there can be. In most instances, specialization leads to increased output and—if we measure well-being by output levels—to increased happiness. (Indeed, we are using the term *well-being* very loosely here.) Self-sufficiency on the part of an individual undeniably means that he foregoes opportunities to consume more than he could by not being self-sufficient. Likewise, self-sufficiency on the part of a nation will lower its consumption possibilities and, therefore, will lower the real-income level of its inhabitants. Imagine life in Delaware, if that state were forced to become self-sufficient!

COSTS OF TRADE

Trade does not come without its costs. If, for example, one state has a comparative advantage in producing agricultural crops, other states may not be able to survive as centers of agricultural production. Farm workers in states that are losing out will suffer decreases in their incomes until they find another occupation.

As tastes, supplies of natural resources, prices, and so on change throughout the world, different countries may find that their comparative advantage changes away from what they have been exporting. One example of this is the production of steel in the United States. Japan has become increasingly competitive in steel products, and United States steelmakers are being hurt. The stockholders and employees in United States steel companies are feeling the pinch from Japan's ability to produce steel products at low prices.

JAPANESE MIRACLE

Japan is a good example of how a nation can benefit from exploiting its comparative advantage and engaging in a large volume of world trade.

Japan's recovery from World War II has been called miraculous. Real income in that country has been growing at an average rate of about 10 percent a year. Foreign trade has grown at an even faster rate. While real incomes doubled between 1952 and 1960, exports from Japan more than tripled. During the early sixties Japan's exports were doubling almost every five years. Japan has used its comparative advantage in manufacturing to expand its export markets in cameras, automobiles, and steel products. One wonders how Japan can become a net exporter of steel products without already having the raw materials needed to make them, but Japan's comparative advantage is in the machining of the steel and not in the exploitation of raw resources to make it. Japan, therefore, imports iron ore and exports cold rolled steel.

Obviously, you can see that many American steel producers would want to fight to *restrict* Japanese imports into the United States. Some industrial spokesmen claim that Japan has an absolute advantage (in the sense of man hours consumed to produce a good) in the production of electronic equipment and steel products. Even in those areas where Japan must consume more man hours than the United States to produce goods, the lower wage rates paid in Japan may still permit Japanese producers to undercut the prices of American producers. In any event, complaints about increased Japanese competition with American producers have produced pressures for hindering free trade among nations. The pressures became so great back in 1971 that President Nixon instituted a 10 percent temporary surtax on all dutiable imports as part of his New Economic Policy. It immediately hurt foreign exporters of cars and electronic equipment.

ARGUMENTS AGAINST FREE TRADE

The numerous arguments against free trade all have their merits. However, most of the time these arguments are incomplete. They mainly point out the costs of trade but do not consider any of the benefits and do not consider possible alternatives for mitigating costs while still reaping the benefits.

Infant Industry Argument

A nation may feel that, if a particular industry were allowed to develop domestically, it could eventually become efficient enough to be competitive in the world. The idea is that if some restrictions were placed on imports, native producers would be given time enough to develop their own techniques; eventually, they would be able to compete in the world market without any restrictions on imports into the United States. The idea has some merit and has been used to protect a number of American industries in their infancy. Such policy can be used to abuse, however. Even after the infant has matured, the protective import-restricting arrangements are often not removed. The people who benefit from this type of situation are obviously the stockholders in the industry that is still being protected from world competition. The people who lose out are consumers who must pay a price higher than the world price for the product in question.

National Security

It is often argued that we should not rely on foreign sources for many of our products because in time of war we would not be able to rely on our own industry. A classic example of this involves oil exploration. For national defense reasons (supposedly), President Eisenhower instituted at first a voluntary, and then a mandatory, oil import **quota** system, thereby restricting the amount of foreign oil that could be imported into the United States. The idea was to create an incentive for more exploration of American oil; thus, in time of war we would have a ready and available supply of oil for our tanks and ships and bombers.

The fact of the matter is, though, that restricting the amount of foreign imported oil merely served to raise the price of oil in the United States. The people who benefit are, obviously, the stockholders in oil corporations; the people who lose out are the consumers of oil products. It has been estimated by various government officials that the oil import quota program costs the consumer a staggering $7 billion a year in the form of higher oil product prices. Also, when looking at the distribution of who pays, you'll find that it is the poor who pay relatively more than rich, since poor people spend a larger proportion of their income on petroleum products than do rich people. Finally, it is absurd to think that we will have more oil for a national emergency when we restrict the amount of foreign oil we presently use. The only possible outcome is that we are now using up more of our own!

Stability

Many people argue that foreign trade should be restricted because it introduces an element of instability into our economic system. It is pointed out that the vagaries of foreign trade add to the ups and downs in our own employment level. If we follow this argument to its logical conclusion, we would restrict trade among our various states as well. After all, the vagaries of trade among particular states sometimes causes unemployment in other states. Things are sorted out over time, but workers suffer during the adjustment period. Nonetheless, we don't restrict trade among the states. In fact, there is a Constitutional stricture against taxing exports among the states.

As regards the international sphere, people somehow change their position. It is felt that adjusting to the vagaries of *international* trade costs more than adjusting to the vagaries of domestic *interstate* trade. Perhaps people believe foreign trade really doesn't benefit us that much, and this is why they argue against it, claiming that the stability of aggregate economic activity is at stake. We should note one difference between the do-

mestic and international situations. Labor is mobile between our states, but it is not mobile between nations. Immigration laws prevent workers from moving to countries where they can make the most money. Therefore, the adjustment costs to a changing international situation may be higher than the adjustment costs to a changing domestic situation.

THE WAY TO HINDER TRADE

We have already mentioned two possible ways of restricting international trade—*quotas* and *taxes*. Taxes on internationally traded items are usually called **tariffs.** First, however, let's talk about quotas.

Quotas

In the quota system, countries are restricted to a certain amount of trade. Take, for example, a quota on the importation of oil into the United States. Let's look at Figure 15–6. Here, we have presented the standard supply and demand graph for the product in question. The horizontal line, P_w, represents the world price line; this line also represents the world's supply of oil to the United States. We can draw this line horizontally because we assumed (somewhat unrealistically) that the United States buys an extremely small fraction of the total world supply; therefore, the United States can literally buy all the oil it wants at the world price. In the absence of world trade, the price would be at the intersection of the domestic supply and demand schedules. The quantity demanded would be determined at that intersection also. However, with world trade opened up, Americans will buy 4 billion barrels of oil in total; domestic oil producers will provide 3.5 billion barrels of this total. The difference between 4 billion and 3.5 billion represents the imports. This is an equilibrium situation. The supply curve is the domestic one below the price P_w but becomes the horizontal

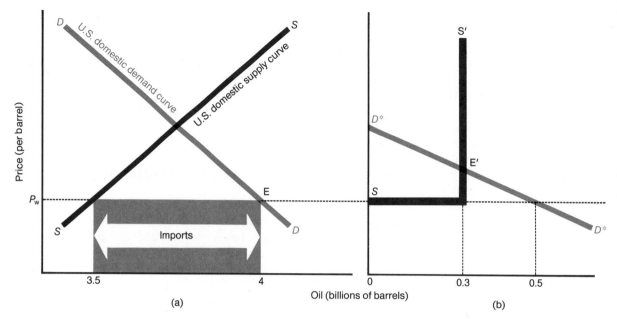

FIGURE 15–6   THE EFFECT OF AN IMPORT QUOTA ON OIL

The world price is established at P_w. We assume that the United States buys a very small part of the total world supply of oil. The United States can buy all the oil it wants at the world price. The supply curve, in effect, is P_w. Our domestic supply curve is SS in the left-hand portion of the graph, and our domestic demand curve is DD. At the world price of P_w, we will reach equilibrium at E. This means we will consume 4 billion barrels of oil, of which 3.5 billion will be produced domestically. The difference is represented by imports. In the right-hand portion of the figure, we have shown the excess demand for oil as $D * D^*$. That is, D^*D^* represents the demand curve for oil imports. At the world price of P_w, the quantity demanded will be 0.5 billion barrels of oil. The government, however, steps in and imposes an import quota of only 0.3 billion barrels. The supply curve remains P_w until it hits the quota line of 0.3 billion barrels. Then it becomes vertical. The new supply curve is then SS'. The new supply curve, SS', intersects the demand curve for imports, D^*D^*, at a new equilibrium of E'. The consumers of oil will end up paying the higher price represented by the vertical distance to E'. The stockholders in domestic oil producing companies will benefit, however.

P_w line at the price of P_w. The intersection of the supply curve and the domestic demand curve is at E, where it will stay without restrictions.

Let's now look at the right-hand portion of the graph. We will draw the excess demand for imports. We put in the world price line, P_w, and we come up with the 0.5 billion barrels of oil imported at the world price. Now we want to see what happens when a quota is instituted. Instead of allowing 0.5 billion barrels of oil to be imported,

the government arbitrarily says that only 0.3 billion barrels may be brought into the United States. We draw a vertical line at 0.3 billion barrels per year. The supply curve effectively becomes the world demand price line until it hits the import quota restrictions at the vertical line. The supply curve then follows the vertical line up; it is now SS'. The new equilibrium point is at E', the intersection of the new supply schedule with the excess demand for imports. We see that at point

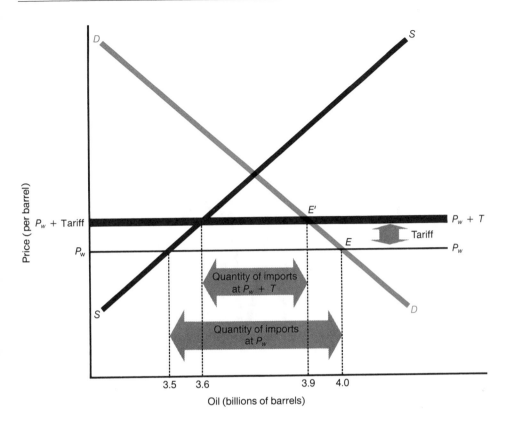

FIGURE 15-7   **AN IMPORT TARIFF**

The domestic supply curve for oil is *SS*. The domestic demand curve is *DD*. At a world price of P_w America can buy all the oil it wants. Equilibrium is established at *E* where the quantity demanded is 4 billion barrels. The quantity supplied domestically is 3.5 billion. The difference is imports, or 0.5 billion barrels. Now the government puts on a tariff, *T*. The price at which Americans can buy oil now is equal to P_w plus the tariff. This shifts the effective horizontal supply curve up to the heavy solid line, $P_w + T$. Now, at this higher price the quantity demanded is at *E'*, or 3.9 billion barrels. The quantity supplied domestically increases to 3.6 billion barrels. Imports, therefore, fall from 0.5 billion barrels to 0.3 billion barrels, as in the arbitrary example used for the import quota set at 0.3 billion barrels. However, in this particular case, it is the U.S. Treasury that reaps the benefits of restricting the supply of imports. In the case of import quotas, it was the stockholders in oil companies who benefited.

E', however, there is a higher price for imported oil. This should indicate that something in the situation has to change. Indeed, it is the price Americans must pay that has to change. You, the consumer, lose. The importers (who get the quotas) and import-substituting industries gain.

Tariffs

We can use our graphic technique to analyze the effect of a tariff. A tariff raises the world price. Let's assume that the tariff is 10 percent of the price of the product entering this country. In Fig-

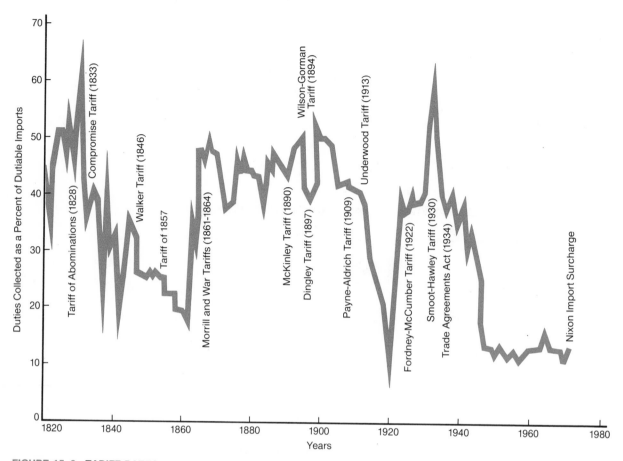

FIGURE 15-8   TARIFF RATES IN THE UNITED STATES SINCE 1820

Tariff rates in the United States have bounced about like a football, and, indeed, in Congress tariffs do represent a political football. Import-competing industries prefer high tariffs. In the twentieth century, the highest tariff we ever had was the Smoot-Hawley Tariff of 1930 which was almost as high as the Tariff of Abominations in 1828. (*Source:* U.S. Department of Commerce.)

ure 15–7, we have drawn domestic supply and demand schedules for oil, with the world price at P_w. In this case, we add a tariff. The tariff, T, is equal to the difference between the world price, P_w, and the heavy horizontal line above it ($P_w + T$). Domestic demanders of oil must now pay the world price plus the tariff. They cannot get oil any cheaper because producers know that everyone

must pay the tariff; no one can escape it. The quantity demanded for oil falls from 4 billion barrels to 3.9 billion barrels because of the higher price. The quantity supplied domestically rises from 3.5 billion barrels to 3.6 billion barrels. The level of imports decreases from 0.5 billion barrels to 0.3 billion barrels, as in the case of an arbitrary import quota system the government has used with oil. However, there are differences. The price is higher; the quantity demanded is smaller; the domestic supply increases, but *the government is now in possession of tariff revenues.* These revenues could be used to reduce taxes or to increase government expenditures on public goods and services. This does not happen with the oil import quota program. There, the beneficiaries of the higher oil price are the stockholders in oil corporations, not the U.S. government treasury.

TARIFF RATES

The tariff rates on goods entering the United States have varied widely in the past 150 years, as can be seen in Figure 15–8. In fact, it is only recently that we have kept a relatively low tariff level on goods entering our country. Perhaps increased awareness of the beneficial aspects of international trade has convinced Congressmen and Chief Executives that the nation as a whole will benefit from reduced restrictions on world trade. The argument apparently was lost on the Nixon Administration when the President imposed his New Economic Policy. In August of 1971, Richard Nixon did not reduce tariffs to encourage more trade, but rather, he *increased* them. As we explain in the next issue, President Nixon's temporary 10 percent surtax on dutiable imports was a response to both exchange rate problems and high unemployment rates in import-competing industries, such as automobiles and electronics.

Definition of New Terms

EXCESS DEMAND SCHEDULE: a demand schedule for imports derived from the difference between the quantity supplied and the quantity demanded domestically at world prices *below* the domestic equilibrium price.

EXCESS SUPPLY SCHEDULE: a supply schedule of exports derived from the difference between the quantity supplied and the quantity demanded at world prices *above* domestic equilibrium prices.

ZERO TRADE POINT: the point on an excess demand and supply diagram where there is no foreign trade. This is at a price where the domestic demand and supply schedules intersect.

ABSOLUTE ADVANTAGE: the advantage that a person or nation has over other people or nations in the production of a good or service. If you have an absolute advantage in doing something, you can do it better than anybody else—absolutely. To be contrasted with comparative advantage.

COMPARATIVE ADVANTAGE: an advantage arising out of relative efficiency. So long as opportunity costs are different for different people or different countries for doing the same job, one will have a comparative advantage. Comparative advantage follows from scarcity of resources.

INFANT INDUSTRY ARGUMENT: an argument in support of tariffs. Tariffs are to be imposed to protect an industry that is trying to get started. Presumably, after the industry becomes technologically efficient, the tariff can be lifted.

QUOTA: a specified number of or value of imports that are allowed into a country.

TARIFF: a tax on imported goods.

Chapter Summary

1. Trade has expanded from a mere $1.3 billion in terms of current purchasing power in the year 1800 to over $300 billion in 1972. Trade rates differ among nations. The United States has one of the smallest amounts of world trade expressed as a percentage of GNP than any country in the world. Trade represents only 5 percent of our GNP, whereas it represents 44 percent of the GNP of the Netherlands.

2. Even though it only represents 5 percent of GNP, we would notice a substantial change in our life style if we stopped world trade.

3. Trade is always voluntary among nations and among people. Therefore, it must benefit everyone concerned.

4. We can draw an excess demand schedule for foreign goods by looking at the difference between the quantity demanded and the quantity supplied domestically at prices below our domestic equilibrium price. The excess demand schedule for foreign goods is a demand schedule for imports.

5. The excess supply schedule of domestic goods is found by looking at the difference between quantities supplied and quantities demanded at prices above our domestic equilibrium price. The excess supply schedule is our supply schedule of exports.

6. Equilibrium trade is established where one country's excess demand schedule intersects another country's excess supply schedule. So long as the zero trade points of two countries are at different prices, there will be trade (in the absence of restrictions).

7. It is important to distinguish between absolute and comparative advantage. A person or country may have an absolute advantage in doing everything. That is, the person or country can do everything better than everybody else. Nonetheless, trade will still be advantageous because people will specialize in the things that they do best. They will take advantage of their comparative advantage.

8. A person finds out his comparative advantage by discovering when he is paid the most. Comparative advantage follows from different relative efficiencies and from the fixed nature of our resources at a point in time.

9. Along with the gains, there are costs from trade. Certain industries may be hurt if trade is opened up. There are numerous arguments, therefore, against free trade.

10. The infant industry argument is used to justify protective tariff. According to this argument, a budding new industry must be allowed to blossom. After it has blossomed and become more technologically efficient, the tariff presumably can be removed, and the new industry can fight its way alone in the world market.

11. There is also a national security argument for tariffs and import quotas. For example, the oil import quota was imposed in the name of national security; presumably by keeping out cheap foreign oil, we increase the incentive for domestic exploration of oil resources. Therefore, in time of war we would have a sufficient amount of gas to put in our bombers and ships!

Questions for Thought and Discussion

1. Do you ever make any trades in which you don't benefit? Why do you make them?

2. "Cheap foreign labor is ruining jobs for Americans. Therefore, we should stop all trade with other countries." Evaluate this statement.

3. If you believe in free trade among nations concerning goods and services, do you also believe in the free movement of human resources? That is, do you think all immigration laws should be repealed?
4. Evaluate Abraham Lincoln's famous quotation at the beginning of this chapter.
5. Can you think of reasons why the foreign trade multiplier might be smaller than the domestic investment multiplier?
6. If every state in the union had exactly the same productivity and efficiency, would there be any trade? Why?
7. Is it possible for a country to lose its comparative advantage in the production of a specific good or service? What happens then?
8. Why would you expect a newly discovered continent to have a comparative advantage in the production of food?

Selected References

Balassa, Bela, Ed. *Changing Patterns in Foreign Trade and Payments.* Rev. Ed. New York: W. W. Norton, 1970.

Pen, Jan. *A Primer on International Trade.* New York: Random House, 1967.

Snider, Delbert. *Introduction to International Economics.* 5th Ed. Homewood, Illinois: Irwin, 1971.

ISSUE XVIII

BEWARE OF THE MULTINATIONALS

The Costs and Benefits of Multinational Investment

Empire Building

Michael Fribourg owns an empire with international sales estimated at almost $3 billion per year. He heads a corporation which includes: vast real estate holdings in Switzerland, Long Island, France, and Morocco; 50,000 head of cattle grazing in Argentina; hybrid grain seed in Latin America; ski resorts in Spain; a nail manufacturing plant in the United States; Oroweat Bread, Polofood Frozen Dinners, and Hilburn Chickens; Wayne Feed, Full-o'-Pep Animal Food; the worldwide Continental Grain Company; Overseas Shipholding Group Incorporated; and—believe it or not—even more. This empire is **multinational**. Fribourg's Continental Grain Company has a worldwide communications system that feeds over 5000 messages per day in and out of its New York headquarters. Some come from the Paris office; others are relayed from various posts in Europe, Africa, Latin America, and the Middle East. The extent of Fribourg's multinational corporation boggles the mind.

The Fribourg empire is just one of a number of burgeoning cor-

poration setups that have become known as multinationals. You are probably familiar with some of them. Certainly, if you have ever traveled abroad you probably saw Coca Cola factories, Pepsi Cola factories, IBM offices, American Express offices, and so on. Pepsi Cola, for example, has over 500 plants located in just about every country in the world. That means when you buy a Pepsi Cola in some far-off land, you're buying an American product that was actually produced and bottled in the country you're in. Ford Motor

Company has 40 foreign-based corporations throughout the world. Over 150,000 Ford Motor Company employees are located in foreign lands. General Motors, IBM, Standard Oil of New Jersey, General Electric, and Chrysler are also included in the list of multinationals. Of the top 100 American corporations, over 60 of them have production facilities in four or more nations. By the beginning of the seventies, the gross revenues obtained in these foreign production facilities owned or controlled by U.S. firms accounted for almost $75 billion. This figure far exceeds the total values of our exports of manufactured goods for the country. In fact, it exceeds all of our exports, including food products and other nonmanufactured goods.

"*Don't be childish, man! Kicking Toyotas is no answer to our balance-of-trade gap.*"

DRAWING BY DONALD REILLY; © 1971
THE NEW YORKER MAGAZINE, INC.

Investing Abroad

One way firms are able to sell abroad is by investing abroad. U.S. direct investments in other countries have grown from a little more than $10 billion in 1950 to almost $80 billion in 1972. Much of that direct investment brought with it control over foreign companies. That is to say, a U.S. company could invest $100 million in a company worth $190 million and have control over all the operations because it held a majority of the stock. When you add the amount of foreign-based assets that American companies own and control, you probably come up with a figure closer to $250 billion in 1972. That is indeed staggering, and for one reason or another it worries foreign countries. They have the notion that we are going to "bury" them, that we are going to take over all of the control of their own production for our benefit instead of theirs. This is a sufficiently important point for us to review here.

Will a Few American Multinationals Dominate?

Concerned academicians have estimated that by the end of the twentieth century, most trade will be dominated by 200 to 300 large corporations, the vast majority of which will be American owned. It is estimated that these corporations will account for over half the world's industrial output. This may seem farfetched; however, international production currently accounts for almost one-sixth of the total value of all world output. International production includes our production in other countries, foreign production in other countries, and foreign production in the United States. The question arises as to whether these large corporations can wield sufficient political power to alter the course of international economics and even international or national politics. Look at the following table taken from Lewis Turner's *Invisible Empires.* On the left side we see the sales of selected multinational corporations and, on

the right side, the GNPs of various countries. Notice that sales of General Motors exceed the GNP of Belgium, Switzerland, Austria, Denmark, Norway, Greece, and Portugal. Even the sales of rather small IBM are greater than the GNP of Portugal. Pretty shocking, isn't it? The thought of corporations that have to be treated as nations has scared many European economists into suggesting that constraints be put on foreign investing in their countries—especially by American multinationals.

The American Challenge

A book written by a noted Frenchman, Jean Jacques Servan-Schreiber, disclosed the amount of American penetration into French markets. Indeed, *The American Challenge* brought home to all of Europe the extent of American penetration into the European industrial scene. Monsieur Servan-Schreiber maintained that over half of Europe's

---

TABLE XVIII-1

MULTINATIONALS ARE BIG

Here we compare the 1967 sales of several large companies with the GNP of some selected countries. (*Source:* Louis Turner, *Invisible Empires* [New York, Harcourt Brace, 1971]. Pp. 135–136.)

COMPANY	SALES IN BILLIONS (1967)	COUNTRY	GNP IN BILLIONS
General Motors	$20.0	Holland	$26.6
Standard Oil (N.J.)	13.3	Switzerland	15.8
Ford	10.5	Denmark	12.2
Shell	8.4	Austria	10.6
General Electric	7.7	Norway	8.3
Chrysler	6.2	Greece	7.1
IBM	5.3	Portugal	4.6

transistor market was accounted for by American multinationals; over 80 percent of its computer markets and almost all of its integrated circuits production was by American-owned companies. He stated: "Fifteen years from now it is quite possible that the world's third greatest industrial power, just after the United States and Russia, will not be Europe, but American industry in Europe." (Servan-Schreiber pointed out that of the world's 500 largest corporations, over 300 are American.) His suggestion for Europe to meet the American challenge was to form equally efficient large pan-European companies that could operate on the same level as the American corporations.

The Japanese Challenge, The Dutch, and the Swiss

America is not the only country with multinationals. In fact, many American multinationals are being challenged by non-American international corporations. Phillips Lampworks operates in 68 countries and is owned by Dutchmen. It has almost 200,000 workers in foreign nations. Japanese companies actually are starting to set up production within the United States and other countries. The Swiss chocolate firm, Nestle, generates over $2 billion of revenues a year,

almost wholly outside of Switzerland. (You can't expect the Swiss to eat that much chocolate, can you?)

There are many European and Japanese firms that have been expanding foreign production bases even more rapidly than the American multinationals. Jean Jacques Servan-Schreiber should have named his book *The Foreign Challenge* instead of *The American Challenge* because our corporations are not alone in their quest for international production bases.

We may wonder why the trend toward multinationals is what it has been. Why is it better to go to a foreign country, invest directly in production facilities, and sell products there rather than merely export American-made products abroad? That's a thorny question, but we'll try to answer it at least partially.

Why Multinationals?

What could entice General Motors to set up production facilities in Spain? What would lead the Board of Directors of IBM to set up a production in Germany? Let's see if we can answer these questions.

Tariff Avoidance

One possible explanation involves the desire to avoid high tariffs. Tariffs are merely taxes that must be paid when imports enter a country. The United States has tariffs, and so, too, do most other countries. If a foreign car comes to the United States, it is taxed a certain rate. If IBM sends a computer to Germany, it is taxed by Germany at a certain rate because it is an import. Thus, if tariff walls are very high, it may be profitable for companies to produce within a foreign country rather than export American-produced goods to that country.

Good Investment Strategy

Perhaps a more fruitful line of inquiry might be to view foreign investment by American corporations as merely an attempt to make money. What governs any firm's attempt to make money? The answer is, of course, the expected rate of return. American companies view direct foreign investment the same way they view expansion investment in the United States. They will look at the potential revenues that can be made; they will look at the potential costs they must incur; and then they will come up with expected profits over time. If the expected profits over time warrant making a direct investment in another country, then we would expect American corporations to increase investment in such a manner.

High Risks Involved

We would expect that the expected profits from direct investment by American companies in underdeveloped countries would have to be considerably higher than the expected profits for a similar investment in the United States. This is so because foreign governments have the habit of expropriating American investments, and American investors want higher profits to compensate for the risk of expropriation. You're probably familiar with what happened to American copper interests in Chile when the Allende government took over. You might even remember when Castro took over Cuba and quickly expropriated American corporations without, of course, much payment in compensation, if any. However, an investment by an American company in England would probably not require as high a profit as an investment in Guatemala or Chile or Nicaragua or Uruguay because the probability of expropriation is much smaller in England.

American direct investment abroad also often faces numerous restrictions. For example, in Mexico it is usually the case that Mexicans must own more than 50 percent of the company that Americans either build or wish to purchase. Usually a certain percentage of top management must be of Mexican nationality.

Economists have done little work in explaining why multinational production emerges. We do not have a successful theory, for example, that tells us why there is more multinational production in glass than in steel, or why there is more multinational production in pharmaceuticals than in machine tools. Where we don't have theory, though, we do have facts; and the facts indicate that multinational production has not been concentrated in underdeveloped countries.

Forgetting the Less Developed?

Foreign investment used to be concentrated in the less developed countries of the world. In the late nineteenth and early twentieth centuries American capital flowed to Latin America, Africa, and the Middle and Far East. Railroads, plantations, and mines were the investments of the day. At the turn of the century, almost 60 percent of American direct investment in other countries was in railways, food stuffs, and mining—most of which was concentrated in the underdeveloped countries of the world. At the beginning of the seventies, however, less than 20 percent of all overseas assets were in railways, mining, and foodstuffs. Less than 40 percent of direct investment was located in underdeveloped countries. Instead, multinational companies have been investing within each other's geographical boundaries, rather than going into the third world. Table XVIII-2 shows the change in the distribution by market and by industrial sector of U.S. foreign investment abroad during the last two decades. The shift is dramatic. Latin America is becoming a never-never land for American investment, and you probably know the reason why. The risks involved are simply too great. The political situations in Latin American countries are too unstable for American investors to take a chance. What good is it to know that you can make a 30 percent profit in Latin America, if a government there takes away all of your assets two years after you invest?

Political Economics

Politics has as much to do with multinational companies as economics. Most foreign nations, especially small ones, are extremely nationalistic. They want to retain control over the production that is done in their countries. They are afraid of Americanization of their industry; they are equally afraid of Japanization or Germanization of their industry. Foreign governments are afraid of the power that American corporations may wield, and they may rightly have something there. There was quite a scandal in 1972 when it was learned that International Telephone and Telegraph (IT&T), a huge multinational conglomerate in the United States, had apparently told the CIA it would go along with any plan that the infamous organization had to prevent the socialist take-over of the Chilean government. When the Chilean government heard this news, it promptly decided that IT&T holdings would be nationalized in that country.

There is a more subtle argument, though, that is worth going over. We should ask ourselves to what extent, for example, an American corporation can actually do harm to a country by direct investment in that country.

Does Direct Investment Do Harm?

Undoubtedly, if an American company goes into France and gains a monopoly in the production of transistors, France will

---

TABLE XVIII-2   WHERE U.S. FOREIGN DIRECT INVESTMENT GOES

Here we see that in the last two decades there has been a shift away from Asia, Africa, and Latin America toward Europe, and also a shift toward more direct investment in manufacturing. (*Source:* U.S. Department of Commerce.)

	1950	1969
Total (millions)	$11,788	$70,763
Percent distribution, by market		
Canada	30	30
Europe	14	30
Latin America	41	20
Asia, Africa, other	15	18
Percentage distribution, by industrial sector		
Manufacturing	31	42
Petroleum	29	29
Transport and utilities	12	4
Mining	9	8
Trade	7	8
Agriculture and other	11	9

suffer due to the monopoly distortion of prices and quantities produced in France. A monopolistic price of transistors will be higher than the competitive price and there will be a restriction in the quantity supplied and demanded. Frenchmen would be better off if a competitive structure prevailed in that industry. But France has no more reason to fear an American monopoly than a French monopoly: both could be equally prosecuted if they occur. Both have exactly the same effects on prices and quantities. The price goes up and the quantity goes down relative to a competitive situation. French, German, Spanish, Italian, and other countries' antitrust laws could be enforced against multinationals as much as against nationals.

The entrance of American capital into a foreign country should, therefore, not be cause for alarm simply because of the possibility of a monopoly. Presumably antitrust laws can be enforced to prevent such monopolization, whether it be American, Japanese, German, French, or whoever.

What about the possibility of Americans taking all the profits out of France? Certainly, that possibility exists. But so what? How do Americans take profits out of France? They export French francs to America, but those exports of French francs are only useful if Americans in turn somehow want to spend money in France. Any profits that are taken out of France will, ultimately, come back to France in the form of American purchases of more French goods in world trade. There is really little meaning to the notion that America can somehow "bleed" a foreign country of its resources.

Monopoly Problems

What about the possibility of Americans pursuing business behavior that is detrimental to the best interests of the foreign countries? This possibility exists, and we have already covered it. The possibility is that Americans could seek to monopolize an industry in another country. This would be detrimental to that country. But what if Americans merely seek to make as much profit as possible? Is this bad for the foreign country in which Americans have directly invested? If so, then surely it would be equally bad for the nationals themselves to pursue similar goals. Yet that's exactly what they do. This is also exactly how we have analyzed business behavior throughout this book. We have assumed that businessmen are out to make money; they're out to maximize profits—to maximize their wealth. Whether an American decides to take $1 million and maximize his return on that million in France or in America makes no difference to the American. It should make no difference to the French either. If the American is successful, the French are better off. After all, the American brings with him over $1 million of capital that the French did not formerly have available. If he is a wise businessman, he will turn a profit. Further, whatever he has produced, the people in France must have wanted. He was able to produce what they wanted with the use of outside American capital. The French real standard of living will go up because of American direct investment that is, in fact, profitable.

Gains to Trade

We can think about it this way. Is it bad for Californians that New Yorkers invest New York capital in California and then spend the profits in New York? Is it bad for Texas if Californians invest in Texas oilwells and then spend the profits in California? The answer to these questions is no. It is perfectly all right for Americans to invest their money in any state in the Union and spend their money in any other state. We live in a mobile society; people move all the time, and capital moves too. Profits are distributed throughout the land and spent throughout the land, and we haven't seemed to suffer as a nation because of this. The world certainly will not suffer if in fact multinationals grow in size and number and if international production increases manyfold. In fact, we would expect that the world will be better off.

Presumably, men invest in other countries because they think the rate of return is higher. That means that world capital will be flowing to areas where the rate of return is highest. This also means that the growth in the real standard of living of the world will be higher than it would have been otherwise. Instead of discouraging multinational expansion, we might expect that philanthropists would want multinational investment to expand.

Definition of New Term

MULTINATIONAL: a company which has direct or indirect investment in many different nations.

Questions for Thought and Discussion

1. What does economics have to say about American imperialism by way of direct investment in foreign countries?
2. Do you think that an increase in multinational companies will lead to more international unrest or less? Why?
3. If there were no political shenanigans involved with large American companies in foreign lands, do you think that foreign governments would be so reluctant to allow direct American investment?

Selected References

Brown, Courtney. World Business. New York: Free Press, 1970.

Rowthorn, Robert, & Hymer, Stephen. International Big Business. New York: Cambridge University Press, 1971.

Servan-Schreiber, J.J. The American Challenge. New York: Atheneum, 1968.

Turner, Lewis. Invisible Empires. New York: Harcourt, Brace & Jovanovich, 1971.

Wilkins, Mira. The Emergence of Multinational Enterprise. Cambridge: Harvard University Press, 1970.

WIDE WORLD PHOTOS

THE CORPORATE PHANTOM

Howard Hughes, Jr.
Industrialist

"THERE HE'D BE, alone in a big suite, room after empty room. No photographs on the bureau, no books, the closets empty, except maybe for a single jacket on a hanger, and a pair of socks thrown on the floor. Usually on one of the beds there'd be a cardboard laundry box with a couple of shirts in it, and piled around it dozens of manila envelopes. I figured these were his filing system, though I never saw him with a piece of paper in his hand." This technician, troubled by a businessman without papers and secretaries, installed some equipment for Howard Hughes. But at least he *saw* Hughes, a businessman who meets his staff in empty hotel rooms and conducts most of his business by telephone.

Howard Hughes, probably the richest man in the United States, should be a very public person, but all that is known about him is what can be gleaned from his associates' statements, reporters' recollections, his letters, and a few carefully staged public statements. Often called the "spook of American capitalism," Hughes has forfeited millions of dollars in court settlements rather than appear in public to protect his own interests.

In sharp contrast to his current life style, Hughes' first 50 years were among the most glamorous of any American industrialist. Born in 1905 in Houston, Texas, Hughes was educated at the Rice Institute and the California Institute of Technology. At the age of 19, he inherited the controlling interest in his father's tool company. After buying out his relatives, he moved to Hollywood to make movies and enjoy a colorful social life. However, his prevailing interest continued to be aviation; he was an award-winning pilot, and during World War II he built the world's largest airplane, the "Spruce Goose." The transformation into a recluse began in 1947 when Hughes was nearly killed in a plane crash. He grew a mustache to hide his scars, and became more introspective and eccentric. He refused an automobile construction deal offered by Henry Kaiser after the war, saying, "no, I don't want to make any more automobiles. I made one once when I was a kid and I ran it for years, but I don't want to go back to doing things I've already done." Even then, Kaiser admitted that getting an opportunity to actually meet Howard Hughes was more important to him than the outcome of the prospective deal.

By 1960, Hughes owned 78 percent of the stock of Trans-World Airlines (TWA). He attempted to arrange a merger between TWA and Northeast Airlines, but refused to appear at hearings of the Civil Aeronautics Board to defend the merger. During the late 1950s, Hughes had become involved in a battle at TWA over the planned purchase of jets. His poor relationship with the company's management was exposed in court in a wild suit-and-countersuit exchange. At the end of the 1960s, Hughes escaped with a profitable stock sale, right before the airline industry's disastrous slump.

Looking for a suitable site for investment, Hughes found that the pollution-free Nevada desert suited his personal tastes, while the almost nonexistent industrial tax structure suited his financial plans. Las Vegas has been aptly called "Howard Hughes's Monopoly set." The development of Hughes Air West, the purchase of several major hotels and casinos, the investment in mining property, and the acquisition of an airport have pushed Howard Hughes's net worth beyond $1.4 billion. Although many mismanagement crises and intracompany power struggles have seriously threatened the cohesion of the empire, Hughes apparently exercises strong control. Hughes Tool and Hughes Aircraft are models of corporate success and growth.

The new Democratic state administration in Nevada press Hughes to appear publicly, the issue being the defense of his gambling licenses. Under Republican administrations, many of these requirements were waived, but Hughes may be forced to relinquish either his privacy or his profitable casino interests. Certainly, Hughes is one of the few Americans who could have inspired the Clifford Irving misadventure. He apparently appeals to something in the American character—perhaps he provides an exciting image in a dull business world. It remains to be seen whether pressures from government and from the private sector will eventually force him to appear in public to protect the Hughes empire. Ordinarily, one might assume that self-interest would force a businessman to sacrifice eccentricity; but Howard Hughes is no ordinary businessman.

Comparative Economic Systems

16

Y OU ARE ALL at least vaguely aware that the economic system in the United States is capitalistic. We haven't really described what capitalism is, nor have we considered in this book alternative economic systems and how our theory would have to be altered in these systems. In this chapter we will outline some basic attributes of each of the currently existing economic systems. We will note whenever possible where theories learned in this book apply equally well to another or all systems. This chapter will not, however, present any modern day criticisms of capitalism, socialism, or communism. Our goal is to develop some feel for how economic decisions are made in different countries in the world today.

THE SPECTRUM OF SYSTEMS

We might want to compare alternative economic systems according to how decentralized their economic decision-making processes are. At the extreme right-hand side of our spectrum, we would find pure free enterprise **capitalism** where all economic decisions are made by individuals without government intervention. On the extreme left-hand side of the scale, we might put pure **socialism,** where most economic decisons are made by some central authority. Somewhere in between would be the mixed economic system we have in the United States. It is neither pure capitalism nor pure socialism, but it is obviously closer to capitalism than to socialism. This spectrum is represented in Figure 16–1. The Soviet economy is an example of a mixed system also: the central authorities make a lot of decisions in the economic sphere but still allow many decisions to be made by individuals. Perhaps one of the most centralized economic systems in existence today is in

FIGURE 16–1 SCALE OF DECENTRALIZATION

On the extreme right-hand side of the diagram we find pure capitalism which no country follows. On the extreme left-hand side is pure socialism, which again no country follows. In the middle are all of the mixed economies in the world. Russia, the United Kingdom, Mexico, and the United States are just a few that are shown, with the United States being closer to capitalism, of course, than any of the others and Russia being closer to socialism.

China. We will delve somewhat more deeply into the economic system of that fascinating country in the following issue.

UNPLANNED VERSUS COMMAND

Some economists like to distinguish between economies on the basis of whether they are planned or command systems. In a **command economy,** such as Russia, the government controls many of the decisions; it makes decisions according to what seems best for society. In an unplanned or decentralized system, individual economic agents acting without government coercion make decisions as to how resources should be used.

WHAT IS AN ECONOMIC SYSTEM?

Before beginning a survey of several existing economic systems, we had best define what we are talking about. We might formally want to characterize an economic system as the institutions which have been chosen and accepted as the means of utilizing national resources in satisfying human wants. Thus, an economic system will consist of all the ways a particular nation uses its resources to satisfy whatever its citizens desire. The institutions referred to here are principally the laws of the nation, but they may also include the habits, ethics, and customs of the citizens of that nation.

It should be obvious that all economic systems are man made; none of them are god given or brought from the stars. All economic institutions are just what human beings have made them. There are continual modifications, for example, of laws and the other institutions that make up the economic system. All of these modifications are man made; the judges, workers, government officials, consumers, and legislators are the ones who change, destroy, create, renovate, and resuscitate economic institutions. All of the institutions that make up our system or, for that matter, any other system are quite flexible. They may be modified by one group of people or another, and, in fact, this is constantly happening. After all, in the Middle Ages, we had a feudal system. In the sixteenth and seventeenth centuries mercantilism was the dominant system. After mercantilism came laissez faire. Institutional change may take time, but in fact it is occurring all of the time. The proof is in our history of constant change.

ECONOMIC THEORY AND ECONOMIC SYSTEMS

As stated, economic institutions are extremely flexible, particularly if one takes into account a long enough time period. However, economic theory may be viewed as somewhat less flexible.

In fact, when we apply economic theory to the study of alternative economic systems, we probably will end up realizing that it is quite *in*flexible. This is good for you, the student; if you have mastered the theory presented in this book in the context of a capitalist system, you will also be able to analyze other types of economic organizations, particularly those that have a money economy.

Let's take a quick look at some of the key economic principles that have been stressed throughout this book. We will find that these principles are the same in just about every system with the exception, perhaps, of pure communism where resources go "to each according to his needs, from each according to his ability." Even in a pure communist system, some of the principles outlined below would still apply. The principle of diminishing marginal returns would be one of them.

Diminishing Marginal Returns

When discussing the law of diminishing returns, we said that, as a rule, for a given (fixed) quantity of land, machines, or other natural resources, additional units of labor would result in a less than proportional increase in output. This, again, is the famous law of diminishing returns. If all factors of production are held constant except one, there will be a less than proportional increase in output when that one variable factor of production is increased. The law of diminishing returns—an economic principle that we have used in the context of our mixed capitalistic system—is equally applicable to every past, present, and future economic system. There is no way for anyone to overcome diminishing returns in the use of factors of production. This principle applies, for example, to giant government-owned farms in the Soviet Union and also to small family farms in the United States. It must be reckoned with no matter where one finds oneself. The principle of diminishing marginal utility must also always be considered.

Diminishing Marginal Utility

At some point, just about every good or service in existence will run into diminishing marginal utility. After some point an increase in the consumption of a good or service will be met with a proportionately smaller increase in the utility derived. This means no matter where you are—be it China, the United States, or Albania—people will respond to lower (relative) prices by purchasing more.

Opportunity Cost

The concept of opportunity cost has been stressed throughout this book, and it can be stressed again in the context of alternative economic systems. Opportunity cost always exists whether explicitly or implicitly. In a socialist or communistic system, the government may decide not to put a price on certain goods, but this does not do away with the fact that the production and distribution of those goods involved an opportunity cost to society. An individual's opportunity cost for working exists, no matter where he is or for whom he works. If he works, he sacrifices leisure and, therefore, incurs an opportunity cost. If he doesn't work, he sacrifices income (usually). He therefore incurs an opportunity cost when he "buys" leisure.

The existence of opportunity cost comes about because resources are scarce. This has to be true in any system one chooses to look at. If resources were not scarce, there would be no need to have an economic system at all; there would be no need to have institutions to regulate the allocation of resources because there would be no question of where they should be used since they would all be free.

It is maintained by many that America has reached an age of abundance and therefore economic theory no longer applies in this country. This, however, is definitely not the case. We still have the problem of scarcity, even though our

real standard of living is relatively high. It is a physical truism that at any moment in time, the total amount of resources is fixed; for this reason, there is always going to be scarcity. There will also always be an opportunity cost for using any resources in existence. View it this way: if we look at the amount of time available, it appears to be infinite because it reaches out into eternity. However, during any particular period in time, you only have a specific amount of time to do whatever you want to do. If you decide to do one thing, you automatically exclude doing anything else. Therefore, every time you decide to use your time in a particular way, you automatically incur an opportunity cost. There is no way out of it. The same is true when you use a resource other than time, unless it is truly free like air in the mountains.

HOW TO ANALYZE ALTERNATIVE SYSTEMS

There are particular questions that must be answered when analyzing different economic systems. The answers to these questions indicate the attributes that each system has. If we want to know how any given economic system works, we must find out:

1. Who is permitted to own which items of wealth?
2. What incentives are presented to people to induce them to produce?
3. What forces determine the individual benefits that people get from producing?
4. Which lines of economic activity may individuals engage in on their own initiative? And what

are they permitted to do with the proceeds of such activity?

Let's take a look at capitalism in theory and see how its economic institutions provide for the answers to the above four questions.

CAPITALISM IN THEORY

The theoretical concept of capitalism is usually associated with the father of laissez-faire economics, Adam Smith, who wrote *The Wealth of Nations* in 1776. Smith described a system where the government had little to do with economic endeavors. Individuals pursued their own self-interest and in so doing—according to his doctrine of the "invisible hand"—maximized the social welfare of the nation. Obviously, capitalism in its purest form has never existed, even though classical writers sometimes described theoretical capitalism as if it did exist.

Difference between Capital and Capitalism

At the outset, we should be careful to distinguish between *capital* and *capitalism*. In this book, *capital* has been used in two senses: one is *money* capital, and the other is *physical* capital. Money capital is the money that businessmen have to come up with, either by borrowing, selling equity shares of stock, or using their own savings, to purchase physical capital with which they can produce goods and services that they later sell, hopefully for a profit. Capital as a term can be applied to both man-made things and to natural, tangible things that are not directly used in consumption. Capital goods assist in the production of other capital goods and of consumption goods. We have also briefly talked about human capital, or the investment in human beings. Human capital is the knowledge, experience, and skills that are embodied in every human being and which aid every human being in producing and making a living.

Capitalism, on the other hand, should not be regarded as an economic system where there is physical capital or where machines are used to produce goods. Obviously, every economic system, regardless of its label, has some sort of capital, if only the ground on which individuals work. Capitalism, however, must be defined by the economic institutions which are in existence. We shall use the following definition:

Capitalism is an economic system where individuals privately own productive resources and possess the right to use these resources in whatever manner they choose, subject to certain legal restrictions.

Notice here that we used the term *productive resources* rather than *capital*. This takes into ac-

count not only machines and land, but also labor services. We see, then, that the definition of capitalism includes (at least implicitly) the right of individuals to use their talents in the manner that they think is best for themselves. One of the most fundamental economic institutions in a capitalist system is private property rights, which we will discuss now.

Private Property

The ownership of property under a capitalist system is usually vested in individuals or in groups of individuals. That is, the state is not the owner of all property, as in some other systems that we might come up with in theory. In the United States, the government does own certain pieces of property. But in general we live under a system of private property rights. Private property is controlled and enforced through a legal framework in the form of laws, courts, and police. Property rights are generally protected under a capitalist system, and under capitalism an individual is usually free to use his private property as he chooses. So long as he is satisfied with a contractual agreement, he is usually allowed to undertake it.

This statement really belongs in the realm of pure capitalism. In our mixed capitalist system, there are numerous government interventions into contracting among individuals, even when private property is concerned. In some states, even if someone is willing, you cannot loan him money at an interest rate which exceeds a stipulated maximum. In some industries, you could not go to work for a wage rate below a specified minimum even if you were willing to do so. You are prevented from using your private property—your personal labor services—in just any manner that you see fit.

The private property system in a capitalistic economy involves not only tangible things, but also intangibles. That is why we have such an extensive system of contracts in the United States, for example.

Under capitalism, the existence of private property rights makes the owners of productive resources the controllers of those resources. If you own a productive resource in a pure capitalist system, no one else but you can decide how it should be used; you are the one who makes the decision. Moreover, in a private property system, any accumulation of wealth which you as an individual amass throughout your life belongs to you and to no one else. You can decide who will get that accumulation of wealth upon your death. We see then that inheritance rights are another key aspect of capitalism in its purest form—and one which provides an incentive for accumulation and conservation of wealth. If people can pass on their wealth to their heirs, they'll be more likely to accumulate wealth than they would be in a situation where it was illegal or impossible to pass on an inheritance to children. In the United States there are inheritance taxes, but there are few restrictions on how inherited wealth can be distributed.

Free Enterprise

Another attribute of a purely capitalistic system is the notion of free enterprise. This is merely an extension of the concept of private property rights. Free enterprise allows individuals to freely select economic activities for whatever resources they own. Free enterprise in an economic system allows individuals to seek whatever occupation they want; there are no restrictions. Again, this is obviously a purely theoretical aspect of a capitalist system.

In the United States, for example, people are not generally free to go into any occupation they wish. Try to become a doctor without first getting admitted to medical school. Try to become a plumber without getting admitted to the plumbers' union. Free enterprise is probably another way of stating laissez faire. As outlined by Adam Smith in his *Wealth of Nations,* laissez faire is a system where each person goes his own way, seeking to maximize his own self-interest. He is free to be as enterprising as he wants. The government does not restrict his actions unless, of course, he physically harms others. In a free enterprise capitalistic system (at least in theory), productive resources are generally supposed to be directed into their best uses. Presumably, workers will go where they can make the most money and, therefore, contribute the most to the social product.

The Role of Government

Even in a purely capitalistic system, there is still a role for government. At a minimum, the government must exist to enforce private property rights. The government protects the rights of individuals and businessmen so that private property remains private and so the control of the property continues to be vested with the owners. Even the father of free enterprise, Adam Smith, described in some detail the role of government in a purely capitalist system. He talked about the need of government for national defense and for eliminating monopolies in restraint of trade.

CAPITALISM—A SUMMARY

We can summarize the attributes of pure capitalism by answering the four questions posited previously.

1. Private individuals are permitted to own and control the use and disposal of all items of wealth.
2. The incentives used to induce people to produce are: wages, rents, interest, and profits, which all are subsumed under the heading of "purchasing power." Production leads to the ability to purchase and consume desired goods or accumulate wealth.
3. The forces determining the individual benefits from production are market forces made up by the collective wants of the entire economy. The government does not decide how much an individual should be paid for his productive

efforts. Rather, this is determined by the forces of supply and demand.
4. Individuals may enter all lines of economic endeavor and they are not required to do anything in particular with the proceeds of such endeavors. They can accumulate and conserve wealth if they wish, or they can consume their rewards if they wish—it is a free enterprise system.

SOCIALISM

Socialism perhaps even more than capitalism carries with it numerous connotations which sometimes cloud the theoretical aspects of the economic system. A good idea of what the word can mean can be had from the following quote.

[Socialism] is both abstract and concrete, theoretical and practical, idealist and materialist, very old and entirely modern; it ranges from a mere sentiment to a precise program of action; different advocates present it as a philosophy of life, a sort of religion, an ethical code, an economic system, an historical category, a judicial principle.*

Obviously, our concern with socialism here is as an economic system. We will not attempt to describe any specific socialistic economy in existence, such as that in England, Sweden, or Russia, but will stick to the theoretical aspects. Generally, socialism can be defined as an economic organization in which society, rather than the individual, owns and manages the means of production. A socialist economy is oftentimes called a command economy because there is an authority, somebody in the government, who commands the means of production, such as land and the capital stock.

One of the most prevalent features in any socialist system is the attempt to redistribute in-

*A comment by A. Shadwell in *Quarterly Review* (July, 1924), p. 2.

come. The government will typically use its taxing powers to reduce inherited wealth and large incomes. A socialist system will usually have "cradle-to-grave" welfare services provided by the collective purse of the government.

Socialism as a Movement

The term *socialism* usually refers to a movement which aims to vest in society, rather than the individual, the ownership and management of all producer goods used in any large scale production. When we call socialism a movement, we are implying that there exist organizations with programs designed to transform the idea into some concrete, socialized economy. Moreover, if we decide that certain property rights—specifically property rights in producers' goods—should be vested in society as a whole, we imply the continued existence of some form of an *organized* society. Generally, the phrase *society as a whole* implies the existence of what we might call a "democratic" organization of society.

If the ownership of the means of production were vested in a relatively small group of people who did not act so as to reflect the wishes of the masses, this particular type of ownership would not be deemed ownership by "society as a whole." Essentially, if the ownership and management of producers' goods are to be vested in society as a whole, then the decisions concerning the use of those goods will be made directly by society rather than by individuals. Socialism then is really concerned with transferring decision-making powers from individuals to society. Most theories of socialism assume that this transference of power takes place only for large scale production, and not for small scale production. Land and tools used personally by their owners will not be subject to decision making by "society as a whole."

Also implicit in the theoretical definitions of socialism is that a socialist economy will lead to increased output for the nation as a whole. In other words, socialists believe in general that, without socialism, *potential* output of the existing productive agents in society is greater than *actual* output.

Economics—The Core of Socialism

Obviously, the heart of socialism is economic. The central issues include who should have the property rights in producers' goods, who should make decisions about the use of these goods, and how real income should be distributed once it is created. To be sure, around this central economic core there will be political, social, religious, and other issues. In fact, many of these issues seem to loom larger than the economic ones in current-day discussions of socialism. The central problem, however, is really how to alter society's methods of producing, distributing, and consuming economic goods. We know—and socialists do not deny—that a change from a capitalistic system to the institutions necessary for a socialistic system will also entail many changes that are not economic—changes that will be social, philosophical, religious, and even psychological.

We should not confuse current ideas on socialism with ideas presented by **utopian socialists**. These persons were a group of French and English theorists in the early nineteenth century, who proposed the creation of self-contained communities where the instruments of production were owned collectively by everyone. The government would be primarily on a voluntary and certainly on a democratic basis. Robert Owen in England and Charles Fourier in France were the principle proponents of utopian socialism.

Key Attributes

Perhaps we can best isolate the key attributes of a socialistic system by answering the four questions outlined previously.

1. While individuals are allowed to own many items of wealth, in a socialistic system the

government owns the major productive re-sources, such as land and capital goods. Individuals can own consumer goods and consumer durables, but they are not allowed to own factories, machines, and other things that are used to produce what society wants.

2. People are induced to produce by the possibility of wages. However, taxation of large incomes in order to redistribute income does reduce some of the incentives to produce a lot.

3. The forces which determine the reward that people get from producing are usually set by the state, and not by the market. That is, supply and demand may not determine people's wage rates. Rather, the government will determine who should be paid what, in which government owned and operated factories.

4. In a socialist system individuals are allowed to enter only certain endeavors. They cannot, for example, set up their own factories. They cannot become entrepreneurs or capitalists, for that is in the realm of state control.

While this summary explanation of socialism is based purely on a theoretical level, it should be pointed out that the varieties of socialist systems in the world today are numerous. The only thing that they seem to have in common is that socialist governments control more factors of production than do capitalistic governments. However, since economic institutions change, we find the trend in some socialist systems is away from government control. The enthusiasm for nationalization of industries seems to be waning in West Germany and in the United Kingdom, for example, but increasing in certain Latin American countries such as Chile.

A CASE STUDY IN AN ALTERNATIVE ECONOMIC SYSTEM

In the next issue we present a case study in a system quite different from what we are used to in the United States. We will not be able to come to any conclusions as to whether our system is better than any other. That is in the realm of normative economics. You may have your own personal feelings; and so, too, may your instructor and your friends. In any event, a detailed study of the institutions which make up our system and other systems is important if any consensus is to be reached on what is the "right" system.

Definition of New Terms

COMMAND ECONOMIES: economies in which economic decisions are commanded by central authorities. The opposite of decentralized economies, such as the United States.

CAPITALISM: an economic system where individuals privately own productive resources and can use them in whatever manner they choose, subject to certain legal restrictions.

SOCIALISM: an economic system in which producers' goods for large scale production are owned and controlled by the state.

UTOPIAN SOCIALISM: an economic system devised by utopians such as Robert Owen and Charles Fourier; systems in which the community would be self-sustained and the instruments of production would be owned collectively by everyone.

Chapter Summary

1. Economists usually like to distinguish economic systems by the degree of decentralization. The most decentralized system is one of pure capitalism, and the most centralized is one of pure socialism. Sometimes the distinction is made in terms of command versus unplanned economies.

2. An economic system consists of all of a nation's different ways of using its resources for satisfying whatever its citizens desire. An economic system involves different institutions, principally the laws of the nation, but additionally it involves habits, ethics, and customs of the citizens of that nation. All economic systems are man made and, therefore, can be changed.

3. Many of the economic concepts we have learned in this text can be applied to any economic system. For example, the law of diminishing marginal returns, the law of diminishing marginal utility, the concept of opportunity cost, and others apply wherever resources are scarce.

4. In order to analyze alternative economic systems, we must answer the following questions: who is allowed to own wealth? What incentives do people have to make them produce? What determines the individual benefits people get from producing? Can individuals engage in any economic activities, and can they do whatever they want with the proceeds of such activities?

5. It is important to distinguish between capital and capitalism. All economies have capital, but a capitalistic system is one in which individuals privately own productive resources and possess the right to use these resources in whatever manner they choose.

6. A key aspect of a capitalistic system is the right to own private property, even for producers' goods for large scale production.

7. The capitalist system is sometimes called the free enterprise system. This is merely an extension of the concept of private property rights. In a free enterprise system, individuals can freely select economic activities for whatever resource they own.

8. Socialism is much less easy to define than capitalism for it means many things to many different people. In general, we will define a socialist system as one in which the major resources for production are owned by the state.

9. In a socialist system individuals can own consumer goods and certain productive resources.

10. We find attempts to redistribute income in socialist systems much more than in capitalistic systems. This redistribution may be done by way of highly progressive taxation, such as occurs in Sweden.

11. Individuals in a socialist system cannot do just anything they want economically. For example, they cannot set up their own factories, nor can they become entrepreneurs, just because they want to.

Questions for Thought and Discussion

1. Is a pure capitalist system impossible? Is a pure socialist system impossible? If your answer is different for these two questions, what accounts for the difference?

2. Since the means of production are owned by the state in a socialist system, would you expect to find less antisocial business behavior in the form of pollution in a socialist system?

3. Is it possible to redistribute income in a capitalist system just as in a socialist system? If so, why have we failed so miserably in the United States at redistributing income?
4. Do you think there would be more innovation in a socialist system than in a capitalist system? Why?
5. "The world is headed in the direction of neither socialism nor capitalism, but rather, a mixture of the two. After a while, all economic systems will be alike." Do you agree?
6. The Soviet Union uses large amounts of capital. In one sense, is the Soviet Union capitalistic?
7. How do you think decisions as to where new capital should be utilized are made in command economies?

Selected References

Grossman, Gregory. *Economic Systems.* Englewood Cliffs, N.J.: Prentice-Hall, 1966.

Preston, Nathaniel Stone. *Politics, Economics, and Power.* New York: Macmillan, 1967. Chapters 3 and 4.

Rima, I. H. *Development of Economic Analysis.* Rev. Ed. Homewood, Ill.: Richard D. Irwin, 1972.

Schumpeter, Joseph A. *Capitalism, Socialism and Democracy.* New York: Harper & Row, 1950.

ISSUE XIX

CHINA

A Case Study of a Vastly Different System

PHOTO BY MARC RIBOUD, MAGNUM

The People's Republic

One-fourth of the world's population lives within an economic system that is vastly different from what we are used to in the United States. Yet the extent to which scientists and researchers have made economic analyses of the Peoples' Republic of China is relatively minute, to say the least. The reason, of course, for this lack of analysis has been the traditional problems of inadequate data and poor communication with economic policymakers in China. Until recently, very few Americans were allowed to enter the Peoples' Republic. Moreover, the number of mainland Chinese traveling outside of their country has been almost zero. Only now after a relaxation of the tensions between the United States and China are we able to get a closer glimpse at how socialism works in the most populous country in the entire world. Moreover, after President Nixon's historic trip in the spring of 1972, potential for trade between the United States and China has opened up and the subject of Chinese economic analysis will henceforth be a growing field of study.

Facts About China

It is difficult to obtain accurate statistics on the Chinese economy. Therefore, what we present here are only estimates—and crude ones at that. The population as estimated by the United Nations approaches 800 billion. Perhaps 80 percent of the entire population derives its livelihood from agriculture. It is estimated that over 70 percent of the people are organized into communes—a topic we will discuss later on in this issue. Chinese gross national product is probably around $150 billion. However, this figure (contrary to the one given in the United States) does not include services, housing construction, water conservation, and land reclamation expenses. Agricultural product constitutes perhaps 40 percent of annual GNP, with industrial product accounting for about 35 percent.

Economic growth has been higher in the industrial sector than in the agricultural sector for some time. It is estimated that the growth in industrial output was about 9 percent per annum between 1962 and 1970. The largest single industrial endeavor is in metal processing, with crude oil, chemical fertilizers, and coal following in that order.

Employment

The Chinese economy is fully employed at all times. There are over 4 million people in the official work force. Workers in theory have complete freedom to change occupations and locations, but this is true mostly in theory. There are internal police regulations and particular quota systems which prevent complete job mobility. For example, university students are generally assigned their future positions while still in school.

Monetary System

The currency in China is denominated in the jenminty or yuan. The so-called official exchange rate is 2.5 yuan to one U.S. dollar. However, yuan are not traded in the world money market. In fact, it is officially a capital offense to remove yuan from the country. The value of the currency in communist China and, therefore, the prices of goods and services are generally highly stable. Cash enters the economy through wage payments and agricultural production sales in free markets. The money supply is regulated through credit rationing and controlled by the Peoples Bank of China. There is relatively little currency held and in circulation. In fact, 85 percent of transactions are done without currency; rather, there's crediting and debiting in bank accounts with the Peoples Bank of China.

Average Food Price

Translated into American currency, food prices per kilogram in 1970 were as follows: rice, 3 to 4 cents; wheat flour, 10 to 12 cents; meat, 40 to 80 cents; poultry, 80 cents to 1 dollar; fruit, 30 to 70 cents. These were the popular prices in urban centers.

Consumption and Investment

Much of the average person's income in China is used for food purchases. In fact, it is estimated that over 50 percent of a wage earner's monthly income goes for food. Many of the items that consumers want to buy are rationed. For example, rice, cotton cloth, most grains, and oils are not sold to anyone who wants to buy them, but rather only to people in terms of how much they have been rationed per family. An average family's monthly ration might be 35 pounds of rice per month, 6 pounds of meat per month, and 8 yards of cloth per month.

There are very few automobiles in China because steel has been diverted for railroad construction. Bicycles, however, are very common, and there is usually one per family in urban centers.

A small portion of a worker's income is placed directly into a welfare fund at each production site. Most of the income that is not paid to workers from industrial and agricultural output is reinvested into the means of production. It is estimated that the annual rate of investment on capital formation is over 20 percent of annual income in China. We would expect, then, that the growth rate in China will accelerate in the future if this large amount of saving and investment continues.

wages in industry were $270 per year and the average wages in agriculture were somewhat less than $200 per year. Chairman Mao Tse-tung is reported to have a salary of over $200 per month, the highest possible level of wages in the entire country.

Economic Planning

After taking power in 1949, the Chinese communists under Mao Tse-tung set about devising plans which would help their devastated country back onto the road to economic well-being. The first five year plan was instituted in 1952. It stressed investment in heavy industry, retention of small scale and handicraft industries, and a land reform in which land was taken from wealthy Chinese and given to poor peasants. Farms at that time were also collectively organized.

In 1958, the second plan was put into effect. It started out with the so-called "Great Leap Forward" which everybody in the world was aware of at that time.

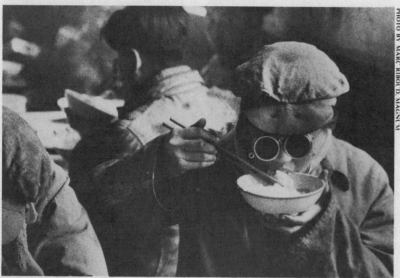

PHOTO BY MARC RIBOUD, MAGNUM

The Great Leap Forward

Chinese leaders planned to increase individual output by over 25 percent per year. Heavy industry was to develop even more rapidly than it had in the last five years. There was going to be more use of labor in order to reduce underemployment of the labor force. Instead of directing all heavy industrial plants from the center of government, there was going to be some decentralization in the sense that local managers would have more control over what their plants bought and sold and what production methods

Wages and Work

Wages in China are not determined by supply and demand as in the United States. Wages are, in fact, fixed and equal throughout a given strata of the labor force. There are nine of these strata or ranks of employees with such categories as teacher, state executive, technician, and so on. Within each rank, there is a division into grades through which promotion can occur. It was estimated that in 1970 the average

In many respects, wages are determined by productivity of individual work forces. Wages in agriculture, for example, are generally determined by the distribution among teams of workers on the basis of the gross income of the crop. Taxes are deducted and welfare fund allotments are taken out. The rest is distributed. If a particular work team has had a relatively excellent production record, the members of it are rewarded by a larger percentage of the gross income of the team.

would be used. Presumably this was going to encourage greater initiative.

From the very beginning there were unexpected and tragic consequences of the Great Leap Forward. The program was just too ambitious. Many products were being produced that were not really wanted in the economy. Many large-scale irrigation projects were undertaken, even though they were poorly planned. The result was often complete fiasco. Steel was being made by many unskilled workers in unsafe, often quite primitive, production environments. Many times, the quality of the produced steel was so poor that it could not be used.

A food shortage began to develop. Many workers were transferred from agriculture to the city to help in the great industrial expansion program. The consequence was too little production of food. Finally, a much needed, new economic policy was instituted.

Agriculture Again

The leaders of China realized that agriculture had to be built up before rapid industrialization could be attempted. There were just too many mouths to feed. Agriculture then became the foundation of the entire economy. It was not until the latter part of

the 1960s, however, that agricultural production per capita reached the level it had attained in the 1950s.

One of the most interesting aspects of the agricultural program in China is the system of collective farming or communal farming. It is vastly different from the capitalist system we are aware of in the United States.

The Commune

In 1958 the Great Leap Forward had as one of its major real innovations of the economy the shift to commune regimes in the agricultural sector. Within a commune, there is generally no cash wage system. Workers are paid with "work points" which can provide a daily income comparable to about 65¢ per day. In the communal system, workers live together at the same site of their work. The work teams are essentially self-governing, and, in fact, it was in the Great Leap Forward that central leaders expressed hope that the communes would take it upon themselves to mechanize and become more efficient without leadership from above.

The communal system of agriculture did not prove to be highly successful as was obvious by about 1960. However, today it still remains as an institution. The func-tional organization of agriculture has reverted, though, to its pre-1958 pattern. Additionally, the central government has now made greater efforts to increase the use of fertilizer by the work teams and to expand the amount of area that is irrigated.

Even on the communes, some individual initiative is allowed. Small families will have plots of land on which they can grow crops for sale in a free market. Additionally, there has been some revival of the so-called "cottage industries." Peasants can trade in homemade goods on a limited scale to what are called consumer cooperatives.

The Attitude of the Working Population

There have apparently been periodic shifts in the attitude of the Chinese working population, and this apparently relates to the general pattern of economic stability. During the Cultural Revolution which started in about 1966, there were rebellions, ad hoc sit-down strikes by workers. This is generally not the case, however. There is a firm, almost Calvinistic work ethic in the Maoist regime, and it has been generally well received. Apparently, there is a strong pride in work with a somewhat less obvious interest in lei-sure than that demonstrated in the United States. The Chinese believe, for example, that the major goal of Americans is a leisure society. They make a mockery of American business executives as victims of a "10,000 aspirin job."

Mao and Economics

The Cultural Revolution which has more or less died down in China did, however, bring with it an overt and extremely caustic disdain for what has been called *economism*. This term is a neologism created by Chairman Mao which has been transliterated into English. It is a pejorative term referring to preserving one's self-interest in economic decision making. It has been used mostly against nonrevolutionary worker groups in the country. Now it is generally applied to all anti-Maoist economic policies of any persuasion.

During the Cultural Revolution, the danger signs of economism were individual initiative except within the narrowest confines, accumulation of personal wealth, and a reluctance to make necessary sacrifices of personal comfort. During the Revolution a ten-point program was launched against economism on the broadest possible front.

Despite the fact that much of

what goes on in China is deemed political, Mao on closer analysis is truly an economic animal. He has been preoccupied with the problems of economic growth, and he has repeatedly emphasized the importance of entrepreneurship and in his writing personally attaches great importance to material incentives. He is, however, referring to an entrepreneur not in the individual sense, but in the collective sense.

Mao's writings emphasize three important economic aspects:

1. Since 1927, Mao has generally been on the side of economic rationality. He has insisted that economic and social policies could not succeed unless they were successful in raising the standard of living. In other words, he believes that economic policy should be geared toward material incentives instead of sociopolitical ones.

2. Like economists working in other underdeveloped areas such as India or Latin America, Mao has emphasized the importance of entrepreneurship in a collective sense. He has attached great value to the collective's willingness to integrate. This was brought out in the Great Leap Forward when he asked that collectives or communes themselves take on the initiative in mechanization.

One of Mao's preoccupations has been the maximization of entrepreneurial qualities within a system of collective or communal work teams.

3. Mao has always insisted that the emphasis of work in economics must be to the end of increasing production. He has also emphasized this in the field of public finance and taxation. He has never thought that state procurement of goods and services should stand in the way of increased production. He would not, for example, allow the type of government confiscatory techniques that Stalin used in Russia because he feels that this would be counterproductive.

China's Economic Realities

Students of China's economics all agree that China is still an underdeveloped country with too many people living on land with low average productivity. Land reclamation in China is very costly. Not since 1957 has there been a major effort to increase the amount of arable land. Mechanization is also costly, and agriculture has been slow to comply.

In order to increase growth, it is important that there be a high rate of saving. China does have a high rate of saving—estimated at over 20 percent a year—but this is not a high *voluntary* rate. In fact, the rate of saving is more forced than voluntary. The government diverts a large amount of resources from the production of consumer goods to the production of producers' goods and military equipment.

China is faced with an indigenous population which has an extremely low level of technical ability. Thus, even though there is a high rate of forced saving, it is not so easy to put these savings into extremely productive endeavors. For a while the Soviet Union provided technical assistance and the needed capital goods to help equip and run large industrial projects. That is no longer the case with the current Sino-Soviet rift still in effect.

China may have difficulties just like other underdeveloped countries, but it has succeeded in one area: the area of income distribution. In the last 20 years the distribution of income has been made more equitable than it was in the past. Even during periods of extreme droughts in the production of agricultural products, there were no famines. No one starved to death, which is something that could not be said for pre-communist China and which, in fact, could not be said for many underdeveloped countries in the world today.

Questions for Thought and Discussion

1. Can and does the U.S. government cause the economy to engage in forced saving?
2. Do you think that China's isolation for two decades helped her economic growth?
3. What do you like about the Chinese economic system? What do you dislike?

Selected References

Richman, Barry M. *Industrial Society in Communist China.* New York: Random House, 1972.

Shaffer, Harry G., Ed. *The Communist World.* New York: Appleton-Century-Crofts, 1967.

Wheelwright, E. L., & McFarlane, Bruce. *The Chinese Road to Socialism.* New York: Monthly Review Press, 1970.

WIDE WORLD PHOTOS

POLITICS AND PRIORITIES

William Proxmire

**Senator, Wisconsin
Chairman, Joint Economic Committee**

WILLIAM PROXMIRE is mainly interested in what the government does with its money. He has been a vigorous opponent of the supersonic transport, wasteful military spending, and high oil depletion tax allowances. Unlike his colleagues in the Senate, however, Proxmire is in a unique position to bring his views to emphatic public attention.

As chairman of the Joint Economic Committee, Proxmire enjoys an unusual platform. The JEC is not empowered to take legislative action, and can only influence public policy by hearings and recommendations to the standing committees which specialize in economic action. Yet, like most Congressional committees, the JEC is a product of its chairman, and, under Proxmire, the Committee meetings have been the site for some of the most crucial government economic policy battles of recent years.

Attracted to the growing Democratic party in Wisconsin, Proxmire first went to Madison to work on a newspaper. He was elected to the state legislature in 1950, and, after three defeats for the governor's chair, was elected to fill the late

Joseph McCarthy's seat in the U.S. Senate.

During the fiscally conservative Eisenhower administration, Proxmire was ridiculed as a big spender. But he did favor elimination of large tax write-offs for industry and wanted to broaden the deduction provisions for low-income tax brackets.

Ironically, it was during the expansionist Kennedy years that Proxmire turned a corner on government spending, and began careful scrutiny of national economic priorities. He fought against the 1965 tax cut, arguing that it would fail to balance the deficit budget. In that same year, he earned the wrath of the Florida Congressional contingent by opposing a huge trans-Florida barge canal system. Only after $104 million had been spent, was the project scrapped as economically unsound. He has also been a steady critic of the cozy relationship between the military and its defense contractors, citing the high number of former military officials who "retire" into defense industries.

Proxmire was appointed chairman of the JEC in 1967 and immediately began studying military spending. In well-publicized, carefully planned hearings, he exposed a $1 billion cost overrun on the C5A military transport plane and seriously damaged the credibility of the Defense Department. Under his leadership, the Committee has been an open platform for critics of the cost-plus system of contract planning, the free use of government facilities by legislators, and the *de facto* subsidies given to defense contractors and agri-

culture through government purchasing and distribution programs. In fact, during January of 1972, Proxmire began a series of JEC sessions on the agricultural parity system and the oil-depletion allowance.

Certainly his most ambitious battle was the fight over the SST. Starting with an anti-SST faction of six votes in the Senate in 1963, Proxmire maintained steady pressure on the issue until, in 1970, the Senate defeated a $290 million appropriation to continue work on the development of an SST prototype. Proxmire simply considered the SST an economically disastrous plan which constituted little more than a subsidy to the aerospace industry at great public expense and slight public benefit. He contrasted the expected cost of the SST with the needs of mass transit and other slimly funded programs.

Despite the furor of big labor and big industry in response to Proxmire's investigations and public statements, the Senator insists that the majority of the American people agree with his long-term view of national economic priorities. There can be little doubt that the subjects which have been pursued by the JEC are now of great public concern—consumer legislation, use of taxpayers' money, and funding of social welfare programs. In addition, Proxmire feels that the JEC is one of the few places in which conflicting interests can be exposed. "You use the committees you've got; the Armed Services committee won't attack military spending."

Military Capitalism

THE AMOUNT OF resources that goes to supporting military armament is staggering. Military spending accounts for perhaps one-tenth of the GNP in the United States. The sheer size and the way in which our government goes about amassing its military might are sufficiently important for us to spend this last chapter on the economics of military capitalism. Before we go into the specific facts concerning the military-industrial complex in the United States, it may be worthwhile to examine armament spending on a worldwide basis.

WORLD MILITARY EXPENDITURES

Back in 1964 when the first estimates of global military spending were made, the U.S. Arms Control and Disarmament Agency revealed that $140 billion was the price tag for that year. From 1965 to 1967, world spending increased at a rate of 13 percent per year. By 1973, despite the fact that the rate of growth has decreased to approximately 5 percent per annum, the estimate of total global spending on military endeavors will reach perhaps $250 billion per year. We see in Figure 17–1 that world military expenditures have been increasing every year for the past ten years. The U.S. Arms Control and Disarmament Agency estimated that from 1964 to 1969, more than $1 trillion was spent for arms and armed forces. That's equal to the gross national product of the United States at the beginning of this decade. It's also equal to more than two years' gross national product for the world's 93 developing countries which have over 2.5 billion inhabitants. During this six-year period, the world's military budget required more money than was spent by all governments on all forms of public education and health care.

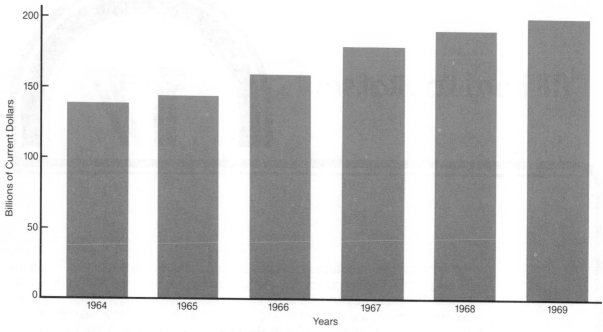

FIGURE 17-1   **WORLD MILITARY EXPENDITURES**

Here we find world military expenditures from 1964 to 1965. Today they probably exceed $250 billion. *Source:* U.S. Arms Control and Disarmament Agency, Washington, D.C.

COMPARISON WITH OTHER PUBLIC EXPENDITURES

No single activity of government uses so much public financing as military preparedness. In some countries, military spending accounts for more than 25 percent of all expenditures of the central government. The second largest expenditure is for education. We see in Figure 17-2 the comparison of military spending for the world with education spending and health spending.

In Figure 17-3, the per capita expenditures are given for military, education, and health by different regions in the world. North America is, for better or for worse, head and shoulders above all the other regions in all categories of expenditure including military.

THE U.S. SITUATION

The estimates of the size of the military budget in the United States vary, but we can be fairly certain that almost 10 percent of the total output of the American economy consists of military services and goods. The allotted defense budget is around $80 billion, or over 30 percent of total federal expenditures. We see in Figure 17-4 that Department of Defense expenditures have been increasing, albeit unsteadily, throughout the past two decades. The somewhat slower amount of military maneuvering in Vietnam slowed down the rise in 1969 and 1970.

The Pentagon, center of all government defense activities, is in itself a small country. In fact, it has been called the largest planned economy

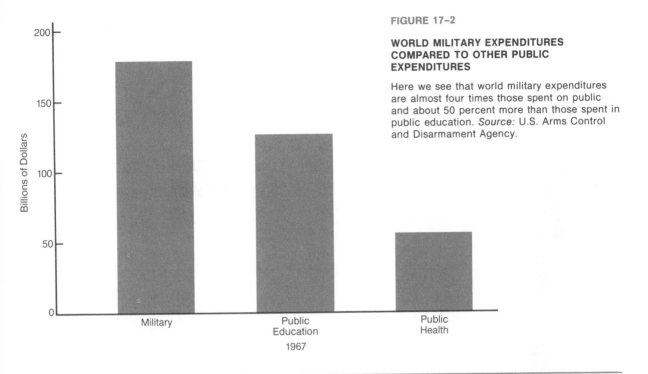

FIGURE 17–2

WORLD MILITARY EXPENDITURES COMPARED TO OTHER PUBLIC EXPENDITURES

Here we see that world military expenditures are almost four times those spent on public and about 50 percent more than those spent in public education. *Source:* U.S. Arms Control and Disarmament Agency.

outside the Soviet Union. Almost 10 percent of all assets in the United States belong to the Pentagon. It owns, for example, around 40 million acres of land, and it controls, directly or indirectly, over 4 million workers. Its budget is only about 25 percent less than the entire gross national product of Great Britain. The Department of Defense is richer than just about any small nation in the world.

THE TRUE COST OF THE MILITARY

We know in economics that the true cost of anything is equal to its opportunity of alternative cost. Hence, the direct *recorded* outlays of the Defense Department do not include the entire cost of the military machine to the American people. We have already discussed one of the major costs that is completely hidden by the particular method the Army uses to obtain military manpower.

The Draft

When discussing the topic of involuntary military servitude, we found that the true cost of the labor component of military spending was equal to the opportunity cost of using that labor—not what the military machine actually paid to its soldiers. If a man is drafted and receives an income from the Army of $1000 a year, but could be making $10,000 a year in the civilian world, the opportunity cost of using this man is $10,000, not $1000. With a draft system, the Pentagon was able to hide from the American public the true cost of defense. Suffice it to say that the cost greatly exceeds what the government actually claims to be paying for labor input into the production of defense.

Other Hidden Costs

Numerous other hidden costs are never brought to public attention. One such cost involves the

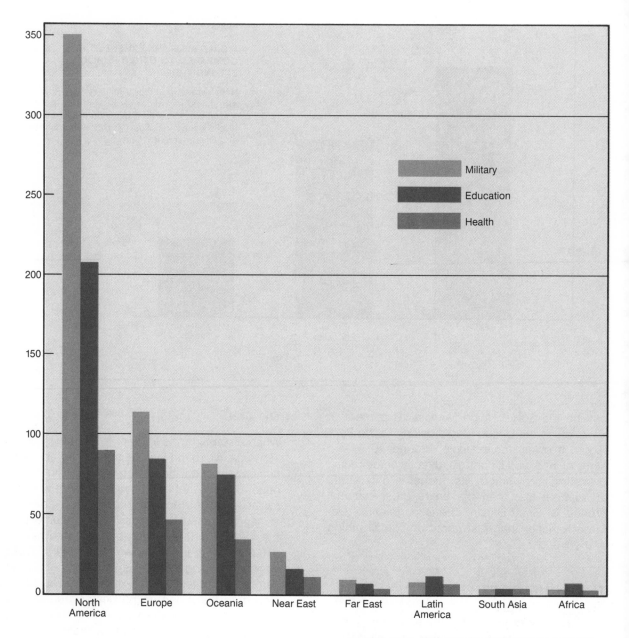

FIGURE 17–3 **PER CAPITA EXPENDITURES FOR ARMAMENT, EDUCATION, AND HEALTH**

Here we show for 1967 per capita expenditures for military, education, and health in different parts of the world. North America is by far the largest spender on military might of anywhere in the world. *Source:* U.S. Arms Control and Disarmament Agency.

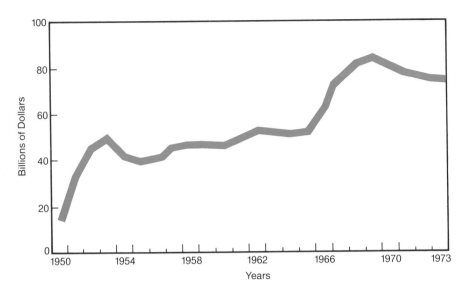

FIGURE 17–4

**NATIONAL DEFENSE
SPENDING IN THE U.S.**

National defense spending in
the U.S. peaked out in 1967
and fell slowly but steadily
from then until 1973. *Source:*
Office of Management and
Budget.

oil import restriction program. Back in 1954, President Eisenhower signed some bills making importation of foreign crude oil subject to certain restrictions. The restrictions were voluntary and then became mandatory. The reason that the importation of foreign oil was restricted, according to the White House, was to protect our national security. It was argued that if we relied on foreign sources of oil, then in time of war these sources would be cut off. We would not have sufficient petroleum to run our military machine. If this is indeed the case, then the $7 billion a year that consumers pay in higher petroleum product prices must be added onto the budget of the Department of Defense. This $7 billion must properly be added on to the true cost of our military machine. In fact, one suggestion for making the true cost of defense known would be to directly subsidize American oil producers so that they would be producing enough oil to satisfy national security requirements. The subsidy would be taken out of the Department of Defense budget and then the American public, Congressmen, and Pentagon managers would know the true cost of this national security action.

There are probably other industries which are given special support, supposedly for national security reasons. We might wish to have, for example, a functioning watchmaking industry so that in time of war we would have people who could make the delicate instruments that go into our guided missiles. If this were indeed the case, then the watchmaking industry might be directly subsidized by the Department of Defense. It is known, however, that we in America have rarely been so open and honest about our national security expenditures. Instead of directly subsidizing watchmakers out of Department of Defense budgets, the government would opt for imposing a tariff on foreign watches so that the price of watches would remain high enough in the United States to support a large domestic watchmaking industry. Consumers would be the ones paying for the support of the watchmaking industry, and the Department of Defense would have none of the costs charged against it.

FIGURE 17–5

GUNS AND BUTTER

It is true: we can't have more guns and more butter at the same time. We have shown here a production possibilities curve. The horizontal axis measures civilian goods, and the vertical axis measures war goods. If we want to have more war goods, we have to sacrifice civilian goods. There is always going to be a trade-off at any point in time. In the long run, however, as we increase our productive capacity, we can have more war goods and more civilian goods. At any moment in time, though, there is a distinct trade-off.

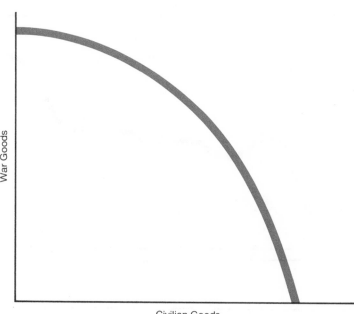

MISLEADING DISCLOSURES

In addition to the hidden costs we have described, other costs are just now coming to light. The Senate Foreign Relations Committee discovered that military assistance to foreign nations in 1971 totaled almost $7 billion. However, in the President's budget message to Congress, the listing under military assistance to foreign nations was only $625 million. Additionally, it was discovered that almost $700 million had been transferred to foreign nations for the purchase of arms under the Food for Peace Program.

The list does not stop here. The United States spent $1.5 billion helping support the South Vietnamese currency; the Pentagon had a surplus weapons stock worth over $17 billion that was never reported previously. One Senator stated: "In some respects, the United States has been transformed from an 'arsenal democracy' to a gigantic discount supermarket with no check-out counters, no store managers—only clerks who blithely deliver to foreign governments of practically any political persuasion whatever they happen to see and like." Indeed, Pentagon capitalism seems slightly different from the capitalism used as a basis for the development of economic theories throughout this book.

THE OVERALL PICTURE

There is no way to deny the common sense notion that you can't have more guns without having less butter. This follows from our production possibilities curve (shown again in Figure 17–5). Here we have put civilian goods on the horizontal axis and war goods on the vertical axis. At any point in time, only one production possibilities curve exists. If we find ourselves on that curve, obtaining increased production of war goods necessarily means decreased production of civilian goods.

Congressmen and Presidents have maintained that we will not have to make the choice between guns and butter, that we will have both more guns and more butter. This, in fact, is true in a growing economy. As we grow we can have more of each because the production possibilities curve will move out to the right. However, at any point in time, it has to be true that the more resources we devote to the production of military armament, the fewer resources we will have left for the production of civilian goods. This is an undeniable fact that no politician can negate merely by stating the opposite.

It is often stated that military expenditures are necessary to bring us from a point inside the production possibilities curve (unemployment) to some point on the frontier itself. However, a dollar is a dollar is a dollar. If, in fact, it is true that military spending will lead to increased employment, the government still has the option of spending those same dollars for other things such as more education, dams, buildings, and other civilian goods. There is no truth to the argument that a large defense sector is necessary to provide for full employment in our economy. The government has numerous ways to spend its money, defense being only one of them.

AGGREGATE EFFECTS OF MILITARY SPENDING

Even though military spending may not be necessary for full employment, currently the military is involved in numerous aspects of aggregate economic activity in the United States. At the height of the Vietnam war in 1968, almost 10 percent of our labor force was employed in defense-related work. The spending of the military machine is highly concentrated. In 1967 a Defense Department study found that 72 employment areas depended on war output for about 12 percent of their employment; 80 percent of these employment areas were small communities with labor forces numbering less than 50,000. The impact of a cutback on military spending to these selected communities can obviously be very detrimental.

Moreover, defense employment is concentrated among very specially skilled people and defense-oriented companies. These scientists and specialized companies often have a hard time finding alternative employment when the military decides to cut back on spending. Everybody knows what happened to the aerospace industry when the government started cutting back on spending in 1969. Lockheed almost went under,

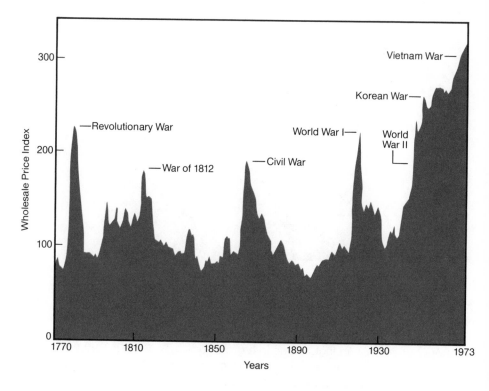

FIGURE 17–6

THE WAR AND INFLATION

In just about every war-time period
in the United States, prices have risen.
Vietnam was no exception. *Source:*
U.S. Department of Labor and U.S. Bureau
of Commerce.

due in part to a reduction in the orders it was getting from the Pentagon. (Lockheed's trouble was also partly due to mismanagement.) Boeing lost out on several military contracts and, coupled with the reduction in commercial jet orders, almost went under too.

The Department of Defense also provides large amounts of revenues to private companies that don't seem to be war related. For example,

Pan American Airways generates over 40 percent of its revenues from military contracts. The military post exchange system (the PX) is the third largest marketing chain in the country, following A&P and Sears and Roebuck. Spending on military housing exceeds federal spending on public housing. In short, the amount of military activity in our domestic economy is indeed large, and one would expect that changes in military spending would have dislocating effects on people and companies throughout these United States. In fact, we saw what happened when the rate of growth of military spending slowed down in the late sixties and actually became negative in 1970 when the Department of Defense budget was $5 billion less than it was the previous year. Many communities experienced big drops in employment because of military cutbacks.

It is often asserted that increased military spending leads to inflation. In fact, looking at the historical record, we find that there does seem to be some relationship between war times and inflation in the United States. As shown in Figure 17-6, World War II seemed to have less inflation than previous wars; however, this is a misleading statement because during World War II there were direct wage and price controls. After controls were lifted, the war-time repressed inflation became actual inflation. Prices jumped up drastically right after the end of the war.

THE MILITARY-INDUSTRIAL FIRM

One of the most outspoken students of Pentagon capitalism, Dr. Seymour Melman, has presented several propositions concerning military-industrial firms. Melman's propositions are as follows.

Proposition One: The military-industrial firm is not autonomous.
Proposition Two: The military-industrial firm is controlled by the state management.
Proposition Three: The military-industrial firm does not minimize costs.
Proposition Four: The military-industrial firm is not a profit-maximizing entity.
Proposition Five: The military-industrial firms as a group lack flexibility for conversion to civilian work.

Professor Seymour Melman's stinging indictment of business practices in defense industries seems to be borne out somewhat by many of the scandals that have so afflicted defense contractors in recent years. We can't say that we weren't warned. President Eisenhower cautioned the nation to beware of the military-industrial complex in his famous farewell address to the nation. In 1961, Eisenhower was thinking of a fairly informal group of high military officers, defense-oriented firms, and Congressmen who would be bound together by an ideology of continual expansion of the military machine. If one looks at the way prime government contracting firms have been able to operate in past years, there might be some argument made in support of the idea of a "complex."

Approximately 22,000 firms are deemed prime contractors with the Department of Defense. These firms in turn subcontract much of their work to smaller enterprises. When all the contractors and subcontractors are added up, there are perhaps 100,000 firms directly or indirectly engaged in supplying the Department of Defense with whatever it wants. There are, however, a few very large firms which supply most of the manufactured goods to the Pentagon. The hundred largest contractors supply almost 70 percent of manufactured goods to the Department of Defense. Many of these firms actually employ government owned capital, such as furniture and office machines and material.

Military Procurement

Though there has been much recent criticism of the way defense contractors manage their firms, we might want to look at some of the incentives they *don't* have for managing these firms correctly. Headed by Sen. William Proxmire, the Joint Economic Committee of the Congress of the United States looked into the economics of military procurement and made a public report in May of 1969. Essentially, the report was a stinging criticism of the problem of "uncontrolled costs." It was attributed to an unmanaged, unshapen military procurement policy. The Joint Economic Committee stated that a set of practices and circumstances exist in the Department of Defense which lead to: *(a)* economic inefficiency and waste, *(b)* a subsidy to contractors, and *(c)* an inflated defense budget.

The circumstances in the Department of Defense which led to these three undesirable results had to do with the following practices.

1. low competition and high concentration among prime defense contractors,
2. allowing contractors to use government owned property,
3. using progress payments to reimburse contractors for up to 90 percent of incurred costs on a pay-as-you-go basis, even if these costs are greatly in excess of original estimates,
4. no uniform accounting standards,
5. voluminous change orders and contractors' claims,
6. the absence of on-going reports to Congress, and
7. the failure of incentive contracting.

Some of the results of careless military procurement have indeed been incredible. The original cost estimates of the F-111 jet fighter ended up being one-third of the actual cost per plane. The cost overruns on the infamous Lockheed C5A jet transport are on the order of $2 billion.

A Symbiotic Relationship

The relationship between prime defense contractors and the Pentagon is indeed close and seems to be getting closer all the time. Congress finally has taken heed of certain practices within industries that lead to some dubious actions on the part of Pentagon officials. Not only does the Pentagon support a large sector of our economy in terms of defense contracts, it supplies a large number of key executives to large defense-contracting firms. Senator William Proxmire of Wis-

consin has criticized the "incestuous hiring" that industry engages in among retired Army colonels and high Pentagon officials.

In 1959 a survey was made by Congress. It brought to light that almost 800 retired officers of the rank of colonel, Navy captain, and above were employed by the largest 100 defense contractors. In 1969 the Defense Department made a similar survey which showed that top former military men working in defense industry firms had jumped to over 2000. In 1969 Lockheed Aircraft had 210; the Boeing Company had 169; McDonald-Douglas Corporation, 141; General Dynamics Corporation, 113; and North American Rockwell Corporation had 104 former military men. You can imagine that something less than hard-nosed business rules would be used in dealings among retired colonels and current colonels running the Defense Department. Moreover, you can expect that colonels looking forward to a cushy retirement job might act differently toward prospective employers than if there was no chance for getting a job after retirement.

The military establishment also has a powerful political arm. The Department of Defense employs almost 350 lobbyists in Capitol Hill. There are some 2850 public relations men in the United States and in foreign countries.

The close relationship between the Pentagon and defense contractors has led one staunch critic, Professor John Kenneth Galbraith, to hypothesize the following.

Where a corporation does all or nearly all of its business with the Department of Defense; uses much plant owned by the government; gets its working capital in the form of progress payments from the government; does not need to worry about competitors for it is the sole source of supply; accepts extensive guidance from the Pentagon on its management; is subject to detailed rules as to its accounting; and is extensively staffed by former service personnel, only the remarkable flexibility of the English language allows us to call it private enterprise. Yet this is not an exceptional case, but a common one. We have an amiable arrangement by which the defense firms, through part of the public bureaucracy, are largely exempt from its political and other constraints.*

*John Kenneth Galbraith, *The Military Budget and National Economic Priorities,* Part 1. Washington, D.C.: U.S. Government Printing Office, 1969, pp. 5-6.

A Question for Thought and Discussion

1. Explain the why of military madness?

Selected References

Benoit, Emile, & Boulding, Kenneth E., Eds. *Disarmament and the Economy.* New York: Harper & Row, 1963.

Bolton, Roger E., Ed. *Defense and Disarmament.* Englewood Cliffs, New Jersey: Prentice Hall, 1966.

Clayton, James L., Ed. *The Economic Impact of the Cold War.* New York: Harcourt Brace, 1970.

Mansfield, Edwin. *Defense, Science, and Public Policy.* New York: W. W. Norton, 1968.

Melman, Seymour. *Pentagon Capitalism.* New York: McGraw Hill, 1970.

Rodberg, Leonard, & Shearer, Derek, Eds. *The Pentagon Watchers.* Garden City, New

Rodberg, Leonard, & Sherer, Derek, Eds. *The Pentagon Watchers.* Garden City, New York: Doubleday, 1970.

Yarmolinsky, Adam. *The Military Establishment.* New York: Harper & Row, 1971.

INDEX

*Numbers in **boldface** indicate pages where terms are defined.*

Abortion, 3f., 12, 15
Absolute advantage, 368, **375**
Accumulation, 348
Acreage restrictions, 122f., **126**
Advertising, 7, 70, 174ff., **180**
Age-earnings cycle, 261, **270**
Agglomeration economies, 322, **329**
Agriculture, 116ff.
Aid to Families with Dependent Children, 280ff.
Airlines, 190
Air pollution, 312
Alcohol, 4ff.
  demand for, 6ff.
  supply of, 5f.
American Basketball Association, 234
American Football Association, 234
American Medical Association, 146ff.
American Stock Exchange, 156
American Telephone and Telegraph, 128, 193
Annuity, 250, **254**
Antitrust policy, 191
Apartment market, 38f.
Assumptions, simple demand-supply model, 15f.
Atomic Energy Commission, 317
Auto, 313, 327f.
Average revenue, 101, **111**
Average total costs: *See* Costs
Average variable costs: *See* Costs
Average vs. margin, 37, 83f.

Backpacking, 306
Bald eagle, 307
Barriers to entry, 104, **111**, 128f., **138**
Baseball, 229
Basketball, 234f.
Bilateral monopoly, 224, **226**
Billboards, 229
Biological Oxygen Demand, 315f.
Biology, 17
Birth control, 336
Birthrights, 341
Brand names, 7
Break-even point, 102, **111**
Budget constraint, 25ff., **32**, 90
Bureau of Narcotics and Dangerous Drugs, 8
Buttonwood Tree Agreement, 155

Ceteris paribus, 46, **59**
Calvert Cliffs, 317
Campfire Girls, 12
Cannabis sativa, 8f., 10

Capital accumulation, 348
Capital gains, 63, **70**
Capitalism, 387, 391ff., **395**
Capitalization, 65, **70**
Capital stock, 247, **254,** 348, 391
Cartel, 166f., **171**
Caveat emptor, **204**
Center for Study of Responsive Law, 207
Charting, 66, **70**
Children, 336f.
China, 398ff.
Civil Aeronautics Board, 190
Civil suits, 95
Civil War, 237
Clayton Act, 192
Club des Hachischins, 9
Club of Rome, 356
Collateral, 272, **279**
Command economy, 388, **395**
Commission on Product Safety, 201
Commodity Credit Corporation, 120
Common property, 294f., **299,** 312
Comparative advantage, 368, **375**
Compensation for innocent, 94
Competition, model of, 97ff.
  nonprice, 158, **161**
  perfect, 16
Compound interest, 252f., **254**
Concentration, industry, 163
  ratio, **171,** 174
Congestion, 322ff.
Conglomerates, 193, **195**
Conservation, 301, **309**
Consumer price index, 144
Consumer protection agencies, 198
Consumer sovereignty, 202, **204**
Consumerism, 198ff.
Contracting, 295
Copulatory economics, 339
Corporation, 76, **86**
Corvair, 201
Cost-benefit analysis, 317, **319**
Cost-of-service regulation, 187, **195**
Costs, 80ff.
  average total, 82, **87**
  average variable, 82, **87**
  external, 261
  of farm programs, 125
  fixed, 81
  historical, 26
  internal, 291f.
  joint, 187, **195**
  marginal, 83, **87,** 100f., 133, 182
  opportunity, 25, 77
  private, 291f., 324

  social, 291ff., **299,** 324
  transportation, 323
  variable, 82, 88
Courts, 94
Crowding, 343
Crude birth rate, 330, 332, **337**
Crude death rate, 330, 332, **337**
Cultural Revolution, 402
Curbstone crowd, 156

Deferments, college, 242
Demand, 15
  in competitive industry, 98
  curve, derivation, 42f.
  curve, kinked, 60
  derived, 214f., 217, **226**
  excess
Depopulation, 344
Depression, Great, 119
Development, 346
Diminishing marginal returns, 77, **87,** 389
Diminishing marginal utility: *See* Utility
Discounting, 249, **254,** 303
Discount rate, 351
Discrimination, 267ff.
Distribution of income, 258, **270**
  marginal productivity theory of, 262
Doubling time, 331, **337**
Draftees, 239
Draft, military, 237ff., 408
  costs of, 240, 408
  exemption, 242
  implicit tax, 244
  lottery, 242
  mercenary, 242
Draft (sports), 230, **235**
Drive-in movie pants, 25
Duopoly, 165
Durable goods, 248

Ecology, 301ff.
  and population, 342
Economic damages, 411
Economic growth, 29
Economic rents, 264ff., **270**
Economic surplus, 265
Economies of mass production, **139**
Economies of scale, 129, **138**
Economism, 402
Education, 272ff.
  financing of, 274ff.
  opportunity cost of, 268, 273
Efficiency, 109, 237ff., 241, 242, 314
Eighteenth Amendment, 4, 8, 15
Elasticity, of demand, 48ff., **59**

of demand for food, 117f.
income, 116f.
for an input or factor of production, 215ff.
and marginal revenue, 133
and price changes, 53f.
in long run, 57f.
of supply, 52, **59**, 117
unit, 51
Electrical conspiracy, 63
Electricity, 183, 313
Equilibrium, 18, **20**
Equilibrium price, 44, **59**
Equilibrium world trade, 366f.
Equities, 63, **70**
Euphoria, 4ff.
Excess demand, 45
Excess demand schedule, 363ff., **375**
Excess supply, 45
Excess supply schedule, 365, **375**
Experience, 264
Exploitation, 266, **270**
Exports, 363
demand and supply of, 363ff.
External costs, 291
External effects, 203, 275
Externalities, 275, 292f., 297

Factor demand curve, 213
Fair trade price, 193
Family Assistance Plan (FAP), 285
Farmers, 116ff.
Fat wienie, 200
Federal Farm Board, 119
Federal Trade Commission, 174, 178
Firm, 76, **86**
Fixed costs: See Costs
Flow, 249, **254**
Football, 234
Ford Motor Company, 256f.
Forests, 305f.
Free enterprise, 392
Free goods, 24

Gains from trade, 367f.
Game theory, 165
Gas, no lead, 313
General equilibrium analysis, 19, **20**
Great Depression, 119
Great Leap Forward, 400f.
Group Health, 152
Growth, economic, 29f., 346ff.
and capital, 349
limits to, 356ff.
and natural resources, 347
and property rights, 353
rates of, 347, 358f.

Hard drugs, 92
Historical costs, 26f.

Human capital, 353
improving market for, 273f.
market for, 273f.
Human capital investment, 247, 268f.

Imperfect competition: See Monopolistic competition
Income, distribution of, 258, **270**
real, 24, **32**
Income elasticity, 114f.
Infant industry argument, 370, **375**
Inflation and regulation, 188
and war, 414
Information, 267
costs, 15f., **20,** 38f., **59**
inside, 64, **70**
about marijuana, 10
perfect, 110, 263
public, 64
about whiskey, 7
Instability in a cartel, 167f.
Institutional constraints, 24f.
Institutional investors, 160, **161**
Intelligence, 263
International trade, 361ff.
arguments against, 370f.
gains from, 367f.
Investment, foreign, 379
human capital, 247, 268f.
ITT, 193

Joint costs, 187, **195**
Joint Economic Committee, 405, 415

Kellogg's cornflakes, 178
Kinked demand curve, 184

Labeling, 201
Labor, demand for, 211ff.
Labor market, 212ff.
unrestricted, 228f.
Lake Erie, 310
Leary vs. United States, 9
Liability, 95
Line, waiting in, 266
Liquor consumption, 6
Lorenz curve, 258, **270**

Mafia, 5
Man-in-the-house rule, 282, **286**
Margin, 92, 110, 200
Marginal analysis, 92f., 200f.
Marginal cost pricing, 109, **111**
Marginal costs: See Costs
Marginal product, 79, **87**, 91, 212, **226,** 262f.
Marginal revenue, 101, **111**, 130
and elasticity, 133
Marginal revenue product, 219, **226,** 233
Marginal utility: See Utility
Marijuana, 3f., 131

demand for, 10
legalization of, 11, 16
prohibition of, 8ff.
supply of, 9f.
Marijuana Tax Act, 9
Market, 31, **32**
Mass production, 129, **139**
Mass transit, 326
Mathematics, 17
McDonald's, 252
Medicaid, 144, 283
Medical care, 144ff.
in Britain, 152
supply of, 146
Medicare, 144, 150, 283
Microeconomics, **32**
Middleman, 5, 37ff., **58**
Military capitalism, 407ff.
Military expenditures, 407ff.
Military industrial firm, 415ff.
Military manpower, opportunity cost, 243
supply of, 238
Miller-Tydings Act, 193
Minimum commission rates, 158f.
Minimum wages, 222, **226**
Mobility, 267f.
Models, 15ff., **20**
bilateral monopoly, 224, **226**
competitive, 16, 97ff.
of the firm, 75f.
oligopoly, 184ff.
monopoly, 16, 127ff.
wealth maximizing, 19, 23f., 80
Monopolistic competition, 169ff., **171**
Monopoly, 16, 36, **58**, 127ff., **138**, 383
bilateral, 224, **226**
natural, 182, **194**
price discriminating, 138, **139**
Monopsony, 220, **226,** 229, 232
Multinational corporation, 378, **384**
Mutual funds, 69, **70**

National Basketball Association, 228, 234
National Defense Education Act, 273
National Electrical Manufacturers Association, 167
National Environmental Policy Act, 317
National Football Association, 234
National Health Insurance, 152
in Britain, 152
Natural monopoly, 182, **194**
selling rights to, 187
New York Stock Exchange, 155
Nondurable goods, 248
Nonprice competition, 158, **161**
Normative economics, 4, 19f., **20,** 23
Nuclear power, 317f.

OASDHI, 282f.
Ocean rights, 308

Office of Economic Opportunity, 278
Oil depletion allowance, 406
Oil import quota system, 370ff.
Oligopoly, 162ff., **171**
Opportunity banks, 275
Opportunity cost, 25f., 77, 243, 268, 285, 368, 389
Over-the-counter market, 63

Parity, 119, **126**
Partial equilibrium analysis, 18f., **20**
Partnership, 76, **86**
Peak-load problems, 324
    and income distribution, 325
    pricing, 325, **329**
Pentagon, 408
Penthouse, 47
Perfect competition, 16, **20,** 103, 110
Performance contracting, 278, **279**
Personal discount rate, 351, **353**
Physics, 17
Pimps, 11
Playboy, 46ff., 339
Political economics, 382
Pollution, 292, 310ff.
Population, 330ff.
    control, 340f.
Positive economics, 4, 19f., **20,** 23
Potential entry, 178
Poverty, 280ff., 283
Preferences, 7
Present value, 249f., **254**
Price, equilibrium, 44, **59**
Price differentiation, 186, **195**
Price discrimination, 138, 150ff., 185
Price elasticity of demand, 48ff., **59**
Price elasticity of supply, 52, **59**
Price fixing, 155
Price index, consumer, 144
Prices, relative, 240, 357
Price supports, 119ff., **126**
Price taker, 97, **111**
Price theory, 23, **32**
Pricing, marginal cost, 109
    peak-load, 325
Private costs, 292, 324
Product group, 169
Production possibilities curve, 25ff., 27, 348
Productivity, 80, **87,** 212, **226**
Product safety, 201f.
Professional sports, 228ff.
Profile bread, 174
Profit, 102, 135f., 170
    accounting, 76, **86**
    economic, 77, **86,** 102, 104, 191
    in long run, 105
    monopoly, 156ff.
Profit maximization, 99ff., 131, 136, 184
Prohibition, 4ff.

Property, common, 294f., **299,** 312
Property rights, 294ff., **308,** 352, 392
Proprietorship, 76, **86**
Prostitution, 11f., 15
Public assistance, 281, 284, **286**
Public goods, 298f., **299**
Psychic returns, 24, **32,** 239

Quality of service, 189f.
Quotas, 370, 371ff., **375**

Radio transmissions, 175
Random walk, 66, **70**
Real income, 24, **32**
Regulation, airlines, 190
    cost of service, 187f., **195**
    and inflation, 188
    of natural monopoly, 185
    rate of return, 188, **195**
Relative prices, 240, 357
Rents, economic, 264ff., **270**
Resale price maintenance, 193, **195**
Research, 159
Reserve clause, 230, **235**
    and distribution of players, 231
Resources, natural, 301ff.
Return, normal rate of, 77
Risk, 266, 381
Rivalry, 36, **58**
Robinson-Patman Act, 192

Safari Island, 308
Safety, product, 202
    costs of, 203
Saving, 248, 351
Scarcity, 23, 25, 302, 358
Schooling, 263
S-curves, 334
Seat, value of, 157, **161**
Second Law of Thermodynamics, 335n.
Sherman Act, 191f.
Shut-down point, 102, **111**
Smog, 310
Social costs, 291ff., **299,** 312, 324
Social insurance, 282
Socialism, 387, 393ff., **395**
Social security, 282f.
Soil bank, 122, **126**
Speak-easy, 5
Specialization, 38, **59,** 322
Sports, professional, 228ff.
Spruce Goose, 386
SST, 406
Stag, 47
Standard Oil, 192
Stock, 249, **254**
Stock broker, 62
Stocks, common, 63
Subsidization, 184, 327
Substitutes, 11, 304

Subways, 326
Sulfur tax, 314
Supply, 15
    curve, derivation, 44
    excess, 45
    of firm, 106
    of industry, 107
    long run, 108
Surcharge, 325
Surplus, **126**
    agricultural, 121

Tariffs, 371, 373ff., **375,** 378ff., 381
Tastes, 7
Tautology, 14, **20**
Tax, and externalities, 293f.
    effect on cost curves, 85
    implicit, 244
    negative, 283ff., **286**
Technical analysis, 66, **70**
Technology, 340
Television repairs, 199
Television transmissions, 175
Temperance Society, 4
Thailand, 261
Theft, 91
Theory, 17, **20**
Theory of games, 165
Thermal pollution, 317
Third-party effects, 203, **204**
Timing of airplane flights, 190
Timing of resource use, 302, 304
Tobacco, 124
Total revenue curve, 99, **111**
Trade, international: *See* International trade
Training, 264
Transactions costs, 15, **20,** 38f., **59,** 296
Truism, 17
Truth in labeling, 201
Turnover costs, 241

Uncertainty, 201
Unemployment, 28
Unemployment insurance, 283
U.S. Arms Control and Disarmament Agency, 407
Utility, 39, **59**
Utopian socialism, 394, **395**

Value of marginal product, 212f., **226,** 229, 243, 263
Variable costs: *See* Costs
Vice, 91
Victims of crime, 95
Vietnam, 237f.
Volstead Act, 4, 6, 15
Volunteer army, 244
Vouchers, 276, 277, **279**

Wages, in China, 400
Waste, municipal, 316
Water pollution, 315ff.
Wealth, 247ff.
    distribution of, 296
Welfare, 280ff.

Wienie, fat, 200
Wild animals, 307f.
Wilderness, 205f.
Wood products, 306
Workfare, 285
World trade: See International trade

Yuan, 399

Zero economic growth, 2, 346, 356ff.
Zero population growth, 2, 330, 339ff.
Zero trade point, 365, **375**

NAME INDEX

*Page numbers in **boldface** type indicate biographical sketches.*

Adams, W., 141, 173, 181
Anslinger, H. J., 13

Backman, J., 181
Baez, J., 264, 265, 266
Balero, R., 327
Barnett, H., 360
Baudelaire, C., 9
Becker, G. S., 267, 271, 279
Balassa, B., 377
Benoit, E., 417
Berki, S. E. 197
Bish, R. L., 329
Bolton, R. E., 417
Boulding, K. E., 341, 360, 417
Brando, M., 264
Brown, C., 384
Brunner, J., 345
Bruton, H. J., 355
Budd, E., 271

Capone, A., 4
Cartter, A. M., 227
Castro, F., 115
Caves, R., 141
Chamberlin, E. H., 169ff, 173
Clark, B. F., 4
Clayton, J. L., 417
Coase, R. H., 300
Cochrane, W. W., 126
Cocker, J., 264
Columbus, C., 17
Commoner, B., 320
Cooper, I. B., 230
Cootner, P. H., 71
Cournot, A., 165
Crutchfield, J. A., 309
Culbertson, J. M., 329

Dales, J. H., 319
Deneuve, C., 264
Dowd, D. F., 355
Durr, F., 329

Dylan, B., 264, 265

Edgeworth, F. Y., 165
Ehrlich, A. H., 309, 338
Ehrlich, P. R., 309, 338, 340, 343, 344, 345
Eisenhower, D. D., 411
Engel, L., 71

Ferman, L. A., 271
Flexner, A., 147, 148, 149
Flood, C., 228, 230
Ford, E., 256
Ford, H., **256**
Fox, The, **320**
Fribourg, M., 378
Friedman, M., **142**
Frisch, R., 15

Galbraith, J. K., **34,** 173, 417
Galenson, W., 227
Gardner, R. L., 348
Goldman, M. I., 319
Goldwater, B., 143
Goode, E., 13
Green, M., 197
Grossman, G., 397

Haber, A., 271
Hagen, E. E., 355
Hall, R. E., 13
Hamilton, D., 287
Hardin, G., 338, 345
Harrington, M., 271
Haynes, W. W., 88
Haywood, S., 228
Heady, E. O., 126
Hechinger, F. M., 279
Hefner, H., 47
Herodotus, 9
Higgins, B., 355
Holmes, O. W., 233
Houthakker, H. S., 126

Hughes, H. R., **385**

Irving, C., 386

Jacobs, J., 329
Johnson, H. G., 355
Johnson, L. B., 35, 115

Kahn, A. E., 197
Kaiser, H., 386
Kefauver, E., 141
Kennedy, J. F., 115, 143
Kershaw, J. A., 287
Kessel, R., 154
Kirkpatrick, M., 174
Kneese, A. V., 300, 319
Knight, F. H., 113
Knowles, J. H., 146
Kornbluh, J. L., 271

Leonard, W. N., 197
Levitan, S. A., 287
Lincoln, A., 361

MacAvoy, P. W., 197
McFarlane, B., 404
McKean, R. M., 300

Maher, J. E., 22
Malthus, T. R., 339, 357, 358
Mansfield, E., 173, 417
Marshall, F. R., 227
Martin, J. P., 96
Meadows, D. H., 360
Melman, S., 245, 246, 415, 417
Miller, J. C., 246
Mishan, E. J., 329, 360
Morgan, J. P., 62
Morse, C., 360
Muskie, E., 320

Nader, R., 198, 205, **206,** 320
Neil, H. B., 161
Neng, S., 9

Netzer, D., 329
Ney, R., 161

Oi, W. Y., 246

Pen, J., 377
Phelps, E. S., 329
Pontecorvo, G., 309
Preston, N. S., 397
Proxmire, W., **405,** 415

Rayack, E., 154
Rees, A., 227
Reuben, D., 13
Richard, M., 11
Richman, B. M., 404
Ridker, R. G., 319
Rima, I. H., 397
Robinson, E. A., 113, 141
Robinson, J., 173
Rockefeller, J. D., III, 340
Rodberg, L., 417

Roosevelt, F. D., 35
Rostow, W. W., 355
Rottenberg, S., 236
Rowthorn, R., 384
Ruttan, V. W., 126

Samuelson, P. A., **114**
Schreiber, A. F., 329
Schultze, C. L., 126
Schumpeter, J. A., 141, 397
Schur, E. M., 13
Schwartz, W., 309
Servan-Schreiber, J. J., 379, 380, 384
Shadwell, A., 393
Shaffer, H. G., 404
Shearer, D., 417
Skolnick, J. H., 96
Smith, A., 93, 198, 322
Snider, D., 22, 377
Soltow, L., 271
Sprinkel, B. W., 71
Stanford, D., 205

Stelzer, I. M., 197
Stigler, G., 171

Theobald, R., 287
Thurow, L., 279
Tinbergen, J., 15
Tomerlin, J., 205
Tse-tung, M., 400, 402
Tullock, G., 96
Turner, L., 379, 384

Vatter, H. G., 271

Weiss, L. W., 141
Wheelwright, E. L., 404
Wilcox, C., 197, 287
Wilkins, M., 384
Will, R. E., 271
Wilson, G., 96

Yarmolinsky, A., 417